D0881174

PROBING THE DEPTHS OF GERMAN ANTISEMITISM

Probing the Depths of German Antisemitism

German Society and the Persecution of the Jews, 1933–1941

Edited by
David Bankier

Berghahn Books
New York–Oxford

Yad Vashem
Jerusalem

Leo Baeck Institute
Jerusalem

Published in association with Berghahn Books

The responsibility for the views expressed in this publication rests solely with the authors.

Language Editor: Heather Rockman
Typesetting: Judith Sternberg
Printing: Daf-Noy, Jerusalem

Printed in Israel

Library of Congress Cataloging-in-Publication data

Probing the Depths of German Antisemitism: German Society and the Persecution of the Jews, 1933–1941/ edited by David Bankier.
p. cm.
Includes bibliographical references and index.
ISBN 1-57181-238-5 (alk.paper)
1. Antisemitism–Germany–History–20th century. 2. Jews–Germany–Public opinion. 3. Public opinion–Germany. 4. Jews–Persecutions–Germany. 5. Germany–Ethnic relations. 6. Holocaust, Jewish (1939–1945)–Causes. I. Bankier, David

DS 146.G4 P75 1999
940.53'18–dc 21 99-056222

Contents

Introduction

Overall Explanations, German Society and the Jews or: Some Thoughts About Context

YEHUDA BAUER

Opening a conference like this presents a difficult problem, that is, if one wants to avoid repeating old clichés. There is the temptation to deal with overarching themes that result from accumulated research, rather than with historiographical descriptions. The best thing one can do with temptation, so say the cynics, is to yield to it. Permit me to follow this prescription.

One of the most fascinating developments in the area that concerns us is the fact that hardly a month, or even a week, passes without another book being published — be it a history, a social-scientific treatise, a literary effort in prose or poetry — that directly relates to the Holocaust. Not only books, but artistic expressions, whether paintings or sculptures, musical works, and of course films and TV productions. The flood is increasing rather than decreasing as time goes on. The Holocaust has become a symbol of evil in our modern society, first and foremost in the so-called western countries, but increasingly also in other areas of the world. Politicians, for instance, will incessantly refer to it, comparing Saddam Hussein, or Arafat, or simply other politicians whom they do not like to Hitler. All comparisons of events considered to be evil will be compared to the Nazi era. The question is why this should be so. The Holocaust was a form of genocide, yet, in this century alone, there were numerous events of genocides and mass murders. Why, then, is attention focused on the destruction of the Jews, and much less so of Cambodians, Tutsi, Gypsies, Armenians, Herreros, or others?

There is no empirical study that I know of which deals with this problem, and we are thrown back into the realm of hypotheses. But as I think this is an important issue, allow me to suggest two possible answers. One seems to be the development of an instinctive realization that in the Holocaust some frontiers, some barriers, were broken. Something unprecedented happened, something which cannot be subsumed under existent categories. That something I think, can be defined under three headings. The first is the global character of the Holocaust; while, as far as I know, practically all genocides or mass murders were localized, this one was not. With the Armenians, the Tutsis, the Cambodian victims, and so forth, the purpose was to eliminate them from a given area, such as Turkish ethnic regions, the area of the Cambodian state, or Rwanda. What happened to Armenians in France or even in Greece, to Khmer in Thailand, or to Tutsis in Zaire, did not come into the purview of the planners of these genocides. But the destruction of the Jews was not to be limited to German, or French, or Polish Jews. It was to take place wherever the German writ ran, and as the ultimate goal was world domination, that meant everywhere.

The second is the purely ideological character of the murder program. With all other genocides, there were pragmatic considerations. The Young Turks wanted to remove the Armenians from the lands they lived on within Turkish ethnic regions in order to create a Pan-Turkic empire, and to eliminate them from their middle-class positions in towns in order to hand these over to ethnic Turks. The Hutus wanted to remove the Tutsis from scarce lands; the Pol Pot regime wanted to remove what they saw as a class enemy that was owning land and houses and engaging in economic and cultural activities inimical, so they believed, to a classless utopia, and so on. But the Jews owned no territory, and contrary to legend did not control the German economy. From the point of view of pragmatic interests the murder of the Jews was, as we all know, counterproductive in the extreme. It was the only genocide I am aware of that was based on purely ideological premises opposed to pragmatic considerations.

Third, the destruction was, in principle, to be total. Every person with three or four Jewish grandparents was sentenced to death for the crime of having been born — and that, as far as I know, is unprecedented. Which does not of course mean that it cannot be repeated.

If all this constitutes one of the reasons why I would suggest that the Holocaust is slowly being seen as something unprecedented and new, the other reason I would suggest is connected with the character of the victim group. What we inaccurately call western civilization is based, after all, on two main pillars: Greece and Rome on the one hand, and Jerusalem on the other. Two hundred, or 250 years ago, if somebody in Europe owned a book it was most likely the Bible, which consisted of the Old and the New Testaments. Both of them were largely written by Jews. The Greeks and Romans are no longer there. The nations that live in these places do not speak the same languages, do not pray to the same gods, and do not practice a continuation of the same social and other practices. But the Jews are still there, with the same basic culture. The National Socialist regime, in its rebellion against all that preceded it, did not act so illogically when it attacked the Jews, the symbol of all they were attacking. The Jewish position in the so-called Christian-Moslem culture is complicated and contradictory. In polite society to this day there is a slight unease when the subject turns to Jews. They are symbol and content at once, and the traditional adversary in the societies in which they live.

These, therefore, are the two main reasons why, I would suggest, the Holocaust exercises an ever-increasing fascination for the western world: the slow realization of its being an unprecedented event; a break in the civilization that produced it; and the fact that the targeted group were the Jews, with their special position in European civilization.

Another issue worth pondering over is the fact that, after a fairly long period, general histories of the Holocaust are again being attempted. Many years ago there stood the "giants," who tried to present these great, all-encompassing histories of the Holocaust and/or of Nazi Germany generally. It was understandable that German historians dealt with the latter topic, and I do not mean Meinecke and Ritter, but rather Karl Dietrich Bracher, Wolfgang Sauer, Martin Broszat, and then later Eberhard Jäckel,[1]and others. Then other historians came along and began to investigate separate areas, from the political and

1 Friedrich Meinecke, *Die deutsche Katastrophe*, Wiesbaden, 1965; Gerhard Ritter, *Die Daemonie der Macht*, Munich, 1948, and: idem, *Europa und die deutsche Frage*, Munich, 1948; Karl Dietrich Bracher, *Zeitgeschichtliche Kontroversen*, Munich, 1984, and *The German Dictatorship*, London, 1982; Karl Dietrich Bracher and Wolfgang Sauer, *Die nationalsozialistische Machtergreifung*, Cologne, 1960; Martin Broszat, "Hitler and the Genesis of the Final Solution," *Yad Vashem Studies,* 13 (1979), pp. 73–126, and *Der Nationalsozialismus*, Stuttgart, 1960; Eberhard

diplomatic, to the military, then economic and social history, and finally ideological and cultural aspects. It is becoming more and more difficult to present overarching syntheses; there is so much material, so much variety. But we have to try to see the overall picture, because society, in its development, is one, and the various aspects we investigate are parts of a whole that changes constantly. The overall *Gestalt,* or *Gesamtdarstellung,* is the goal to strive for. The difficulty is that our interpretations must change and develop because we change, just as our own starting point, our *Sitz im Leben*, changes and influences us. We try our best to minimize that unless we are extreme relativists; relativism, however, is a cul-de-sac, and if one adopts that, no history can be written in any case.

In the history of the Nazi era, the Holocaust is, I think, the most difficult subject to approach. There, too, we had the early giants: Gerald Reitlinger,[2] and then Raul Hilberg,[3] and the less well-known, such as Joseph Tenenbaum.[4] They all approached the Holocaust as a German project, the Jews being the unfortunate victims — the object and not really the subject of history. The question was — how, and then why, did the Nazis do it? There was antisemitism of course, but that was something the non-Jewish society had developed over millenia. Then it became racist and ended in Hitler, though it did not end with him and is alive and well in many parts of the world. Was antisemitism the result of a continuity stretching from early Christianity — and perhaps even earlier — to the Nazis, or was Nazi antisemitism something radically new, and if so, why? In Israel, these different approaches were represented by scholars such as Shmuel Ettinger[5]and Shulamit Volkov.[6] And again the questions arose: why did the non-Jews develop

Jäckel, *Der Tod ist ein Meister aus Deutschland*, Hamburg, 1990, and *Hitlers Weltanschauung*, Stuttgart, 1981.

2 Gerald Reitlinger, *The Final Solution*, London, 1956.

3 Raul Hilberg, *The Destruction of the European Jews*, Chicago, 1961.

4 Joseph Tenebaum, *Race and Reich*, New York, 1956.

5 Shmuel Ettinger, *Hakayyam vehamishtane baantishemiut shel dorenu*, Hebrew University, 1968; idem, "Antisemitism of Our Time," *The Jerusalem Quarterly,* 23 (1982), pp. 95–113.

6 Shulamit Volkov, Kontinuität und Diskontinuität im deutschen Antisemitismus, *Vierteljahreshefte für Zeitgeschichte*, 35 (1985), pp. 221–243.

this hatred, how did it develop, and what was its influence on Germany specifically, because *Der Tod ist (war), ein Meister aus Deutschland,*[7] and not *aus Frankreich,* or *aus Amerika.* However, anti-Jewishness is very ancient, the Nazi regime was a unique phenomenon in history up to our times, and the Holocaust has unprecedented features within that. So antisemitism, it was and is said, cannot be the answer to the *why* of the Holocaust, because you supposedly cannot explain something unique and unprecedented by a phenomenon that has been around for many centuries. The question "why the Jews?" was answered by the retort: because they were hated — hated as outsiders, as middlemen, as capitalists, as Bolsheviks, as foreigners. This, in reality, is a kind of circular argument: they are hated because they are identified as people who are hated. Yes, there was a historical background as well. But people hate strangers, or capitalists, and so forth — and Jews were strangers, so Jews were hated. Yet French, Russians, Czechs, Danes, and others were strangers, capitalists, and Bolsheviks, too. And the Germans did not like French, Czechs, Russians, or Poles for many centuries, and vice versa. So why the Jews and not the others? No real answer was given, and for the reasons I just stated the question seemed to be a secondary one.

The main problems to which answers were sought were structural on the one hand, or ideological on the other. What made the Holocaust possible? Was it the Nazis', or Hitler's, intentions, perhaps as early as 1919, or 1924, to work towards a radical, murderous solution? Or was it a progressive radicalization of German society, against the background of social, political and economic crises, that made the murder of the Jews into a consensual project initiated largely from the middle ranks of the bureaucracy and the intelligentsia? Was it so-called "modernity," understood as a culture of cost-effectiveness, rationalization of the use of resources and of bureaucratic procedures, against the background of so-called "national interests"?

The "modernity" argument was put forward by Zygmunt Bauman, the structural model by a number of important academics such as

7 By Paul Celan, and see, e.g., John Felstiner, "Paul Celan's Todesfuge," *Holocaust and Genocide Studies*, 1 (1986), pp. 249–264.

Karl Schleunes,[8] Hans Mommsen,[9] Goetz Aly,[10] and others, and the intentionalist one by, for instance, Eberhard Jäckel.[11] I would argue that they all renewed in a way the effort to arrive at an overall interpretation, and that while they contributed a great deal to our understanding, their effort was less than successful in the end. Bauman failed to explain why modernity did not produce a Nazi-like regime and a murderous ideology in other modern countries, such as the United States, Britain or France. On the other hand, one wonders why murderous regimes developed in less-than-modern countries like Cambodia or Rwanda; or why the U.S. developed a murderous policy towards the American Indians in the nineteenth century when modernity was just emerging, and abandoned it in the twentieth when modernity flowered. Having first said that the Holocaust was caused by modernity, he concludes that both modernity and antisemitism were necessary factors leading to the Holocaust.[12] Not, I think, a very insightful statement, though Bauman adds an important addition to our analysis of modernity and of the disjunction between modernity and morality.

The structuralist argument uncovered some very important elements in Germany that led to the mass murder. These began with the complicated development of bureaucratic policies in the twenties and thirties, and the problems created by them, followed by the involvement of mid-level academic bureaucrats who tried to rearrange policies in accordance with principles of economic and social rationalization as they understood them — as discussed by Goetz Aly and Susanne Heim,[13] and ending with reordering of populations in occupied Poland, as described by Aly in his brilliant book *Endlösung*.[14] The problems this raises are not founded in lack of further research, though undoubtedly

8 Karl Schleunes, *The Twisted Road to Auschwitz*, Chicago, 1970.

9 Hans Mommsen, *From Weimar to Auschwitz*, Oxford, 1991.

10 Goetz Aly, *Endlösung*, Frankfurt, 1995.

11 Eberhard Jäckel, *Hitler in History*, London, 1984; and *Der Tod ist ein Meister aus Deutschland*, Hamburg, 1990.

12 Zygmunt Bauman, *Modernity and the Holocaust*, Oxford 1989, p. 94. He explains that the Holocaust was a "short circuit (one almost wishes to say, a chance encounter), between an ideologically obsessed power elite and the tremendous facilities of rational, systemic action developed by modern society".

13 Goetz Aly und Susanne Heim, *Vordenker der Vernichtung*, Hamburg, 1991.

14 See above, note 10.

research may well uncover additional important factors. The problems are intrinsic. The simplest is this: why did the radicalization occur *after* the main economic and social crises were resolved by the Nazi regime in the first years of its rule? If radicalization was the result of accumulated crisis-related problems, then surely their partial solution should have weakened the drive towards murder. And if, as Bauman suggested, murderous policies were the result of the deadly combination of modernity and dictatorship, then why did it not happen in a dictatorship such as Italy, or even, in the form of planned genocide, in communist Russia where mass murder took a completely different form?

Another issue is the character of the bureaucratic machinery itself. If it was, as Raul Hilberg has argued, a machinery following precedent,[15] why did it radicalize? And if it did, who gave it the push towards radicalization, why was that push given, and why did the machinery not only accept being pushed but showed drive, initiative and inventiveness in pushing further? Is it possible that Hilberg, as he so often said, did not want to ask large questions for fear of coming up with small answers? He never asked the question of who gave the push and why. The *Vordenker*, and the population experts so convincingly described by Aly, operated in Poland. Does that explain the deportation of the Jews of Corfu or Narvik to their deaths? Does it even explain why the Jews of the Pripjet Marshes in Belorussia were shot into ditches? And why did the *Vordenker* choose the Jews for elimination, and not all bald-headed men and left-handed women, in the name of economic and social rationalization and reduction of overpopulation? Yes, Aly does refer to racial ideology as the background. But how important was that background? Did it motivate the policies, or was it just a point of reference? Who decided on policies — the *Vordenker*, or the top echelon bureaucrats appointed by Hitler personally, his immediate entourage, or Hitler himself?

A fascinating problem seems to be emerging as we examine these matters. At least some very important mid-level bureaucrats in the German administration in Poland seem to have come to the conclusion, in late 1941 and early 1942, that since the Jewish ghettoes — originally

15 Raul Hilberg, *The Destruction of the European Jews*, Chicago, 1961.

intended only as holding pens for some future deportation — were becoming a permanent fixture, perhaps the Jews in them should be utilized for labor. The German-Soviet war had increased the need for more Polish laborers who were being brought to Germany by persuasion and, increasingly, by brutal force. To keep up with the economic tasks in Poland and the East generally, Jews might be useful. But they were starving, and starving people cannot work productively. So these bureaucrats thought that it might be worthwhile giving them a bit more food, and squeeze labor out of them. Indeed, there are indications of a slight improvement in the economic situation in quite a number of ghettoes in early 1942. If this line of research leads to confirmed results, the structuralist argument would suffer a serious reversal, because the decision to murder the Jews was taken in Berlin, by the center, and not by the local bureaucracy that was beginning to follow a quite different line. If these findings are confirmed, it would not be the mid-level structure that gave the push towards murder in the name of cost-efficiency and overall consensus; they were looking for a non-murderous way out. It would then be the ideological decision-makers at the center who acted contrary to the mid-level people and who decided on murder. These lines of argument are being developed by Christopher Browning, and it will be interesting to see where they might lead us.[16]

The intentionalist argument, too, seems to be faulted. There is, after all, not the slightest proof that the murder of any ethnic group, including the Jews, was actually planned before 1939. Jäckel's argument about a Hitler intention in 1924 is equally unprovable. The pure intentionalist argument is quite obviously fallacious in that it ignores the elements discussed by the structuralists, whose importance has been proven in the last few decades of research. And although the intentionalist-structuralist controversy is passé by now — and no serious scholar today, including of course those I have mentioned, will argue for the original, contradictory, positions — it is worth pondering the very basis of these arguments.

There is a crucial moral problem there, I would suggest. We cannot deal with the Nazi period in the spirit of *auditur et altera pars*. One

16 I am most grateful to Prof. Browning for sharing some of his thoughts on this with me. Yisrael Gutman, *The Jews of Warsaw,* Bloomington, 1982, p. 101 hints at similar conclusions.

should certainly also try to look at situations the way National Socialists saw them, but there is no way a western-type academic can adopt that point of view in the manner, say, that a historian of the French Empire can take Napoleon's side. It is not the only historical situation that has that peculiarity, to be sure. You cannot identify with Genghis Khan, or with Idi Amin either. But when you deal with Nazism, another aspect arises: if you adopt a structuralist point of view, you claim that German society became a murderous community, which is true, but which leaves the responsibility nowhere. If everyone was responsible, nobody was. One may surmise that the mid-level bureaucrats were responsible. But they were a part of an existing system, so the system is responsible and not the individual bureaucrat. If you adopt the strictly intentionalist line, then everyone was guided by their superiors who identified with the ideology. But *they* were not responsible because they received their guidance from Hitler, and he was not responsible either because he was, not clinically, but morally, mad. This is a rephrasing of the argument of Emil Fackenheim, of course, and I think he is right.[17]

Apparently, then, in order to approach the Holocaust one has to adopt a mixture of the different points of view. The problem is where you put your emphasis. And the question is, are we already at a stage where this is possible?

At this point one has to introduce the "G" word. Daniel J. Goldhagen burst upon the scene with the argument that, a), by the early 1940s most of German society had become a natural recruiting ground for willing murderers, and b), the reason for that being what he calls "eliminationist antisemitism," which had become an accepted general norm in German society from the mid-nineteenth century at least.[18] The first statement is true and has been argued for decades by most Israeli historians and many others, in different forms. The second statement is patent nonsense. German society was split in a number of ways, and no general eliminationist norm valid for the whole society is observable. What *is* observable is that radical antisemitism became prevalent in important sections of the German and, especially, the Austrian elites, but this is not what happened in France, for instance.

17 Emil Fackenheim, "Concerning Authentic and Unauthentic Responses to the Holocaust," *Holocaust and Genocide Studies*, 1 (1986), p. 111.

18 Daniel J. Goldhagen, *Hitler's Willing Executioners*, New York, 1996.

In France, radical antisemitism among the elites experienced a serious setback with the defeat of the anti-Dreyfusards. In Russia, murderous antisemitism among the elites was crushed by the defeat of those elites in World War I. Not so in Germany and Austria; this was proposed recently in a more or less essayistic form by John Weiss[19]and seems to me to be fairly self-evident; but the reasons why this should be so have not, to my knowledge, been sufficiently addressed. However, Nazi, murderous, antisemitism did not develop in the elites; it developed elsewhere, because in the German lands the elites were split. Thus one cannot point to a uniform antisemitism of the murderous kind; one can only say it existed, among other forms, and the Nazi variety took root among disaffected intellectual middle classes and not predominantly among the elites. Yet, while Goldhagen's explanation may be totally mistaken, he did point to where the emphasis of research should lead — namely to the motivations, of elites and of others. Quite correctly, in my view, he pointed to antisemitism as the main issue, though he disregarded all the others in that monocausal way for which he was, I think rightly, criticized. It is becoming increasingly clear that by the mid-thirties most sections of German society had adopted the discourse of Nazi ideology with its radical and radicalizing antisemitic contents; the reason why has not been sufficiently dealt with.

There seems to be little doubt that bureaucratic leadership groups were absolutely convinced of the correctness of an extreme racist worldview, and especially of an increasingly murderous approach to the Jews. This includes the groups examined by Ulrich Herbert,[20] and recently by Yaakov Lozowick,[21] within the SS, but also the Wehrmacht elites as shown by Hannes Heer and others. Wolfgang Gerlach has shown the same for the Confessing Church,[22] and others have done similar work on other segments of German society. The *Vordenker* were part of that picture. Their motivation was not only careerism, or economic and other rationalizations, but a worldview of which careers and rationalizations were constitutive elements. The German officials in

19 John Weiss, *Ideology of Death*, Chicago, 1996.

20 Ulrich Herbert, *Best*, Bonn, 1996.

21 Yaakov Lozowick, *Unusual Bureaucrats*, Ph.D. thesis (unpublished), Hebrew University (Hebrew), 1996.

22 Wolfgang Gerlach, *Als die Zeugen Schwiegen*, Berlin, 1987.

charge of Polish ghettoes, other civilian authorities in German cities and villages, their counterparts in various countries of occupied Europe, and the directors of the *IG Farben* and other industrial concerns, held similar worldviews in which antisemitism with a murderous potential played a part. But then, how do we explain the fact that on 6 November 1932, 293 out of a total of 584 representatives were elected to the *Reichstag* which represented parties that did not accept that worldview, namely Social Democrats, Communists, Liberals and Catholics? Another forty-two represented the collapsing center and were infected by radical antisemitism and radical nationalism, but were neither *DNVP* nor Nazi. How then do we explain that in 1932 half or more of the German people voted the way they did, but seven or eight years later most of them had indeed evolved into potential mass murderers generally, and especially murderers of any Jew they could lay their hands on? Goldhagen does not ask the question, and when you don't ask a question you are not likely to come up with an answer. But it is not just Goldhagen who does not ask the question.

To that question there may be two kinds of answer. One has to do with the way ideological dictatorships act. Were most people in the USSR convinced ideological communists in, say, 1926? Hardly, I would think. Yet in 1941, millions believed that the survival of their national groups within the Soviet Union was assured with the communist regime, and millions of soldiers went to their deaths shouting "For Fatherland, for Stalin." Communism became the "glue". There was a consensus and, mark you, not only among the Russians, but the Kalmycks, Tadjiks, Kazakhs, and even among many Ukrainians and Belorussians. Is that the result only of propaganda, of a cleverly directed educational system combined with terror? Is that not also connected with the persuasiveness of an utopian ideology which really convinces? Is utopia not a most powerful motive force which explains why the pieces fall into place, why the elites, the *Vordenker*, and the ordinary people reacted positively to the consensus desired by the regime's leaders; why there was a meeting of initiatives from below and from above? I do not know of any utopian ideology that has not led to mass murder. The Nazis promised a new Germany, a wonderful new *Volksgemeinschaft,* that would allow for both equality and private initiative, a return to natural morality, to an ideal family with fixed roles for every member, and so on. They promised this to a nation whose social structures had disintegrated and in the throes of personal and communal lack of security, a people not only devastated by terrible and recurring economic crises, but who suffered military defeat and humiliation. Utopia was offered and utopia, as I said, equals murder, once that becomes feasible.

I wonder whether a second answer may not lie in a model that seems to hold true for modern societies. This was introduced to me by Ian Kershaw, orally, and it really underlies the contributions of other colleagues as well. It goes something like this: A potentially murderous, genocidal quasi-elite or elite gains power, not because of its potentially genocidal program, but because of a host of social, economic, cultural and political factors that it utilizes to gain ascendancy. The intellectual elites in the society — bureaucracy, army, churches, the professions, and most importantly, the academics — quickly identify with the genocidal elite, again not because of the potentially genocidal program but because of the utopian elements in the ideology. Perhaps also, as things develop, because of the initial successes of the genocidal elite after it has gained power. A consensus will arise, based on identification with the regime, which will lead to enthusiastic cooperation and to independent initiatives in line with the consensus. And if the ruling elite then wishes to translate its genocidal potential into reality, it will be able to count on the unstinting support of the intellectuals. With the support of these intellectual elites, general society — the workers, the peasants and the lower middle classes — will naturally follow. There will be no dearth of willing executioners, if that is what is needed.

Recently, in a discussion, my colleague Saul Friedländer expressed his surprise that I thought this model was new. All of us have long thought in these terms, he said. Being an admirer of his work, I sought to check it out. Indeed, in an impressive volume called *Nazi Germany and the Jews: Years of Persecution*,[23] he uses this approach. But nowhere have I found the theory spelled out. Perhaps I did not look hard enough. It does provide at least a challenge, a possible way of explaining why German society — or any society — could become what German society became.

But there is a hitch there, precisely because the Nazi genocide of the Jews was *not* like the mass murder committed in Soviet Russia,

23 Saul Friedländer, *Nazi Germany and the Jews*, vol. 1, London, 1997.

Cambodia, or Rwanda, not to speak of Bosnia or Nigeria. It has a different quality. It brings us back to the Jews. None of the authors I mentioned earlier deals with the Jews as such, except as poor and pitiful victims. Only Leni Yahil did, in her comprehensive textbook volumes about the Holocaust.[24] Yet what was done to the Jews is different from what was done to Poles, Gypsies, Serbs, Russians or the handicapped, by the Nazis, and different to what was done to Cambodians, Tutsi, Ibo or Bosnian Muslims. Not in terms of brutality and sadism — there you can find horrible parallels — but in terms of motivations and aims. A quasi-religious, Manichean ideology marked all Jews as defined by the Nazis — wherever there would be German influence, i.e., everywhere in the world as sentenced to death, in the name of what Friedländer, I think rightly, calls "redemptive antisemitism." Because once you have killed all Jews, that is, once you have killed Satan, humanity will be redeemed. That is the crucial center piece of the utopia.

In order to understand that, one has to deal with the Jews. You have to study their culture and civilization to see why a modern, genocidal utopia would zero in on that particular target. You will then discover, I believe, that the place of the Jews in traditional Christian and Moslem society was a necessary, but of course not a sufficient, background to a secularized, anti-Christian, murderous ideology, and why that ideology became so central to the Nazi regime. You can and should, I think, incorporate all the other factors — the crises, the particular German background with its elites, its social history, its political history. I do think one can begin to write an overall history, but you cannot write it without dealing with the Jews. They were not only victims; they were a community which was, in some significant ways, central to the self-understanding of European, and not just German society. Which is why they became the target of an unprecedented onslaught that has changed the western, and now increasingly also the non-western world's perception of itself. In other words, at the core of National Socialism lies not bureaucracy or modernistic structures — all of which were there, to be sure, and contributed — but a purely ideological desire to overturn, not just a regime or a system, but the basic order of the world. All the other changes that people aspired to were connected to

24 Leni Yahil, *The Holocaust*, New York, 1990.

accepted subdivisions of societies — elites, classes, ethnic or religious divisions. The Nazis wanted something completely new and totally revolutionary. They wanted to reorder humanity according to what they called "races," with themselves at the top of course. In order to do so they had to rebel against the society they came from, against all of what we inaccurately call western civilization. No one had ever tried to do something like that. National Socialism was a total rebellion. I have hinted already why that rebellion might have targeted the Jews as its main, utterly hallucinatory, enemy. The unique features of the Holocaust derive from the unique features of the Nazi regime, and from the unique position of the Jews in western civilization.

What we propose to study at this meeting is, I suppose, largely what we mean by *Alltagsgeschichte*. But, as Friedländer pointed out in his controversy with Martin Broszat,[25] you cannot deal with the day-to-day life in Nazi Germany as you would with a parallel effort regarding, say, Switzerland. National Socialist Germany was ruled by a criminal, murderous regime, and the day-to-day life of its citizens was colored by this, even in the most trivial circumstances. Social welfare, medicine, neighborly relations and so on took place in the framework of a regime devoted to murder and genocide, and when you describe the *Alltag* without reference to that, you are in danger of trivialization of what should never be trivialized. In other words, there is a moral problem here. Yet, of course, day-to-day life must be studied, and when the framework of the murderous regime is remembered this becomes a crucial element in an overall explanation. I think, hope and expect that that is what we are aiming to do in this volume.

25 Martin Broszat and Saul Friedländer, "A Controversy About the Historicization of National Socialism," *Yad Vashem Studies,* 19 (1984), pp. 1–48.

Party and State Antisemitic Policy

Acquiescence?

HEIDE GERSTENBERGER

"hält man sich die Ohren zu,
hört man kein Stöhnen mehr."

Karl Kraus, *Dritte Walpurgisnacht*[*]

Public Opinion and the Government of Modern Societies

In the last decades of the eighteenth century, revolutionaries in North America and France established that public opinion should be considered the only legitimate basis of government. After having successfully served as the rallying battle cry against the domination forms of the *ancien régime*, this principle soon underwent severe practical restrictions. The question of who should by right belong to the legitimating public became one of the focal points of political controversy. Furthermore, it became obvious that the mechanisms that transformed individual opinions into public opinion functioned not only as technical transmissions but as processes of selection. In the course of time, channels of selection have become integral parts of modern parliamentary systems. Today we are accustomed to the fact that electors can only choose between programs and persons that have been decided upon by political parties, the constitutional fiction being that parties preselect interests and opinions of the electors. We also tend to assume that the presidencies of associations represent the opinions of their members, and though we all know that the choice between the opinions published via the media is restricted by economic power,

* "Those who shut their ears will no longer hear the moans." Karl Kraus, *Dritte Walpurgisnacht*.

we usually accept the main traits of published opinion as representing the main opinion traits of the population. Politicians, however, have learned to be a little more cautious. They tend to refer themselves to public opinion polls. That these can also be used to influence opinions has often been shown. In summary, not only historians and political scientists, but everyone living in a modern parliamentary democracy is aware that governments, though dependent upon reelection, do not have the consent of the majority of the governed for each of their measures nor for each of their major political strategies. Likewise, it is known to be not only possible but even probable that published opinion differs in many respects from the opinion held by a majority of the population.

As long as we do not feel that the politics of a government are violating our most important interests or fundamental principles, we might decide to vote for another party at the next election or not to vote at all. Most of us leave it at that. If we do not approve of certain political decisions we often say so in private or in the realm of those restricted public spheres in which we lead our daily lives. Sometimes, but not always, we try to make our disappointment known to the wider public. If we aspire to formulate all of this in theoretical language, we could do so by generalizing Niklas Luhmann's analysis of the function of law for modern societies. In his opinion, its legitimating function is not achieved by the results of legal processes but by the formal processes that precede the legal decisions.[1] I propose the hypothesis that the mere existence of selective channels for public opinion constitutes the main precondition for the acceptance of differences between politics, published opinion, and the opinions of the population. Seen in this light, every dictatorship in one of the modern nation-states has to be considered a structural paradox. None has ever been established without postulating that it acted in the true interests of the nation, on behalf of the people. However, by prohibiting, destroying or at least severely restricting the processes which in parliamentary democracies constitute public opinion — namely, the plurality of parties, the freedom of

1 Niklas Luhmann, *Rechtssoziologie*, Opladen, 1983, especially pp. 262–267. The fact that this analysis belongs to an earlier stage in the development of Luhmann's theoretical conceptions does not have to concern us here.

elections, the press and other media, as well as the right to autonomously organize in order to further one's interests — dictatorships paradoxically make themselves directly dependent upon the opinions of the governed. In other words,[2] by doing away with the institutional and legal preconditions for the compromises inherent in the political reality of any parliamentary system, they make themselves politically very vulnerable. If there are no channels that publicly form and transmit opinion, then the opinion of each and everyone is — at least in principle — the basis for government. Consent becomes a much more crucial issue. We all know the instruments and measures used to counterbalance this vulnerability: first of all propaganda, secondly political theater in the form of parades, symbols, special language or special gestures — all designed to act out public consent — and thirdly terror. The transformation of the public effects its displacement. From the sphere of civil society it is transferred into the sphere of government. This obviously lessens its capacity to legitimize government. The attempt to integrate society as well as government into a movement, to mould them together in activism, is one of the strategies to counteract this danger. Historically, the Nazi leaders were not the first to realize that this strategy made it difficult to curb the atrocities of activists, and that it was not wise to declare that these were practiced with the consent of the government.

Public Opinion and Nazi Government

It has been convincingly argued that popular enthusiasm and the willingness to accept official Nazi propaganda already started to diminish in the summer of 1934.[3] From that time on the great public events might have functioned mainly as the means to reconfirm the activists' belief in

2 To prevent misunderstandings it might be advisable to state that the very broad concept of dictatorship used here to point to some divergences from parliamentary regimes should not be considered as aiming at one more concept of totalitarianism.

3 Ian Kershaw, *Popular Opinion and Political Dissent in the Third Reich: Bavaria*, Oxford, 1983; David Bankier, *Die öffentliche Meinung im Hitler-Staat*, Berlin, 1995, Introduction.

the importance of their role,[4] while at the same time officially regulating its expression. David Bankier talks of a gap between officially staged opinion and the opinions of the population, Klaus-Michael Mallmann and Gerhard Paul use the term *zweite Öffentlichkeit* (secondary public).[5] It was this secondary public, or rather the various expressions of opinions in the different social, religious and local contexts of everyday life, that the Nazi leaders wanted to know about. Not being able to fully free themselves from the requirement of the consent of the governed, they needed to be informed of a public opinion whose undisturbed expression they were eager to prevent.

The hypothesis that the dynamics of anti-Jewish policy was to a large extent shaped by reports on opinions and behavior has been convincingly developed.[6] I will take this very haunting hypothesis as a starting point and try to supplement it by proposing an analytical concept which might help to explain the relationship between the nonofficial public sphere and anti-Jewish policy, without falling into the trap of postulating that modern antisemitism in Germany had always aimed at the physical destruction of the Jews.[7] In doing so I refer myself to theoretical and historical research in the function of the

4 Gerhard Paul, "Zur Sozialgeschichte von Verfolgung und Widerstand am Beispiel des Saarlandes (1935–1945)," in: *Terror, Herrschaft und Alltag im Nationalsozialismus*, Brigitte Berlekamp and Werner Rühr, eds., Münster, 1995, p. 41.

5 Bankier, *Die öffentliche Meinung*, p. 36; Klaus-Michael Mallmann and Gerhard Paul, *Herrschaft und Alltag. Ein Industrierevier im Dritten Reich*, Bonn, 1991, p. 339; "informal public" p. 352; In one of his essays Gerhard Paul even uses the term *"Gegen Öffentlichkeit,"* which suggests the *intention* of critique. Gerhard Paul, "Zur Sozialgeschichte," p. 41.

6 See: Otto Dov Kulka, "Die Nürnberger Rassengesetze und die deutsche Bevölkerung im Lichte geheimer NS Lage-und Stimmungsberichte," *Vierteljahrshefte für Zeitgeschichte,* 32 (1984), pp. 582–624, passim; David Bankier, *Die öffentliche Meinung*, op.cit., passim. In the first years of the regime, critique from foreigners and its potential effect on economic relations was also taken into consideration. See for example Günter Plum, "Wirtschaft und Erwerbsleben," in: *Die Juden in Deutschland 1933–1945*, Wolfgang Benz, ed., Munich, 1988, p. 274f.; Albert Fischer, *Hjalmar Schacht und Deutschlands "Judenfrage,"* Cologne, 1995.

7 Quite obviously the hypotheses developed in this paper do not fit into the interpretation of Daniel Jonah Goldhagen, *Hitler's Willing Executioners. Ordinary Germans and the Holocaust*, London, 1996.

public sphere[8] in modern societies.[9]Let me sum up where I think we stand.

One after another, the legends regarding the relative immunity to National Socialism of the inhabitants of certain towns, for example the Hansa-towns, of certain social groups, especially the workers,[10] or of certain leading individuals,[11] have been destroyed by closer scrutiny.[12] Today we are aware of many of the reasons for the wide acceptance of the regime. One is the populism of the *Gauleiters*, their *Sozialismus der Tat* (practical socialism),[13] which sometimes fulfilled long-standing

8 The German term "Öffentlichkeit" is very difficult to translate into English, there being no English term to signify a collective subject consisting of those who act in a certain public sphere. This possible meaning of the German term is to be remembered when I talk of secondary or primary public(s).

9 To a large degree this research has been prompted by the study of Jürgen Habermas, *Strukturwandel der Öffentlichkeit*, Frankfurt am Main, 1990. See for example the contributions in: *Habermas and the public sphere*, Craig Calhoun, ed., Cambridge, MA., 1992 (especially the contributions of the editor and of Nancy Fraser). The historical and analytical concept of the public sphere to which I refer is developed in: Heide Gerstenberger, *Die subjektlose Gewalt. Theorie der Entstehung moderner Staatsgewalt*, Münster, 1990.

10 See Ulrich Herbert's summary of research into the relationship between workers and National Socialism, "Arbeiterschaft im 'Dritten Reich.' Zwischenbilanz und offene Fragen," *Geschichte und Gesellschaft,* 15 (1989), pp. 320–360. I do not, however, agree with Herbert in one of his central arguments. In stating that the politics of racial hygienics aimed at disciplining "the workers" (p. 335), he assumes that workers then (or ever), felt that those who were discriminated against, criminalized and persecuted as being "asocial" belonged to them. See also Martin Röther, "Lage und Abstimmungsverhalten der Arbeiterschaft: Die Vertrauensratswahlen in Köln 1934 und 1935," *Vierteljahreshefte für Zeitgeschichte,* 39 (1991), pp. 221–264, who stresses that concentration on the material conditions of one's own private life guided the political attitudes of workers.

11 One of the latest examples is an analysis of the attitudes and politics of Hjalmar Schacht who has long been viewed as somebody principally opposed to anti-Jewish policy. See Albert Fischer, *Hjalmar Schacht.*

12 See also the summary review by Bernhard Hey, "Regionen, Kommunen, Personen unter dem Nationalsozialismus, Sammelrezension," *Westfälische Forschungen,* 38 (1988), pp. 319–325. In this contribution Hey discusses the results and the shortcomings of several local studies on towns in Westphalia.

13 Mallmann and Paul, *Herrschaft und Alltag*, chapter III.1; Frank Bajohr, "Gauleiter in Hamburg. Zur Person und Tätigkeit Karl Kaufmanns," *Vierteljahrshefte für Zeitgeschichte,* 43 (1995), pp. 267–295.

demands, such as for example the equal distribution of working hours among the harbor workers of Hamburg.[14] Many of these workers were glad to once more find employment, others were delighted that for the first time in their lives they could take a vacation. Many were content that the regime pledged to do away with the humiliation of the Versailles peace treaty.[15] Many Germans experienced or could hope to experience social advancement. We have come to realize that neither spontaneous nor coordinated endeavors to defend old traditions, religious practices, preferences of cultural expressions,[16] or economic interests should be assembled under the term *Resistenz*[17] because this suggests that any diversion from the principles upheld by Nazi propaganda expressed reservation about the regime as such. Instead, we have slowly come to accept that Nazism existed in a German society that in many respects

14 Klaus Weinhauer, *Alltag und Arbeitskampf im Hamburger Hafen. Sozialgeschichte der Hamburger Hafenarbeiter 1914–1933*, Paderborn, 1994, chapter II.8 and passim; this is also confirmed by the ongoing research of Frank Broeze who has scrutinized the archives of Hapag Lloyd.

15 Bernd Stöver, *Volksgemeinschaft im Dritten Reich. Die Konsensbereitschaft der Deutschen aus der Sicht sozialistischer Exilberichte*, Düsseldorf, 1993, pp. 173–184.

16 As a recent addition to Hans Dieter Schäfer's pioneering study, *Das gespaltene Bewusstsein. Deutsche Kultur und Lebenswirklichkeit 1933–1945*, Munich, 1981, see Volker Dahm, "Nationale Einheit und partikulare Vielfalt. Zur Frage der kulturpolitischen Gleichschaltung im Dritten Reich," *Vierteljahreshefte für Zeitgeschichte,* 43 (1995), pp. 221–265.

17 The concept was first developed by the members of the research project "Widerstand und Verfolgung in Bayern." Its central elements (originally contained in vol. IV of the publication of its results), have been reproduced in Martin Broszat, *Nach Hitler*, Munich, 1987, pp. 68–91. I refrain from citing the extensive literature that has been provoked by the use of this term, but would like to call attention to Ian Kershaw's remark that the fact that *"Resistenz"* is not easily translated in other languages without suggesting resistance, i.e., opposition, should have made us cautious. See Ian Kershaw, "'Widerstand ohne Volk?' Dissens und Widerstand im Dritten Reich," in: *Der Widerstand gegen den Nationalsozialismus,* Jürgen Schmädeke and Peter Steinbach, eds., Munich, 1994, p. 783; Recent publications have gone much further in stressing mass loyalty. See for example. Klaus-Michael Mallmann and Gerhard Paul, "Resistenz oder loyale Widerwilligkeit? Anmerkungen zu einem umstrittenen Begriff," *Zeitschrift für Geschichtswissenschaft,* 41 (1993), pp. 99–116; Bernd Stöver, "Loyalität statt Widerstand," *Vierteljahreshefte für Zeitgeschichte,* 43 (1995), pp. 437–471.

was less strictly dominated than we used to think.[18] The latest blow to the cornerstone of any interpretation that considers Nazism as a system totally alien to the German society has come from the research into the functioning of observation and terror. Mann, Gellately, Mallmann and Paul have shown that the Gestapo and the other institutions involved in observation and persecution were much less overpowering than had been assumed, that they had to and could rely on denunciations. All of these authors have demonstrated that the institutions of persecution were made use of to resolve conflicts of everyday life. We have to conclude that to a considerable extent control of the German population was exercised by itself.[19]

Persecution and Secondary Public Spheres

In addition, I would now propose the hypothesis that it was not only Nazi propaganda nor the endeavors to lead a more or less undisturbed private life[20] which furthered what German historians have called *die Hinnahme*, the acquiescence with Nazi anti-Jewish policy,[21] but that the

18 This hypothesis is developed by Reinhard Mann who refers to interpretations of Erwin K. Scheuch. See Reinhard Mann, *Protest und Kontrolle im Dritten Reich*, Frankfurt am Main, 1987, Introduction.

19 See also: Gerhard Paul, "Zur Sozialgeschichte von Verfolgung und Widerstand am Beispiel des Saarlandes (1935–1945)," in: Berlekamp and Röhr, *Terror,* pp. 32–76; Ludwig Eiber, though confirming many of the findings of Mann, Gellately and Mallmann and Paul hesitates to follow them in their very radical hypothesis. Ludwig Eiber, "Zur 'Effektivität' der Gestapotätigkeit und der Funktion der Gestapo im faschistischen Terrorsystem," in: Berlekamp and Röhr, *Terror,* pp. 187–189.

20 Bernd Stöver takes these endeavors to be the main reason for the acquiescence, Bernd Stöver, *Volksgemeinschaft*, p. 125 and passim.

21 The concept of *"Hinnahme"* (acquiescence), represents a first step in the retreat from the concept of *"Resistenz,"* but the authors who make use of it still hold that *passivity* was the main characteristic in the behavior of the population and they tend to interpret passivity as constituting non-action. This however contradicts any sociological concept of action. In the social sciences it has long been established that doing nothing is to be considered a form of action. Sociological analysis therefore refrains from probing into the motives and tries to evaluate the consequences of actions. In trying to explain the objective consequences of acquiescence in the very first measures of anti-Jewish policy (however this may have been motivated), I simply apply concepts of sociological theory to the analysis of the functioning

secondary public sphere, in other words all the scattered and restricted publics of everyday life, had their part in furthering this acceptance. Widespread antisemitism was a precondition for the persecution of individuals who either conceived of themselves as being Jewish, or by the criteria of the new regime were declared as belonging (fully or in half), to a Jewish race. It does not explain the development from antisemitism to state-organized mass murder. Any such explanation, unsatisfactory as it will always remain, must take into account what we have come to learn about the functioning of western societies in the twentieth century.

There were social, and in particular professional groups whose members were convinced that Jews endangered or prevented them from becoming economically and socially successful. Since this is well known we usually do not seek further explanation for the fact that individuals belonging to these groups made use of the advantages that were offered to them through the persecution of Jews. However, one of the results of the current international debate on analytical concepts in social history is the insight that individuals do not simply function according to their economic or social positions,[22] and that interests and attitudes, therefore, should not be considered simple reflexes of social positions. Instead, interests are always the result of an interpretation of these positions. Individuals interpret their position in life, their hopes and their needs by taking into consideration what they know or assume to be thought legitimate by "everybody." This "everybody" can be the anonymous authority of the general public, be it officially regulated or not. Most often, however, the most important body of reference is

of the Nazi regime. One of the main advocates of the analytical concept that interprets the behavior of the population as *"Hinnahme"* is Alf Lüdtke. See for example Alf Lüdtke, "Die Praxis von Herrschaft: Zur Analyse von Hinnehmen und Mitmachen im deutschen Faschismus," in: Berlekamp and Röhr, *Terror,* pp. 226–245. In his contribution to this volume Lüdtke has overcome the shortcomings of this interpretative concept. He now stresses the active contribution inherent in the practices of everyday life.

22 Much of this debate has been provoked by the work of E.P. Thompson. For a critical evaluation of his analytical concepts and for summaries of the debate see the contributions in: Harvey Kaye and Keith McClelland, eds., *E.P. Thompson. Critical Perspectives*, Cambridge, 1990.

one or other of the public spheres in which we lead our daily lives, ranging from school class to church congregation, to the workplace.[23] In fact, sociologists have told us that the professional group is the most important reference group for modern man.[24] Public opinion, in other words, is not only to be conceived of as the legitimating body for government, but also as the legitimating authority that is relevant in the process of constituting one's interests. It is, therefore, one of the main preconditions for behavior.

The possible relevance of this for research into the dynamics of anti-Jewish policy might be illustrated by reference to an event at the University of Göttingen. On 12 April 1933, almost immediately after the law of the Restoration of the Professional Civil Service had been enacted, the local paper printed the announcement that every university teacher would receive a questionnaire to be completed and returned as soon as possible in order to enable the minister to solve *die Judenfrage* before the commencement of the next term. Everyone seems to have complied. Twenty-eight of the professors at this university were removed from their posts in 1933, six by telegram already on 25 April. No traces of any protest have been found. On 17 April, Prof. James Franck, winner of the Nobel prize in physics, asked the responsible Prussian minister to relieve him of his duties. Newspapers all over Germany made this move known, and the local newspaper in Göttingen printed Franck's statement that he did not want to make use of the privilege accorded to those Jewish public servants who had fought for Germany in the war. There was only one action of solidarity from a university colleague. It came from Prof. Ewald in Stuttgart. In Göttingen, forty-two members of the faculty hastened to publish a statement declaring Franck's resignation to be an act of sabotage. After the death of Prof. Franck in 1954, many letters that he had received from individuals all over Germany who had wanted to let

23 That there were also workers who denounced their colleagues to the Gestapo has been noted, for example, by Ludwig Eiber, "Zur Effektivität," p. 187.

24 Most pointedly Pierre Bourdieu who in his theory of social practice proposes that the main traits of the behavior and thinking of modern man are shaped by the social class to which he belongs, interpreting "class" as consisting of the informal collectivities of the members of professional groups. See for example Pierre Bourdieu, *Le sens pratique*, Paris, 1980.

him know their esteem and their solidarity were found. It is because of these letters that I choose the "removal" of James Franck from a German university as an example. He might have valued them for their consoling virtue. Many others have reported that any sign of pity, solidarity or esteem helped them through some of their days or weeks.[25] For historians they prove that although we do not know if this was always prompted by an attitude devoid of traces of antisemitism,[26] there were in fact individuals who disagreed with this specific measure.[27] But the university as a body, including all the colleagues not approving of the new law, remained silent. Victor Klemperer, professor in Dresden until April 1935, again and again noted in his diary that he found it simply incomprehensible when close acquaintances abruptly ended any contact with him after his dismissal.[28] Franck must have had similar experiences.

In 1933 the SA was terrorizing the German population. Although its gangs most often tormented individuals who were known to be "left", among them numerous Jews, it is possible that many others were afraid. At Göttingen, as in most other universities, the percentage of students who openly declared their favor for the new regime was high. Whatever the motivations of those who acquiesced in the first official anti-Jewish measures in 1933, the university public, by not insisting on humanity, on professional standards, or on its traditional autonomy, had

25 In the account of her life in Germany from 1933 to 1945, Else R. Behrend-Rosenfeld reports many instances of help and solidarity, stating that she thought it even more important to report them than to try to convey her suffering. *Ich stand nicht allein. Erlebnisse einer Jüdin in Deutschland 1933–1944*, Cologne, 1949, p. 262.

26 There are numerous examples of individuals criticizing one specific measure and at the same time expressing their own antisemitism. For some typical examples see the solidarity expressed with Kurt Hahn, the founder of the Salem-school, after his dismissal in March 1933. See Ruprecht Poensgen, "Die Schule Schloss Salem im Dritten Reich," *Vierteljahreshefte für Zeitgeschichte,* 44 (1996), pp. 25–54.

27 Volker Dahm, "Kulturelles und geistiges Leben," in: *Die Juden in Deutschland 1933–1945*, Wolfgang Benz, ed., Munich, 1988, pp. 194–197; Konrad Kwiet and Helmut Eschwege, *Selbstbehauptung und Widerstand. Deutsche Juden im Kampf um Existenz und Menschenwürde 1933–1945*, Hamburg, 1984, p. 43.

28 For example on 19 October 1935, five and a half months after his dismissal: *"Nicht einer von all den romanistischen Kollegen hat mich aufgesucht; ich bin wie eine Pestleiche."* Victor Klemperer, *Ich will Zeugnis ablegen bis zum letzten. Tagebücher 1933–1941*, Berlin, 1995, vol. I, p. 223.

already missed its opportunity to set limits to government strategies. Even more important is the impact this behavior must have had for the possible development of the nonofficial public sphere. In matters of anti-Jewish policy it had its back broken before it even had a chance to develop as a "secondary public" in the sense of Mallmann and Paul. After having experienced the rejoicing of some and the acquiescence of others, after having noticed that those who became professors because leftist and Jewish colleagues were forced to leave without arousing the disapprobation of their colleagues, who would in the years to come have felt it necessary to think twice before unreservedly bending to any official request? The loss of humanity might sometimes be an individual affair. Most often it is a social process.[29]

Analysis of modern organizations has shown that every social organization, every institute, school, office or workshop has a spirit of its own.[30] Once developed it is transmitted to newcomers, integrating them into a social climate that seems to be quite immune to changes in formal organization and rules. In 1933–34 the Nazi movement was successful not only in formally regulating the activities of social institutions that were allowed to continue functioning, but also in decisively shaking their spirit. Many Christian congregations, especially those of the Catholic church, fostered dissent against the regime. However, after their overwhelming acquiescence with the first measures of anti-Jewish

29 The debate of recent years has furthered the realization that this was the case in the concentration camps and in the *Einsatzgruppen.* There is much more reluctance to accept that the same mechanisms work in the practice of everyday life. See especially: Christopher R. Browning, *Ordinary Men*, New York, 1992. In part this concept of interpretation has also been made use of by Wolfgang Sofsky, *Die Ordnung des Terrors: Das Konzentrationslager*, Frankfurt am Main, 1993. Sofsky, however, fell into the trap of assuming a dynamics of "absolute power," which once set in motion is no longer the outcome of concrete social processes but rather irrationalism set loose.

30 See for example Michel Crozier, *Le phénomene bureaucratique*, Paris, 1964; Michel Crozier and Erhard Friedberg, *L'Acteur et le Systéme*, Paris, 1977, especially Part III; almost all the contributions in Stephen Fineman, ed., *Emotion in Organizations*, London, 1993; A very radical critique of concepts that assume the rationality and total instrumentality of organizations is contained in: Theodor M Bardmann, *Wenn aus Arbeit Abfall wird. Aufbau und Abbau organisatorischer Realitäten*, Frankfurt am Main, 1994.

policy,[31] nothing less than a spiritual revolution could have enabled the church to regain the capacity to develop into a secondary public sphere that could have functioned as something like a collective backing of dissent against anti-Jewish policy.[32] As it was, individuals had to rely on their own faith, morality and courage and on support from close friends.[33]

From autobiographies and from sources produced via oral history we have learned that, at least in the thirties, there were still some schools in Germany whose staff somehow managed to deal with the order of having students greet them with *"Heil Hitler,"* while not demanding the same from Jewish students. In most schools, however, this order was immediately applied to either force Jewish students to conform or to exclude them from the social collective by prohibiting their use of the official greeting.[34] Although Wolfgang Klafki, in his summary of research into the construction of adolescent identity during the Nazi period, stated that children and youngsters prior to reaching puberty were to the greatest extent influenced by their parents, research on the effects of the institutional climate would lead us to assume that the spirit of a school legitimized some forms of behavior

31 There is an extensive literature on the attitudes of the churches. For short summaries see: Ian Kershaw, *Popular Opinion*, pp. 246–247, Kwiet and Eschwege, *Selbstbehauptung*, p. 42; Heinz Hürten, "Selbstbehauptung und Widerstand der katholischen Kirche," in: Schmädeke and Steinbach, *Der Widerstand*, pp. 240–254 and Jochen-Christian Kaiser,"Protestantismus, Diakonie und 'Judenfrage' 1933–1941," *Vierteljahreshefte für Zeitgeschichte,* 37 (1989), pp. 673–714.

32 See: Jonathan Sperber, "Commentary on Christians and Anti-Semitism," *Central European History,* 27 (1994), pp. 349–354. Sperber comments on several contributions to the topic, contained in *Central European History,* 27, Nr. 3.

33 This statement does not contest the interpretation that resistance to the regime, most often developed in a social context that furthered dissent (see for example: Klaus-Michael Mallmann and Gerhard Paul, *Das zersplitterte Nein,* Bonn, 1989, p. 9), but points to the fact that this social context was usually not identical with the formal organizations in which people led their daily lives. For a very fine example of a social analysis of opposition see: Onno Poppinga, Hans Martin Barth and Hiltrud Roth, *Biographien aus dem Widerstand*, Frankfurt am Main, 1977.

34 See for example the contributions of Marcel Reich-Ranicki, Wolf-Dietrich Schnurre and Walter Jens, in: *Meine Schulzeit im Dritten Reich, Erinnerungen deutscher Schriftsteller,* Marcel Reich-Ranicki, ed., Cologne, 1988; Wolfgang Keim, *Erziehung unter der Nazi-Diktatur,* Darmstadt, 1995, vol. I, chapter III.2; Clemens Vollnhals, "Jüdische Selbsthilfe bis 1938," in: Benz, *Die Juden*, pp. 330–338.

while delegitimizing others. Hannah Arendt, Raul Hilberg, Zygmunt Bauman and many others[35] have attempted to show that persecution and mass murder were not dependent on extraordinarily cruel personalities, because these were to a large extent developed and organized in the normal forms of rationalized modern society[36] — and in many respects the Germany of the thirties was an extraordinarily modern society. I still agree with general elements of this interpretation, but we do have to be very clear about the fact that the working of any modern organization is not sufficiently grasped by reference to its formal structures.[37] From organizational analysis we have learned that these function amid a special climate, amid internal and external personal networks. If individuals not considered as fierce haters of Jews drew up lists of so-called non-Aryans and evaluated their property as they would have prepared statistics on dog owners, this was not only because of their compliance to orders but also because the nonofficial public sphere in which they operated did not prevent their indifference to the content of their work. For departments of public services as well as for the representative bodies of towns, which in 1933 and 1934 moved quickly ahead with rules discriminating against Jews,[38] the way

35 Already in 1939 Sebastian Haffner wrote that those who were willing to take a closer look at the perpetrators had to prepare themselves for a surprise because the perpetrators did not fit together with their outrages. Sebastian Haffner, *Germany: Jekyll and Hyde. 1939 — Deutschland von innen betrachtet* (first published in London in 1940), Berlin, 1996, p. 3.

36 Hannah Arendt, *Eichmann in Jerusalem*, New York, 1964, especially chapters II & III; Raul Hilberg, *Die Vernichtung der europäischen Juden*, Berlin, 1982, especially chapter III; Zygmunt Bauman, *Modernity and the Holocaust*, New York, 1989, pp. 25ff and passim; see also Michael Zimmermann, "Eine Deportation nach Auschwitz. Zur Rolle des Banalen bei der Durchsetzung des Monströsen,"in: *Normalität oder Normalisierung?,* Heide Gerstenberger and Dorothea Schmidt, eds., Münster 1987, pp. 84–96; That these structures were also present in France is demonstrated in: Bernd Zielinski, *Staatskollaboration. Vichy und der "Arbeitseinsatz" für das Dritte Reich*, Münster, 1995.

37 The present paper tries to grasp more precisely what I was already aiming at in: Gerstenberger and Schmidt, *Normalität oder Normalisierung?*

38 There are numerous examples for such acts of obedience that had not yet officially been asked for. See for example Geschichtswerkstatt Tübingen, *Zerstörte Hoffnungen, Wege der Tübinger Juden,* Stuttgart, 1995, p. 105 for the decree issued by the city council of Tübingen as early as May 1933 prohibiting individuals of "foreign race" from visiting the public swimming pools. See also Ursula Büttner,

back would have been very long. Bureaucratization and legalization of discrimination and persecution developed in partialized public spheres that as early as 1933 forsook their capacity to foster dissent against the persecution of Jews.

Historians have convincingly demonstrated that the critique of blatant acts of violence, present in secondary public spheres and reported to Nazi leaders, furthered the legalization of persecution. That the existence of critique is well documented does not shake the conclusion that acquiescence with official anti-Jewish policy was imbedded in the secondary public spheres. Neither is this conclusion contradicted by many of the instances of reported and otherwise documented nonconformist behavior. If peasants all over Germany went on to deal with Jewish livestock traders until it was made impossible in 1938, this was because these traders offered better prices and still had the money to make immediate payment. Many of those who continued to buy in Jewish shops seem to have done so for economic reasons.[39] Some, of course, used their shopping practices to manifest dissent and solidarity. Sometimes this even seems to have been the collective practice of a secondary public. In Tübingen the rather poor winegrowers, all of whom lived in the so-called lower town, continued to frequent the textile shop of Leopold Hirsch as long as it remained in existence.[40] This behavior was probably prompted not only by economic considerations but also by a stubborn insistence upon the right to decide for oneself where to buy.

On the whole, the partialized secondary public spheres did not function as legitimizing instances for nonconformist, let alone dissenting

ed. *Die Deutschen und die Judenverfolgung im Dritten Reich*, Hamburg, 1992 (containing: Ursula Büttner, "Die deutsche Gesellschaft und die Judenvernichtung — ein Forschungsproblem," pp. 7–30 as well as: Ursula Büttner, "Die deutsche Bevölkerung und die Judenverfolgung," pp. 67–88); Günter Plum gives examples of boycott against shops before March 1933; See: Günter Plum, "Wirtschaft und Erwerbsleben," in: Benz, *Die Juden*, pp. 273–275.

39 Kershaw, *Popular Opinion*, p. 245; Many instances of nonconformist behavior (i.e., serving Jews, trading with them, taking down antisemitic notices in tourist villages, opposing the closure of a "Jewish shop"), were reported to the Social Democrats in exile. See: Stöver, *Volksgemeinschaft*, pp. 152–253; see especially: Günter Plum, "Wirtschaft und Erwerbsleben," in: Benz, *Die Juden*, pp. 297–313.

40 Geschichtswerkstatt Tübingen, *Zerstörte Hoffnungen*, p. 131.

behavior against anti-Jewish policy. If we still permit ourselves to think that the majority of Germans did not support what Nazis termed the "Final Solution,"[41] it is not easy to refute that a majority would have agreed to a reversal of the emancipation which would have made Jews members of a permanently discriminated minority.[42] When leading Nazi activists decided that any such development was not to be considered an adequate realization of their aims, not only official public opinion but also partially dissenting secondary public opinion had long robbed Jews of the protection accorded to men, women and children perceived as fully belonging to the social collective.

Those who acquiesced in the first anti-Jewish measures did not thereby acquiesce in all the atrocities that were to come. But in refraining from voicing and demonstrating dissent against anti-Jewish measures, at least in the nonformal publics in which they lived their daily life, they preconstituted social conditions for the radicalization of anti-Jewish policy.

Everyday Life and Persecution

This essay is neither about the active proponents of persecution nor about those who actively tried to oppose it, but about those who afterwards felt they could rightfully state that they had not been involved. Seen in the light of research into the functioning of modern

41 See also Stöver, *Volksgemeinschaft*, pp. 262–270, who refutes the interpretation that Hitler and other Nazi leaders were successful in convincing the population that the regime had gone so far in its measures against Jews that there was no way back. For the latter interpretation see Bankier, *Die öffentliche Meinung,* p. 219. In any case, by 1941 the mass of the population had become so insensitive to the fate of Jews that most people did not even want to know what happened to the Jews who had been deported.

42 In one of the memoranda of the SD (dated 24 May 1934) that have recently come to light in Russian archives, it is formulated very clearly that "Jews and Germans" should incessantly be taught that the final goal was the emigration of all Jews living in Germany. The SD thought it necessary that the reduction of Jews to the state of members of a discriminated minority should not be conceived of as being a permanent solution. See: Michael Wildt, ed., *Die Judenpolitik des SD 1935 bis 1938*, Munich, 1995, p. 66.

states in general as well as into the functioning of Nazi government, this conviction has to be refuted. The government of modern societies is not dependent on the active support of the majority of its citizens, but only on the absence of massive open dissent. Those who did not feel compelled to speak up, to offend against regulations, or to refuse compliance with directions of their superiors have therefore to be considered as having been involved.

In a recent publication on the history of consciousness in Germany during the 1930s, Helmut Arntzen stated *"Gleichzeitig sucht sich aber — und mit Erfolg — die Alltagsmentalität zu erhalten",*[43] thereby suggesting that daily practices and structures have a life of their own, that their reproduction under different political regimes should be considered autonomous from the intentions of the people involved. But social practices, be they ever so firmly embedded in the past of a social collective, are not reproduced by any dynamics inherent in themselves but only by the behavior of social actors. Continuation of the usual practices of everyday life did not simply happen, it was the result of collective behavior. In shaping the climate of most informal publics it not only produced the conditions for the governing of the German population, it also provided the legitimation for those who refrained from publicly voicing dissent.

Many of us who grew up in Germany after the end of the Third Reich have time and again asked themselves how they would have behaved. We used to imagine all types of crucial situations in which one would have had to choose between courage and cowardice, humanity or villainy. Those of us who have gone on to study the functioning of National Socialism have since learned that though these crucial situations did occur, the social preconditions for the functioning of the regime and its policies of persecution were produced in rather undramatic forms. When, in 1933, most of the "secondary publics" acquiesced with the first measures of discrimination, their members might have felt they were merely in the process of defending the normal functioning of their daily life. However, when this practice became imbedded in most of the informal publics in which people led their daily life, it also tended to shape the attitudes and behavior of

43 Helmut Arntzen, *Ursprung der Gegenwart. Zur Bewusstseinsgeschichte der Dreissiger Jahre in Deutschland,* Weinheim, 1995, p. 7.

individuals. Attitudes towards the politics of the regime were not a given fact, nor were they simply changed by specific political measures. Instead, they were fostered by the climate in the "secondary publics" to which individuals belonged. It is not possible to know exactly what would have happened had the members of some of the leading institutions and many others not acquiesced in the first measures of anti-Jewish policy, or if the reports on the secondary opinion had sounded differently. This, however, cannot soften the impact of the knowledge that the behavior of Germans gave power to a government that was to organize mass murder. In the midst of persecution the defense of normality becomes political involvement.[44]

44 When critique — especially from members of the Roman Catholic Church — had become public the "euthanasia program" was officially stopped, but it continued secretly and was even intensified. See Ernst Klee, *"Euthanasie" im NS-Staat*, Frankfurt am Main, 1983, Chapters VIII & X. Recently Nathan Stoltzfus argued that the success of the public protest by "non-Aryan" wives against the deportation of their husbands shows what might have been possible had there been more public protest. Nathan Stoltzfus, "Widerstand des Herzens. Der Protest in der Rosenstrasse und die deutsch-jüdische Mischehe," *Geschichte und Gesellschaft,* 21 (1995), pp. 218–247. Although Christof Dipper correctly states that this particular success can only be explained by the very specific political and local conditions within which it occured, [Christof Dipper, "Schwierigkeiten mit der Resistenz," *Geschichte und Gesellschaft,* 22 (1996), pp. 409–416], this should not be seen as a successful refutation of the whole strain of Nathan Stoltzfus' argument. Much more haunting is the thought of what would have happened if not only the members of the court in Breslau but all the judges and lawyers in Germany had gone on strike as soon as the order came through that Jews were no longer to be admitted as judges and lawyers. For the Breslau strike see: Günter Plum, "Wirtschaft und Erwerbsleben," in: Benz, *Die Juden,* p. 285.

The Double Consciousness of the Nazi Mind and Practice

LENI YAHIL

I

In 1962 the Dutch writer Harry Mulisch published a report of the Eichmann Trial. A year later it was published in German as *Strafsache 40/61*[1]. He began his report with a photographic trick under the caption "Eichmann's Two Faces." First he presented the photograph of Eichmann that had been taken on 8 June 1960 shortly after his capture, then divided it up, doubling each half of the face into a complete face, and showed these two new pictures, one beside the other. The effect is riveting. One is the intent face of a man who has made up his mind to carry out his purpose, and in spite of the harsh look in his eyes it is not repelling. The other shows the pleading expression of someone who has lost his way in life and is without orientation. It makes you shudder. Mulisch concludes that the right half shows how Eichmann's deeds affected him, while the left half reflects the man who committed them.[2] Fest observes a similar phenomenon as portrayed by two death masks of Himmler: "One of them shows a face twisted into a grotesque grimace, brutal, curiously impudent. ... The other is an inexpressive, rather calm face with nothing frightening about it."[3] I think that Mulisch (whose father had left Vienna for Holland after World War I) saw deeper than Hannah Arendt. He too saw the "banal" man but he distinguished between the banality of this man's face and

1 Harry Mulisch, *Strafsache 4061, eine Reportage,* Cologne, 1963.

2 Ibid, p. 16

3 Joachim C. Fest, *The Face of the Third Reich, Portraits of Nazi Leadership*, New York, 1970, p. 111.

what lay behind it — the moral devastation wrought by the crimes he committed. (This shall be discussed later.)

My thesis is that the Nazi regime undertook, and to an astonishing degree succeeded, to impose its revolutionary concept on German society. This concept annulled the moral ground on which human society was and — fortunately still — is built and which guides the conscience of the individual as well as the law regulating national and international statute, notwithstanding the differences in theories and politics. In the international realm this fact was recognized and "genocide" was universally declared a crime against humanity.

This declaration separated normal human society from the one the revolutionary Nazi regime implemented in Germany. This process is characterized by a certain phenomenon whereby a "double consciousness" is created in the population at large — one being of the persisting normative structure of the society, and the other of the revolutionary concept of the Nazi regime based on its ideology and expressed in totalitarian and terrorist practices. This split affected the structure of German society as a whole, but mainly found expression in the individuals who belonged to the two opposite and competing currents both in their consciousness and in their activity.

There existed in the modern world, however, a factor that did not conform to the normative structure of human society: antisemitism. The age-old hatred of the Jewish people had changed its motivation according to the political, social, cultural and religious elements that shape the ever-changing character of human society. However, through all the different historical periods, the persistence of the Jewish people's existence seemed to negate the nature of the ever-changing normal human society. Since, in the course of the nineteenth century, this phenomenon's motivation was combined with a racist doctrine, Jew-hatred became the modern antisemitism.[4] Thus, antisemitism was, one might say predestined to serve as the tool to implement the change into a radical, immoral, racist society.

4 I am of the opinion that it is not justified to apply the modern notion of antisemitism to the whole of Jewish history, see my article: "Holocaust and Antisemitism in Historical Perspective" in: *Major Changes within the Jewish People in the Wake of the Holocaust*, Yisrael Gutman, ed., Jerusalem, 1996, pp. 199–241.

Some statements of Hitler hint at this assumption. In his speech to the *Reichstag* on 30 January 1937 celebrating the day of his ascension to power, he prophesied that just as the acknowledgment of the existence of the solar system had changed the basic concepts of the world, National Socialist racial theories would transform the historical consciousness of the past and future of mankind. According to Rauschning, Hitler told him: "I know perfectly well ... that in the scientific sense there is not such a thing as race. ... I as a politician need a conception which permits the order which has hitherto existed on historic bases to be abolished and an entirely new and antihistoric order enforced and given an intellectual basis." But he needed antisemitism not only as an ideological basis for a morality-deprived society, but also as a tactical device. When asked by Rauschning if he thought it was necessary to destroy the Jew, Hitler claimed that otherwise it would be necessary to invent him because "it is necessary to have a tangible enemy, not merely an abstract one."[5]

Hitler was not the only, and perhaps not even the decisive, exponent of the concrete concept of a racial society and the means to implement it. It is to the credit of Ulrich Herbert that, in his voluminous biography of Werner Best, he exposes the historical, social and theoretical sources of the *völkisch* ideology that was conceived by the academically trained intellectuals who formed the highest echelon of Himmler's and Heydrich's SS state. Moreover, it was they who conceived the materialization of the scheme — namely, the organization and implementation, step by step, of the "Final Solution": first segregation and concentration, then expulsion, and finally — wherever the army created the opportunity — the massive extermination of the symbolic enemy, the Jew. The symbolic, even mythical character of the Nazis' murderous antisemitism as the rationale for the fight for racial supremacy became especially clear during the war, which set out to prove Germany's might and mastery. In addition, it was also a tactical and political device to activate, direct, and exploit the all pervasive antisemitism not only as a means to lay hands on the Jews but also to perfect its domination over the subdued or collaborating states. In that respect the vicissitudes in

5 Hermann Rauschning, *Hitler Speaks*, London, 1939, pp. 229, 234.

Germany's relations with the "independent" Slovak State concerning both aspects in dealing with the Jewish question are especially telling.[6]

The cadres of trained perpetrators, ranking from the upper echelon over the *Schreibtischmörder* to those carrying out the orders in the field and moving the millions, were indispensable. The cardinal question is: how was this established, and, even more important, how did people, raised in a normative society turn into mass murderers?

Herbert quotes the characterization given of Otto Ohlendorf by a judge at the Nuremberg Trials, who concluded that the transformation of the university professor into a mass murderer can be explained only by a psychic defect, a split of the personality, what Robert Louis Stevenson described in his book *Dr. Jekyll and Mr. Hyde.*[7] Hannah Arendt, in her book *Eichmann in Jerusalem,* advised the Israeli court on which arguments the judges should have based their death sentence, relating to Eichmann's "inner life" as possibly differing from his deeds. The Israeli court's sentence, however, expressly rejected such a defense argument saying: "...we have found, that the accused acted out of an inner identification with the orders that he was given and out of a fierce will to achieve the criminal objective."[8] Here the consciousness and actions of Eichmann, just as those of Ohlendorf, Best and thousands of others with varying responsibilities, are conceived as one and in conformity with the revolutionary racist regime that these men undertook to establish. There was wholeness in their concept, and their mentality was not in disorder; on the contrary, logic, rationality and intuition directed their activity. Their mind and practice were tied together in pursuing the existentialist goal. It is not a question of psychology but of an existentialist entity, where psychic drives such as ambition, competition, brutality, sadism, craving for riches, sexuality and many more, not to speak of murder, were not inhibited and regulated by

6 The literature on this subject is quite differentiated, and only part of it is mentioned here: Ladislav Lipscher, *Die Juden im Slowakischen Staat 1939–1945*. Munich, 1980, Yehuda Bauer, *Jews for Sale? Nazi-Jewish Negotiations. 1933–1945*, New Haven, 1994.

7 Ulrich Herbert, *Best, Biographische Studien über Radikalismus, Weltanschauung und Vernunft 1903–1989*, Bonn, 1996, p. 14.

8 Hannah Arendt, *Eichmann in Jerusalem, a Report on the Banality of Evil*, New York, 1963, p. 255; *The Trial of Adolf Eichmann, Record of the Proceedings in the District Court of Jerusalem,* Jerusalem, 1994, vol. V, p. 2218.

the accepted rules and statutes of a traditional society. Nor were they guided by moral considerations. Their deeds were not judged according to any moral code of "right" and "wrong." Justification was measured by the yardstick of success or failure in promoting the Nazi racial regime.

There is a story about an SS officer, stationed in Russia, who wrote in a report concerning killings that their deeds could not be used by the outside world as propaganda against Nazi Germany because people would not believe it — and we know that he was right.[9] This man was conscious of the fact that there was a crevasse between the reality which they originated and that of the rest of mankind. They did not conceive of themselves as criminals or consider their atrocities as crimes. They cut themselves off from humanity, while, according to normal human mores, their actions were crimes against humanity, of a nature and scale never seen before. Thus their evil is the flagrant contradiction of normality. Hannah Arendt was taken in by the "banal normality-face" of Eichmann. She did not understand that this face belonged to what may be called "Nazi-normality" of those who identified with the system. She judged him as "banal" in accordance with the standard evaluation of normal society: "The trouble with Eichmann was precisely that so many were like him, and that the many were neither perverted nor sadistic, that they were, and still are terribly and terrifying normal."[10] She had no inkling of the possibility of two normalities — one of the society to which she together with all mankind belonged, and the other which the Nazi regime had put side by side to and even infiltrated into the existing German society with the intention of spreading it all over the world. The Nazi leadership knew, as did that officer, that they stood on different ground and that defeat would result in them being judged by the norms of that human society which Hitler meant to abolish.

The rank and file, however, were not conscious of their unique position. Standing trial after the war, one of the drivers of the gas vans at Chelmno, a man by the name of Laabs, was asked what his reactions were at the time. He gave the rather unusual answer: "One gets used to it after a while. It's like crushing a beetle." But later on he said:

9 Report 13 June 1943, *Nazi Conspiracy and Aggression*, vol I, p. 1001.
10 Hannah Arendt, *Eichmann in Jerusalem,* p. 253.

"If people had only known then what would happen now."[11] These people attained the Nazi normality without recognizing that they had discarded their former normal or banal existence and adopted a new one in its place. Eventually, when they were captured after returning to the original normative society and brought to court, they were surprised, even flabbergasted.

And here lies the crucial question: The Nazis, both leadership and followers, had been raised and continued to conduct their private and social life within the very society they wanted to change. How was that done, how could it be done, and what were the consequences for the society and for the individual? Moreover, how did they create the illusion that made masses of people slip from their original social normality into the delusive Nazi orbit, "getting used to it" without difficulty and accepting it as "normal"? In other words: what eventually turned "ordinary Germans" into "Hitler's willing executioners"?

II

Clearly, I cannot give a complete and comprehensive answer to the riddle. I can only try to sketch the direction of my thinking and indicate some points of my analysis. I assume that the revolutionary process proceeded simultaneously on three levels.

One, the Nazi concept was systematically introduced into the existent society by the performance of novel, exciting, and grandiose rites in public; by creating its own symbols; by tirelessly spreading its theories, convictions and lofty goals; and by using any kind of communication to establish contact with the population of all social strata. This propagandistic activity was complemented by legislation, which did two things: it legitimized the developing Nazi regime and laid the ground for its final racist and authoritarian structure. This target was of special significance in the organization of the young generation and the

11 Quoted in Leni Yahil, *The Holocaust, The Fate of European Jewry 1932–1945*, New York, 1990 (pbk.ed. 1991), p. 703, note 10. The answer was unusual. The question was put to every defendant, but most replied, following the advice of their lawyers, that they had misgivings in order to attain *Befehlsnotstand* as an argument in their favor.

implementation of reform in the educational system. Alongside these measures for constructing a new face to society, the true governmental instruments — namely, the threatening totalitarian police apparatus and the military force — were installed. In the economic sphere the racist aspect was apparent in the attempt to destroy the economic base of Jews through boycotts and explicit "Aryanization" of their property. At the same time, economic activity focused on the preparations for war.

Two, the above is not new and has been described and analyzed extensively ever since National Socialism overpowered the Weimar Republic. However, the process at which I hinted was accompanied by an additional phenomenon, one that evoked less interest and was even less investigated. This is the fact that the German people in general did not change their traditional way of life immediately, but continued, certainly during the thirties but even during the first years of the war, to live as they had always done. The Nazi rulers did not disturb the way of life of the masses; on the contrary, they did much to improve it. They not only overcame unemployment, they improved the situation of the worker and his work conditions, even providing for his recreation under the slogan "Strength through Joy." (Hitler went so far as to promise each worker a Volkswagen, but this never materialized.) The regime opened institutions of higher learning to youngsters who had never dreamed of studying. They built large housing projects, continuing them even during the war, and advertisements called on the people to invest in saving schemes so that they could build their homes after the war. Moreover, the inflow of American culture, including electrical gadgets, that had started during the Weimar period was not stifled but even intensified. American films, swing and jazz were extremely popular, as was the very much advertised *Coca Cola* whose production continued during the war until the shortage of raw material reduced its manufacture. Writers such as Thomas Wolfe, Faulkner and Hemingway had quite an audience, and books like *Gone with the Wind* and *Northwest Passage* became bestsellers. There was even a trend to retain in society a "non-political region," a "sphere free of the State" as part and parcel of the National Socialist regime. This Janus-like phenomenon of two faces of society — one reflecting the traditional way of life, and the other the revolutionary racist scheme — was unified by the Führer. In his personality, Hitler not only represented both, but cast his authority on both, thus belying the inherent contradiction. This unification closed the rift, eliminated moral conflict, and, easing the passage from the one to the other, made it possible to live both ways at one time. Thus the illusion of a harmonious world was created in which a man could be a loving parent to his own children while sending masses of other helpless children to their death, carrying out the orders based on the racist principle of the children-loving Führer. This double consciousness became the order of the day — a new, seemingly natural attitude of the rulers and the ruled. In other words, it became "banal." This Hannah Arendt sensed. But at her time it was probably not yet possible to analyze the double form of the society and the double consciousness it created. She was a sociopsychological philosopher, not a historian. Historical research of the Holocaust was still in its infancy, only beginning to establish the horrifying facts by the use of professional methods. There was virtually no possibility of verifying the roots in an objective manner, let alone clarify basic contradictions. The facts Hannah Arendt learned from Raul Hilberg's pioneering historic work that was published at the time she wrote her book, and she believed it endorsed her understanding. It took twenty years until a German professor of literary history, Hans Dieter Schäfer, published a book in 1981, *Das Gespaltene Bewusstsein, Deutsche Kultur und Lebenswirklichkeit 1933–1945*, that described the controversial reality of German society.[12]

The book is divided into two parts. The first deals with the writing of some young authors and poets who were under the Nazi spell, and relates to the cultural trends, personal utterances, especially in diaries, and literary evidence that reflects the reactions of those writers who remained in Germany and lived in the so-called 'inner emigration' and those who went into exile. The second part describes and analyzes the "split consciousness." Here he accuses the researchers and the media dealing with the Third Reich of identifying the terror system with the comprehensive reality of the Hitler state and of not probing into the very controversial reality. During the years since this book first appeared, much has been done to correct such a simplistic picture of

12 Hans Dieter Schäfer, *Das Gespaltene Bewusstsein, Deutsche Kultur und Lebenswirklichkeit 1933–1945,* Ullstein Sachbuch, Frankfurt/M–Berlin–Wien, February 1984 (new edition).

German society, but it seems to me that the inner contradiction that he points to has not been sufficiently emphasized.

One example of "double consciousness" which I noticed by chance in Victor Klemperer's diary demonstrates this point. On the significant date of 31 March 1933, he notes that he and his wife had gone to watch an American film some days before. There they happened to sit beside a young couple, a soldier, ("almost a boy") and his girl. Following an advertisement for a Jewish-owned firm shown on the screen before the film, they discuss the question of the boycott. The soldier thinks it necessary and right, but the girl objects and claims that in a Jewish store the same merchandise is much cheaper, and she does not accept his argument that the quality is inferior or less reliable than German merchandise. During the newsreel the boy applauds enthusiastically when Hitler and Hindenburg appear, but Klemperer adds: "*Nachher bei dem gänzlich amerikanisch jazzbandischen, stellenweise deutlich jüdelnden Film klatschte er noch begeisterter.*"[13] This minor incident demonstrates that there was no connection between this soldier's emotional affiliation with the Nazi world, including antisemitism, and his otherwise spontaneous positive reaction to such imported elements of modern American culture, certainly not suspecting Jewish influence on it.

Three: of special importance is the third level of the inner controversy, which is perhaps the most significant and telling. On this level the two main structures merge and even contradict each other. Among Hitler's peers it is Himmler who was probably the most aware of the problematic character of the twofold consciousness and the ensuing conflicts. This is evident from his reaction in January 1942, when he realized the extent to which American "swing" had taken hold of German youngsters. Forwarding a document of the *Reichsjugendführer* Axmann dealing with the "swing youth" of Hamburg, he declared in his attached letter:[14] "*Meines Erachtens muss das ganze Übel radikal ausgerottet werden. Ich bin dagegen, dass wir hier nur halbe Massnahmen treffen.*" He goes on to propose detailed instructions:

13 Victor Klemperer, *Ich will Zeugnis ablegen bis zum letzten, Tagebücher 1933–1941*, Berlin, 1995, p. 17.

14 Printed in Detlev Peukert, "Heinrich Himmler und der Swing," *Journal für Geschichte*, 6 (1980), pp. 53–56.

The initiators (*Rädelsführer*), boys and girls, and hostile teachers who support them, are to be incarcerated in a concentration camp. (The existence of special camps for youngsters up to the age of eighteen is here obvious). The treatment has to be especially harsh, starting with beatings and leading to exhausting drill and hard labor for both, boys and girls. Actually the intention was to destroy also the future adult life of those people, one way or the other. Himmler considered this brutal praxis necessary in order to avoid *"ein gefährliches Umsichgreifen dieser anglophylen Tendenz."* This "danger" was very real in his eyes as he had received similar reports from other big cities in Germany. After 1940 the public dancing festivities with hundreds of young participants were forbidden. Goebbels tried to introduce a more restricted type of dancing connected to cultural events and suiting the *völkish* ideology, which his ministry arranged, but the young people moved their swing parties into closed circles that met in private dwellings, using mass-produced grammophone records of jazz music and popular American songs. It did not take long for this oppositional spirit to find its expression in a relaxed personal attitude as well in sexual behavior. But this behavior of mostly middle-class youth remained restricted to these clubs. It was an expression of private needs, and its individualistic character did not turn into a blatant opposition to the regime. The longing for personal freedom did not spread over into the public realm.

Here we have to take into account the power of the regime's terror. At school or as apprentices in a workplace these young people had to behave in conformity with the official attitude, often having to join Nazi youth organizations and activities. We have here a clear case of "double consciousness" — since these youngsters must have been aware of the fact that they lived in two definitely contrary spheres, but most seem to have adjusted themselves quite easily to this situation in spite of the dangers involved.

Much more evident and complicated is the confused behavior of the adult population. For more than fifteen years this issue has been dealt with in Germany, expressed in descriptions and research of local conditions and the behavior of people in their daily life.[15] Using this approach

15 An early analysis of the problem is Detlev Peukert's, *Alltag unterm Nationalsozialismus*, Beiträge zum Widerstand 17, Informationszentrum Berlin, 1981, see note 18.

the researcher tries to describe the regime "from below;" that is, he has to deal with the multifaceted subject of the peoples' reactions to the National Socialist attempt to implement this revolutionary, streamlined system and concept into the traditional society that was politically, culturally, socially and religiously divided. The distinguished professor of public law Carl Schmitt elaborated on the principles of the new government in the first issue of a new publication called *Der deutsche Staat der Gegenwart* (The German State in Present Time) under the title *Staat, Bewegung, Volk,* which was published in December 1933.[16] According to him these three elements are combined in a political unit, which is led by the movement carrying the other two. In this threefold structure the roles are divided between the state representing the fixed political element, the movement being the politically dynamic element, and the people that constitute the *a-political* part (his emphasis). The people, however, have to grow under the protection and in the shadow of the political decision *(So lässt sich ... das Volk als die im Schutz und Schatten der politischen Entscheidungen wachsende unpolitische Seite betrachten*, my emphasis L.Y.).[17] The whole treatise was meant to clarify the new structure of the state as differing from the democratic constitution of the Weimar Republic. However, not by chance does it lack a clear definition of what is meant by the a-political character of the people and how it should grow under the influence of the movement to become the projected unified *Volk*. Relatively simple for him is the statement that the members of the civil service are now part and parcel of both the *Volk* and the Nazi party (the only one that now exists), because of this "organic" structure of the administration under the direction of the political leaders belonging to the movement. But, the decision which case or subject has to be considered a-political depends on the decision of the political leaders. Thus, at least theoretically, no independent aspect of their lives would be left to individuals, groups, or organizations, and — as is especially emphasized — no form of self-government would be allowed. How these directives were handled in practice, we know today quite well. What is important with regard to the problem I have raised is the question, to what extent did people

16 Carl Schmitt, *Staat, Bewegung, Volk, Die Dreiteilung der politischen Einheit*, Hamburg, 1933.

17 Ibid, p. 12.

accommodate to these demands, and if and in what manner did they retain some conscious and practical independence.

Detlev Peukert, relying on the public opinion reports and publications of the Social Democratic party in exile, attests to a deep dissent in the population due to economic hardships and the many instances of National Socialist tampering with the private sphere of people's lives and established habits. Nevertheless, he comes to the conclusion that beneath the superficial criticism, the widespread attitude of the people revealed signs of acquiescence and even of basic consensus. He then proposes the antithesis: "We are confronted by a contradiction that in the same public opinion reports and apparently also in the same population segments the signs of disapproval and approval are mixed in an indifferentiated way" (*die Indizien für Missstimmung und Zustimmung unentwirrbar gemischt sind* — my italics L.Y.).[18] He goes on to explain that the criticism is usually directed against the lower grades among the party officials, while the consensus is tied to the Führer. The "Führer-Myth" was not only the product of Nazi propaganda but also the focus for consensus with the regime. This existential situation the author calls split of consciousness (*Bewusstseinsspaltung*). The consensus included terror acts as –for instance the murder of the SA in the summer of 1934 — or any other violent actions, as long as they guaranteed "law and order," emanated from the state's vital needs, were ordered by the Führer, and implemented by his paladins. Moreover, Peukert emphasizes that even people who belonged to the resistance could not help but acquiesce to a certain degree to the regime's system in order to survive; they were, *nolens volens*, influenced by it because of fear of persecution, their own impotence, and the small compromises they had made in order to survive. The records of Helmuth James von Moltke, Ulrich von Hassell, and others of this circle, not to mention Kurt Gerstein the supplier of killing gas, tell such stories.

18 Peukert, *Alltag*, p. 8f. This sector is based mainly on his treatise, and the respective pages will be given in brackets in the text.

III

As described earlier, Himmler was determined to eradicate the tendency of youngsters who tried to escape the behavioral confines that Nazis prescribed as appropriate. But he was apparently also conscious of a hidden conflict in the SS men between their murderous occupation and their otherwise normal private life in the traditional society and families in which they had been raised. He related to this conflict very clearly in his infamous speech at Poznan. I wish to quote from the English translation of Reitlinger who was, I think, the first who drew attention to it.

> I also want to talk to you quite frankly on a very grave matter. Among ourselves it should be mentioned quite frankly and yet we will never speak of it publicly ... I mean the evacuation of the Jews, the extermination (*Ausrottung*), of the Jewish race. It is one of the things it is easy to talk about. "The Jewish race is exterminated." ... and then they come, eighty million worthy Germans, and each one has his decent Jew. Of course, the others are vermin, but this one is *ein prima Jude*. ... Most of you must know what it means when a hundred corpses are lying side by side or five hundred or a thousand. To have stuck it out and at the same time — apart from exceptions caused by human weakness — *anständig geblieben zu sein*, that is what made us hard. This is a page of glory in our history, which has never been written and is never to be written.[19]

In this short excerpt of his rather long speech before a dozen high-ranking SS and police leaders and more than a hundred additional SS officials, Himmler revealed three of his notions.

(1) To ourselves we have to admit that the task we are carrying out contradicts normal human relationship with other human beings; this can be observed in the approach of any German to any Jew in whom he sees a fellow human being and not a monster that has to be annihilated.

(2) We have to handle two clearly incompatible types of behavior — acting as mass murderers *"und dabei anständig zu bleiben"* and living as normal people in a normal human society.

(3) The way out of this insoluble conflict is that one day [he probably meant after the victory of Germany] there will prevail only the

19 Gerald Reitlinger, *The Final Solution, The Attempt to Exterminate the* Jews *of Europe 1939–1945*, London, 1968, p. 317f.

> one, the National Socialist society, but it will not maintain any record how this was attained.

He concluded by trying to encourage himself and his followers, proclaiming their — of course secret — glory.

Out of this concept he tried — without success however — to cover up the traces of the *"Ausrottung"* and not, as it is mostly supposed (also by Hannah Arendt), out of a guilty conscience and fear of discovery that had been awakened by the defeat.[20] He started with these actions in the summer of 1942 long before defeat was even envisioned. The commander who supervised the gruesome act of exhuming the corpses from the mass graves and destroying them completely was one of the most brutal and notorious officers of the SS, Paul Blobel, who had commanded the massacre at Kiev. Once an architect in the city of Solingen, his rise from a poor socioeconomic background was strengthened by raising a well-situated family. However, at the time of the economic crisis at the end of the 1920s he joined the *NDSAP* and quickly became a forceful member of the SD, from where he was later called to head the Einsatzgruppe 4a. Sentenced to death at the Nuremberg Trials he declared to the court that he could face his wife and children "with a clear conscience."[21] Evidently he belonged to the category of those among Hitler's devoted minions who not only implemented the racist order but identified with it to the degree that they included their family in the system.

Himmler, on the other hand, as much as he was willing to attain this goal even by brutality, nevertheless was, in some instances, unsure where to draw the line between the traditional and the revolutionary practices. In such cases he had recourse to the Führer. Such an instance occurred when he witnessed for the first time the medical experiments performed on human beings in Dachau, and felt the need to ask for Hitler's decision. The answer was in principle when the state interest is concerned the use of human beings in experiments is to be allowed (*"dass grundsätzlich, wenn es um das Staatswohl geht,*

20 Arendt, *Eichmann*, pp. 253f.

21 For more details see Michael Okroy, "Vor 50 Jahren in Nürnberg der Einsatzgruppenprozess und Paul Blobel," *Tribüne, Zeitschrift zum Verständnis des Judentums*, 142 (2. Quartal 1997), pp. 21–32.

der Menschenversuch zuzulassen ist").[22] Since then Himmler was not troubled any more by scruples about the experiments.

The literature about human experiments — undertaken for so-called medical "research" and, of course, "euthanasia" or mercy killing, the fictitious name under which the criminal process of mass murder was perpetrated — provides us with the most instructive material on the phenomenon of the inversion of medical ethics, as formulated in the physician's age-old oath. These doctors, at the same time, treated their patients — in hospitals or in their private practice — in the normal way, making every effort to restore their health and whenever possible save their lives. Thus, they acted on two completely reversed levels. Their behavior exemplifies the clearest case of double consciousness, because they switched — mostly without great difficulty — from the one approach to its contrary, dealing with each in full capability and consciousness. If we describe the ethical aberration of those who implemented the National Socialist ideology as layers of a pyramid whose base is Hitler's command to transform Germany into a racist society, the Nazis' medical establishment is the apex of that pyramid. There are, however, signs that at the beginning the organizers of the "euthanasia" project had some difficulty persuading physicians to take part in this criminal undertaking, and they succeeded only by presenting Hitler's written order turning the criminal act into a "legal" one, based on the Führer's law-setting authority.[23] It is unclear whether the legal argument was the decisive factor or whether there were also moral hesitations. We do know, however, that the cases of leading physicians who protested and excluded themselves from the euthanasia massacre were extremely rare.

The doctors who committed these crimes generally lived in two worlds — acting as intentional murderers, and at the same time leading a "banal" life in normal society in which they established families, raised

22 Alexander Mitscherlich und Fred Mielke (Hrsg.), *Medizin ohne Menschlichkeit*, Heidelberg, 1949, p. 132.

23 This argumentation for the rare fact, that Hitler gave this order in writing is provided by Lothar Gruchmann, "Euthanasie und Justiz im Dritten Reich," *Vierteljahrshefte für Zeitgeschichte*, 20 (1972), p. 271, quoted by Karl A. Schleunes, "Nationalsozialistische Entschlussbildung und die Aktion T4" in: *Der Mord an den Juden im Zweiten Weltkrieg*, Eberhard Jäckel and Jürgen Rohwer, eds., Stuttgart, 1985, p. 75.

children and relaxed with their friends. How did they oscillate so easily between the two tracks? It seems that sometimes they separated them, other times mixed them. One physician, Dr. Friedrich Mennecke, would write letters to his wife before going out to Buchenwald to select victims for euthanasia, telling her what he was eating and how he was spending his free time, but also relating how his work was going. One morning he wrote: *"Auf geht's zum fröhlichen Jagen."*[24] Eventually, the two tracks could not be kept apart and due to pressure Hitler was forced to cancel euthanasia officially, as he had announced it officially (but this time not in writing). However, the action nevertheless proceeded, secretly, as the so-called 'wild euthanasia,' in hidden quarters at his disposal. No longer needed, the official institutional equipment, including machinery and personnel, was transferred to the east to implement the "final solution of the Jewish question."

It seems that even far from German soil the people who were engaged in mass murder needed to assure themselves that there also existed a normal world which they had to adjust to their exceptional deeds for the *"Staatswohl;"* moreover, this was probably the intention and policy of the *RSHA*. One has to ask why they allowed commanding officers and other SS officials to bring along their families, to whom they could return in the evening from the extermination camp, and listen to classical music in a pleasant and comfortable dwelling. How could the wives of ordinary men in the Reserve Police Battalion 101 visit their husbands at the places of their murderous activity. Perhaps it was intended to prevent the men's estrangement from their families and ensure those families' association with the process in the making? The strange behavior of the policemen, which Goldhagen described so vividly, can only be understood on the assumption that the Nazis handled the two parallel but contradictory realities with the intention of bringing them to complete conformity.

How was this achieved and how did the people, ordinary men and women, manage not only to live in a twofold reality but, in order to achieve that, develop a double consciousness — one normal and banal and the other criminal and devoid of morality?

24 quoted in Yahil, *Holocaust*, p. 310

Investigating the phenomenon "Hitler," in his book *Hitler in History,* Eberhard Jäckel juxtaposed him, and the Germans. His analysis starts with a Hitler statement from *Mein Kampf*: "The basic foundation for establishing authority is always popularity." And Jäckel adds: "He immediately qualified that sentence and saw 'in power ... in force' the other principal basis of all authority."[25] Here the Janus head of Hitler's governmental system is already visible. When he established his supreme leadership, he became the only one who ruled over German society as well as over the parallel, partly hidden, sphere of force. He created a strong but very human image of himself. Baby kissing and other popularity-seeking acts as well as deceit and lies are used not only in dictatorial regimes. The difference is that in democratic constitutions the basic evaluations of the ruling and the ruled rest on the same base, while in Hitler's view the people as such were of no consequence. "In general," says Jäckel, "the relationship of the Germans to Hitler rested on deception, conscious deception on his part and self-deception on their part. ... They rewarded his deception with trust."[26] This trust held the double-faceted reality together, but it destroyed the sense of true reality, a fact observed by many who tried to evaluate and analyze the Third Reich, among them also Hannah Arendt. The Führer myth had to replace the confrontation with reality.

Contrary to Carl Schmitt's theoretical statement that the "unpolitical" sphere depends on the leaders' political decisions, Schäfer shows that the authorities were forced to tolerate, through compromise, the public's longing for American "swing" for instance, yet on the other hand resorted to the most drastic measures in order to shape society according to their political intentions. Hence evolved the "split consciousness." The outcome of this complex situation is characterized by Schäfer in his extensive description of the internal dissolution of the German society-structure.[27] Among the very negative consequences, he describes the flight into apathy, petrification, and what he calls *"Wahndenken"* (phantom thinking.) He concludes that this absolute paralysis of the

25 "Hitler and the Germans" in Eberhard Jäckel, *Hitler in History*, University Press of New England, Hanover, 1984, p. 89.

26 Ibid.

27 Schäfer, pp. 188–206, passim; his observations are of interest, his psychoanalytic interpretations doubtful.

capability to confront reality developed mainly during the war, but had its roots in the 1930s.

This hallucinatory concept found expression in different types of behavior and generated specific pragmatic consequences. In the revolutionary sphere, directed by the National Socialist ideology and its racist component, "the solution of the Jewish question" through the annihilation of the Jewish race became the symbolic focus of war victory. The more victory eluded them and the threat of defeat became increasingly real, the more the Nazis clutched at the focal symbol, killing the remaining Jews or sending them on death marches. Hitler himself passed on to posterity the symbol of racist victory in his testament before admitting defeat by suicide.

In this rather short sketch of the problem of double consciousness that developed in German society under the Nazi regime, I have tried to indicate some principal viewpoints but also to hint at the immense variety in the behavior of individuals and specific groups of the population. It became clear, however, that this behavior was not unified, moreover it underwent serious changes and developments in the course of the twelve years both in the general population and inside the Nazi cadres. Many questions remain unanswered, and some were not even touched upon.

The Mixed Marriage: A Guarantee of Survival or a Reflection of German Society during the Nazi Regime?

BEATE MEYER

Until emancipation of the Jews in the mid-nineteenth century and the introduction of civil marriage, marriage between Christians and Jews was prohibited.[1] In the twentieth century, the number of mixed marriages increased considerably — a sign not only of the assimilation of Jews, but also of the declining significance of religion in marriage. The city of Hamburg, whose example will be used in this essay to illustrate the interplay of external pressure and internal breakdown of mixed marriages during the Nazi regime, provides as early as the 1920s the most "unfavorable picture" from the Jewish point of view — in other words, the most mixed marriages —followed by Berlin and Breslau.[2] By 1933 the percentage of mixed marriages in the Hanseatic city had risen to more than 57 percent of all Jewish weddings. Whereas the average in Germany fell to 15 percent in 1934[3], the numbers dropped in Hamburg to only 32 percent despite restrictive measures introduced by the registry offices.[4] When the Nazis came to power,

1 The increase of mixed marriages until 1933: Kerstin Meiring, *Zwischen zwei Welten: Studien zur christlich-jüdischen Mischehe in Deutschland, vom 19. Jahrhundert bis zum Ende der Weimarer Republik*, Ph.D. Dissertation, University of Bielefeld, 1995, p. 123ff.

2 *Zeitschrift für Demographie und Statistik der Juden*, 3–4 (1924), p. 79.

3 Jeremy Noakes, "The Development of Nazi Policy toward the German-Jewish 'Mischlinge' 1933–1945," *Leo Baeck Institute Year Book,* 34 (1989), p. 291.

4 Baruch Zwi Ophir, "Zur Geschichte der Hamburger Juden 1919–1939," in: *Juden in Preussen — Juden in Hamburg*, Peter Freimark, ed., Hamburg, 1983, pp. 89ff.

there were approximately thirty-five thousand couples living in mixed marriages in Germany.[5] This development had been causing the Jewish communities in the cities much concern since it generally meant that the next generations were lost to the community.[6] The ban on mixed marriages laid down by the Nuremberg Laws finally put an end to a development that had been prevalent for almost eighty years.

Far more Jewish men than women married non-Jewish partners. Those Jews living in mixed marriages were more likely to have come from long-established Hamburg families than from among Jewish immigrants from Eastern Europe, who as a rule still had stronger ties to their religion.[7] Jewish women living in mixed marriages were no longer recognized as members of the Jewish community; Jewish men, on the other hand, were only excluded from Orthodox associations but were allowed to remain in the community.[8] The mixed marriage very often led to conversion to Christianity, and in Hamburg conversion was usually to the Protestant Church. By 1940, when emigration was no longer possible and the mounting pressure against Jews, accompanied by the destruction of their economic existence, had already led to a sharp rise in the divorces rate, 972 couples were living in mixed marriages — 623 with Jewish men and 349 with Jewish women.[9]

5 Ursula Büttner, *Die Not der Juden teilen*, Hamburg, 1988, p. 14. In 1939 it was estimated that there were between 20,000 and 30,000 mixed marriages in the areas of Germany and the Protectorate of Bohemia and Moravia (see Bruno Blau, "Die Mischehe im Nazireich,"*Judaica* 4/48, p. 48; and Eberhard Röhm, Jörg Thierfelder, *Juden-Christen-Deutsche*, Stuttgart, 1995, vol. 3/II, 1938–41, p. 112.)

6 Arthur Ruppin, "Die Verbreitung der Mischehe unter den Juden," *Zeitschrift für Demographie und Statistik der Juden,* 4 (1930), p. 58.

7 Dora Weigert, "Die jüdische Bevölkerung in Hamburg," *Zeitschrift für Demographie und Statistik der Juden,* 5–7 (1919), pp. 66–112.

8 Ina S. Lorenz, "Das 'Hamburger System' als Organisationsmodell einer jüdischen Grossgemeinde. Konzeption und Wirklichkeit," in: *Jüdische Gemeinden und Organisationsformen von der Antike bis zur Gegenwart*, Robert Jütte and Abraham P. Kustermann, eds., Vienna, pp. 221–255. The exclusion of women later meant that they could not be included as members of the religious society in the compulsory organization *Reichsvereinigung der Juden in Deutschland (RVJD)* until 1943. They were protected because they had changed their names and addresses and were much more difficult to trace than the men.

9 Leo Lippmann, *"...'Dass ich wie ein guter Deutscher empfinde und handele.' Zur Geschichte der Deutsch-Israelitischen Gemeinde in Hamburg in der Zeit vom*

The term "mixed marriage" now no longer referred to marriages between members of the Jewish community and non-Jews, but, according to the National Socialists, to relationships in which one partner fitted their "racial" definition of a Jew. From a National Socialist viewpoint, Jews who had entered into a marriage with *"Deutschblütige"* (German-blooded), were even more undesirable than other Jews, as they posed a direct threat to the *"deutschen Blutsverband."* Accordingly, any future mixed marriage should be forbidden in order to prevent *"Blutmischung"* (The mixing of blood), and the effects on the *"deutschen Blutsverband,"* should as far as possible be made undone. This is why specialists of "racial science" were so eager to know where a couple had originally come from, and on what grounds they had entered into a mixed marriage. In 1937, one of the leading racial-hygienists, Otmar Frhr. v. Verschuer, publicly posed the question: "What kind of people were they, on both the German and the Jewish side, who entered into mixed marriages?"[10] Statistics had long shown that wealthy Jewish men married non-Jewish women who were "often below their rank."[11] Verschuer's question led to the first large-scale investigation on the subject, which was carried out by the anthropologist Alexander Paul.[12] He had documents on 1,115 male and 670 female Jews that the Reich Ministry of the Interior had put at his disposal.[13] Paul, a convinced racial-hygienist, investigated the class that

Herbst 1935 bis zum Ende 1942," Finanzbehörde Hamburg, ed., Hamburg, 1993, p. 41.

10 Otmar Freiherr von Verschuer, "Was kann der Historiker, der Genealoge und der Statistiker zur Erforschung des biologischen Problems der Judenfrage beitragen?," in *Forschungen zur Judenfrage,* vol. II, Sitzungsberichte der zweiten Arbeitstagung der Forschungsabteilung Judenfrage des Reichsinstituts für Geschichte des neuen Deutschlands vom 12. bis 14. Mai 1937, Hamburg, 1937, p. 219.

11 Dora Weigert, "Die jüdische Bevölkerung in Hamburg,"*Zeitschrift für Demographie und Statistik der Juden,* 5–7 (1919), p. 85. See also Meiring, *Welten*, p. 228ff.

12 Alexander Paul, *Jüdisch-deutsche Blutsmischung. Eine sozialbiologische Untersuchung*, Berlin, 1940.

13 These family documents were probably attached to applications for marriage permits submitted by "*Mischlingen ersten Grades*" (persons with one Jewish parent), who had hoped to be allowed to marry "German-blooded" partners with the permission of *Reichsausschuss zum Schutze des deutschen Blutes* ("Reich Committee for the Protection of German Blood").

the prospective couple belonged to, as well as the allegedly hereditary diseases. Although his study is unacceptable because of its racist, pseudoscientific character[14] and the proposed political consequences of exclusion of the offspring, it is very precise and subtle with respect to the social classes of the mixed marriages. In short, he reached the conclusion that Jewish men who entered into a mixed marriage came, as a rule, from the upper or upper middle classes (mostly from the merchant class), and generally married much younger women of a lower social status. While a mixed marriage offered male Jews the opportunity of integration into non-Jewish society, the attraction of marrying a Jew for non-Jewish women was that it meant a step up the social ladder. On the other hand, when Jewish women married non-Jewish men (on the whole this was less common), both man and woman usually came from the same social background and there was no great difference in their ages. Although both partners in the marriage came from a higher class, the marriage seldom meant social advancement for the Jewish woman. It seems that Jewish women chose non-Jewish partners more for emotional than materialistic reasons.

Even if the motivating force for entering into a mixed marriage did not influence to any considerable extent every decision made in married life, it was given a new relevance after the National Socialists came to power, since the measures taken against the Jews, especially the destruction of their economic existence, had just as much effect on Jews in mixed marriages as on other Jews. In the first five years of the Nazi regime, precisely those marriages contracted for materialistic reasons broke up very quickly, although the divorce rates from this period are not known.

A woman living at that time recollected in an interview[15] the break-up

14 The terms that Paul uses in his investigation indicate his convictions as an advocate of the pseudo-science of racial theory and racial hygiene; for example, *Kaufmannssippen* ("merchant tribes"), *Juwelierssippen* ("jeweler tribes"), etc. He pleads for a comprehensive model for the exclusion of the offspring from the German community. Because of the rigidity of this model it was not carried out.

15 All interviews quoted were compiled and archived (FZH/WdE), as part of the project *Hamburger Lebensläufe — Werkstatt der Erinnerung* in the *Forschungsstelle für die Geschichte des Nationalsozialismus in Hamburg* (now: *Forschungsstelle für Zeitgeschichte*). The names given are aliases. FZH/WdE 009, Interview with Irene Heuermann (9 June 1988).

of such a marriage. When her parents married her mother converted to Judaism (this was more an exception than the rule). Her father, a wealthy merchant, supported his wife's relatives for some years and provided a comfortable life for his family. Severe anti-Jewish measures, however, brought about a serious decline in his business. Her mother's relatives suggested clubbing together to buy a sewing machine so that the mother could take in work and earn enough money to feed the family. She vehemently rejected the proposition: "How could I stoop to that!" Her husband's arrest during *Kristallnacht* and subsequent internment in KZ Sachsenhausen clearly indicated to her that he would be stigmatized as a criminal in addition to the decline in social status that he had already experienced. Both strengthened her in her resolution to seek a way out of a marriage whose material foundation had crumbled. She filed a petition for divorce while her husband was making emigration plans. Through obtaining the divorce and leaving the Jewish religious community, she was able to return to her *deutschen Blutsverband.*

This "offer" to the "German-blooded" women was included in categories of "privileged" and "non-privileged" mixed marriages that were formulated by Hitler in the winter of 1938 and promulgated by Göring.[16] The intention was to lure these women into divorces while they were still reeling under the shock of *Kristallnacht* and "Aryanization." Even if the majority of "German-blooded" women did not choose to take advantage of this "offer," the repressive atmosphere had a destabilizing effect on mixed marriages. Thus, the roles played by the individual members of a family underwent a change during the first five years of the Nazi regime. Jewish husbands were scarcely in a position to play their traditional male role of breadwinner, and most of them were no longer able to represent the family in public. They were obliged to sign over their assets to their wives or children, entrust them with the daily running of their companies, let them deal with the authorities, burden them with negotiations concerning rent and/or visas, etc. The wives, as a rule, were ill-prepared to take on these tasks,[17]

16 Bundesarchiv (BA), Reichsministerium des Innern 5519 (343–345), Letter (Geheimer Schnellbrief), of Göring, to the Minister of the Interior and others, 28 December 1938.

17 The 60 interviews conducted by the author in which *Mischlinge ersten Grades*

as their upbringing and married life until then had been dictated by the traditional male and female roles. If they wanted to earn money, they were obliged to resort to "a woman's capabilities," like sewing for example, which meant it was impossible to maintain their previous standard of living. A man living at that time describes how this change affected family life:

> Yes, but there were many ..., you couldn't call them "quarrels." The family's morale was steadily broken. Although my father was very authoritarian, he was not a strong man ..., he was otherwise mild, gentle, especially with children. And anyway, my mother didn't understand anything about such things [earning money, B.M.]. Of course, she stood by my father. There was no question about it. Nevertheless, the pressure from outside — the pressure on those people who had to live under such circumstances — made family life difficult. One wrong word led to a quarrel ... The relationship between my parents was no longer as peaceful as it used to be. We were short of money and then finally we were short of food. Eventually my father no longer received full rations, which meant we had even less food.... There was a lot of unrest which actually had nothing to do with my parents. It was a result of the pressure from outside.[18]

The Jewish husbands found it difficult to come to terms with the loss of their position and reputation in society; their wives had to provide them with the emotional support they needed, especially when they were plagued by depression and thoughts of suicide.[19] Another person interviewed summarized the effect that the drop in status had on her family: "My father was always very depressive; he constantly thought about suicide and kept on saying if it weren't for him, if he were out of the way, then it would be easier for all of us. Of course, we all suffered under these circumstances because we always wanted to cheer him up and unfortunately we weren't very successful."[20] In many families, it was left to the wives alone to earn the money as well as to come to terms emotionally with the pressure from outside; they, in turn, tried to share this responsibility with their adolescent children.

talk about their personal experiences reveal that only about 10% of the non-Jewish mothers were employed before 1933.

18 FZH/WdE 052, Interview with Dennis Berend (5 May 1993), Transcript, p. 7.

19 Dissertation of the author on "*Jüdische Mischlinge*," Hamburg, 1999.

20 FZH/WdE 010V, Interview with Hermann Iversen (21 May 1990), Transcript, p. 8.

If, on the other hand, the wife was Jewish, her husband's professional status determined to what extent racial discrimination affected their life. In the civil service, racial discrimination was particularly severe and either prevented the husband from being promoted or even brought about his dismissal. This could well mean hard times for the family. Someone who was self-employed, however, was neither forced to give up his business nor was his Jewish wife affected by such dramatic events as *Kristallnacht*, but was "merely" subject to social discrimination.

In the winter of 1938, as already mentioned, Hitler classified mixed marriages as either "privileged" or "non-privileged."[21] "Privileged" meant that for the time being a family was allowed to stay where they had been living, and that the family property could be transferred to the non-Jewish partner or the children. "Privileged" was either a marriage without children where the wife was Jewish, or a marriage in which the husband was Jewish and their children had not had a Jewish upbringing. If, however, the husband was Jewish and there were no children, if the non-Jewish wife had been converted or if the children had been brought up in the Jewish faith, then the marriage was "non-privileged." The married couple lost not only the right of residence in non-Jewish districts and power over the family property, but in addition were treated like Jews who were emigrating; in other words, they lost both their citizenship and their property. Jews living in "privileged" mixed marriages were exempt from wearing the yellow badge.[22] When the *Sicherungsanordnung für Vermögen* (blocking of accounts), was revised according to the status: In the case of the husband being Jewish, his assets and those of his wife and their non-Jewish children were "saved" by the state of Germany. However, in the case

21 The term "privilege" is not used by Göring, he acquired the administrative jargon to define the exceptions for certain mixed marriages.

22 "Polizeiverordnung über die Kennzeichnung der Juden" from 1 September 1941, §3; Hilberg adds that Jews who were married to *Mischlinge* were also regarded as having "privileged" marriages. See Raul Hilberg, *Die Vernichtung der europäischen Juden,* Frankfurt, 1990, vol. II, p. 445f. "Privileged" mixed marriages could only be the result of one's biological and not adopted children. Staatsarchiv Hamburg (StaHH), Jüdische Gemeinden, Abl. 1993, Ordner 20, Letter of *RVJD* Berlin to *RVJD* Hamburg, 7 May 1940.

of the wife being Jewish, the *Sicherungsanordnung* affected only her.[23] If an exception had been made and the "German-blooded" husbands in mixed marriages were allowed to stay in the Wehrmacht,[24] their wives were exempt from forced labor,[25] which they were initially summoned to (as were all Jews), at the beginning of 1939.[26]

The government granted such "privileges" in order to placate the "German-blooded" relatives as the measures taken against the Jewish population were becoming more and more radical. The categories of "privileged" and "non-privileged" mixed marriage were never legally protected, but for each measure taken against the Jews this status allowed exceptions to be made.

While the Jewish men in mixed marriages had to be in constant touch with the *Reichsvereinigung der Juden in Deutschland (RVJD)*, because of their status, Jewish women were to a great extent protected by their "German-blooded" husbands. These husbands, however, after their wives had been obliged to do forced labor, found that their role as protectors was gradually dwindling. In 1940/41 discussions took place in Hamburg's Jewish community about the critical financial situation. The topic of the discussions was whether or not to regard Jewish women living in mixed marriages as members of the community (again). However, it was not possible simply to dispense with the religious principles that had led to their expulsion. Moreover, attempts to induce these women to pay the membership fees met with little,

23 StaHH, Oberfinanzpräsident 10 (Devisen- und Vermögensstelle), Enactment (Allgemeiner Erlass No. 23/40 D.St.), of the Reichswirtschaftsminister to the Oberfinanzpräsidenten, 9 February 1940, p. 1.

24 The "German-blooded" husbands of 25,000 Jewish and "half Jewish" women were discharged from the Wehrmacht on 8 April 1940. See Noakes, "Development," p. 331.

25 Paul Sauer, *Dokumente über die Verfolgung der jüdischen Bürger in Baden-Württemberg durch das nationalsozialistische Regime 1933–1945* , Stuttgart, 1966, vol. II, p. 374. For further special regulations see Büttner, *Not*, p. 44ff.

26 Letter of the Präsident der Reichsanstalt für Arbeitsverwaltung und Arbeitslosenversicherung to the Präsidenten der Landesarbeitsämter a.o., 20 December 1938, in: Dieter Maier, *Arbeitseinsatz und Deportation. Die Mitwirkung der Arbeitsverwaltung bei der nationalsozialistischen Judenverfolgung in den Jahren 1938–1945*, Berlin, 1994, p. 30f.

if any success. Consequently, the plan was shelved.[27] In 1942 those people living in mixed marriages who were members of the *Jüdischen Religionsverband* (religious association), and in 1943 the remaining people who were — according to Nazi definition — Jewish, were forced to join the *RVJD*.[28]

Until early 1945, those Jews living in "privileged" mixed marriages had been exempted from the deportations that began in October 1941; the deportation of those living in "non-privileged" marriages was deferred initially, unless either divorce or the death of the "Aryan" partner had ended the marriage. In this case, other reasons had to be found for deferring the deportation; one reason often used was that the son was on active military service, another was that the child was still a minor. Since decrees were issued that prohibited *Mischlinge* from serving in the armed forces after 1941/42, this excuse often served the purpose of drawing attention to the son, with the result that, after his discharge from the Wehrmacht, his mother was deported.[29] Even after divorce, Jewish women were still to a certain extent protected if they had young children who had not had a Jewish upbringing. The age at which a child ceased to be a protection for his mother was lowered from eighteen to sixteen years.[30]

In 1942, the participants at the Wannsee Conference and subsequent conferences discussed the future fate of the *Mischlinge* and the twenty-eight thousand mixed marriages in the area of Germany and the Protectorate of Bohemia and Moravia.[31] They considered the possibility

27 StaHH, Jüdische Gemeinden, Beiakte zu C 6 (Mischehen), note Löffler to Lippmann, 10 March 1941, pp. 4–7. The author would like to express her thanks to Dr. Ina S. Lorenz for this information.

28 Büttner, *Not*, p. 45 und StaHH, Senatskanzlei, Hans Martin Corten, *Bericht über die Organisationen der Juden in Hamburg vor und nach dem Waffenstillstand,* undated report (probably winter 1945).

29 In the case of the son being granted an exemption and remaining in the *Wehrmacht*, according to a "*Führerentscheid*" (decision by the "Führer"), the "privilege" still held if the only son died a *Heldentod* (hero's death), in the war. BA, Reichsjustizministerium 455, Letter of Lammers, to the Minister of the Interior, 4 March 1941.

30 Lippmann, *Geschichte*, p. 92.

31 Hilberg, *Vernichtung,* p. 436. Report of the Wannsee Conference on 20 January 1942, written by Adolf Eichmann according to instructions form Reinhard Heydrich,

of compulsory divorce,[32] and in the event that the "German-blooded" partner refused, whether he should also be sent to a ghetto.[33]Since there was resistance from the Ministry of the Interior to the idea of a deportation without a divorce, and the Ministry of Justice was opposed to compulsory divorce,[34] a final decision was not reached. Hitler was asked to find a solution, but he postponed making a decision until after the war. The majority of people in mixed marriages owe their lives to the fact that this decision was deferred. Nevertheless, even without compulsory divorce and deportation, the chances of survival for individuals or small groups lessened in the face of the Gestapo's activities.

Yet, when the Gestapo arrested Jews living in mixed marriages in Berlin in February 1943 as part of the *Fabrik-Aktion,* the public protests by the "German-blooded" wives and other relatives apparently were successful. This has been given considerable attention by postwar researchers.[35] The people concerned soon came to the conclusion that the Gestapo was intent on gradually including "privileged" mixed marriages in the deportations. In reality, this action was an attempt by the Gestapo to radicalize anti-Jewish policy and they simply employed methods of public raids that were quite routine in the East.[36] Moreover, there was an unusually large number of people from the world of art and letters among those arrested, which caused an uproar and united the women in their protest. In addition, the arrests only served the purpose of registration and not deportation — a fact that came to light

published in Kurt Pätzold and Erika Schwarz, *Tagesordnung: Judenmord. Die Wannsee-Konferenz am 30. Januar 1942*, Berlin, 1992, pp. 108f.

32 Report "Besprechung über die Endlösung der Judenfrage" on 6 March 1942 in Pätzold and Schwarz, *Judenmord,* p. 111 and p. 118.

33 Letter of Staatssekretär im Reichsjustizministerium Franz Schlegelberger to the participants of the Wannsee Conference from 5 April 1942, in Pätzold and Schwarz, *Judenmord*, p. 126f.

34 Uwe D. Adam, *Judenpolitik im Dritten Reich,* Düsseldorf, 1972, p. 325.

35 Kwiet assumes, for example, "that similar actions could have changed the course of National Socialist policy as regards the Jews." Konrad Kwiet, "Nach dem Pogrom: Stufen der Ausgrenzung," in: *Die Juden in Deutschland 1933–1945*, Wolfgang Benz, ed., Munich, 1988, p. 594.

36 Christof Dipper, "Schwierigkeiten mit der Resistenz,"*Geschichte und Gesellschaft*, 22 (1996), pp. 409–416.

upon new investigations. Indeed, the result was fully acceptable to the state.[37]

In Hamburg and elsewhere,[38] however, the Gestapo adopted a less dramatic approach that could be adapted to each individual case. The men were sometimes required to report to the Gestapo, while others were picked up less conspicuously. The action stretched over a period of some days and primarily affected men who had formerly been self-employed and who were fairly well known but not linked with influential groups. According to reports made by the wives and children, the women in Hamburg tried everything to get their husbands released, but their attempts were unsuccessful. There were not enough of them, they were not united and they let themselves be intimidated. "Your husband is being sent to Auschwitz, just pretend that you haven't got a husband any more," was the reply that one wife was given by the man responsible when she asked for help. He advised another woman not to bother any more because her husband was not going to come back — nobody ever returned from Auschwitz. He had already made the note "Auschwitz" on his file cards.[39] The people arrested were taken to Hamburg's police prison in late March 1943, and around the end of April or beginning of May 1943[40] were sent to Auschwitz where they were murdered.[41] For the Gestapo the action was a double success:

37 Wolf Gruner, *Der Geschlossene Arbeitseinsatz deutscher Juden,* Berlin, 1997, p. 319.

38 Ibid., p. 317. Gruner refers to arrests at work and following a summons from the Gestapo in Berlin, Breslau and Dresden. Dipper refers to simultaneous arrests in Darmstadt, which did not lead to a public protest either (see Dipper, "Schwierigkeiten," p. 411). The authorities carried out the arrests of 12 Jewish husbands in "privileged" mixed marriages during the period March to May 1943. The person responsible was supposed to have received the information from his superiors that, according to a new directive against Jewish partners in mixed marriages, unlimited internment could be applied for. He was sentenced after the war, just like the person responsible in Hamburg. See Urteil 2a Ks 1/49, appearing in Irene Sage-Grande et al., eds, *Justiz und NS-Verbrechen. Sammlung deutscher Strafurteile wegen nationalsozialistischer Tötungsverbrechen 1945–1966*, Amsterdam, 1981, vol. 22, pp. 658–682.

39 FZH, Sign. 12 S, Urteil des Landgerichts Hamburg (50), 35/50 14 Ks 56/50, pp. 8–11.

40 FZH, Sign. 35363, Zu- u. Abgangslisten des KL Fuhlsbttel, 31. December 1942 to 8 May 1943.

41 Only one prisoner was able to escape since he was working outside.

those people who until then had been protected were seized for the first time, and it intimidated those mixed-marriage families that had not been affected by the arrests.

If Jewish husbands had been interned, extra pressure was put on the wives to obtain a divorce. In certain cases the Gestapo fixed a deportation date irrespective of the divorce plans.[42] The "legal position" was that deportation had precedence over a prison sentence or custody, with the result that the prisoners were transferred to Auschwitz.[43] This increased the pressure on the wives to file petitions for divorce. In many cases they were also persuaded by relatives who were anxious about their own careers, privileges or political ambitions.

The housing policy of the Nazis constituted an additional form of pressure on mixed marriages. By mid-April 1942, not only Jewish married couples but also couples living in "non-privileged" mixed marriages had been assigned to *Judenhäuser*. This also applied to "Aryan" wives who now found themselves in cramped quarters in blocks marked with the Star of David.[44] The housing situation deteriorated even further following the air raids on Hamburg in the summer of 1943, when the Gestapo demanded that more houses be vacated. The *RVJD,* which was responsible for carrying out these orders, sent notices to those homes that had been rented by Jewish husbands. As regards those mixed-marriage families whose houses had been bombed, the *RVJD* found them accommodation with other mixed-marriage families,[45] where families were segregated according to the sex of the Jewish partner. This meant that the rooms in which those families with Jewish husbands lived became overcrowded — and what was more, they could be given notice to vacate their accommodation by the *Amt für Raumbewirtschaft* (administration of living space), or on the Gestapo's orders at any time. This was much more difficult if the rooms in

42 For example, the court decisions 5 U 82/1942, 3 b R 234/1941, p. 5f can be found in the archives of the Hamburg District Court (ALH).

43 Jews who were to be "evacuated" (deported), were to have the execution of their sentence suspended, and if they were in custody they were not to be charged, except if the death penalty was expected. BA, Reichsjustizministerium 1238, Letter of the Minister of Justice to the Attorney General, a.o., 16 April 1942.

44 StaHH, Jüdische Gemeinden, Rutschbahn 25, UA 27–45.

45 StaHH, Jüdische Gemeinden, Abl. 1993, Ordner 26, Max Plaut, report of the discussion, 4 October 1943.

which the mixed-marriage family lived were rented by or belonged to a "German-blooded" man. The situation did not deteriorate further until October 1944 when the "German-blooded" husbands also had to do forced labor.

Every new measure against the Jewish population — and even more so, every arrest — confronted the "German-blooded" wife once more with the question whether or not she should accept the "offer" of a divorce with all its privileges of a "member of the German people" with full rights or continue to bear the growing repression. Taking one Hamburg family as an example, Ursula Büttner describes vividly the difficult conditions under which most of these marriages were kept intact.[46]

My article sets out to examine the minority of mixed marriages that broke up because of external pressure and internal disintegration. To this end, 130 decisions on divorces made by the Hamburg District Court from 1937 to 1945 were analyzed.[47] Most researchers have estimated the divorce rate among mixed marriages to be at a level of 7–10 percent,[48] these divorces were not categorized according to sex.[49] However, this estimate takes into account only those divorce proceedings that began in late 1941 and were completed in 1942. More than one-third of the court decisions made in Hamburg are dated between 1942 and 1945. In my opinion, the estimated number of divorces involving mixed marriages should be revised upwards to over 20 percent.[50]

From a National Socialist viewpoint, a married couples' first duty was to serve the "national community" and secure its continued existence

46 Büttner, *Not*.

47 The 130 decisions analyzed here were random samples and were found with the help of index entries in the archives of the Hamburg District Court (ALH); they are however not identical to the unknown number of mixed marriages in Hamburg that ended either in divorce or annulment.

48 Büttner refers to 7.2% (97), mixed marriages that were divorced in Baden-Württemberg and 9.9% (123), in Hamburg. See Bttner, *Not*, p. 298.

49 The general divorce rate in Germany in 1939 was 38.3 (per 10,000 marriages), which dropped to 30 per 10,000 marriages in 1940. See Dirk Blasius, *Ehescheidung in Deutschland*, Göttingen, 1987, p. 211. The divorce rate for mixed marriages was at a similar level per 1,000 marriages (see Table 1).

50 Unfortunately, since figures from Berlin, Breslau or Frankfurt do not exist, we cannot compare the divorce rate.

with respect to "purity of blood" and race.[51] This was contained in the new Marriage Law of 6 July 1938, although some concessions were made to those conservatives who still believed in the indissoluble bond of matrimony and privacy of married life. National Socialist judges had already created a new situation *de facto* by reinterpreting existing laws in the years between 1933 and 1938. They had defined the belonging to the Jewish race as a *personal* characteristic, the effect or significance of which would be explained to Germans when the National Socialists seized power.[52] Those who had been "enlightened" in this way should be entitled to demand an annulment within a certain period. This interpretation of the law produced a new legal reality that was incorporated in the Marriage Law of 6 July 1938. At the same time as this radicalization *de facto* was taking place, the members of the Academy for German Law were working on fundamental changes in the German legal system. The main issue was the introduction of the principle of irretrievable breakdown which was to replace the question of culpability. The hard-line racists defined marriage as "a long-term relationship between two persons who are of healthy blood, of the same race and of opposite sex, for the purpose of preserving and promoting the common good ... and for the purpose of procreating racially equal children of healthy blood and for the purpose of rearing them to be diligent *Volksgenossen*."[53] In the case of a childless marriage, the couple should obtain a divorce in order to enter into another marriage for the purpose of having children. In reality though, after protracted discussions the final law was a middle-of-the-road compromise in accordance with Hitler's own wishes. The new Marriage Law combined the principle of irretrievable breakdown with the question of culpability. That is, in cases of adultery, refusal to procreate, and other serious

51 Gabriele Czarnowski, "Der Wert der Ehe für die Volksgemeinschaft. Frauen und Männer in der nationalsozialistischen Ehepolitik," in: *Zwischen Karriere und Verfolgung. Handlungsräume von Frauen im nationalsozialistischen Deutschland*, Kirsten Heinsohn et al., eds., Frankfurt am Main, 1997, pp. 78–95.

52 Hans Wrobel, "Die Anfechtung der Rassenmischehe," *Kritische Justiz,* 16 (1983), pp. 354ff. Ingo Müller also provides a general overview , *Furchtbare Juristen*, Munich, 1987, pp. 97–105. Marius Hetzel, *Die Anfechtung der Rassenmischehe in den Jahren 1933–1939,* Tübingen, 1997.

53 Friedrich Mössmer, chairman of the committee, quoted according to Blasius, *Ehescheidung*, p. 195.

marital offenses, the question of culpability still applied. One of the new provisions was the "dissolution of the household" on the grounds of an irretrievable breakdown, which was possible after three years of separation. These rules applied to all couples seeking divorce. In addition, the government created another possibility for couples in mixed marriages to annul the mixed marriage — and by doing so, the judges continued their application of the principle that the non-Jewish spouse was not enlightened on the effects of the "racial difference." Those "German-blooded" partners who wanted a divorce (primarily non-Jewish wives), could now have their marriages annulled on "racial grounds" without having to prove the partner's neglect of marital duties or a breakdown of the marriage. The period within which they could file for annulment was one year; in other words, it would have expired in 1939. The judges, however, always found new reasons in the subsequent years for extending the period. They accepted that the non-Jewish partner had not understood the consequences of the "difference in races" until the arrests of *Kristallnacht*, the compulsory wearing of the yellow badge, or the commencement of deportations — even if they did not apply to mixed marriages. Finally, even the United States' entry into the war was supposed to have made the effects clear to the "German-blooded" partner.

The judges standardized the ruling on marriage annulments at a steering committee meeting in 1942. They decided, contrary to the wording of the law, that the petition for annulment of a marriage could be filed after each drastic measure taken against the Jewish population. Moreover, they ruled that a divorced Jewish woman had no right to alimony.[54] Of the 130 judgments passed, 29 were marriage annulments. The highest annual figure was reached in 1943 with 17 petitions for annulment. Most of the petitions were against Jewish men who had been interned for breaking one (or several), of the anti-Jewish

54 Minutes from a meeting of the judges' steering committee of the Hamburg District Court on 20 May 1942 appearing in: Helge Grabitz, "In vorauseilendem Gehorsam ...Die Hamburger Justiz im 'Führer-Staat'," in: *"Für Führer Volk und Vaterland... ." Hamburger Justiz im Nationalsozialismus*, Justizbehörde Hamburg, ed., p. 57f. Hamburg's district court judges also reached similar conclusions on 16 June 1942, see Reginald A. Puerschel, "Trügerische Normalität. Die Rechtsprechung in Ehe- und Familiensachen der Landgerichte Hamburg und Altona," *ibid.*, p. 413.

regulations. The grounds for having a marriage annulled were generally insubstantial; for example, the "German-blooded" wife had only just become aware of the "difference in races," or, it had been impossible to predict the state's current attitude towards Jews. It is hardly possible to find any differences in the 1943 petitions between the sexes. It was more urgent for the petitioners and the judges that the divorce be granted as quickly as possible. After 1943, the decisions made were fairly arbitrary. While some judges tried to maintain the level of radicalness that had been reached, others saw that the war was being lost and they returned to former procedures. This lack of uniformity is illustrated by the following two examples of annulment proceedings initiated by "German-blooded" husbands:

- A sergeant[55] stationed in Cholm-Lublin wished to have his marriage to his Jewish wife annulled on the grounds that: "He had already been obliged to resign his position as a political leader [of the NSDAP, B.M.] because of his wife's race. Now, in the war, he had witnessed how his comrades had been brutally murdered by Jews while he himself had only been lightly wounded. These experiences had made it clear to him that he could not continue his marriage with her."[56] It was certainly not true that Jews murdered German soldiers in the area around Lublin. It is however true that precisely in this area, which was originally planned as an enormous ghetto for Jews, the SS and the Wehrmacht had over the years massacred thousands of Jewish inhabitants and slave laborers who had been transported there. Mass shootings, gassings in wagons, and finally mass deportation to Sobibor and Treblinka were features of everyday life there during this war of extermination.[57] The soldier was a confirmed National Socialist and the reason for his divorce

55 The petitioner had in the meantime reached the rank of *Feldwebel*, which was the highest army rank open to "*jüdisch Versippte*" (someone related to a Jew by marriage). See order of the Oberkommando der Wehrmacht (OKW), from 20 January 1940, in: *Die Sondereinheiten in der früheren deutschen Wehrmacht*, bearbeitet im Personenstandsarchiv II des Landes Nordrhein-Westfalen (22c), Kornelimünster from 14 October 1952, p. 49.

56 ALH, 8 R 54/44.

57 Dieter Pohl, *Von der "Judenpolitik" zum Judenmord: der Distrikt Lublin des Generalgouvernements 1939–1944*, Frankfurt am Main, 1993.

could have been that since he knew about the murder of the Jews he could no longer bear being married to a member of this group. The sight of this person would remind him every day of his terrible guilt. After his annulment, he refused to pay his wife any alimony whatsoever. She became chronically ill and had to be put in a nursing home. What followed was a bitter dispute between the social welfare office and the *RVJD* about who should pay for her care since nobody felt responsible for her.[58]

Another "German-blooded" husband, perhaps encouraged by the court rulings, filed a petition for annulment or divorce on the grounds of an irretrievable breakdown. He had already been dismissed by the postal service in 1937 and discharged by the Wehrmacht in 1943 on account of his marriage. He wanted to sue for divorce on the grounds of "racial difference," but lost his suit! The judge was of the opinion that the time limit for contesting the validity of his marriage had expired; moreover, he had long since experienced the disadvantages of having a Jewish wife. He had not produced evidence that his wife had committed a matrimonial offense; on the contrary, it was likely that he wanted to marry another woman.

The majority of mixed marriages were, however, not annulled as the hard-line racists would have liked; rather, divorces were obtained on the grounds of serious matrimonial offenses. That applied to both "privileged" and "non-privileged" marriages.[59] There were also "normal" divorces; some were obviously conjoint, while other couples continued their marital quarrels in the court. In these cases (as with other divorces), the judges based their decisions in the first place on whether and which gender-specific, marital duties had been violated. Couples in which both partners wanted a divorce often used the argument that the "German-blooded" partner had refused to have sexual intercourse

58 StaHH, Jüdische Gemeinden, Abl. 1993, Ordner 12, correspondence between the lawyer Dr. Haas and *RVJD* (Heinemann), 12 June 1944, 14 and 24 July 1944.

59 Fifty nine marriages with offspring and 56 childless marriages were annulled or ended in divorce; in 15 other divorces it was not discernible whether or not children were involved. Since as a rule marriages with offspring were "privileged," the divorce rate for the two categories should be nearly the same.

because of *rassischer Abneigung* (racial aversion).[60] Such behavior was evidence of the "racial awareness" desired by those in power, and the judges could therefore regard this as a violation of marital duties.

Another example of the violation of marital duty was given by a Jewish husband, who stated that his wife's "completely uneconomic behavior" and her personal insults such as "dirty old Jew" had wrecked the marriage.[61] The court regarded this behavior as a clear violation of the duties of a wife and found the woman guilty. In the prewar period, the judges still had a definitive picture of exactly what constituted matrimonial offense and required proof of such offenses. Nevertheless, the kind of offenses showed that the discrimination against the Jews had long become a part of the marriage partnership. By the time war broke out, Jewish partners had also started filing petitions for divorce if they could no longer endure everyday married life. They did not at that time have to weigh the strain of being married against the fear of being deported.

These court decisions were still influenced by efforts to give the impression of gender-specific criteria and persecution measures. From 1939 more and more anti-Jewish measures were imposed, and the Jews themselves were blamed for being hit by such measures and for their marriage coming to an end. Examples of this are given below:

- Among the men with previous convictions arrested in the *Juni-Aktion* in 1938[62] there were also Jews who lived in mixed marriages. Some of their wives filed petitions for divorce. The arrests were adjudged to be due to destruction of the marriage by the arrested husbands.[63]
- If a Jewish husband lost his job, he was blamed for the divorce for failing to fulfill his duty of supporting his wife.[64]

60 ALH, 4 R 260/37.

61 ALH, 6 R 185/37.

62 Wolfgang Ayass, "Ein Gebot der nationalen Arbeitsdisziplin." Die Aktion "Arbeitsscheu Reich" 1938, *Beiträge zur nationalsozialistischen Gesundheits- und Sozialpolitik* no. 6, *Feinderklärung und Prävention*, Berlin, 1988, p. 59.

63 ALH, 7 R 40/39, 5b R 41/40, 7 R 40/39, 3 R 94/39, 5b R 41/40.

64 ALH, 4 R 28/42.

- If Jewish husbands were arrested and interned for breaking anti-Jewish regulations, the civil court ruled that: "The defendant made himself guilty of dishonorable conduct by an act against the State which he has already confessed to. His conduct has irreparably destroyed his marriage."[65] In another case the court went even further and surmised that, owing to the husband's "bad conduct," he would most likely be taken directly from the police prison to a concentration camp and that would mean the end of his marriage anyway.[66]

Gender-specific grounds disappeared gradually from the court rulings. The administering of justice shifted from a chaotic juxtaposition of the most varied criteria to a divorce procedure that as a matter of principle assumed that the Jewish partner was to blame. This process virtually ended in 1942. Thereafter, there were at best "non-political" decisions if the couple had been separated for at least three years or if there were elements of an offense, for example if adultery could be proved.

Adultery remained grounds for divorce in both the old and the new marriage law. The facts were obvious since the injured party filed a petition for divorce, but it was essential that *Rassenschande* had not been committed, because the Nuremberg Laws had made extramarital sexual intercourse between Jews and *Deutschblütige* an offense requiring public prosecution. This accounts for the judgments following *Rassenschande*-proceedings among decisions relating to divorce case.[67] However, in other cases, wives denounced their Jewish husbands so that it would be easier for them to obtain a divorce.[68] While the district court still regarded such legal proceedings as a breach of marital fidelity, the higher regional court praised the *Volksgenossin* for having acted (albeit unintentionally), in the interests of the public.[69]

65 ALH, 8 R 462/42.

66 ALH, 2 R 382/42.

67 Hans Robinsohn, *Justiz als politische Verfolgung. Die Rechtsprechung in "Rasseschandefällen" beim Landgericht Hamburg 1936–1943*, Stuttgart, 1977. Robinsohn calculated that Hamburg (in comparison with Frankfurt and Cologne), had the highest persecution coefficients and concluded that "Hamburg had by far the most severe practice of persecution" (p. 21).

68 ALH, 11a R 401/39.

69 ALH, 6 U 420/37.

In addition, the Marriage Law of 6 July 1938, as already mentioned, made it possible for a couple to obtain a divorce without any question of culpability after being separated for three years. Some couples obviously saw this as an opportunity to obtain a divorce on the grounds of mutual consent. In the prewar period, mixed-marriage couples who had been living apart for several years also availed themselves of this law. Nevertheless, the separation was often the result of persecution. For example, the wife of a Jewish man had refused him access to their home after he had been released from a concentration camp in 1938. In 1942 he received his deportation orders as a person from a "non-privileged" mixed marriage who had separated from his wife. His wife seized this opportunity to file her petition for divorce. Apparently he asked his wife to delay her petition in order to defer his deportation. When his wife turned down his request he refused to consent to a divorce. But the court dismissed his interventions since "the respondent is a *Volljude* and therefore a member of a race that belongs to the sworn enemies of the new Germany and now fights on the side of our foes."[70] After her husband had been released from the concentration camp, the woman could not have been expected "to live like husband and wife again just because the respondent is Jewish."[71] The court made short work of it (so as not to delay the impending deportation), and granted the divorce on the grounds of a separation lasting several years.

Just as a long internment in a concentration camp had led to a three-year separation, in other cases it was the emigration of the Jewish partner: some of the Jewish spouses, mostly the men, had emigrated alone if their wives had not wanted to follow them into the economic uncertainty of a foreign country. In the judgments of these divorces after a three-year separation, every "racial" reason, which was not required by this criterion, is missing. Only rarely was the reality of a marriage apparent through the veil of insubstantial reasons. Often only the address of the Jewish spouse, given as somewhere abroad, "address unknown," a concentration camp or a *Judenhaus* — reflects the reason for the separation.[72] In the case of the Jewish partners being interned, they were taken from the concentration camp and brought

70 ALH, 11b R 286/41.

71 ALH, 11b R 286/41.

72 Locations of the Jewish spouses at the time of the divorce included 59 residing in Hamburg or elsewhere in Germany, 28 imprisoned in a jail or concentration camp,

before the judge; in the case of them having emigrated, the petition was sent to them via the consulate, or during the war simply inserted in the *Reichs-und Staatsanzeiger*.

There were, also, conjoint divorces during the Nazi regime — those that took place under extreme pressure and those that occurred as a result of bad advice given not only by the Gestapo, but also by representatives of the *Reichsvereinigung*, for example, Max Plaut, chairman of the organization in Hamburg. Some of the wives who had been subjected to pressure by the Gestapo asked for his advice in such a tricky situation. Who else could they have turned to? Lawyers, acquaintances and representatives of the *Reichsvereinigung* unanimously advised the wives to obtain a quick divorce and made every effort to ensure this happened as speedily as possible, especially if the Jewish husband had been interned. By doing so, they all helped to accelerate his deportation. In a report made after the war, the daughter of a Jew murdered in a concentration camp describes her mother's dilemma as follows:

> Members of the Gestapo, employees of Jewish centers as well as other victims of persecution told my mother time and time again that if she did not have her marriage dissolved, it would have severe consequences for my father. If this state of *Rassenschande*, as it was made out to be, did not change, then my father would be sent to a concentration camp where, they thought, he would probably die. If the marriage were dissolved, then my father could expect better treatment. He would at the worst be evacuated. We had already heard from the relatives of people evacuated that it ... was more a question of rehousing. It had been possible to send post after some months and those evacuated were also allowed to receive parcels.[73]

Relatives did not know that Theresienstadt often was only a stopover on the way to KZ Auschwitz.

Of the 130 divorces investigated, there were 103 Jewish men and 27 Jewish women involved (Table 1). Many of them had been married for decades (Table 2). More than a third of the petitioners filed for divorce

25 had emigrated, 6 were living in a *Judenhaus* in Hamburg, 6 had emigrated with their non-Jewish spouses, 2 lived in a nursing home or hospital, 2 lived with the non-Jewish spouses in occupied eastern territories, and 2 whose whereabouts were unknown.

73 Archives of the Justizbehörde Hamburg, Eheanerkennungsverfahren 346 E 1 i/3/5, Letter of G.W. to Landesjustizverwaltung Hamburg, 5 August 1956, p.1f.

when it was obvious that the Jewish partner would be deported (Table 1). More than 70 percent of those who remained in Germany after their divorce were murdered, that is, sixty-three men and six women. At the end of the war there were still 647 Jews in Hamburg, more than half of whom were women (358 women to 289 men).[74]

Pressure from all sides was put on those couples seeking a divorce (though mainly on the "German-blooded" wives) — pressure from employers, clerks at the employment exchange, professional associations, welfare workers, landlords, the Gestapo, neighbors, and superiors in the Wehrmacht. At least the representatives of the *RVJD*, the lawyers (including the Jewish legal advisers), and often the family played a supportive role. Apart from the authorities already mentioned, people involved in the persecution included the non-Jewish wives and, to a much lesser extent, the non-Jewish husbands. An objection has to be raised here against Nathan Stoltzfus who, in an attempt to locate a potential for resistance in the German people, defines the low divorce rate for mixed marriages in general and the much-cited protest by the wives of those Jews arrested in the *Fabrik-Aktion* in the *Rosenstrasse* in particular, as "acts of political opposition."[75] External factors may well have prejudiced the decision to divorce, for example, the forced move to a *Judenhaus*, or the husband's internment and the inescapable fate of "evacuation," added to the decline in social status and the economic hardships during the war. Moreover, the women were often confronted with the dilemma: whether or not to accompany their husbands on the final journey, having already suffered the difficult years from 1933 to 1942–43. Divorce seemed to be the only way of surviving. However, the decision to renounce one's partner was mostly taken by non-Jewish women, who, although not perpetrators, by doing this nevertheless became involved in the process of exclusion and persecution and consequently assumed a role they did not like to be reminded of when the

74 FZH, Sign. 6262, Report on the Jewish Community of Hamburg, undated (probably summer 1945), p. 1 and 3. The New York newspaper *Aufbau* published lists of Jews who had survived in Hamburg. See *Aufbau* of 20 and 27 July 1945.

75 Nathan Stoltzfus, "Widerstand des Herzens. Der Protest in der Rosenstrasse und die deutsch-jüdische Mischehe," *Geschichte und Gesellschaft*, 2 (1995), p. 221. See also Nathan Stoltzfus, *Resistance of the Heart. Intermarriage and the Rosenstrasse Protest in Nazi Germany*, New York, 1996.

war was over.[76] Indeed, far more "German-blooded" women obtained divorces from their Jewish husbands than "German-blooded" husbands from their Jewish wives — even after taking into consideration the proportionally larger number of such marriages with Jewish husbands. The initial materialistic reasons for the marriage, and the high level of pressure exerted on these marriages at an early stage by the Gestapo and non-Jewish society had a negative effect on the marriage. In contrast, the emotional reasons for the marriage between "German-blooded" men and Jewish women, together with the lower level of pressure that was exerted at a later stage from the surroundings, probably had a stabilizing effect that sustained the marriage. However, even if a couple fought to keep their marriage intact in order to give the Jewish partner protection, this was by no means a guarantee that he or she would not be deported. A small number of people living in both dissolved and intact mixed marriages had on several occasions been deported to Theresienstadt between the summer of 1943 and January 1945, yet, more than two hundred people — mostly living in "privileged" mixed marriages — were deported from Hamburg to Theresienstadt in February 1945.[77]

The protection offered by a "privileged" mixed marriage was always only temporary even if many people survived in this constellation. In many marriages the external pressure led to internal disintegration. It evoked both the wish to struggle through together, to save the other one, to escape the persecution, just as much as it evoked base feelings. A "privileged" mixed marriage was no guarantee of survival — it was merely a reflection of German society.

76 A law "Gesetz über die Anerkennung freier Ehen rassisch und politisch Verfolgter" of 23 June 1950 (*Bundesgesetzblatt*, p. 226), enabled, among other things, the revision of divorces after the war. It is certainly no coincidence that 22 women from Hamburg (all "German-blooded" except for one Jewish woman), but no divorced man made applications which secured for them benefits and the right of inheritance.

77 Gruner, *Arbeitseinsatz*, p. 328. In Hamburg, this deportation, declared throughout the *Reich* as "labor in another area," affected — after exemptions and postponements — 128 men and 66 women mainly from "privileged" mixed marriages. Fortunately, almost all of them survived the late deportation.

Table 1. Duration of Marriage among divorced mixed couples

Length of marriage	**Number of divorces**
0–5 years	12
6–10 years	38
11–15 years	25
16–20 years	19
21–25 years	15
26–30 years	12
More than 30 years	4
No data	5
Total	130

Table 2. Divorces among "racially mixed marriages" in Hamburg 1937–45

Year	**Number of** divorces	**Jewish** men	**Jewish** women	**Total of** mixed marriages
1937	4	3	1	
1938	20	16	4	
1939	22	19	3	
1940	14	9	5	972
1941	19	15	4	1,036
1942	21	17	4	1,122
1943	23	20	3	
1944	6	3	3	874
1945	1	1	—	647
Total	130	103	27	

Public Welfare and the German Jews under National Socialism

On Anti-Jewish Policies of the Municipal Administrations, the German Council of Municipalities and the Reich Ministry of the Interior (1933–1942)[1]

WOLF GRUNER

Our historical understanding of the situation of German Jews during the first years of National Socialist rule is influenced by the image of emigrating attorneys, physicians, civil servants and academicians who, as a result of the ensuing persecution, closed down their chancelleries and practices or were compelled to give up their positions in government or the universities. In fact, they comprised the first groups that were removed from their professional positions by, for example, the Law for the Reestablishment of the Professional Civil Service. Yet the myth that was behind it all, that of the well-to-do German Jews — which even appears to be untenable prior to 1933 — remains.

In reality, the world economic crisis and the exclusionary measures that began in 1933 set into motion a massive process of impoverishment within the Jewish population which very rapidly outpaced the proportion of the unemployed and dispossessed.[2] In 1936, in spite of the economic upward trend and a significant decrease in the population as a result of emigration, over 37,000 German Jews were unemployed —

1 This article is an overview of the first results of a larger research project on this subject. The study will be published in the near future.

2 Compare S. Adler-Rudel, *Jüdische Selbsthilfe unter dem Naziregime 1933–1939*, Tübingen, 1974; Avraham Barkai, *Vom Boykott zur "Entjudung,"* Frankfurt am Main, 1988.

far more than at the beginning of the Nazi dictatorship which continued to be overshadowed by the world economic crisis.[3]

How did German society react to this social problem which increasingly intensified with each new measure of discrimination? From the vantage point of their ideology, it was unthinkable for the National Socialists to expend government resources on the Jews. Yet at the same time, all needy Germans had a legal right to social services in accordance with the Public Welfare Ordinance (*Reichsfürsorgeverordnung).* At first, public welfare could not and was not to be withheld since abject poverty hindered the emigration efforts of individuals, and in the eyes of the National Socialists emigration meant successful expulsion. Moreover, a situation where tens of thousands of people were forced to live without money and work over long periods also meant an internal political risk for the Nazi leadership.

The increased economic dependency of thousands of Jews subjected the overall National Socialist plan to unanticipated contradictions precisely within the framework of this explosive social sphere. For this reason, the process of impoverishment — a fact rarely been appreciated until now — played an increasingly significant role in the strategy discussions within the National Socialist leadership and at the ministerial level. Hitler, in contrast to other authorities, calculated precisely the negative social ramifications of his policy from the very beginning, issuing a directive in 1935 that new measures should be avoided were they to result in "Jews burdening the public sector."[4]

However, this was only intended to apply to the central levels. The contradiction between the duty to provide public welfare and an overriding will to exclude the Jews was increasingly settled by the cities and municipalities to the disadvantage of the needy. Jewish welfare recipients apparently suffered discrimination and isolation at the hands of welfare offices long before there were centralized regulations. Clear developments, mechanisms and contradictions in the politics of persecution can be demonstrated by the study of the sociopolitical

3 Clemens Vollnhals, "Jüdische Selbsthilfe bis 1938," in: *Die Juden in Deutschland 1933–1945*, Wolfgang Benz, ed., Munich, 1988, p. 374.

4 See speech of Walter Gross (Head of the *NSDAP-Rassepolitisches Amt*), 25 September 1935, about a talk with Hitler on "Judenpolitik;" cited by Philippe Burrin, *Hitler und die Juden*, Frankfurt am Main, 1993, p. 48.

treatment of the Jewish needy. In this regard, diverse institutional interests appear to have influenced such policy, more seldom to have acted as a hindrance to it than to hinder it. Exclusion was not — as shall be demonstrated — simply implemented from above, but rather developed as the result of a process that involved an interplay between local and central levels; a process one might call "trial and error."

A more precise analysis of policy creation under National Socialism may be made based on the extensive source materials available for both the federal and the municipal levels which deal with operations within the public welfare apparatus — at least in the sphere of social policy. In the following, I will sketch the process leading to the exclusion of German Jews from government welfare programs, focusing on the responsible institutions — namely, the cities and their public welfare administrations and the Reich Ministry of the Interior. Secondly, I will illustrate the significance and function of the German Council of Municipalities (*Deutscher Gemeindetag*), for planning this persecution. Finally, I will summarize the questions regarding the persecution of Jews between 1933 and 1942 that arose out of the events thus presented.

The First Local Exclusionary Measures in Public Welfare (1933–Summer 1937)

Although some researchers in the 1980s equated Nazi social policy with racist policy,[5] opinions up to now have generally put social and political treatment of Jewish and non-Jewish Germans on an equal footing until November 1938.[6] For example, in their three-volume history of public welfare for the poor in Germany, Sachsse and Tennstedt claim that only

5 Gisela Bock, *Zwangssterilisation im Nationalsozialismus,* Opladen, 1986; Detlev Peukert, *Volksgenossen und Gemeinschaftsfremde*, Cologne, 1982; Detlev Peukert, "Zur Erforschung der Sozialpolitik im Dritten Reich," in: *Soziale Arbeit und Faschismus*, Hans-Uwe Otto and Heinz Sönker, eds., Frankfurt am Main, 1989, pp. 36–46.

6 See e.g., Paul Sauer, *Dokumente über die Verfolgung der jüdischen Bürger in Baden-Württemberg durch das nationalsozialistische Regime 1933–1943*, Stuttgart, 1966, part II, p. 130. See also Schoen, who followed Adler-Rudel; Paul Schoen, *Armenfürsorge im Nationalsozialismus*, Weinheim-Basel, 1985, p. 102.

from 1938 did racial criteria "seep into" all sectors of social security.[7] This in no way corresponds to the facts discovered years ago from the studies done on Frankfurt am Main,[8] Munich[9] and Hamburg,[10] and recently on Berlin[11] and other cities in the Third Reich.[12] Racism and antisemitism in many areas had resulted in unequal treatment of German Jews by government welfare organizations long before the 1938 pogrom.

Shortly after Hitler became Chancellor first municipal initiatives to target Jewish personnel ocurred also in the field of welfare. In Berlin, civil servants and doctors were being dismissed or relieved of their duties even weeks before the notorious Law for the Reestablishment of the Professional Civil Service on 7 April 1933. Following the dismissals entailed by this law, the municipal administration in 1933 and 1934 was above all concerned with cutting subventions made to the welfare activities of Jewish homes and institutions.[13]

In 1935, well in advance of federal legislation, measures had already been taken in some cities to remove certain supplemental benefits from the Jewish poor who should have been fully supported through the public welfare system. In this context, non-local Jewish residents were

7 Christoph Sachsse and Florian Tennstedt, *Der Wohlfahrtsstaat im Nationalsozialismus. Geschichte der Armenfürsorge in Deutschland*, Stuttgart, 1992, vol. 3, p. 276.

8 Kommission zur Erforschung der Geschichte der Frankfurter Juden, ed., *Dokumente zur Geschichte der Frankfurter Juden*, Frankfurt am Main, 1963.

9 Peter Hanke, *Zur Geschichte der Juden in München zwischen 1933 und 1945*, Munich 1967.

10 Angelika Ebbinghaus et al., eds., *Heilen und Vernichten im Mustergau Hamburg*, Hamburg, 1984, pp. 65–67; Uwe Lohalm, "Hamburgs öffentliche Fürsorge und die Juden 1933–1939," in: *Die Juden in Hamburg 1590–1990*, Arno Herzig, ed., Hamburg, 1991, pp. 499–514.

11 Wolf Gruner, *Judenverfolgung in Berlin 1933–1945. Eine Chronologie der Behördenmassnahmen in der Reichshauptstadt,* Berlin, 1996; Wolf Gruner, "Die Reichshauptstadt und die Verfolgung der Berliner Juden 1933–1945," in: *Jüdische Geschichte in Berlin,* Reinhard Rürup, ed., Berlin, 1995, pp. 229–266.

12 See the chapter "Vom betreuten Individuum zur verfolgten Gruppe. Juden im Fürsorge- und Arbeitsrecht bis Sommer 1938," in: Wolf Gruner, *Der Geschlossene Arbeitseinsatz deutscher Juden. Zur Zwangsarbeit als Element der Verfolgung 1938 bis 1943*, Berlin, 1997, pp. 31–40.

13 Gruner, *Judenverfolgung*, pp. 17–33.

one of the first groups targeted by the municipal administrations. Up to 1935 the high unemployment and the economic pressures that this created, together with the prospect of better chances of emigration, intensified the migration of Jewish families from the country into the cities as well as from smaller to larger towns. Jews who moved to Frankfurt am Main only received seventy percent of public welfare benefits,[14] and in Berlin, in contrast to "Aryan" immigrants, they were principally assigned to asylums for the homeless.[15]

Though the National Socialists used the Nuremberg Laws to relegate German Jews to second-class citizens in the fall of 1935, there were no further regulations in the social sphere. Although Jews were not yet entirely excluded from public welfare, they were being increasingly separated. In October 1935 Erich Hilgenfeldt, the official representative of the German Winter Relief Organization, used the new political situation to exclude Jews from their list of the needy, there being no individual legal entitlement to the benefits provided by this organization. Hilgenfeldt forced the Jewish welfare institutions to establish a separate and controlled system of relief assistance.[16]

In the meantime, those cities responsible for social welfare had to expend more and more welfare resources for the rapidly growing number of unemployed and impoverished Jews. Individual welfare offices reacted to this reality created by the persecution by proposing that this group be generally disadvantaged within the scope of the welfare program.[17] In summer 1935,[18] Berlin demanded from the German Council of Municipalities for all Jewish welfare offices to be placed under official control in order to prevent "a misuse of public welfare funds" through their activities.[19] In October, at the insistence of the local *Gauleiter*, the town of Königsberg urged the German Council

14 *Dokumente zur Geschichte der Frankfurter Juden*, VIII 3, p. 372: Wohlfahrtsamt an Bürgermeister Frankfurt am Main, 12 December 1935.

15 Landesarchiv Berlin, Rep 214, Acc. 794, no. 13, unnumbered: Verfügung Spiewok (OB/Landeswohlfahrts-und-jugendamt), 17 July 1935.

16 Vollnhals, "Selbsthilfe," pp. 399–406; Barkai, *Boykott*, pp. 107–111.

17 Uwe-Dietrich Adam, *Judenpolitik im Dritten Reich*, Düsseldorf, 1972, pp. 191–192.

18 On the history of the German Council of Municipalities since 1933 see Horst Matzerath, *Nationalsozialismus und kommunale Selbstverwaltung*, Stuttgart, 1970. On the German Council of Municipalities and Public Welfare see Schoen, *Armenfürsorge*, pp. 88–92.

19 Oberbürgermeister Berlin an Deutscher Gemeindetag (DGT), 17 July 1935, and

of Municipalities to impose stricter standards in assessing the neediness of Jews entitled to support.[20]

In order to find a way to limit the number of Jewish applicants for welfare support, the Reich Ministry of the Interior at the end of 1935 implemented a suggestion made by the Council of Municipalities: namely, to instruct the welfare associations that henceforward social support for the Jewish poor will be dependent upon supplementary support being granted by Jewish welfare offices.[21] This provided local offices with the possibility of denying assistance if other forms of support were not declared. In addition they were provided with the means to control Jewish facilities. But except for individual sociopolitical provisions — Jews still had to pay radio license fees and no longer received marriage loans — there was no centralized regulation for the next one and a half years.

For this reason, some of the municipal administrations launched their own initiatives. In May 1937 Karl Fiehler,[22] the Mayor of Munich, announced that Jews were to be assisted in accordance with the laws, but under no circumstances was it necessary to put Jews "on an equal footing with Aryan comrades at all levels of social security." Voluntary services provided by welfare offices, such as loans, credit assistance and convalescence support, should be "refused on principle."[23] Since Mayor Fiehler (who participated in 1923 in the Hitler putsch in Munich), served also as the chairman of the German Council of Municipalities and head of the *NSDAP-Hauptamt für Kommunalpolitik* (Main Office

DGT an Reichsinnenministerium (RMdI), 25 July 1935; cited by Adam, *Judenpolitik,* p. 191.

20 Oberbürgermeister Königsberg an DGT, 15 October 1935; cited Ibid., p. 191.

21 Dienstblatt der Stadt Berlin, 1935 Part VII, p. 325, no. 407: RMdI-Erlass (without date), in Verfügung Spiewok (Landeswohlfahrtsamt), 28 November 1935.

22 Born 31 August 1895, following a commercial apprenticeship, he did military service in the First World War. And after 1919 he was employed in the Munich Municipality. From 1924 to 1933 he served as honorary city councillor; from 1927 to 1930 was head of *NSDAP-Ortsgruppe* in Munich, and from 1933 to 1945 was Mayor of Munich and Member of the Reichstag. He died in 1969.

23 Yad Vashem Archive, Jerusalem (hereafter YV), M1DN, no. 85,fol. 63: Verfügung Oberbürgermeister München, (Wohlfahrts- und Stiftungsreferat), 21 May 1937.

for Municipal Policy), from 1933, his opinion not only carried a certain weight, its influence extended to other cities as well.[24]

A Discussion in the German Council of Municipalities (June 1937)

In November 1935 and in April 1936 also the welfare associations that formed the Northwestern German Committee for Welfare discussed the discrimination topic.[25] The common demand for new guidelines for the "treatment of non-Aryans" was finally brought to the German Council of Municipalities. Its functionaries were instructed to ensure that the Reich Ministry of the Interior come up with a corresponding regulation.[26]

The social plight of tens of thousands of Jews, until then considered acceptable, was now also being discussed in the ministries, although at first exclusively as a possible hindrance to their expulsion. At a meeting in the Reich Ministry of the Interior on 29 September 1936, by way of preparation for a ministerial conference, it was agreed that the ultimate goal of the *Judenpolitik* would be reached "when there are no longer any Jews in Germany." It was a matter of determining the pace and extent of the individual measures. Also considered was the issue of "implementing the emigration compulsorily." Despite a basic consensus, there were some voices among the higher ministry officials that warned against "the formation of a Jewish proletariat" and the consignment of Jews to assistance for the poor.[27]

In view of the demands made on the Reich Ministry of the Interior via the German Council of Municipalities in 1936, the ministerial department responsible for municipal interests suggested in May 1937,

24 On his career as Mayor see Helmuth M. Hanko, "Kommunalpolitik in der Hauptstadt der Bewegung 1933–1935," in: *Bayern in der NS-Zeit*, Martin Broszat et al., eds, Munich, 1981, vol. 3, pp. 392–442. On his other careers see Matzerath, *Nationalsozialismus,* pp. 186, 251.

25 Lohalm, "Hamburgs öffentliche," p. 507.

26 Ibid., p. 507.

27 Hans Mommsen and Susanne Willems, eds., *Herrschaftsalltag im Dritten Reich. Studien und Texte*, Düsseldorf, 1988, pp. 445–452, document 13: Vermerk Stuckart.

on the basis of the growing discrepancy between the acute consequences of the persecution of the Jews and the interests of the cities themselves, that "the future treatment of the Jews in the public welfare system" be put as a question of general principle on the agenda of the next meeting of the German Council of Municipalities and its responsible Welfare Committee.[28]

The internal political role played by the German Council of Municipalities during the period of National Socialism has been underestimated until now. In research accounts of the history of the German Council of Municipalities under National Socialism, there has been an overemphasis on both the reduction of municipal self-administration functions after 1933 and minimization of the political and legal latitude granted to the towns and municipalities represented in this institution. The consensus until now has been that with the help of the Reich Ministry of the Interior the state virtually put the Council of Municipalities out of action.[29] However, a thorough examination of social policies under National Socialism shows that the *Gleichschaltung* of leading organizations in the German Council of Municipalities created a body that played an active part in the development of policies which were related to domestic affairs and persecution under National Socialism. This applies in particular to welfare, the labor market and the housing market, as well as to the anti-Jewish policy in these sectors, which is of primary interest here.

The mayors and municipal civil servants of the communities and cities represented in the German Council of Municipalities and its specialized committees discussed the implementation of decisions made by the central government as well as persecutory initiatives developed at the local level. The Reich Ministry of the Interior, which also acted as a supervisory organ for the German Council of Municipalities as it had done for the municipalities since 1935, could support or, if necessary, curtail the latter through the German Council of Municipalities.

Taking part in the meeting of the German Council of Municipalities on 10 June 1937 in Heidelberg, at which the treatment of Jews in the welfare system was discussed, were not only the vice president Ralf

28 Staatsarchiv Hamburg, 351–10 Sozialbehörde I, VT 12.25, unnumbered: RMdI an Martini, 24 May 1937.

29 Matzerath, *Nationalsozialismus,* pp. 104, 218, 435.

Zeitler[30] and other functionaries from the Council of Municipalities, the representatives of various towns and municipalities,[31] but also Ministerial Counsel Fritz Ruppert of the Reich Ministry of the Interior. Brief accounts of the session have already been provided by research articles, but without an analysis of its significance and context.[32] Oskar Martini, the main speaker and vice president of the Social Services Administration in Hamburg, was thoroughly prepared. Not only had he acquired material from other cities on their welfare practices, but he had also met with Lösener, head of the section on Jews at the Reich Ministry of the Interior, who intimated to him the intentions of his ministry.[33] Martini first provided an overview of the current legal status of the Jews and of the so-called *Mischlinge*. He then stated that although many aspects of the welfare system could be regulated in accordance with the spirit of National Socialism, "a series of questions" remained open "which could only be regulated by means of federal legislation."[34] Based on the demand to place Jews within the framework of legislation regarding foreigners, as it was expressed in the party program of the NSDAP, it followed that "Jews [would have to] be equated with foreigners in the welfare system." Monthly cash supports should be calculated "based on the standards which apply to public welfare for foreigners." Hence, privileged welfare categories,

30 Born 7 October 1903 in St. Petersburg. Studied economics and law; from 1931 was a member of the SA, from May 1932 a member of the NSDAP, and from June 1933 vice-manager, and later vice-president of the German Council of Municipalities, from 1945 he was the director manager of a hospital in Hamburg; he died in Hamburg in 1953.

31 These included city councillors: Dr. Fischer-Defoy (Frankfurt am Main), Plath (Nuremberg), Spiewok (Berlin), and guests Claes (Mayor of Braunschweig), Dr. Conti (Berlin), and Duntze (Ministry of the Interior in Baden).

32 Adam, *Judenpolitik*, pp. 190–192; Gruner, *Geschlossener Arbeitseinsatz*, pp. 33–35; Lohalm, "Hamburgs öffentliche," p. 508.

33 StA Hamburg, 351–10 Sozialbehörde I, VT 12.25, unnumbered: Stadtrat Plank (Nürnberg), an DGT, 24 May 1937; Ibid., Bericht aus München (undatet), Ruppert (RMdI), an Martini, 24 May 1937.

34 StadtA Göttingen, Sozialamt, Acc. no. 407/77, no. 47/1, unnumbered: Bericht über die Konferenz des DGT-Wohlfahrtsausschusses, 10 June 1937 in Heidelberg, p. 13; compare Adam, *Judenpolitik*, pp. 190–191.

such as *Gehobene Fürsorge,*[35] would also be eliminated in addition to voluntary welfare services. Moreover, it was demanded that all Jewish recipients of welfare benefits be required to do *Pflichtarbeit* (unpaid mandatory labor).[36] With regard to the housing of the handicapped and mentally ill in nursing homes and mental homes (so-called closed welfare), in the future Jews would be segregated from the others. Similarly, Jewish children in need of special education were to be accommodated separately in Jewish institutions.[37]

The conference discussion revealed that, in fact, diverse discriminatory tactics had been employed by the various municipal welfare authorities up to this point. The welfare office in Nuremberg was already paying twenty percent less in benefits and services to its Jewish inhabitants, similar to the practice in Frankfurt am Main. On the other hand, Berlin and Munich had eliminated all the "supplementary," i.e., non-obligatory, welfare services. The Leipzig authorities made cuts by reducing public services when supplementary aid was given by Jewish support centers to Jews in need.[38] Forced compensation of benefits to Jewish public welfare recipients in isolated groups through *Pflichtarbeit* was a customary practice in Duisburg,[39] Hamburg,[40] Berlin,[41] Göttingen[42] and Leipzig.[43] These different approaches, which became clear in the course of the discussion, prompted Ministerial

35 *"Kriegesbeschädigte"* and *"Kleinrentner"* within this privileged class received higher welfare benefits than the average recipient in the *"Allgemeine Fürsorge."*

36 On *Pflichtarbeit* as an instrument of persecution see Gruner, *Geschlossener Arbeitseinsatz*, pp. 34–37.

37 StadtA Göttingen, Sozialamt, Acc. no. 407/77, no. 47/1, unnumbered: Bericht über die Konferenz des DGT-Wohlfahrtsausschusses, 10 June 1937 in Heidelberg, pp. 13–16.

38 Ibid., pp. 22–23. StA Hamburg, 351–10 Sozialbehörde I, VT 12.25, unnumbered: Stadtrat Plank (Nürnberg) an DGT, 24 May 1937; Ibid., Bericht aus München (undatet); Ibid., Vorlage für Martini, 4 June 1937.

39 Günther von Roden, *Geschichte der Duisburger Juden*, Duisburg, 1986, p. 854.

40 StA Hamburg, 351–10 Sozialbehörde I, VT 12.25, unnumbered: Vorlage für Martini, 4 June 1937.

41 StadtA Göttingen, Sozialamt, Acc. no. 407/77, no. 47/1, unnumbered: Konferenz, 10 June 1937, pp. 22–23.

42 Ibid., p. 16 (handwritten note).

43 StadtA Leipzig, AFS, no. 1939 vol. 3, fol. 124, 175: Verwaltungsberichte der Arbeitsfürsorge 1936–1937.

Counsel Ruppert to call for a collection of material and ideas in order to draft a uniform legislation, which the conference participants from all the institutions considered necessary.[44] A year later the municipal representatives provided this material to the Reich Ministry of the Interior to draft the ordinance designed to exclude Jews from the social welfare system.

The procedure described here certainly characterizes more than an individual case, as evidenced by debates of this type that took place at the central administration of the German Council of Municipalities in Berlin, its provincial bodies or specialized committees. In addition to the discussions which will be described in the following, the municipalities also discussed after 1933 the separation of Jewish scholars in public schools,[45] in 1939 the "eviction" of Jews,[46] and in 1942 the wage rates for compulsory labor performed by German Jews in public sector companies.[47] In all these cases city mayors with the help of the German Council of Municipalities used this opportunity to coordinate their own practices with procedures elsewhere at very little expense. Functionaries from the Council of Municipalities presented themselves at the Reich Ministry of the Interior as advocates of the cities with the result that local opinions acquired real weight in the shaping of central policy.

The Preparation for a Central Exclusionary Regulation (Autumn 1937—Summer 1938)

In spite of the discussion described above and the interests of the Reich Ministry of the Interior that were expressed, nothing happened in fact

44 StadtA Göttingen, Sozialamt, Acc. no. 407/77, no. 47/1, unnumbered: Konferenz, 10 June 1937, pp. 20–24.

45 Compare YV, M1DN, no. 92, fol. 9: Preussischer Gemeindetag Berlin an Magistrat Frankfurt am Main, 21 July 1933; Ibid., fol. 20–21: DGT Berlin an Preuss. Minister für Wissenschaft, Kunst und Volksbildung, 17 October 1934; Ibid., fol. 23: Artikel in *Der Gemeindetag*, 15 April 1935.

46 Bundesarchiv Berlin, formerly in Koblenz (hereafter BAK), R 36 DGT, no. 902, unnumbered: Protokoll der 6. Tagung der Süddeutschen Arbeitsgemeinschaft für Wohlfahrtspflege am 27. 1. 1939 in Bad Dürkheim, p. 3.

47 Gruner, *Geschlossener Arbeitseinsatz*, pp. 297–298.

because the exclusionary measures were supposed to be incorporated into a comprehensive National Socialist restructuring of the welfare system.[48] Only in 1938, as Hamburg began to restructure the guideline rate for the welfare system in its region, did the Reich Ministry of the Interior recommend that Jews be excluded from the progressive levels of welfare support in order to prevent them from benefiting from the planned improvements in service.[49] This meant *de facto* that for the first time Jews were not only disadvantaged, but their social status was diminished by a federal instruction.

Shortly afterwards, the Reich Ministry of the Interior announced that for the time being there would not be a uniform regulation for Jews at the national level. However, local welfare authorities could take informal measures themselves.[50] On 24 March the Reich Ministry thus granted the district welfare associations permission to reduce the level of welfare payments to Jews when supplementary support was given by Jewish welfare offices by exactly the amounts of the latter,[51] as Leipzig was in fact already doing. In general, at this time the welfare practices with regard to German Jews in many cities were characterized by increasingly stringent criteria and by isolation. The Jewish homeless were by now either being handed straight over to the local Jewish communities for support (in Chemnitz, Dresden, Munich and Nuremberg), or accommodated away from "Aryans" in municipal shelters on separate premises (Cologne, Leipzig).[52] In order to introduce separation in the treatment of the needy, the Berlin welfare offices from April 1938 started keeping records as to which of their current claimants were Jewish. For the separate medical treatment of

48 Notiz Zengerling (DGT), über Gespräch mit Ruppert (RMdI), 12 November 1937; cited by Adam, *Judenpolitik*, p. 192. Compare Institut für Zeitgeschichte ed., *Akten der Parteikanzlei der NSDAP (AdP),* Munich, 1983, Part I, vol. 2: Microfiche, no. 10312468: RMdI-Schreiben, 16 August 1938.

49 Geheimes StA Preussischer Kulturbesitz Berlin-Dahlem, I.HA, Rep. 151, no. 2311, fol. 242: RMdI an Reichsstatthalter Hamburg, 5 February 1938.

50 Adam, *Judenpolitik*, p. 192.

51 Dienstblatt der Stadt Berlin, 1938 Part VII, p. 116, no.106: Verfügung des Landeswohlfahrtsamtes, vom 31. 3. 1938 unter Bezug auf den RMdI-Erlass vom 24. 3.1938.

52 LA Berlin, Rep. 142 DGT, no. 1–2–6–1, unnumbered: DGT-Umfrage, 5 February 1938, pp. 1–7.

the more than 10,000 Jewish men and women receiving social support, the Berlin authorities at first admitted just twenty Jewish doctors, who were also required to take on all manner of special duties.[53] Roma and Sinti, so-called wanderers, or others alleged to shy away from work were discriminated against in the same fashion and often together with the Jews.[54]

At a meeting of the East German Committee for Welfare in Königsberg on 23 April 1938, once again the complaint was voiced about the lack of a legal foundation for the "elimination of non-Aryans from higher-level welfare."[55] One month later the German Council of Municipalities at the meeting of its Welfare Committee in Würzburg on 25 May presented its own guidelines. On the one hand, the support for "Aryans" was to be lifted. On the other, individual support for Jews and foreigners — as in the city-state of Hamburg since the beginning of the current year — was to be restricted to the level of *Allgemeine Fürsorge* (general welfare).[56]

As the Reich Ministry of the Interior informed the Ministry of Labor and the Führer's Deputy towards the end of July 1938, the new guidelines developed by the German Council of Municipalities served a public welfare system that was run on the principles of National Socialism. According to Secretary of State Pfundtner, the Reich Ministry of the Interior supported the suggestion in particular "from the sociopolitical perspective." However, owing to the heavy financial burden that it would place on the town and municipal authorities, the Reich Ministry would be publishing the directive requested by the Council of Municipalities solely as a recommendation, especially a centralized anti-Jewish regulation was now imminent anyway.[57]

The number of dispossessed Jews increased more rapidly than ever as a result of measures taken in the economic sector at the beginning of 1938. Consequently, the prevailing stance at the Reich Ministry of the

53 Gruner, *Judenverfolgung*, pp. 47–49: Entries of 30 March, 26 and 27 April 1938.

54 Compare Michael Zimmermann, *Rassenutopie und Genozid. Die nationalsozialistische "Lösung der Zigeunerfrage,"* Hamburg, 1996, pp. 81–84.

55 Brandenburgisches Landeshauptarchiv Potsdam, Pr. Br. Rep. 55 Provinzialverband, VII a, no. 10, fol. 8: Auszug aus Niederschrift über die Sitzung, 23 April 1938.

56 BAK, R 36, no. 933, fol. 146, 146 B: Niederschrift zur Sitzung am 25. 5. 1938, Anlage A: Richtlinien für die Bemessung der Leistungen der öffentlichen Fürsorge.

57 Ibid., no. 1118, unnumbered: RMdI an Reichsarbeitsministerium, 27 July 1938.

Interior shifted accordingly, and in August the Reich Ministry together with the Council of Municipalities drafted an ordinance designed to exclude Jews entirely from the national social welfare system. Only in "emergency cases," for instance if benefits could not be assured through Jewish voluntary welfare work, were German Jews to receive state benefits at a much reduced level by being equated in the future with foreigners.[58] This draft went much further than the previous demands of reduced payments to Jews made by various local authorities. A central decision taken within the context of a generally radicalized persecution.

The Anti-Jewish Welfare Ordinance and its Application by German Cities (Autumn 1938—Summer 1939)

After the November pogrom in 1938, which did not succeed in accelerating the expulsion of German Jews to the extent desired, the Nazi leadership began to reorient and pursue a new parallel strategy of persecution — namely forced emigration, and forced separation of those remaining. In the long run, as predicted by Heydrich at the first central strategy session on 12 November, after the pogrom, "countless Jews" would remain in the country anyway. As a result of the many measures discussed and decided by the ministers at this conference — especially expropriation, special taxes and a prohibition on trading — Jews who remained behind would be long-term unemployed and thus be "proletarianized."[59] The new dependence on the welfare system of the Third Reich by rapidly growing numbers of Jews who were unable to emigrate was to be countered with all-encompassing isolation. This new radical strategy to separate German Jews in the areas of education, economy, labor, the housing market, and public welfare was served by numerous ordinances published by the Nazi authorities until the summer of 1939. As a result, a mandatory Jewish organization was

58 *AdP*, Part I, vol. 2, Microfiche, no. 10312468–72: RMdI-Schreiben, Verordnungsentwurf, 16 August 1938.

59 *Der Prozess gegen die Hauptkriegsverbrecher vor dem Internationalen Militärgerichtshof*, Nuremberg, 1948, vol. XXVIII, Dok. PS-1816, p. 534: Protokoll der Ministerkonferenz, 12 November 1938.

founded to create a separate school and welfare system. Thus for the Jews, this policy meant not only separation from German society but a further upheaval — living in a controlled and isolated "forced community"(*Zwangsgemeinschaft*).[60]

A few days later Minister of the Interior Frick, Minister of Labor Seldte and Minister of Finance Graf Schwerin von Krosigk issued the long-discussed decree pertaining to welfare. Based on the Ordinance on Social Welfare for Jews issued on 19 November 1938, German Jews were allowed the welfare resources of exclusively Jewish institutions. Jews were to be granted public benefits only in the most extreme emergencies, and even then only the "barest necessities."[61] For the implementation of this decree a special apparatus was set up. The public welfare system was instructed jointly by the Ministries of Labor and the Interior that from January 1939 it would be responsible for keeping a statistical record of Jews in the whole of Germany. The local and district welfare associations supplied the pertinent data to the Reich Department of Statistics, according to which Jewish Germans were identified from 1939 as a separate group by the "Reich Welfare Statistics Express Service" (*Schnelldienst der Reichsfürsorgestatistik*) to be issued on a quarterly basis.[62] At the local level, welfare offices segregated Jewish welfare recipients systematically in special offices or at specific hours. In Berlin at the beginning of December 1938, Mayor Lippert personally demanded the establishment of special consultation days and departments for Jews.[63] And following the pogrom, Hamburg's welfare authorities introduced special hours for dealing with Jews, but towards the end of December 1938 the decision was made to set up a separate department, the *Sonderdienststelle B für Juden*, which opened in February 1939.[64]

Separate offices were also set up by employment authorities. Following the new persecution strategy after the pogrom these offices

60 For the first description and analysis of this complex anti-Jewish policy after 1938 see Gruner, *Geschlossener Arbeitseinsatz*, pp. 58–62 and 334–335.

61 *Reichsgesetzblatt,* 1938 I, p. 1649: Verordnung über die öffentliche Fürsorge für Juden.

62 Dienstblatt der Stadt Berlin, 1939 Part VII, S. 25, no. 27: Verfügung Behagel (Landeswohlfahrtsamt), 21 January 1939.

63 Gruner, *Judenverfolgung*, p. 61: Entry 3 December 1938.

64 StA Hamburg, 351–10 Sozialbehörde, StA 26.19, vol. 1, unnumbered: Sitzung des Beirats der Sozialverwaltung, 22 December 1938, p. 4; compare Ibid. Sitzung,

organized segregated compulsory labor (*Geschlossener Arbeitseinsatz*) not only for Jews who were unemployed but also for those who claimed welfare support. The Reich Institute for Employment and Unemployment Insurance (*Reichsanstalt für Arbeitsvermitlung und Arbeitslosenversicherung*) had ordered this measure on 20 December 1938, as the National Socialist state had "no interest" in supporting Jews who were fit for work "from public funds without receiving anything in return."[65] This step had its origins in the policy of separate mandatory labor that had been applied to Jews by welfare offices since the mid-1930s.

It was as if the anti-Jewish welfare ordinance was a long-awaited start signal — a whole series of city administrations (Breslau, Chemnitz, Düsseldorf, Cologne and Munich), stopped providing welfare assistance to Jews.[66] As for Berlin, the German capital, even though ordered by Mayor Lippert as early as the beginning of December 1938, the exclusion of Jews from public welfare was not immediately put into practice. The reason for this lag was that the Jewish community would have been overwhelmed if it had to provide for such a large number of dependants, as was officially confirmed by a trustee specially appointed by the capital after the pogrom.[67] In other towns as well, for example Frankfurt am Main, Jewish welfare was now controlled by local authorities.[68] Whether public welfare still intervened on behalf of Jews in need was determined by the local authority, as well as by the financial situation of the local Jewish community.

Also in December 1938, the municipal welfare office in Munich proposed to Fiehler, Mayor of Munich and Chairman of the German

21 November 1938, p. 8. Documents published by Ebbinghaus et al., *Heilen und Vernichten*, pp. 65–67. Compare Lohalm, "Hamburgs öffentliche," p. 510.

65 See in general, Wolf Gruner, *Der Geschlossene Arbeitseinsatz.*

66 Statistisches Reichsamt, *Die offene Fürsorge im Vierteljahr Januar/März 1939. Ergebnisse des Schnelldienstes der Reichsfürsorgestatistik*, Berlin 1939, p. 8. Compare *Dokumente Frankfurter Juden*, VI 44, p. 321: DGT-Konferenz in Berlin, 1 March 1939.

67 LA Berlin, Rep. 214, Acc. 794, no. 13, unnumbered: Verfügung Behagel (Landeswohlfahrtsamt) 29 December 1938. Compare Gruner, "Reichshauptstadt," pp. 240–242.

68 *Dokumente Frankfurter Juden*, p. 323, VI 46: Bericht Rechnungsprüfungsamt, 23 June 1939.

Council of Municipalities, that the ruling whereby the support of local Jewish residents is the responsibility of the voluntary Jewish welfare organizations also be applied to "Jews by race."[69] On 7 January 1939 Munich decreed that on principle all the Jewish poor — including non-members — were to be referred to the Jewish community.[70] The outcome of such severe measures was the subject at the South German Welfare Committee meeting of the German Council of Municipalities on 27 January 1939 in Bad Dürkheim. The members discussed how the town authorities were to behave when Jewish offices asked for help in meeting the costs they could not cover themselves.[71] The chairman of the association, a councilor from Nuremberg, maintained that on no account should the solvency of the local office be allowed to serve as a gauge. The central leadership of the Jewish welfare system, he claimed, would have to secure the support through a redistribution of funds or, if necessary, through aid from abroad. In order to get this point across on a national scale, a report was to be given at the German Council of Municipalities in Berlin.[72]

Along with the exclusion of Jewish Germans from the so-called "open welfare" system, which provided regular support to those who were in need but were not independent, there was much discussion on the treatment of Jewish Germans in the "closed welfare" system, which provided for the ill and handicapped in nursing and mental homes. Based on a survey conducted in Prussia, where the majority of those responsible for welfare declared themselves in favor of physical segregation of patients, the executive president of the German Council of Municipalities, Jeserich, asked the Minister of the Interior on 26 January 1939 for a ruling on what direction regional welfare associations should follow with regard to Jews who were mentally

69 YV, M1DN, no. 109, fol. 157–161: Vorlage Dezernat 6 für OB München, 13 December 1938.

70 Ibid., no. 121, fol. 30–31: Rundschreiben OB/Dezernat 6 München, 7 January 1939.

71 BAK, R 36, no. 902, unnumbered: Protokoll der 6. Tagung der Süddeutschen Arbeitsgemeinschaft für Wohlfahrtspflege am 27. 1. 1939 in Bad Dürkheim, pp. 1–6.

72 Ibid.; compare YV, M1DN, no. 162, fol. 107: Vermerk des OB/Dezernats 6 München zur 6. Tagung.

ill.[73] In the journal *Volksgesundheit*, the managing director of the Hamburg-Langenhorn Institution publicly demanded that "all mentally ill Jews" be concentrated in an institution for which the "Jewish community in Germany" was to take financial responsibility.[74]

The exclusionary process, which was considerably accelerated as the result of constant communication among the members of the German Council of Municipalities, took on new dimensions in the spring of 1939. In Berlin the regional welfare office, together with its trustee, decided that from May the Jewish community would have to take responsibility for the costs and organization of "closed welfare" in its entirety and for the feeding and clothing aid given in "open welfare," not only for its own community members, but also for "all Jews in need (Jews by race)," of both German and foreign nationality as well as all stateless Jews. The regional welfare office would, for the time being, continue to make cash payments for "open welfare," but these would be reduced to thirty Reichsmarks, including thirty percent for rent costs that had previously been paid additionally.[75] As early as the Bad Dürkheim meeting of the South German Welfare Committee of the German Council of Municipalities on 27 January, a representative of the city of Munich had called for the general introduction of such "special reduced rates for Jews," as practiced in his own city.[76]

Municipal authorities that still had to provide funds for the Jewish poor because of the financial difficulties of their Jewish communities increasingly demanded compensation payments from other Jewish communities in the Reich.[77] At the beginning of June 1939, the German Council of Municipalities implemented a regulation pertaining to the joint liability of all Jews in Germany for those Jews who required

73 BAK, R 36, no. 1842, fol. 32–33 and 39: DGT Berlin an RMdI, 26 January and 23 February 1939.

74 Ibid., fol. 37: Vermerk Zengerling (DGT Berlin), 27 February 1939.

75 Dienstblatt der Stadt Berlin, 1939 Part VII, S. 146, no. 143: Verfügung Steeg (OB/Landeswohlfahrtsamt), 12 May 1939; LA Berlin, Rep. 214, Acc. 794, no. 13, unnumbered: Verfügung Steeg (OB/Landeswohlfahrtsamt), 3 June 1939. Compare Gruner, *Judenverfolgung*, p. 66: Entry 12 May 1939.

76 YV, M1DN, no. 162, fol. 194–198: Koreferat des OB/Dezernat 6 München zur 6. Tagung der Süddt. Arbeitsgemeinschaft für Wohlfahrtspflege am 27. 1. 1939 in Bad Dürkheim (undated).

77 BAK, R 36, no. 1022, fol. 26, 26 B: DGT Sachsen an DGT Berlin, 17 May 1939.

social support, such that in the event of local Jewish welfare institutions running out of funds they should "fall back upon the umbrella organization."[78] The formal establishment of such an institution, the Reich Association of Jews in Germany (*Reichsvereinigung*), on 4 July 1939 had the effect of a catalyst; this mandatory organization was obliged to organize and finance a separate Jewish welfare system.[79]

This fact was used by many cities and municipal authorities, such as Essen and Wuppertal, as the last pretext in order to discontinue providing any kind of support.[80] A survey by the German Council of Municipalities in the Rhineland gives a clear picture of the process of exclusion in "open welfare" during the first six months of 1939. Of sixteen town boroughs in the region only a single welfare office was still paying its regular allowance to Jews, and this only if the local Jewish community was not able to meet the costs itself.[81] Things were not all that different in the large local districts of Thuringia and Saxony: Erfurt had stopped making the payments, and in Leipzig only a few districts were still paying. Only Dresden was still providing support.[82] The number of Jewish families receiving public assistance fell from over 10,000 in March 1939 to 6,500 in September.[83]

Shortly before the war began the German Council of Municipalities announced to its members, in conjunction with the Reich Ministry of the Interior, that public welfare should now "be freed of supporting the Jews without further delay."[84]

78 Ibid., fol. 29: DGT Berlin an DGT Westfalen/Lippe, 9 June 1939.

79 Compare Barkai, *Boykott*, pp. 171–172.

80 Statistisches Reichsamt, Die *offene Fürsorge im Vierteljahr Juli/September 1939*, Berlin 1939, p. 8.

81 Kurt Düwell, *Die Rheingebiete in der Judenpolitik des Nationalsozialismus vor 1942*, Bonn, 1968, pp. 286–293, Anhang V: DGT-Umfrageergebnis in der Rheinprovinz, 22 August 1939.

82 Statistisches Reichsamt, *Die offene Fürsorge im Vierteljahr April/Juni 1939*, Berlin 1939, p. 8; *Deutschland-Berichte der Sozialdemokratischen Partei 1934–1940*, Salzhausen 1989, vol. 1939, p. 924.

83 Statistisches Reichsamt, *Die offene Fürsorge im Vierteljahr Januar/März 1939,* Berlin 1939, p. 2; Idem, *Die offene Fürsorge im Vierteljahr Juli/September 1939,* Berlin 1939, p. 2.

84 BAK, R 36 DGT, no. 1022, fol. 50: DGT Berlin Brief auf Anfrage DGT Dresden, 25 August 1939.

Welfare Associations, the German Council of Municipalities and the Reich Security Main Office in Conflict (Autumn 1939—End of 1942)

Apparently, the pressure exerted by the municipalities increased after Poland was overrun. Several weeks later the *Reichsvereinigung* was obliged to assume the costs after November 1939 for any Jews in need of nursing care who were still in public clinics and institutions (i.e. closed welfare).[85] Although this was still not the case with open welfare, as the Reich Ministry of the Interior informed the German Council of Municipalities at the beginning of December,[86] the few welfare offices still making payments to Jews were applying even more rigid criteria in assessing the neediness of the Jewish poor. By the end of December 1939 the district welfare associations were making regular support payments to just 5,192 Jewish families, of whom four-fifths lived in Berlin.[87] By contrast, the *Reichsvereinigung* counted a total of 52,000 Jews in need of support in Germany.[88] In other words, almost one in three Jewish Germans by this stage required support, which now had to be raised predominantly by the *Reichsvereinigung* and its district offices.[89]

As early as spring 1940 the local authorities began a new round of discussions on the exclusion of Jews. At issue was whether — once the Jewish welfare offices completely take over the responsibility for social costs — they would provide for all Jews or only for members of the *Reichsvereinigung*. On 10 April 1940 Fiehler, head of the German Council of Municipalities, appealed to the staff of the deputy of the

85 Enacted since 1 November 1939; Bundesarchiv, former Abt. Potsdam (hereafter BAP), 75 C Re 1, no. 761, fol. 138–140: Cohn (RV/Fürsorge), an Oberpräsident/Landesfürsorgeverband Breslau, 18 April 1940. Compare Nordrhein-Westfälisches Hauptstaatsarchiv Düsseldorf, RW 53, no. 413, unnumbered: Rundschreiben Oberpräsident/Rheinprovinz, 23 September 1940.

86 BAK, R 36, no. 1022, fol. 66: RMdI-Brief vom 4. 12. 1939 mit Erlass.

87 Statistisches Reichsamt, *Die von den Bezirksfürsorgeverbänden laufend in bar unterstützten Parteien am 31. Dezember 1939,* Berlin 1940, pp. 2, 5.

88 Arbeitsbericht der Reichsvereinigung der Juden in Deutschland für das Jahr 1939, (Berlin 1940), p. 32.

89 On the change of conditions based on the war reform of labor legislation see Gruner, *Geschlossener Arbeitseinsatz*, pp. 113–116.

Führer for a "satisfactory legal clarification" of this question.[90] In addition he asked that Rudolf Hess use his influence to assign the same treatment to "persons in any way interrelated to Jews (at least if they belong to the Jewish religious community!), that Jews were receiving with regards to their legal entitlement to welfare."[91] Thus, in the summer of 1940, before the *Reichsvereinigung* took over full responsibility for supporting the Jews, the Rhineland regional department of the German Council of Municipalities claimed that "radical help can only be given if the solvency of the *Reichsvereinigung* is established by the German Council of Municipalities in Berlin or the Reich Ministry of the Interior."[92]

Yet it was neither the German Council of Municipalities nor the Reich Ministry of the Interior that had the authority at the time, but rather the RSHA.[93] On 12 September 1940 at a Berlin meeting of the chairmen of the German Committees for Welfare, Ministerial Counsel Ruppert of the Reich Ministry of the Interior announced:

> It has not yet been possible to order a complete exclusion in accord with the office for the supervision of Jewish wealth as the financial solvency of the *Reichsvereinigung* has not yet been clarified. As regards this point, however, an investigation is in progress. Should the complete solvency of the *Reichsvereinigung* be established, then a tightening of the measures decreed is envisioned, entitling the welfare associations to discontinue all support to Jews immediately. Up until this point, however, the current regulation will have to stay in force.[94]

This clear statement, however, was contradicted by Preiser, representing the German Council of Municipalities, who publicly told the Rhineland regional department in Düsseldorf that he believed the *Reichsvereinigung* to be capable of payment not only for closed welfare but also open welfare.[95]

90 YV, M1DN, no. 109, fol. 34: Fiehler (OB München), an Stab StdF München, 10 April 1940.

91 BAK, R 36, no. 1022, fol. 79: 2. Brief Fiehler (OB München), an Stab StdF München, 10 April 1940; compare YV, M1DN, no. 109, fol. 30–33.

92 NW-HStA Düsseldorf, RW 53, no. 413, unnumbered: Vermerk DGT Düsseldorf, 7 September 1940.

93 Compare NW-HStA Düsseldorf, RW 53, no. 413, unnumbered: Vermerk DGT Düsseldorf, 17 September 1940.

94 BAK, R 36, no. 1023, fol. 17–18: Vermerk DGT Berlin, 10 October 1940.

95 NW-HStA Düsseldorf, RW 53, no. 413, unnumbered: Vermerk DGT Düsseldorf,

At the same time, welfare associations in the Rhineland and Silesia were now pressuring the *Reichsvereinigung* to backdate their payments for the housing of Jews in public nursing and mental homes to as far back as the beginning of 1939. In Silesia, at least, they were successful.[96] It was only on 12 December 1940 that the Reich Ministry of the Interior ordered the isolation of mentally impaired Jews in the Bendorf-Sayn institution in the district of Koblenz.[97]According to demands by various welfare associations and cities in the German Council of Municipalities since 1938, all Jewish patients had to be isolated in that single facility maintained by the *Reichsvereinigung*.

While all the large cities had handed over the entire responsibility for welfare to the Jewish agencies by the end of 1939, this only took place in the capital one year later. By the end of 1940, Berlin too joined the fray, and the city welfare administration reneged on its obligation to provide support for over 3,000 more needy Jewish families.[98] After this it became the exception in Germany for Jewish families to take advantage of public welfare services.

But the success of the exclusionary measures taken since 1933 was not enough for the local welfare authorities. Now attention focused on the Jewish partners in "privileged mixed marriages." Since these individuals were not members of the *Reichsvereinigung*, they had to be supported by the state welfare associations. In addition, the welfare authorities started to increasingly train their sights on the "German-blooded" partners in these mixed marriages. In early 1941 the German Council of Municipalities was in agreement with the town authorities that both groups should be induced to join the *Reichsvereinigung*.[99]

17 September 1940; compare BAK, R 36, no. 1022, fol. 124: DGT Düsseldorf an DGT Berlin, 8 January 1941.

96 NW-HStA Düsseldorf, RW 53, no. 413, unnumbered: Rundschreiben Oberpräsident der Rheinprovinz, 23 September 1940; BAP, 75 C Re 1, no. 761, fol. 138–140: RV/Abt. Fürsorge (Cohn), an Oberpräsidenten/LFV in Breslau, 18 April 1940. BAK, R 36, no. 1022, fol. 96: Oberpräsident/LFV Schlesien an DGT Berlin, 29 August 1940; Ibid., fol. 99: RV/Abt. Fürsorge an Oberpräsidenten/LFV Schlesien, 4 June 1940; Ibid., fol. 117: Vermerk des DGT Berlin, 29 October 1940.

97 Reichsministerialblatt der inneren Verwaltung, 1940, p. 2261.

98 Gruner, "Reichshauptstadt," p. 245.

99 YV, M1DN, no. 109, fol. 242: Schlüter (DGT) an OB/Wohlfahrtsamt München, 2 April 1941.

On 9 May 1941 the Munich welfare office appealed to the Reich Ministry of the Interior to come to a decision as to whether German Jews could be forced into membership of the *Reichsvereinigung* by denying them all financial support.[100] Mayor Karl Fiehler also brought his full weight to bear as head of the Council of Municipalities and likewise pressed the Ministry for a verdict on the matter.[101] Although the RSHA could have blocked such new initiatives out of concern for the *Reichsvereinigung*'s budget and ability to operate,[102] it had already lost the battle. By summer 1941 no more than 250 Jewish families were still being supported by German state welfare associations — so few that once the deportations had begun in autumn 1941 the quarterly Reich Welfare Statistics discontinued its "Jew Category" both in the big cities and in the separate German states.[103]

For Jews, this meant that their welfare offices were in need of funds to an unprecedented degree in order to be able to finance both closed and now also open welfare. Along with the increased funds given to the Jewish communities and district offices by the *Reichsvereinigung*, funds were also taken from the so-called "Emigration Contribution" which was actually earmarked for helping Jews leave the country.[104] Financial restrictions were certainly also a reason for a new general regulation on welfare guidelines, passed by the Ministries of Labor and the Interior on 31 October 1941, instructing the *Reichsvereinigung* to reduce the allowances made by Jewish welfare institutions to twenty

100 BAK, R 36, no. 1022, fol. 150–151: OB/Wohlfahrtsamt München an RMdI, 9 May 1941; compare YV, M1DN, no. 109, fol. 90: OB/Wohlfahrtsamt München an Ruppert (RMdI), 9 May 1941.

101 BAK, R 36, no. 1022, fol. 149: Vorsitzender des DGT und OB München an DGT Berlin, 22 May 1941; Ibid., fol. 150–151: OB München/Wohlfahrtsamt an RMdI, 9 May 1941 (draft); Ibid., fol. 154–155: DGT an RMdI, 10 June 1941.

102 Until October the Ministry of the Interior made no decisions on this matter; BAK, R 36, no. 1022, fol. 156: DGT Berlin an Fiehler (October 1941).

103 Statistisches Reichsamt, *Die offene Fürsorge der Bezirksfürsorgeverbände im Halbjahr April–September 1941*, Berlin 1941, pp. 6–7; Idem, *Die von den Bezirksfürsorgeverbänden in bar unterstützten Parteien am 31 Dezember 1941,* Berlin 1942, pp. 2–5.

104 See Wolf Gruner, "Poverty and Persecution: The Reichsvereinigung, the Jewish Population and Anti-Jewish Policy in the Nazi State, 1939–1945," *Yad Vashem Studies*, 27 (1999), pp. 23–60.

percent below the local level for general welfare.[105] In Berlin as a result, the community was only permitted to pay an average of RM24 to the needy instead of the previous RM30.[106] Nonetheless, following the deportations that had begun in autumn 1941, the number of people receiving welfare benefits from the *Reichsvereinigung* declined at an ever-quickening rate. From autumn 1942 onwards, the receiving of welfare benefits from Jewish offices even became one of the Gestapo's criteria in its selection of Jews for deportation.[107]

Finally, in December 1942 the Reich Ministry of the Interior forbade government welfare associations from providing social services to Jews.[108] By this stage there was no longer any state support necessary or possible — even in emergency cases. The exclusion of Jews in the welfare sector was formally completed with this act, even though this could hardly have any further effect since this goal had largely been attained by the welfare authorities years before.[109]

Exclusion from Public Welfare Services as a Dynamic Process — Initial Conclusions

A few months after the pogrom in November 1938 the chairman of one of the district committees responsible for public welfare recommended to all mayors in the Idar-Oberstein district that public assistance services to German Jews be terminated with the following justification:

> I have become familiar with a number of cases where public welfare has been terminated by the administrative authorities months ago. Nevertheless, I have not learned of any case where a Jew has starved to death. In local mayors'

105 Reichsministerialblatt der inneren Verwaltung, 1941, p. 1951. Compare BAP, 75 C Re 1, no. 759, fol. 1: Vermerk der RV/Abt. Fürsorge, 19 August 1942.

106 BAP, 75 C Re 1, no. 759, fol. 2: Tabelle mit Richtsätzen der RV-Bezirksstellen als Anlage zum Vermerk (19 August 1942).

107 BAP, 75 C Re 1, Film 52407–23, fol. 83: Notiz Henschel (RV), über Rücksprache bei Gestapo Berlin, 28 September 1942.

108 Reichsministerialblatt der inneren Verwaltung, 1942, p. 2377.

109 The decree affected only the group of "*Geltungsjuden.*"

> reports I have read that they continue to be well-dressed and appear to be well-nourished.[110]

In light of the foregoing descriptions, the attitude of this civil servant cannot be regarded as an isolated incidence but rather has to be seen as a more or less institutionalized rule. The frequent efforts by local welfare offices to treat the Jewish poor worse than "Aryan needy"can be traced back to the mid-1930s. Scarce evidence of resistance can be found to these efforts. This behavior may be seen as part of a general sociopolitical reorientation. The public welfare associations gradually abandoned the principle of "care for the individual"[111] which originated in the period of the Weimar Republic, and reorganized their policies based on racist criteria into National Socialist "care for people" (*Volkspflege*), from which German Jews and other groups were excluded.[112] The antisemitic exclusionary process continued until the November 1938 pogrom, without ever having been sanctioned by law from the Reich government or covered by ministerial decree. Moreover, the cities and their respective welfare offices, in carrying out their practices, did not even cause a conflict of interests between the local and federal levels.

The municipalities not only planned how exclusion from public welfare services would be carried out, they also discussed the social and political ramifications of such measures. The German Council of Municipalities served as the forum for these questions, all of which were relevant for municipal authorities throughout the country. This is where local exclusionary plans and ideas could be presented by local mayors and were coordinated by the German Council of Municipalities. With the aid of the communication and coordination that existed within the German Council of Municipalities, the National Socialist

110 NW-HStA Düsseldorf, RW 53, no. 413, unnumbered: Rundschreiben Kreisausschuss, 1 April 1939.

111 On the principles of the "*Reichsfürsorgeverordnung*" (1923), see Schoen, *Armenfürsorge,* pp. 28–31.

112 See on a similar thesis Schoen, *Armenfürsorge*, p. 96. For an analysis of the "*Volkspflege*" concept see Hans-Uwe Otto and Heinz Sönker, "Volksgemeinschaft als Formierungsideologie des Nationalsozialismus," in: *Politische Formierung und soziale Erziehung im Nationalsozialismus*, Hans-Uwe Otto and Heinz Sönker, eds., Frankfurt am Main, 1991, pp. 50–77.

administration was able to break through the traditional vertically structured hierarchy of the civil service apparatus in order to realize their political strategy for domestic policy. The Reich Ministry of the Interior thus made direct studies of the locally developed models of discrimination and their practical application. The Reich Ministry developed its Exclusionary Ordinance of November 1938 based on this experience and later groundwork. After antisemitic policy on the state level was thoroughly redefined following the pogrom in 1938 and the complete isolation of the remaining Jews in a "forced community" was achieved, the significance of the German Council of Municipalities as a source of ideas and proposals for the government waned considerably but, nonetheless, remained relevant for certain issues.

As the "legal" attempt by many cities to unload their responsibility for welfare services failed in 1939–40 due to the financial problems of Jewish welfare institutions and the veto powers exercised by the then controlling Gestapo, the Council of Municipalities coordinated local initiatives after the anti-Jewish ordinance was passed. However, from the end of 1938 the weight of the Council of Municipalities had shifted with regard to centralized discrimination in the social sphere, just as the fronts between the institutions that were involved. At this point, the Reich Ministry of the Interior, the German Council of Municipalities, and the municipalities with their respective welfare associations were commonly opposed to the RSHA and the Gestapo. The latter controlled the separate Jewish welfare system. The former not only pressed for a quick takeover of welfare organization and costs through the *Reichsvereinigung*, but also insisted on rapid exclusion of other groups such as Jews in "mixed marriages." The RSHA was reticent on this point due to its more general view of the persecution policy. It was interested in the functioning of the Jewish mandatory organization and wanted to avoid any financial or organizational encumbrance to the *Reichsvereinigung*. This selective conflict of interests led to absurd reproaches — seen from today's vantage point — such as that expressed by the leadership of the German Council of Municipalities. It was said that Reinhard Heydrich "apparently was interested in securing the greatest possible protection of the privileged Jews."[113] The German

113 YV, M1DN, no. 109, fol. 118: DGT Berlin Zeitler an Fiehler, 13 October 1941.

Council of Municipalities as an institution may thus be described as a functional relay between local and state persecution planning in the social sphere.

The above description of the development of persecutory strategies in the social welfare system provokes a rethinking of "familiar" topographies such as the often stated difference between the NSDAP and the rest of society, or that of a quasi natural distance between the administrative authorities of the old school and the prevailing ideology, or even the conception that local authorities were only involved in passive implementation of decisions made by the Nazi leadership. Thus several questions arise: How can the often-observed precursory activism on the part of individual civil servants be explained? What is actually reflected here — radical ideology, bureaucratic estrangement or simply zeal? Clearly, several factors played a role — the forced antisemitism that derived from the new social reality after 1933, new concepts of racism, and traditional authoritarian views of the relationship between the state and the individual.[114] Not to be underestimated is also the internalization of administrative interests in the behavior of their members of staff.

At the same time the Nazi party positioned its personnel. A key figure in this regard was the chairman of the German Council of Municipalities. Functionaries like Karl Fiehler who occupied multiple positions incorporated varying group interests in one person, such as those of the cities, the state and the party. Thus the NSDAP was able to target its discriminatory intentions much more effectively to municipal affairs; at the same time municipal interests could influence central policy creation within the leading committees of the NSDAP than was possible via a local NSDAP organizational group.

It is clear from the developments presented here that the process of exclusion in the area of public welfare services can neither be explained in terms of exclusive state orchestration nor spontaneous local developments. It would be more accurate to speak about a mutual dynamic interaction. An increasingly radical public consensus developed in favor of the exclusion from German society of the weakest

114 On the "*Gleichschaltung*" of the female welfare staff see Emilija Mitrovic, "Fürsorgerinnen im Nationalsozialismus," in: *Opfer und Täterinnen*, Angelika Ebbinghaus, ed., Hamburg, 1987, pp. 14–36.

section of the Jewish population — the Jewish poor. It was precisely this rapidly growing group, created as a result of persecution and consequently dependent on the Nazi regime, and unable to emigrate because of the lack of financial resources, that constituted an essential hindrance to the policy of expulsion. This development was one of the cardinal reasons for the National Socialist leadership's decision of a new double strategy of persecution in 1938 — forced expulsion and isolation of the remaining Jews in a "forced community."

Nazi Antisemitic Policy on the Regional Level

Local Administration and Nazi Anti-Jewish Policy

UWE LOHALM

In the research on the deprivation, segregation and persecution of the Jews in National Socialist Germany, little attention has been paid to the behavior and acts of certain departments of the Reich and local administrations that were not themselves directly involved in the persecution that was taking place. Likewise, little has been written about the fate of the Jews among the people for whom these administrative bodies were responsible.[1] This also applies to public welfare administration and the lot of the Jewish welfare recipients, although their number was constantly multiplying as a result of the growing repression.[2] If at all, reference is made to the exclusion of Jews from the *Winterhilfswerk* (winter aid) from 1935 onward and from public relief as ordained by the November decree of 1938. Until

1 Ursula Büttner, "Die deutsche Gesellschaft und die Judenverfolgung — ein Forschungsproblem," as well as the general summary by Horst Matzerath, "Bürokratie und Judenverfolgung," in: *Die Deutschen und die Judenverfolgung im Dritten Reich*, Ursula Büttner, ed., Hamburg, 1992, pp. 2–29 and pp. 105–129.

2 Contrary to studies on Jewish self-help at that time: Salomon Adler-Rudel, *Jüdische Selbsthilfe unter dem Naziregime 1933–1945 im Spiegel der Berichte der Reichsvertretung der Juden in Deutschland*, Tübingen, 1974; David Kramer, "Jewish Welfare Work under the Impact of Pauperisation," in: *Die Juden im nationalsozialistischen Deutschland. The Jews in Nazi Germany 1933–1943*, Arnold Paucker, ed., Tübingen, 1986, pp. 173–188; Clemens Vollnhals, "Jüdische Selbsthilfe bis 1938," in: *Die Juden in Deutschland 1933–1945. Leben unter nationalsozialistischer Herrschaft*, Wolfgang Benz, ed., Munich, 1988, pp. 314–411; Jüdisches Museum der Stadt Frankfurt am Main, ed., *Zedaka. Jüdische Sozialarbeit im Wandel der Zeit. 75 Jahre Zentralwohlfahrtsstelle der Juden in Deutschland 1917–1992*, Frankfurt am Main, 1992; Esriel Hildesheimer, *Jüdische Selbstverwaltung unter dem NS-Regime. Der Existenzkampf der Reichsvertretung und Reichsvereinigung der Juden in Deutschland*, Tübingen, 1994.

then Jews had the right to expect the same degree of support from the state as non-Jews. In effect, this order, together with the tenth decree of the Law of German Citizenship of 4 July 1939, through which the *Reichsvereinigung der Juden in Deutschland* came into being, brought about a fundamental legal change in the relationship between public relief and the Jews.[3] But in practice this was even more complicated than the general differentiation typical of the period just before and after the November decree, and to a certain extent more contradictory than might be expected. Long before 1938, local welfare offices, confronted with antisemitic claims, began to discriminate against Jews with their own measures, yet without infringing on the basic legal position of Jews in the welfare system. In this essay, I will use the example of the Hamburg Welfare Office[4] to demonstrate the participation, reaction and activities of a local administration within the framework of National Socialist antisemitic policies, and will end it by drawing some basic conclusions.

Exclusion of Jewish Employees and Suppliers

Like all public administrative departments, the Hamburg Welfare Office had to deal with the consequences of the Law on the Reestablishment of the Professional Civil Service, passed on 7 April 1933. According to this legislation, numerous civil servants, employees and workers were forced to leave the employ of the state.[5] In case where the regulations

3 *Reichsgesetzblatt* (hereinafter *RGBl*), 1938 I, p. 1649, and 1939 I, pp. 1097–1099.

4 At this stage it is important to point out that the Welfare Office experienced several changes in its structure and its titles between 1933 and 1945. It existed as a Welfare Office until autumn 1933, it was then integrated as a Welfare Body into an intermediate office known as the Health and Welfare Office, again from autumn 1936 onward existed as an independent Welfare Office, and in April 1938 took on the title of Social Administration Office. Uwe Lohalm, "Wohlfahrtspolitik und Modernisierung. Bürokratisierung, Professionalisierung und Funktionsausweitung der Hamburger Fürsorgebehörde im Nationalsozialismus," in: *Norddeutschland im Nationalsozialismus*, Frank Bajohr, ed., Hamburg, 1993, pp. 387–413.

5 On the application of the *Berufsbeamtengesetz* in Hamburg, Uwe Lohalm, "Hamburgs Verwaltung und öffentlicher Dienst im Dritten Reich," *Zeitschrift des Vereins für Hamburgische Geschichte,* 82 (1996), pp. 167–208, especially 190–196: Until 31 May 1934 a total of 83 Jewish civil servants had to leave the employ of

of §3 (retirement of "non-Aryan" civil servants) could not be applied, dismissals were effected with the help of alleged political unreliability (§4) or under the pretext of administrative simplification (§6). There were also some additional dismissals due to pressure from newly employed National Socialist colleagues,[6] or as a result of denunciation from outside, which was typical of the SA.[7] However, unlike the situation in most other departments, this law affected a much larger staff which was involved in the day-to-day matter of providing relief to those in need. These personnel included people who were working in addition to their normal professional duties, such as doctors in various official departments and numerous contractually bound doctors in the decentralized offices, the so-called *Wohlfahrtsstellen* (welfare offices)[8] as well as a large number of honorary social workers on the advisory boards,[9] and male and female nurses. Among these, all who were Jewish were urged, as inconspicuously as possible, to voluntarily relinquish

the state as a resulf of §3. Furthermore, there were still numerous Jews among those dismissed for political reasons or on the grounds of restructurization of the administration.

6 See the case of the war-disabled Julius Plaut, who was dismissed in May 1934 because of alleged differences of opinion with National Socialist colleagues. The authorities adhered to this dismissal even after intervention by the victim with the *Reichsstatthalter* and in the *Reichskanzlei*. Staatsarchiv Hamburg (hereinafter StA Hamburg), Senatskanzlei-Personalabteilung I, 1934 Ma 1/200.

7 SA-Untergruppe Hamburg to Senator von Allwörden, 29 March and 9 June 1933, StA Hamburg, NSDAP, B 202.

8 Leitender Oberarzt der Wohlfahrtsbehörde Dr. Kurt Peter to SA-Untergruppe Hamburg, 19 March 1933, StA Hamburg, NSDAP, B 202; Letter of Dr. Johannes S. to Martini, 30 June 1933, StA Hamburg, Sozialbehörde I, AK 40.16. A final legislation was not passed until spring 1935, according to which no Jewish doctors should be employed as medical officers for the Welfare Authorities with effect from 1 July 1935, although the Association of Health Insurance Schemes in Germany had expressly announced their disapproval. This involved a total of about 100 doctors. Vermerk Martini, 25 March 1935, and Notiz Leitender Oberarzt, 14 Mai 1935, StA Hamburg, Sozialbehörde I, GF 10.11and 14.54; see also StA Hamburg, Jüdische Gemeinden, 297, vol. 22, Minutes of the Meeting of the Board on 20 March and on 9 July 1935.

9 D.G. Wolfsberg to Wohlfahrtsbehörde, 27 May 1933, StA Hamburg, Sozialbehörde I, KO 13.12, vol. II.

their honorary positions.[10] Most welfare officers solved this problem by combing through their lists to find supposedly Jewish-sounding names. They then contacted the honorary area representatives and proceeded to address the individuals in question. At first it was not compulsory to present proof of one's descent.[11]Most bowed to this pressure, even those who could rightfully claim to remain in office having fought on the front in World War I.[12] Only two expressly resisted this unreasonable pressure. Nurse Magdalene Hirsch protested in a letter dated 1 May 1933:

> For the past 3 years I have spent the best part of my spare time serving the Welfare Office and have dedicated myself as best I could to the sector allotted to me. I have fulfilled my official duties to the best of my knowledge and ability. If today the new civil laws demand my dismissal from duty, then the officials should renounce their confidence in me and remove me from my position. I will not quit my service to the needy in my area voluntarily.[13]

The Welfare Office reacted by dismissing her without even a letter of thanks. Following this, another three Jews remained in honorary service for a short time only. From then on, each newly proposed applicant was to submit an explanation concerning his or her "Aryan" ancestry.[14]

Secondly, the welfare offices were under extreme pressure from individual tradespeople and professional organizations to reject Jewish-owned firms that supplied relief services. They referred to the first public appeal for boycotting and to the antisemitic laws, and pointed out that the slogan "The state authorities only buy from Germans"[15] had been published in the press in June 1933, relating to a former decree of the Reich's Minister of Finance. On the other hand, the official

10 Präses der Wohlfahrtsbehörde an die Leiter der Wohlfahrtsstellen, 25 April 1933, StA Hamburg, Sozialbehörde I, VG 12.13.

11 Berichte der einzelnen Wohlfahrtsstellen, May 1933, StA Hamburg, Sozialbehörde I, EO 31.16.

12 Ergebnis der Rundfrage betr. nichtarische ehrenamtliche Wohlfahrtspfleger, 30 May 1933, StA Hamburg, Sozialbehörde I, EO 31.16.

13 StA Hamburg, Sozialbehörde I, EO 31.16.

14 Ergebnis der Rundfrage betr. nichtarische ehrenamtliche Wohlfahrtspfleger, 30 May 1933, and Verwaltungsabteilung an die Leiter der Wohlfahrtsstellen, 30 May 1933, StA Hamburg, Sozialbehörde I, EO 31.16 and VG 12.13.

15 *Hamburger Nachrichten* No. 260, 7 June 1933; see also *Hamburger Anzeiger* No. 129, 6 June 1933.

government policy of the Reich initially sought to keep the economy free of any antisemitic activities. Viewing economic recovery as the primary task and that unemployment be "given priority above all other considerations," the Reich forbade any form of ideologically motivated interference in the economy.[16] This directive was also adhered to by the Reich later on.[17] However, the Reich often felt compelled to point out the obvious facts to the state authorities.[18] The welfare offices were thus confronted with a difficult decision — to choose between public pressure and official policy. To make matters worse, the Hamburg Senate took no clear stand behind the Reich regulations and even issued a secret advisory that contradicted government policy.[19] Also, employees in public services had been urged from the very beginning to buy in German shops only and thus demonstrate their obligation towards the state.[20] The Welfare Office and its individual committees

16 See the "Richtlinien über die Vergebung öffentlicher Aufträge" concluded by the Reichskabinett on 1 July 1933, which were sent to all the ministries and local governments together with a letter by the Minister of Economics dated 19 July 1933. StA Hamburg, Sozialbehörde I, WA 10.18; as well as the letter from the Minister of Propaganda dated 9 June 1933 and from the Minister of Economics dated 8 September 1933 to the German Industrie- und Handelstag, StA Hamburg, Finanzdeputation IV, VuO IIA 1be. In general on this problem see Avraham Barkai, *Vom Boykott zur "Entjudung." Der wirtschaftliche Existenzkampf der Juden im Dritten Reich 1933–1943*, Frankfurt am Main, 1988.

17 This was mainly carried by the Minister of Economics and by the Ministry of Foreign Affairs.Vertraulicher Runderlass des Reichs- und Preussischen Ministers des Innern vom 18. April 1935 mit einem Bericht über eine Besprechung der betroffenen Reichsministerien und des Beauftragten des Stellvertreters des Führers am 15. November 1934 in Berlin. StA Hamburg, Senatskanzlei-Präsidialabteilung, 1935 A 35.

18 The Reich Minister for Internal Affairs emphasized in his letter dated 17 January 1934 that it would be critical to extend the "deutsche Ariergesetzgebung" to areas in which it did not apply. This applies "in particular as the National Socialist government has repeatedly explained, to free trade." The letter was distributed by the Senate to all Hamburg authority offices. StA Hamburg, Senatskanzlei-Präsidialabteilung, 1935 A 35.

19 Vertrauliches Schreiben des Regierenden Bürgermeisters an die Senatoren, 22 October 1934, StA Hamburg, Senatskanzlei-Präsidialabteilung, 1935 A 35.

20 Ersuchen des Senats, 17 March 1933, StA Hamburg, Senatskanzlei-Personalabteilung I, 1933 Ja 10. Whereas later in Hamburg's neighboring towns such as Wandsbek, clear instructions were given which prohibited any kind of business and private contact for employees of public services under threat of

reacted to this in a completely inconsistent manner. But nowhere did anyone protest that existing relationships with Jewish businessmen be maintained.

In March 1933 the Guild of Shoemakers in Hamburg, Altona and the surrounding areas petitioned the authorities, complaining about the alleged preference given to Philipp Jacob for the supply of orthopedic shoes and promising to supply the authorities with a list of other competent companies.[21] In his answer the president of the Welfare Office, Oskar Martini, protested vehemently against the complaint. But he accepted, without any limitations, the list promised to him by the Association, which of course no longer included the Jewish company Philipp Jacob. He even went so far as to publish the list in a "register of all companies approved for the supply of ready-made orthopedic shoe products with effect as from 1 July 1933."[22] He adhered to this decision even when one welfare office reproached him, maintaining they could not do without that particular supplier in that sector. This prompted his decree on 21 July 1933 that the Philipp Jacob firm "being a non-Aryan company could no longer be considered suitable for supplying to the welfare office."[23]Shortly afterwards the authorities were sent the new regulations from the *Reichskabinett* with the command of the Senate to "strictly enforce them."[24] Following this, on 12 August 1933 the individual welfare offices were instructed to allow the needy to decide for themselves where to buy the approved items. As a supplement to

disciplinary measures, in Hamburg general instructions were simply given as it was assumed "that every civil servant is aware that he should basically not get involved in business with any Jews." Oberbürgermeister von Wandsbek Ziegler to Hamburgisches Staatsamt, 6 October 1937, and Vermerk Toepffer/Staatsamt, 25 October 1937, StA Hamburg, Senatskanzlei-Personalabteilung II, 265. According to a judgment passed by the Reichsarbeitsgericht on 22 September 1937, which met with a lengthy response in the general press, to buy goods from a Jewish shop represented a good reason for immediate dismissal. *Der Gemeindetag,* 32 (1938), p. 481.

21 Letter, 20 March 1933, StA Hamburg, Sozialbehörde II,021.50–1.

22 Schreiben Martinis, 24 March 1933 and Verzeichnis, StA Hamburg, Sozialbehörde II, 021.50–11.

23 Aktenvermerk Meyer, 11 July 1933, and Aktenvermerk Dunkel, 21 July 1933, StA Hamburg, Sozialbehörde II, 021.50–11.

24 Senat an alle Behörden, 22 July 1933, StA Hamburg, Sozialbehörde I, WA 10.18.

this a further circular, dated 14 November 1933, stipulated that the amount should be reimbursed to the needy person "even if the supplier is a non-Aryan."[25] However, this new instruction did not lead to Philipp Jacob being reinstated in the list of suppliers to the Welfare Office. This was finally decided in a report by the Board of Trade which, upon an inquiry from the authorities, certified "that Jacob, in a manner typical of the peculiarities of his race, has made it his practice to gain access to the authorities and suppress other companies. In view of the present circumstances it is time to strike Jacob from the list of suppliers and give preference to other companies that had no access before."[26]

Whereas the advance made by the Shoemakers' Guild represented a unanimous initiative, the opticians' trade took only individual action which did not even meet with the approval of its Guild.[27] Here too, attention was drawn to Jewish competitors whose inclusion in the list of suppliers to the welfare office would no longer be tolerated. How is it possible it was asked, that Jewish companies continue to supply to the relief departments? The main target of these attacks was Campbell, an old established optical firm whose Jewish owner was unjustly charged by the district attorney for crimes against the German economy and was forced to flee the country. An optician who opened up a shop on the Mönckebergstrasse, the main shopping street in Hamburg, wrote on 31 May 1934 in his application for a license to operate a business that the two nearest opticians were "non-Aryans" and that a warrant for the arrest of one of these men had been issued on charges of treason.[28] Another shop owner emphasized his long-standing membership of the NSDAP and went on, "It is a ridicule of our National Socialist state when Jews and their associates are allowed unswervingly to continue to supply and I am still barred from doing so." He did not want to be "ranked behind the Jews whose inferiority has at last been notoriously proved by their fleeing from prosecution and being wanted by the

25 Rundschreiben Nr. 44, 14 November 1933, StA Hamburg, Sozialbehörde I, WA 10.18.

26 Gewerbekammer to Fürsorgewesen, 3 and 28 May 1934, StA Hamburg, Sozialbehörde II, 021.50–11.

27 Anträge 1933/34, StA Hamburg, Sozialbehörde II, 021.50–3.

28 Letter to Fürsorgeamt, 31 May 1934, and Niederschrift, 6 June 1934, StA Hamburg, Sozialbehörde II, 021.50–3.

district attorney."[29] The Welfare Office, which had granted only some applications, placed both these opticians on the list of those allowed to supply the welfare offices, but did not strike Campbell from their rolls.[30] Instead, they negotiated with the Opticians' Guild to clarify the admission procedures for suppliers to welfare recipients, but the question of the admission of "non-Aryan" firms as suppliers remained open and was excluded from the contract finally signed between the authorities and the Opticians' Guild in April 1935. According to this agreement, licenses were to be granted exclusively to members of the guild, which at that time still included some Jewish businesses.[31]

Thirdly, the NSDAP and its organs had already insisted that the welfare administration do something about this state of affairs. The most vociferous was the SA, which demanded an explanation from the welfare authorities. Its new National Socialist president, Dr. Friedrich Ofterdinger, explained apologetically to the SA leaders that the Welfare Office was still "dependent on the Jewish junk dealers" for the supply of textiles as it was not possible "to manage entirely without these gentlemen. It seems that up to now no Aryan has been born who is suitable for this dirty business. On the other hand it is not unimportant to the authorities whether we buy a second-hand but good suit for 15 RM from a junk dealer or one for 30 RM in an Aryan clothing shop."[32] The welfare office noted a steady increase in this pressure during 1935.[33] For example, in July 1935 the liaison officer between the *Gauleitung* and the Senate, Dr. Hellmuth Becker, passed an official inquiry onto the welfare administration. In August of the same year the *Gauamtsleiter* of the National Socialist National Welfare, Wilhelm von Allwörden, also a senator, declared that licenses to all suppliers "without reference

29 Letters to Fürsorgebehörde, 22 May and 4 July 1934, StA Hamburg, Sozialbehörde II, 021.50–3.

30 Verfügung, 7 June 1934, and Liste der vom Fürsorgewesen zugelassenen optischen Geschäfte, July 1934, StA Hamburg, Sozialbehörde II, 021.50–3.

31 Vertrag, 30 April 1935, StA Hamburg, Sozialbehörde II, 021.50–3.

32 Ofterdinger to SA der NSDAP Brigade 12, 4 January 1935, StA Hamburg, NSDAP, B 202.

33 This fits into a generally accepted activation of antisemitic economic propaganda in spring and summer 1935. Helmut Genschel, *Die Verdrängung der Juden aus der Wirtschaft im Dritten Reich*, Göttingen, 1966, pp. 109–113; Barkai, *Vom Boykott zur "Entjudung,"* pp. 67–69.

to their racial descent" was no longer possible.[34] In the same month, the director of the relief department complained to the head office that the party and party organizations were constantly accusing him and his staff of paying bills owed to Jewish suppliers. He therefore suggested marking the licenses with the following proviso: "Payment will not be reimbursed if the goods are purchased from a Jewish supplier."[35] Scrutiny of the authorization procedure, revealed that the decentralized welfare offices as a rule, paid the bills presented by recipients even when the supplier was a Jew. The welfare recipients of one office were told not to buy in Jewish-owned shops. Another office warned that bills owed to Jews would no longer be paid. The welfare offices then requested lists of Jewish-owned businesses similar to the list of doctors that already existed.[36] In its general conclusion, the Hamburg Welfare Office stated that the issue of licenses to supply welfare recipients should observe the guidelines issued by the Reich government in July 1933. However, clarification of the matter was urgent as "public opinion [was] not consistent with the state's administrative regulations."[37] Alfred Richter, the senator for Internal Affairs, and the Hamburg *Staatsamt* tried to find a solution that would satisfy the whole of Germany. At the same time, in September 1935, the *Staatsamt* once again confirmed the regulation for Hamburg whereby non-Aryan businesses were to be excluded when

34 Becker to Präsident der Gesundheits- und Fürsorgebehörde, 25 July 1935; Vermerk Martini about talks with von Allwörden, 19 August 1935, StA Hamburg, Sozialbehörde I, WA 10.18.

35 Wohlfahrtsstelle VI to Wirtschaftsabteilung, 26 August 1935, StA Hamburg, Sozialbehörde I, WA 10.18.

36 Aktenvermerk Gotte, 23 August 1935, and Niederschrift der Dienstbesprechung der Wohlfahrtsstelle VII, 28 August 1935, StA Hamburg, Sozialbehörde I, WA 10.18 and VG 20.10. The Personalabteilung put "Verzeichnisse jüdischer Ärzte" at the disposal of the Fürsorgeabteilung but forbade any posting. Letter of 26 November 1936, StA Hamburg, Sozialbehörde I, AW 50.10. — In Prussia the Minister of the Interior had already announced to the Bezirksfürsorgeverbände in a circular dated 7 November 1933 that he had no objection to an "exclusion of non-Aryan doctors from treating the needy." *Ministerial-Blatt für die Preussische innere Verwaltung*, as of 1936 *Ministerialblatt des Reichs- und Preussischen Ministeriums des Innern* (hereinafter MBliV), 1933, p. 1335.

37 Gesundheits- und Fürsorgebehörde to Senator der Inneren Verwaltung, 21 August 1935, StA Hamburg, Sozialbehörde I, WA 10.18.

placing orders for public services.[38] However, both offices initially deferred their efforts owing to the still unswerving attitude of the responsible ministries of the Reich; they could not ignore the latest orders of the Minister of Economics dated 4 November 1935 in which it was unmistakably stated "that until a new regulation has been issued regarding the position of Jews in the economy, all measures taken by lower-ranking offices against Jewish businesses are prohibited."[39] This also put an end to all other agreements between the welfare administration and the Association of Second-Hand and Junk Dealers, in which non-Aryan dealers were excluded from the list of suppliers to the needy, which the authorities had accepted without hesitation.[40] The significance of this complex of questions on the welfare policy at that time is reflected by the Health and Welfare Office report on the political situation dated 1 October 1935: "With the period covered by this report only one issue has arisen which is of particular importance and of general interest. It is the question of the placing of orders by the authorities with Jewish businesses and companies."[41]

The question of licensing Jewish businesses came up again in 1937 with the incorporations of districts resulting from the *Gross-Hamburg-Gesetz*. The permits issued by the welfare office of Harburg-Wilhelmsburg from April 1933 already bore the statement: "Does not apply to Jewish shops, warehouses and penny-bazaars." This welfare office was not willing to comply with the attitude in Hamburg that this was illegal. The departmental head responsible, Paul Prellwitz, declared: "I am convinced that an interpretation of this kind would not be understood by anybody in the public except the Jews and would therefore request that this matter be looked into and the actions of the

38 Staatsamt to Senator der Inneren Verwaltung, 4 September 1935. Once again, it was pointed out that in accordance with the secret letter of the Regierender Bürgermeister "there is no doubt, that any order cannot be given to non-Aryan businesses." StA Hamburg, Senatskanzlei-Präsidialabteilung, 1935 A 35.

39 StA Hamburg, Sozialbehörde I, WA 10.18. Letters of Senator Richter and Senator Ahrens, 2 and 5 October 1935, StA Hamburg, Senatskanzlei-Präsidialabteilung, 1935 A 35.

40 Wirtschaftsabteilung, Büsing, to Sonderreferent Brandt, 18 February 1936, Ofterdinger to Senator der Inneren Verwaltung, 13 March 1936, and Staatsamt to Senator der Inneren Verwaltung, 16 April 1936, StA Hamburg, Sozialbehörde I, WA 10.18.

41 StA Hamburg, Senatskanzlei-Präsidialabteilung, 1935 A 35.

corresponding economic department be adapted to suit the prevailing opinion."[42] The matter was referred for further consideration to the Office for Trade, Shipping and Commerce, which, after consulting the *Reichsstatthalter* Karl Kaufmann, passed the resolution in December 1937 that the whole of Hamburg should henceforward adopt the Harburg policy.[43] From then onward the finance department of the Welfare Office was extremely busy. To ensure that all Jewish suppliers were registered, it turned to the various guilds, the retail department of the Chamber of Industry and Commerce, as well as the Association of Second-Hand Dealers. These bodies carried out surveys among their members and provided the Welfare Office with lists of their "non-Aryan" members.[44] On behalf of the welfare administration and the Office for Trade, Shipping and Commerce, the chairman of the guild or trade association then notified the firms listed that, as of 1 March 1938, they would be barred from supplying the welfare offices. Any inquiries as to the instigator of these regulations would remain unanswered.[45] On 2 March 1938 the welfare offices received the order to print the following stipulation on the purchase permits: "Not valid for purchases from Jewish companies."[46] On 1 April 1938, the first lists of licensed suppliers that excluded all Jewish companies were issued.[47]

Hamburg's policy in this sector had therefore forerun the policy of the Reich by several weeks. Not until 17 March 1938 did the Minister

42 Prellwitz to Martini, 16 October 1937; see also Industrie-und Handelskammer Harburg-Wilhelmsburg to Behörde für Handel, Schiffahrt und Gewerbe, 22 April 1937, StA Hamburg, Sozialbehörde I, WA 10.18.

43 Aktenvermerke Martini, 7 December 1937, and Büsing, 9 December 1937, StA Hamburg, Sozialbehörde I, WA 10.18.

44 See the correspondence of the Wirtschaftsabteilung betr. Ausschliessung nichtarischer Geschäfte von der Belieferung der Fürsorgebehörde, December 1937 until February 1938, StA Hamburg, Sozialbehörde I, WA 10.18.

45 Vermerk Büsing, 25 February 1938, StA Hamburg, Sozialbehörde I, WA 10.18.

46 Rundschreiben der Verwaltungsabteilung über den Ausschluss nichtarischer Optiker, 24 February 1938, and Vermerk Büsing, 2 March 1938, StA Hamburg, StA Hamburg, Sozialbehörde II, 021.50–3, and Sozialbehörde I, WA 10.18.

47 Liste der zugelassenen Lieferanten für Brillen, künstliche Augen und Brillenreparaturen ab 1. April 1938 as well as Dienstvorschrift über die Schuhversorgung, 5 July 1938. The latter listed once again all Jewish shoe shops which were no longer licensed to supply. StA Hamburg, Sozialbehörde II, 021.50–3, and Sozialbehörde I, VG 28.67.

of Finance rectify the still valid regulations of the Reich cabinet dated 14 July 1933 by issuing a secret decree which stipulated as follows: "When placing orders for public contracts it should be made sure that Jewish companies do not participate." The social administration department was not informed of this decree until 31 May 1938 in a confidential message from the town treasurer.[48] When on 14 July 1938 the Reich Minister of the Interior issued a circular on the "Enforcement of the Third Ordinance of the Citizenship Law" dated 14 June 1938 concerning the exact registration and listing of all Jewish commercial businesses, the head of the economic department simply remarked: "Within our social administration, nothing is to be done for the time being. The commercial enterprises in question are already registered and have been excluded from the allocation of orders."[49]

Marginalization and Segregation of the Jews

Of the measures taken to segregate the Jews mentioned so far, the real clients of the Welfare Office — the welfare recipients — were not directly affected. But the bureaucracy of the welfare administration was familiar with ways of segregating Jews long before November 1938, even though these were mostly special measures taken by the Reich in which the welfare authority was only additionally involved or which it carried out in its capacity as administrator. This already began in 1933 when the welfare offices were asked to be consultants for the granting of loans to young married couples; from 1 July 1937 they were solely responsible for the processing of all applications.[50] From the very beginning these loans were only granted to persons who could offer a guarantee that they would "wholeheartedly support the national State." According to a decree by the Minister of Finance on 5 July 1933 these did not include non-Aryan marriage partners.[51] This Aryan

48 StA Hamburg, Sozialbehörde I, WA 10.18.

49 Vermerk Büsing, 1 August 1938, StA Hamburg, Sozialbehörde I, WA 10.18.

50 Dienstverordnungen über Ehestandsdarlehen, 7 June 1935 and 28 June 1937, StA Hamburg, Sozialbehörde I, EF 30.14.

51 Durchführungsverordnung über die Gewährung von Ehestandsdarlehen, 20 June 1933, *RGBl* 1933 I, pp. 377–379, and Uwe Dietrich Adam, *Judenpolitik im Dritten Reich*, Düsseldorf, 1972, p. 74.

clause also found its way into the stipulations for granting radio license reductions and exemptions that the Minister of Posts had decreed on 25 March 1935 and that, after the passing of the Nuremberg Laws, only required corresponding indemnification. The Welfare Office had always processed these applications on behalf of the Reichspost.[52] Moreover, Jewish citizens were expressly excluded from the National Socialist state allowances for large families. Even before the Reich government became involved in 1935, the Senator for Internal Affairs, Richter, had stipulated on 8 December 1933 who should get parental assistance in the form of single lump sums. These were to be paid by the welfare offices to particularly large families, provided these were "healthy and of Aryan descent."[53]Similar stipulations were made by the Minister of Finance on 26 September 1935 concerning the granting of single allowances to large families. The welfare offices were also commissioned with the processing of these applications.[54]The regulations published by the Minister of Finance on 24 March 1936 for granting regular parental assistance limited the beneficiaries to citizens of the Reich, as defined by the Reich Citizenship Law. Although initially only the Revenue Offices were commissioned with such matters, the welfare offices were later integrated into the system.[55] The Reich's new regulations for low-income pensioners intervened in the practice of the welfare system in a even stricter way than the previous measures. This meant that from the beginning this category of persons constituted the immediate clientele of the welfare offices. The low-income pensioners — whose numbers increased in 1934, still without any limitations[56] — received

52 *Amtsblatt des Reichspostministeriums* 1935, pp. 149–152; Dienstvorschrift über die Befreiung von Rundfunkgebühren, 8 April 1935, and Nachtrag, 11 August 1936, StA Hamburg, Sozialbehörde I, AF 11.20.

53 Dienstvorschrift über Beihilfen an besonders kinderreiche Familien, StA Hamburg, Sozialbehörde I, StA 27.71.

54 Verordnung des Reichsfinanzministers, 15 September 1935, and Durchführungsbestimmungen, 26 September 1935, *RGBl* 1935 I, p. 1160 and pp. 1206–1208, and Auszug aus dem Protokolle des Senats, 21 October 1935, StA Hamburg, Sozialbehörde I, AF 84.25.

55 *RGBl* 1936 I, pp. 252–254, and Rundschreiben des Landesfürsorgeamtes an alle Wohlfahrtsstellen, 2 June 1938, StA Hamburg, Sozialbehörde I, VG 28.67.

56 Verordnung über die Fürsorgepflicht, 13 February 1924, and Gesetz über Kleinrentnerhilfe, 5 July 1934, *RGBl* 1924 I, pp. 100–107, and 1934 I, pp. 580–581.

special Christmas bonuses from the Reich from 1936 that were payable by the welfare offices. Jews and the so-called *Geltungsjuden* (those counted as being Jews) were excluded from these special bonuses. The same stipulations were also applied with regard to eligibility for regular assistance from the Reich which the *Reichsarbeitsminister* initiated in March 1938.[57] Finally, in 1939, the welfare offices were to decide who was to be awarded *Mutterschaftskreuze* (motherhood medals) the processing of these applications also being the responsibility of the social administration department.[58]

But also in its own employment and administrative sector, the Hamburg Welfare Office had ways of relegating Jews to a special role among the relief recipients. This development was marked by two trends — the gradual reduction of public support, and the segregation of Jews from other welfare recipients. The first independent initiatives were taken as early as 1933 and 1934. The Nuremberg Laws of 15 September 1935 were even more stringent. The Hamburg Welfare Office thus began as early as 1933 to limit support for Jews to the legally permissible level and to exclude them from all other supplementary benefits in preventive care.[59] This applied in the first instance to Jewish schoolchildren, whose school meals were no longer subsidized. Also, needy Jewish teenagers were no longer granted public support for higher education or professional training schemes.[60]Even at the beginning of April 1933 the kosher kitchens of the Jewish Community were excluded from the "food for the unemployed" scheme supported

57 Erlasse des Reichsarbeitsministers über die Reichssonderzuschüsse für Kleinrentner, 20 November 1936 and 15 November 1937, *Reichsarbeitsblatt* 1936 I, p. 317, and 1937 I, p. 309, as well as Rundschreiben des Reichsarbeitsministers, 25 March 1938, StA Hamburg, Sozialbehörde I, FR 34.20.

58 Verordnung des Führers und Reichskanzlers über die Stiftung des Ehrenkreuzes der Deutschen Mutter; Satzung des Ehrenkreuzes der Deutschen Mutter; Durchführungsverordnung über die Stiftung des Ehrenkreuzes der Deutschen Mutter, 16 December 1938, *RGBl* 1938 I, pp. 1923–1926. See also Irmgard Weyrather, *Muttertag und Mutterkreuz. Der Kult um die "deutsche Mutter" im Nationalsozialismus*, Frankfurt am Main, 1993, especially pp. 55–84.

59 §3 Reichsgrundsätze über Voraussetzung, Art und Mass der öffentlichen Fürsorge, 4 December 1924, *RGBl* 1924 I, p. 766.

60 Vermerk Martini, 1935, about talks with representatives of the Deutsch-Israelitische Gemeinde, 21 August, and Bericht Dunkel, 3 June 1937, StA Hamburg, Sozialbehörde I, AF 10.22 and VT 12.25.

by the welfare authority.[61] Later, the welfare offices proceeded to credit money allotted for Jewish welfare support — at first partly and then fully — to the Fund for Public Assistance. Although according to a decision made in February 1935 by the political leader of the Health and Welfare Office, Dr. Friedrich Ofterdinger, that only 50 percent should be counterclaimed in normal cases, the welfare department expressly confirmed the legality of this practice in August 1935.[62] The Welfare Commission of the Jewish Community therefore turned to Vice President Martini. Owing to the increasingly depleted finances of the Jewish Community and the rise in the number of assistance cases, the community asked the Welfare Office to allow needy Jews to draw full assistance once more, to waive extra payments by the community for special ritual needs regarding food and accommodation, and to facilitate the formalities for emigration by prepaying the assistance that would otherwise continue to accrue.[63] However, the authorities saw no reason for such "preferential treatment," deciding instead that the Jewish needy were only eligible for the normal benefits granted by the Welfare Office. They viewed the contributions paid by the Jewish community as a special moral obligation in keeping with the principles laid down by the Reich on 4 December 1924 concerning the conditions, type and extent of public assistance, with the result that these were charged fully against any amounts of public assistance.[64] This regulation, which was enforced also in other places, was not expressly approved by the Minister of the Interior until spring 1938 and was passed on to the responsible offices in a strictly confidential letter from the Council of German Municipalities.[65] On the whole the Hamburg Welfare Office

61 Sitzung des Vorstandes der Gemeinde on 13 April 1933, StA Hamburg, Jüdische Gemeinden, Protokollbuch, p. 483.

62 Aktenvermerk Abteilung II/1, 17 February 1939, and Bericht der Abteilung II/1 an die Verwaltungsabteilung, 26 February 1939, StA Hamburg, Sozialbehörde II, 046.00–1.

63 Sitzungen des Vorstandes der Jüdischen Gemeinde on 3 September and on 11 November 1935, StA Hamburg, Jüdische Gemeinden, 297, vol. 22, Protokollbuch pp. 211 and 241.

64 Vermerk Martini about talks with representatives of the Deutsch-Israelitische Gemeinde, 21 August 1935, and Stellungnahme der Abteilung II, 28 August 1935, StA Hamburg, Sozialbehörde I, AF 10.22.

65 Letter of the Deutscher Gemeindetag, 31 March 1938, StA Hamburg, Innere Verwaltung, A VII 26. Up to this time only the general instructions given by the

was able in this way to reduce the amount of public benefits paid to Jews to the legally stipulated minimum payments.

After the promulgation of the Nuremberg Laws, the welfare administration adopted special procedures in the field of extended medical and recuperative care that should have been regulated by legislation. Henceforth such care would only be granted when the Jewish community paid at least half or even two-thirds of the additional costs.[66]From autumn 1935 needy Jews who moved to Hamburg were only offered "closed care," which meant that in the case of families the women, children and men were accommodated in separate asylum homes,[67] according to the examples set by Berlin and Bremen. Unemployed Jewish welfare recipients were no longer placed in salaried jobs; instead, as persons on the dole, they would merely be given *Pflichtarbeit* (obligatory jobs for the unemployed). However, the low extra premiums for this work were taken into account towards their general benefit payments. In addition, Jews employed in *Pflichtarbeit* outside of their communities were not given money to travel home, as were their German colleagues. Needy Jews received no extra money towards their rent, nor were monthly allowances paid any longer to Jewish residents of convalescent or old aged homes.[68] In 1937 they were excluded from the list of recipients of the new Christmas bonus introduced by the president of the Welfare Office.[69] Finally, even the board allowances for Jews in closed care were considerably reduced.[70] On the issue of assistance for Jewish

Minister of the Interior for the Reich and for Prussia were valid. According to these the payment of public assistance could only be made upon the presentation of a certificate from the Central Welfare Office for the Jewish Community as to whether and to what extent the needy person in question could claim benefits through this organization. Rundschreiben des Deutschen Gemeindetages an die Landes- und Provinzialdienststellen, 22 November 1935, Bundesarchiv Koblenz (hereinafter BA Koblenz), R36/2765.

66 Bericht Dunkel, 3 June 1937, and Bericht Ärztliche Abteilung, 4 June 1937, StA Hamburg, Sozialbehörde I, VT 12.25.

67 Niederschrift der Dienstbesprechung der Abteilung II am 1. Oktober 1935, StA Hamburg, I, AF 10.22.

68 Bericht Ruccius, 3 June 1937, StA Hamburg, Sozialbehörde I, VT 12. 25.

69 Anweisung für die Auszahlung der Weihnachtsspende des Herrn Präsidenten an Privatheime und Stifte, December 1937, StA Hamburg, Sozialbehörde I, AK 20.24.

70 Kurzbericht der Sozialverwaltung für den Monat Oktober 1938, StA Hamburg, I, VT 29.11.

emigration the welfare offices were noncomittal, and only after the Ministry of the Interior declared its interest in the emigration procedure in October 1938 did they become more active. But even then the authorities were only prepared to intervene in a supportive manner and to give "the needy Jews the chance to emigrate by giving them a one-off relief payment," provided the Jewish community or even the *Reichsvertretung* paid a similar contribution.[71]

With the suspension of welfare and fringe benefits and the reduction of the legal minimum payments,[72] the Jewish needy were completely segregated from the rest of the relief recipients during the years 1933-38. This was intensified after the introduction of the Nuremberg laws in autumn 1935, but to a certain extent it had already begun. For example, the *Jugendamt* (youth office), a department within the Welfare Office since 1933, pleaded with the audit bureau and the finance department in September 1934 to continue to grant public support to two Jewish children's homes. Their argument went as follows: "...from the racial point of view, supporting two Jewish institutions is a better solution because, consequently, the other children's homes can be kept free of Jewish children" which will guarantee that "the racial instinct of our children will not be suppressed by being together with Jewish children."[73] In keeping with this, the youth office also began in 1934 to arrange guardianships, guided by the principle "that only guardians of Jewish race may be proposed for Jews. To allow a Jew educational influence on other children, even if these are not of pure Aryan descent, would be purely irresponsible."[74] A similar regulation for the whole

71 Niederschrift über die Leitersitzung am 26. Oktober 1938, StA Hamburg, Sozialbehörde I, VG 24.36.

72 The group of Jewish war-disabled was at first spared all these cutbacks imposed on the Jewish needy. They were considered as belonging to exactly the same category as the other relief recipients but could hardly be placed in any paying job because of other restrictions. See the debate on the "Application of the disabled laws to the non-Aryan disabled" during the working conference of the German Head Welfare Offices on 27 and 28 September 1938 in Lübeck. Tagungsbericht, Bundesarchiv, Abteilungen Potsdam (hereinafter BA Potsdam), 39.01 RAM, 9465.

73 Rechnungshof to Finanzverwaltung einschliesslich Anlage, 5 October 1934, StA Hamburg, Finanzdeputation IV, DV VC 21e I.

74 Vizepräsident der Gesundheits- und Fürsorgebehörde to Deutscher Gemeindetag, 7 December 1934, BA Koblenz, R36/1442.

of the Reich was published in a circular dated 17 October 1938.[75] In the autumn of 1935, in almost all sectors of relief for the needy — be it family support, aid for the unemployed, for education, for accommodation in homes, hospitals or with foster parents — extensive measures were introduced that were designed to segregate the Jews from the rest of the population. And in cases where the segregation could not be completely achieved, it was carried out in principle.

In the files of Jewish welfare recipients a note was made about each individual's "racial affiliation." Some welfare offices marked the cover of the files with the title "Jew."[76] This was often done without consulting the person involved but based on the contents of the files and the individual's physical appearances, with the result that many entries were incorrect.[77] During the winter of 1935-36 the Jewish relief recipients were dealt with separately with regard to fuel supplies, since this was organized in cooperation with the general *Winterhilfswerk*, which in turn refused any further supplies to Jews.[78] The issue of segregation of Jews from other patients during admission to hospital, at the expense and at the request of the authorities, had been under discussion by higher political bodies since summer 1935. But at first, for purely financial reasons, all welfare patients were exclusively admitted to state-owned hospitals.[79] By summer 1936 the welfare authorities changed their strategy: to ensure a total segregation, Jewish welfare recipients were to be admitted solely, except in cases of emergency, to the Jewish Hospital. The authorities also stopped all payments for non-Jewish patients in the Jewish Hospital.[80]

75 *MBliV* 1938, p. 1722.

76 Niederschrift über die Dienstbesprechung der Abteilung II am 1. Oktober 1935 and Niederschrift über die Dienstbesprechung der Wohlfahrtsstelle VII am 4. Dezember 1935, StA Hamburg, Sozialbehörde I, AF 10.22 and VG 20.10.

77 See, for example, the complaint lodged to the Reichsstatthalter, 12 March 1936, StA Hamburg, Senatskanzlei-Präsidialabteilung, 1936 Pb 671.

78 In contrast to the others, the Jewish relief recipients received a sum of money which was transferred to them via the Post Office. Dienstvorschrift, 18 October 1935, StA Hamburg, Sozialbehörde I, NSV 22.35.

79 Correspondence of the Senator der Inneren Verwaltung Richter with the Präsident der Gesundheits- und Fürsorgebehörde, August and September 1935, StA Hamburg, Innere Verwaltung, A IV 11.

80 Vermerk Leitender Oberarzt Dr. Jahn, 29 July 1936, StA Hamburg, Innere Verwaltung, A IV 11. This also occurred a long time before a decree was given by the

The *Arbeitsfürsorge* (work relief office) set up special places of work in 1935 for Jewish relief recipients only, where the men were made to do backbreaking excavation work.[81] Almost all the Jewish unemployed welfare recipients, numbering between 60 and 110, were engaged "solely in obligatory work." Female recipients were allowed to sew in the workhouses of the Welfare Office — in segregated rooms.[82] About thirty Jewish women were employed in the sewing room but in January 1939, "for reasons of employment policy" were sent to do agricultural and horticultural work instead.[83] The difficulties involved in employing Jews led to efforts by the work relief office in autumn 1937 to arrange jobs for Jewish relief recipients — despite the prohibition of such — in *Notstandsarbeiten* (work for the unemployed) in surrounding areas. The first attempt with the Lower Saxony State Employment Office met with little success,[84] but the scheme succeeded in collaboration with the Nordmark State Employment Office. Thus in 1938 and 1939 the Work Relief Office dispatched Jews to work in two-three labor camps in the region of Stade. Here too they were made to work separately and under special regulations. In these camps, near Buxtehude, there were up to ninety Jewish unemployed relief recipients forced to do heavy excavation work.[85]

Minister of the Interior on 22 June 1938 demanding a physical segregation of the Jews "from sick people of German or similar blood." Landesarchiv Berlin, DGT, 3–10–11/72. Of all cities with large Jewish populations Cologne had been admitting Jewish welfare patients only to the local Jewish hospital since 1933 and therefore endangered the existence of the hospital by limiting the number of patients in this way. Kurzbericht über die Sitzung der jüdischen Krankenanstalten Deutschlands in Berlin am 12. June 1933, in Mary Lindemann, *140 Jahre Israelitisches Krankenhaus in Hamburg. Vorgeschichte und Entwicklung*, Hamburg, 1981,pp. 61 f.

81 Jahresbericht 1936 der Abteilung VIIb, 4 January 1937, and Protokoll der Dienstbesprechung der Wohlfahrtsstelle XIII, 7 December 1935, StA Hamburg, Sozialbehörde I, VG 54.36 and VG 20.10.

82 In this connection a remark by Ingeborg Hecht, *Als unsichtbare Mauern wuchsen. Eine deutsche Familie unter den Nürnberger Rassengesetzen*, Hamburg, 1984, pp. 82f.

83 Jahresberichte der Arbeitsfürsorge 1936, 1937 and 1939, StA Hamburg, Sozialbehörde I, AW 50.83, AW 50.84, AW 50.86.

84 Arbeitsfürsorge to Arbeitsamt Bassum, 27 October 1937, and to Arbeitsamt Hamburg, 1 November 1937, StA Hamburg, I, AW 40.30.

85 Bericht des Vermittlungsdienstes der Arbeitsfürsorge für Juli 1938; Vermerk

Ever-greater segregation was also the case for Jewish recipients in *Geschlossene Fürsorge* (closed care). Since there was insufficient room in homes for old people, the convalescent and the handicapped, the Hamburg welfare administration — despite the increase in the number of state care homes — still had to depend on private old aged homes. From 1935 — as for children before — the authorities exercised a consciously manipulated policy on admissions.[86] Church institutions also changed their previous policies and, allegedly in consideration of the revised tax laws of 1936, resolved to no longer take in "non-Aryans" via their charitable trusts or to move elsewhere those they had already taken in. Thus, from August 1937, the Alsterdorfer Institutions gradually dismissed their Jewish charges, most of whom were admitted to a care home belonging to the state welfare institutions.[87] Already in summer 1936 most institutionalized Jews were concentrated in a single home at the institution in Farmsen.[88] The segregation within charity

Reinstorf, 17 December 1938, and Jahresbericht der Arbeitsfürsorge für 1939, StA Hamburg, Sozialbehörde I, AW 12.28, AW 40.30 and AW 50.86; as well as Kurzberichte der Sozialverwaltung, June and July 1938, StA Hamburg, Sozialbehörde I, VG 29.11. In Wohlerst, one of the camps near Buxtehude, the then 18-year-old Heinz Rosenberg did forced labor from March 1939 until he was dismissed in August 1939 with severe stomach trouble and sent home where he finally found work as a storekeeper. Heinz Rosenberg, *Jahre des Schreckens ... und ich blieb übrig, dass ich Dir's ansage*, Göttingen, 1985, p. 12. See also Wolf Gruner, "Terra incognita? — Die Lager für den "Jüdischen Arbeitseinsatz" (1938–1943)," in Büttner, ed., *Die Deutschen und die Judenverfolgung*, p. 133.

86 Bericht Ruccius, 3 June 1937, StA Hamburg, Sozialbehörde I,VT 12.25.

87 Niederschrift über die Besprechung in den Staatlichen Wohlfahrtsanstalten am 10. November 1937 and Niederschrift über die 30. Amtsleitersitzung am 30. November 1938, StA Hamburg, I, VG 23.08 and VG 23.01; about the fate of the Jews among the inmates of the Alsterdorfer Anstalten, see Michael Wunder, Ingrid Genkel, Harald Jenner eds., *Auf dieser schiefen Ebene gibt es kein Halten mehr. Die Alsterdorfer Anstalten im Nationalsozialismus*, Hamburg, 1987, pp. 155–167.

88 Vermerk Sonderreferent Brandt, 10 July 1936, StA Hamburg, Sozialbehörde I, VG 29.10, vol. II. The mentally handicapped inmates among them probably belonged to the first transport of Hamburg mentally handicapped taken to the extermination camp Brandenburg within the scope of the National Socialist scheme for extermination of the sick on 23 September 1940. Peter von Rönn, "Die Entwicklung der Anstalt Langenhorn in der Zeit des Nationalsozialismus," in: *Wege in den Tod. Hamburgs Anstalt Langenhorn und die Euthanasie in der Zeit des Nationalsozialismus*, Klaus Böhme and Uwe Lohalm, eds., Hamburg, 1993, pp. 70 f.

homes was difficult. Many had been founded with money donated by German Jews and had admitted people irrespective of their religion.[89] Here, too, the possibility of bringing together all "non-Aryans" in one home was considered in October 1938.[90] In negotiations with the Board of Trustees it was hoped to achieve "a complete isolation of Jews from those of German blood."[91] The Hamburg youth office openly praised the Nuremberg laws, which confirmed their policy of a strict separation of children in homes or living with foster parents.[92] In January 1936 the youth office developed a set of "general rules for the accommodation of full Jews and other 'non-Aryan' foster children," which planned to allot children according to their *"Rasseanteilen"* (racial share).[93] By the end of November 1938 almost all the Jewish infants in its charge had been removed from the state homes; later those termed *Mischlinge* of the first degree according to "certification by a racial biologist" were to follow.[94] Furthermore, during 1937 the youth office investigated all cases of adoption granted under their guidance to determine whether any "Aryan" children were living with Jewish adoptive parents. The youth office intended to free "German-blooded children from Jewish influences and Jewish names," even if this involved "hardship or human tragedy." This was to be done before a national law was passed on the matter.[95]

89 Angela Schwarz, "Jüdische Wohnstifte in Hamburg," in: *Die Juden in Hamburg 1590 bis 1990. Wissenschaftliche Beiträge der Universität Hamburg zur Ausstellung "Vierhundert Jahre Juden in Hamburg,"* Arno Herzig, ed., in cooperation with Saskia Rohde, Hamburg, 1991, pp. 447–458.

90 Niederschrift der Beiratssitzung am 27. Oktober 1938, StA Hamburg, Sozialbehörde I, StA 26.19b.

91 The words of the Beigeordnete der Sozialverwaltung Martini at the 3rd Ratsherrenberatung on 2 November 1938, which was not open to the public. StA Hamburg, Ratsherrenkanzlei, 20.

92 Jugendamt to Fürsorgebehörde, 4 June 1937, and Bericht der Jugendamtspflegerin der Wohlfahrtsstelle XIII, 3 June 1937, StA Hamburg, Sozialbehörde I, VT 12.25.

93 StA Hamburg, Sozialbehörde II, 361–00.00.

94 Bestandsaufnahme vom 6. Dezember 1938, StA Hamburg, Jugendbehörde I, 359c.

95 Jugendamt to Landgerichtsdirektor Dr. Matthaei, 19 June 1937, StA Hamburg, Jugendbehörde I, 244; Runderlass des Reichsministers des Innern über die gerichtliche Aufhebung von Kindesannahmeverhältnissen, 20 September 1938, *MBliV* 1938, pp. 1597–1600.

On the other hand, *Familienfürsorge* (family care) did not show any signs of strict segregation until 1938. The social workers also had nothing out of the ordinary to report to the advisory bureaus, although there were isolated signs of surprise or displeasure. In summer 1937 one social worker reported:

> It is unavoidable for social workers, despite a large degree of reticence, to often come into the closest contact with Jewish families. In Aryan circles in the district, surprise is often expressed that Jews are still being supported and their children still being cared for. Many don't like the idea of first negotiating with Jews and then maybe going into their homes. Often, if it so happens that I first have dealings with Jews in the street, I notice the disapproving looks and you have to be careful as to what course the negotiation takes.

Here, too, the desire for "strict separation" was expressed, and the chief welfare worker of one office always made sure that Jewish mothers and their children be called in for appointments "possibly before or after official office hours."[96] The obvious distancing of the public and personnel from the Jews can also be observed in reports by official and honorary social workers on their custodians. For example, from autumn 1938 character reports by the Alcoholics Advisory Service contained more and more remarks on the Jewish descent of custodians, as well as entries with anti-Jewish stereotypes, such as a patient who made "a typical Jewish, drunken and dissipated impression."[97]

For the Hamburg Welfare Office, the fundamentally changed regulations for relief support to Jews was already on the calendar in January 1936.[98] In spring 1938, when the Hamburg welfare administration was in the process of reviewing their rules and guidelines to make them more consistent, especially regarding the principles of National Socialism, the position of Jews was entirely reformulated.[99] Four groups of welfare recipients were defined, each to receive a different amount of welfare

96 Bericht der Familienfürsorgerin and Bericht der Oberfürsorgerin of the Wohlfahrtsstelle XIII, both 2 June 1937, StA Hamburg, Sozialbehörde I, VT 12.25.

97 Vermerk Trinkerfürsorge, 13 October 1938, StA Hamburg, Arbeits- und Sozialfürsorge, 216.

98 Letter Abteilung II, Völcker, to Martini, 18 January 1936, StA Hamburg, Sozialbehörde I, VG 30.44. Similar considerations had also been taken since the middle of 1936 in the Welfare Office in Munich. Peter Hanke, *Zur Geschichte der Juden in München zwischen 1933 und 1945*, Munich, 1967, pp. 264.

99 Parallel to this, meetings were held within the welfare administration committee

benefits. As part of this redivision "non-Aryans" were grouped with foreigners in the third category, *Allgemeine Fürsorge* (general welfare). This group was reserved for those who could not be classed as "worthy" *Volksgenossen*, and included also socially difficult people, "who lack the will or the strength to free themselves from public welfare."[100]

Embedded as it was in general politics and the sociopolitical development, and yet mostly still acting independently, the Hamburg welfare administration had by 1938 initiated a segregation of the Jews from the generally practiced welfare system. It had forced them into the stigma of a specialized group and placed them in a category with other similarly lowly regarded minorities such as Gypsies and the so-called asocials who could only expect very limited support. Thus, before 1938, local welfare policies were generally "far ahead" of those of the national or Reich's jurisdiction. This was, however, an untenable position, and finally the national government was ordered to make its policy consistent with that being carried out by local authorities. After all, the legal equality of Jews and Germans had often been violated through the political-ideological adjustment of the local welfare offices. Indeed, this had started long before November 1938, when it occurred as part of the total elimination of Jews from the economic life of the nation and the plundering of their wealth, all of this resulting from national legislation.

Expulsion of the Jews from Public Welfare

The first initiatives towards a consistent legislation throughout the Reich came from some local welfare offices and were presented via the Council of German Municipalities to the Reich government. Some welfare organizations had taken similar steps as early as the summer of 1935.[101] The decisive step was taken a few months later by the

of the German Council of Municipalities to discuss this issue. Niederschrift über die Sitzung des Wohlfahrtsauschusses des Deutschen Gemeindetages am 25. Mai 1938, StA Hamburg, Sozialbehörde I, VT 12.21, vol.II.

100 Dienstvorschrift über die Grundsätze der Fürsorge, 26 March 1938, StA Hamburg, Sozialbehörde I, AF 10.20.

101 Adam, *Judenpolitik im Dritten Reich*, pp. 191f.

Nordwestdeutsche Arbeitsgemeinschaft für Wohlfahrtspflege (Northwest German Working Group for Welfare), an alliance within the Council of German Municipalities to which the county welfare unions of northwestern Germany belonged and whose head had been the Hamburg man, Oskar Martini, for many years. During their conference in November 1935 on the incentive of the head of the Welfare Office in Bremen, Wilhelm Kayser, this group discussed the welfare handling of the Jews. The results of the conference were passed on by Martini to the Council of German Municipalities, with a request to the Ministry of the Interior to issue general regulations for the treatment of "non-Aryans" in the public welfare system.[102] The Ministry of the Interior, however, passed the debate back to the Council of German Municipalities and requested Oskar Martini to put the matter forward for discussion at the next meeting of the welfare committee of the Council of German Municipalities. The latter had already appointed Martini as responsible for this issue since he was the actual initiator of the idea.[103] Due to the lack of appropriate legislation within the Reich, Martini's proposals at the conference on 10 June 1937 in Heidelberg were based on the party program of the NSDAP,[104] and ended up with the suggestion that Jews in Germany be classed with foreigners as far as welfare was concerned. This meant that in cases of poverty, Jews would be granted only the absolutely essential subsistence, i.e., accommodation, food, clothing, care and nursing, and funeral costs. Jews should be excluded from any

102 Niederschriften über die Sitzungen der Nordwestdeutschen Arbeitsgemeinschaft on 22 November 1935 and on 3 April 1936, StA Hamburg, Sozialbehörde I, VT 22.90.

103 Deutscher Gemeindetag, Schlüter, to Martini, 22 May 1937, and Reichs- und Preussisches Ministerium des Inneren, Ruppert, to Martini, 24 May 1937, StA Hamburg, Sozialbehörde I, VT 12.25. I first indicated the significance of the communal administration offices and their top leadership, of the German Council of Municipalities as well as of the special role played by the Hamburg vice president and later town councillor Oskar Martini in the development of an antisemitic welfare policy in Uwe Lohalm, "Hamburgs öffentliche Fürsorge und die Juden 1933 bis 1939," in: *Die Juden in Hamburg 1590 bis 1990*, pp. 499–514.

104 As already stated, in the material put at Martini's disposal by the Wohlfahrtsamt Munich: "The first and foremost rule should be that all orders should be interpreted according to National Socialist ideology. This is recorded in the party program of the NSDAP." Deutscher Gemeindetag, Zengerling, to Martini, nebst Anlagen, 31 May 1937, StA Hamburg, Sozialbehörde I, VT 12.25.

other benefits, such as recuperation for employment, employment suitability for minors and the handicapped, maternity benefits, and higher and preventive welfare benefits. Special relief should be available to Jewish recipients only where it was a matter of general interest, for example in cases of infectious diseases and threatening decrepitude. The neediness of any Jew should be carefully inspected and the current benefit payment by the Jewish Community fully deducted from the public welfare benefits. On the whole this meant that the Jews were reduced to the level prescribed for public assistance that existed before 1924. In the debate that followed both the details and the basic principles met with wide approval. It even became apparent that reductions in benefits and special conditions in welfare care already existed in the welfare systems in the cities of Berlin, Frankfurt am Main, Leipzig and Nuremberg, exactly as in Hamburg.[105] *Ministerialrat* Fritz Ruppert from the Ministry of the Interior summarized the unanimous opinion of the welfare committee — he expressly adopted this point of view as being his own — that legislation was necessary and that it would be most appropriate to consider Jews equal to foreigners with regard to the type and extent of relief due to them.[106]

Despite the general agreement among the welfare experts of the Council of German Municipalities and the Ministry of the Interior officials responsible for this matter, it took more than a year until the ministry submitted a proposal for a Decree on Public Welfare for Jews, in August 1938.[107] The contents of this proposal were

105 The same applied to the city of Munich, which had sent corresponding material on this issue to the Council of German Municipalities in advance. Their consultant, Friedrich Hilble, was originally intended to be the speaker too but died immediately before the conference with the result that Munich was not represented at all. See note 104.

106 Niederschrift über die Sitzung des Wohlfahrtsausschusses des Deutschen Gemeindetages on 10 June 1937, now published in Uwe Lohalm, *Fürsorge und Verfolgung. Öffentliche Wohlfahrtsverwaltung und nationalsozialistische Judenpolitik in Hamburg 1933 bis 1942*, Hamburg 1998, pp. 84–94.

107 However, in the meantime talks had been held between representatives of the Reich and the Prussian Ministry of the Interior and the chairman of the Working Group for Welfare Care in the German Council of Municipalities in order to work out new "Richtlinien für die Bemessung der Leistungen der öffentlichen Fürsorge," which had been discussed and resolved during the meeting of the Welfare Committee of the German Council of Municipalities on 25 May 1938 in Würzburg. After that

closely modelled on recommendations by the Council of German Municipalities and already contained, with the exception of a special regulation for war-injured Jews, all the clauses of the legislation that was to be passed later.[108] This was finally published simultaneously by the Reich Ministers of Labor, Finance and the Interior on 19 November of that year.[109] The main thrust of the decree was that needy German and stateless Jews, as well as so-called *Geltungsjuden*, were to be completely struck from the rolls of the welfare system. Furthermore, these people were excluded from grants to recipients of low pensions. The public welfare system would step in only if the Jewish welfare agency appeared to be pressed by excessive demands. The decree also put limitations on the amount of aid the Welfare Office could pay. Only war-injured Jews were exempt at first from these new regulations. The legislation that was passed by the Reich on 1 January 1939 merely defined the general framework. Although a decree to carry out legislation followed on 25 May 1939, it only stipulated support for those Jews who were living with non-Jews as a family unit.[110] This meant that the formulation of concrete regulations was left to the local area welfare associations; for example, deciding on the type and exact extent of the proportion to be carried by public welfare, determining the scope of the Jewish welfare organizations, and controlling the withdrawing of income and assets. A discussion was held on this topic on 1 March 1939 in the Council of German Municipalities in Berlin with *Ministerialrat* Ruppert and representatives of the cities involved, namely Berlin, Breslau, Frankfurt am Main, Hamburg and Munich.[111]

the Jews were excluded from the "gehobenen Fürsorge" (higher level of welfare) which was to be reserved for "valuable members of the public" and placed in the same category as foreigners who were to receive benefits according to the rates of the general relief fund. Niederschrift über die Sitzung des Wohlfahrtsausschusses des Deutschen Gemeindetages am 25. Mai 1938, StA Hamburg, Sozialbehörde I, VT 12.21, vol. II.

108 Reichsminister des Innern, Stuckart, 16 August 1938, Akten der Parteikanzlei, Teil I, vol.2, Microfiche Nr. 10312468–72.

109 *RGBl* 1938 I, p. 1649.

110 Runderlass des Reichsarbeitsministers und des Reichsministers des Innern, 25 May 1939, *MBliV* 1939, pp. 1297–1300.

111 Bericht des Dezernenten des Fürsorgeamtes Frankfurt, Werner Fischer-Defoy, über die Teilnahme an einer Besprechung des Deutschen Gemeindetages in Berlin am

As a result of this discussion, Breslau and Munich refused any further benefits to Jews upon the validity of the new legislation,[112] whereas other cities such as Hamburg applied regulations of this kind only to certain sectors. That the expulsion of Jews from the public welfare system was generally regarded as the target is made apparent by a letter from the Council of German Municipalities dated 25 April 1939, which states: "Basically one can proceed on the assumption that the welfare organizations have fulfilled their duties which result from the decree of 19 November 1938 if they succeed in excluding the Jews completely from their welfare system."[113] The policy of the German government only insisted that pauperized Jews not become a financial burden on the public welfare system. They clearly and repeatedly demanded that Jewish welfare agencies be excluded from the "Aryanization" program and that as an absolute priority poor Jews be urged to emigrate.[114]

The expulsion of needy Jews from the public welfare system was put into effect just when the distress of the Jewish citizens was drastically

1. März 1939, 3 March 1939. This particularly emphasized that the regulations valid in Frankfurt, where the welfare office had already set up a special department for dealing with the Jews since 1 October 1936, were particularly recommendable examples. Printed in Kommission zur Erforschung der Geschichte der Frankfurter Juden ed., *Dokumente zur Geschichte der Frankfurter Juden 1933–1945,* Frankfurt am Main, 1963, pp. 320–322.

112 Similar regulations had been introduced by the cities of Düsseldorf and Cologne. See on this topic and for the whole Rhine province a collection of the results of a survey by the Deutscher Gemeindetag dated 22 August 1939 on benefits to the Jews, BA Koblenz, R36/1022, also printed in Kurt Düwell, *Die Rheingebiete in der Judenpolitik des Nationalsozialismus vor 1942. Beitrag zu einer vergleichenden zeitgeschichtlichen Landeskunde*, Bonn, 1968, pp. 286–293. Supplementary for Breslau Moshe Ayalon, "Jewish Life in Breslau 1938–1941," *Leo Baeck Institute Year Book,* 41 (1996), pp. 323–345, especially pp. 333–336; for Munich Hanke, *Zur Geschichte der Juden in München*, pp. 266 f.

113 Deutscher Gemeindetag to Fürsorgeamt der Stadt Mainz, 25 April 1939, BA Koblenz, R36/1022.

114 See the two major discussions on the Jewish issue on 12 November 1938 with Hermann Göring (Stenographische Niederschrift in *Der Prozess gegen die Hauptkriegsverbrecher vor dem Internationalen Gerichtshof*, Nürnberg, 1948, vol. 28, pp. 499–540) and on 16 December 1938 with the Minister of the Interior Wilhelm Frick (Niederschrift in Forschungsstelle für Zeitgeschichte in Hamburg — hereinafter FZH — Archiv Fsc. 11/K7), as well as letters from Göring to the Reichsminister dated 28 December 1938 and to the Minister of the Interior dated 24 January 1939 (printed in Paul Sauer, ed., *Dokumente über die Verfolgung der*

intensified: less and less money was available to the Jewish communities because of the exclusion of their members from the economic life of the cities and because so many Jews had emigrated. Although the number of Jews living in Hamburg had been reduced by half from 1933 to 1939, the number of those considered as needy rose drastically at first and then remained almost unchanged at a high level. Whereas about 2,600 persons received additional assistance from the Jewish *Winterhilfe* during 1935-36,[115] their number increased during 1936-37 to about 3,600 and in 1937-38 to 3,900, and remained at a similar level with 3,700 in 1938-39. This meant that the proportion of welfare recipients in the whole Jewish population was doubled from less than 20 percent in the winter of 1935-36 to just under 40 percent in winter 1938-39.[116] The running expenses of the Jewish Community from 1936 to 1939 also doubled due to welfare needs; in 1936 it equalled 40 percent of the total budget, but rose to 80 percent by 1939.[117] These figures were therefore quite contrary to the general development in public welfare, which showed a significant reduction in both the number of people involved and the related expenses.[118] The number of needy Jews who were also supported by public welfare in the period before 1939 could not be determined. Not until the welfare legislation for Jews was passed

jüdischen Bürger in Baden-Württemberg durch das nationalsozialistische Regime 1933–1945, Stuttgart, 1966, vol. II, pp. 83 f. and 119 f.).

115 *Israelitisches Familienblatt* 38. Jg., Nr. 3, 16 January 1936.

116 In 1935 there were about 15,000 Jews in Hamburg. During the census of May 1939 there was still a total of 10,131 Jews in Hamburg according to the Nuremberg Laws. *Aus Hamburgs Verwaltung und Wirtschaft* 1939, No.1, p. 17.

117 Abrechnung und Revisionsbericht der Deutsch-Israelitischen Gemeinde in Hamburg, 15 July 1938, StA Hamburg, Finanzdeputation IV, VuO IIC 6c III; Bericht der Abteilung Fürsorge der Reichsvereinigung der Juden in Deutschland, 19 July 1939, printed in Günther B. Ginzel, *Jüdischer Alltag in Deutschland 1933–1945*, Düsseldorf, 1984, pp. 222–225, as well as Leo Lippmann in, Finanzbehörde Hamburg, ed., *"..dass ich wie ein guter Deutscher empfinde und handele." Zur Geschichte der Deutsch-Israelitischen Gemeinde in Hamburg in der Zeit vom Herbst 1935 bis zum Ende 1942. Zwei Berichte*, Hamburg, 1993, pp. 35–123.

118 Uwe Lohalm, "Der öffentliche Umgang mit der Armut. Zur nationalsozialistischen Fürsorgepolitik in Hamburg 1933 bis 1939," in: *Hamburg in der NS-Zeit. Ergebnisse neuerer Forschungen*, Frank Bajohr and Joachim Szodrzynski, eds., Hamburg, 1995, pp. 231–258, especially pp. 238–244.

on 1 January 1939 were Jews also registered statistically as a special category.[119] At that time the Hamburg Welfare Office was continually supporting 860 Jews in open care. Their numbers decreased steadily in the months that followed. When war broke out it was only 318, and 274 by 1 December 1939.[120]On this point Hamburg's public welfare was supporting a total of 36,500 full-relief recipients.[121] At the end of 1938 there were eighteen Jews in closed care and 22 in permanent state-care homes one year later.[122] No statistics are available on the number of Jews who received once-only benefits or special payments, or those who were living in private homes. If one bases one's assumptions on the general ratio of full-relief recipients to the other relief recipients, there must have been about 200 to 300 additional Jewish beneficiaries, so that at the end of 1938 more than a thousand Jews were receiving assistance from public welfare in Hamburg.

For Hamburg's welfare policy, the national ruling merely meant another leap forward on what was already the beaten path. It brought a new objective to recent acts aimed at culling Jewish welfare recipients once and for all. Before the administration could fulfill the general guidelines, the separation of Jews from other recipients was ordered in the sector of open care: Jews were to report to the welfare office twice a week at a special time in order to avoid a situation in which "Aryan" Germans would have to share the waiting room with Jews.[123] Once

119 Erhebungsbogen des Statistischen Reichsamtes "Reichsfürsorgestatistik für das Rechnungsjahr 1939," StA Hamburg, I, Stat 20.10, vol. XII.

120 Vierteljährlicher Schnelldienst der Reichsfürsorgestatistik für Hamburg, January-September 1939, StA Hamburg, Sozialbehörde I, Stat 20.11; as well as Statistik über Barleistungen im Stadtbezirk Rechnungsjahr 1938, 1–15.1.1939; Rechnungsjahr 1939, 16–31.8.1939, and 1–30.11.1939; StA Hamburg, Sozialbehörde I, Stat. 20.34, and Finanzdeputation IV, VuO IIC 6b VII B. These figures differ slightly from the official figures published in *Aus Hamburgs Verwaltung und Wirtschaft*, January–July 1939.

121 Meldung der Abteilung IA1/3, 9 January 1940, StA Hamburg,I, Stat 10.30.

122 Aufstellung vom 14. Oktober 1938 and Statistik vom 1. Januar 1940, StA Hamburg, Amt für Wohlfahrtsanstalten I, 19, and Sozialbehörde I, VG 54.56.

123 Remarks of the head of the Landesfürsorgeamt Herbert Völcker at the Leitersitzung on 30 November 1938, StA Hamburg, Sozialbehörde I, VG 24.36; Martini gave his opinion in the very same way at the Beiratssitzung on 21 November 1938, StA Hamburg, Sozialbehörde I, StA 26.19 b; see also Niederschrift über die 33. Amtsleitersitzung on 1 December 1938, StA Hamburg, Sozialbehörde I, VG 23.01.

again, the level of support was expressly adjusted to the lowered rate of the general relief scheme. The Jews' right to protest was curtailed by the ordinance that appeals against decisions should from then on be decided by the heads of the authorities. Even at the end of November 1938 the files of Jews who had received continual support were inspected yet again.[124] Furthermore, the administration developed a plan whereby the various sectors of welfare support were to be transferred gradually to the *Jüdische freie Wohlfahrtspflege* (Jewish Welfare Agency). The scheme was to begin with closed care (in institutions and homes) of the elderly, the convalescent, and orphans or foster children. This was to be followed by medical and hospital care.[125] The transfer of open care would be handed over to this Jewish agency last of all, with the view that Jews might be able to do some "useful work" and that the physical labor might "encourage them to emigrate."[126]

The talks that took place on 13 December 1938 between the Social Administration (the former Welfare Office), the Jewish Community, and the boards of trustees of the foundations resulted in the complete separation between the administrative departments as well as between the residents of the trust homes. The Social Administration made it the responsibility of the Jewish Community to take in all the Jewish residents of three of the nine foundation homes that had rooms for a total of 183 residents, which at that time represented double the amount required, with the explanation that "in future one could reckon with

124 Bericht über die Tätigkeit des Fürsorgeprüfdienstes im Geschäftsjahr 1938/39, 24 May 1939, StA Hamburg, Sozialbehörde I, VG 20.33.

125 A similar step-by-step transfer of welfare duties was carried out in Berlin: from 1 May 1939 the Jewish community was also initially made responsible for closed care; by the end of 1940 it was forced to take on the complete welfare of the Jewish citizens. Rundschreiben des Oberbürgermeisters an die Bezirksbürgermeister, 12 May 1939, and Vermerk Deutscher Gemeindetag, Seyffert, 10 October 1940, BA Koblenz R36/1022 and 1023. For the activities of the welfare administrations in Berlin after the Verordnung über die öffentliche Fürsorge für Juden came into force see Monika Schmidt, "Ausgrenzung der Juden," in *Kommunalverwaltung unterm Hakenkreuz. Berlin-Wilmersdorf 1933–1945*, Bezirksamt Wilmersdorf von Berlin, ed., Berlin, 1992, pp. 161 f., and Wolf Gruner, "Die Reichshauptstadt und die Verfolgung der Berliner Juden 1933–1945," in *Jüdische Geschichte in Berlin. Essays und Studien*, Reinhard Rürup, ed., Berlin, 1995, p. 240.

126 Martini at the Beiratssitzung on 22 December 1938, Niederschrift, StA Hamburg, Sozialbehörde I, StA 26.19 b.

a higher degree of poverty within the Jewish Community and these were mainly institutions founded with Jewish money anyway." They also supplied additional funds to the three homes in order to ensure longer-term financing of these institutions. The other foundations — which were to become victims of "Aryanization" — were to contribute financially towards these three. In return for this the Jewish Community was forced to declare that this marked the completion of all the prerequisites for a complete takeover of the closed care scheme.[127]

On 22 December 1938, the Social Administration finally released a service instruction that was to regulate every aspect of public welfare for Jews as of 1 January 1939. It transferred the problem of caring for Jews in homes and institutions to the Jewish Welfare Agency, as previously planned.[128] Only the needy with certificates from the Jewish Community confirming that they were not receiving any or sufficient support from the Jewish welfare agency remained in open care. The same low rate, equivalent to the lowest level of the *Allgemeine Fürsorge* (general welfare) was to apply to everyone, except for those who had been severely wounded in the war. In addition, there were to be stricter deductions which would apply even to those with little wealth or a low income. Without any consideration of age, needy Jews were to do forced labor for which they would receive remuneration reduced by one-fifth. Health care, preventive or otherwise, was no longer provided for — unless this was in the public interest. The treatment of Jewish welfare recipients would be carried out by a professional staff who were to keep a constant eye on their Jewish charges "to a greater extent

127 Niederschrift der Besprechung am 13. Dezember 1938, StA Hamburg, Jugendbehörde I, 359c. In July 1942 the Jewish religious society was contractually obliged to give up the three homes as the objectives of the foundations had "become impossible" because of the deportations. Lippmann, *"dass ich wie ein guter Deutscher empfinde,"* p. 118. The issue of the allotment of residents and the administration of Jewish and similar foundations had already been a concern of the Bezirksfürsorgeverbände (county welfare associations) in other cities such as Frankfurt am Main and Munich since 1936 without achieving any general legislation on the subject. The question was not decided until a corresponding circular was issued (but not publicized) by the Minister of the Interior on 8 May 1939 with a view to distinct separation. Landesarchiv Berlin, DGT, 1–2–6/1.

128 A similar ruling was adapted into the 10th decree of the Reich Citizenship Law dated 4 July 1939 a short time later. *RGBl* 1939 I, p. 1097.

than usual." Finally, all administrative work involving Jewish welfare recipients was to be conducted in one office only which would be responsible exclusively for Jews. This office began its activities on 6 February 1939.[129] At the same time the Jewish welfare care scheme also took on the expenses for the accommodation of the Jewish needy in foundations or homes.[130]

In further negotiations, in which the financial administration, the employment office and the Gestapo[131] participated, the Social Administration put the burden of the complete welfare care of Jews upon the Jewish Community beginning on 1 April 1939. The financing was to be secured by expropriating Jewish property and foundation assets. In preparatory talks with the financial administration and the Gestapo, both of which showed keen interest in certain property belonging to the Jewish Community, representatives of the Gestapo claimed that dissolving ownership of these properties would put the Jewish Community in a position to be able to take on the welfare of the needy Jews, especially in view of the fact that "in about 3 or 5 years most Jews will have emigrated anyway."[132] At a meeting in which all parties took part, the Jewish Community expressed its doubt about the plans that the Social Administration had announced, claiming that a transfer of all the welfare work would mean such high costs both in administration and capital that the assets would be used up within a very short time with the result that all welfare work would again fall within the responsibility of the state. The Hamburg financial administration backed this argument,[133] and the distribution of responsibilities remained as it was previously, at least for some time.

129 Dienstvorschrift über die öffentliche Fürsorge für Juden, 22 December 1938, and amendment, 1 January 1939, StA Hamburg, I, VG 28.67 and AF 33.21.

130 Rundschreiben an alle Dienststellen, 6 February 1939, StA Hamburg, Sozialbehörde I, StW 31.22.

131 On 13 March 1939 at the 8th Conference of the Nordwestdeutsche Arbeitsgemeinschaft für Wohlfahrtspflege, Martini expressly recommended for the "not always easy inspection of the efficiency of the Jewish communities, a close cooperation with the Gestapo." Tagungsniederschrift, StA Hamburg, Sozialbehörde I, VG 22.90, vol. IV.

132 Niederschrift einer Besprechung on 25 January 1939, StA Hamburg, Finanzdeputation IV, DV IB 2g VB1; and Niederschrift der Beiratssitzung on 23 March 1933, StA Hamburg, Sozialbehörde I, VG 26.19 b.

133 Niederschrift einer Besprechung on 22 March 1939 and letter of Kämmerei to

In fact the Social Administration even insisted on being reimbursed by the Jewish Community for all expenses accrued by them in execution of their duties towards the welfare of Jews — these amounted to about RM 350,000 per annum in open care according to the figures of January 1939[134] backdated to 1 April 1939, plus a 10 percent surcharge for the administrative costs involved. The property of the Jewish Community — which would be bought by the city of Hamburg in the course of the so-called "Aryanization" program — would be the form of payment. The amounts were never in fact paid out, but were charged against the welfare debts of the social administration.[135] In other respects too, the social administration profited directly during this time from the intensified plunder policy of the Reich government. When Jews were forced by a new decree to surrender any objects they possessed that were made of gold, platinum or silver as well as jewels and pearls,[136] the Social Administration immediately stipulated that the full proceeds from the sale of these objects should be reckoned against any amounts of welfare relief paid out. In return it declared its willingness to carry, upon corresponding application, the cost of the name changes ordered by the Reich government on behalf of any Jews without income or those being continually supported from public funds.[137]

Meanwhile, the new arrangements for distribution of welfare duties did not last long. In July 1939 the Reichsvereinigung der Juden in Deutschland was founded and declared the official carrier of the Jewish

Sozialverwaltung, 5 April 1939, StA Hamburg, Finanzdeputation IV, VuO IIC 6c III.

134 Martini to Stadtkämmerer Nieland, 27 February 1939, StA Hamburg, Finanzdeputation IV, DV IB 2g VB1.

135 Sozialverwaltung to Behörde für Handel, Schiffahrt und Gewerbe and to Jüdischer Religionsverband, both 22 June 1939, StA Hamburg, Finanzdeputation IV, VuO IIC 6c III. In December 1938 the Senate led the social administration to believe they would be paid for the purchase of the Talmud Torah School which would cover the welfare expenses that had accrued to them. Niederschrift über die 97. Amtsleitersitzung on 15 December 1939, StA Hamburg, Sozialbehörde I, VG 23.01.

136 Dritte Anordnung auf Grund der Verordnung über die Anmeldung des Vermögens von Juden, 21 February 1939, *RGBl* 1939 I, p. 282.

137 Niederschrift der Leitersitzung on 7 March 1939, StA Hamburg, Sozialbehörde I, VG 24.36.

Welfare Agency.[138] Hamburg began removing all German Jews from the public welfare rolls, including the so-called *Geltungsjuden* and stateless Jews, whose numbers had now increased to include the Jews from the Protectorate of Bohemia and Moravia, as well as Polish Jews now in the city. The support of these individuals was to pass to the *Jüdische Religionsverband.* This action began in Hamburg on 30 November 1939, long before the Ministries of the Interior and Labor formally and finally decreed the same regulation on 21 December 1942.[139] This applied to 380 individuals in continuous open care. The Social Administration, however, reserved the right to keep control of the Jewish welfare administration.[140] The special office for handling Jews was closed again after only ten months of service.[141] But it took almost a year before the financial details were finally clarified. In a letter dated 18 October 1940 the social administration informed the finance department "that a further transfer to the *Landesfürsorgeamt* (Provincial Welfare Office) of proceeds from the sale of Jewish property is no longer necessary because the Provincial Welfare Office has already squared up with the Jewish Community in the meantime."[142] According to national welfare statistics in the period that followed up to the end of the detectable records in March 1941, there were still between ten and eighteen Jews registered in the public welfare system in Hamburg.[143] In the social administration's annual report for the financial year 1940-41 the extent of administrative work involving the welfare of the Jews is

138 Zehnte Verordnung zum Reichsbürgergesetz, 4 July 1939, *RGB1*, pp. 1097–1099.

139 *MBliV* 1942, pp. 2377/8.

140 Protokoll der Sitzung des Vorstandes des Jüdischen Religionsverbandes Hamburg on 7 November 1939, StA Hamburg, Jüdische Gemeinden, 985 c.

141 Dienstvorschrift über die Geschäftsverteilung, 30 November 1939, and Dienstvorschrift über die öffentliche Fürsorge für Juden, 1 April 1940, and Rundschreiben an alle Dienststellen, 30 November 1939, StA Hamburg, Sozialbehörde I, StW 31.22.

142 StA Hamburg, Finanzdeputation IV, DV IB 2g VB1.

143 Schnelldienst der Reichsfürsorgestatistik, 31 December 1939 until 31 March 1941, StA Hamburg, Sozialbehörde I, Stat 20.11. During this time still about 8,000 Jews lived in Hamburg of which just under a third were over 65 years old and even older. Amtsleitersitzung on 18 December 1941, StA Hamburg, Sozialbehörde I, AF 44.23, vol. I. At the same time the Jewish Community was continually supporting more than 500 persons in open care. Lippmann, *"dass ich wie ein guter Deutscher empfinde,"* p. 76.

described as follows: "The amount of work connected with the welfare of the Jews is low in figures. It proves to be difficult as a result of the new laws. It is necessary to carry out extensive inquiries in order to clarify the state of affairs."[144]

Thus, shortly after the outbreak of World War II, all welfare support of needy Jews by the state and the community in Hamburg officially ended. Segregation and marginalization of Jewish welfare recipients was almost total. Those few still receiving support, as well as the remaining funds allotted to their support would be reduced even more in the years to come. So it was that in August 1940 foreign Jews, and in August 1941 Jewish widows or wives of "Aryan" men from marriages that had been dissolved, were referred to the Jewish Community for support.[145] So it was that former Jewish relief recipients received no ration coupons for clothing from January 1940 onward and from 1 April 1940 were excluded from subsidies of fat for people with low income.[146] So it was, as of December 1941, that severely disabled Jewish war veterans had their privileges and rate reductions revoked by the railway companies or when dealing with government officials.[147] Finally, the Minister of Justice sent out a circular dated 5 March 1942 which deprived the needy Jews of their right to legal aid. In Hamburg the social administration was responsible for dealing with applications for eligibility.[148] Only badly injured war veterans[149] and Jewish marriage partners in so-called privileged mixed marriages remained in the care

144 StA Hamburg, Sozialbehörde I, VG 54.40.

145 Rundschreiben an alle Dienststellen, 7 August 1940, and Deckblatt zur Dienstverordnung vom 1. April 1942, StA Hamburg, Sozialbehörde I, StW 31.22.

146 Rundschreiben des Landesfürsorgeamtes, 20 March 1940, StA Hamburg, Sozialbehörde I, AF 34.22, vol. III.

147 Niederschrift über die 99. Amtsleitersitzung on 5 January 1940 and Nachrichtenblatt der Sozialverwaltung Nr. 3, 17 January 1942, StA Hamburg, Sozialbehörde I, VG 23.01 and VG 27.11. In Hamburg the social administration had already canceled travel supplements for the seriously war disabled when the welfare directive for Jews came into force. This was done in strict interpretation of the national legislation as being a special regulation beyond the scope of public welfare. Amt für Kriegsbeschädigte und Kriegerhinterbliebene to Einspruchsstelle des Reichsstatthalters, 27 April 1939, StA Hamburg, Senatskanzelei-Präsidialabteilung, 1939 S III 740.

148 FZH, Archiv Fsc. 6263

149 With his letter dated 13 February 1943, the Labor Minister informed the Deutscher Gemeindetag that the badly disabled war veterans were included in the takeover

of the Social Administration,[150] which tried to get rid of this group by urging the individual welfare recipients to voluntarily join the *Reichsvereinigung der Juden in Deutschland.*[151] The Jewish welfare recipients had reached the last stage before the final destruction of any chance of livelihood. In the meantime the deportations to the camps in the east had already begun in Hamburg.[152]

Conclusion

As far as public welfare was concerned, Hamburg's community welfare administration had operated according to the tenor and spirit of National Socialism from the outset. It not only accepted the creation of a completely new welfare group, the Jews, but also contributed of its own accord and finally actively practiced discrimination and segregation. And in cases where it did not take an active part, it conscientiously adhered to the guidelines that it received. This was carried out in the individual departments with varying intensity. In an administration whose most sacred duty is the care of the weak and those in need, no protest worth mentioning was made. The behavior

of the needy Jews by the Reichsvereinigung as stipulated in the decree of 21 December 1942. BA Koblenz, R36/882.

150 See Deckblatt zur Dienstvorschrift vom 1. April 1942, StA Hamburg, Sozialbehörde I, StW 31.22. The same was stipulated a short time after this by a decree from the Minister of the Interior dated 20 July 1942. Deutscher Gemeindetag, Schlüter, to Oberbürgermeister von München. Fiehler, 14 September 1942, Yad Vashem Archives, File M1DN/109.

151 Karminski to Eppstein, 9 May 1942, on the occasion of an inquiry of the Jüdische Kultusvereinigung Hamburg, BA Potsdam, 75C Rel, Nr. 4. See in contrast the decision of the Minister of the Interior dated 20 July 1942, whereby it was not feasible to demand of Jews living in "privileged mixed marriages" that they join the Reichsvereinigung with the sole purpose of gaining through their membership the right to be supported by the Reichsvereinigung. Rundschreiben des Deutschen Gemeindetages an die Reichsgau-, Landes- und Provinzialdienststellen, 14 September 1942. BA Koblenz, R36/883.

152 The first transport left Hamburg on 25 October 1941 in the direction of Lodz. Übersicht der Deportationstransporte 1941–1945 in *Hamburger jüdische Opfer des Nationalsozialismus. Gedenkbuch*, Jürgen Sielemann, ed., Hamburg, 1995, p. XVII.

of the Hamburg welfare administration was not unique. In comparable cities such as Berlin, Breslau, Frankfurt am Main, Cologne, Munich and Nuremberg, very similar developments were taking place. These cities were able to support each other and accelerate their actions by exchanging information and by coordination within the Council of German Municipalities.[153]

The process of segregating Jews from the other needy, and the gradual reduction of their means of survival, indeed paralleled the general development of the segregation of Jewish citizens from the *Volksgemeinschaft*. But, as has been shown, no special impetus on the part of the government or the party leadership was required to set this policy in motion, even if the final decisive course was set by them.[154] Generally speaking, this process developed from a combination of various factors. From "above," there were legal directives from the regime. From "outside," there was the political activism of the NSDAP and its organs as well as the economic and social pressures exerted by the public, and from "inside," there was community self-interest and activity on the part of the authorities. This process was borne by the public administration employees — just as much through their individual willingness and personal keenness to put the radical National Socialist anti-Jewish ideals into effect as through the administrators' mainly unconditional adaptation to the new social and administrative norms and through a specific bureaucratic conscientiousness.[155] This process steadily escalated. It must be added that the events of the years 1935 and 1938 represent no hiatus; rather they were an additional

153 Responsible and therefore taking full part was Department III, Health Service, Welfare Care and Social Politics under the leadership of deputy mayor Georg Schlüter.

154 The results of this study make it necessary to contradict Horst Matzerath's general theory that in putting National Socialist Jewish politics into practice the local administrations were bound to cooperate; "the actual initiative" having come only from the highest state and party leaderships. Matzerath, "Bürokratie und Judenverfolgung," p. 118. In contrast, Peter Hanke was correct in 1967, but was too biased by reference exclusively to Munich on the one hand and the legislation of the Reich on the other: "Action taken by the town administration was constantly ahead of any decree of important laws which were passed in individual cases, in fact, merely upon the example of the action already taken by the city of Munich." Hanke, *Zur Geschichte der Juden in München*, p. 270.

155 See Lohalm, "Hamburgs Verwaltung und öffentlicher Dienst," pp. 190–208.

impetus which finally resulted in the complete expulsion of Jews from German society. Here was expressed a high degree of acceptance — both passive and active — of anti-Jewish prejudice and the goals of the National Socialists in a closed *Volksgemeinschaft*.

The Germans: "An Antisemitic People" The Press Campaign After 9 November 1938

HERBERT OBENAUS

I

The pogrom of 9–10 November 1938 gave rise to a variety of tactical and strategic considerations by the German government and National Socialist party offices. The discussions that took place in the Ministry of Propaganda — which in some respects played a pivotal role in the events, due largely to its minister, Josef Goebbels — were of particular significance. On the one hand, the ministry was obliged to document the "wrath of the people" following the assassination of Ernst vom Rath; on the other hand, it was also responsible for manipulating the population by influencing the press and molding opinion. Concerning the events themselves, the main issue was what kind of picture the press was conveying to both a national and an international readership. In the ministry, this prompted several questions: Could it be satisfied with the reactions of the population to vom Rath's murder? What explanation could be given for the people's obvious distance to the events surrounding 9 November? Should the press make greater efforts to influence the opinions prevalent among the population? Should special strategies for the press be developed and pursued after 9 November 1938? Moreover, since the pogrom proved to be a turning point in the regime's policies towards German Jews and marked the beginning of a qualitative change, how should the press react to these changes?

Press activity was also conducted on a second level, that of the

NSDAP, which had its own press service, the *Nationalsozialistische Partei-Korrespondenz (NSK).*[1] As was the case with Goebbels' ministry, the propaganda activity of the party was organized both in party headquarters as well as in local and regional offices; the Gau propaganda offices were for the party what the Reich propaganda offices were for the ministry.[2] The press activity of the party was closely connected to that of the Ministry of Propaganda, and after 9 November the party's press service was faced with the same tasks as the ministry. But it remains to be asked whether it pursued its own path, developed its own propagandistic content and offered its own solutions.

In addition to the activity of the ministry and the party, both of which released information to influence the press, the activity of the journalists in the various divisions of the press should also be investigated. One of the particular strengths of the National Socialist news organization was that it could limit itself to general guidelines or to individual specific directives, and was confident that either way the prescribed political line of thought would be adhered to. Yet on occasion, journalists were granted some scope for their own creative activity. If they violated the rules, they were disciplined according to a graduated scale of punishment.[3] The National Socialist propagandists could rely on the loyalty of the press. Nevertheless, it remains to be

1 It was published in 1938 with the publisher's information, "Commissioned by Wilhelm Weiss; responsible for the reports from the Reichspressestelle: Dr. Otto Dietrich, *Reichspressechef* of the NSDAP. The editor-in-chief responsible for the remaining contents was Helmut Sündermann. Deputy editor-in-chief was Wilhelm Ritgen." For more information on the *NSK*, which was established on 14 January 1932 in Munich and published in Berlin after 1 May 1933, see: Peter Stein, "Die NS-Gaupresse 1925–1933. Forschungsbericht — Quellenkritik — neue Bestandsaufnahme," *Dortmunder Beiträge zur Zeitungsforschung,* 42 (1987), pp. 55 ff.

I would like to thank Rebecca L. van Dyck for the translation of my contribution.

2 Ernest K. Bramsted, *Goebbels und die nationalsozialistische Propaganda 1925–1945*, Frankfurt am Main, 1971, pp. 167–175, which describes the complicated distribution of tasks and the resultant tension between Goebbels and Dietrich. After 1937, the branches of the Ministry of Propaganda were called *Reichspropagandaämter*; before that they were called *Landesstellen*.

3 Refer to Kurt Koszyk, *Deutsche Presse 1914–1945. Geschichte der deutschen Presse Teil III. Abhandlungen und Materialien zur Publizistik*, Berlin, 1972 , vol. 7, p. 372, according to which a breach of the rules could lead to court proceedings under the *Schriftleitergesetz* (Editor-in-Chief Law), or the *Reichskulturkammergesetz*

investigated how each of the directives was adhered to, and whether the press independently contributed to the objectives set by the ministry. This cannot be tackled within the scope of the present study; rather, pertinent questions can be addressed by examining the divisions of the press at the local level. In order to accomplish this I have consulted newspapers from the northwestern area of Germany.

II

To begin with, it is necessary to trace the steering activity of the Ministry of Propaganda during the weeks after the pogrom, as well as the intensification of the persecution of Jews.[4] Within what context and from what perspective did the ministry wish to see the subject of the Jews handled? Further, it must be asked what the intention was of each point discussed. Previous investigations have already shown that the Ministry of Propaganda was aware of the population's detachment from — and even its censure of — the pogrom.[5] Were the reasons for this detachment analyzed, and what attempts were made to understand the population's reactions? It can be shown that the ministry responded by developing a coordinated political concept and intensifying its antisemitic policy. Constructed by the Ministry of Propaganda, this concept — which will be discussed in detail further on — placed the Jew in the context of German national history, and by the misuse and distorted interpretation of historical facts attempted to prove the validity of antisemitism. The party's press service adopted this concept and consistently pursued it in the subsequent weeks.

(Reich Chamber of Culture Law). Compare Norbert Frei and Johannes Schmitz, *Journalismus im Dritten Reich*, 2nd edition, Munich, 1989, pp. 30–35.

4 For the steering of the press during the pogrom itself, refer to: Wolfgang Benz, "Der Rückfall in die Barbarei. Bericht über den Pogrom," in: *Der Judenpogrom 1938. Von der "Reichskristallnacht" zum Völkermord*, Walter H. Pehle, ed., Frankfurt am Main, 1988, pp. 13–51 (specifically pp. 15–19). Also Wolfgang Benz, "Der Novemberpogrom 1938," in: *Die Juden in Deutschland 1933–1945. Leben unter nationalsozialistischer Herrschaft,* 3rd edition, Wolfgang Benz, ed., Munich, 1993, pp. 499–544, and pp. 505–521, a section with the heading "Die Inszenierung des Pogroms und die Regie der öffentlichen Meinung."

5 Jürgen Hagemann, *Die Presselenkung im Dritten Reich*, Bonn, 1970, pp. 126 f.

At the Reich press conference on 17 November 1938, fundamental directives regarding the journalistic treatment of the "Jewish question" were issued. (This date may have been deliberately chosen, being the day of vom Rath's funeral.) This was preceded by a conference under the chairmanship of Hermann Göring, who had received instructions from Hitler to "uniformly combine" the policies with respect to the German Jews and "to carry them out either way" (*sie so oder so zur Erledigung zu bringen).*[6] It was at this conference, attended by many people including the two other main protagonists Goebbels and Heydrich, that the strategies were decided upon for the forced emigration of Jews, and the exclusion from German society of those Jews unfit for emigration and their subsequent transportation into a forced community.[7] It was the responsibility of the Ministry of Propaganda to support and justify these policies both in their execution and in their heightened radicalism and irrevocability.

The chief spokesman of the Ministry of Propaganda was *Ministerialrat* Alfred-Ingemar Berndt, who served as director of the press department;[8] he was supported by *Oberregierungsräte* Dr. Wilhelm

6 Minutes of a meeting held in the Reich Ministry of Aviation on 12 November 1938. *Der Prozeß gegen die Hauptkriegsverbrecher vor dem Internationalen Militärgerichtshof, 14. November 1945 — 1. Oktober 1946*, XXVIII, Nuremberg, 1948, pp. 499–540.

7 Two further "strategy conferences" of National Socialist leaders in the subsequent weeks were concerned with the continuation of the policies against German Jews; see Wolf Gruner, "Lesen brauchen sie nicht zu können.... Die 'Denkschrift über die Behandlung der Juden in der Reichshauptstadt auf allen Gebieten des öffentlichen Lebens' vom Mai 1938," *Jahrbuch für Antisemitismusforschung,* 4 (1995), pp. 305–341 (specifically pp. 306 and 313, including footnote 80). For the individual measures, Joseph Walk, *Das Sonderrecht für die Juden im NS-Staat. Eine Sammlung der gesetzlichen Maßnahmen und Richtlinien —Inhalt und Bedeutung. Motive — Texte — Materialien*, Karlsruhe, 1981.

8 Berndt, born in 1905, was appointed head of the department in April 1936. When it was divided into domestic and foreign departments in April 1938, Berndt headed the domestic department until Hans Fritzsche, born in 1900, became his successor in December 1938; see Koszyk, *Deutsche Presse*, p. 363. Berndt is described as Goebbels' protegé; see Bramsted, *Goebbels*, p. 124.

Ziegler[9] and Hans Fritzsche.[10] Berndt announced that every newspaper must "print a series of articles ... within the next ten days" on "the role of the Jews in Germany." The articles that the Ministry of Propaganda had in mind focused on Jews from the time of Bismarck's Reich until Hitler's takeover of the government in 1933. The literary allusions later provided by Ziegler also referred to this period. The period after 1918 was considered particularly important, as "the revolution brought the Jews to the top everywhere ... The Council of the People's Delegates (*Rat der Volksbeauftragten*) consisted solely of Jews, ... until 1933 there were Jews everywhere, only Jews."[11] The "information campaign" of

9 Ziegler, born in 1891, frequently wrote articles on contemporary history. From 1919 to 1932 he worked for the *Reichszentrale für Heimatdienst* and was a member of the *Deutsche Volkspartei*. Upon joining the Ministry of Propaganda in 1933, he took over the department concerned with the "Execution of a Uniform Reich Propaganda in the Areas of Foreign, Defense and Jewish Policy." According to Kürschner's German Calender of Literature for 1943, Ziegler was a *Ministerialrat* in the Ministry of Propaganda. In 1941 he was appointed honorary professor for modern — specifically postwar — history in the Department of Foreign Sciences of the University of Berlin. Ziegler was the director of the Institute for the Study of the Jewish Question run by the Ministry of Propaganda. Helmut Heiber, *Walter Frank und sein Reichsinstitut für Geschichte des neuen Deutschlands*, Stuttgart, 1966, pp. 600 ff.

10 The spokesmen's expositions have been very well documented. On the one hand, there is the report on the press conference written and signed by Kurt Metger of the German News Office. This report, no. 568/38, written in the form of a letter, was headed "Strictly confidential! For information only! Must remain secret!": Bundesarchiv Koblenz, ZSg. 110/11/125r. On the other hand, there is the telex sent by the Berlin office of the *Frankfurter Zeitung* to the head office in Frankfurt: Ibid., ZSg. 102/13/30v. This topic is again taken up in the press conference of 19 November. A telex was also sent in this regard: ibid., ZSg. 102/13. In the following, I rely in particular on Metger, who wrote coherent reports. The shorter and less precise wording of the telex is only mentioned to supplement the reports. For the records, see *NS-Presseweisungen der Vorkriegszeit. Edition und Dokumentation*, Hans Bohrmann, ed., vol. 1, revised by Gabriele Toepser-Ziegert, Munich, 1984, pp. 53–59. The press directives for 1935, which have not yet been published, go into more detail about Kurt Metger; compare ibid., p. 53, footnote 143. Incidentally, I would like to thank Ms. Toepser-Ziegert for her friendly advice and support. In addition to the press directives from 17 and 19 November extracted from archives, I have also cited press directives from the subsequent weeks as they appear in Hagemann, *Presselenkung*.

11 Telex version.

which Berndt spoke was meant to be conducted not only by the press, but also radio and film, and ultimately "in all areas." Accompanied by the laughter of those present, he announced that dialogues would be aired on radio, for example "between the editors in chief of the *Frankfurter Zeitung* and the *Stürmer*."[12] However, Berndt also coupled his address with the warning that over the course of the following few days, newspapers would be "very closely observed" with respect to their compliance with the ministry's directives.[13]

One of the key phrases of the information campaign was the "subversive activity" of Jews, of which Ziegler spoke while drawing on antisemitic literature. Subversion had occurred both in the labor movement — he mentioned the names Marx, Engels and Singer — as well as in the liberal movement — he referred to Bamberger and Lasker. In the labor movement, Ziegler said, the Jews were generally responsible for tendencies that were "negative, hostile to the state, oppositional;" in liberalism, the Jews represented the "typical enemies of the Reich." And these included of course Jewish bankers — broadly referred to as the "court Jews" (*Hofjuden)* in the Wilhelminian era. The "politics of Judaism" became clearly discernible within the context of the escalating crisis during World War I: the Jews had come out "firstly against a strong national authority, and secondly against the nation's will to resist external forces." This tendency, Ziegler remarked, was even more noticeable during the November Revolution. "The Jews have triumphed all along the line, and now it turns out that Jews are at the top everywhere: ... in the Council of the People's Delegates — Hugo Haase and Otto Landsberg; in Munich — Eisner; in Dresden — Gradnauer, Lipinsky und Fleissner. ... Everywhere radicalism breaks through and triumphs, there are Jews there as supporters of radicalism." Referring each time to antisemitic literature, Ziegler's casting of blame extended also to the Treaty of Versailles and the "epoch of the policy of

12 For details on the special role of the *Frankfurter Zeitung* during the Nazi period see Bramsted, *Goebbels*, pp. 191–213.

13 It was said that "over the last few days, many tips have been received," of which the newspapers, however, had "not yet used even 5%." It is interesting to note that Berndt's warning was also included in the telex version, which was overall much shorter.

fulfillment."[14] Further literary references followed, this time pointing to the role of Jews in economics, culture and crime.[15] In his crowning conclusion, Ziegler recommended that newspapers look into the role of Jews as assassins. It came as no surprise then that the shots fired by Herschel Grynszpan at vom Rath were denounced shortly after as typically Jewish.

As Berndt had already implied, the information campaign was broadly structured and was meant to encompass all media. It was the main focus of the propaganda activity of the winter.[16] Great importance was attached to antisemitic press activity after 9 November; this is

14 In this regard he referred to one of his own publications: Wilhelm Ziegler, *Versailles, die Geschichte eines missglückten Friedens*, Hamburg, 1933. The 4th edition was published in 1937.

15 The "basic" literary source was the book *Die Juden in Deutschland*, edited by the Institut zum Studium der Judenfrage, Munich, 1936. See footnote 9, above, for information on the institute. As a source of information on the role of the Jews in the labor movement, Ziegler mentioned *F[ritz] O[tto] H[ermann] Schulz, Jude und Arbeiter. Ein Abschnitt aus der Tragödie des deutschen Volkes*, edited by the Institut zum Studium der Judenfrage in conjunction with the Antikomintern, Berlin, 1934. For Maximilian Harden he referred to Walter Frank, *Geist und Macht. Historisch-Politische Aufsätze*, Hamburg, 1938, as well as to J. Keller and Hanns Andersen, *Der Jude als Verbrecher*, Berlin, 1937. In addition, Fritzsche mentioned Alfred-Ingemar Berndt, *Gebt mir vier Jahre Zeit! Dokumente zum 1. Vierjahresplan des Führers*, 5th and 6th edition, Munich, 1938, which contained a "lot of material on the Jews in Germany." The book by Keller and Andersen had already found its way into several editorial offices even prior to the press conference of 17 November. Thus in its edition of 12/13 November, the *Stader Tageblatt* made reference to the publication by Keller and Andersen in an editorial on the assassination of Ernst vom Rath. Wolfgang Fehrmann, "Die Waffe des Juden ist der Mord! Im ewigen Hass gegen das deutsche Volk," ibid. The author concerns himself with the character stereotype of the Jews as "fundamentally and basically criminal," their tendency "to murder," which in turn "corresponds to their negation of the rules and their anarchistic mentality, both of which stem from an inherent tendency towards Bolshevism." That previous August, the Institute for the Study of the Jewish Question had already pointed out the high proportion of Jewish criminals. The *Helmstedter Kreisblatt* published an article on this topic on 11 August 1938: "Die Juden in der Kriminalistik. 50mal soviel Rechtsbrecher aus dem Judentum."

16 As per the press conference of 24 November 1938: Hagemann, *Presselenkung*, p. 149. In the press conference of 25 November 1938, the participants were "reminded of the Jewish question, as will daily be the case from now on," ibid., p. 143.

demonstrated also by the status it received in Josef Goebbels' journal. He spoke of "our campaign against the Jews in the press,"[17]and an "antisemitic crusade" in newspapers, on radio, and in political assemblies.[18] At the end of November he noted that Hitler was "very satisfied with the campaign against the Jews in the press."[19]

The ministry's press conference was dominated by the tendency to portray the Jews as a threat to the German state, economy and society. To this end, the entire cache of antisemitic prejudices and stereotypes was emptied. Interesting is that compared with political prejudice, the prejudice of subversive activity diminishes considerably in the areas of the economy and culture. More important than this rather speculative evaluation is the campaign's intention to increasingly indoctrinate the German people and stir up antisemitic sentiment through the newspaper. The attempt to demonstrate the subversive activity of Jews relates to the period of contemporary history as it was perceived from the perspective of the year 1938, beginning with the founding of Bismarck's Reich, a decisive national occurrence at the time. The telex version of the press conference also included a general statement to the effect that more should be written about the Jews "of earlier times, of prewar times." However, the literary references provided by Ziegler essentially related to contemporary history. The emphasis on contemporary history was paralleled with a reduction of Jewish history in Germany to the years subsequent to the founding of the German Reich. Previous periods — that of the often ostracized and persecuted ethnic-religious minority in the Middle Ages and early modern times, and the dynamic process of Jewish emancipation and assimilation within the framework of German civil society — were not even mentioned.

The antisemitic interpretation of contemporary history was intended to justify the pogrom of 9 November as well as the subsequent measures to exclude and repress the Jews. Furthermore, this view

17 Taken from Joseph Goebbels' diaries. Entry of 17 November 1938: Elke Fröhlich, *Die Tagebücher von Joseph Goebbels. Sämtliche Fragmente*, part 1, vol. 3, Munich, 1987, p. 535.

18 Fröhlich, *Tagebücher*, p. 537, entry of 18 November 1938.

19 Fröhlich, p. 540, entry of 24 November 1938. After this date, Goebbels no longer mentioned the "campaign against the Jews" in his journals. Hagemann, *Presselenkung*, p. 127, justifiably refers to "anti-Jewish propaganda" as the "topic of the winter of 1938–39."

of German history legitimized also the justification of the National Socialist takeover in 1933. In the end, the press campaign was meant to leave readers with the belief that history proved the compelling necessity of policies aimed against the Jews. On 19 November, in the first critical review of the campaign's progress, it was said, "in all newspapers, the series of articles must conclude with the clear message: German people, you have now been able to read how and where the Jews have harmed you!" Once the information campaign was underway, to behave as a friend of Jews was characterized as opposition to the regime. Thus, the historical line of reasoning and the urgent appeal to the German people immediately turned into an incitement for denunciation. Where there was a "national comrade" who did not support the suppression of the Jews, it was clear "that he was one of those who has still not comprehended the situation, one of those people who always say no. Make a note of him: those are the men who turn their backs on the Führer."

The intent to increase the weight of antisemitism as an ideology of integration is shown by the determination to impose an antisemitic interpretation of contemporary German history. The campaign was consistently directed toward those who continued to evade this ideology. Berndt announced that the "German philistine" *(Spiesser),* was to be attacked within the framework of the campaign. By this he meant "the one percent of the people who have said "no" in the elections during the years since the government's takeover by Hitler. The *Spiesser* were those people who "again sympathized with the Jews" they must "be silenced ... within ten days." Upon closer examination of who was meant by "the *Spiesser*," one can recognize the followers of the major political groups prior to 1933; expressly named were the followers of Stresemann and Schleicher. In addition, the sceptics of Hitler's rule were referred to as those "who were frightened by the invasion of the Rhineland." According to Berndt, those Germans who rejected the antisemitic policies on the basis of their pre-National Socialist socialization and attitudes were the *Spiesser.* However, it quickly became obvious to the organizers of the campaign that by the mere mention of opponents of antisemitism, they were taking a risk. According to the press conference of 17 November, under no circumstances was one allowed to "create the impression, by means of headlines, that large parts of the population did not agree with the measures against the Jews."

It can be inferred from the campaign that, on the whole, antisemitism was regarded as insufficiently entrenched in the German population to have the desired integrating effect. In view of the tolerant or even friendly tendencies toward Jews that he had himself observed, on 24 November Berndt went so far as to acknowledge this lapse, declaring that the impression not be allowed to arise "that only the party and the state are antisemitic."[20] Above and beyond this, the ministry was quite aware that it was the violence of the pogrom that met with disapproval, even repudiation. Contemporary reports reveal that the population particularly objected to what it considered "senseless" destruction, including the attack on private property.[21] For this reason, the instructions to the press emphasized that on the one hand, "in Germany ... under all circumstances, the issue of the Jews" would be solved "once and for all," yet on the other hand, "under no circumstances" would "acts of violence continue to take place." In this respect, the press directive categorically declared that the rejection of violence be particularly emphasized in consideration of domestic sentiments.[22]

Yet another aim of the press directive of 17 November was to increase the population's support of the government's antisemitic policies. The Ministry of Propaganda wanted the information campaign on the role

20 Hagemann, *Presselenkung*, p. 149.

21 William Sheridan Allen, "Die deutsche Öffentlichkeit und die 'Reichskristallnacht' — Konflikte zwischen Werthierarchie und Propaganda im Dritten Reich," in: *Die Reihen fest geschlossen. Beiträge zur Geschichte des Alltags unter dem Nationalsozialismus*, Detlev Peukert and Jürgen Reulecke, eds., Wuppertal, 1981, pp. 397–411, specifically pp. 402 ff. David Bankier, *Die öffentliche Meinung im Hitler-Staat. Die "Endlösung" und die Deutschen. Eine Berichtigung*, Berlin, 1995, pp. 118–122.

22 Wording of the telex. The rioting associated with the pogrom "continued until 13 November in some places." Benz, *Rückfall*, p. 32. In the press conference of 14 November 1938, Hans Fritzsche makes reference to the statement Goebbels had made the previous day "that from now on, the antisemitic demonstrations against Jewish shops must come to an end." In a matter of "a few weeks," there would not be any shops left anyway. Two days prior to that, an interview on the same subject had been granted to a representive of Reuter, Joseph Wulf, *Presse und Funk im Dritten Reich. Eine Dokumentation*, Frankfurt am Main, 1989, p. 104.

of Jews in contemporary German history to be embedded in a complex of news that turned attention towards the treatment of Jews in other countries. "In the long term, perhaps in the next week," as never before, it was considered necessary to emphasize any event "that somehow demonstrates that foreign powers refuse to permit entry to the Jews," mistreat them,[23] or incarcerate them in concentration camps. On the subject of concentration camps, Berndt cited the British policy during the Boer War, when twenty thousand women and children starved to death: "Women and children of a civilized people, not niggers."[24] Thus the actions of the British in South Africa served as an example to the German people, who were undoubtedly aware of the fact that following the events surrounding 9 November Jews had been sent to concentration camps. Another example cited was the United States, which — "unlike any other country" — had solved the "issue of race" by "blocking the entry of unpleasant races by means of immigration laws."[25] Australia, too, exemplified a country that refused to admit Jews because they were considered "foreign bodies." Berndt said, "They want to force an overpopulated Germany to keep these parasites in the country, when there is room enough in the whole world to accommodate them." He demanded that this behavior be characterized as antisemitic, as the "antisemitism of the others." What the Ministry of Propaganda achieved by drawing a parallel between the German policy towards Jews with that of other countries was that all were shown as being confronted with the same problem.[26] It was charged that many countries had attempted to rid themselves of, or keep out, Jews. Thus antisemitism was depicted as the underlying trend of world politics.

23 Repeated during the press conference of 18 November 1938: Hagemann, *Presselenkung*, p. 149.

24 On this occasion, the *Berliner Lokal-Anzeiger* is praised for having published an article the previous day on "English colonial methods." The atrocities committed by the English during the Boer War, in Palestine and in the American War of Independence had already been denounced in the press conference of 15 November 1938 and compared with "a couple" of windowpanes that had been broken on 9 November, Hagemann, *Presselenkung*, p. 148.

25 Wording of the telex.

26 A call for describing in detail the antisemitism of other governments had already appeared in a press directive dated 17 May 1938, Hagemann, *Presselenkung*, p. 146.

The message to the German newspaper reader was: We do not stand alone in our antisemitism.[27] In this regard, the *NSK* adhered to the line of the Propaganda Ministry, and in December 1938 published a special issue on the echo and effect in many different countries around the world that had resulted from the persecution of Jews in the German Reich. Here, too, the central message was that "defense movements" against Jews existed in all countries.[28]

The Ministry of Propaganda's argument to placate the German population had a realistic core: the suppression of Jews in Germany did in fact trigger off antisemitic attitudes in the governments of other countries. In January 1939, the Foreign Office informed all diplomatic representatives of the Reich that in the Scandinavian countries, Holland and France, to where many German Jews had immigrated, "a significant increase of antisemitism could be noted." The Foreign Office was confident it could develop a political concept out of this situation. It generated the idea that in the future, an "international solution to the Jewish question" would be possible, which could begin from the mutual understanding among all peoples that the Jews pose a threat.[29]

27 Hagemann, *Presselenkung*, p. 126, writes, that the "emphasis of the unfriendly treatment of the Jews in other countries" was to be understood as "justification of the rioting during the 'Reichskristallnacht'."

28 "Der Feind aller Völker," *NSK* issue no. 289. There is no date for this issue. It either appeared with no. 288 on 9 December 1938, a Friday, perhaps on 10 December 1938, a Saturday, or else together with no. 390 on 12 December 1938, a Monday.

29 Series *Der Prozess gegen die Hauptkriegsverbrecher vor dem Internationalen Militärgerichtshof* 32, Nuremberg, 1948, pp. 234–245. Circular directive by the Foreign Office to its agencies abroad, 25 January 1939: *Akten zur deutschen auswärtigen Politik 1918–1945*, Series D (1937–1945), Volume 5, Baden-Baden, 1953, no. 664. The circular directive was signed by Legationsrat 1st Class Emil Johannes Schumburg. For more information on his career with the Foreign Office see, *Akten zur deutschen auswärtigen Politik 1918–1945. Aus dem Archiv des Auswärtigen Amtes*, Supplement to the series A-E, Göttingen, 1995, p. 506. A statement issued by the Office of the Reichsführer SS and Chief of the German Police on 19 april 1944 says that Schumburg had been "a kind of liaison officer to the RSHA for some time." SS Officer's File, Bundesarchiv Berlin, PK (formerly BDC), Schumburg, Emil, d.o.b. 14 May 1898. The close link to the practice of expelling the Jews is evident by the direct reference made to the looting of the Jews before their expulsion as beneficial to foreign policy. Thus, the Foreign Office emphasized that "the poorer and therefore more burdensome the immigrating Jew is for the immigration country, the more strongly the host country will react, and

Antisemitism became an exportable item; the domestic antisemitic policy of the National Socialists expanded into a concept of world policy. In this regard, the work of the Ministry of Propaganda appears to have been meshed with foreign policy; in other words, domestic antisemitic activism would give German diplomacy a leading role in world policy.

However, the press conference of 17 November was dominated by ambivalence. A deliberate concession to the German population's hierarchy of values was made, thus recognizing that antisemitism might have to assume a subordinate position in situations where values associated with property and order had been deviated from.[30] In the antisemitic perspectives of politics, however, no concessions were made. The National Socialists did not waiver from the basic idea that liberation from "Jewish rule" represented one of the central tasks of German politics, which was to be pursued on an equal level with the other main objectives of Germany's struggle for a hegemonic position within Europe. However, since this also required that the population's hierarchy of values be acknowledged, the use of violence — as in the pogrom of 9 November — was expressly ruled out. In future, the solution to the "Jewish question" would be sought by means of laws and ordinances. It was believed that by making this concession, the status of antisemitism could be secured against the possible reordering of the hierarchy of values.

III

Aside from the swaying of the press by the Ministry of Propaganda, a close look at the press activity of the NSDAP, which was conducted by the Reich news office of the NSDAP and its press service *NSK*, reveals some coordination between the two institutions, at least regarding the

the more desirable the effect will be in the interest of German propaganda." There are indications that in the winter of 1938–39, both Hitler and Himmler had hoped to be able to "export" German antisemitism: Hermann Graml, *Reichskristallnacht. Antisemitismus und Judenverfolgung im Dritten Reich*, Munich, 1988, pp. 189f.

30 Compare Allen, *Deutsche Öffentlichkeit*, p. 402.

dates of publication of certain news items. For example, the day after the Ministry of Propaganda's press conference, the *NSK* published a special issue on the subject of "Judah's Debt of Guilt in Germany." It comprised thirty-nine pages and contained a plethora of suggestions for antisemitic accusations and attacks, which were in part identical with the press directives but contained independent elements as well.[31]

In an introductory article in its special issue, the *NSK* attempted to portray contemporary history as an uninterrupted series of attacks on the German people by Jews, which "had caused embitterment to spread to such an extent, that a logical reduction of the tension can only be achieved by means of the total elimination of the Jews not only from politics, but also from the German economy and cultural life."[32] Reminiscent of the Ministry of Propaganda's press conference, an array of stereotypes was used. Everywhere the Jews were presented as enemies of the Reich and of humanity. They were typical assassins, criminals and murderers; the henchmen of foreign powers who "stab in the back" (*Dolchstoss*); the covert rulers of the economy, culture and science; "separatists;" the architects of economic boycotts, the malicious agitators in German emigrant circles; black marketeers, controllers of the press, destroyers of the German soul through modern literature. "On the stage and on the screen, speculation over the lower instincts"[33] — Jews everywhere were described as undermining culture and morals. Individual social groups, for instance farmers, were portrayed as being suppressed by Jewish financial backers.[34]

31 Fritzsche announced that the special issue would be "published somewhat later than usual and only be finished in the course of the morning." He recommended "making broad use" of the special issue, which was then published on 18 November 1938 as issue no. 270. The contributors to the special issue were listed on the last page; however, the individual articles are not expressly attributed to them (with the exception of the article written by J[örg] R[ehoff], p. 13). The *NSK* issue no. 279, dated 29 November 1938, announced that the "great" special issue, which had sold out in the meantime, would be reissued.

32 "Israels Feldzug gegen das Reich," ibid., p. 3.

33 Ibid., pp. 27 f.

34 "Judas wirtschaftliches Schuldkonto: Gauner, Lügner, Spekulanten, Diebe," ibid., pp. 28 f. Central in this regard are the articles: "Judenmanöver in der Landwirtschaft: Ernte ohne Saat," pp. 32 f., and "Bauerngüter in jüdischer Hand: Raubzug gegen deutschen Boden," ibid., pp. 33 f.

The press service of the NSDAP was better at managing the routine and detailed press coverage of antisemitic topics. An example is their review of the book *Bagatelles pour un massacre*, written by the French antisemite Louis Ferdinand Céline, upon the publication of its German translation.[35] On the day before the ministry's press conference, the *NSK* had already raised a topic that was to gain significance for the foreign policy strategy of the National Socialists — namely the reserve with which many Jews who were driven out of Germany were admitted into foreign countries.[36] Other articles dealt with the financial circumstances of those Jews still living in Germany, circumstances which were depicted as splendid.[37]

In comparison with the press conference of the Ministry of Propaganda, the articles of the party's press service reflect a somewhat different character, as seen in the openness with which they pronounced a more intense persecution of Jews for the future. True, Berndt had requested representatives of the press to "always emphasize that for us, the problem of the Jews is naturally now going to be finally solved once and for all;" at the same time, however, he declared that violent action had ended. In this regard, the special issue published by the *NSK* adopted an opposite standpoint, one that was knowingly meant to deviate from the Ministry of Propaganda's placating gesture. Under the headline "What did not work with kindness must work with harshness: The clear separation," the party's press service claimed that up until that point, "the separation of the racially different Jews from the German people, also with the aim of spatial separation by means of migration," had been conducted "in a strictly legal way." The measures had been carried out in "as tolerable a way as possible." However "this German position was not understood" and the German Jews had begun "to forget the seriousness of the situation." After the murders of Wilhelm Gustloff and Ernst vom Rath, "patience had come to an end," and "what remained unreachable in kindness" would now be regulated

35 The German title: *Die Judenverschwörung in Frankreich*, Dresden, 1938; see also *NSK* issue no. 267 dated 13 November 1938.

36 "Keiner will sie haben ... 'Judenauslese' in den Vereinigten Staaten," *NSK* issue no. 269 dated 16 November 1938.

37 "Wie lebt der Jude in Deutschland? Die Lüge vom 'armen Juden'," *NSK* issue no. 268 dated 15 November 1938.

"with harshness and inconsiderateness." The policies regarding the Jews would be "mercilessly carried through."[38] In fact, legal action was claimed to have guided the politics of the past; in contrast, a future policy of severe and merciless harshness was proclaimed. The *NSK* spoke openly about what had been avoided at the press conference. At the end of December, looking back at the "politics of justice," it was said that the year 1938 had "brought forth the legal foundation for the complete elimination of the Jews from all areas of life of the German people."[39]

To assess how the antisemitic campaign was conducted in the provinces and states after 9 November, one would have to analyze an extensive collection of material, including film and radio, and not least, the speeches at political assemblies.[40] For example, the series of lectures on "Judaism and the Jewish Question," presented in January 1939 in the main lecture hall of the University of Berlin by the Reich Institute for the History of a New Germany, are of central importance.[41] An exhibition called "The Wandering Jew," presented in Berlin and other towns, was also presumably related to the campaign.[42]

A complete investigation of the reactions to the press directives of 17 November would require extensive analytical work which cannot be

38 *NSK* issue no. 270, p. 18.

39 "Grossdeutsche Rechtspolitik 1938," *NSK* issue no. 304 dated 29 December 1938, supplement: "Das Deutsche Recht."

40 The conference of the Reichspropagandaamt Ost-Hannover, held in Luneburg on 9–11 December 1938, is an example of such a meeting. Dr. Wilhelm Ziegler of the Reich Ministry of Propaganda gave a lecture on the topic "The Solution of the Jewish Problem." "Die Lösung des Judenproblems. Vortrag von Pg. Wilhelm Ziegler auf der Presse- und Propagandatagung in Lüneburg," *Cellesche Zeitung*, 12 December 1938.

41 See Heiber, *Walter Frank*, pp. 627–630. The opening lecture given by Walter Frank, which was also broadcast on radio, was on the subject "Dreyfus — the Wandering Jew." A further nine speakers from the Institute held talks at the university every evening. According to Heiber, attendance "was unusually high, considering this was a scientific lecture series," ibid., p. 628.

42 Hans Timner, "Zwei Welten. Dem ewigen Ahasver gegenüber — Gedanken bei einem Rundgang durch die aktuellste Ausstellung," *NSK* 285 (6 December 1938), pp. 4f. For more on the traveling exhibition, which was also shown in Dresden on 24 March 1939 after shows in Munich, Vienna, Berlin and Bremen, see: Victor Klemperer, *Ich will Zeugnis ablegen bis zum letzten. Tagebücher 1933–1941*, 5th edition, Berlin, 1996, p. 467 including footnote. The poster announcing the exhibition appears in: *Wir schritten durch eine schweigende Stadt. Material für*

accomplished within the framework of this article. However, several important tendencies are discernible. The ministry soon realized that some regional and local newspapers were not able to carry out an information campaign in the form of a series of articles.[43] Indeed, many provincial newspapers did not react to the directive "within the next ten days" as promptly as the ministry had desired. All the same, samples taken from local newspapers in northwestern Germany show that they did comply with the ministry's directive, for instance the *Stader Tageblatt*[44] and the *Helmstedter Kreisblatt*.[45] In contrast, other newspapers — like the *Achimer Kreisblatt* — were unable to produce anything beyond short antisemitic news items[46] or aphorisms, like one of Martin Luther's comments on the Jews.[47] Instead of a series

Schulen: Für die Opfer der Reichspogromnacht 1938 und über die Bremer Juden 1933 bis 1945, 3rd edition, Bremen, 1991, without pages.

43 Press conference of 22 November 1938: Hagemann, *Presselenkung*, p. 149. Berndt reported on the Minister's dissatisfaction.

44 Ibid., 21 November 1938; ibid., 24 November 1938: "Israels Feldzug gegen das Reich. Revolte, Versklavung, Kriegshetze, Boykott und Mord" (with the key words "Jewish subversive activity" during the First World War, sabotage by Jewish Bolsheviks, the signing of the Treaty of Versailles by Jews, organization of an economic boycott, as well as propaganda against Nazi Germany), and 25 November 1938: "Jüdischer Raub! Das Bauerntum einst in Judas Klauen" ibid., 26/27 November 1938: "Mit Stumpf und Stiel ausgerottet. So wurde Literatur im jüdischen Sumpf gemacht" (the central theme is "the Jewish control of German cultural life in its entirety").

45 "Der Affe des Menschen," *Helmstedter Kreisblatt*, 19–20 November 1938 (with the key sentence: "There is no community between the Jews and the Europeans!"); "Aus dem Ghetto in die Welt," 21 November 1938; "Raffsucht als Leitmotiv," 22 November 1938; "Mitleid ist Verrat. Nicht als Verfolger des Judentums führen wir diesen Kampf, sondern als Wahrer unseres Volkstums," 30 November 1938.

46 "Jüdische Schiebungen von riesigem Ausmass Jüdischer 'Diamantenklub' schmuggelt für 150 Millionen RM Diamanten," 18 November 1938; "Lieder, auf die wir verzichten. Jüdische Autoren" (proof that many traditional German songs had been composed by Jews), "Allein in Berlin 200 jüdische Millionäre. Der Bluff mit den ausgeplünderten Juden — Zahlen gegen Märchen," 17 November 1938.

47 "Luther entlarvt die Juden," 22 November 1938. In general, Martin Luther was very useful. Compare, e.g. "Ein Wort Martin Luthers," *Helmstedter Kreisblatt*, 23 November 1938. Also Ernst Ludwig Ehrlich, "Luther und die Juden," in: *Antisemitismus. Von der Judenfeindschaft zum Holocaust*, Herbert A. Strauss and Norbert Kampe, eds., Frankfurt, 1985, pp. 47–65.

of articles, sometimes individual articles on topics suggested by the ministry were published.[48] Incidentally, many newspapers published articles on the stereotypical Jewish criminal, on the great number of Jewish millionaires, or on the "antisemitism of the others,"[49] — topics that were meant to be discussed on a secondary level.

By making reference to local society and history, the anti-Jewish campaign in the regional organs of the press took on a special character. When the *Stader Tageblatt* published a report in a farming region on the "underhanded and vulgar methods with which the Jew gets his hands on the farmer," this of course carried a lot of weight. The article spoke of Jewish land speculation and Jewish food profiteers, affirming "that in the World War, the Jews shattered the German nutritional economy in order to break Germany's power of resistance." Thus it was not difficult for National Socialism to begin rebuilding on the rubble of the farming community, in particular during the years of inflation and the Great Depression.[50] Local news also confirmed the stereotype of the Jew as criminal.[51]

IV

Unlike the Ministry of Propaganda, regional newspapers did not restrict their anti-Jewish campaign to contemporary history. The *Helmstedter*

48 A later article can presumably be attributed to a suggestion by the Ministry of Propaganda: "Kriminalität des Judentums. In Deutschland stellten die Juden 73 v. H. an den abgeurteilten Verbrechen," *Stader Tageblatt*, 24 November 1938.

49 "Antijüdische Massnahmen in aller Welt," *Helmstedter Kreisblatt*, 17 November 1938, with the subheadings: "Konzentrationslager in Belgien, Antisemitische Welle in Amerika." Further news in brief: "Wie die Juden die Völker aussaugten" — "Ein Aufruf der Antijüdischen Sammelbewegung Frankreichs" — "Das 'arme' Volk Israels" (with a report on Jewish large property owners in Berlin, who had been registered in accordance with the regulation dated 26 February 1938). This continued with a collective report under the heading: "Überall werden die Juden abgewiesen. Immer neue jüdische Abwehrmassnahmen,“ 18 November 1938. "Politik der verschlossenen Tür. 650 000 Juden aus Deutschland auswanderungsbereit, USA will sie nicht," 26 December 1938.

50 "Jüdischer Raub! Das Bauerntum einst in Judas Klauen," *Stader Tageblatt*, 25 September 1938.

51 "Gerechte Strafe für jüdische Betrüger," *Stader Tageblatt*, 12 December 1938.

Kreisblatt, for example, printed excerpts from medieval city chronicles indicating a separation of Jews from non-Jews, and further, the repeated acts of violence against Jews. "As is again the case today," Jewish physicians were not allowed to treat non-Jewish patients.[52] This newspaper attempted to portray the persecution of the Jews, as recorded in German cities in the Middle Ages, as a phenomenon of historical continuity that was common in medieval Europe, including England and France.[53] The Jews were also accused of having practiced ritual murder.

In general, in the decentralized press campaign, reports written from a local historical perspective gained special importance. The *Stader Tageblatt*, for example, reprinted an ordinance passed in 1825 by the State Bailiff of Stade which dealt with permitting Jews to marry and their right of residence. The wording of the ordinance was preceded by a short introductory remark that placed the stereotype of the "cunning Jew," who understood how to squeeze himself through the loopholes of the law, into a contemporary context.[54] Regional history also furnished cases that were meant to clearly demonstrate the Jewish proclivity to crime. Many newspapers in the northwestern area of Germany cited the robbery of the Golden Plaque, a particularly precious altar ornament, that had been stolen by a band of thieves from Saint Michael's church in Luneburg in 1698 and offered for sale in Hamburg by Jewish fences.[55] The *Stader Tageblatt* supplemented this news with a report on the

52 "Juden im Mittelalter. Aus Chroniken der deutschen Städte," *Helmstedter Kreisblatt*, 6 December 1938.

53 Oskar Trautmann, "Was alte Chroniken erzählen. Judenaustreibungen in alter Zeit — Unschuldig verfolgt? Nein — schuldig geworden!," *Helmstedter Kreisblatt*, 13 January 1938.

54 "Die Juden im Jahre 1825. Eine Verordnung der Landdrostei Stade," *Helmstedter Kreisblatt,* 22 November 1938.

55 "Jüdischer Räuberstreich vor 240 Jahren. Jüdische Gangsterbande beraubte die Goldene Tafel," *Stader Tageblatt*, 15 December 1938." Jüdischer Räuberstreich vor 240 Jahren. Nickel List u. Co. raubten die Goldene Tafel," *Helmstedter Kreisblatt*, 20 December 1938. For the historical context showing a case of antisemitic journalism in 1699 see: Hans-Dieter Schmid, "Das schwer zu bekehrende Juden-Hertz. Jüdische Unterschicht und christlicher Antisemitismus am Beispiel des Celler Stadtpredigers Sigismund Hosemann," in: *Christen und Juden. Ein notwendiger Dialog*, Peter Antes et al., eds., Hanover, 1988, pp. 39–60.

current trial of a Jewish physician in Hamburg, and a brief report on "thirty Jewish millionaires," also in Hamburg.[56]

Continuing to look at the course of the news campaign in the northwestern area of Germany, the important role of a series of articles published at the end of 1938 by the *Niedersächsische Tageszeitung*, the main organ of the NSDAP in Hanover, particularly stands out.[57] The author of the series, who pompously claimed to "present the first coherent account of the history of Judaism in Lower Saxony," was Dr. Hans Mauersberg from the Gau Office of Racial Policy.[58] In the series, the details of German-Jewish history were put into a context that spanned centuries. This history had always been affixed the antisemitic interpretation that the German forefathers had no choice but to treat the Jews harshly, as they could not have otherwise held their ground against the Jewish claims to power. Mauersberg explained that in the twelfth and thirteenth centuries, a large number of Jews had settled in the large and small cities of Lower Saxony, but that in the fourteenth and fifteenth centuries — as had already occurred in cities in the Rhineland — they were expelled in several phases. Mauersberg attributed this sequence of events to the resistance of the local population against Jews who

56 "Und heute!," ibid.; "30 jüdische Millionäre in Hamburg," ibid.

57 Hans Mauersberg, born in 1910, received his doctorate from the University of Berlin. His dissertation carried the title *Besiedlung und Bevölkerung des ehemals hennebergischen Amtes Schleusingen*, Würzburg, 1938. He subsequently wrote *Beiträge zur Bevölkerungs- und Sozialgeschichte Niedersachsens. Studien zur Volkskörperforschung Niedersachsens. Veröffentlichungen aus dem Rassenpolitischen Amt der NSDAP, Gau Südhannover-Braunschweig*, vol. 1, Hanover, 1938. The director of the Rassenpolitisches Amt was Hans-Helmut Rehkopf, who co-published this series of works with Mauersberg. Mauersberg qualified as a university lecturer in 1962 at the University of Munich. His main areas of work are given as economic, population and social history: *Kürschners Deutscher Gelehrten-Kalender,* 11th edition, Berlin, 1970, p. 1891; 12th edition, Berlin, 1976, p. 2028.

58 "Die Geschichte des Judentums in Niedersachsen. Im 12. Jahrhundert kommen sie als 'Emigranten,' erringen bedeutende Macht und werden wieder vertrieben," *Niedersächsische Tageszeitung*, 28 December 1938; "Wie die Juden sich wieder im Lande breitmachten. Das Wiedererstarken des Judentums in Niedersachsen vom Beginn der Neuzeit bis zur Emigration," *Niedersächsische Tageszeitung*, 29 December 1938; "Judas Weg zum Höhepunkt seiner Macht. Die Emanzipation des Judentums und ihr Durchbruch zur Macht im 19. Jahrhundert," *Niedersächsische Tageszeitung,* 30 December 1938. All articles included antisemitic drawings by Rolf Wilde. I occasionally rearranged the quotes.

were beginning to gain control over "Lower Saxony's economy." With the tone of voice of a storyteller skilled in conveying important lessons from the past, Mauersberg explained: "the people" came to their senses "and expelled the strangers from the country not only by means of their persecution, but also by means of state laws. They were kept away from commercial life and gradually also from trade by means of ordinances implemented by the community of guilds. ... At the onset of the sixteenth century," there was nothing left "of the former Jewish positions of power in the cities of Lower Saxony."

However, persecution and other restrictive measures were "not successful in exterminating the Jews," continued Mauersberg. "Unbroken in their urge for conquest and inspired by an even stronger will to recapture territory once lost," with the privileges granted the Jews by the princes governing the territories of Lower Saxony, in the seventeenth century they were allowed to resettle and to establish a regional rabbinate with its center in the new town of Hanover. By the end of the eighteenth century, the Jews "had again so much strengthened their positions, that these ... constituted the centers from which — in continuance of the emancipatory efforts of the nineteenth century — they would seize the decisive power of the people in the first third of the twentieth century." With its ideals of equality and fraternity, the French Revolution had led the "German people" to accept the notion of "tolerating a new position of Jewish power within Germany's boundaries," and, upon enactment of the law of 30 September 1842 in the Kingdom of Hanover, taking a step towards emancipation. Mauersberg did recognize the general social movement that gave rise to this development; however, he stresses that within the framework of this movement the Jews had "worked for themselves." Starting out from their emancipation, the Jews then "lined up for their triumphal march to rule over the German people," in order to erect "the strongholds of their foreign rule" in the villages and cities, at the University of Göttingen, as well as "in the offices, department stores and administrative offices." These strongholds were not won back until the National Socialists stepped into power. Mauersberg summed up his series of articles by stating that "the up and down" of Jewish rule in Lower Saxony must be considered a warning for the future. He closed with the firm injunction that after their expulsion by means of "persecution" and the enactment of "state laws," the return of the Jews "to power" must be prevented.

Based on antisemitism, Mauersberg's articles provided a comprehensive interpretation of the regional history of German-Jewish relations. In this historical interpretation, the persecution of Jews in the late Middle Ages became a focal point and was made to serve as a benchmark for current policy making. The pogroms of the Middle Ages became models for contemporary National Socialist politics and represented a treasure chest of experience worth digging up. The repeated references to past pogroms served to validate the politics of the present. Mauersberg thus set a standard for the news campaign of the winter of 1938–39.

An article on the local history of the Jews published in the *Celler Beobachter*, a supplement to the *Niedersächsische Tageszeitung* for the town of Celle, showed that this standard had lent antisemitic journalism a new quality, which was quite in line with the radicalization of the press after 9 November.[59] The author of the article was Otto von Boehn, archivist of Celle. Despite the fact that it was also printed in a supplement to the main organ of the Hanover NSDAP, the version of the article printed in the *Celler Beobachter* did not include any mention of the takeover of power by the Jews or their subsequent expulsion. Nonetheless, references to antisemitic stereotypes are obvious. The article says, for example, that the Jews in Celle had restricted themselves "almost solely to commercial activity ... as was the case throughout Germany," and that they had avoided "any kind of physical labor." The article emphasized the numerous restrictive regulations by which Jews were required to abide, for example when establishing a business. The expulsion of "begging Polish Jews" in the year 1825 was also mentioned. Yet, von Boehn made no reference to "the Jew" in the singular, an otherwise stereotypical expression officially used by the NSDAP when referring to Jews as a social group.[60] The editors of the

59 Peter Stein, *Die nordostniedersächsische Tagespresse. Von den Anfängen bis 1945. Ein Handbuch*, Stade, 1994, p. 157.

60 "Die Geschichte der Juden in Celle," published in five episodes with alternating subheadings: "Schon 1530 'Zwei Jodden' — Man weiss nicht, woher sie kamen — Kontrolle über Kontrolle," *Celler Beobachter*, 10 January 1939; "Hauserwerb und Belastung des Besitzes durch Steuern und Abgaben," ibid., 11 January 1939; "Handel und Erwerbsverhältnisse: 'Kommerziell' bevorzugt — Was war jüdische Handelsware? — Einheimische und fremde Juden — Eine interessante Statistik,"

Celler Beobachter attempted to heighten the anti-Jewish character of the text by the use of subheadings.[61] They also considered it necessary to provide a commentary. In a preliminary remark, they made reference to the restrictive regulations in the town of Celle emphasized by von Boehn, and added that

> Three hundred years ago, our ancestors kept the Jews extraordinarily short, and they will have well known why. It was the distortion of the notion of freedom by the French Revolution that first emancipated the Jew to such a degree, that he could again begin the old game of gaining control over people by poisoning their intellects and with the help of money. ... What we are experiencing now is the reaction to this.

The editors' closing remark resounded with meaning: "Let us learn from the past."

In their preliminary remark, the editors of the *Celler Beobachter* implied what they expected from an article on the history of the

ibid., 12 January 1939; "Religiöser Gegensatz — Judentaufen — Die Sabbatruhe — Schulen und Synagogen — Wenn zwei heiraten wollten," ibid., 13 January 1939; "Der Judenfriedhof — Kultur und Kunst — Liberalist Salomo Philipp Gans," ibid., 14/15 January 1939. Von Boehn, who held the job title of Retired State Garden Inspector, had been commissioned in 1935 by the City of Celle — at the request of the State Academy for the Cultivation of Race and Hygiene in Dresden — to write his article. The Academy had planned to publish a history of the Jews in German cities, which, however, was never realized. See "Innerstädtische Korrespondenzen im Stadtarchiv Celle 1 D 23a." Heiber mentions the State Academy, p. 423. Von Boehn's article, by the way, was reprinted in *Zur Geschichte der Juden in Celle. Festschrift zur Wiederherstellung der Synagoge*, Celle, 1974, pp. 9–15. This book, published by the City of Celle, cited the source of the article: the *Celler Beobachter*. The following comment, characteristic for the city's self-image, appeared on p. 16: "It is typical of the attitude of the population of Celle towards the Jews in the period after 1933 that such an article could have been written — a careful and objective article that strictly adheres to the records of the City Archives — above all, however, that it could have been published in its original form in a daily newspaper." After a number of objections, this passage was removed from a later edition of the publication without comment.

61 One of the subheadings, for example, read "Konkurrent 'Billig' ist da!" (trade disagreements between Jewish and non-Jewish businessmen in Celle during the 17th century). Another subheading read "Die üppigen Judenweiber" (the focus was on the wide hoop skirts that had to be removed at "school" as they took up too much space).

Jews; it should demonstrate "that what is happening today to the Jews in Germany and in other countries is definitely nothing new or unheard of." Again we meet with the line of thought that portrays the actions of 9 November and the weeks thereafter as an established and proven practice based on experience. The Ministry of Propaganda's press conference had placed emphasis on actions against Jews in other countries; by referring to medieval and early modern history, these actions would be viewed as being in accord with the past. This placed new demands on articles meant to serve the purposes of antisemitic indoctrination. Although the reader might approve of the restrictions against the Jews as enumerated in a traditionally antisemitic text like the one written by von Boehn, there was, however, another step that Mauersberg clearly espoused in his article — persecution and expulsion. After 9 November, readers were expected to identify with this next step, which could be associated with both violence and legal measures.

Lessons of the past were to be applied to the present. The press conference of 17 November had already aspired to this.[62] In the local and regional press, a geographical point of contact was now added to the temporal one — contact between past and present places and regions. This resulted in combining the strength of both the local and regional worlds and the lives of the people therein, which had always contained elements of history and which expressed itself as local or regional history — *Heimatgeschichte*. This helped to create a feeling of closeness to, and familiarity with one's own home town.[63] Local and regional history provided antisemitism with an extraordinarily useful

62 See Dr. Wilhelm Ziegler in the conference of the *Reichspropagandaamt Ost-Hannover* from 9–11 December 1938: "What is happening today in Germany and in other countries ... is not occurring for the first time in the history of Judaism and other people:" "Die Lösung des Judenproblems. Vortrag von Pg. Ziegler auf der Presse- und Propagandatagung in Lüneburg," *Cellesche Zeitung*, 12 December 1938.

63 Everhard Holtmann and Winfried Killisch, *Lokale Identität und Gemeindegebietsreform. Der Streitfall Ermershausen. Empirische Untersuchungen über Erscheinungsformen und Hintergründe örtlichen Protestverhaltens in einer unterfränkischen Landgemeinde*, Erlangen, 1991, pp. 48–50. On the connection between political interests and political concern on the one hand, and the affinity with and feelings for the *Heimat* on the other hand, see: Heiner Treinen, "Symbolische Ortsbezogenheit. Eine soziologische Untersuchung zum Heimatproblem," *Kölner Zeitschrift für Soziologie und Sozialpsychologie* 17 (1965), pp. 73–97, 254–297.

vehicle that penetrated social spheres not usually conducive to political propaganda. The planners of the press campaign in the Ministry of Propaganda had obviously overlooked this aspect of history. It did not lie directly in their field of vision, as their conception of the campaign, including instructions to the press, encompassed the entire Reich. However, the turn towards regional history was eagerly taken up by the provincial press, which had always represented an area of journalism in which antisemitic attitudes and stereotypes were common. With a certain amount of autonomy, the local and regional press took advantage of particularly favorable opportunities for propagating antisemitic positions. The powerful effect this had is attested to by notes on a conversation held at the time between the technician Karl Dürkefälden and his father. Dürkefälden's father, who ran a small farm east of Hanover, had read the article written by Mauersberg in the *Niedersächsische Tageszeitung*. When, at the beginning of January 1939, he was asked by his son if Jewish shops had also been destroyed in Peine during the pogrom, he evaded the question with the reply: "Didn't you read what havoc the Jews used to create here?" This was precisely the effect the newspaper article was designed to have.[64]

After 9 November, the press service of the NSDAP went its own way in the antisemitic manipulation of national history. It was also confronted with the thorny question: to what extent would the population help to implement the anti-Jewish policies of the National Socialists, and how far did these policies correspond with the will of the population. The *NSK* wrote: "The crudest instrument of foreign agitation is wanting to create the impression that there is a rift between popular National Socialist leadership and the German people by asserting that antisemitism is a party slogan meant to trigger off a racial struggle in which the people have no interest."[65] In order to refute claims of a division between leadership and the people, the *NSK* published a series of articles that were meant to "prove that the German people are an

64 Herbert and Sibylle Obenaus, eds., *"Schreiben, wie es wirklich war ... Aufzeichnungen Karl Dürkefäldens aus den Jahren 1933–1945,"* Hanover, 1983, p. 90.

65 "Antisemitisches Volk. Die deutsche Geschichte widerlegt Auslandshetze — Zur neuen NSK — Artikelserie," *NSK* 282, (2 December 1938), pp. 3ff. The article carries the initials of the deputy editor-in-chief of the *NSK* W[ilhelm] R[i]tg[en]; see footnote 1, above.

antisemitic people." In accordance with National Socialist ideology, the enmity between Germans and Jews, which had been proven many times in the history of Germany, could be accounted for by race: "Based on the laws of his race and his natural instinct, the German has had a sharply defensive and rejective attitude towards Judaism in all epochs." It had always been the "racial sensitivity" of the Germans that had compelled them to "separate" themselves from the Jews. Finally, a close connection between Germans and National Socialist ideology was derived from the historical enmity towards Jews, based on a "fundamental" antisemitic "philosophy." National Socialism was the fulfillment of everything the people had ever wanted. Or, in the words of the *NSK*: "With all of their characteristics, the German people were finally united and revived in the National Socialist idea."[66]

The *NSK* series began with an article on the "Laws passed by the Germanic kings pertaining to the Jews." On the one hand advocating the policy of separation from the Jews, the article also castigated the church's obstruction of the "Germanic defense movement," This was a reference to the fact that the church had repeatedly attempted to overcome Judaism by means of baptism, thus "disregarding ... the primary racial difference" and driving "a wedge between the leaders and the people."[67] Another article began with the early Middle Ages when the economic status of the Jews had made them indispensable to the princes and town dwellers, but hated by the country people.[68] The article applied the same image of the Jews to the late Middle Ages, its

66 Ibid.

67 "Antisemitisches Volk (I): Die Judengesetze der Germanenkönige. Abwehr und Erkennung der Judengefahr in frühester Zeit. Das 'Westgotische Gesetz' verbot Ehen mit Juden," ibid., pp. 4 f.

68 "Antisemitisches Volk (II): H[einz] Ballensiefen, "Nackt möget ihr ausziehen!" Wachsende Volksauflehnung gegen die Juden im frühen Mittelalter — Schutzbriefe als Dokumente völkischen Widerstandes gegen die Ausbeuter — Die Gunst der Fürsten ergaunert," *NSK* 283, (3 December 1938), pp. 3. In 1941, Ballensiefen worked for *SS-Standartenführer* Franz Alfred Six in Office VII, "Ideological Research and Evaluation," of the RSHA. His department VII B 1 was responsible for "Freemasonry and Judaism." In 1944 — he had received his doctorate and been promoted to the rank of *SS-Hauptsturmführer* in the meantime — his field of activity was in Hungary. Here, among other things, he controlled the Hungarian Institute for the Research of the Jewish Question, which he had co-founded: Jürgen Matthäus, "Weltanschauliche Forschung und Auswertung." Aus den Akten des Amtes VII im Reichssicherheitshauptamt," *Jahrbuch für Antisemitismusforschung,*

central theme now being the "exploitation of the people by profiteers." This gave rise to hatred by the people, though it was again and again "made inactive" by Jews, who "cleverly" manipulated "the balance of power between municipality, princes and the emperor," playing one against the other. The author follows this up with the politically unambiguous comment:

> Despite all of the good and right approaches, the removal of the Jews from the life of the people failed. The people did not have a leader whom they sustained with their spirit, they did not have a united Reich necessary for uniformly and effectively carrying out all measures. The foundation for the successful solution of the Jewish issue in the Third Reich lies in the existence of these prerequisites.

The author does not fail to make the point that in the Middle Ages, intellectuals also joined the barricades against the Jews. He places particular emphasis on Martin Luther.[69]

For the German principalities of the early modern era, the court Jew is portrayed as the determining social element. Noted too are the efforts made by the line of princesses and princes from Maria Theresa to Frederick the Great to limit the influence of Jews; however, the argument is somewhat weakened by the author's acknowledgment of the usefulness, time and again, of the court Jews to the princes. Nevertheless, the author seeks recourse in the politically explicit rule that the bad or good treatment of the Jews was dependent on the strength or weakness of a prince.[70]

Then the article states, the Enlightenment came "to the aid" of the Jews. Prussia modeled its Emancipation Edict of 1812 on France's granting the Jews citizenship with equal rights following the Revolution. The edict was drawn up by State Chancellor Hardenberg, who was

5 (1996), pp. 287–330, specifically pp. 290 f. The documents published herein also deal with Ballensiefen's scientific work.

69 "Antisemitisches Volk (III): Volksempörung gegen Judenpest. Wie stand das deutsche Volk im Mittelalter zur Judenfrage? — Gemeinsame Auflehnung gegen schamlose Ausbeutung — Völkischer Instinkt weckte drastische Massnahmen," *NSK* 284 (4 December 1938), pp. 5ff.

70 "Antisemitisches Volk (IV): H[einz] B[allensiefen], Könige gegen Hofjuden. Deutsche Fürsten beschränken 'jüdische Rechte' — Jeder starke König war Judengegner, jeder schwache Judenknecht — 'Ich kenne keine ärgere Pest'," *NSK* 286 (7 December 1938). pp. 5f

"dependent on the Jews because of financial difficulties." The author further adds that the people "had had no time to defend themselves against this outrageous attack on their existence. The wars of liberation required their effort." Not until after the Vienna Congress and the end of the war were the people in a position to protest against the emancipation of the Jews and to "ardently" demand "returning the Jews to their old legal positions." With its anti-emancipatory tendencies, the restoration — this concept is not used in the article — thus appears in a positive light.[71] The last article in the *NSK* series outlines further steps taken towards granting the Jews equal status as citizens up until the constitution of the *Norddeutscher Bund*. Again, the names of the main authorities opposed to emancipation are mentioned — Otto von Bismarck, Heinrich von Treitschke and Richard Wagner. The antisemitic "people's movement" at the close of the nineteenth century was also doomed to failure. "The attempt to achieve success by parliamentary means was hopeless from the start. The powerful social democracy, overrun by Jews, voted down all motions for the formation of a party." The enmity of the people against the Jews only found "fulfillment in the legislation of the Third Reich ... National Socialism paid complete tribute to the public feeling for the first time in that it made racial knowledge the foundation of its Jewish legislation and carried through with the separation of blood. Thus the struggle that the German people had led against the foreign intruders for centuries had finally come to an effective close."[72]

V

The series of articles on the "antisemitic people" was part of the effort to persuade the German population to adopt the attitude towards

71 "Antisemitisches Volk (V): H[einz] B[allensiefen], Staatsbürgerrechte gegen Volkswillen. Volksauflehnung gegen die Judenemanzipation — Auch getarnt stets erkannt — Jüdische Ausbeutung der Freiheitskriege," *NSK* 288 (9 December 1938), pp. 4ff.

72 "Antisemitisches Volk (VI): H[einz] B[allensiefen], Erfüllung nach jahrhundertelangem Kampf. Von Judas Sieg zu seiner Bezwingung durch den Nationalsozialismus. Religiöse Tarnung und rassische Erkenntnis — Die Sprecher des Volkswillens im 19. Jahrhundert," *NSK* 291 (13 December 1938), pp. 1ff.

Jews that was desired and hoped for by the party. The interpretation of national history as one governed by a fundamental philosophy of hatred towards Jews — a history also dominated by antisemitism, pogroms and expulsion — was supported by a historical construction that assessed Jews in terms of a continual division between the elite and the people, and ultimately it was the people who always knew how to correctly assess them. Only now and then did the leading figures, (one or another prince) comprehend the people's real attitude towards the Jews. The National Socialists cleverly point this angle in 1933 — that it was the "national longing" (*völkische Sehnsucht*) of Germans to attain their "ultimate separation" from the Jews.[73]

With its appeal to "antisemitic people," the press campaign had reached a certain climax; the one-sidedness and simplifications of the campaign achieved a high degree of credibility through its official pronouncement by the party. It combined important points of criticism — for example the church's position on baptism of Jews — with praise of a strong nation, which implied praise for the National Socialist state. National history thus became the teacher of the nation, and the National Socialists the executors of the lessons to be extracted from history.

The antisemitic manipulation of German history was nothing new. It had a long tradition. Even in the articles published by Mauersberg and the *NSK* and their foundation in regional and national history, respectively, was no exception. It is noteworthy that both series of articles started out from different concepts. Mauersberg kept with tradition by using the stereotype of the Jewish quest for power, which focuses on the subordination of the non-Jewish environment. For this reason it can be said that he endeavored to provide a comprehensive interpretation of German-Jewish history from the Middle Ages to the modern era. This stands in contrast to the *NSK*'s concept, which worked more intensely with the social construct of "the people" and attributed them with special knowledge about, and experience with, Jews. The *NSK* could support this concept by drawing on the change that occurred in German historiography at the time, that is, viewing history from a national point of view.[74] By mystifying the people, the *NSK* could be considered more modern, and at the same time more National

73 *NSK* 282 (2 December 1938), pp. 3f.

74 Karen Schönwälder, "Akademischer Antisemitismus. Die deutschen Historiker in der NS-Zeit," *Jahrbuch für Antisemitismusforschung*, 2 (1993), pp. 200–229,

Socialistic than Mauersberg. Both concepts existed simultaneously and did not contradict each other; they merely complemented historical material in different ways. They could both interpret the "abnormality" of the pogrom of 9 November 1938 as the "normality" of the German treatment of the Jews, and ultimately refer to the seizure of power in 1933 as an act of liberation through which German history reached fulfillment.

Convincing newspaper readers of the correctness of Nationalist Socialist policies towards Jews was not the sole aim of steering the press. Above and beyond this, its task was to deal with the problem of how the central German ideology of integration — nationalism — stood in relation to the central element of National Socialist ideology — antisemitism. M. Rainer Lepsius claimed that "the Third Reich ... was founded much more on belief in German nationalism than on agreement with the National Socialist ideology."[75] If one continues this train of thought, this could well have given rise to the fear that an essential element of National Socialist ideology — antisemitism — would be pushed into the background during the weeks and months of the unification of Austria and the Sudetenland with the German Reich. The central role of antisemitism in Nazi ideology, especially its function of combining "antagonistic parts ... for instance anti-bolshevism and verbal anticapitalism," made action necessary.[76] In this respect, the pogrom and its consequences were possibly a welcome occurrence in order to consciously emphasize antisemitism in a period of national enthusiasm. From a propagandistic point of view, it was now simply a matter of amalgamating both ideologies, a task for which history

specifically pp. 213 f. For more details on this topic, see: Karen Schönwälder, *Historiker und Politik. Geschichtswissenschaft im Nationalsozialismus*, Frankfurt am Main, 1992.

75 M. Rainer Lepsius, "Das Erbe des Nationalsozialismus und die politische Kultur der Nachfolgestaaten des 'Großdeutschen Reiches'," in: *Kultur und Gesellschaft*, Max Haller, Hans-J. Hoffmann-Nowotny and Wolfgang Zapf, eds., commissioned by the German, Austrian and Swiss Society for Sociology, Frankfurt am Main, 1989, pp. 247–264, specifically pp. 253f.

76 Hans Mommsen, "Die Funktion des Antisemitismus im 'Dritten Reich.' Das Beispiel des Novemberprogroms," in: *Antisemitismus. Von religiöser Judenfeindschaft zur Rassenideologie*, Günther Brakelmann and Martin Rosowski, eds., Göttingen 1989, pp. 179–192, specifically p. 184.

lent itself. An investigation of the sources shows that this issue was acknowledged and realized by the Ministry of Propaganda, as well as by the party's press service.

At the Ministry of Propaganda's press conference, the predominance of both ideologies in the creation of integration can be clearly demonstrated by referring to the character of the "*Spiesser*." According to the Ministry of Propaganda's descriptions, he represented a group of people who combined National Socialism with a traditionally antisemitic attitude, but who more or less tolerated the Jews — at least not denying them their right to exist. The Ministry of Propaganda attacked the "*Spiesser*" as the most dangerous adversary to the radically antisemitic consensus, one who questioned the policy of excluding Jews from German society.

In contrast to the suggestions made by the Ministry of Propaganda, the party's press service was quite clear on the question of competing ideologies. Like the ministry, the *NSK* deliberated as to how it should handle those who eluded the anti-Jewish campaign after 9 November — namely, those whom Berndt had called the "*Spiesser*." The *NSK* carefully adhered to the advice that under no circumstances would it convey the impression that the group of "those who said no" was large. Accordingly, they used the term "a handful of political late-risers" who would not "hear or see or read anything." In keeping with Berndt, this group was described as bourgeois, liberal and individualistic. They asked themselves, "What have the Jews got to do with me?" in order to avoid having to give an opinion on the issue, just as one had once said: "What have the others got to do with you? You cast your ballot just like Gustav Stresemann. *(Was gehen Dich die andern an, Du wählst wie Gustav Stresemann.*) The others," the *NSK* continued, "were us Nazis and 'other people'." The party press service then began to refer more frequently to this group as "intellectuals —with an 'educated' vocabulary." They were also called "bourgeois intellectuals" and "outsiders." Elsewhere they are noted as those people whose advancement was made possible — and whose "pensions" were secured — by the National Socialist state. Without question, a part of the social elite referred to here profited from National Socialism, yet did not help — or only partially helped — to support the persecution of Jews. The *NSK* wanted both to defame opponents of the persecution of Jews as a minority outside of the national community and to arouse hostility against intellectuals and educated people, indeed against the old elite in its entirety. At the same time, it was claimed that National Socialist policies were supported by the wide majority of the people.[77]

Following this fairly clear characterization of that part of the social elite that profited from National Socialism, yet kept its distance from the core area of National Socialist ideology — radical antisemitism[78] — the *NSK* discussed in great detail and depth the subject of competition between the central ideologies of integration of nationalism and National Socialism. The *NSK* claimed that it was indeed "not difficult" to be proud of national successes, "when the squadrons of the Luftwaffe thunder over the Zeppelin Lawn in Nuremberg, or when our young Wehrmacht march through the streets, or when ten million Germans return home to the Reich cheering emphatically and thankfully."[79] National sentiment grew naturally after the Treaty of Versailles was signed upon rearmament, and the annexation of Austria and the Sudetenland turned the German Reich into the Great German Reich. However, in addition, it was necessary that the people develop an understanding of "the political process" which reinforced the exclusion of Jews from German society. Opponents to the persecution of Jews — those nationalists who lacked a sense of the correctness of National Socialism, in particular radical antisemitism — were denied membership in the "national community ... Today, the 'simple' national comrade, who sees the last mask torn from the Jew's face and who trusts that the leaders are doing everything for the benefit of the people ... may rightfully refuse to tolerate being bothered by a few frightened burgher souls standing on the fringe."[80]

The competition between the two ideologies of integration, which was criticized by the authorities responsible for steering the press, may be the point of departure for a critique of the view held by Daniel Jonah Goldhagen of the dominance of an eliminatory antisemitism. In

77 Ernst Günter Dickmann, "Was gehen mich die Juden an? Der Volksgenosse und die Judenfrage — Gründliche Aufklärung bis zum letzten Mann," *NSK* 280 (30 November 1938), pp. 2ff.

78 For more details on the consequences of this distance, see Mommsen, "Funktion des Antisemitismus," p. 183.

79 Mommsen, "Funktion des Antisemitismus," p. 3.

80 Ibid.

his opinion, "well before the Nazis came to power ... a virulent and violent 'eliminationist' variant of antisemitism" had developed, "which called for the elimination of Jewish influence or of Jews themselves from German society."[81] The discussion that ensued after 9 November shows that even at this time, which coincided with the greatest successes of domestic and foreign policy, National Socialist propaganda was still concerned with the population's acceptance of its antisemitic program, that was geared towards the exclusion of Jews from German society. In any case, it is doubtful whether one can speak of an "acceptance" of this ideology in the political consciousness of the people. In my opinion, doubts about whether this ideology was accepted are indeed valid, because while insisting that the anti-Jewish policy be accepted — one could also say, while courting the self-image of the Germans as an "antisemitic people" — only the liberal and national conservative elite were being addressed. Or, to put it in the words of the *NSK*: it was the "last remaining, footsore rearguard of Stresemann's Foot Guard."[82] These were the only ones criticized for their lack of understanding of "the political process" of complete separation from Jews. Other social groups, above all the working class, were not mentioned at all, although in this circle, too, only limited approval of an eliminatory antisemitism could be expected.[83] And finally, complete silence prevailed with regard to that part of the population that had no interest whatsoever in the fate of the German Jews.[84] The reason for the failure to mention working-class people and other groups with nonconforming opinions

81 Daniel Jonah Goldhagen, *Hitler's Willing Executioners. Ordinary Germans and the Holocaust*, London, 1996, p. 23. A further analysis of Goldhagen can be omitted here as his notions of the "ordinary German," which are strangely similar to those of an "antisemitic people," have already been analyzed in depth: Ruth Bettina Birn and Volker Riess, "Das Goldhagen Phänomen oder: Fünfzig Jahre danach," *Geschichte in Wissenschaft und Unterricht*, 49 (1988), pp. 80–95.

82 *NSK* 265, p. 2.

83 See Mommsen, "Funktion des Antisemitismus," p. 183, who writes that among the working class, antisemitism plays "virtually no role whatsoever." See Rosemarie Leuschen-Seppel, "Arbeiterbewegung und Antisemitismus," in: *Antisemitismus. Von religiöser Judenfeindschaft zur Rassenideologie*, Günther Brakelmann and Martin Rosowski, eds., Göttingen 1989, pp. 77–96.

84 Compare the list of social groups that criticized the anti-Jewish politics of the regime: Ian Kershaw, "German Popular Opinion and the 'Jewish Question,' 1939–1943: Some further Questions," in: *Die Juden im Nationalsozialistischen Deutschland / The Jews in Nazi Germany 1933–1943*, Arnold Paucker, ed., Tübingen, 1986, pp.

undoubtedly lies in the calculation that to criticize other social groups would lead to the collapse of the "vanishing minority." As mentioned above, this minority was said to consist of the one percent of "those people who had said no" in the elections after the National Socialists took power and who did not support the persecution of Jews and their exclusion from German society. Thus no doubt is cast on the strength of the support for the regime in 1938; however, there was obviously more support on a national level and less for the core area of National Socialist ideology — antisemitism.

After 9 November, however, the policy pursued regarding German Jews was certainly intended to be eliminationist. The press campaign in the winter of 1938–39 coincided with the redirecting of propaganda efforts towards the immediate preparation for war after the Munich conference, which would have suggested to the leaders of the NSDAP that antisemitic activities be intensified.[85] The campaign was intended to prepare the population — with a wealth of incisive measures — for what was still in store for German Jews. By introducing historical and regional dimensions, the campaign revitalized the traditions of German antisemitism with a high degree of urgency. It openly pronounced relentlessness and harshness. The purpose of this turn in the campaign was to confront the Germans with their national history and to force them to acknowledge this history — to acknowledge it as their own historical and national identity, and at the same time acknowledge antisemitism in its barbaric variant, that is, eliminationist antisemitism. With this new clarity of concepts and language — but also with the clarity of the interpretation of history and its praise for the barbarity of the pogroms in Germany during the Middle Ages — it was consistent that, ultimately, Hitler would openly pronounce the future prospects for the Jews. In his speech before the German Reichstag on 30 January 1939, he declared that should a world war again occur, the result would be "the extermination of the Jewish race in Europe."[86]

365–86, specifically pp. 369 f., 383. See also Bankier, *Öffentliche Meinung*, pp. 123–138.

85 Reference to this can be found in Mommsen, "Funktion des Antisemitismus," p. 186.

86 Max Domarus, *Hitler. Reden und Proklamationen 1932–1945*, Munich, 1965, vol. 2, p. 1058.

Violence against Jews in Germany, 1933–1939

MICHAEL WILDT

On 10 April 1933 Victor Klemperer noted in his dairy: "...surrounded by baiting, misery, trembling fear. A cousin of Dember, physician in Berlin, picked up in the middle of office hours, brought to the Humboldt Hospital, in his shirt sleeves and badly beaten, died there, 45 years old."[1] Immediately after the Reichstag elections on 5 March 1933, which marked the starting point of the National Socialist *Machtergreifung*, throughout Germany, the SA and other NSDAP organizations gave free rein to their antisemitic hatred.

What followed was a litany of arbitrary and vicious attacks against Jews. In Breslau, SA men kidnapped the theater director Paul Barnay and beat him with rubber clubs and dog whips so severely that he had to be hospitalized. In Straubing, a Jewish wholesaler who had been abducted was later found, his corpse ridden with bullets. In Königsberg, after a synagogue had been set on fire and arson attacks carried out on several Jewish shops, a Jewish businessman was also kidnapped and so brutally mistreated that he later died in the hospital. In Wiesbaden, several troops of young people marched through the city, breaking the shop windows of Jewish businesses and beating the owners. In Magdeburg, National Socialists attacked a small hotel that was frequented by Jewish guests, fired several shots and injured a number of them with knives. Disturbances on the Kurfürstendamm in Berlin on 6 March escalated into bloody hunts. The German correspondent of *The Manchester Guardian* reported on 10 March: "Many Jews were beaten by the brown shirts until blood ran down their heads and faces.

1 Victor Klemperer, *Ich will Zeugnis ablegen bis zum letzten. Tagebücher 1933–1941*, Berlin, 1995, vol. I, p. 20.

Many fainted and were left to lie in the streets, until they were picked up by friends or passersby and brought to hospitals."[2]

It has become common to adopt Raul Hilberg's scheme — definition-expropriation-concentration-extermination[3] — and assume a purposive development of National Socialist policy against the Jews, a development which progressed through a series of discrete, well-defined and unambiguous phases. This leads, first, to the problematic impression that there was an equally well-defined and linear antisemitic policy of the National Socialist regime.[4] Second, this scheme reflects a "top-down" perspective, which characterizes the persecution of Jews as a series of repressive acts perpetrated by the state and defines politics as actions of the state, at the same time it disregards the practice of societal antisemitism, the antisemitism of neighbors, co-workers, clients, acquaintances, and relatives. Third, and most importantly, this perspective loses sight of the antisemitic violence to which the Jewish population of Germany was subjected from the very start of the National Socialist regime.

Physical violence is not one of the preferred themes of historiography, in particular since influential theories of modernization and civilization such as those of Norbert Elias and Max Weber have assumed that the role of physical violence will wane with the spread of civilization.[5]

2 On the cases mentioned here cf. Comité des Delegations Juives, ed., *Das Schwarzbuch. Tatsachen und Dokumente. Die Lage der Juden in Deutschland 1933*, Paris, 1934, pp. 495–499.

3 Raul Hilberg, *The Destruction of the European Jews*, Chicago, 1961.

4 For a critical perspective on this question, see: Karl A. Schleunes, *The Twisted Road to Auschwitz. Nazi Policy toward German Jews, 1933–1939*, Urbana/Ill., 1970. Essential analyses of antisemitism and National Socialist persecution of the Jews are provided by: Uwe Dietrich Adam, *Judenpolitik im Dritten Reich*, Düsseldorf 1972; Hermann Graml, *Antisemitism in the Third Reich*, Oxford, 1992; Wolfgang Benz, ed., *Die Juden in Deutschland 1933–1945. Leben unter nationalsozialistischer Herrschaft*, Munich, 1988; more recently, the excellent book by Saul Friedländer, *Nazi Germany and the Jews*. Vol. 1: *The Years of Persecution, 1933–1939*, London, 1997.

5 On this topic, see in particular Thomas Lindenberger and Alf Lüdtke, eds., *Physische Gewalt. Studien zur Geschichte der Neuzeit*, Frankfurt am Main, 1995. Note also Bernd Hüppauf, ed., *War, Violence and the Modern Condition*, Berlin, 1997; and Hamburger Institut für Sozialforschung, ed., *200 Tage und 1 Jahrhundert. Gewalt und Destruktivität im Spiegel des Jahres 1945*, Hamburg, 1995.

However, in contrast to the notion of modernity as an age increasingly free of violence, not only the seventeenth and eighteenth but also the nineteenth and, in particular, the twentieth century must be viewed, as Thomas Lindenberger and Alf Lüdtke have asserted, "on a worldwide scale as virtually pervaded and 'saturated' with violence."[6] Violence directed against Jews was not an invention of National Socialist rule. Antisemitic acts of violence occurred under German Imperial rule — one example is the anti-Jewish riots in Berlin's *Scheunenviertel* — as well as in the Weimar Republic.[7] Nonetheless, the National Socialist takeover in 1933 was a watershed, since it marked the end of the German government's adherence to legal norms which had offered Jews some measure of protection in the preceding years. Of central importance was the Presidential Decree for the Protection of the Nation and the State, which issued on 28 February 1933, abolished all basic rights laid down by the Weimar Constitution. The state's antisemitic policies not only disenfranchised the Jews, they also aimed to stigmatize and isolate them socially. Jews were outlawed, considered free game (*vogelfrei*), and protected by neither the Code of Civil Law nor criminal law; they were a minority that could be subjected to violence with no threat of punishment to the perpetrators.

In this essay, I will trace the increasing constriction of the walks of life of the Jewish population, the constant threats, and the daily antisemitic violence in the years before the war, by describing events in Treuchtlingen, a small town in Franconia for which an unusually rich collection of sources is available.[8] I will focus not only on the physical mistreatment and attacks initiated by the SA and the HJ, but,

6 Lindenberger and Lüdtke, *Physische Gewalt*, p. 19.

7 Dirk Walter, *Antisemitische Kriminalität und Gewalt in der Weimarer Republik*, PhD dissertation submitted to the University of Freiburg, 1997.

8 Both extensive reports of former Jewish citizens and official documents pertaining to Treuchtlingen are available. My own research in Treuchtlingen uncovered various files in the municipal archives which supplement the information provided by official regional and federal sources. Thus, this especially dense collection of source material provides an opportunity of reconstructing the history of violence against the Jewish residents of one locality. Moreover, the study appears to be of broader significance, since examples from other regions and localities confirm that Treuchtlingen was not a "special case." This contribution is thus a preliminary study for a larger research project which I have begun, focusing on day-to-day antisemitic violence in Germany in the years 1933 to 1939. I wish to thank Christine

no less important, on the bystanders and observers who increasingly became participants and perpetrators. Contrary to the impression created by sweeping hypotheses such as that postulating an "eliminationist antisemitism" (Goldhagen), inherent in the Germans, we still know little about the intensity and the violent nature of antisemitism in the German population.[9] Instead of providing facile explanations, I feel it is essential to first analyze the actual, concrete, daily practices: Who participated in violence against Jews? What were the prerequisites for the disintegration of civil values and legal norms in daily life? Who was the driving force, who heated things up, who attempted to stem the tide? How did violent actions spread, taking hold of bystanders and transforming them into perpetrators? How does violence change when limits are no longer set? When does murder become "normal"?

Treuchtlingen in the Early Years of the National Socialist Regime

Today, the small town of Treuchtlingen in middle Franconia uses advertising to attract guests to its thermal spa. Situated in the Altmühl Valley not far from Nuremberg, its population in 1933 numbered about 4,200, 119 of whom were Jews. The history of Treuchtlingen's Jews reaches back to the Middle Ages, with the first document mentioning Jewish residents dated 1349. The first synagogue was built early in the eighteenth century and furnished with precious Torah shrine curtains and other valuable ritual artifacts; a ritual bathhouse was added in 1780. At the same time, the Jewish community bought farmland at the foot of the Schlossberg for use as a cemetery, which also served the

von Oertzen, Gesine Krüger, Karin Orth, Axel Dossmann and Ulrich Prehn for suggestions, comments and criticisms.

9 See the work of Werner Jochmann, especially: *Gesellschaftskrise und Judenfeindschaft in Deutschland 1870–1945*, Hamburg, 1988; also the studies of Ian Kershaw, "The Persecution of the Jews and German Popular Opinion in the Third Reich," *Yearbook of the Leo Baeck Institute,* 26 (1981), pp. 261–289; David Bankier, *The Germans and the Final Solution. Public Opinion under Nazism*, Oxford, 1992; and Sarah Gordon, *Hitler, Germans and the "Jewish Question,"* Princeton, 1984.

neighboring Jewish communities of Ellingen, Pappenheim, and Markt Berolzheim.[10]

Immediately after Hitler's takeover in 1933, the police searched the home of the head of the local branch of the *Centralverein deutscher Staatsbürger jüdischen Glaubens (C.V.)*, and confiscated money, documents, and membership lists.[11] In June of the same year, the town council of Treuchtlingen ordered that the Jewish community vacate the schoolhouse at very short notice. The community took legal action against the town's decision but was forced to vacate in early 1935 and ordered to build a new schoolhouse.[12] Treuchtlinger Jews were the victims of physical attacks as early as 1933. Babette Gutmann, the Christian wife of Leo Gutmann, a Jewish livestock dealer, recounted after the war that armed SA watchmen were deployed in front of the couple's house shortly after the *Machtergreifung*: "From that time on, we were constantly boycotted, not only in business matters but also in private life. Windows were often smashed at night. The personal attacks escalated from year to year, we couldn't show ourselves in public, were molested in public with curses like 'Yid' (*Jud*), Jewish pig *(Judensau)*, etc."[13] Hermann Kahn, who left Treuchtlingen in 1935, reported that he was attacked in his own home by members of the Hitler Youth in

10 Cf. Baruch Z. Ophir and Falk Wiesemann, eds., *Die jüdischen Gemeinden in Bayern 1918–1945. Geschichte und Zerstörung*, Munich, 1979, pp. 232–234; also Michaela Schröttle, *Beiträge zur Geschichte der Judengemeinde von Treuchtlingen*, thesis in pedagogy submitted to the University of Augsburg, 1974, pp. 52–82.

11 On the C.V. cf. Arnold Paucker, *Der jüdische Abwehrkampf gegen Antisemitismus und Nationalsozialismus in den letzten Jahren der Weimarer Republik*, Hamburg, 1969; Avraham Barkai, "Der C.V. im Jahre 1933: Neu aufgefundene Dokumente im Moskauer "Sonderarchiv," *Tel Aviver Jahrbuch für deutsche Geschichte*, 23 (1994), pp. 233–246; Hans Reichmann, "Der Centralverein deutscher Staatsbürger jüdischen Glaubens," in: *Festschrift zum 80. Geburtstag von Rabbiner Dr. Leo Baeck*, London, 1953, pp. 55–73.

12 The new school was in fact never built, but the Jewish community attempted to provide regular lessons for the Jewish children, who were forced to leave the town's school in December 1936. In the spring of 1937 the Jewish community's teacher Salomon Frank was still teaching 13 pupils, cf. Ophir and Wiesemann, *Die jüdischen Gemeinden in Bayern*, p. 232.

13 Babette Gutmann to Bayrisches Landesentschädigungsamt, 24 April 1954; Treuchtlingen Municipal Archives (hereafter TMA), 063/27.

December 1934. All his furniture was demolished and he was beaten, sustaining two knife wounds.[14]

In April 1934, the Treuchtlinger *Sanitätsrat* Dr. Goppelt sent a long letter to the *Landkreisamt* (Rural District Office) of Weissenburg, decrying the anti-Jewish attacks in his town. He reported on several cases in which the windows of Jewish homes and shops were broken, the hat of an 89-year-old man was knocked from his head, and antisemitic signs had been put up at the town's borders. The *Sanitätsrat* emphasized the fact that he was by no means "a friend of the Jews" (*Judenfreund*), and described these events as "mischief" and "silly boys' pranks" but went on to convey his concern about the morals of young people and the prosperity of local businesses.[15] Goppelt may have emphasized conservative disquiet about the potential loss of values expressly for those he assumed would be reading his letter, while he was in fact more concerned about the dignity and well-being of his Jewish fellow citizens. Nonetheless, he chose to formulate his warning such that it would not be considered an expression of sympathy for Jews which would put him in danger of being branded a "friend of the Jews." The *Bezirksamt* Weissenburg passed Goppelt's letter on to the *NSDAP Kreisleiter*, enclosing a comment about the difficulties encountered in replacing Jewish livestock dealers with Christian ones. The *NSDAP* officer answered vehemently: "All of these honorable circles have apparently thought it in keeping with the dignity of a cultivated state when year in, year out, tens of thousands of German farmers have lost their homes and farms. No one got up and lamented, 'these poor German people.' But if someone touches a hair on the head of a Jewish pig, a cry goes up from every nook and cranny, 'Our poor Jews!'."[16]

14 Paul Schanz, attorney of Hermann Kahn, to Bürgermeisteramt, 4 February 1957; TMA, 063/26.

15 Goppelt's letter is quoted from Steven M. Lowenstein, "The Struggle for Survival of Rural Jews in Germany 1933–1938: The Case of Bezirksamt Weissenburg, Mittelfranken," in: *Die Juden im Nationalsozialistischen Deutschland. The Jews in Nazi Germany*, Arnold Paucker, ed., Tübingen 1986, p. 117.

16 Lowenstein, "Struggle for Survival," p. 118. In fact, the boycott of Jewish livestock dealers in Bavaria, which the NSDAP pursued vehemently and in part with physical force, was only successful when enforced with governmental measures. The traditional trading relations were lucrative for the farmers and there was a lack of sufficient and competent Christian dealers to replace the Jewish traders: Falk Wiesemann, "Juden auf dem Lande: die wirtschaftliche Ausgrenzung der jüdischen

As far as we can ascertain from the files, Goppelt received no answer to his letter.

The possible disclaimer that the acts of violence which Goppelt reported were everyday village rowdyness and could hardly be termed antisemitic must be taken seriously. However, the fact that Goppelt found these events significant enough to warrant writing a long letter of complaint elevates them above the level of daily village life. These actions were directed not at any old man on the street but at Jews in general. Thus these early actions were antisemitic in nature and their brutality beyond the usual village roughing about, at least as far as Hermann Kahn's report is concerned. A second possible disclaimer — namely that SA attacks were by no means unusual or worthy of notice, violence as such being a unifying and constitutive element of the SA,[17] — is unconvincing. The violence that Treuchtlinger Jews faced was not directed at political rivals who were more or less on an equal footing, as in the street battles with Communists. The cases of antisemitic violence reported by Babette Gutmann, Hermann Kahn and Goppelt were attacks against defenseless persons who had been declared a threat, a "cancer in the body of the German people." Jews were not rivals who had to be defeated, they were "pests" who should be "eliminated." Violence against Jews met unarmed civilian victims, whose possibilities of defending themselves were increasingly limited due to state disenfranchisement.

Murder was, from the outset, a part of antisemitic violence as the examples cited at the beginning of this paper illustrate. On 1 April 1933 during the boycott against Jewish shops, the son of a Jewish businessman in Kiel shot an SS man, gave himself up to the police and was imprisoned; an enraged mob forced its way into the prison and killed the boy in his cell with thirty shots.[18] The series of murders of SA leaders on 30 June 1934 also offered an occasion for antisemitic

Viehhändler in Bayern," in: *Die Reihen fast geschlossen. Beiträge zur Geschichte des Alltags unterm Nationalsozialismus*, Detlev Peukert and Jürgen Reulecke, eds., Wuppertal, 1981, pp. 381–396.

17 On violence by the SA cf. the work of Thomas Balistier, *Gewalt und Ordnung. Kalkül und Faszination der SA*, Münster, 1989, especially pp. 146–160; Sven Reichardt, *Gewalt im SA-Milieu. Sozialhistorische Untersuchungen zum Berliner SA-Sturm Charlottenburg, 1926–1932*, Berlin, (MA thesis), 1994.

18 Dieter Hauschildt, "Vom Judenboykott zum Judenmord. Der 1. April 1933 in Kiel,"

violence, including murder. In the Silesian town of Hirschberg, Jewish shops were attacked, the shop windows shattered, and the owners dragged from their homes and beaten. SS men arrested a lawyer who had participated in court cases against National Socialists, as well as a businessman and a married couple, and shot all of them at night, supposedly "while trying to escape."[19] A pogrom that took place in Gunzenhausen, less than twenty kilometers from Treuchtlingen, illustrates how quickly and fatally antisemitic violence could break out and, like in Kiel, take hold of a crowd in the early years of the National Socialist rule.

On Palm Sunday, 26 March 1934, the local SA leader Kurt Bär made an inflammatory speech, that incited a number of Gunzenhausen citizens to march to the homes of their Jewish neighbors, use brutal force to drag more than thirty of them to the local jail, and there savagely beat them. One Jewish man was reportedly found hanged in a shed, another purportedly drove a knife into his own heart before the mob got hold of him.[20] For weeks the anti-Jewish climate in Gunzenhausen remained at such a fever pitch that the police reinforcements brought in were not released until early May. In the meantime Jewish businesses, in particular the Strauss tavern where the pogrom had started, were repeatedly attacked and demolished at night. Kurt Bär was found guilty of disturbing the peace by the Regional Court Ansbach and in July 1934 shot the Jewish tavern owner Strauss and his son, apparently in revenge for his arrest. Strauss died soon after from the gunshot wounds.[21]

In Kiel as well as in Gunzenhausen, violence was initiated by SA and/or SS men but soon spread to crowds and sometimes culminated in murder. The disposition to violence was apparently so high among those who were initially only bystanders that only a spark was needed to

in: *"Wir bauen das Reich." Aufstieg und erste Herrschaftsjahre des Nationalsozialismus in Schleswig-Holstein*, Erich Hoffmann and Peter Wulf, eds, Neumünster, 1981, pp. 335–360.

19 *Der gelbe Fleck. Die Ausrottung von 500,000 deutschen Juden*. With an introduction by Lion Feuchtwanger, Paris, 1936, pp. 40–43.

20 Ian Kershaw, "The Persecution of the Jews."

21 Halbmonatsbericht Regierungspräsident von Ober- und Mittelfranken, 21 July 1934, documented in: *Bayern in der NS-Zeit,* Martin Broszat, Elke Fröhlich and Falk Wiesemann, eds., Munich, 1977, p. 440.

inflame them. The National Socialist state intervened in Gunzenhausen, sent police reinforcements and put Kurt Bär to trial, but apparently with the intention mainly of reiterating its monopoly on the use of force rather than the desire to protect the life and well-being of Jews. Antisemitic riots in Berlin in the summer of 1935 — in the course of which the SA and HJ attacked Jewish ice-cream cafés, chased away customers, and pasted boycott flyers on the windows — also brought the police to the scene. According to the report of the Berlin Gestapo, the police attempted to "energetically nip [these actions], in the bud" and posted individual policemen in front of "especially threatened businesses." However, these policemen were in a difficult position, as the chronicler noted with regret, since "most of the population did not understand" their activities. The police were reportedly greeted with expletives such as "Jew-slave" (*Judenknecht*), and the like.[22]

In March 1936, youths in Treuchtlingen disrupted a Jewish funeral singing loudly and throwing stones at the mourners. The youths were warned by the local gendarme and their teacher following a police complaint filed by the Jewish community, but no punishment was meted out.[23] The fact that — three years after the Nazis came to power and two years after the pogrom in the neighboring town of Gunzenhausen — the Treuchtlinger Jews appealed to the local authorities to restore law and order is characteristic of the trust that many German Jews still had, if not in the reign of constitutional law then at least in the state's ability to guarantee "public order." Perhaps from a local perspective, the hope that appeals to state powers would prove successful was not as illusory as an analysis of the national development would make them appear. The devaluation of the codes of criminal law may have proceeded more slowly in the minds of local officials than the new National Socialist rulers wished — especially when these officials were older experienced civil servants in rural communities who were generally used to doing their jobs on their own. Without a doubt, the reaction of the Jewish community can be viewed as proof that the Treuchtlinger Jews did

22 Staatspolizeistelle Berlin to Reichs- und preussische Ministerium des Innern, 22 August 1935; Osobyi Archives Moscow (hereafter OAM), 500/1/379, fol. 108–113. On antisemitic violence in the summer of 1935 see also Friedländer, *Nazi Germany and the Jews*, pp. 125–128, 137–139.

23 Lowenstein, "Struggle for Survival," p. 118.

not consider themselves helpless victims but in fact tried to defend themselves. "Until early 1938, complaints to the gendarmes led to brief periods of peace," wrote Moritz Mayer, a Jewish businessman, in a report written in 1939, "later on, complaints were also useless."[24]

Despite the short-term success of these petitions, they were, in the long run, ineffective in checking increasing National Socialist pressure. Acting on a suggestion of the National Socialist mayor Andreas Güntner, the town council of Treuchtlingen voted to prohibit Jews from moving to Treuchtlingen, declared the Christian cemetery off-limits to them, and denied Jewish livestock dealers access to the markets in Treuchtlingen.[25] At a public rally, Günther threatened the Jews: "I won't rest until the whole pack is brought to its knees." He publicly denounced Treuchtlinger citizens who were employed by Jews as "*Judenknechte*."[26] In September 1936 the windows of the synagogue and of a house in which Jews resided were smashed; a month later train passengers pushed Jewish travelers from Treuchtlingen and Gunzenhausen off the train and used force to stop them from riding the train.[27] Moritz Mayer recounted in his memoirs that for years before the pogrom of 1938 "it was nearly impossible to let the children walk down the streets by themselves. And adults were also subjected to abuse by school children."[28]

24 Moritz Mayer's as yet unpublished report, which was written in 1939 after his emigration to Palestine and can be found in the Yad Vashem Archives (hereafter YVA), Record Group 033/80, is a very unique source. Mayer describes in detail and with reference to a specific locality the increasing persecution from the perspective of the victims. His perspective is thus diametrically opposed to the standpoint from which the antisemitic politics of the Nazi regime is usually described, i.e., using the regime's own documents and sources.

25 Extract from the Beratungsbuch der Stadt Treuchtlingen, 20 December 1935, and Bekanntmachung, 24 December 1935; TMA, 063/5.

26 Judgement of the Landgericht Nürnberg-Fürth, 9 Mai 1946 (KLs 16/46); TMA 063/19.

27 Ophir and Wiesemann, *Die jüdischen Gemeinden in Bayern*, pp. 232–233.

28 Memoirs of Moritz Mayer, YVA, Record Group 033/80.

Radicalization 1937–38

At the NSDAP party convention in Nuremberg in September 1937, Hitler gave a demagogic, incendiary speech, assailing the "rulers of Jewish Bolshevism" and invoking his racist worldview, according to which the Jews were "neither mentally nor morally superior but rather in both respects an inferior race, through and through."[29] Two months later he revealed to a small circle of his high-ranking military leaders that he was determined to wage war, and planned, his first goal, to subjugate Czechoslovakia and Austria in a Blitz action.[30]It is against this background that the increasingly brutal course was taken against German Jews: With the preparations for war in Germany, the Jews became "natural" enemies who supposedly intended to undermine this German venture.[31] Furthermore, Jewish assets were coveted as a resource for financing armaments; "Aryanization" and preparations for war were closely interconnected. In early 1933 there were approximately 50,000 Jewish businesses in the German Empire; in July 1938 only 9,000 remained, 3,600 of them in Berlin.[32]

The Colonial Trading Company A. Meyer & Co. in Treuchtlingen, owned in part by Moritz Mayer, was also a victim of this expropriation campaign. The boycott promoted by the Nazis took effect as early as 1933.[33] In late 1937, the public salt factory in Munich (*Salinen München*), made known that it would no longer deliver salt to the Jewish-owned firm and the Southern German Sugar Factory (*Süddeutsche Zuckerfabrik*), sent a similar letter in mid-1938. Customers took advantage of the situation; many who had previously bought on credit refused to pay, arguing that the NSDAP had banned

29 Max Domarus, *Hitler. Reden und Proklamationen 1932–1945*, Munich, 1965, vol. I, p. 729.

30 Minutes of a meeting in the Reichskanzlei on 5 November 1937, in: *Internationaler Militärgerichtshof (IMG), Der Prozess gegen die Hauptkriegsverbrecher in Nürnberg 14.11.1945—1.10.1946*, Nuremberg 1948, vol. 25, pp. 403–413.

31 Cf. Adam, *Judenpolitik*, pp. 166–203; Ludolf Herbst, *Das nationalsozialistische Deutschland 1933–1945. Die Entfesselung der Gewalt: Rassismus und Krieg*, Frankfurt am Main, 1996, pp. 200–217.

32 Avraham Barkai, *From Boykott to Annihilation. The Economic Struggle of German Jews,* Hanover, N.H, 1989, pp. 67–69.

33 Memoirs of Moritz Mayer, YVA, Record Group 033/80.

purchases in Jewish shops. It was reported that in the neighboring town of Pleinfeld a Jewish clothing dealer was beaten and chased out of town after he tried to collect money from debtors.[34] Josef Engl, a resident of Treuchtlingen who worked at the Jewish owned Neuburger Hardware Store, recalled the situation after the war:

> SA men were posted in front of the shops, they even photographed people who went in and out of the Jewish stores. I am thinking in particular of the A. Neuburger Hardware Store, across from the town hall. It caused me personally a lot of trouble, I was declared a Jew-slave. (...), Certain gentlemen from the police had at the time no qualms about occasionally roughing one up."[35]

Every purchase in a Jewish shop, every greeting from a Christian neighbor, every chat with a Jewish citizen was reported to the mayor, who, as Moritz Mayer writes, "immediately ordered such "offenders" to his office. They were then denied public contracts, subsidies, etc. In May 1938, all barbers and hairdressers in the town decided to stop serving Jewish customers. A few tradesmen had already done so earlier."[36]

The year 1938 has quite appropriately been termed the "year of fate" for German and Austrian Jews.[37] On 12 March 1938, the eve of the invasion by German troops, Austrians in Vienna and elsewhere launched brutal antisemitic rampages. Jewish businesses were looted, Jewish citizens were arbitrarily arrested, driven from their homes and beaten, and looting and stealing of Jews was the order of the day.[38] As documented by well-known photographs, Viennese Jews were forced to scrub a sidewalk with their toothbrush jeered by a mocking crowd. In

34 Norman Klinger, *Die Geschichte der jüdischen Gemeinde Ellingen von 1933–1938*, Schülerwettbewerb Deutsche Geschichte 1980/81, Körber-Archiv 000448.

35 Quoted from Schröttle, *Beiträge*, pp. 104–105.

36 Memoirs of Moritz Mayer, YVA, Record Group 033/80.

37 "The year 1938 represents an historical turning point for the fate of Jews." These were the opening words of the working report of the *Reichsvertretung der Juden in Deutschland* published in early 1939. Quoted from Avraham Barkai, "Schicksalsjahr 1938," in: *November 1938. From "Reichskristallnacht" to Genocide,* Walter H. Pehle, ed., New York, 1991, p. 95.

38 Cf. Hans Safrian and Hans Witek, *Und keiner war dabei. Dokumente des alltäglichen Antisemitismus in Wien 1938*, Vienna, 1988. The memoirs of the famous writer Carl Zuckmayer entitled *"Als wär's ein Stück von mir"* include a moving account of this evening of 11 March 1938.

Berlin, antisemitic activities also flared up again in the early summer of 1938. In early May, Jewish businesses were smeared with paint during the night, a local synagogue was damaged, and shop windows were broken in several neighborhoods. On 10 June, Goebbels called on the police to "persist in constantly harassing the Jews,"[39] a day later violent attacks on Jewish businesses swept through Berlin, accompanied in part by looting. Jewish-owned businesses in Magdeburg were also smeared with paint, and in Frankfurt am Main shop windows were smashed, synagogues damaged and Jewish shop owners physically assaulted.[40]

In general local police did not intervene against the perpetrators, and the police central office in Berlin chose to exploit the violent climate to its own ends. In early June the *Reichskriminalpolizeiamt* (Federal Criminal Police Bureau), issued a decree signed by Heydrich stating that, in the week of the 13th to 18th June, every district office of the Criminal Police (*Kriminalpolizeileitstelle*), had to "arrest and keep in preventive custody at least two hundred able-bodied (*arbeitsfähige*), male persons (asocial persons)," as well as "all male Jews in the District of the Criminal Police (*Kriminalpolizeileitstellenbezirk),* who had previously been sentenced to a prison sentence of more than one month."[41] In the course of this June campaign, more than 10,000 people, including 1,500 Jews, were arrested and hauled to concentration camps. One of the victims was Louis Freimann, a Jewish businessman from

39 Goebbels noted on 11 June 1938: "Spoke to 300 police officers in Berlin about the Jewish question. I am really heating things up. Away with all sentimentality. Our motto ist not law but persecution." Elke Fröhlich, ed., *Die Tagebücher von Joseph Goebbels, Sämtliche Fragmente, Teil I Aufzeichnungen 1924–1941*, Munich, 1987, vol. III, p. 452.

40 Fernschreiben SD Leipzig to SD-Hauptamt, 22 June 1938 and SD-OA Fulda-Werra to SD-Hauptamt, 23 June 1938; OAM 500/1/645, Bl. 10, 11. — Hitler apparently halted further rampages personally with an eye to foreign policy considerations. A note from the SD Main Office states that a decision of the *Gauleitung* and the *Polizeipräsident* of Berlin, which was preceded by "a personal message of the Führer from Berchtesgaden," prohibited further activities starting with 21 Juni, 5 p.m. Stabskanzlei SD-Hauptamt to Abteilung II 112, 22 June 1938; OAM, 500/1/645, as well as the corresponding notes in Goebbels' records dated 21 June and 22 June 1938; cf. Fröhlich, *Tagebücher*, vol. III, pp. 461–463.

41 Reichssicherheitshauptamt — Amt V, ed., *Vorbeugende Verbrechensbekämpfung — Erlasssammlung*, n.p. n.d. [Berlin 1943], pp. 81–82; cf. Wolfgang Ayass, *"Asoziale" im Nationalsozialismus*, Stuttgart, 1995, pp. 139–165.

Treuchtlingen who was taken to Dachau and released only after he promised to leave Germany.[42] According to a letter from Güntner to the commander's office at the Dachau concentration camp, Freimann wanted to emigrate to Palestine "which would be welcomed by the local police."[43] The June action thus revealed the intentions of the police and the SS, intentions that were pursued on a much larger scale a few months later in November 1938: namely to utilize terror and concentration camp detention as a means to force Jews to emigrate and relinquish their property to Aryans, so-called *Arisierung*.

For Moritz Mayer and his brother Albert, the pressure on their business increased so drastically that by early 1938 they began to consider giving it up and leaving Treuchtlingen. The archives of the town include a contract between Moritz Mayer and the town of Treuchtlingen dated 13 April 1938, documenting the sale of farmland (0.245 hectar), to the town for a price of RM 2,485, the payment of which Mayer confirmed with a receipt on the same day.[44] The projected sale of the Mayers' business together with the entire property at 16 *Hindenburgstrasse* (today *Hauptstrasse*) to the Rüdiger & Cirus company of Mittelgründen in the summer of 1938 was not finalized however because the Trade Association for Oils and Fats (*Fachgruppe Öle und Fette*), in Berlin refused to transfer the consignment of oil, it had previously delivered to the Jewish businessman Mayer, to the proposed "Aryan" owners.[45]

42 In the case of the Jewish horse dealer Hermann Lang, who was also singled out for arrest, the *Bezirksamt* Weissenburg first requested an order from the criminal police (*Kriminalpolizei*), stating that the 65-year-old Lang should be arrested in spite of his advanced age. Although Mayor Güntner termed both men "capable of working," the police apparently refrained from arresting Lang; *Bezirksamt* Weissenburg to *Bürgermeister* Treuchtlingen, 16 June 1938 with note of the *Schutzpolizei* Treuchtlingen, 18 June 1938; TMA 063/5.

43 Güntner to *Kommandantur* KZ Dachau, 22 July 1938; TMA 063/5. Louis Freimann emigrated in 1939 to Philadelphia in the USA.

44 TMA 063/14.

45 TMA 063/3.

The November Pogrom in Treuchtlingen

After the wave of riots and arrests in June 1938, the climate in Germany remained charged with violence. On 20 and 22 September in Beveringen, Neuenkirchen and Fürstenau, synagogues were broken into, their furnishings destroyed and Jewish cemeteries desecrated.[46] Also on 20 September, NSDAP members forced three Jewish families to leave Bechhofen in Central Franconia. The SD reported: "They [the Jews, M.W.] were brought out of their houses, kicked and driven through the village, some of them barefoot. After being called upon to do so, the children also participated in the demonstration."[47] In early October, the SD *Oberabschnitt Süd-West* reported antisemitic rallies in various localities in Württemberg, during which windows were shattered and Jews threatened.[48] In Vienna in mid-October, SS gangs also attacked hundreds of Jewish businesses and destroyed and looted schools, synagogues, and houses.[49]

In Nuremberg, Munich, and Dortmund, the synagogues were demolished and the act made into a public spectacle; the Jewish communities were obliged to pay the costs of demolition. Of note is the reference contained in a telegram from the SD *Oberabschnitt Süd*:

> Due to the remark a Jew made to a Sudeten German, to the effect that the whole world was being mobilized because of the negligibly small group of Sudeten Germans, disturbances broke out in Melrichstadt during the night of 30 September /1 October 1938. Investigations to date reveal that, following the complete demolition of the synagogue, windows of Jewish houses were smashed and one Jewish shop window was looted.[50]

It almost appears as if the extreme tension that the threat of war evoked among the German population was vented in local pogroms against Jews. The Munich agreement neither calmed the violent climate nor resolved the tense situation or broke the will of the National Socialists

46 Meldung SD-Oberabschnitt West, 24 September 1938; OAM, 500/1/630, fol. 3.

47 Meldung SD-Oberabschnitt Süd, 11 October 1938; OAM, 500/1/630, fol. 6.

48 Meldung SD-Oberabschnitt Süd-West, 6 October 1938; OAM, 500/1/630, fol. 5.

49 David Bankier, *The Germans and the Final Solution. Public Opinion Under Nazism*, Oxford, 1992, pp. 82–3.

50 SD-Oberabschnitt Süd to SD-Hauptamt Berlin, 4 October 1938; OAM, 500/1/630, Bl. 7.

to wage war. Until today, the vehemence and brutality of the November pogroms remain inexplicable. Riots on such a scale do not occur on demand unless the pent-up energy required for a pogrom already exists, awaiting a command to be unleashed. Perhaps the violent atmosphere of the year 1938 and the international tensions that brought Europe to the brink of war were vented in the November pogrom.

In Treuchtlingen, signs of the approaching November pogrom were already perceptible weeks earlier. According to Moritz Mayer, the animosity of local residents increased discernibly during the September crisis:

> Jostling from young and old, stone-throwing, window-shattering, dismounting of the window shutters during the day were not uncommon. Restlessness and nervousness increased when we heard from several Jewish communities (Leutershausen, Ellingen, etc.) that the Jews had been forced to leave their homes on sacred holidays, abandoning all their possessions, and to sell the synagogues for ridiculous prices (sometimes just a few marks).[51]

The mayor of Treuchtlingen declared that it was forbidden for the Jewish community to celebrate the *Hoschana Rabba* feast with the reading of religious texts — the traditional *Tikkun* — in the home of a community member.[52] In Leutershausen the windows of a house in which Jews lived and the windows of the synagogue were broken and cow dung piled in front of the synagogue door. Two days later a group of town citizens forced its way into Jewish homes, demolished all the household contents, and assaulted the residents. About fifty people broke into the synagogue and destroyed everything inside.[53] The local NSDAP chapter in the neighboring village of Windsbach reacted to the violence in Leutershausen with a specially prepared flyer:

> In the past few weeks the Jew has been determined to bait some of the peoples of the world into engaging in an awful war. The German nation was to be wrestled to its knees and destroyed. Millions of people were to be slaughtered

51 Memoirs of Moritz Mayers, YVA, Record Group 033/80.

52 Ophir and Wiesemann, *Die jüdischen Gemeinden in Bayern*, p. 233.

53 Report SD-Oberabschnitt Süd to SD-Hauptamt Berlin, 20 October 1938; OAM, 500/1/630, fol. 15–17; see also Ophir and Wiesemann, *Die jüdischen Gemeinden in Bayern*, pp. 195–196. Most of the approximately 20 Jewish citizens of Leutershausen then fled in panic from the village. Of those remaining, seven left Leutershausen by mid-December and in February 1939 the last Jewish resident moved to Munich.

> and murdered. Cities and villages of the German *Gaue* were to be destroyed. More than one hundred thousand German families would have thus experienced unspeakable suffering. That was the will of the Jew. (...), This is our undaunted will: Windsbach must be free of Jews in short order.[54]

The pogrom in Treuchtlingen began in the early morning hours of 10 November 1938.[55] Shortly before midnight, the SA *Standartenführer* Georg Sauber of Weissenburg was instructed by telephone to report to Nuremberg where he was to receive from SA *Gruppenführer* von Obernitz the order to destroy the synagogues and arrest all male Jews. Sauber then drove to Treuchtlingen to personally convey the relevant orders to the local *Sturmbannführer* Peter Engelhardt. The SA men of Treuchtlingen were woken after which they reported between 3:00 and 4:00 A.M. to the assigned meeting place — the fire company, which was close to the synagogue. While the men were still being divided into groups and receiving orders from Engelhardt to drive the Jewish citizens of Treuchtlingen out of their homes and demolish their belongings, other SA members were already setting fire to the synagogue. One witness recalls how the men stood in front of the house of the cantor Moses Kurzweil, which was attached to the synagogue, and shouted: "Jew, open up, come out, we're setting fire to your house, otherwise we'll burn you up!" They broke down the door and forced their way into the synagogue, which was soon in flames. The fire company arrived at the scene but their efforts went into protecting the surrounding "Aryan" houses, leaving Treuchtlingen's synagogue to burn to the ground.

Awakened by the noise and the fire alarm, more and more citizens of the town gathered in front of the burning synagogue and marched with the SA gangs to Jewish homes. Although SA men formed the core group

54 Quoted from Report SD-Oberabschnitt Süd, 25 October 1938; OAM, 500/1/630, fol. 31.

55 The following description of the pogrom in Treuchtlingen is based on the investigation results, evidence and eyewitness reports found in the court records of the trial before the Landgericht Nuremberg-Fürth, Mai 1946 (KLs 16/46), TMA 063/19. For summaries of the events of the November pogrom, see: Wolfgang Benz, "Der Novemberpogrom 1938," in: Benz, *Die Juden in Deutschland*, pp. 499–544; Hermann Graml, *Antisemitism*; Pehle, *November 1938*; Dieter Obst, *"Reichskristallnacht." Ursachen und Verlauf des antisemitischen Pogroms vom November 1938*, Frankfurt am Main, 1991.

of the rampaging mob, the citizens of Treuchtlingen participated in the destruction, inciting the SA attackers, verbally abusing their Jewish neighbors, and looting the shops. After the war, in 1946, fifty-two women and men were tried before the *Landgericht* in Nuremberg-Fürth for deeds committed that night in Treuchtlingen. Thirty-nine were found guilty of disturbing the peace, some in connection with theft, intimidation, deprivation of liberty and dangerous bodily injury, and sentenced to prison sentences of up to two years; among them were five women who received sentences of between three months and two years.[56] The November pogrom in Treuchtlingen was not the work of isolated SA gangs but rather the rampage of an entire town. Those who did not become perpetrators looked the other way and did not find the courage to resist. The reports mention only a few people who tried to help the victims.[57]

Moritz Mayer reports in his memoirs:

> On 10 November between 4 and 5 A.M. I heard footsteps in the garden. When I looked out of the window, 8 to 10 men (S.A.), heavily armed with axes, hatchets, daggers, and revolvers were standing there. By the time I had awakened my wife and my 11 year old son, there was already a man in the bedroom, ordering us to go to the cellar and starting to smash everything to bits: the washbasin, mirror, window, furniture, doors etc. After we (including my sister-in-law and daughter), had been in the cellar for a short time, I was called upstairs. My

56 The heavy sentences for women may reflect a patriarchial view of women, equating womanhood with nonviolence. Thus, violent women deserve especially severe punishment, since, according to this male perspective, they act contrary to their "feminine nature." The court opinion asserts that: "The defendants [Mrs. A. and Mrs. H.] lack not only the innate sensitivity of feminine emotion, they have, on the contrary revealed a coldness of feeling, even an emotional coarseness, which precludes a milder judgement of their deeds and demands strict punishment." On the topic of the treatment of female Nazis defendants, see Insa Eschebach, "'Ich bin unschuldig.' Vernehmungsprotokolle als historische Quellen. Der Rostocker Ravensbrück-Prozess 1966," *Werkstatt Geschichte,* 12 (1995), pp. 65–70.

57 One such experience is related by Bernhard Tachauer, who later emigrated to Canada, and who was forced to flee head over heels and without a penny in his pocket from the antisemitic mob in his home in Marktbreit, in the rural district of Kitzingen. On his way to Munich, he had to wait at the train station in Treuchtlingen: "My thanks go to the station chief on duty during the night of the 9 November 1938. He didn't betray me to the police but instead let me board the train without a ticket and even made arrangements with the train conductor to allow me to ride all the way to Munich." *Treuchtlinger Kurier*, 19 and 20 November 1988.

> daughter wanted to accompany me but was shoved back. I was screamed at. "You scoundrel, you know that you've been free game since 12 o'clock tonight, give us your documents." Before I could unlock the desk, I was hit so hard in the face that my eyeglasses fell and broke, my right eye swelled up and the pupil damaged. The doctor later explained that I could have lost my vision by this blow. I was then thrown into the corner and pieces of furniture were thrown at me at random. The fact that I retained only three minor wounds and was not seriously injured must be termed extreme good fortune. In the meantime, the entire house was being laid in ruins as described above. In the kitchen, the dishes were smashed down to the last piece; in the cellar, my wife had a full tin can thrown at her head; the women were themselves forced to smash wine bottles and canning jars. After the SA came the plebs, then the school youths; each party continued destroying and stealing.[58]

Other Jewish citizens of Treuchtlingen suffered similar treatment at the hands of the mob. According to the findings of the *Landgericht* Nuremberg, an SA man entered the home of the Gutmann family and threatened one of the sons with a pickaxe. The other men wrecked the furnishings of the rooms on the groundfloor, over turned cupboards and smashed dishes. Gutmann's non-Jewish wife and sons appealed for help to Mrs. A. and Mrs. H. pointing out that they were Christians, but the two women laughed derisively. These women later had to stand trial for their crimes. The mob charged into Albert Neuburger's hardware store, which was close to the burning synagogue, and looted the shop. As a witness later reported in court, everything was destroyed, the shop windows completely plundered, items inside had been thrown helter skelter and the witness and other residents of Treuchtlingen had to climb around and over the merchandise. Laundry baskets full of wine bottles were dragged out of Neuburger's cellar. Personal belongings, especially clothes and hats were thrown down the steps of the home of the Weinmann family. According to the evidence collected at the later trial, HJ youths trampled on the furniture and battered away at an overturned laundry cupboard in a frenzy. People stole cloth, suits, and the like from the shelves of the Bacharach's textile store. The sum of RM 3,000 was stolen from the Hänlein family. A horde of residents of Treuchtlingen gathered in front of the house of Dr. Meyerson, an ophthalmologist, and cheered on the SA rowdies inside. One women reputedly called out: "That is not nearly enough, bring him out, the

58 Memoirs of Moritz Mayers, YVA, Record Group 033/80.

Jew-pig!" The home of the Meyersons was also ransacked and Dr. Meyerson was accused of having clandestine contact with a radio broadcasting station in Strassbourg, taken to the town hall and beaten. He committed suicide a few days later; his wife died shortly afterward in early 1939.

Albert Meyer was stabbed in the cellar of his house, and SA men shoved a bottle with a broken neck into the mouth of his young daughter and demanded that she drink from it. An old man was so badly beaten that he and his wife reported to the local police station in Treuchtlingen on the morning of 11 November and asked to be placed in protective custody as they feared further assaults.[59] Many Treuchtlingen Jews, especially women and children, fled in panic to the train station to escape the inferno, some only scantily dressed and with only as much as they could carry. On the way there they were pursued and beaten. Moritz Mayer and his wife were allowed to pack some linen and clothing and then "had to go through a cordon formed by the mob, accompanied by its derisive laughter, to the train station. Numerous members of the community were already there, others had already left on earlier trains."[60] On the morning of 10 November, the mob was still not satisfied and attempted to prevent the husband of Mrs. G. — a woman who worked as a housekeeper for the Meyersons — from going to work, shouting: "Pull him off his motorcycle, the Jew-slave." The pogrom finally subsided at about ten o'clock.[61]

There are still no exact figures on the extent of the destruction, looting, rape and murder in Germany during those few days.[62] Certainly,

59 Gendarmeriestation Treuchtlingen to Bezirksamt Weissenburg, 11 November 1938; YVA, M1DN/203, fol. 295. The two elderly people were in fact transferred to the prison in Weissenburg and released a week later on 19 November.

60 Memoirs of Moritz Mayers, YVA, Record Group 033/80.

61 Judgement of Landgericht Nürnberg-Fürth, 9 May 1946 (KLs 16/46), TMA 063/19.

62 Heydrich himself estimated the damage in a letter to Göring on 11 November, naming totally unrealistic figures of 815 wrecked businesses, 29 department stores which were set fire to or otherwise sacked, 171 demolished residential homes, 191 synagogues that had been set fire to, 76 of which were completely destroyed. Furthermore, 11 buildings of Jewish communities were set fire to, 36 Jews killed and an equal number injured. Heydrich to Göring, 11 November 1938; documented in, *Nazi Conspiracy and Aggression*, Washington, D.C., 1946, vol. V, p. 854 (3058-PS). One day later, Heydrich was already reporting more than 7,500 wrecked businesses; Stenographic, fragmentary minutes of the meeting in the *Reichsluftfahrtministerium*,

many more than a hundred people were murdered,[63] not including the many Jews who died in concentration camps in the subsequent weeks and months. The mayor of Treuchtlingen reported to the Fire Insurance Office in Eichstätt on 15 November that the synagogue and the attached house of the cantor Moses Kurzweil were completely destroyed by fire and that all Jewish properties, altogether twenty-one houses or apartments, had been destroyed.[64] The *Bezirksamt* Weissenburg reported on 11 November that of ninety-three Jews who had been residents of Treuchtlingen, only three people who were over sixty years old (two men and a women) remained in the town. Four Jews were under arrest, the others had left the town.[65]

Reports from other localities indicate that the events in Treuchtlingen were by no means unique. In Lünen, SA and SS men even drove the Jews they arrested directly through the fire into the burning synagogue. In Saarbrücken, the 130 Jewish men who had been arrested were lined up in marching formation, one had a drum hung around his neck, another was given a kettle-drum, and they were forced to parade through the streets, singing and drumming as they went. Upon arrival at the synagogue, they were made to dance and kneel and sing religious songs. On the way back to the train station the men, clad only in pyjamas, nightshirts or trousers, were sprayed on this November morning with water from the municipal street sprinkler until they were soaking wet. In Meppen, Jewish men were driven through the streets, ordered to lie on the street in front of the SA *Standartenhaus* and kiss the ground, while the SA men kicked them and walked on them.[66] This type of

12 November 1938, documented in: *Nazi Conspiracy and Aggression*, Washington, D.C., 1946, vol. IV, pp. 425–457 (1816–PS).

63 Arno Hamburger reports that in Nuremberg alone 26 persons were murdered or were so terrified that they committed suicide; Arno Hamburger, "Die Pogromnacht vom 9. auf den 10. November 1938 in Nürnberg," in. *"Niemand war dabei und keiner hat's gewusst." Die deutsche öffentlichkeit und die Judenverfolgung 1933–1945*, Jörg Wollenberg, ed., Munich, 1989, pp. 21–25.

64 *Bürgermeister* Treuchtlingen to *Brandversicherungsamt* Eichstätt, 15 November 1938; TMA 063/9.

65 *Bezirksamt* Weissenburg to *Staatspolizeileitstelle* Nürnberg, 11 November 1938; YVA, M1DN/203, fol. 293.

66 Obst, *Reichskristallnacht*, pp. 284–285.

brutal cruelty occurred publicly; in smaller localities the local party functionaries staged the rounding up of Jews for deportation as parades through the town or village. The victims often had to carry signs or banners with slogans such as "We are the murderers of vom Rath," "We are wretched Jews and have betrayed the Fatherland," and "The exodus of the Jews." They also had to sing folk songs, like "*Muss i denn zum Städele hinaus," Nun ade mein lieb Heimatland*" or "*Das Wandern ist des Müllers Lust.*" The procession was usually accompanied by a horde of onlookers; for the victims the march to the train station was like running the gauntlet. In Frankfurt, the Jewish captives arrived at the South Train Station to find themselves awaited by a jeering crowd which proceeded to chase them with clubs and sticks. In some places entire school classes were summoned to witness the spectacle and spit at or beat the victims.[67]

Detention in Concentration Camps

The Mayer family of Treuchtlingen fled to Munich. Moritz and his brother were arrested there and sent to the Dachau concentration camp. During the night of 9 November, Heydrich and Gestapo head Müller, had ordered the arrest in concentration camps of thirty thousand particularly well-to-do, Jewish men. By 16 November about thirty-six thousand Jewish men had been subsequently arrested throughout the German Reich and most of them sent to the concentration camps in Dachau, Buchenwald and Sachsenhausen.[68]

The former attorney of the *CV*, Hans Reichmann, who was arrested on 10 November in Berlin and deported to Sachsenhausen, describes in his memoirs the "welcome" that the SS members had prepared for the Jewish prisoners:

> Forty or fifty of these fellows are lurking around the gate, grinning. "Get off the truck! Will you get moving! You skunks, you pack of scoundrels, you

67 Ibid., pp. 297–307.

68 The arrests and concentration camp detention of the "November Jews" have hardly been researched to date. Cf. in particular Heiko Pollmeier, *Die Inhaftierung deutscher Juden im November 1938*, MA thesis submitted to the Technische Universität, Berlin, 1995.

> Jew-pigs!" At the same time, blows rained down, everyone inside the dark truck tumbled head over heels and tried to jump off the truckbed. Energetic help was provided. Zealous arms reached into the truck and dragged out whoever they could grab. Whoever fell to the ground and got hurt was kicked. All the while there was jeering, screaming, tugging, beating and twenty or thirty times the cry was repeated: "Will you get moving, you skunks!" In this turbulent melee, bank director Lux of Beuthen took an unfortunate fall and broke his leg. (...), Immediately after this "reception" I saw a gaunt man whose face had a gaping wound from his eye to his chin.[69]

Moritz Mayer reported from Dachau that when they arrived they were made to stand for hours in the cold, clad only in a shirt, socks, trousers, and a drill jacket: "SS men watched over us and if they saw that someone wasn't standing at attention properly, they would slap his face and poke him."[70]

Thousands of new prisoners were crowded together in the existing barracks. In Dachau and Sachsenhausen, the beds had been removed and the floor was covered with straw on which the men had to lie like sardines next to each other. In Buchenwald, a provisional camp was hastily erected with five barracks, each of which was to house two thousand prisoners. Here there was neither straw nor blankets; there were only two provisional latrines and washing was nearly impossible.The daily labor duty for prisoners in Sachsenhausen was aimed more at degrading the prisoners and ruining their health than pursuing economic goals. "This labor," as Wolfgang Sofsky wrote, "was intended to disable the people and break their resistance. It was not a means of survival but rather one of absolute power and terror."[71] In the Sachsenhausen camp, work in the dreaded brick factory in particular meant severe and senseless torment for the prisoners. The train lorries and the grading rollers, which weighed tons, had to be pulled by hand. Since there were neither wheelbarrows nor shovels, the prisoners were forced to button their jackets in the back and to carry sand in their

69 Michael Wildt, ed., *Hans Reichmann, Deutscher Bürger und verfolgter Jude. Aufzeichnungen über Pogrom und Konzentrationslager, 1937 bis 1939,* Munich, 1997, pp. 121–122.

70 Memoirs of Moritz Mayer, YVA, Record Group 033/80.

71 Wolfgang Sofsky, *The Order of Terror: The Concentration Camp*, Princeton, New Jersey, 1997, p. 167.

aprons. When SS men appeared they purposely accelerated the work pace until the prisoners collapsed from exhaustion.

But the terror of the concentration camp lay not solely in such cruelty, equally important was the arbitrariness and the knowledge that one was at the absolute mercy of the captors. The punishments to which prisoners were subjected were not sanctions for transgressions against some code handed down by the SS, which at least would have offered some opportunity of avoiding punishment. In fact, the SS men made a joke of punishing prisoners for "misdeeds" that were unknown to them. Moritz Mayer recounted that in Dachau an old man was ordered to say his name but he forgot to add *Schutzhäftling*. He was slapped so hard that he fell and when he was released soon after, he died two days later. A sixty year old man with a bladder ailment asked to use the latrine and was beaten so severely by the SS that his lifeless body was carried from the *Appellplatz*. Another prisoner who had apparently died of a heart attack during roll call was left lying on the ground.[72]

Dispassionate statistics speak an unambiguous language: from 1933 to 1936 the SS killed between 21 and 41 prisoners per year in Dachau; in 1938 they killed 276. In September 1938 twelve people died, in October 1938 ten. In November, following the internment of the Jewish captives, the number jumped to 115 and reached 173 deaths in December.[73]No other group of prisoners faced the drastic and brutal treatment as the Jews.[74]

Expropriation

Initially, the detention of the Jewish men arrested in November 1938 was not intended to continue for a long period. Rather, the aim was to open the way for the expropriation of Jewish assets and pressure the Jews into leaving Germany. Müller and Heydrich emphasized in their telex to all Gestapo offices in the Reich that, above all, well-to-do Jews

72 Memoirs of Moritz Mayers, YVA, Record Group 033/80.

73 Statistics quoted from Karin Orth, *Die "Konzentrationslager-SS" — Sozialstrukturelle Analysen und biographische Studien einer nationalsozialistischen Funktionselite*, PhD dissertation submitted to Hamburg University, 1997, p. 155.

74 Cf. among others Falk Pingel, *Häftlinge unter SS-Herrschaft. Widerstand, Selbstbehauptung und Vernichtung im Konzentrationslager*, Hamburg, 1978, p. 94.

were to be arrested. On 16 November Heydrich ordered that the arrests be halted and that all Jews over the age of 60 and those who were sick or handicapped be released.[75] Jews whose presence was required at *Arisierungsverhandlungen* (Aryanization negotiations), were also to be released: "*Arisierungsverhandlungen* must not be disrupted by preventive detention of business owners or partners. In the interests of desirable *Arisierungen*, such cases are to be dealt with liberally."[76]

Mayor Güntner sent a letter to Karl Beck from Treuchtlingen, then a Jewish prisoner in the Buchenwald camp:

> I hereby inform you that I will purchase your property at 30 *Kirchenstrasse* for the municipality. The purchase price for the property and the existing store furnishings has been set at RM9,000 by the *Kreisleitung*. (...), In order to complete the transaction with the signing of a notarized sales contract, you must name an authorized representative. *Stadtsekretär* Willy Röder has been appointed to transact the business of the local Jews. You are at liberty to also authorize him as your representative. Otherwise you must come here as soon as possible, to which end you may request leave at the commander's office of the concentration camp.[77]

The wife of Moritz Mayer was warned that her husband would not be discharged from the Dachau camp until his brothers and sisters, who lived abroad, released their mortgages on the property. In fact, Moritz Mayer was released earlier than many others but had to sell the house, the property, and the warehouse shares which were owned by the trading company, his brother Albert, and himself. But Moritz and Albert Mayer did not return to Treuchtlingen. They lived with their families for a short time in Munich before leaving Germany in

75 Heydrich to all Stapostellen, 16 November 1938, documented in: Kurt Pätzold, ed., *Verfolgung, Vertreibung, Vernichtung. Dokumente des faschistischen Antisemitismus 1933–1941*, Leipzig 1983, pp. 183–184 (Document no. 144).

76 Rundverfügung Staatspolizeistelle Kassel, 17 November 1938; documented in: Wolf-Arno Kropat, *Kristallnacht in Hessen. Der Judenpogrom vom November 1938. Eine Dokumentation*, Wiesbaden, 1988, pp. 172–173 (Document no. 63).

77 Güntner to Beck, 5 December 1938; TMA, 063/9. Presumably because of the police order of 12 December 1938, which ordered the release of all Jewish prisoners over 50 years of age, the 52-year-old Beck was set free and contacted Güntner on 16 December from Frankfurt where friends had taken him in. Güntner ordered him to appear on 20 December. Beck's property was finally "sold" in March 1939 to Heinrich Distler. Karl Beck succeeded in emigrating to the USA.

February 1939 for Palestine. Before their departure they authorized an "Aryan" businessman in Weissenburg to represent them in further sales transactions.

In the meantime, after the first attempts of local officials in the summer of 1938 to find a new "Aryan" owner for the Meyers' wholesale and retail food business had failed, Willi Schmidt of Duisburg announced his interest. In March 1939, the first sales contract was nullified on Schmidt's application and the value of the business reappraised, not surprisingly, the new figure was lower than the first. The *Landrat* in Weissenburg informed the parties concerned at the end of October 1939: "the reduction of the purchase price was justified due to the belated ascertainment of defects and the need for repairs on the buildings."[78]The purchase price was not paid in cash but instead transferred to a special, blocked account at an exchange bank; access was only possible with special permission of the *Oberfinanzpräsidenten* in Nuremberg. Moritz Mayer recounted that he was granted a sum of RM14,000, of which RM2,500 was immediately deducted for the damage caused on 10 November. Thus, Mayer was required after the fact to pay for the destruction of his own property by others. The *Regierungspräsident* in Ansbach decided in June 1939 that the "Aryan" buyer should pay the government a "compensation fee" of RM3,500[79] — a common token payment demanded by those in power in return for lucrative business takeovers.

In early December 1938, the mayor of Treuchtlingen reported to the *Bezirksamt* in Weissenburg that there had been six Jewish businesses in the town until early November: three textile stores, Neuburger's hardware store, Meyer's food business, and Karl Beck's mothball factory. All businesses were shut down on 10 November.[80] Since *Arisierung* meant not only the expropriation of property but also the elimination of competition,[81] the mayor proposed that the three textile

78 *Landrat* Weissenburg to Etschel, München, and Schmidt, Treuchtlingen, 27 October 1939; YVA, M1DN/198, fol. 586.

79 *Anordnung Regierungspräsident* Ansbach, 14 June 1939; YVA, M1DN/198, fol. 670.

80 *Bürgermeister* Güntner to *Bezirksamt* Weissenburg, 3 December 1938; YVA, M1DN/203, fol. 315.

81 Götz Aly and Susanne Heim have pointed out this aspect in: *Vordenker der Vernichtung. Auschwitz und die deutschen Pläne für eine neue europäische Ordnung*,

stores be closed, but "the other three business [should be] maintained in their entirety in the interests of the town and the public" — with new owners.[82] Meyer's grocery business was deemed "essential for securing the supply of small businesses in Treuchtlingen and surroundings, since this is a wholesale business of considerable size, which provides wares for numerous small businesses from Treuchtlingen and surroundings." Moreover, "An urgent public need" was established for the continued existence of the hardware and machine trading business formerly owned by A. Neuburger which had been bought by the hardware dealer Fritz Ehrentreich, "since even in recent times, mechanics, carpenters and other tradesmen were forced to purchase hardware such as metal fittings, cast iron, etc., in the Jewish store Neuburger, as these wares were not available in other stores, including those in Donauwörth and Weissenburg." Karl Beck's mothball factory was also seen as "a far from unimportant enterprise, which is supposed to be only (sic), unique in the entire Reich." The town was thus "interested in maintaining this plant and having an Aryan continue its operation."[83]

The town's wishes were fulfilled. The textile stores that had belonged to David Bacharach, Wilhelm Bürger, and Ludwig Herz remained closed and their wares distributed among the "Aryan" shops in Treuchtlingen. Ludwig and Helene Herz' house and land were sold at a forced auction on 18 December 1940 to the shoemaker August Feistner from Treuchtlingen for a price of RM1,500.[84] The tailor Hans Lepp opened a new clothing store in the former shop of David Bacharach; Bacharach's real estate was bought by the baker Karl Dörner.[85] Albert Neuburger's house and property were acquired by his former employee Josef Engel. The house and property of Dr. Siegfried Meyerson was purchased by members of the Schuderer family from

Hamburg, 1991; cf. in particular pp. 21–49. See also Frank Bajohr, *"Arisierung" in Hamburg. Die Verdrängung der jüdischen Unternehmer 1933–1945*, Hamburg 1997.

82 *Bürgermeister* to *Bezirksamt*, 3 December 1938, YVA, M1DN/203, fol. 315.

83 *Ibid.*

84 Zuschlagsbeschluss Amtsgericht Weissenburg, 18 December 1940; YVA, M1DN/198, fol. 563.

85 *Bürgermeister* Treuchtlingen to *Landrat* Weissenburg, 21 June 1939; YVA, M1DN/198, fol. 686.

Nuremberg, who thanked the party for the lucrative transaction by transferring RM3,000 as a "*Arisierungsgabe*" to a special account of the NSDAP — Gau Franken, earmarked the *Judenkonto*.[86] The town itself eventually became the new owner of most of the land formerly owned by the Jewish community of Treuchtlingen. The neighboring community of Pappenheim bought the new Jewish cemetery, nearly one hectare in size, for RM800.[87] Those citizens of Treuchtlingen who did not manage to acquire one of the Jewish properties were also provided for. In early December the mayor announced that "on Thursday, 8 December 1938, starting at 2 P.M. in the afternoon, at the address 30 *Kirchenstrasse*, various pieces of used furniture will be sold at cheap prices."[88] Mayor Güntner could proudly report to the *Landrat* in Weissenburg "that Treuchtlingen has been Jew-free since 10 November 1938."[89]

Conclusion

The murders and violent excesses of 9 and 10 November 1938 forced tens of thousands of German Jews to flee. From 1933 to the end of 1937 between 126,000 and 129,000 Jews had left Germany, in 1938 between 33,000 and 40,000 fled, in 1939 another 75,000 to 80,000.[90] Those who stayed behind were robbed of their last possessions. Unemployed and impoverished, they were then called up for forced labor. On 30 January 1939 Hitler threatened the Jews that if it came to war the result would not be the "Bolshevization of the earth" but the "extermination of the Jewish race in Europe." In March 1939, Germany invaded and occupied the rest of the Czechoslovak Republic, a clear breach of the

86 *NSDAP Gau* Franken to the Economics State Ministry, Munich, 12 October 1939; YVA, M1DN/198, fol. 727.

87 *Kaufvertrag*, Urk. Rolle Nr. 466, Notar Dr. C. Johanny, 14 May 1943; YVA, M1DN/198, fol. 610–612.

88 *Bekanntmachung*, 7 December 1938; TMA 063/4.

89 *Bürgermeister* Treuchtlingen to *Landrat* Weissenburg, 29 June 1939, YVA, M1DN/203, fol. 352.

90 Ino Arndt and Heinz Boberach, "Deutsches Reich," in: Wolfgang Benz, ed., *Dimension des Völkermords. Die Zahl der jüdischen Opfer des Nationalsozialismus*, Munich, 1991, p. 34.

Munich Agreement, followed six months later by the German invasion of Poland. In the shadow of war, the "solution of the Jewish problem" became systematic mass murder.

Physical violence, assault, and riots with fatal consequences were part of the practice of National Socialist politics against Jews — not only after but also before 1939. The "deregulation" of German society under the Nazi dictatorship and the unleashing (*Entgrenzung*) of violence, whose perpetrators did not fear punishment but on the contrary were encouraged by the Party when the victims were Jews, clearly fostered an antisemitism that had previously existed in many people's minds only. Terror "from above" was supported by increasing and expanding antisemitic violence "from below," violence that a growing portion of the population participated or at least tolerated. Antisemitism does not merely "happen," it must be thought of and then implemented. Even before the November pogrom the climate in German society was charged with violence. Attacking Jews, destroying their homes and synagogues, beating, injuring, or even killing people was no longer the work of only a few. The pogrom in Treuchtlingen gives us an idea of how many "normal Germans" were involved in the violent assaults against Jews in 1938.

Of the ninety-two Jews who still lived in Treuchtlingen in mid-1938, forty-eight were deported and murdered, among them the Bacharach, Hänlein, and Herz families. Fourteen Jews from Treuchtlingen managed to escape to the United States; these included Karl Beck, Louis Freimann, Siegfried Weinmann, and Albert Neuburger and his family. Wilhelm and Rosa Bürger emigrated to France and ten Jewish citizens of Treuchtlingen succeeded in emigrating to Palestine, among them Albert and Moritz Mayer and their families. The Christian-Jewish Gutmann family remained in Augsburg and survived the Nazi regime. There is to date no trace of other former Jewish residents of Treuchtlingen.

In the late fifties, following an initiative of then-mayor and Social Democrat Hans Döbler, the Jewish cemetery was restored. A memorial and a plaque recall the fate of the Jewish community of Treuchtlingen, a sign in the Uhlengasse marks the site where the synagogue formerly stood. None of the surviving former Jewish citizens of Treuchtlingen returned to the town. There is no Jewish community in Treuchtlingen today.

The Policy of Expropriation

The Minister of Economics and the Expulsion of the Jews from the German Economy

ALBERT FISCHER

Hjalmar Schacht lived from 1877 to 1970. During this time he was twice president of the Reichsbank, the first time as a left-wing liberal from 1923 to 1930 and again as a follower of Adolf Hitler from 1933 to 1937. In addition, he served under Hitler as Minister of Economics from 1934 to 1937 and as Minister without Portfolio until 1943.[1] Schacht was thus one of the dominating figures in the field of economic policy and the prime mover of the National Socialist economic upturn.[2] Not only was he a powerful figure in the economy during the first years of the Hitler regime, he played a significant political role as well. In 1936 the *New York Times Magazine* called him "dictator no. 2" after Hitler, the "dictator no. 1."[3]

Hjalmar Schacht's political role has always been a subject of dispute and controversy — with one exception: for decades there had been widespread agreement that Schacht had opposed Nazi antisemitism, in particular that he had prevented the expulsion of the Jews from the German economy. The business world was considered to have been a so-called refuge in which, despite the Nuremberg laws, the Jews were

1 Amos E. Simpson, *Hjalmar Schacht in Perspective* (Studies in European History. No. XVIII), The Hague, 1969; Edward N. Peterson, *Hjalmar Schacht. For and against Hitler. A Political-Economic Study of Germany 1923–1945*, Boston, 1954.

2 Loc. cit. Furthermore: Harold James, *The German Slump. Politics and Economics 1924–1936*, Oxford, 1986; Harold James, "Hjalmar Schacht. Der Magier des Geldes," in: *Die braune Elite II. 21 weitere biographische Skizzen*, Ronald Smelser et al., eds., Darmstadt, 1993, pp. 206–218.

3 Emil Lengyel, "Schacht Challenges the Nazi Hotheads," in *New York Times Magazine*, 1 September 1935.

able to continue comparatively unmolested until the second half of the thirties, almost until Schacht stepped down as Minister of Economics.[4] In the postwar years Schacht himself claimed again and again that this was the case. Once he even said that he would feel embarrassed to admit the extent to which he had helped the Jews in Germany.[5]

However, in the 1980s an Israeli historian, Avraham Barkai, refuted that view. He maintained that Schacht could not have done much for the Jews who were working in industry and commerce, nor for the Jews in general.[6] But Barkai did not support this view with specific research on the Jewish policy of the head of the central bank. He announced this as hypothesis that should be further investigated. Soon afterwards other historians, such as Reinhard Rürup and Werner Mosse for example, called for a more detailed investigation of Schacht's role in relation to the Jews.[7]

This article takes up the challenge, and poses, examines and attempts to answer the following questions. Firstly, what was Schacht's attitude towards the Jews in principle? Did he actually want to help them? Secondly, did he fight for the Jews to the extent he afterwards claimed? In other words, how far did he act if he really wanted to help them? Thirdly, did he achieve any notable results? If he did help the Jews, was he successful? The investigation only covers the years up until the dismissal of Schacht as Reichsbank President in January 1939. The investigation does not deal with the war years and the mass extermination of the Jews. It is limited to examining the extent to which Schacht opposed the expulsion of the German Jews from their jobs and from the country prior to January 1939.

4 Uwe D. Adam, *Judenpolitik im Dritten Reich*, Düsseldorf, 1972, p. 173. Willi A. Boelcke, *Die deutsche Wirtschaft 1930–1945*, Düsseldorf, 1983, p. 210; Rolf Puppo, *Die wirtschaftsrechtliche Gesetzgebung des Dritten Reiches*, Konstanz, 1987, p. 274; Karl A. Schleunes, *The Twisted Road to Auschwitz. Nazi Policy toward German Jews 1933–39*, London, 1972, p. 217.

5 Hjalmar Schacht, *76 Jahre meines Lebens*, Bad Wörishofen, 1953, p. 590.

6 Avraham Barkai, *Vom Boykott zur "Entjudung." Der wirtschaftliche Existenzkampf der Juden im Dritten Reich*, Frankfurt am Main, 1988, p. 73.

7 Reinhard Rürup, "Das Ende der Emanzipation: Die antijüdische Politik in Deutschland von der 'Machtergreifung' bis zum Zweiten Weltkrieg," in: *Die Juden im nationalsozialistischen Deutschland. The Jews in Nazi Germany. 1933–1943*, Arnold Pauker, ed., Tübingen, 1986, pp. 97–114; p. 110, n. 54.

The source of the research material was the Central State Archives at Potsdam in the former German Democratic Republic, which houses the files of the Reichsbank and the Ministry of Economics. The Federal Archives at Koblenz, the Foreign Office records and some municipal archives in the Federal Republic of Germany were made use of as well. The records of the International Military Tribunal held at Nuremberg, those of the de-Nazification Chamber at Ludwigsburg, and the records of American archives at the Institute of Contemporary History in Munich were also consulted.

The investigation revealed that Avraham Barkai was correct in his assumption. Schacht neither fought for the Jewish minority to the extent claimed, nor did any efforts on his part really contribute to protecting the Jews. And, most importantly, not only was Schacht *unable* to achieve as much as he himself claimed, he actually did not *want* to oppose Nazi policy. In fact, from time to time he even helped to tighten those laws discriminating against the Jews.[8]

This is not as surprising as it may seem since Schacht was never the champion of the German Jews as he is portrayed by his biographer Pentzlin, for example.[9] According to his own confessions, he was not. Even in Schacht's post war writings, antisemitic resentments surfaced again and again. And in 1953 he was still complaining about Jewish overrepresentation in the spheres of culture, justice, administration, and medicine in the Weimar Republic. He called this "the break-in of an alien spirit into the spirit of the host nation,"[10] and he concluded: "If they [the Jews] had been a little bit less urgent in these things, no one would have done anything to them."[11]

The fact is that Schacht did not oppose the expulsion of the Jews from the civil service, the bar and the medical profession at all. He kept silent at cabinet meetings.[12] He implemented the racial laws in his Ministry of Economics and at the Reichsbank, although he was

8 The whole investigation has already been published in German: Albert Fischer, *Hjalmar Schacht und Deutschlands "Judenfrage." Der "Wirtschaftsdiktator" und die Vertreibung der Juden aus der deutschen Wirtschaft*, Cologne, 1995.

9 Heinz Pentzlin, *Hjalmar Schacht. Leben und Wirken einer umstrittenen Persönlichkeit*, Berlin, 1980, p. 14.

10 Schacht, *76 Jahre*, p. 450

11 Institut für Zeitgeschichte, Munich, Sp. 1/12, Stuttgart, F.1/89.

12 Konrad Repgen and Hans Booms, eds, *Akten der Reichskanzlei. Regierung Hitler*

not obliged to do so. That is to say he personally arranged and signed the decrees that ordered the dismissal of Jews and of those Germans married to Jews.[13] Furthermore, Schacht justified the antisemitic policy in public and made light of it to the international community.[14] As he had justified the laws and edicts of the early years of the Third Reich, so he energetically defended the Nuremberg Laws.[15] In November 1935 he declared to the Saxonian Chamber of Commerce:

> I welcome the [racial] classification that is realized by the Nuremberg laws. ... I welcome ... that the Jew won't be a citizen of the Reich any more, that he is being repelled back into his isolation from which he has pushed out of to dominate the German people in an impertinent and impudent manner, that he is being repelled into his ghetto. That is completely right and justifiable. If we had 600,000 Chinese people in Germany today who presumed to occupy our theaters, our press, our culture, we wouldn't tolerate it and would put them into a Chinese ghetto. ... So we have to agree to the Jewish policy of the Führer and, you may be surprised to hear, that of Julius Streicher as well. The race problem will be solved by the Nuremberg Laws and by throwing the Jews out of the administration, the theaters and so on.[16]

By the time of this statement Schacht had gone a long way in the sphere of Jewish policy. He had begun his career as a pronounced pro-Jew and, having entered the political arena as a founder and executive member of the left-wing liberal German Democratic Party (GDP),[17] he

1933–1938, part 1, 1933/34, vol. 1, 30 January to 31 August 1933, documents no. 1–206, Boppard, 1983.

13 Bundesarchiv, Abt. Potsdam (hereafter BAP), 25.01, Deutsche Reichsbank, no. 7237, 7238, 7251.

14 See for example: Gerhard L. Weinberg, "Schachts Besuch in den USA im Jahre 1933," in *Vierteljahreshefte für Zeitgeschichte,* 11 (1963), pp. 166–180; Edwin Black, *The Transfer Agreement. The Untold Story of the Secret Agreement between the Third Reich and Jewish Palestine*, New York, 1984, pp. 115–116; Hjalmar Schacht, "German Trade and German Debts," *Foreign Affairs*, October 1934, pp. 1–5; p. 4.

15 *Der Prozess gegen die Hauptkriegsverbrecher vor dem Internationalen Militärgerichtshof. Nürnberg. 14. November 1945—1. Oktober 1946*, Nuremberg 1947–49, vol. 36, doc. 450-EC, p. 525.

16 BAP, 25.01, Deutsche Reichsbank, no. 7169.

17 Lothar Albertin, *Liberalismus und Demokratie am Anfang der Weimarer Republik. Eine vergleichende Analyse der Deutschen Demokratischen Partei und der Deutschen Volkspartei*, Düsseldorf, 1972, pp. 95–96, 179.

had taken over the chair of the Reichsbank President as the candidate of the left.[18] The fact that the GDP fought for the rights of the Jewish minority more than any other political party meant that Schacht for many years had been exposed to the barrage of insults and ridicule of right-wing demagogues. They had called him an "obedient pupil of Jewish bankers,"[19] and claimed that he was a Hungarian Jew whose real name was "Hajum Schachtel"[20] or a Danish Jew "Chaim Schachtel."[21]

Schacht supported the "Aryanization" outside industry and commerce without qualification. Moreover, his commitment to the Jews in the business world was not as significant as claimed either by himself or by his followers afterwards.[22] He did indeed try several times to check antisemitic encroachments. He mentioned them in ministerial meetings. He issued decrees regarding the matter. He rebuked local authorities.[23] However, Schacht's ministry and the Reichsbank helped the Jewish firms too infrequently and too halfheartedly to warrant the claim of being a defender of the Jews.

This is clearly illustrated in three incidents that occurred in the banking sphere; each reflects the daily, routine, harassment of Jewish banks as well as the attitude of Schacht's ministry and the Reichsbank. The banking sphere is especially relevant, for two reasons. Firstly, it was under Schacht's control, or better under his responsibility. As Minister of Economics, as President of the Reichsbank, and as chairman of the supervisory authority for the credit system he was in a very strong position.[24] Secondly, the importance of the Jews in the private banking sector was considerable — not in the banking system as a whole but in

18 Helmut Müller, *Die Zentralbank eine Nebenregierung. Reichsbankpräsident Hjalmar Schacht als Politiker der Weimarer Republik*, Opladen, 1973, p. 36.

19 Alfred Rosenberg, *Dreissig Novemberköpfe*, Berlin, 1927, p. 239.

20 Quoted by Norbert Mühlen, *Der Zauberer. Leben und Anleihen des Dr. Hjalmar Horace Greeley Schacht*, Zürich, 2nd edition, 1938, p. 31.

21 Document Center, Berlin, B 328, Hjalmar Schacht.

22 Hjalmar Schacht: "As long as I was minister of Economics not a single act of injustice was done to the Jews in the business world" (IMT, doc.NI-406, p. 37). See furthermore: Schacht, *76 Jahre*, p. 404. Hjalmar Schacht, *Abrechnung mit Hitler*, Hamburg, 1948, p. 13.

23 Fischer, *Hjalmar Schacht*, pp. 113–209.

24 Christopher Kopper, *Zwischen Marktwirtschaft und Dirigismus. Bankenpolitik im "Dritten Reich" 1933–1939*, Bonn, 1995, pp. 71–74.

the private banking sector. For example, the large joint-stock companies that still exist in Germany today were founded by Jewish bankers: The *Deutsche Bank*, the *Dresdner Bank* and the *Commerzbank*. Before 1900 half of the leading positions in the limited companies were held by people of Jewish origin, and in 1928 this figure was still at least ten percent.[25] In 1930 fifty percent of sole trader and partnership private banks were still Jewish owned.[26]

The first incident occurred in the autumn of 1935. The Saxon state withdrew the financial administration of the state lottery from a large private bank because its owners were Jewish. The bank had administered the lottery for 75 years. It was not without good reason that the management of the bank feared the deleterious effects on its reputation and concern among its clients if the revocation were to be published. The bank therefore asked the Reichsbank to prevent publication of this decision. But the Reichsbank's Board of Directors ignored the request. "We won't do anything about it," remarked one director, and the Jewish bankers found themselves on their own.[27]

The second incident was the declaration by the newspapers of Lübeck that they would publish the usual joint Christmas greetings of the local banks, only if the Jewish banks remained excluded. The local banking association protested. Schacht's ministry, however, remained silent, tacitly accepting the advertising ban on Jewish banks.[28] One might add that these newspapers generally refused to accept advertisements from Jewish firms.[29]

The third incident occurred in the autumn of 1936 and is particularly illuminating of Schacht's role inside his ministry. The President of the Hamburg Law Society had proposed revoking the registration of a lawyer because he had begun working for the Warburg Bank. Schacht's subordinates were strongly opposed. They drafted a letter to the Minister of Justice, demanding "that the aspects of the racial

25 Jakob Lestschinsky, *Das wirtschaftliche Schicksal des deutschen Judentums. Aufstieg Wandlung Krise Ausblick*, Berlin, 1932, p. 91.

26 Alfred Marcus, *Die wirtschaftliche Krise des deutschen Juden. Eine soziologische Untersuchung*, Berlin, 1931, p. 48.

27 BAP, 31.01, Reichswirtschaftsministerium, no. 15514.

28 Loc. cit.

29 Bundesarchiv, Koblenz (hereafter BAK), R 2, Reichsfinanzministerium, no. 4863. Furthermore: Uwe Westphal, *Werbung im Dritten Reich*, Berlin, 1989.

question should come second to the economic aspects in the struggle for the preservation and fostering of our foreign relations." They further protested with detailed complaints against the harassment of (Jewish-run), companies dealing with foreign countries. For Schacht, however, such wording was definitely going too far and he had these remarks as well as the quoted sentence completely deleted. The critical letter was never sent.[30]

Table 1. Private Bankers in Germany 1 January 1936[31]

Total Assets (Millions RM)	**Number**		**Total Assets (1,000 RM)**	
	"Non-Aryan"	**"Aryan"**	**"Non-Aryan"**	**"Aryan"**
0–0,1	71	117	3,146	5,742
0,1–0,5	133	227	33,965	59,056
0,5–1,0	54	97	37,796	68,340
1,0–10,0	72	112	217,871	276,242
10,0–50,0	10	17	181,871	342,867
50,0–	5	0	512,123	0
	345	570	986,772	752,247
	915		1,739,019	

The implications of these individual incidents become more significant when seen in the broader context. By the time Schacht was dismissed as President of the Reichsbank in 1939, the Jews had been completely driven out of the banking world.[32] During the first three years after Hitler's seizure of power, almost a quarter of the 1,300 private bankers had given up banking. The vast majority of the more than 300 closed banks had been Jewish owned.[33] After 1935 the "selection process" continued, as can be seen from Table 1 and Figure 1. The table shows

30 BAP, 31.01, Reichswirtschaftsministerium, no. 15514.

31 BAP, 25.01, Deutsche Reichsbank, no. 6790.

32 Albert Fischer, "Jüdische Privatbanken im "Dritten Reich," *Scripta Mercaturae, Zeitschrift für Wirtschafts-und Sozialgeschichte,* 28 (1994), p. 1–54, p. 37.

33 Ibid., p. 17.

that in 1935 half of the private banking firms were still Jewish, and the diagram illustrates the extent of the "Aryanization" during the years 1936 and 1937. According to the balance sheets one-third of the banks were "Aryanized," another one-third entered into "Aryanization" negotiations.

Figure 1. Jewish Private Banks — Total Assets January 1936 to April 1938 (%)[34]

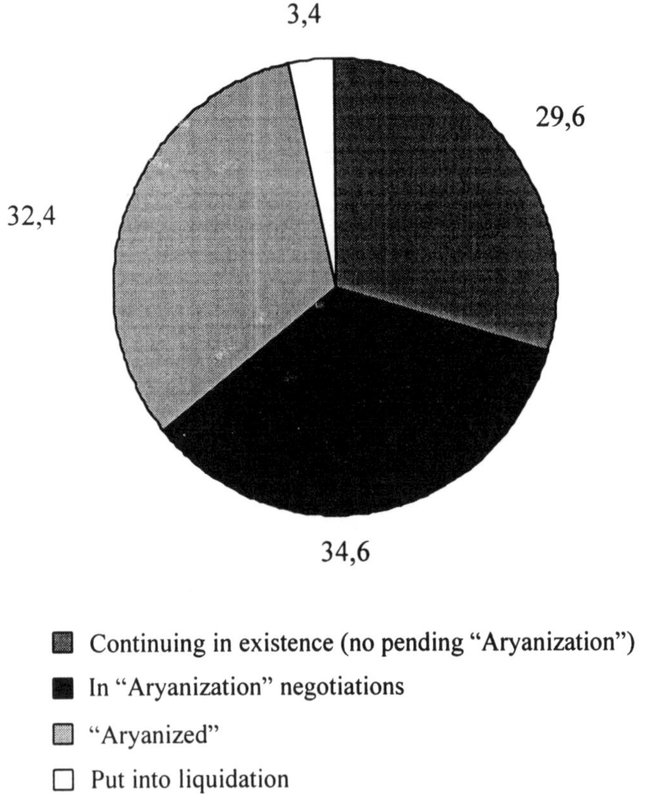

34 BAP, 25.01, Deutsche Reichsbank, no. 6581, no. 6791.

Unfortunately there are no data for November 1937, the month when Schacht was dismissed as Minister of Economics. But the aforementioned secret figures provided by Reichsbank statisticians are evidence enough, even though they continue beyond Schacht's period in office, until the spring of 1938. This is explained firstly by the fact that Schacht remained Reichsbank President until 1939 and was thus responsible for the banking system; Secondly, a significant number of the "Aryanization" procedures that were completed after Schacht left had already been initiated. Thirdly, and most importantly, the closure of the Jewish banking firms had begun long before the statistical registration in 1936. As already mentioned, almost half of them had to close during the first three years of Hitler's leadership. Incidentally, looking beyond the banking sphere to the economy as a whole, we find a similar picture: By the summer of 1935 a quarter of *all* Jewish enterprises had already been "Aryanized" or put into liquidation.[35]

Doubtless Schacht was not enthusiastic about the "Aryanizations." He was only interested in a sound economy, and the persecution of Jewish firms jeopardized this. However, when considering Jewish businesses overall and not only select and famous firms, it is important to recognize that Schacht and his officials, even if they really tried, were simply unable to halt the process. Konrad Fuchs captures the essence of the situation in his monograph on the Schocken company. He claims that even if Schacht had remained minister the Jewish owners would have taken the same measures that they took after his dismissal, because "the reasons which had required a certain consideration for the Jews in business life had lost their relevance."[36]

The staying or leaving of Hjalmar Schacht would not have affected the "Aryanization" process. "Private Aryanization" had already taken place during Schacht's period of office. The state increased its involvement not because of Schacht's dismissal. The state increased it because the factors that had earlier prevented it — namely depression and unemployment on the one hand and dependence on trade with Western Europe and the United States on the other hand — no longer existed. By 1937 there was full employment, and foreign trade had decreased

35 Barkai, *Vom Boykott*, p. 80.

36 Konrad Fuchs, *Ein Konzern aus Sachsen: das Kaufhaus Schocken als Spiegelbild deutscher Wirtschaft und Politik 1901 bis 1953*, Stuttgart, 1991, p. 237.

and shifted significantly to other countries.[37] Thus the economic risks against completing the "Aryanization" process had become calculable and Schacht was now dispensable. The reasons which had both brought Schacht to power and required some consideration for the Jewish enterprises no longer existed. The minister's dismissal should be viewed, therefore, as a result of the economic and political development in general, and not as a cause.

Moreover, an essential point is that the fundamental course had been changed, with Schacht's approval, long before his dismissal. At an executive meeting on 20 August 1935 he had made it clear that he basically accepted the Nazi objectives. He had no objection to either reducing the influence of Jews in the business world or to expelling them from it. His only stipulation was that it should take place gradually, and through the enactment and use of laws. Basically, damaging effects on the economy were to be avoided.[38] A year later, in September 1936, a year before Schacht left the Ministry of Economics, his Ministry and the Ministry of the Interior had come to an agreement that the question regarding the complete expulsion of all the Jews from Germany had to be tackled. From this time on the only economic activity to be allowed to the Jews was that which was absolutely necessary for them to earn their living.[39]

The Ministry and the central bank acted accordingly. In 1936 the Ministry of Economics agreed to a marking of Jewish firms. It instructed, in full agreement with the Nazi party and the Ministry of the Interior, which firms should be classified as Jewish and which not.[40] At the same time the Reichsbank recorded the racial ownership of all German export businesses.[41] Later on Schacht himself gave the order to

37 René Erbe, *Die nationalsozialistische Wirtschaftspolitik 1933–1939 im Lichte der modernen Theorie*, Zürich, 1958, pp. 72, 76, 82, 100.

38 BAK, R 18, Reichsministerium des Innern, no. 5513. Institut für Zeitgeschichte, Munich, F 71/2 and IMT, doc. NG-4067/II. *Die jüdische Emigration aus Deutschland 1933–1941. Die Geschichte einer Austreibung*, Frankfurt am Main, 1985, no. 131, pp. 71–72; *Akten der Partei-Kanzlei der NSDAP*, Munich, 1983, no. 21251.

39 BAK, R 18, Reichsministerium des Innern, no. 5514.

40 Hans-Joachim Fliedner: *Die Judenverfolgung in Mannheim 1933–1945.* Vol. 2. *Dokumente*, Stuttgart, 1971, no 117b, p. 194.

41 BAP, 25.01, Deutsche Reichsbank, no. 7252.

prohibit Jewish banks from selling and purchasing foreign currencies.[42] It is no surprise then that the Reichsbank finally decided to curtail its business with Jews as much as possible and under no circumstances to undertake any new business with them.[43]

There are some other notable points. Firstly Schacht was convinced that his actions always had the approval of Adolf Hitler. Not only the chancellor explicitly encouraged the head of the central bank to keep up his relations with Jewish high finance.[44] It is important to note here that generally there was no discord between Schacht and Hitler or the party's headquarters at Munich; there were conflicts between Schacht and other individual Nazis such as Goebbels, some Gauleiters and the leader of the German Labor Front, Robert Ley, but never with the Nazi party as a whole. In fact, Schacht's statements were nearly always preceded by similar or identical statements from the party's headquarters or by a Nazi minister, or Schacht insured himself by consulting party officials before voicing his opinion.[45]

No, Schacht did not risk any real conflict with Hitler or with the headquarters of the Nazi party. Neither was he the only politician who occasionally opposed the antisemitic terror. His predecessors within the Ministry of Economics, Hugenberg, Schmitt, and other important Nazi figures such as Rudolf Hess or Wilhelm Frick did so, too.[46] Their dissent was based not on pro-Jewish motives but on economic ones: In the first years after the *Machtergreifung* they agreed completely with Schacht that absolute priority should be given to Germany's economic recovery. Hitler had himself ordered the party to stop and to prevent all encroachments on banks (March 1934). "A banking crisis," he had said, "would deal a deathblow to the economic upturn which would make everything else fail."[47]

This is precisely the point: the priority of the economic targets, and less a demand for justice, was Schacht's motive for sometimes

42 Fischer, "Jüdische Privatbanken", p. 30.

43 BAP, 25.01, Deutsche Reichsbank, no. 7259.

44 *Der Prozess gegen die Hauptkriegsverbrecher*, vol. 12, p. 490.

45 Fischer, *Hjalmar Schacht*, p. 224.

46 Helmut Genschel, *Die Verdrängung der Juden aus der Wirtschaft im Dritten Reich*, Göttingen, 1966.

47 *Akten der Reichskanzlei*, vol. 2, doc. 320, p. 1197/n. 3, p. 1198.

intervening in favor of Jewish companies. Problems in economic policy, or better in the economic sphere in general, would reflect on the Minister of Economics — Hjalmar Schacht. The words with which he concluded his complaint about the harassment of some banks in March 1933, when he was only the central banker, speak for themselves: "My request [for stopping this harassment] is strictly limited to the area of banking... because I am not responsible for other economic spheres."[48] In the summer of 1934 he was appointed Minister of Economics. From this time on he was responsible for the whole economy, and because of this he occasionally asked to speak. Had he been Minister of Finance or Minister of Agriculture he most likely would have kept his silence as Schwerin von Krosigk or Eltz-Rübenach had done because in this case he *would not have been responsible* for the economic sphere.

Finally, the point should be made that Hjalmar Schacht was quite willing to take measures against the Jews if those measures could serve to improve or stabilize the economy. It was Schacht who excluded the Jews from the foreign exchange markets in order to limit the selling of Reichsmarks by emigrating Jews.[49] It was Schacht who later forbade the Jews nearly any foreign currency transactions.[50] Jews who survived the Third Reich complained bitterly about this measure.[51] Schacht was also responsible for making the flight of capital punishable by death from 1936 on, and tightening the foreign exchange laws to such a degree that Jewish property could be legally confiscated.[52] The common denominator of these measures was the objective of a prospering economy. Sometimes the economic policy worked in the Jews' favor, for example when Schacht, fearing damage to foreign trade, opposed the antisemitic terror, and sometimes it worked directly against them such as in the case of the foreign exchange policy.

The fact that Schacht helped Jews in certain individual cases should not be overlooked. He especially supported his long-standing friends in high finance.[53] These efforts are without doubt indeed commendable.

48 BAP, 31.01, Reichswirtschaftsministerium, no. 15514.

49 Adam, *Judenpolitik*, p. 148/n. 24. BAP, 31.01, Reichswirtschaftsministerium, no. 16928.

50 *Reichsgesetzblatt* I, 1936, p. 525.

51 Institut für Zeitgeschichte, Munich, Sp. 1/5, Ludwigsburg, p. 463.

52 Reichsgesetzblatt I, 1936, pp. 999–1001.

53 Institut für Zeitgeschichte, Munich, Sp. 1/4, Ludwigsburg, p. 330.

However, firstly one should note that his activities were quite limited. He had already told Max Warburg in 1934 that he would not be able to do a lot for the Jews.[54] Later he would shrug his shoulders, leaving to their fate even those Jews who personally appealed to him for help.[55] Secondly, his position was not very different from those of his colleagues. Other members of the regime acted in a similar way. Schwerin von Krosigk, the Minister of Finance, helped some of those Jews who turned to him;[56] and even Hermann Göring supported his Jewish friends.[57] So Schacht's effort in individual cases has to be acknowledged, but within the Nazi government he was not the only one who helped Jews. It should be repeated that his behavior and actions were not so different from those of his contemporaries as has been claimed, and *if* it was different then it was different for economic reasons.

On balance one has to say that the often-mentioned restraining role of the Ministry of Economics, the Reichsbank and especially of Hjalmar Schacht, was a quite small one. Of course Schacht and his subordinates were not the driving forces of the "Aryanization" process, and they certainly opposed any acts of violence such as *Kristallnacht*. A prosperous economy would not be able to withstand violence, boycotts and the like. Nonetheless, we have to note that they helped the Jews only somewhat more than did other government institutions.

Finally, not only had Schacht done everything within his power to help Hitler attain the chancellorship, he was also responsible for the famous economic upturn and for eradicating mass unemployment. Thus he made an important or even vital contribution to the popularity of Hitler and to the internal stabilization of the regime. Unintentionally so he cleared the way for all that followed.

54 Max M. Warburg, *Aus meinen Aufzeichnungen*, New York, 1952, p. 154. Lutz Graf Schwerin von Krosigk, *Staatsbankrott. Die Geschichte der Finanzpolitik des Deutschen Reiches von 1920 bis 1945*, Frankfurt am Main, 1974, p. 221.

55 Henry Bernhard, *Finis Germaniae. Aufzeichnungen und Betrachtungen*, Stuttgart, 1947, p. 221.

56 Stefan Mehl, *Das Reichsfinanzministerium und die Verfolgung der deutschen Juden 1933–1943*, Berlin, 1990, p. 21.

57 Manfred Funke, *Starker oder schwacher Diktator? Hitlers Herrschaft und die Deutschen*, Düsseldorf, 1989, p. 54. Alfred Kube, *Pour le mérite und Hakenkreuz. Hermann Göring im Dritten Reich*, Munich, 1986, p. 204.

The "Aryanization" of Jewish Companies and German Society: The Example of Hamburg[1]

FRANK BAJOHR

I

The process of eliminating the Jews from the economy in Hamburg began in the spring of 1933 with an apparent paradox. On the one hand the situation was marked by an eruptive antisemitism "from below," which, independent of government initiatives, urged that the elimination of the Jews be speeded up. In the course of uninhibited riotous antisemitism, SA men smashed the windows of Jewish businesses, sealed off the entrances to Jewish-owned department stores and attacked Jewish passers-by.[2] Arbitrary house search warrants, violent trespassing, and boycott campaigns against department stores and "penny bazaars," which were intended to enforce the immediate dismissal of Jewish employees were the order of the day in the spring of 1933. Antisemitic campaigns were also organized by numerous middle-class professional associations, which excluded Jews from membership without being ordered to do so and partly against the vote of the head of their associations. These courses of action were particularly apparent in

1 The following accounts are based on my dissertation *"Arisierung" in Hamburg. Die Verdrängung der jüdischen Unternehmer 1933–1945*, 2nd edition, Hamburg, 1998. Indispensable source of background information on the history of "Aryanization" continues to be Helmut Genschel, *Die Verdrängung der Juden aus der Wirtschaft im Dritten Reich*, Göttingen, 1966, and Avraham Barkai, *Vom Boykott zur "Entjudung". Der wirtschaftliche Existenzkampf der Juden im Dritten Reich 1933–1943*, Frankfurt am Main, 1987.

2 On the topic of violent demonstrations by the Hamburg SA units see also OSOBY (The Special Archive in Moscow), 721.1.2339, p.47.

professional associations of, for example, solicitors, estate agents and market traders, who even before 1933 had complained about the "overcrowding" of their professions and demanded limitations by the state regarding membership requirements.[3] The National Socialist *Kampfbund für den gewerblichen Mittelstand* declared boycotts on deliveries to Jewish companies and organized "Brown Masses" in Hamburg which introduced the products of the middle-class economy and warned against buying in Jewish shops.[4]

But even without such organizational directives "from above," middle-class businessmen organized boycott campaigns against their Jewish counterparts such as Beiersdorf by means of newspaper advertisements, pamphlets and stickers ("Whoever buys Nivea articles is helping to support a Jewish company") and joined forces in antisemitic groups (namely, *Interessengemeinschaft "Deutsche Marke"* — the "German Trademark" Combine; and *ADEFA — Arbeitsgemeinschaft deutscharischer Fabrikanten der Bekleidungsindustrie* — the Working group of German Aryan Manufacturers in the Clothing Industry).[5]

On the other hand, the new National Socialist rulers in Hamburg kept tactically aloof in the first years of their rule. They even stepped in to protect hard-pressed Jewish firms and took action against middle-class radical antisemites. For example, the head of the Hamburg Tailors' Guild was relieved of his office for "endangering economic peace" when he led an antisemitic campaign against a mail-order fabric business in an association magazine.[6] In some individual cases the Hamburg

3 On the topic of anti-Jewish activities by solicitors, estate agents and market dealers see *Hamburgischer Correspondent*, 7 April 1933; Staatsarchiv Hamburg (hereafter StAHH), Staatsamt, 106, Letters from the representative of Hamburg in Berlin to the Hamburger Staatsamt dated 30 November 1933; Letter of Jakob Boldes to the Ministry of the Interior dated 19 January 1934, Bundesarchiv, Abteilung Potsdam (hereafter BAP), Reichwirtschaftsministerium, 13862, pp. 68–71.

4 *Hamburger Tageblatt*, 9 September 1933.

5 On antisemitic campaigns of this type, in particular against the Hamburg Beiersdorf AG, see Frank Bajohr and Joachim Szodrzynski, " 'Keine jüdische Hautcreme mehr benutzen.' Die antisemitische Kampagne gegen die Hamburger Firma Beiersdorf," in: *Die Juden in Hamburg 1590–1990*, Arno Herzig, ed., Hamburg, 1991, pp. 515–526.

6 StAHH, Justizverwaltung I, II Ba Vol.2, No.6, letter from the deputy NSDAP- Gau Economic Consultant to Dr. Breiholdt dated 31 August 1934.

representative in Berlin represented the interests of Jewish companies in the institutions of the Reich right up to 1937.[7] Along these lines the *Hamburger Wirtschaftsbehörde* declared to the *Reichspressestelle* of the NSDAP in 1933 that antisemitic campaigns were damaging to its economic policy which was "responsible for the upkeep of job opportunities in Hamburg."[8]

The reasons for this preliminary tactical restraint lay in the economic structure and the economic situation of Hamburg — a port and a commercial center. Firstly, the National Socialist rulers of Hamburg feared that the antisemitic activities were endangering trade relations of the Hamburg economy. The relentless reports in the international press about the excesses of antisemitism "from below" had alarmed them. *Gauleiter* Kaufmann, in a conversation with Hitler in November 1934 concluded that "Hamburg is attracting the attention of the whole world," its port forming an "open boundary" which strongly favors "foreign propaganda."[9] The National Socialists so feared of foreign boycott campaigns that the Hamburg Senator for Economic Affairs, for example, withdrew the prohibition against Jewish butcheries after Jewish dockworkers in North Africa had refused to unload ships from the port of Hamburg.[10]

Until 1938 Hamburg was officially recognized as an economically "depressed area." Contrary to the trend in the Reich, the unemployment figures in Hamburg declined slowly due to the National Socialist policy of armament and self-sufficiency, which was favorable for industry and agriculture but damaging to Hamburg's foreign trade. Almost 42.5% of those employed in Hamburg were working in the trade and transport sector (the average in the Reich was 16.9%),[11] which was suffering from stagnation of foreign trade under the National Socialists. The

7 See StAHH, Staatsamt, 106, letter from the representative of Hamburg in Berlin to Hamburgisches Staatsamt dated 31 March 1937.

8 Company archives of the Beiersdorf AG, Section 130, letter from the Behörde für Wirtschaft to the Reichspressestelle of the NSDAP dated 6 October 1933.

9 Quoted from StAHH, Staatsamt, 91, protocol of the representative of Hamburg in Berlin dated 2 November 1934.

10 Archives of the Institut für die Geschichte der deutschen Juden, Hamburg, 14–001.2, Memoirs of Max Plaut, "Die jüdische Gemeinde in Hamburg 1933–1943" (taken from a tape recorded interview from 1973), p. 5.

11 *Die Volks-, Berufs- und Betriebszählung vom 16. Juni 1925, Statistik des Hamburgischen Staates*, Hamburg, 1928, Book XXXIII, Part 2, p. 82, Übersicht

result was dissatisfaction and dissonance among the people. This was particularly evident in the results of the plebiscite on 19 August 1934 when over twenty percent of the citizens of Hamburg voted against a merger of the offices of the Reich Chancellor and the Reich President to be under Hitler, their "no" votes constituting twice the average number of "no" votes throughout the Reich. *Gauleiter* Kaufmann described the election results as "the most bitter disappointment during my long term of activity within the party."[12]

In this context any offensive action against the more than 1,500 Jewish companies in Hamburg would have worsened the economic crisis and endangered the stability of National Socialist rule, which the latter were eager to prevent. Thus, until 1936–37 the main feature of Hamburg's policy towards the Jews was a certain tactical restraint, in particular when compared with other regions and cities such as Munich where the National Socialists had already taken more radical steps than in Hamburg. This meant that the Jewish businesses in Hamburg were able to hold their own for much longer than in other places. Avraham Barkai estimated that until 1938 sixty to seventy percent of Jewish businesses throughout the Reich closed down.[13] According to figures produced by the NSDAP-*Gauwirtschaftsberater* (Gau Economic Consultant), the number of Jewish business in Hamburg decreased by only twenty percent during the same period. Even if the latter figure is most certainly too low,[14] the Jewish businesses in Hamburg were in a better position than in most other cities in the first years of National Socialist rule[15] — paradoxically not least because the economic situation in Hamburg was quite unfavorable on the whole.

67 (Die Wohnbevölkerung in 20 deutschen Grossstädten im Jahre 1925 nach Wirtschaftsabteilungen).

12 Quoted from a letter from Kaufmann to Rudolf Hess dated 27 August 1934, Bundesarchiv Koblenz (hereafter BAK), R 43 II/1344, p. 59.

13 Barkai, *Boykott,* p. 123.

14 The Hamburg Gau Economic Consultant did not produce an overall list of Jewish business in Hamburg until 1935–36 so that in his statistics those Jewish businesses that had been liquidated or sold by then were not mentioned.

15 This is also confirmed by one of the leaders of the Hamburg Advisory Service for Jewish Economic Aid, Dr. Ernst Loewenberg. In his memoirs he reports that the "Aryanization" of Jewish businesses in Hamburg was only effected "slowly" and that the wave of emigration began later "because here the living conditions were

II

While basic antisemitism was widespread among middle-class businessmen and repeatedly exhibited in individual "wild" acts, the economic leadership circles of the major Hamburg traders and the Chamber of Commerce were differentiated in their attitude towards antisemitism and the National Socialist policy vis-a-vis the Jews. This meant that the Hamburg Chamber of Commerce, despite its formal *Gleichschaltung,* did not support the anti-Jewish policy actively at first. Until 1937 it maintained its independence, characterized by a mixture of passivity and distance. For example, it continued to use a Jewish firm for printing its information sheets despite strong opposition from the Gestapo and the Hamburg *Wirtschaftsbehörde.* In reply to subsequent reproaches, the Chamber of Commerce explained that it had to "remain free in its economic decisions."[16] Furthermore, not wanting to get involved in boycott campaigns it rigorously refused to provide information about Jewish companies and did not participate in the systematic listing of Jewish businesses. There is every indication that behind this attitude was a certain amount of hidden scepticism regarding the National Socialist race policy, which was unofficially expressed by some members of the Hamburg bourgeoisie. Several times the National Socialist *Hamburger Tageblatt* polemized against the lack of "race-consciousness" among the city's bourgeoisie and publicly accused individuals of "pro-Jewish behavior."

In July 1935 the party organ of the Hamburg NSDAP denounced the wife of a lawyer in public. She had expressed her anger about the virulent antisemitic placards in the window of an "Aryan" shop and had told the owner "that certain ladies do not like this and would not buy in such shops."[17] Under the heading "Lawyer's wife stood up for the Jews," the *Tageblatt* commented:

better than in any other place in the Reich." See the autobiography of Dr. Ernst Loewenberg (private possession), pp. 46, 81.

16 Comment by Reg. Dir. Köhn dated 14 November 1934 on a conversation with Präses Hübbe, StAHH, Deputation für Handel, Schiffahrt und Gewerbe II, S XIII, A 1.24.

17 Quoted from "Frau Rechtsanwalt nahm Juden in Schutz," *Hamburger Tageblatt*, 23 July 1935.

> You have to take a deep breath in a case like this in order to remain calm. The fact that things like this can still happen today goes to prove to us quite unmistakably that in particular certain "gracious"circles do not or do not want to understand National Socialism. Presumably the latter is correct and only possible because these "certain people" have discourse with the Jews, because they also have the money required to cultivate a nice society in a big way. Yes, in these "certain circles" the people are judged only by their purses. If these are in order, all other things are of no importance, not to mention the question of race.[18]

In March 1935 the mayor of Hamburg, Krogmann, in a speech to the merchants of the East Asia Association, reacted to criticism of racial policies. Before this audience, Krogmann censured those who "believed they could deny the term 'race' and in particular that of the Aryans." He considered the "Jewish issue" to be of "very great importance." To assuage any doubts that might arise, Krogmann assured the merchants that National Socialism would proceed with the "Jewish issue" in a "very much more humane way than was generally the case in world history."[19] Although a remark of this kind was an outright mockery of reality, the consul general of the South African Union congratulated the mayor on his remarks which he thought were "particularly fortunate." The consul general emphasized that it was correct to publicly oppose the "doubters" among the businessmen: "It is true that these old chaps can't get things into their heads very easily."[20] The consul general's comments about the "old chaps" gives us to understand that it was the older businessmen in particular who had misgivings about the National Socialist policy towards the Jews. Deeply rooted in their bourgeois world of status, which was so dominant in the *Kaiserreich* and which prized *Tüchtigkeit* (efficiency) of the individual so highly, they tended to renounce ideologies such as antisemitism which were hardly compatible with their pragmatic entrepreneurial self-image. Furthermore, in their eyes, steps taken against Jewish businesses represented an inadmissible intervention by the state in the economy, and, hence, a potential threat to their own position. And finally, many actions of the anti-Jewish

18 Ibid.

19 Quoted from StAHH, Staatliche Pressestelle I–IV, 7050, Vol. II, manuscript of the speech by Krogmann dated 9 March 1935, p. 2.

20 StAHH, Familie Krogmann I (Carl Vincent Krogmann), C 15, III/3, letter from the consul general of the Union of South Africa to Krogmann dated 11 March 1935.

policy, such as organized boycotts, were regarded by them as "politics of the street" and were rejected with a great deal of indignation. Thus, for example, the Hamburg banker Cornelius Freiherr von Berenberg-Gossler, although a member of the NSDAP, condemned the boycott of 1 April 1933 as being "outrageous" and "medieval," and he confided in his diary that the anti-Jewish activities left him feeling quite ashamed.[21]

Appraisal of and objection to the policy towards the Jews were often apparent within Hamburg's bourgeois families and usually followed a generational pattern. Dr. Eduard Rosenbaum, corporation counsel of the Chamber of Commerce and himself a Jew, had already recognized before 1933 that there were definite differences of opinion between the older and younger businessmen in their attitude towards the National Socialist ideology. The younger businessmen no longer thought in terms of "status" but of "race." When asked by the older businessmen after the *Reichstag* elections in July 1932 what they could do to stop the spread of the NSDAP, he replied: "Just take a look at what your sons are reading."[22] According to Rosenbaum's observations, the way of thinking of the younger businessmen was increasingly influenced by the intellectual right-wingers in the Weimar Republic. In particular, the members of the *Kriegsjugendgeneration,* who had been raised in the bourgeois world but found that world of privilege increasingly compromised by the current crisis and decay, were quite open to ideas which, in their fathers' eyes, appeared to be heresy: beginning with the "national planned economy," as propagated by the magazine *Die Tat*, and extending to racial antisemitism.

A typical representative of this *Kriegsjugendgeneration* was the new National Socialist president of the Chamber of Commerce, Hermann Victor Hübbe, born in 1901, who strongly objected to the "corrosive influence of Jewry."[23] He forced Eduard Rosenbaum, already mentioned above, to take early pension with the remark that it must be tough to

21 Diary of Cornelius Freiherr von Berenberg-Gossler (private possession), entries from 31 March and 1 April 1933: "I am ashamed in the face of my friends because of the steps taken by the Nazis against the Jews."

22 Quoted from Hans Bielfeldt, "Politik und Personalia im Dritten Reich," *Staat und Wirtschaft. Beiträge zur Geschichte der Handelskammer,* Hamburg, 1980, p. 157.

23 Letter from Hermann Victor Hübbe and Dr. Haage to the Reichs- und Preussische Wirtschaftsministerium dated 9 April 1936, Archiv Forschungsstelle für Zeitgeschichte in Hamburg (Archiv FZH), 227–11.

"belong to such a rootless race." His father Anton Hübbe, on the other hand, made no secret of his scepticism towards the National Socialists, and as early as 1931 financed the printing of his publication *Haltet das Tor offen*[24] (Keep the Gate Open) which protested against the Hamburg National Socialists and their economic policy. After 1933 he kept up relations with Jewish friends such as the banker Max Warburg, until the National Socialists photographed the meetings and denounced Hübbe in public.

Generational differences of opinion about antisemitism occurred also within other families, for example the family of businessman Witthoefft. Franz Heinrich Witthoefft, born in 1863, had played an important political role in the 1920s as *DVP-Deutsche Volkspartei* (German People's Party) representative in the National Assembly and as a senator in Hamburg. Although in the final phase of the Weimar Republic he veered over to the National Socialists, joined the NSDAP, and as a member of the "Keppler-circle" belonged to the most prominent sponsors of the National Socialists in the commercial world in Hamburg, he was not an antisemite and rejected the anti-Jewish policy after 1933. He made every effort to support Jewish scientists, withdrew in anger from the Rotary Club when it introduced the "Aryan clause," and reported to Max Warburg at the beginning of 1934 "that many things have come up which are quite different to what we would have liked them to be."[25] His son Peter Ernst on the other hand, a confirmed antisemite, opposed the "braying of the international Jewry" and justified the steps taken against the Jews "because they have gone a little too far with their impertinence."[26]

It would miss the point to characterize these differences of opinion as a "generational conflict," especially in view of the fact that within the generation of older businessmen very few engaged themselves on

24 *Haltet das Tor offen!*, Hamburg, 1931, StAHH, Familie de Chapeaurouge, U 91; excerpts from the brochure published by Werner Jochmann, *Nationalsozialismus und Revolution. Ursprung und Geschichte der NSDAP in Hamburg 1922–1933. Dokumente*, Frankfurt am Main, 1963, pp. 341–347.

25 StAHH, Arnold Otto Meyer, 3, Vol. 1, Letter of condolence from Witthoefft to Max Warburg on the death of Carl Melchior and Aby Warburg (undated, beginning 1934).

26 StAHH, Arnold Otto Meyer, 12, Peter Ernst Witthoefft to F.H. Witthoefft dated 3 November 1933.

behalf of the persecuted Jews. Among the few that did was the above-mentioned Cornelius von Berenberg-Gossler who, in direct negotiations with SS leaders Karl Wolff and Reinhard Heydrich, achieved the release of his friend Fritz Warburg from Gestapo arrest in April 1939.[27] But efforts of this kind were the exception. On the behavior of most businessmen, banker Alwin Münchmeyer's self-critical conclusion was: "We did nothing and we didn't think anything of it."[28]

The older merchants expressed reservations only when the closure of Jewish businesses threatened their own position or was understood to be a potential threat. In January 1939 *Gauleiter* Kaufmann discounted these reservations by stating in a speech in the presence of the Chamber of Commerce:

> The Aryanization has somewhat disconcerted one or the other of the Hamburg Aryans. I have heard rumors that elderly gentlemen have been quite seriously pondering the problem when this kind of Aryanization would befall them. One can only think, express and expect such a thing if one is not familiar with this racial problem or is not certain of one's own race. Therefore such statements are so childish — please excuse this expression — that they should really be the cause of some serious concern. I would like to ask you, whenever you meet upon such misgivings, to expel such whims from these gentlemen with most refreshing clarity and, if the effect can be intensified by it, to refer to my words, for, whoever is diligent, will remain, economically speaking, he who he was before.[29]

The "elderly gentlemen" expressed their scepticism about the "Aryanization" because it tarnished their ideal of economic order. With the actual expropriation of a business — an individual's lifework — the National Socialist state effected a serious intervention in private property which contradicted the bourgeois value of security. Many therefore interpreted "Aryanization" as the forerunner of an imminent "brown Bolshevism."

Around 1937–38, however, the Hamburg Chamber of Commerce abandoned its restrained attitude towards the economic elimination of

27 Diary of Cornelius Freiherr von Berenberg-Gossler (in private possession), 1939, entry dated 18 April 1939.

28 Quoted from Stefanie von Viereck, *Hinter weissen Fassaden. Alwin Münchmeyer — ein Bankier betrachtet sein Leben,* Hamburg, 1988, p. 136.

29 Kaufmann's speech before the Handelskammer Hamburg dated 6 January 1939, Archiv FZH, 12 (personnel file Kaufmann).

the Jews. It openly took sides with the "Aryan" buyers and supported their efforts to retroactively extricate themselves from contractual commitments to Jewish property owners. Accordingly, in an initiative on behalf of the Ministry of Economics, the Chamber of Commerce ordered that all "Aryanization" contracts drawn up before 1938 be retroactively subject to the same restrictive conditions as for the sale of businesses after 1938.[30] This meant that any payment agreement on the value of a business — the so-called "goodwill" fee — be declared invalid.

Violent attacks on Jews and Jewish companies continued to evoke strong objections from the economic sector and Hamburg's bourgeoisie, as reactions to the November 1938 pogrom demonstrated. Even Hamburg *Gauleiter* Kaufmann felt himself compelled to refer to the pogrom publicly as an "undignified solution."[31] By this time the economic elimination of the Jews was neither questioned nor merely passively accepted; it was in fact actively supported.

This change in behavior can be attributed to several factors: Firstly, the National Socialist regime, through its national and foreign political "successes," had consolidated in 1938 that not only the majority of the population but also the Hamburg economy reckoned with a long term of National Socialist rule. Secondly, the consequences of the economic crisis had been overcome to such an extent by this stage that Jewish businesses were no longer considered necessary to the economy. Thirdly, the situation of the Jewish companies in 1938 could be compared with that of a sinking ship, that is, the dynamics of the elimination procedure had reached a point where this had become irreversible. Fourthly, the Chamber of Commerce was by then institutionally involved in the process of "Aryanization" by its appointment of consultants and experts. Finally, the National Socialist expansion after 1938–39 had opened a new, lucrative dimension for certain sectors of the Hamburg economy through the "Aryanization" of Jewish companies in the annexed areas. This procedure began with the annexation of Austria in 1938 when Hamburg companies participated

30 Archiv FZH, 227–11, letter from Dr. Haage to the Berlin office of the Chamber of Commerce, 11 May 1939.

31 Quoted from Archiv FZH, 12 (personnel file Kaufmann), speech by Kaufmann before the Hamburg Chamber of Commerce on 6 January 1939.

in the "Aryanization" of Jewish transit traders and continued in the occupied areas of Eastern and Western Europe.

These changes in policy that surfaced in 1937–38 marked an overall growing decline in moral standards which reached a climax during the Second World War when certain Hamburg trading companies became deeply involved in the expansion and destruction policy of the National Socialists.

III

While acknowledging the escalation and increased radicalization in the economic elimination of the Hamburg Jews, one should not point solely at the supposed "change of course" in the Ministry of Economics at the end of 1937 or the legally enforced "Aryanization" after April 1938. The main reason, I believe, was the introduction in 1936–37 of draconian measures in the foreign currency policy, a factor hardly considered by researchers until now. The establishment of the *Devisenfahndungsamt* (foreign currency search office) under the supervision of Heydrich on 1 August 1936,[32] the intensification of foreign currency regulations and the extension of the *Devisenprüfungsdienst* (foreign currency inspection service) led to the elimination of numerous Jewish import and export companies in Hamburg from the beginning of 1937.[33] Even vague suspicions incited the *Devisenstelle des Oberfinanzpräsidenten* (foreign currency office) to withdraw the powers of disposal of Jewish company owners and to "aryanize," or preferably liquidate their businesses. The legal basis for the anti-Jewish activities was clause 37a which was adopted into the foreign currency regulations in December 1936.

32 BAK, R 58, 23a, p. 163f., circular from Heydrich to all State Police Offices dated 22 September 1936; StAHH, Oberfinanzpräsident, 4, circular from the Reichsstelle für Devisenbewirtschaftung to the presidents of the Landesfinanzämter-Devisenstellen dated 16 September 1936.

33 On the topic of "Aryanizations" as a result of currency regulations, also see: Archiv des Wiedergutmachungsamtes beim Landgericht Hamburg (Archiv WgA LGHH), Z 21664 (Jacoby, Zucker-Export), Z 2869–1 (Metallwerk Peute), Z 2660 (Arnold Bernstein Schiffahrtsgesellschaft m.b.H.), Z 995–1 (Julius Lachmann, Im- und Export), Z 3190–1 (Messrs. J. Jacobi & Co., Ex- und Import), Z 193–1 (Dammtor Lombard, Weiss & Sander).

This new regulation provided for the compulsory administration in trust upon suspicion of flight of capital and thus enabled the actual expropriation of the Jewish company. From December 1936 to October 1939 the Hamburg foreign currency office granted as many as 1,314 securing orders (*Sicherungsanordnungen*) against Jews, based on clause 37a.[34] The files from the foreign currency search office, which are still available almost in their entirety in the Hamburg State archives, provide an impressive documentation as to how far removed the daily behavior of this institution of the "Normative State" was from normative constitutional principles. The foreign currency search office demanded *Entlastungsbeweise* (exonerating evidence) from the accused Jews, used fictive confessions and false interrogation protocols that found their way into official files while the true facts were put away in so-called "secret files," denounced to the Gestapo those solicitors who had taken on Jewish clients, and applied clause 37a of the foreign currency regulation such that the effect was the same as an overall elimination of Jewish import and export companies in Hamburg.[35]

The behavior of the foreign currency search office indicated that the radicalization of the anti-Jewish policy was not simply a matter of the "Prerogative State" overpowering the bureaucratic "Normative State." Ernst Fraenkel's analysis of the "Dual State," which first appeared in 1940 and in which he tried to demonstrate the limited range of activity of the "Normative State" by using the foreign currency search office as an example,[36] does not take into account the radicalization processes in the "Normative State" itself, which tended to withdraw itself from its norm-bound behavior, and considered this to be a act of freeing itself from constitutional restrictions. To simply apply Fraenkel's analysis to the anti-Jewish policy in National Socialism[37] would fail to account for the much more complex reality.

34 StAHH, Oberfinanzpräsident, 10, Report from the Oberfinanzpräsident to the Ministry of Economics dated October 1939.

35 Compare in detail Bajohr, "*Arisierung*," Chapter IV.

36 Ernst Fraenkel, *Der Doppelstaat*, Frankfurt am Main, 1974, p. 99.

37 According to Uwe Dietrich Adam, *Judenpolitik im Dritten Reich*, Düsseldorf, 1972, p. 359, who interpreted the radicalization of the anti-Jewish policy as "*den äusseren Widerschein des Kampfes zwischen dem totalitären Anspruch des Nationalsozialismus mit den Rudimenten der normenstaatlichen Ordnung*." (p. 359).

The Jewish lawyer Dr. Friedrich Rosenhaft, reporting after 1945 on the attitude of the Hamburg foreign currency search office, stated that after 1933 this had "got completely into the track of illegal acts of power and terror." It had used the complex system of tax and foreign currency regulations to "excessively exaggerate" marginalia and to transfer the monetary penalties incurred into "a significant source of income for the state." The investigation offices had kept "success statistics," informed courts and state attorneys in a prejudiced manner, and applied more and more intensive methods "in order to take their victims by surprise during those first 'unexpected' attacks and soften them to such an extent that they were prepared to deliver 'declarations of submission'." This judgement is confirmed when analyzing the Hamburg foreign currency files, which were marked throughout by a virulent antisemitic tone. They spoke of "Jewish lack of scruples,"[38] "twisted Jewish language," "Jewish black marketeers"[39] and "shady dealings" with which "emigration-willing Jews take advantage of the facilities in our economic life in a shameless manner in order to illegally transfer Jewish capital" and therefore "to sell off the assets of the German people at throw-away prices."[40] The president of the *Landesfinanzamt* went so far as to claim that a Jewish suspect belonged "to the Jewish existences which know no fatherland, but bestow their presence on countries in which they believe they can line their pockets at the expense of the host country." He was therefore "a people's parasite from which Germany should be freed, which would be a gain for the Reich and its economy."[41]

This hotchpotch of antisemitic arguments in the files of the *Devisenstelle* cannot merely be interpreted as reactions to the "illegal" attempts of some Hamburg Jews who tried to retain some of their assets prior to them being completely expropriated. The numerous examples of anti-Jewish slander point rather to the fact that the behavior of the

38 StAHH, Oberfinanzpräsident, Str 629, p. 96, report by the Devisenstelle dated 21 January 1939.

39 Ibid., R 1936/276, p. 35, report by the president of the Landesfinanzamt to the Minister of Finance dated 2 May 1936.

40 Ibid., Str 678, Vol. 1, pp. 10, 17, report from the Devisenstelle dated 27 October 1939.

41 Quote from Ibid., R 1936/276, Sh. 1f., 38, President of the Landesfinanzamt Unterelbe to the Minister of Finance dated 2 May 1936.

financial bureaucracy towards the Jews was determined by antisemitic ideological convictions.

IV

Despite the central role of the "Normative State" authorities in the process of the economic elimination of the Jews, no state institution such as the *Devisenstelle* or the *Wirtschaftsbehörde* took over the leading role in the "Aryanization" but — at least in Hamburg — a party organization, namely the *Gauwirtschaftsapparat* of the NSDAP. From 1936 it established itself as an institution for the approval of "Aryanization applications."[42] Its activity meant the end of contractual freedom for Jewish owners and led to drastic decreases in value of businesses for sale since the "goodwill" fee was no longer in effect. In his approval procedure, the Gau Economic Consultant adhered to certain guidelines: Among the applicants he gave preference to young businessmen and NSDAP members; the formation of corporations should be avoided, and "Jewish influence" should be completely eradicated, which, also implied the immediate dismissal of any Jewish employees. Finally, he insisted "that the Jew should not receive an unreasonably high price"

42 The participation in the "Aryanization" by the Gau Economic Consultant considerably varied from one Gau to another. For example the Gau Economic Consultant in Baden founded a commission in February 1936 with the approval of the Baden Ministerpräsident which from then on was to process any queries relating to the activities of Jews in the economy. Apart from the Gau Economic Consultant the Treuhänder der Arbeit as well as two higher government officials from the Finance- and Economics Ministry in Karlsruhe were members of the commission. This meant that although the Gau Economic Consultant had enforced his right to participate in the "Aryanizations," he had to take into account the ministerial bureaucracy which pulled the brakes on a radicalization of the "Entjudung" even afterwards (see Hans-Joachim Fliedner, *Die Judenverfolgung in Mannheim*, Stuttgart, 1971, pp. 114, 144). In South Westphalia the Gau Economic Consultant had the right to only check "Aryanization" agreements, whereas the actual decisions were made by the mayors and local police authorities (see Gerhard Kratzsch, *Der Gauwirtschaftsapparat der NSDAP. Menschenführung — "Arisierung" — Wehrwirtschaft im Gau Westfalen-Süd,* Münster, 1989, pp. 150f, 180). In Hamburg on the other hand, the Gau Economic Consultant played a hegemonial role in the approval of "Aryanizations" (see Bajohr, *"Arisierung,"* Chap. IV).

and therefore often reduced the agreed purchase price at the expense of the Jewish owners.[43]

The Gau Economic Consultant maintained his leading role in the "Aryanization" without any legal sanction. He commissioned experts and surveyors or appointed trustees to Jewish companies without legal authorization. This should in fact have been the task of the Chamber of Commerce or the *Oberfinanzpräsident.* In particular, the Hamburg Chamber of Commerce and the city treasury allowed the Gau Economic Consultant to continue with the "Aryanization" at his own discretion. They tried to redirect the "revolutionary" energies of the *Gauwirtschaftsapparat* to "Aryanization" in order to limit its activities in other sectors such as economic planning and the allotment of industry.

The Hamburg Gau Economic Consultant and his colleagues who were involved with "Aryanization" almost all originated from the *Kriegsjugendgeneration* born after 1900. When the National Socialists came into power the first Gau Economic Consultant, Dr. Gustav Schlotterer, was 26 years old, his successor Carlo Otte was 24 and his successor Dr. Otto Wolff 25; the economist Karl Frie, later head of the "Aryanization department" was 19 years old, and the lawyer in charge of "Aryanization contracts," Dr. Arthur Kramm, was 25. This group consisted almost entirely of ideologically oriented, academic upstarts from the lower middle class who had already joined the NSDAP in their youth. Some of them had been awarded honorary leading positions in the SS. They had little practical experience in the world of economics and some had even graduated straight from university into responsible positions. Their origin, age, experience and self-esteem significantly differentiated them from the traditional dignitary type of Hanseatic businessmen. On the whole they represented an ideologically motivated, specifically National Socialist economic elite.[44] Also characteristic of this group was the particularly intense antisemitism of the

43 On the publicly announced approval principles of the Gau Economic Consultant see *Hamburger Tageblatt*, 2 December 1938.

44 Whether this characterization of the Hamburg Gau Economic Consultant can be generalized or is merely typical of Hamburg must remain open due to the lack of empirical comparative studies. Gerhard Kratzsch arrives at another result in his study of the Gau Westfalen-Süd. There the personnel of the *Gauwirtschaftsapparat* comprised "*gutsituierte Unternehmer und Kaufleute, Geschäftsführer der Industrie-*

Kriegsjugendgeneration, which was widespread in the national student movements in the Weimar Republic and later played an important role in the persecutional body of the National Socialists.[45]

V

The main beneficiaries of the "Aryanization" in Hamburg were by no means the established Hamburg commercial enterprises. Rather, the buyers of Jewish businesses were predominantly those who saw "Aryanization" as the opportunity to establish themselves. These included former employees, up-and-coming traders who until then could not join the state-controlled foreign trade system, people changing their profession or coming from related sectors of the same profession, as well as those seeking their fortune in the wake of National Socialism who were described by Max Warburg as "disgusting subordinates."

It was the middle-class economy that profited most from the "Aryanizations" since the liquidation of Jewish companies reduced the pressure of competition. Consequently, Hamburg's highest middle-class functionary, Christian Bartholatus, leader of the *NS-Hago* (National Socialist trade organization), announced triumphantly in January 1939 that 2,000 shops were standing empty in Hamburg which, among other reasons, was mainly due to the liquidation of Jewish retail businesses.[46] The Jewish chain store enterprises (*Filialbetriebe*) in Hamburg were not "Aryanized" as a whole, but in the interests of the middle class were

und Handelskammern, Werksdirektoren, Betriebs- und Sparkassenleiter." See Gerhard Kratzsch, "Die 'Entjudung' der mittelständischen Wirtschaft im Regierungsbezirk Arnsberg," in: *Verdrängung und Vernichtung der Juden in Westfalen,* Arno Herzig et al., eds., Münster, 1994, p. 97.

45 On the significance of the *Kriegsjugendgeneration* see also Ernst Günther Gründel, *Die Sendung der Jungen Generation. Versuch einer umfassenden revolutionären Sinndeutung der Krise,* Munich, 1932; Ulrich Herbert, "'Generation der Sachlichkeit'. Die völkische Studentenbewegung der frühen zwanziger Jahre in Deutschland," in: *Zivilisation und Barbarei. Die widersprüchlichen Potentiale der Moderne,* Frank Bajohr et al., eds., Hamburg, 1991, pp. 115–144; Ulrich Herbert, *Best. Biographische Studien über Weltanschauung, Radikalismus und Vernunft 1903–1989,* Bonn, 1996.

46 *Hamburger Fremdenblatt,* 11 January 1939.

split up and sold separately.[47] In addition, the principles of the NSDAP Gau Economic Consultant concerning the approval of "Aryanizations" were directed at middle-class interests with the aim of "avoiding the formation of corporations" and "encouraging the younger generation." Thus the prevailing view among researchers that "Aryanization" encouraged the development of corporations in the German economy and proved to be disadvantageous for the bourgeoisie[48] needs correcting. The impressive "Aryanizations" of individual Jewish large-scale enterprises have — so it seems — tended to direct research one-sidedly to the relationship between "Big Business and Aryanization."[49] It is important therefore not to overlook the fact that since most Jewish businesses belonged to the middle-class sector, "Aryanization" should be considered on the whole as an internal change in ownership within the middle class.

Furthermore, corruption and nepotism were central phenomena of the "Aryanizations" in Hamburg. Numerous functionaries in the Hamburg NSDAP enriched themselves from Jewish property, and the *Gauleiter* used the "Aryanizations" as welcome sources of income by demanding from owners and buyers "Aryanization contributions" which he put towards the financing of the NSDAP and his minions.[50]

The buyers of Jewish companies represented a thoroughly diverse spectrum — from avaricious exploiters bent on completely plundering Jewish property to sympathetic businessmen willing to pay a fair price. According to their behavior the buyers of Jewish property can be divided typologically into three groups:[51]

47 This applies in Hamburg to Jewish chain store enterprises such as Bottina Schuh GmbH, Speiers Schuhwarenhaus, Korsetthaus Gazelle, Fiedlers Strumpfläden. See also Bajohr, *Arisierung*, Chap. V.

48 For example Helmut Genschel, *Verdrängung,* p.213.

49 Peter Hayes, "Big Business and 'Aryanization' in Germany," *Jahrbuch für Antisemitismusforschung*, 3 (1994), pp. 254–281.

50 For numerous examples, such as the preferential treatment of NSDAP-Kreis- and Ortsgruppenleiter, see Bajohr *"Arisierung"*, Chap. VI. On the nepotism of the Hamburg Gauleiter also see Frank Bajohr, "Gauleiter in Hamburg. Zur Person und Tätigkeit Karl Kaufmanns," *Vierteljahrshefte für Zeitgeschichte*, 2 (1995), pp. 267–295.

51 This character description was developed on the basis of the restitution files of the Wiedergutmachungsamt at the Landgericht Hamburg and on a sample of just

The first group of active and unscrupulous profiteers comprised about forty percent of all buyers. Typical of their conduct was the fact that apart from the discriminatory rules of the "Aryanization," they personally approached Jewish owners in order to reduce the purchase price even further and to shamelessly exploit the predicament of the owner to their own advantage. They were not satisfied with the undervaluation of inventory and warehouse stocks and the elimination of the "goodwill," and often introduced themselves to the owners as representatives of the NSDAP[52] in order to intimidate them and to make clear that they would not be accepted as equal partners for negotiations. Many blackmailed the Jewish owners, threatening them with denunciation or, with the intervention of the Gestapo, had their passports suspended,[53] refused to fulfil contractual commitments, or turned up in party uniform and prohibited the owners' entry into their own businesses.[54] Particularly well represented in this group were members of the NSDAP and employees of Jewish companies. Many of the "Aryanizations" did not take place until 1938–39, when the accelerated expropriation of the Jewish businesses provided increasing possibilities for the buyers to enrich themselves on the plight of these Jews.

The second group of buyers of Jewish property, which also constituted about forty percent, can aptly be characterized by the term "sleeping partners." They raked in their personal profit in the course of the "Aryanizations" — through the devaluation of inventory and stocks — but did not expose themselves and made every effort to ensure that the transfer of property was conducted, at least outwardly, according to correct procedures. The most conspicuous feature about their behavior was their inconspicuousness. They appeared to refrain from deriving their own advantage yet made no attempt to pay the Jewish owners an appropriate and fair compensation. Since many of these buyers believed that these were "normal" transfers of property,

under three hundred individual cases altogether in which sufficient information was available concerning the behavior of the "Aryan" buyers.

52 Archiv WgA LGHH, Z 9879/2894 (Textilgeschäft Martin Josephs), Z 2889 (H.W. Almind Nachflg.).

53 Ibid., Z 3103 (Chemische Fabrik Rothschild & Leers).

54 Ibid., Z 2588 (Messrs. H.J. Luft).

they did not recognize the claims of the former Jewish owners in the compensation proceedings after 1945.[55]

The remaining twenty percent — the smallest group — can be described as well-meaning and sympathetic business people who tried to pay the Jewish owners appropriate compensation. Many buyers in this group were personal friends of Jews. Many had not thought of buying property until they were persuaded to do so by Jewish friends. On closer look, this type of buying contract clearly demonstrates that there were cases where buyers and Jewish owners had joined in a silent alliance against the approval authorities. They often tried to disguise the "goodwill" —which was prohibited — in other, artificially increased assets[56] or to pay secret amounts to the Jewish owners.[57] Such transactions were well-intentioned, but as a result of the rigid National Socialist tax and contributions policy they only seldom fulfilled their purpose of suitably compensating the Jewish owners. Many Jewish owners therefore preferred to completely reject suitable remuneration and to meet a secret agreement with the buyer, who defined the purchase as an act of trustee management that would be annulled at the end of the National Socialist rule.[58]

A few buyers took steps that were illegal in the eyes of National Socialist law. For example, they gave the Jewish buyers outstanding receivables from abroad which were not mentioned in the contract of sale,[59] or paid them a secret monthly pension which was also not listed in the transfer documents.[60] One buyer even personally smuggled Swiss watches and gold chains to Amsterdam and arranged for the "goodwill" to be brought in a briefcase to another country in order to suitably compensate the Jewish owner.[61] Even during the repressive

55 The regulations for the *Wiedergutmachung* were often regarded as being "immoral and illegal" and many buyers at that time even described themselves as being the real victims of the political situation. For example see Ibid., U 3350–1 (Inselmann & Co.), letter from Julius Mehldau to the Landgericht Hamburg dated 17 February 1953.

56 Ibid., Z 1124 (Spedition S. Dreyer Sen. Nachf. GmbH), Z 13410 (Julius Engländer & Hinsel).

57 Ibid., Z 13984 (H. van Pels & Wolff).

58 Ibid., Z 2185–1 (Walter Benjamin).

59 Ibid., Z 14281/14292 (Wilhelm Haller).

60 Ibid., Z 6051 (Blankenstein & Bosselmann).

61 Ibid., Z 15172–1 (Julius Hamberg).

conditions of National Socialist rule it was still possible, if the buyer was willing, to achieve a fair solution for the Jewish owners. However, such acts not only put the buyers at a considerable personal risk, but also threw significant light on the reversal of moral basic principles by "Aryanization": He who felt obliged by the traditional principles of a businessman's code of honor and who refused to gain profit from the innocent predicament of others, i.e., preferred to remain honest, was forced to turn "criminal" and violate current laws. It was this moral dilemma of well-meaning buyers that finally disclosed the immorality of the "Aryanization." Moreover, the behavior of the third group of buyers made it clear that even in the course of "Aryanization" a minimum standard of morals could be adhered to. The buyers moved of course within a framework dictated by National Socialism, but remained as acting subjects who actively influenced the atmosphere and conditions of the transfers of property. This meant that the responsibility for repression and discrimination was not limited to the National Socialists but included also the buyers, and with them German society as a whole.

The Attack on Berlin Department Stores (Warenhäuser) After 1933

SIMONE LADWIG-WINTERS

Georg Wertheim, the head of one of the four largest German department store chains in the 1920s and 1930s, noted in his diary: "1 January 1937 — the store is declared to be 'German'."[1] This entry marks the forced end to his activities in the business that he and his family had worked hard to build up.[2]

Roots

In 1875, Georg's parents, Ida and Abraham Wertheim (who sometimes went by the name Adolf), had opened a modest shop selling clothes and manufactured goods in Stralsund, a provincial town on the Baltic Sea. An extensive network of family members ensured a low-priced supply of goods. In 1876, one year after the shop opened, the two eldest sons Hugo and Georg (aged 20 and 19 respectively), went to work in the

1 In addition to archival material of the Deutsche Bank, available in the Bundesarchiv, Abt. Potsdam (in the meantime moved to Berlin-Lichterfelde) for the first time in the wake of reunification, I was able to use the copy of Georg Wertheim's diary in the Archiv Stürzebecher (cited in the following as: Wertheim, *Diary*). I am grateful to Georg Wertheim's son for permission to use this material. The unpublished diary has three parts: a family history that must have been compiled around 1905; a chronological diary that notes important business events but focuses primarily on personal events such as travel, illness, and the like; and some comments by Georg Wertheim on his relationship to Kaiser Wilhelm II.

2 This article is based on my dissertation, which goes into greater depth on the complex of problems discussed here; see Simone Ladwig-Winters, *Wertheim — ein Warenhausunternehmen und seine Eigentümer. Ein Beispiel der Entwicklung der Berliner Warenhäuser bis zur "Arisierung,"* Münster, 1997.

shop following their apprenticeships in Berlin. Three younger sons later joined them. The business was called "A. Wertheim" after the father, who increasingly withdrew from active management of the business. Guidelines were introduced into the business that had been known outside of Germany for some time but were innovative in German retailing. These included: "low profit margins with high sales and quick inventory turnover; a broad and varied selection of merchandise; fixed prices (price tags on the goods); viewing of merchandise without a personal, psychological obligation to buy; exchanges — even a right to return goods and above all, payment in cash."[3] Particularly the last was an important innovation, because trade in Germany until then had been based extensively on the principles of borrowing and haggling. With the new business methods, which other businessmen soon began to implement as well, the small shops experienced a rapid upturn and were soon able to expand their product assortment until they became small *Warenhäuser*, or department stores.

Wertheim's growth was part of a broader development in German retailing. Following the Industrial Revolution it had become necessary to modernize trade. Mass products were being produced that also had to be sold on a mass scale. The *Warenhaus* — the site where mass products were sold — was the retail equivalent to the factory in the production area. Other forms of large-scale retail enterprises emerged as well, such as single-price variety stores, junk shops, mail-order businesses, consumers' cooperatives, and another sort of department store, the *Kaufhaus*. A careful distinction was drawn between the *Kaufhaus* and the *Warenhaus*. Both aimed at high sales, particularly in Berlin, the capital of the newly founded German Reich which was growing by leaps and bounds. However, the *Kaufhaus* concentrated on one sector, usually clothing, while the *Warenhaus* stocked a wide variety of goods.

3 Peter Stürzebecher, "Warenhäuser," in: *Berlin und seine Bauten*, Architekten- und Ingenieurverein zu Berlin, ed., Berlin, 1978, part VII, vol. A, p. 4.

Beginnings

Wertheim was the first store of its type to open for business in Berlin. Previously, only *Kaufhäuser* had flourished in the capital, such as N. Israel, Rudolph Hertzog, and Gebrüder Gersons. Wertheim met with grand success in Berlin as well. Business was so good that in 1893 and 1894 a building was constructed on the *Oranienstrasse* in Kreuzberg to accommodate a new *Warenhaus*. Three additional buildings were to follow, including one on the *Leipziger Strasse* that caused a public sensation. Criticism — much of which was antisemitic in tone — soon accompanied this success. Nearly all the founders of *Warenhäuser* happened to be Jews. Attempts were now made to defame the *Warenhaus* as a new type of business. The pejorative term "bazaar" was applied to it, although the practice of fixed prices contradicted the stereotype of "oriental" trading. Nor did the so-called socialist danger that allegedly emanated from the *Warenhäuser* have any basis in reality.[4] The merchants of the commercial middle class and their various professional associations used these tactics in an effort to prevent further expansion of the *Warenhäuser*.

This went so far that in 1900 Prussia (and other German states), introduced a tax that only *Warenhäuser* had to pay. This tax applied to the sales of *Warenhäuser* that had an annual income exceeding RM 400,000. *Kaufhäuser*, some of which achieved significantly higher sales, were exempted from this measure. In addition, a variety of building and fire-code regulations were instituted that went far beyond the usual degree of safety precautions for public buildings.[5] The working conditions of employees were also attacked, for reasons of health and as a purported danger to morality. Ironically, A. Wertheim had made extraordinary efforts to set especially high social standards. The company was the first to introduce Sunday as a day of rest for all employees. In spite of these efforts, Wertheim was attacked in the press.[6] And in light of the company's prominence in Prussia, the *Warenhaus* tax was to be seen as a "lex Wertheim."

4 Dr. F. Wollny, "Die Frage der Warenhäuser," in: *Berliner Fragen — Etwas auf dem Weg in das neue Jahrhundert*, Berlin, 1901, pp. 110–111.

5 Stürzebecher, "Warenhäuser," p. 8.

6 Wertheim, *Diary*, pp. 26, 27.

In fact, with its department stores, Wertheim had created a new concept of shopping that went along with changing consumer behavior. There had developed "a body of consumers able and willing to buy above the line of necessity."[7] Bright, airy, and lavishly designed stores with correspondingly decorated wares, and friendly salespeople who went out of their way to help the customer transformed shopping into an experience. The "democratization of consumption"[8] had been a necessary precondition for expanding the clientele of department stores. Wertheim's outstanding success was due to its presenting an astute mix of mass products and luxury articles. And every customer was warmly welcomed — as long as he or she was a potential shopper.

Indeed, the vehement agitation contributed in part to this success, since customers were curious as to what was really happening — and were exceedingly impressed, as Wertheim's growth in sales attests.[9] The business prospered, sales space underwent further expansion, and more personnel had to be added. Competition increased too, as other enterprises such as Hermann Tietz and Jandorf opened stores in Berlin.

The Warenhäuser Flourish

Though Wertheim remained the top *Warenhaus* in Germany throughout the first decade of the century, the ranking within this sector changed during the 1920s. Now the enterprises with the highest sales were Karstadt and Hermann Tietz (which had been founded by Oscar Tietz with the financial backing of his uncle Hermann Tietz), followed by Leonhard Tietz, Wertheim, and Schocken.

7 David Landes, *The Unbound Prometheus*, Cambridge, Mass., 1969, p. 243.

8 For a detailed account of this, see Klaus Strohmeyer, *Warenhäuser*, Berlin, 1980, p. 80; see also Ladwig-Winters, *Wertheim*, p. 37.

9 According to Georg Wertheim's sales account book, which can be found in the Archiv Stürzebecher, sales rose from RM 1.3 million in 1890, the first year business was conducted in Berlin, to RM 33.6 million in the year 1901!

Ranking of the German *Warenhäuser*, Late 1920s and Early 1930s[10]

	Stores	Employees (1930)	Sales (1928), in RM
Karstadt	91	23,428	300 million
Hermann Tietz	18	16,458	300 million
Leonhard Tietz	40	15,000	190 million
Wertheim	7	10,450	128 million
Schocken	18	5,067	88 million

Concentration had advanced. The most dramatic break occurred in 1927 as the result of the takeover by Hermann Tietz of Adolf Jandorf's business, including the KaDeWe. The takeover effort and its defense significantly depleted capital. In addition, the tax burden placed tremendous pressure on these companies.[11] Serious problems ensued in all *Warenhäuser*, that were further exacerbated by the world economic crisis, which led to the collapse of several banks and a major decline in purchasing power.

In addition to this, increased antisemitic tendencies marred public life again in the 1920s. The NSDAP agitated against the *Warenhäuser* and called for a boycott. In the wake of the inauguration of the first Reichstag that included delegates from the NSDAP, Wertheim was physically attacked. Stones shattered the display windows.[12] The *Warenhäuser* took legal steps to defend themselves,[13] but legal tactics could do nothing to hinder the discussion that was already underway

10 The information in this table was drawn from a variety of sources; on Hermann Tietz, its sales, and its number of stores, see Hermann Tietz, *Warenhäuser — ein Spiegelbild volkstümlicher Verkaufsstätten*, vol. 31 of the Industrie-Bibliothek, Berlin, 1928, p. 83. The information was derived from other information, since this source is very reticent in providing particulars. For Wertheim, the information was taken from the sales book. Otherwise, see Heidrun Homburg, "Warenhausunternehmen und ihre Gründer in Frankreich und Deutschland oder: eine diskrete Elite und mancherlei Mythen," *Jahrbuch für Wirtschaftsgeschichte* (1992), p. 208.

11 In 1932, the Wertheim company applied to defer its payments on its tax debt, but the application was rejected; Bundesarchiv, Abt. Potsdam (hereafter BAP), R 80 Ba 2 P 5200, Doc. 16, Georg Wertheim's statement to the banks from the year 1936.

12 Wertheim, *Diary,* p. 72.

13 The protective society of the larger businesses (*Schutzgemeinschaft der Grossbetriebe und verwandter Gruppen e.V.*), made the various decisions jointly; see BAP

on prohibiting the expansion of large retailers.[14] In December 1932, an emergency decree did in fact impose a general ban on the establishment, expansion, or relocation of variety stores.[15] The law took no heed of the fact that large retailers accounted for a very small proportion of retail sales.

Retail Sales 1928[16]

	Germany		USA	
	in billion RM	**% of total sales**	**in billion RM**	**% of total sales**
Small and Specialty Shops	28.2	80.6	105.0	56.7
Hawkers, Junk Dealers, and Street Markets	2.2	6.3	4.2	2.3
Department Stores	1.5	4.3	29.4	16.0
Co-ops	1.4	4.0	0.84	0.4
Mail-order Firms	0.35	1.0	6.72	3.6
Other	1.35	3.8	38.64	21.0
Total	35.0	100.0	184.8	100.0

In the above table, the variety stores are categorized as "other." With respect to the *Warenhäuser*, however, it must be clearly emphasized that they never attained more than a 4.8% share of retail sales before 1933. Nevertheless, the abolition of the *Warenhäuser* constituted Point 16 of the NSDAP program.

Reichswirtschaftsmininsterium (RWM), P 13859, Doc. 3–18, entitled "Der Boykott in der Judikatur."

14 ADGB-Restakten, Archive of the former Historische Kommission zu Berlin, NB 430, Doc. 004 from 3 March 1932, "Arbeitsbericht des Vorläufigen Reichswerberates."

15 Heinrich Uhlig, *Die Warenhäuser im Dritten Reich*, Cologne, 1956, p. 207.

16 ADGB-Restakten, Historische Kommission zu Berlin, NB 429, Doc. 014, n.d.

Attacks on the Warenhäuser Intensify

After the National Socialist seizure of power in 1933, these businesses — together with Jewish shop owners, physicians, and lawyers — came under ever harsher attack from propaganda and calls for boycotts. During the nationwide boycott of 1 April 1933, the Warenhäuser remained closed for the entire day, although customers stood at their doors demanding entry.[17]

The members of the executive board of the Association of German Department Stores (e.V.) had to resign their posts at the end of March due to enormous pressure.[18] Their successors took office with the aid of Emil Georg von Stauss, a representative of the Deutsche Bank.[19] They, in turn, had already been replaced in May by persons who had stronger ties to the National Socialist party. The public — including the international community — was led to believe that business was proceeding completely as usual, even after 1 April 1933.

The *Betriebszellen* (*NSBO*), the local National Socialist representatives within each large enterprise, ordered on 1 April that the *Warenhäuser* deposit two months' salary as security for each non-Jewish employee.[20] Had this demand been implemented, all *Warenhäuser* would have immediately had to file for bankruptcy.[21] Since this was to be avoided at all costs, officials quietly dropped this demand, and substituted it by a declaration that did not require compliance under labor law.[22]

In the following months, an unofficial struggle broke out within the party over the "*Warenhaus* question." The creditor banks demanded a clear resolution. Hess[23] ordered a halt to the harassment of *Warenhäuser* in order to preserve the thousands of jobs that they

17 Ladwig-Winters, *Wertheim,* pp. 111–126, 161.

18 Interview with Ulrich A. Tietz, son of the chief executive Leonhard Tietz, in November 1994, New York; see also Uhlig, *Warenhäuser im Dritten Reich*, p. 76.

19 Uhlig, *Warenhäuser im Dritten Reich*, p. 76; but also BAP R 80 Ba 2 P 24404, Aktennotiz Stauss/Frank from 13 March 1933.

20 Comité des Délégations Juives, ed., *Das Schwarzbuch*, Paris, 1934, p. 365.

21 *Das Schwarzbuch*, p. 366.

22 Supplement to the *Hannoverschen Anzeiger*, 2 April 1933.

23 *Central Verein Zeitung,* 23 November 1933.

provided. Even then, attacks continued to occur, especially in the provinces, and in Breslau above all.[24]

In September 1933, the Ministry of Economics issued a definition for "*Warenhaus*" in contrast to "*Kaufhaus*." According to this definition, a *Warenhaus* was "a marketing outlet ... in which goods of many types that do not belong together, including groceries, are offered for sale."[25] The presence of a grocery department or cafeteria gradually became the decisive criterion as to whether an establishment was a *Warenhaus*, or only a significantly less attractive *Kaufhaus*. Despite this regulation, for many years official policy remained unclear as to whether *Warenhäuser* as such, or only those belonging to Jews, were to be treated as an undesirable retail branch.

After the *Gleichschaltung*, not only *Warenhäuser* but also Jewish businesses of all sorts were forbidden to place advertisements in the press. This had far-reaching consequences, as customers could no longer keep abreast of special sales. For despite all the political agitation, *Warenhäuser* remained business enterprises, interested above all in selling their merchandise. And they managed to do this in the face of all opposition. By 1933 a shopping ban had not yet been enforced and even "persons in uniform" — that is, National Socialist party members — continued to patronize the *Warenhäuser*.[26] When fanatical salespeople denounced uniformed party members for shopping at *Warenhäuser* or refused to serve them, this was deliberately played down by management and by the Ministry of Economics. The propaganda apparently had not yet affected party members to the extent that they would refrain from shopping in *Warenhäuser*.

In general, the April boycott cannot be said to have caused the collapse in sales that might have been anticipated. Beginning in 1930, monthly sales in the *Warenhäuser* continually declined in comparison to the months of the preceding year. Only in April 1933 did they reach

24 See Chronologie, Ladwig-Winters, *Wertheim*, p. 457–458.

25 BAP, RWM 31.01 P 13862, Doc. 363, 11 September 1933. This ruling was reaffirmed on 16 December 1933 with a circular of the Ministry of Economics; see Uhlig, *Warenhäuser im Dritten Reich*, pp. 100–101.

26 BAP, RWM 31.01 P 13860, Doc. 59, 1 September 1933. In a circular, Schmitt, the Minister of Economics, came out against a shopping ban for National Socialist party members; see the documents of the Ministry of Economics.

practically the same level as the year before.[27] While the *Warenhäuser* attained between 94% and 97% of the previous annual figure during 1933 (the exact figures vary depending on their source, the Institute for Research on the Business Cycle or the Research Office for Trade),[28] Wertheim's Berlin stores suffered an additional decline of about 10 percent.[29] Still, this development turned around, at least for Wertheim, by 1935.[30] When the *Warenhäuser* are compared with the *Kaufhäuser*, the *Kaufhäuser* come out ahead, at least until the end of 1936.[31] This may appear to be evidence of the effectiveness of the propaganda against *Warenhäuser*. Yet, there are other compelling reasons why the *Warenhäuser* performed poorly. For example, in the summer of 1933 the Ministry of Finance issued guidelines for granting low interest loans to newlyweds (*Ehestandsdarlehen*), authorized by the Law for the Promotion of Marriage.[32] These loans were awarded in the form of purchase coupons instead of cash; Jewish businesses and *Warenhäuser* (irrespective of whether the owner was considered to be Jewish), however, were not permitted to redeem these coupons. In addition, special tax breaks were instituted for businesses that handed out Christmas bonuses in the form of purchase coupons. I.G. Farben, for one, took advantage of this arrangement; but these coupons, too, fell under the regulation that prohibited them from being redeemed in Jewish businesses or *Warenhäuser*. It is nearly impossible to estimate how much income was lost in this way. One source, a letter from the Ministry of Economics to the Ministry of Finance, dated 29 January 1934, criticizes this regulation and approximates a sales volume of RM 135 million for the year 1934.[33] The importance of the measure can be

27 *Einzel-Handel — Amtliches Organ des Handelsschutzverbandes der Pfalz*, vol. 34, pp. 52–54, in BAP, RWM 31.01 P 9227, Doc. 15–17.

28 *Einzel-Handel*, vol. 34, pp. 52–54; however, skepticism is justified regarding these numbers.

29 Ladwig-Winters, *Wertheim*, p. 163.

30 Ibid., p. 206.

31 *Wirtschaftsblatt der Industrie- und Handelskammer zu Berlin*, 22 August 1936, vol. 23/24, p. 1122.

32 Enacted 1 June 1933 (RGBl. I, S.326).

33 BAP, RWM 31.01 P 13862, Doc. 332, response on 27 April 1934 of the Ministry of Finance to the letter of the Ministry of Economics (30 January 1934)! Total sales for the branches of merchandise affected by this were estimated at RM 2.4 to 2.5

assessed on this basis alone. Sources further indicate that the total for 1933 clearly exceeded RM 135 million.

Moreover, the purchase coupons plainly directed consumption toward durable goods (e.g., furniture, ovens). Also, public authorities invested more heavily than before in merchandise from the photography, communication, and vehicle industries, which previously had been sold in part through the *Warenhäuser*. Since such sales were illegal, these stores lost considerable income due to political manipulation.

"Aryanization" of the Hermann Tietz Group

The conflict surrounding the *Warenhäuser* soon affected their ownership status as well. The Hermann Tietz Group was the first in which changes in management occurred in response to pressure from the creditor banks. At the beginning of 1933, the group needed an additional loan to the tune of RM 14 million. The business had experienced declines in sales of up to 41 percent (in Dresden), during that year, with particularly severe losses in its many provincial stores due to the fact that fixed costs remained relatively high.[34] After an initial agreement with the consortium of banks involved — which comprised the Akzept — und Garantiebank, Deutsche Bank und- Disconto-Gesellschaft, Dresdner Bank, Hardy & Co. und Commerz-und Privat-Bank[35] — approval of the loan was made contingent on Hertie, a newly founded company led by Georg Karg, becoming part of the management for procuring credit and the "establishment of Aryan predominance in management."[36] Karg, in turn, was dependent on the banks since he could offer security

billion; see P 13861, Doc. 244–248, manuscript of a letter of the RWM, 30 January 1934.

34 BAP, R 80 Ba 2 P 5218, Doc. 42, appendix to a report for Hertie advisory board members (*Beiratsmitglieder*), dated 3 January 1934.

35 Uhlig, *Warenhäuser im Dritten Reich*, p. 116; and BAP R 80 Ba 2 P 11482, 25 January 1935.

36 Contract from 29 July 1933; Appendix 7 of the claim for reparations (*Klage auf Wiedergutmachung*), filed in 1948.

only in the amount of RM 50,000.[37] A family member in management, Hugo Zwillenberg, was forced to leave the business immediately. In the following months, auditing firms examined the various businesses of the group. During this time, the remaining brothers, Georg and Martin Tietz,were personally responsible for the property and obligations of the group. By mid-1934, after almost a year, the entire property had been accounted for, and Georg and Martin Tietz were forced to resign. The family members, who had built up the giant group, received a total of about RM 1.2 million as compensation for the whole enterprise. During this entire time, their opponents had searched for ways to saddle the two brothers with continued liability without conceding them any decision-making power. In 1934, however, they came to the conclusion that this was not possible, and the two were pushed to resign.[38] The loan had been disbursed already in 1933.

Hitler's Role

Many historians have commented on this loan[39] because it is believed that Hitler was involved in the decision to grant it to Hermann Tietz. This has often been taken as evidence that Hitler assumed direct responsibility for all crucial decisions in the economic sector. However, it seems in fact that Minister Schmitt, new at his post, wanted to cover himself by implicating Hitler, since criticism was expected given the general rabble-rousing propaganda against the *Warenhäuser*. However, the decision had already been made: liquidation of Hermann Tietz was out of the question on account of the 14,000 jobs that would thus have been eliminated, but also in light of the further consequences for industrial and agricultural suppliers[40] and — above all — for the

37 BAP, R 80 Ba 2 P 11482, articles of incorporation (*Gesellschaftsvertrag*), 24 July 1933.

38 Ladwig-Winters, *Wertheim,* pp. 149–158.

39 The central source on this point is Uhlig, *Warenhäuser im Dritten Reich*, pp. 115–119. All other authors cite this source.

40 The volume of these deliveries had come to RM 132.8 million in 1932; see Uhlig, *Warenhäuser im Dritten Reich,* p. 115.

creditor banks.[41] Hitler had no alternative but to assent to the loan that assured the company's continued existence.

Events at Wertheim

The events at Hermann Tietz also affected the Wertheim Group. This group, too, was wholly owned by family members. After a dispute in 1908, the brothers Georg, Franz and Wilhelm Wertheim owned the majority share in the business until the early 1930s. Following Franz's death in 1933, his heirs held the majority of shares along with the brothers Georg and Wilhelm. Both Georg Wertheim and his brothers had been baptized many years earlier. After having repeatedly defended the business against antisemitic attacks during its early years, he converted to Christianity in 1906, shortly before his marriage to Ursula Gilka, a Christian.[42] From then on, his circle of friends and advisers had undergone a clear change; one of the most important of these, from the late 1920s, was Emil Georg von Stauss, member of the executive board and later of the supervisory board at the Deutsche Bank.[43] Emil Georg von Stauss was an enigmatic character of the Weimar and National Socialist periods, albeit one who has rarely been given his due in historical studies.[44]

41 BAP, R 80 Ba 2 P 5218, Doc. 124, "Motivbericht."

42 Wertheim, *Diary*, pp. 33.

43 The highly informative files of the Deutsche Bank in the Bundesarchiv Potsdam on the process of "Aryanizing" Wertheim consist mainly of the personal collection of Emil Georg von Stauss. As the person in the center of events, he carefully recorded and filed the most important details. The precise documentation ends with his death in 1942, so it is scarcely possible to reconstruct the dramatic events between 1942 and the war's end, as well as during the postwar period.

44 His role was first appreciated in the OMGUS documents (Office of Military for Germany, United States Finance Division — Financial Investigation Section); see *Ermittlungen gegen die Deutsche Bank*, 1946/47, reprinted Nördlingen, 1985, especially pp. 45–47. Later, Henry A. Turner also devoted attention to him in *German Big Business and the Rise of Hitler*, New York, 1985. Recently his position was portrayed in a more critical light (albeit only to a limited extent), in Harold James' commemorative publication on the Deutsche Bank; see *Die Deutsche Bank 1870–1995*, Lothar Gall, Gerald D. Feldman, Harold James, Carl-L. Holtfrerich, Hans E. Büschgen, eds., Munich, 1995, especially p. 352.

Stauss had made the acquaintance of Göring and Hitler by the early 1930s.[45] Although he never became a member of the NSDAP,[46] he supported its activities in numerous ways. After the seizure of power, his involvement focused on the economic reorganization of industry in line with National Socialist policy. He was integrated into decision-making processes at Daimler-Benz, BMW, Lufthansa, Bergmann Elektrizität, and Bayerische Stickstoff, usually as a member of the supervisory board. At the same time, he was always closely connected to "nationalistic and militaristic elements,"[47] though this was scarcely perceptible in his language, for instance, which until the end retained a clearly business-like style. In the name of Daimler-Benz, Stauss made a donation to the "*Ahnenerbe*,"[48] yet he seems not to have subscribed to the racist elements of National Socialist policy himself. He always maintained good relations with prominent economic figures who were Jews, such as his colleague Oscar Wassermann at the Deutsche Bank. His friendship with Georg Wertheim continued, he had spent a seaside vacation in 1928 with the Wertheim family. After 1933, he did not sever his relationship with Georg Wertheim who was officially redefined as a Jew under the new regime, even though from 1934, Stauss also held the office of vicepresident of the Reichstag. Thus his activities at Wertheim were presumably motivated by personal interests.[49] At the same time, it cannot be wholly denied that he viewed the continuing existence of the *Warenhäuser* as sensible and necessary since they could serve as centers for distributing goods in case of war. In addition, personal, material interests cannot be completely ruled out as another motive for his involvement.

45 BAP, R 80 Ba 2 P 57, Doc. 91, *Der Abend*, 18 October 1930.

46 BAK, Aussenstelle Zehlendorf (former Berlin Document Center), see Personalakte Franz von Papen (1080076713), for a query from a representative of the Führer to the Reich Treasurer of the NSDAP, from the year 1938, as to whether various representatives, including Stauss, had become members by then. Since no party member's card existed at that time, it seems reasonable to conclude that he did not join the NSDAP. However, this illuminates only the formal level, because Stauss did support the substance of NSDAP policy.

47 OMGUS, in *Ermittlungen gegen die Deutsche Bank*, p. 46.

48 BAK, Aussenstelle Zehlendorf, 29 November 1939, Akte Ahnenerbe (8260001465).

49 Wertheim, *Diary,* p. 69.

Both Stauss and Arthur Lindgens, an independent attorney with close contacts to Bormann and other powerful National Socialist officials, assumed important positions within the Wertheim group at an early stage. Georg Wertheim hoped that these persons could protect the business from the external attacks. When SA troops attempted to close the Wertheim store in Breslau, Stauss did indeed manage to keep it open under police protection.[50] But although Stauss and Lindgens seem to have been welcome within the higher echelons of the National Socialist party, they could not completely shelter the Wertheim enterprise and Georg Wertheim personally. Nor is it clear whether they truly wanted to offer complete protection. In the end, Georg Wertheim did not succeed in keeping his properties. His son, Albrecht, who has spoken on his memories of these years,[51] believes that the *Betriebszellen* exacerbated the further marginalization of his father. Georg Wertheim was unofficially barred from entering his own stores, and after 1934 he never again visited them; however, he remained chair of the supervisory board until 1937, although he no longer personally participated in its meetings.

In the wake of the events at Hermann Tietz, Georg Wertheim transferred his own shares and some of the shares that had belonged to his deceased brother to his non-Jewish wife Ursula, who then owned the majority of shares of the company.[52] In 1934, internal power struggles within the party had absorbed so much energy that the leaders of Wertheim began to hope that they had passed the peak of the persecution. Very few Jews were employed by the company, most of whom were veterans of World War I and virtually all had converted to Christianity. The hope was that the company could continue to do business by maintaining an inconspicuous business style.

50 BAP, R 80 Ba 2 P 24404, Notation Stauss 11 and 13 March 1933; see also Ladwig-Winters, *Wertheim*, p. 113–114.

51 The author conducted a number of interviews with him, in Berlin and at his home in Switzerland.

52 Ladwig-Winters, *Wertheim*, pp. 189–195.

Policies Aimed Against the Warenhäuser in General

Agitation against the *Warenhäuser* continued. However, the party had come to accept certain of them as "German." These included — in addition to the "Aryanized" Hertie, formerly Hermann Tietz — the Karstadt group, which had worked toward an agreement with party leaders very early on with the goal of becoming exempt from boycott measures.[53] These two enterprises now had an urgent interest to distinguish themselves from other *Warenhäuser*. The importance of the remaining *Warenhaus* groups, such as Wertheim and Schocken, made it necessary to develop regulations for *Warenhäuser* in general. The *Warenhäuser* largely rejected the definition put forth by the Ministry of Economics, which offered an escape route — namely, abolish the grocery departments and cafeterias and the *Warenhaus* would be declared a *Kaufhaus*. Moreover, the leading creditor banks insisted that their debtors continue to do business without disruption, in order to secure trouble-free repayment of their loans. This influence ensured that such special events as the "White Week" and end-of-season close-out sales could take place in 1934 and 1935, too.[54] As had already occurred at Hermann Tietz, the banks and the National Socialist party headquarters in Munich jointly engaged auditors to investigate the personnel situation, that is, the participation of Jews in management.[55]

In the meantime, the lower ranks of the National Socialist organizations continued to take action against the *Warenhäuser*. The grocery departments and the cafeterias, which constituted regular sources of income for the *Warenhäuser* because they were independent of seasonal fluctuations, were a particular target of attention. The main point of criticism was that the large purchase orders placed by the *Warenhäuser* had the effect of setting agricultural prices. For the *Warenhäuser* these were especially vulnerable points. The unions had in their possession an assessment of this situation, the origin of which is unclear. The

53 Rudolf Lenz, *Karstadt. Ein deutscher Warenhauskonzern 1920–1950*, Stuttgart, 1995, pp. 173, 176.

54 Ladwig-Winters, *Wertheim,* pp. 141–142.

55 At Wertheim, this was the *Deutsche Revisions- und Treuhandgesellschaft*; Ladwig-Winters, *Wertheim*, p. 203.

overall conclusion of this report favored retaining the *Warenhäuser*.[56] One can assume that the National Socialist party had obtained access to this political evaluation in May 1933 at the latest, when the unions were forced to disband. Now, it was used against the *Warenhäuser*. In the process, lies regarding allegedly poor hygiene, for instance, stirred up public opinion in the hope of creating a taboo against touching the merchandise. Press reports spread the rumor that a banana saleswoman in the grocery department of a *Warenhaus* had had leprosy. Among many other provocations, there were also demands that butchers working in these departments no longer be listed in the Register of Craftsmen.[57] The Ministry of Economics intervened, stipulating that the grocery departments and cafeterias be allowed to continue doing business in the large cities, with a few exceptions. These departments played an important role in supplying the population with food, also they could flexibly integrate into their operations the rationing regulations, which grew ever more complicated. Thus, with respect to preparing for a war, they were essential distribution channels for the population.

In sum, while a tendency toward retaining the *Warenhäuser* dominated at the highest political levels, they continued to suffer antisemitic attacks from the lower and middle levels. The attacks came in waves: in 1933 they were extremely severe, but they diminished in intensity in 1934, only to increase again in 1935. They lessened before and during the Olympic Games in Berlin in 1936. Meanwhile, the transfer of individual companies went on unabated.

Policies Directed against Wertheim

In early 1936, the denunciation of a former employee in Breslau was used as a pretext to close all of Wertheim's book departments.[58] These departments had been subjected to special supervision by the Ministry of Propaganda. And like all booksellers, the *Warenhäuser* had to comply with the order to destroy forbidden books. Wertheim alone

56 ADGB-Restakten, Archiv Historische Kommission, NB 430, Doc. 021, n.d. under the title: "Das Warenhaus in der deutschen Volkswirtschaft."

57 Ladwig-Winters, *Wertheim,* pp. 142–143.

58 BAP, R 80 Ba 2 P 5200, Doc. 78/81/96, 1936.

burned 2,500 books between October 1934 and January 1936. However, this cooperative behavior was in no way rewarded. In Breslau, the head of Wertheim's book department had taken it upon himself to sell to store employees at a cheap price those books that were no longer allowed to be borrowed from public libraries but had not yet been banned. The Ministry of Propaganda took this as an excuse to order that all of Wertheim's book departments be closed down. Stauss was called in, and he managed to avert the closing. However, economic reasons alone persuaded the National Chamber of Culture (*Reichskulturkammer*), to withdraw the order and insist only on a penalty, in the form of Wertheim making a "voluntary" donation of RM 24,000 to the German Schiller Foundation.[59]

During this ostensibly quiet period, Georg Wertheim and his son had the opportunity to visit Schacht, the current Minister of Economics, in his office. Schacht told them: "You have to howl with the wolves."[60] But he offered no other helpful advice.

For the Wertheim Group — with four stores in Berlin, one in Stralsund, one in Rostock, and one in Breslau — sales between 1933 and 1937 were surprisingly good.[61] Compared to sales for 1933, which had fallen to RM 54,594,454, the lowest level since 1924 (RM 75,308,433), and only 45 percent of the sales in 1928, Wertheim's sales increased steadily in Berlin — roughly 3.4% between 1933 and 1935, in 4.4% 1936, and about 5.3% in 1937. In absolute figures, sales went from RM 54,617,867 in 1933 to RM 64,118,565 in 1937, with an overall increase of RM 9,500,698, or 17.4%. Wertheim's growth contrasted dramatically with the situation of the stores recognized to be "German," namely Hertie and Karstadt. While sales fell for Hertie and Karstadt until 1935 and then slowly began to recover,[62] Wertheim maintained its sales (except in 1933), and even improved them. It is probable that antisemitism was responsible for the drastic changes in the structure of staff and management at both Karstadt and Hertie. Thus, their employees, who required National Socialist approval before being

59 BAP, R 80 Ba 2 P 5200, Doc. 138, 7 November 1936.

60 Interview with A. Wertheim, 1987.

61 According to an internal report on Wertheim's sales. No figures exist for the year 1934.

62 BAP, R 80 Ba 2 P 5200, Doc. 88, Bankenkonsortium to Wertheim, 27 July 1936.

hired, were less experienced and knowledgeable. In contrast, customers kept returning to Wertheim because nothing seemed to have radically changed: the name, most of the staff, the store's self-presentation, and the owner remained the same.

Wertheim's Valuable Property

Nonetheless, the creditor banks demanded higher earnings and interfered with concrete business decisions, demanding, for instance, that inventories be reduced. Real estate was to be sold off at prices far below market value, and here Stauss again played an important role. He was the coordinator for purchasing a piece of land for the new Reich Chancellory.[63] It is fairly likely that the proximity of various Wertheim properties in the *Voss Strasse*[64] to the government district substantially influenced the decision to build at this site. Stauss knew that Wertheim could be easily pressured to sell. With the cooperation of the banks involved, all these properties were severely undervalued, with the low prices enforced by a constant threat of outright expropriation.

Throughout this whole transaction it is notable that Stauss, who defended the business against attack by lower level National Socialist functionaries and fed Georg Wertheim information about upcoming government measures, behaved disloyally toward Wertheim for the sake of his bank and the party. To clarify: Wertheim had to sell a number of properties to pay off some loans. But when a chance arose to open a new credit line with another bank, Stauss delayed and blocked the negotiations. Wertheim was therefore unable to repay the necessary sum and was at the mercy of its creditors.[65]

By then Georg Wertheim had no property and no power to direct the business. His other brother had died in 1934 and the widow, Martha, attempted to hang on to her shares. His colleagues on the board and

63 BAP, R 80 Ba 2 P 5200, Doc. 42, 6 February 1934.

64 The properties were located at Voss Str. 7/8/9/13/14/17/18, see Zentrales Grundbucharchiv Hohenschönhausen, Berlin, which contains the land register entries for these properties.

65 BAP, R 80 Ba 2 P 5201, Doc. 156, 5 May 1938, Stauss to Wintermantel and Wieland, Deutsche Bank.

in management seldom asked him for counsel. The shares his wife Ursula held had to be put into a trust (*Kuratorium*), with Stauss as trustee. During this period Ursula Wertheim showed little interest in the business. She viewed her social life, which revolved around traveling, as more important.

Beginning in 1936, pressure mounted to transfer all shares to "Aryan" individuals. All shares held by family members had to be transferred to non-Jewish shareholders. The most influential figures on the board and trust apparently felt no responsibility for long-time colleagues or the Wertheim family. In not one case were the "small shareholders" — the nieces and nephews of the Wertheim brothers — able to negotiate a fair price for their shares. Most of those who owned shares worth approximately RM 100,000 were preparing to emigrate, but the company showed no interest in making this easier for them. Only when political pressure made the transfer of shares necessary did the company or a group of its leaders (which included Lindgens and Stauss) buy these shares.[66]

Stauss conveyed to Georg and Ursula Wertheim the National Socialist party's demand that they divorce.[67] To keep the property in the family, Georg Wertheim readily agreed. At the end of 1938 they divorced.

Conditions of "Aryanization"

By late 1937 and early 1938, the "Bureau Hess" had determined out three criteria that would have to be met before Wertheim could be considered "Aryanized." The Ministry of Economics, in turn, notified Wertheim of these conditions, although this ministry had already recognized the enterprise as "German." This notification is the only written version of the criteria for "Aryanization" that I found during my entire research. The conditions were comparable to those that had been applied at Hermann Tietz in 1934, namely non-Jewish ownership, non-Jewish employees, and a new name.[68] Concerning the ownership of Wertheim, a gradual transfer of shares from Jewish to non-Jewish members of the

66 On these events, see Ladwig-Winters, *Wertheim,* pp. 229–296.

67 Interview with A. Wertheim, 1987.

68 BAP, R 80 Ba 2 P 5205, Doc. 37, 9 March 1938.

family had taken place, until finally, in 1938, the last Jewish co-owners were eliminated. Secondly, Jewish managers — of which there had only been two — were forced to leave at the end of 1936 and 1938.[69] The number of Jewish employees at lower levels was reduced over several years, and in early 1938, the last thirty-four had to give up their jobs in the company. More than half of them had worked at Wertheim for over fifteen years. The files of the Deutsche Bank include a list of their names.[70] Thirteen of these thirty-four employees were later deported and killed; for most of them, the place of death is unknown. In contrast to Schocken, where dismissed employees received severance pay,[71] the sources give no hint of comparable measures at Wertheim. And thirdly, the company name: after long discussions among the Ministry of Economics, Stauss, and top officials of the party, the new name decided upon was *AWAG*, an acronym for *Allgemeine Warenhandelsgesellschaft A.G.* (General Retailing Corporation), not A. Wertheim A.G. as most customers believed.[72]

The company stayed in business and a good many of its loans were repaid. This was the situation when Georg Wertheim died on 31 December 1939, nearly blind and still refusing to emigrate. He had been hit hard by the 1938 pogrom, his divorce, and the fact that his only son had been drafted into the military. In December 1939 he sent his daughter a farewell letter.[73] Georg Wertheim was cremated on 4 January 1940 and is buried in a Christian cemetery in Berlin.

The Founding Family Loses their Property and Fights to Survive

Most Jewish members of the family were able to emigrate, others survived underground in Berlin, but three family members were killed in Auschwitz. Only one "non-Aryan" wife emigrated with her husband. The others distanced themselves from the family's troubles, agreed to

69 Ladwig-Winters, *Wertheim*, pp. 281–282.

70 BAP, R 80 Ba 2 P 5205, Doc. 29, 16 December 1937.

71 Avraham Barkai, *Vom Boykott zur Entjudung*, Frankfurt a.M., 1988, p. 94.

72 BAP, R 80 Ba 2 P 5201, Doc. 261, 6 August 1938.

73 Wertheim, *Diary*, p. 85.

divorce, and took over their relatives' property, behaving more like legal owners than trustees. A year after Georg Wertheim's death, Ursula Wertheim, who still held the clear majority of shares, married Arthur Lindgens, who was a member of the supervisory board of Wertheim/AWAG.

Conclusions

Looking at the overall development of the company, one can conclude that the arbitrary threats of early 1933 were so menacing that the climate was quickly prepared for the takeover of important businesses, under pressure from Germany's leading banks. Ideological aims, such as subjecting the *Warenhäuser* to the control of local authorities, turned out to be unfeasible in light of the stores' economic importance and of their creditors. Officials in the highest ranks of the National Socialist party took an interest in the controversy. In the early phase, a fragile balance existed between the German banks and top officials in the party.

Local authorities, such as in Breslau, tried to work against this balance, but they remained at a disadvantage, at least until the beginning of the war. The local chambers of industry and commerce were not involved in the process. The newly installed directors and owners of the businesses enjoyed the backing of the party. Auditing agencies played an important part in this redistribution as well. On order of the party, the auditors helped to assess the value of an enterprise. They always did this in a politically biased way, to the disadvantage of the legal owner.

As Laak has noted,[74] "Aryanization" in the business sector involved the greatest number of persons in antisemitic persecution, as a step toward total elimination. But until 1938 the disappearance of Jews from the sphere of big business was a "welcome effect" (even in the

74 Dirk van Laak, "Die Mitwirkenden bei der "Arisierung." Dargestellt am Beispiel der rheinisch-westfälischen Industrieregion 1933–1940," in: *Die Deutschen und die Judenverfolgung im Dritten Reich*, Ursula Büttner, ed., Hamburg, 1992, pp. 231–257, especially 249.

view of society as whole), but only a secondary one.[75] The parties involved in the takeovers were motivated less by ideology than by profits. As the case of Hermann Tietz illustrates, the redistribution benefited only a limited number of private persons, not to mention the creditor banks. Though the course of events differed at Wertheim, their consequences were similar.

Contrary to what Genschel has argued,[76] the term "insidious" (*schleichend*), is a misleading characterization of this process of selection and persecution. The main difference between the later, official "Aryanization" by decree following the 1938 pogrom and the stage before it was the private initiative that gave impetus to the process. In choosing the term *schleichend*, Genschel describes how people lost their property. This marginalized the important question of who profited. In addition, for those people affected by it, "Aryanization" meant complete selection and exclusion, which was gradual only in a few exceptional cases. An examination of large-scale retail enterprises shows that their takeover occurred during the first phase, which was driven by the actions of private persons. The party and the state only created a framework for these individuals' activities.

In the case of the Hermann Tietz takeover, the new owner was simply interested in enriching himself. In the case of Wertheim, the motivations are less obvious. Here the legal owner tried to keep the enterprise in the family. But loyalties within the family shifted along with external political changes. It was shortly before he died that Georg Wertheim finally realized he could do nothing constructive for the enterprise. The Wertheim family represents here, in a microcosm, a phenomen that occurred in society at large during the National Socialist period.

75 Avraham Barkai, "Max Warburg im Jahre 1933. Missglückte Versuche zur Milderung der Judenverfolgung," in: *Juden in Deutschland. Emanzipation, Integration, Verfolgung und Vernichtung*, Peter Freimark et al., ed., Hamburg, 1991, p. 391.

76 Helmut Genschel, *Die Verdrängung der Juden aus der Wirtschaft im Dritten Reich*, Göttingen, 1966.

Popular Attitudes to Nazi Antisemitism in Wartime

The German Population and the Jews: State of Research and New Perspectives

OTTO DOV KULKA

The new methodological approach I wish to introduce into the study of the attitude of the German population toward the Jews in the Third Reich transcends the chronological boundaries of the Third Reich itself. Indeed, a connection might be found with currents and trends in German society before 1933, and in particular after the so-called *Stunde Null*, the zero hour of 1945. This new approach pays tribute to the late Martin Broszat, who criticized the isolation — or as he put it — the insularity — that marked the study of the Hitler period in German history up to recent years.[1]

But first let us deal with the period within the chronological boundaries of the Third Reich. The National Socialist regime, as we now know, did not accept at face value the monolithic image of state and society that it portrayed in the mass media and projected to the world. The authorities established secret internal reporting systems to provide reliable information about the prevailing popular mood and about activity being conducted by the different sectors of the population. The most important reports were those prepared by the security services of the SS (the SD), the Gestapo, the district governors, the party, and its

1 Martin Broszat, "Eine Insel in der Geschichte? Der Historiker in der Spannung zwischen Bewerten und Verstehen der Hitler-Zeit", in: idem.,*Nach Hitler. Der schwierige Umgang mit unserer Geschichte*, Munich, 1988, pp. 208–215. For an example of the empirical implementation of his theoretical postulates cf. Broszat et al., eds., *Von Stalingrad zur Währungsreform. Zur Sozialgeschichte des Umbruchs in Deutschland*, Munich, 1988; for a critical historiographical survey of this trend in German historiography, particularly after the reunification, see Ian Kershaw, *The Nazi Dictatorship. Problems and Perspectives of Interpretation*, London, 1993, ch. 10.

various organizations. The reports were written on different levels — local, district, and regional — and finally compiled at a national level.

Much of this material has been preserved in various archives, but for a long time was completely ignored. Only at a relatively late stage did researchers become aware of its importance as a paramount source for studying the social history of the Third Reich, encompassing, as it did, the German society's attitude toward the Jews and toward the regimes' anti-Jewish policy. Since then, several sections of those sources have been published, some of them national in scope, others on specific regions and mostly limited to particular periods of the Third Reich.[2] A comprehensive collection of this source material on the Jewish aspect is now being undertaken as a joint German-Israeli project at the universities of Stuttgart and Jerusalem. It is based, *inter alia*, on systematic research in the previously partially inaccessible archives of the former German Democratic Republic.[3]

2 A detailed description of the publications and research up to the mid-1980s is included in the first, methodological, part of my article, "Die Nürnberger Rassengesetze und die deutsche Bevölkerung im Lichte geheimer NS-Lage- und Stimmungsberichte,"*Vierteljahrshefte für Zeitgeschichte,* 32 (1984), pp. 582–600. For further source publications among them on the national level: Heinz Boberach, ed., *Meldungen aus dem Reich. Die geheimen Lageberichte des Sicherheitsdienstes der SS 1938–1945*, 17 vols., Herrsching, 1984; or on the regional level: Thomas Klein, ed., *Die Lageberichte der Geheimen Staatspolizei über die Provinz Hessen-Nassau 1933–1936*, Cologne, 1986, cf. Heinz Boberach, "Quellen für die Einstellung der deutschen Bevölkerung zur Judenverfolgung. Analyse und Kritik," in: *Die Deutschen und die Judenverfolgung im Dritten Reich*, Ursula Büttner, ed., Hamburg, 1992, pp. 31–49.

3 For a critical discussion of the research problems concerning the Jewish aspect, see O.D. Kulka and A. Rodrigue, "The German Population and the Jews in the Third Reich. Recent Publications and Trends of Research on German Society and the 'Jewish Question,'" *Yad Vashem Studies,* 16 (1984), pp. 421–435; Ian Kershaw, "German Popular Opinion and the 'Jewish Question,' 1939–1943. Some further Reflections," in: *Juden im Nationalsozialistischen Deutschland — The Jews in Nazi Germany 1933–1943*, Arnold Paucker, ed., Tübingen, 1986, pp. 365–388; idem, "German Popular Opinion during the Final Solution: Information, Comprehension, Reactions," in: *Comprehending the Holocaust. Historical and Literary Research*, Ascher Cohen et al., eds., Frankfurt am Main, 1989, pp. 145–158. Some additional problems are dealt with in: Hans Mommsen, "Was haben die Deutschen vom Völkermord an den Juden gewusst?" in: Walter Pehle, ed., *Der Judenpogrom 1938. Von der "Reichskristallnacht" zum Völkermord,* Frankfurt, 1988, pp. 176–200; Hans Mommsen and Dieter Obst, "Die Reaktion der deutschen Bevölkerung auf die

One of the basic findings that has emerged from these sources is that beneath the cover of totalitarian uniformity the social, political and religious structures of the previous period were preserved, thus revealing also the public's heterogeneous view of the government's ideology and policy. Among the categories of surveillance and reporting, the subject of the regime's "ideological enemies" (*Weltanschauliche Gegner*) — Marxism, liberalism, "political churches," the conservative opposition, and the Jews — occupies a significant place.With respect to the Jews, the reports also provide current information on the attitude of different groups in the population toward them and toward the different stages of the government's policy on the so-called "solution of the Jewish Question."

The following is a concise summary of the findings on the population's reactions during two periods:

a) The 1930s until the outbreak of the war, centering around racist legislation and the exclusion of Jews from various spheres of life in the German state and society.
b) The war years, which witnessed the mass deportation and the extermination — what is known as the "Final Solution."

Reactions in the 1930s were relatively intensive and can be divided into several main types:

1. Much of the population viewed the racial legislation as a possible permanent solution of social, cultural and biological segregation and isolation, but conditional on the preservation of public law and order.
2. Others, especially those from radical party organizations such as the SA, criticized the government's antisemitic policy for being "too moderate" and launched a series of violent anti-Jewish initiatives, most of which were local in character, with the aim of

Verfolgung der Juden 1933–1943," in: *Herrschaftsalltag im Dritten Reich. Studien und Texte*, Hans Mommsen and Susanne Willems, eds., Düsseldorf, 1988, pp. 374–421; Ursula Büttner, "Die deutsche Bevölkerung und die Judenverfolgungen 1933–1945," in: *Die Deutschen und die Judenverfolgung im Dritten Reich*, Ursula Büttner, ed., Hamburg, 1992, S. 67–88; David Bankier, *The Germans and the Final Solution. Public Opinion under Nazism*, Oxford, 1992, pp. 1–13.

accelerating and radicalizing "the solution" of the Jewish Question "from below."

3. Overt criticism in the opposite direction, based on religious, social or economic grounds, was voiced by people with a religious orientation (*konfessionell gebundene Kreise*) — the Marxist left, the liberal bourgeoisie and intellectuals, and some representatives of big business.
4. Another segment of the population — whose weight and standing on the social and political map are difficult to assess — apparently took no position on the Jewish issue. Some of their reactions, though certainly not the majority, derived from an attitude of passivity or equanimity toward the regime's ideology and policy in general. In any case, the reports contain no explicit mention of the motives behind their passive stand on the Jewish issue.

The overall picture, we may venture with a certain degree of risk, shows a continuation of the standpoints that existed in the Weimar period, the difference being that before 1933 they related to the rapidly expanding National Socialist movement and party, whereas after 1933 the reactions were to the concrete policy of a regime.

A different impression emerges from the reports on the population's mood and attitudes (*Stimmungsberichte*), during the war years. The dominant line is almost total silence regarding the Jews — a particularly striking finding given the extremist official propaganda which portrayed the Jews of Germany and world Jewry as being directly responsible for the war and its tribulations. This attitude of passivity and disinclination to react is all the more pronounced in light of the diverse reactions that continued to be expressed on foreign policy, religion, the economy, and indeed on all spheres of everyday life. People were critical of the continuation of the war, the corruption of the administration, and the food supply policy; and there were even protests, some of which were successful, such as against the killing of the incurably ill — the so-called "mercy killings" or euthanasia program — against orders to remove crucifixes from schools, and others.

In fact, reports in several archives, written mainly on the local or regional level, indicate that there were some sporadic reactions to the policy regarding the Jews. In the first years of the war there were calls for a more radical policy, similar to that implemented in the occupied territories in the east, to be introduced in Germany itself. Later, there were some reports that mentioned, along with broad popular support, some protests against the mass deportations and exterminations in the east and condemning them as inhuman and criminal. But such voices are rare in the mass of reports from all parts of Germany that cover all areas of life during the war years. The only exception was a brief period in the first half of 1943; at that time, in the wake of the Germans' defeat at Stalingrad and the intensification of the massive bombing raids against German cities, growing concern was voiced that the German people would suffer a fate similar to that of the Jews. I quote one example:

> The shock of Stalingrad has not yet faded completely. In many circles there are fears that the large number of prisoners who fell into the Russians' hands there will be executed in retaliation for the mass executions of Jews which the Germans perpetrated in the east, as people say.[4]

Other reactions link the Allies' devastating raids on the major cities in Germany with a conspiracy of reprisal by the Jews, the operators of the western war machine, against German policy toward their brethren in occupied Europe.[5]

At that time, the spring and early summer of 1943, the German public was subjected to a massive propaganda campaign in which the Nazis utilized all the communications media at their disposal, condemning the atrocities and mass murders perpetrated by the Bolsheviks. This followed the disclosure of what is known as the "Katyn Affair." As will be recalled, retreating German forces discovered a mass grave containing the remains of several thousand Polish officers who had been executed in 1940 in a forest near the village of Katyn at Stalin's order. By association, the issue of mass murder, which the campaign

4 Monatsbericht (Lagebericht), des Regierungspräsidenten in Augsburg, 10.4.1943, I Allgemeine politische Lage und öffentliche Sicherheit, A Volksstimmung und Haltung, p. 1. Bayerisches Hauptstaatsarchiv (further on BayHStA), StK 106 703 (cf. Kulka, "'Public Opinion' in National Socialist Germany and the 'Jewish Question,'" *Zion. Quarterly for Research in Jewish History,* 40 (1975), pp. 186–290 (Hebrew with English summary; documentation in German, pp. 260–290), p. 250; facsimile ibid., opposite p. 207).

5 Bericht des SD-Abschnittes Halle, 22.5.1943, Bundesarchiv Koblenz (in the meantime moved to Berlin) (further on BA), NS 6/404.

made the theme of open everyday conversation, also evoked the mass extermination of the Jews. The following is a typical reaction described in one of the reports:

> The propaganda exploitation of the incident in the course of several weeks led to heightened concern of the part of family relations for the fate of the soldiers who are missing or being held captive by the Russians. The Katyn propaganda also generated inquiries about the treatment of the Jews in Germany and in the territories of the east.[6]

Another report quoted remarks about "the hypocrisy of the German propaganda position," this in light of a prevailing view that "Poles and Jews were liquidated on a far greater scale by the German side."[7]There are also extremely caustic statements, albeit very rare, which are attributed to Christian religious circles, such as the following quotation, apparently part of a sermon:

> The National Socialists have no right to get worked up by the bestial slaughter. The SS employed similar methods of carnage in the war against the Jews in the east. The despicable and inhuman behavior of the SS toward the Jews cries out for the Creator to punish our nation. If these murders do not engender harsh acts of revenge against us, then divine justice no longer exists. The German people has taken on itself a blood guilt for which it cannot expect mercy and compassion.[8]

In retrospect, it can be inferred from these, and several other similar reactions that the mass exterminations were general public knowledge — particularly the mass murders that had been perpetrated in the preceding two years, since the invasion of the Soviet Union in June 1941.[9] This constitutes the background to the fears expressed about the possible implications for the fate of the German people.

6 Report from Augsburg (as in note 4), 10.5.1943, BayHStA, StK 106 703.

7 SD-report of 19.4.1943, in, Heinz Boberach, ed., *Meldungen aus dem Reich. Auswahl aus den geheimen Lageberichten des Sicherheitsdienstes der SS 1939–1944,* Neuwied, 1965, p. 383.

8 Parteikanzlei IIB4, Auszüge aus Berichten der Gaue u.a. Dienststellen, Zeitraum: 2.5.43–8.5.43, BA, NS 6/409.

9 Cf. also Kershaw, "German Popular Opinion during the Final Solution" (as in note 3), p. 152; idem, *The "Hitler Myth." Image and Reality in the Third Reich*, Oxford, 1987, p. 246; Hans-Heinrich Wilhelm,"The Holocaust in National Socialist Rhetoric and Writings. Some Evidence Against the Thesis that Before 1945 Nothing Was Known about the 'Final Solution'," *Yad Vashem Studies*, 16 (1984), pp. 95–127;

With the fading of the Katyn Affair, which in the view of many policy makers had become a propaganda liability, the dominant line of silence on the Jewish Question returns in the reports, although public criticism of the conduct of the war and the various other issues continues to be voiced.

The research literature offers various interpretations of the passive stand, or general silence, regarding the "Final Solution." There is general agreement that in contrast to the intensity which marks the diverse opinions that were expressed about the treatment of Jews in concrete, everyday matters during the 1930s, a kind of depersonalized attitude toward them evolved during the war period. Overall, the background to this was the Jews' complete isolation and their gradual disappearance from the German social landscape — indeed, their transmutation into an abstraction, induced by propaganda on the "removal of the Jews," "the utter elimination of the Jewish Question," the relentness war of annihilation against "the Jewish Bolshevism" and the "world Jewish plutocracy," and so forth.

The major area of disagreement concerns two interpretations of that underlying depersonalization. One interpretation holds that the silence or general passivity toward the fate of the Jews was the result of indifference, of not knowing or not wishing to know, or, alternatively, of a repression of such knowledge. The second interpretation views the absence of a pronounced reaction and the general passivity toward the physical annihilation of the Jews as the expression of a broad consensus on the government's policy, a kind of tacit agreement that there was no need to take an active stand on the subject. This analysis views the emerging passive orientation as the cumulative effect of the German population's gradual internalization and assimilation of the claims and content of the war propaganda on the country's "life and death struggle" against the driving force behind its enemies.[10]

The most urgent problem confronting research on this subject is whether additional sources and other indications can be found to help

Goetz Aly, "The Universe of Death and Torment," *Yad Vashem Studies,* 26 (1997), pp. 365–376.

10 For a more detailed description of the different interpretations, see Kulka and Rodrigue (as in note 3), pp. 432–435.

solve this terrible enigma. Besides the systematic surveillance and reporting on public opinion, we have various other sources from the period, including diaries,[11] letters,[12] memoirs,[13]a handful of underground leaflets,[14] and documents of church leaders[15] and anti-Hitler

11 The most illuminating examples of diaries dealing with this question are: Herbert and Sibylle Obenaus, eds., *"Schreiben, wie es wirklich war!" Aufzeichnungen Karl Dürkelfäldens aus den Jahren 1933–1945*, Hannover, 1985; and Ulrich von Hassell, *Vom anderen Deutschland. Aus den nachgelassenen Tagebüchern 1935–1944*, Frankfurt am Main, 1984.

12 The most important among them are the collected and partially published letters of German soldiers from the occupied territories in the east, including: Ortwin Buchbender and Reinhold Sterz, eds., *Das andere Gesicht des Krieges. Deutsche Feldpostbriefe 1939–1945*, Munich, 1982 (Juden: pp. 168–173); Jürgen Reulecke and Anatoly Golovchansky, eds., *"Ich will raus aus diesem Wahnsinn." Deutsche Briefe von der Ostfront 1941–1945,* Wuppertal, 1991; Walter Manoschek, *Das Judenbild in den Soldatenbriefen, 1933–1944*, Hamburg, 1995; Alf Lüdtke, "The Appeal of Exterminating 'Others.' German Workers and the Limits of Resistance," *Journal of Modern History,* 64 Supplement, (1992), pp. 546–567 (based on the letters of German soldiers to their employers during Word War II, preserved in the Staatsarchiv, Leipzig).

13 Some relevant examples and their critical evaluation are found in: Büttner, "Die deutsche Bevölkerung" (as in note 3).

14 Cf. Inge Scholl, *Students against Tyranny. The Resistance of the White Rose, Munich 1942–1943*, Middletown, Conn., 1970. For a critical evaluation of these most important documents of their kind, reprinted on pp. 78–79, see Kulka and Rodrigue (as in note 3), pp. 434–435.

15 Among the many publications on the so-called *Kirchenkampf* (church struggle), only a few relate to the Jewish subject. See, for example, in Joachim Beckmann, ed., *Kirchliches Jahrbuch für die evangelische Kirche in Deutschland (1933–1944),* Gütersloh, 1948; Heinrich Hermelink, ed., *Kirche im Kampf. Dokumente des Widerstands und des Aufbaus in der Evangelischen Kirche Deutschlands von 1933–1945*, Tübingen, 1950; Peter Matheson, ed., *The Third Reich and the Christian Churches*, Grand Rapids, Michigan, 1981. The most interesting on our subject are the letters of Bishop Theophil Wurm, sent during the war years to various representatives of the government, including Hitler, in, Gerhard Schäfer, ed., *Landesbischof Wurm und der nationalsozialistische Staat 1940–1945*, Stuttgart, 1968. For an extensive survey of the publications concerning the churches and the "Jewish Question" in the Third Reich, cf. Kulka,"Popular Christian Attitudes in the Third Reich to National Socialist Policies towards the Jews," in: *Judaism and Christianity under the Impact of National Socialism 1919–1945*, Otto D. Kulka and Paul R.Mendes-Flohr, eds., Jerusalem, 1988, p. 251f., n. 1.

conspirational groups.[16] However, their sporadic and subjective character cannot serve as a foundation either to affirm or to refute one of the two comprehensive interpretations.

Such a foundation, surprisingly, might be found outside the period itself — beyond that "zero hour" of 1945. It appears that not only the regime of the Third Reich, but also the Allied occupation authorities, especially the Americans, wanted to create for themselves reliable sources of information about public opinion, which during the transition from the Nazis' totalitarian rule to a western occupation regime would not find open expression through the normal modes of communication. Accordingly, the Allied Forces introduced a western-style system of public opinion surveys,[17] and I draw here on some of the findings that can be extracted from those sources:

In October 1945, only months after the fall of the Nazi regime, it is reported that 20 percent of those questioned "went along with Hitler on his treatment of the Jews," while a further 19 percent were generally in favor but felt that he had gone too far.[18] A later general survey on the attitude toward National Socialism reveals that in August 1947, 55 percent of the population still believed that "National Socialism was a good idea badly carried out."[19] It goes without saying that these

16 Cf. the documentation in the study by Christof Dipper, "German Resistance and the Jews," *Yad Vashem Studies,* 16 (1984), pp. 51–93; and now also the extensive study of Chaim Rosen, *National Conservative Opposition in the "Third Reich" and their Attitude towards the Anti-Jewish Policy and the "Final Solution" 1938–1945*, Doctoral Thesis submitted to the Hebrew University of Jerusalem, 1997 (in Hebrew with English summary).

17 Anna J. Merritt and Richard Merritt, eds., *Public Opinion in Occupied Germany. The OMGUS Surveys 1945–1949*, Urbana, 1970.

18 Anti-Semitism in the American Zone, ODIC Opinion Surveys Headquarters, OMGUS/APO 757, Report Number 493, 3 March 1947 (UNNRA Archives, RG-11-66,516). On the findings of the October 1945 opinion survey, see p. 3: "Previous studies." For an analysis of the historical context, cf. Ze'ev Mankowitz, *The Politics and Ideology of the Holocaust Survivors in the American Zone of Occupied Germany 1945–1946*, Doctoral thesis submitted to the Hebrew University of Jerusalem 1987, (in Hebrew), pp. 357f., English summary p. 51; Frank Stern, *The Whitewashing of the Yellow Badge. Antisemitism and Philosemitism in Postwar Germany*, Oxford, 1992, ch. 3: "OMGUS Research on Antisemitism and Policy Making," pp. 111–132; idem, *Jews in the Minds of Germans in Postwar Period. The 1992 Paul Lecture*, Indiana, 1993.

19 Merritt and Merritt (as in note 17) p. 32.

replies were given in a situation which no longer left room for the assumption that people were ignorant of the whole truth about the horrors of the concentration and death camps. It is equally clear that in this period responses indicating identification with the ideas and policies of Nazism were not opportunistic. If, nevertheless, these were the results of the surveys, it is obvious that the interpretation that the German population was generally indifferent to the genocidal policy against the Jews does not pass the test of the confrontation with the additional sources. It is also plain enough that identification with the "Final Solution" was quite widespread among the public in the Third Reich.[20]

In terms of the implications of research which broadens the perspective to include the periods that preceded and followed the Third Reich, several additional conclusions can be drawn. In both cases — after 1933 and after 1945 — there was a kind of asymmetry between the regime's declared norms of ethics and politics and the attitudes of the population. For, following the establishment of the totalitarian regime in the Third Reich, a great many of the pretotalitarian structures and attitudes survived and Nazi norms were only internalized gradually. Moreover, under the newly imposed democracy, the bulk of the German population continued to identify with previous attitudes, even after the nature of the crime of genocide had been revealed, only slowly acquiring the alternative ideas of a liberal democracy.

I shall conclude by recalling my introductory methodological note. In that context it is perhaps not superfluous to observe that the findings and theses which I have adduced here must not remain a purely scientific

20 In addition to the findings of the above-mentioned scholars, see also the analysis and conclusions of Martin Broszat in his study "Zur Struktur der NS-Massenbewegung," *Vierteljahrshefte für Zeitgeschichte,* 31(1983), pp. 53–76. I quote here from the closing section of this essay on pp. 74–76 where he speaks on the causes of the passive attitude "of the great majority of the German population during the last years of the war [...] The underlying inhuman conception, especially with regard to the fanatic hatred of the Jews, was also expressed publicly by the leadership on almost every occasion and there certainly was a social sounding ground (*Resonanzboden*) for these ideas [...] Here apparently the awareness of a shared responsibility for and complicity in the excesses and crimes of the regime played a role as well." *(Hier spielte offenbar auch das Bewusstsein herein, dass man mitverantwortlich hineinverwickelt gewesen war, in die Exzesse und Verbrechen des Regimes.)*

exercise to reveal asymmetry between the components of social and political history. It is also essential to be aware of the appalling dynamic that could close one particular gap in this asymmetry.

Popular Attitudes to National Socialist Antisemitism: Denunciations for "Insidious Offenses" and "Racial Ignominy"

CHRISTL WICKERT

In this essay, the term "denunciation" is given to mean the reporting of real or supposed offenses by accusers acting on their own, without official instruction. The files of the NSDAP, the Gestapo, and of judicial authorities reveal that this practice reached unimaginable dimensions during the National Socialist period. Numerous regional and local histories, although undertaken independently of one another, have repeatedly encountered this phenomenon.[1] For there was no simpler method of resolving private quarrels than to accuse a personal enemy or competitor of having made statements critical of the regime.

According to the most recent investigations, the power of the Gestapo was based less on a perfected apparatus of persecution and more on the voluntary work of accusers.[2] Their actions, however, cannot be seen as a sign of conformity with Nazi ideology, but is traceable instead to

1 Gisela Diewald-Kerkmann, *Politische Denunziation im NS-Regime oder die kleine Macht der "Volksgenossen,"* Bonn, 1995, p. 35, 131; Bernward Dörner, "Alltagsterror und Denunziation. Zur Bedeutung von Anzeigen aus der Bevölkerung für die Verfolgungswirkung des nationalsozialistischen 'Heimtücke-Gesetzes,'" in: *Alltagskultur, Subjektivität und Geschichte. Zur Theorie und Praxis von Alltagsgeschichte*, Berliner Geschichtswerkstatt, ed., Münster, 1994, pp. 235–253, 260; Klaus-Michael Mallmann and Gerhard Paul, "Allwissen, allmächtig, allgegenwärtig? Gestapo, Gesellschaft und Widerstand," *Zeitschrift für Geschichtswissenschaft,* 41 (1993), p. 988; Inge Marssolek and Reneé Ott, *Bremen im Dritten Reich. Anpassung — Widerstand — Verfolgung,* Bremen, 1986, pp. 90 ff., 192.

2 Klaus Michael Mallmann and Gerhard Paul, eds., *Die Gestapo. Mythos und Realität*, Darmstadt, 1995.

envy, prejudice and revenge. The majority of accusers lived in the same neighborhoods, worked in the same profession or, indeed,were related to the accused. The Gestapo sought to use denunciation in order to fulfill its claim to universal surveillance, but in reality the phenomenon represented a self-surveillance. The omnipresent antisemitism of Nazi society is reflected in denunciations, but was often instrumentalized by accusers. "Aryans" were charged with behaving "like Jews," or of having contacts with Jews even when no substantiation could be produced. Jews were accused of anti-regime statements or action which could lead to long investigations even when the authorities suspected the accusation to be false.

Since offenses occurred primarily in the nonpublic sphere, the apparatus of official persecution depended on support from the population. The accusers served as a transmission belt between regime and society. The aim was not only security against criticism, but integration into the *Volksgemeinschaft*. Practice, however, fully contradicted the aim. Since, as noted, accusers and accused often came from the same personal and professional circumstances, it is reasonable to suppose that the accusations stemmed from personal conflicts, from lack of sensibility for the problems of others, and from lack of social cohesion. A massive increase in false accusations led to a huge expenditure of bureaucratic effort, which (at the latest, during the war), overloaded the Gestapo and judiciary. For this reason, the problem of denunciation was the subject of instructions to judges, who were made aware of the ambivalence of the phenomenon and instructed to drop false accusations.[3]

The *Gesetz gegen heimtückische Angriffe auf Staat und Partei* (Law against Insidious Attacks on State and Party), of 20 December 1934 criminalized criticism of the regime. Under this law, officials and party organizations were charged with reporting every anti-regime statement, action, or behavior to the Gestapo, and to encourage, record

3 The lack of social cohesion was stressed as early as 1947 by Erich Kordt, for whom the willingness to provide mutual support in the face of danger and distress was never less than in the years 1933–45. Kordt, *Wahn und Wirklichkeit. Die Aussenpolitik des Dritten Reiches. Versuch einer Darstellung,* Stuttgart, 1947, p. 45; compare a collection of denunciatory letters against Jews in Vienna in 1943–44, R. 2, Folder 7, NSDAP Vienna District, Rassenpolitisches Amt, Yad Vashem Archives; Heinz Boberach, ed., *Richterbriefe. Dokumente zur Beeinflussung der Deutschen Rechtsprechung 1942–1944,* Boppard, 1975, p. 168 ff.

and transmit reporting by the public. Without denunciation as a support for the Gestapo the law could have scarcely been implemented.[4]

Rassenschande (racial ignominy), proceedings provide striking examples of accusers seeking not only to harm the accused, but to veil their own motives. Denunciations — which for the accused were associated with physical and psychic danger — were not evidence that the population really adhered to Nazi antisemitism. Rather, accusers used antisemitism to their own advantage. In so doing, they indirectly nullified the regime's propaganda. Nonetheless, from the Nazi point of view, these people were less dangerous than those who helped Jews. The latter, to be discussed at the end of this essay, withdrew themselves completely from National Socialist ideology; without denunciations their attitudes and actions would never have been recorded officially. To stand firm and help Jewish relatives, neighbors, acquaintances and friends was evidence of loyalty to earlier views. Such solidarity ran counter to the regime's efforts to breed a National Socialist *Volksgemeinschaft*, and to undertake the selecting out and annihilation of whole categories of human beings. From the National Socialist perspective, these people were mounting active resistance. That individuals had to risk their lives to help others characterized National Socialism as a terror regime. Since radical antisemites constituted a minority in the German population, the Nazi racial program could be realized only through terror.

Heimtückevergehen (Insidiousness)

According to my research, offenses against the *Heimtückegesetz* were actually misdemeanors of "little people." This does not shed so much light on the views of women and men from the lower classes as it does on the character of the accusers, who generally came from this class. (Up to 50 percent of those who denounced women were women.)

4 Robert Gellately, *The Gestapo and German Society: Enforcing Racial Policy 1933–1945*, Oxford 1990; Gisela Diewald-Kerkmann, *Politische Denunziation*; Diewald-Kerkmann, "Denunziantentum und Gestapo. Die freiwilligen 'Helfer' aus der Bevölkerung," in: *Gestapo, Mythos und Realität*, pp. 288–305.

Antisemitic suspicions were given free rein by the Nuremberg laws of 1935. Anyone could put them to use.[5]

"Such is the fate of all enemies of the people. The wife of a mining engineer arrested for insult and slander of the *Volksgemeinschaft* and state," ran the headline of the Essen *Nationalzeitung* on 10 August 1935. The article reported that 41-year-old Annemarie P. (her full name was cited!), had asked for a particular sort of chocolate in a sweets shop but it was not available. The customer then told the saleswoman that one could get such a chocolate bar at any time in the Hugo Wilhelm shop. When the branch manager Anne B. pointed out that Wilhelm was a Jew, Annemarie P. was alleged to have answered, while standing in the doorway: "Such silliness, this Jewish agitation. They should finally stop it. So long as you don't go to bed with a Jew, you can shop there." Three weeks elapsed before the branch manager reported the incident to the Gestapo. Two days later, the just cited article appeared in the *Nationalzeitung*, describing the case in detail. We may ask: Why did Anne B. wait so long to denounce her customer? Perhaps Mrs. P. had not returned to the shop. Perhaps the two women had met by chance on the street and had quarreled. Perhaps Mrs. P. had simply ignored Anne B. We do not know the answers and the files give no clues. The accuser requested anonymity since many of her customers were friends of Mrs. P.'s family and she feared they would no longer patronize the shop. During the interrogation it was insinuated that Annemarie P. had expressed the hope "that the men, who today sit in the government, disappear." The case excited further commotion when, on 29 August, the *Nationalzeitung* complained that none of the "bourgeois newspapers" had involved themselves with the case, despite its admonitory significance. On 6 September 1935 the *Neue Tagebuch*, published in Paris, took the occasion to comment on the spreading antisemitism of the German Reich. Entitled "Frau P.s Grenze" (Mrs. P.'s limits), the commentary asserted: "The world finally knows the difference between National Socialist and conservative nationalist opposition to Jews. With the one, the store is the limit, with the other, at first the bedroom." Following a court-ordered psychological

5 See Robert Gellately, *The Gestapo and German Society*, pp. 40 ff; idem., "The Gestapo and German Society: Political Denunciation in the Gestapo Case Files," *Journal of Modern History*, 60 (1988), 654ff.

examination of the accused, she was acquitted by the Special Court in Dortmund.[6] Annemarie P. was no real opponent of National Socialism; that she confirmed in her interrogation. Her remarks can be categorized as moderately antisemitic, yet her attitude did not prevent her from "shopping at the Jews" and publicly proclaiming so. This incident served as a warning in Essen, in order to gain public approval of the anti-Jewish laws and to encourage people to denounce those who did not unwaveringly go along with that policy.

The following incident exemplifies the effects, during the war, of dissatisfaction over the shortage of living space, caused both by regulation and bomb attacks. Instead of rousing anger against the government, it was vented rather at landlords. Two sisters, Julia and Theodora W., 56 and 58 years old, were alleged by their tenants to have engaged in insidious talk, to have listened to enemy radio and to have helped Jews. The accusers had been forcibly quartered with their families. The denunciation had been preceded by various quarrels over rent payments, and complaints by the landladies of unnecessary noise. Already in 1934, both the accused had appeared in official files as suspected or convicted of *Heimtücke*. They had lost their professional positions (Theodora as teacher, Julia as musician), after the Nazis assumed power and lived from the rental income of the house, which belonged to their brothers who resided in Canada and the Netherlands. All the tenants in the house were interrogated. They expressed merely the suspicion of political unreliability and complained mainly about the exorbitant rent "which one normally knows from Jews." The accusation that the sisters helped Jews was dropped by the Gestapo due to lack of evidence. The proceedings against Theodora — who had served a two-year jail term for "insidious offenses" — were withdrawn. Julia was the main object of the tenants' accusations and anger, but in August 1938 the Special Court dismissed the proceedings against her on health grounds. On 4 March 1944 a female tenant, goaded by a fellow roomer, tried once again to open the case against the sisters, claiming that they listened to enemy broadcasts and had contacts with Jews. The tenant's animosity had been roused by the landladies' complaints of noise made by her five children. The accuser sought to resolve the problem through

6 Hauptstaatarchiv Düsseldorf (hereafter HStAD), File RW 58–46645.

a denunciation. "If Mrs. Sch. and Mrs. H. assert this," Julia testified to the Gestapo on 11 April 1944, "they are asserting untruths. They were angry because they have to vacate the apartment in our house. They are merely taking revenge on myself and my sister." The accusers had not been moved by National Socialist antisemitism to report alleged contacts with Jews, but were making calculated use of that antisemitism to get rid of two unloved landlords.[7]

The case of the two sisters clearly reflects the decision-making power of the Gestapo: as soon as striking evidence of personal conflicts emerged, cases were either dropped or court-imposed punishments remained comparatively mild. A certain respect for legal procedure was thus observable in the Gestapo apparatus even in wartime. However, the accusers who had registered the denunciations were not called to account for their false assertions.

If the accused were Jews — whatever the offense — the Gestapo would conduct a more thorough investigation in every case. The Gestapo opened a file on Essen resident Else Davidson, a Jewish woman suspected of *Heimtücke*. The file was not closed until her transportation to an extermination camp in 1942. On 12 October 1935, Else went, as she did every month, to the customs office to collect a package of mending sent by her daughter Dora, who had emigrated to France via the Netherlands. She took the roughly 12 kilogram package and hauled it to the family's radio business on Schlageterstrasse 12. Twenty minutes later the customs official who had served her appeared, accusing her of having walked away unauthorized. With the help of her apprentice Anni Schlomm, the package was taken back to the customs office, where Else Davidson complained about having to pay a customs tax of 0.75 Reichsmark on a self-sewn handbag, which was three times the value of the item. The customs inspector O. reported her for an "offense due to insidious attacks and damage to the reputation of the party." From 7 to 9 January 1936 she was interrogated in *Schutzhaft* (protective custody). The witness Anni Schlomm confirmed in several inquiries that Else's behavior had been absolutely correct. O. could not be interrogated as he had been called to a military exercise. After the chief prosecutor's office had confirmed that her action had not fulfilled

7 Files RW 58–49047, 29797 (Theodora W.) and RW 58–63358 (Julia W.), both in HStAD.

the conditions of an "insidious offense," Else had to apologize before being released: "If I behaved in a somewhat too brusque way, I regret this and ask understanding for my excitement. I certainly did not have any intention of stepping on anyone's toes." After six months her postal surveillance was rescinded. Until 1942 nothing more was registered in her file. Fortunately for her, the Gestapo did not know that the sender of the packages, Dora Davidson, was active in the Communist exile resistance. On 22 April 1942, together with her younger daughter Lotte and her son-in-law Josef Grüner, Else was transported with her husband Julius to Izbica, where all trace of her has been lost.[8]

The quick release of Else Davidson in 1935 owes presumably to the decision-making authority of the Gestapo official in charge of the inquiry. Also, it should not be forgotten that the anti-Jewish policy was consciously moderated because of the Olympic Games scheduled to be held in Berlin in 1936. Else was helped, moreover, by the loyalty of her apprentice Anni Schlomm. That the customs inspector O. made a trivial incident into a police action betrays radical antisemitism, for everyone in Essen knew that the owner of the radio business on the Schlageterstrasse was Jewish.

The Gestapo was empowered to act on its own authority, and without specific sanction of National Socialist laws and regulations. Thus, after the outbreak of war, all accusations or suspicions against Jews — even against *Mischlinge* and those in mixed marriages — were life threatening. On 1 September 1941 the Fischer Sheet Metal Company of Düsseldorf-Oberkassel filed an accusation with the regional Gestapo headquarters in Düsseldorf against the 39-year-old Jewish woman Henny (Sara) Stern. She was charged with *Heimtücke* and (another specifically National Socialist offense) *Arbeitsverweigerung* (work refusal). She was said to have used unsorted rivets for the assembly of cans and to have screamed at the shop foreman when he apprised her of this error. She was alleged, moreover, to have already shown herself "unwilling," and had tried to keep her "racial comrades" from working. A warning by the Labor Office at the end of 1940 effected no change in

8 HStAD, Files RW 58–52491, 26889. Author's interviews with Dora Davidson (now Schaul), 26 August 1991 and 28 February 1992. In 1992 Dora Schaul, with the help of the author and the staff of the Essen Old Synagogue, succeeded in locating and visiting Anni Schlomm (now Zimmermann).

her attitude toward work. When reading the accusations, one can only suspect that they had been considerably inflated. In all likelihood the accused woman had used the wrong rivets due to oversight or fatigue resulting from hard work. Had she not been Jewish, her errors would not have constituted a case for the Gestapo. At most, she would have been sent to a *Arbeitserziehungslager* (work instruction camp), and later released. Instead, she was sent to the concentration camp Ravensbrück. The order committing her there was dated 28 October 1941. Evidence in her files refers to a *Haftprüfungstermin* on 16 January 1942. After this, she is last mentioned in connection with the transfer from her estate of 21.85 *Reichsmark* to the state finance department. This transfer was carried out by the Prisoner Property Administration on 14 September 1942. The exact date of her death cannot be ascertained from the files.[9]

The foregoing *Heimtücke* cases stemmed from daily situations that had principally little to do with antisemitism. In every society and at any time, differences may arise while shopping, in dealings with public officials, at work, and in contacts with neighbors. But in Nazi Germany, antisemitic prejudices, regulations and laws inserted themselves into such conflicts and set in motion the apparatus of persecution. From the present standpoint, it seems absurd to examine Annemarie P.'s mental condition. Nonetheless, the fact that she, as well as the sisters W. were acquitted by the courts demonstrates that principles of due process remained partially in force. Jews like Else Davidson could also profit from this. In the 1940s, however, the situation had changed radically, as confirmed by the example of Henny Stern.

Offenses of Rassenschande

The application of the *Rassenschande* provisions of the Nuremberg laws, which went into effect in 1935, shows clearly that persecution was

9 Christl Wickert, "Frauenwiderstand und Dissens im Kriegsalltag," in: *Widerstand gegen den Nationalsozialismus*, Peter Steinbach and Johannes Tuchel, eds., Berlin, 1994, pp. 411–425; Wolf Gruner, "Terra incognita? — Die Lager für den 'jüdischen Arbeitseinsatz' (1938–1943), und die deutsche Bevölkerung," in: *Die Deutschen und die Judenverfolgung*, Ursula Büttner, ed., Hamburg, 1992, pp. 131–160. The Stern case is documented in file RW 58–61530, HStAD.

carried out unevenly against Jews and non-Jews and demonstrates how a law was used to implement Nazi racial policy. This led the Gestapo to investigate all denunciations, even those that seemed initially to be unfounded.

I wish to single out examples of *Judenliebchen* (Jew lovers). Non-Jewish women and girls who went out with Jews were marked with this label. Charges of being a *Judenliebchen* could lead to totally different consequences. It is striking that accusations of "Jew loving" can be traced back to other periods. They arose from conflicts that National Socialist organizations and the Gestapo were not supposed to know about.

On 15 March 1939 the 26-year-old domestic servant Maria M. was denounced to the Gestapo by the daughter of a neighbor, who called her a *Judenliebchen* and "enemy of the people." Because it became known — as noted specially in her files — that she had been involved in a sexual relationship with a Jew since 1931, she was arrested immediately. She was accused of listening to *Feindsender* (enemy radio), and of having made various anti-state remarks about the extramarital affairs of Goebbels, Hitler's war mania, the senselessness of anti-Jewish actions, etc. Six months earlier, she had already received official admonishment for the spreading of such "rumors." In 1936 she had successfully protected her lover from conviction on *Rassenschande*; as a result of her exonerating testimony during interrogation the investigation was dropped. In her interrogation on 15 March 1939, she handled herself once again with pronounced skill. She did not reject all the accusations categorically. For example, "after thorough admonishment," she admitted to continuing the liaison after promulgation of the Nuremberg laws. When the Gestapo then searched for her friend, he had already gone into hiding. The interrogations probed into the details of sexual practices, and clearly demonstrate that the interrogators ascribed to Jewish men a sexual lack of control verging on rape, and assumed, according to Hitler's ideas, that Aryan women agreed to the liaison only under pressure or due to promises made to them by their Jewish partners. Maria M. disputed these insinuations. Protective custody was imposed with the argument: "She praises the Jew Simon as an honorable man. ... She is to be regarded as guilty of offenses under the law against insidiousness. She might have made her insidious utterances out of anger, because the Law for

Protection of German Blood and Honor foiled her intended marriage with the Jew." Neighbors who testified before the Gestapo said that she stood "politically under the influence of the Jew Simon." On 13 September 1939 the Special Court in Düsseldorf sentenced Maria M. to eight months in prison for *Heimtücke*; the five and a half months of investigative custody were reckoned as part of the sentence. The accusation of *Rassenschande* was not mentioned.[10]

Another example is demonstrated by a letter to Düsseldorf *Gauleiter*, Florian, in which the writer claimed that her neighbor, 48-year-old clerk Elisabeth Schu., had an earlier liaison with a Jew and had even gone on vacation with him in the summer of 1935 (*before* enactment of the Nuremberg laws). In the words of the denunciation: "She might dispose now of a very large sum of money. ... The Jew has emigrated. This last information is to be regarded with caution because I don't know myself whether it is completely true." The Gestapo ordered postal surveillance, without result, and the case was dropped.[11] As was typical of *Rassenschande* denunciations, the accusers were mostly neighbors or colleagues who reported to the Gestapo and set the persecution in motion. It is worth noting that the Düsseldorf Gestapo did not research into the circumstances of the accuser, although presumably competition and envy triggered her denunciation.

Upon reading Gestapo *Rassenschande* files, I was struck with the way in which interrogations (whereby confessions were sometimes extracted for offenses that never occurred), became increasingly harsher as the war progressed. Gestapo officials clearly assumed that sexual relations with Jewish men were always characterized by perverse practices. The interest of investigating officials in the details of sexual practices was focused mainly on German female partners who were supposed to have regarded this as a special form of degradation. Such procedures document the National Socialist aim of making sexuality and intimacy into public issues, in order to subordinate them to the propagated goal of the *Volksgemeinschaft*.

10 HStAD, File RW 58–4781.

11 HStAD, File RW 58–46589.

Excursus: "Judenhelfer"

To have helped Jewish neighbors, friends, family members (or indeed strangers), to flee, or to have hidden, fed and cared for them, were typical acts of family welfare. Women, especially, played such sex-traditional roles in traditional settings. "These acts," wrote Richard Löwenthal, "are maybe the strongest evidence that civil courage in face of a totalitarian dictatorship can have a political quality, even when not conducted in service of a particular political goal."[12]

The example of two sisters-in-law, Johanna and Maria F. from Düsseldorf, indicates the danger that was involved in helping threatened fellow citizens. In agreement with her brother-in-law and sister-in-law, the widow Johanna F. had taken in a Polish Jew. With a falsified German passport, she attempted to help him flee to the Netherlands, disguised as her husband. She was anonymously denounced by an acquaintance. The 53-year-old Johanna was sentenced to four months in prison for violation under §1, clause 11 of the passport regulations of 6 April 1923, and pardoned by decree issued on 9 September 1939. After serving a six month sentence, the 52-year-old Maria F. was detained for a further five months in protective custody. The two sisters-in-law gave helpfulness and sympathy as reasons for their behavior. It remains open as to whether they argued this consciously or were so unpolitical that they did not know the dangers that could arise from their action.

After each boycott day that was declared against Jewish shopowners, the schoolmistress of the Schubarth-Schmidt Gymnasium for girls in Düsseldorf sent flowers to the parents of her Jewish students as an expression of sympathy.[13] The housemaid Martha Schumacher experienced the November pogrom in the house of the druggist Oskar Altmann and his wife Margarete. Although forbidden to Aryans, she helped the family to clear the damage. "I have been associated with the

12 Kurt R. Grossmann, *Die unbesungenen Helden*, Berlin, 1961; Heinz David Leuner, *When Compassion was a Crime. Germany's Silent Heroes 1933–1945*, London, 1966; Sarah Gordon, *Hitler, Germans and the "Jewish Question,"* Princeton, NJ, 1984; Pearl M. and Samuel P. Oliner, *The Altruistic Personality*, New York, 1988; Eric Silver, *The Book of the Just*, London, 1992; Richard Löwenthal, "Widerstand im totalen Staat," in: *Widerstand und Verweigerung in Deutschland 1933–1945*, Richard Löwenthal and Patrik von zur Mühlen, eds., Bonn, 1982, p. 22.

13 Leuner, *When Compassion was a Crime.*

Altmann family for a long time and feel that what was done to them was greatly unjust, although I do not understand why all this has to happen." The Altmanns then began to make preparations to emigrate; their daughter Gertrud was already safe in Geneva and their sons Paul and Günter were living in London and Milan respectively.[14]

Through two anonymous denunciations sent to *Gauleiter* Florian on 2 March 1943, the Gestapo learned that Anna W., a 35-year-old saleswoman at the former Jewish dress shop Brenninkmeyer, had remained in touch with her Jewish foster parents, although the father was a "full Jew," and despite a warning issued the previous year. She received another warning and was forced to leave her position, although no fault could be found with her work. The Employment Office assigned her a new job and the Gestapo did not pursue the matter further.[15]

In 1942 the 23-year-old Jewish woman Erna Putermann knocked on the door of her non-Jewish friend, the seamstress Frieda Adam: "They have taken my mother today," she told her. Frieda Adam answered: "Then you stay here." Until the end of the war the two friends, along with the three Adam children, shared the two-room apartment located on Schönhauser Allee in the Berlin district Prenzlauerberg.[16] That these two friends would remain in contact for many years, despite the Berlin wall that separated them, is proof that sometimes friendship was foremost. As the war continued, Frieda Adam became aware of the increasing danger of her situation, including the risk to her children, but she persisted, even crossing the limits into open resistance against Nazi antisemitism.

Whether this recognition of the hopelessness of the Jewish situation derived from a totally human response or was based on existing personal contacts, there *were* people who elected to help others.[17] They put themselves into danger because they were acting consciously — whether from personal or political-oppositional motives — in non-conformity with antisemitic stipulations. This unverifiable source of

14 HStAD, Files RW 58–61948 (Gertrud Altmann), 61954 (Oskar Altmann); author's interview with Martha Schumacher, Düsseldorf, 8 June 1991.

15 HStAD, File RW 58–45964, pp. 6, 17. For labor allocation during the war see Wickert, "Frauenwiderstand und Dissens im Kriegsalltag," pp. 421–423.

16 Martina Voigt, "Flucht und Hilfe in Berlin," cited in *Die Zeit*, 1 April 1994, p. 15.

17 Nechama Tec, *When Light Pierced the Darkness,* New York, 1986.

support by non-Jews has been neglected by research because they, even in retrospect, did not want to play up what they viewed as self-evident action.

In closing, I would like to stress the following:

1) Without denunciation, it would have been impossible to control the observance of National Socialist prohibitions in the private sphere. Without denunciation it would not have been possible to keep Jewish citizens under such constant surveillance and to make their daily lives increasingly difficult, until the situation was resolved by emigration or by transport to extermination camps.
2) A close reading of Gestapo files reveals that not every attitude or action of individuals (whether accusers or Gestapo officials), which may appear at first glance as a reaction for or against the policy of antisemitism, was in fact determined by that factor alone.
3) The individual Gestapo official who recorded and investigated accusations had decision-making and operational authority. This helps explain why the same offense could have very different consequences, independent of the letter of National Socialist law. Until the start of the war, accusations did not automatically mean greater danger for Jews than for *Volksgenossen*.[18] In the 1940s, however, almost every accusation against Jews led to imprisonment in a concentration camp. The available documents show no evidence of differing treatment of accused Jews by individual officials.
4) Contact between Germans and Jews during the National Socialist period was increasingly restricted through laws and regulations, but there was never a legal requirement to report supposed offenses. Although *Volkgemeinschaft* ideology presumed the expectation that any form of non-conformity, dissent and opposition ought to be reported, it was left solely to personal judgment whether or not to report the statements and actions of others.

18 Accusation, however, resulted in Jews being committed to files, thereby making it easier to register them for removal to extermination camps. For many Jews, an accusation prompted them to step up efforts to emigrate, which saved their lives.

5) Denunciations with antisemitic content often veiled the real motives stemming from pure self-interest. Antisemitism was a means to other ends. The Gestapo apparatus became active even when officials had reason to assume that an accusation was rooted in personal conflicts.
6) Assistance to threatened Jews did not always arise out of a conscious resistance to National Socialism and its antisemitic state doctrine. Rather, simple ethical or humane impulses played the determining role. Nonetheless, from the standpoint of the regime, such assistance constituted active opposition and, therefore, entailed deadly risk.

German Work and German Workers: The Impact of Symbols on the Exclusion of Jews in Nazi-Germany

ALF LÜDTKE

The Limits of "Class"

The perplexing question remains: Why did hundreds of thousands of Germans either perpetrate or become accomplices of discrimination, exclusion and, finally, extermination of the European Jewry? Why did millions of Germans, in fact the overwhelming majority of the population, stand by and keep silent, and, sometimes even applaud? In this paper I will examine the attitude and role of the workers — were they actively involved in this discrimination? Were they indifferent? Or, did they oppose the Nazis' treatment of the Jews; perhaps even help them?

Research on the role and behavior of industrial workers has for a long time revolved around class. Whatever the vantage point, the working class(es), appeared as victims. The specifics of argumentation did not change the general line. Whether villains like Hitler, Himmler or Goering or ideologies like "economic antisemitism" (a favorite of the late 1950s), were presented as decisive factors, or whether historians emphasized the "collapse" of the Weimar political system or focused on the (seeming), logic of capital, or if they alluded to the "polycratic" system of National Socialist domination — all coincided in portraying the workers as conquered by these respective agents operating from "outside" of this social class. At least implicitly, these views shared the assumption that workers "structurally opposed" Nazism. Only in the late 1970s did fresh research begin to offer alternative perspectives. Internal blind spots and the deficiencies of left political organizations before and after 1933 became a topic.[1] Others scrutinized the social and cultural differences between various sociocultural milieus, especially between workers from Protestant or Catholic background (omitting Jews, however), between urban workers and peasant-workers, and also between generations.[2] At the same time the publication of hitherto ignored material invited new readings. Particularly important were the detailed reports by illegal correspondents of the Social Democratic Party (SOPADE), about a broad array of facets of everyday life under Nazism between 1934 and 1940.[3]

This research finally dismantled what had been left of the projected heroism of the workers. This research left no doubt that the imagery of the working class as valiant heroes of resistance had been a political, or for that matter an ideological construction by political functionaries of the left. Even more, this image had also shaped the expectations and, perhaps, anxieties of Nazi authorities.[4] Most workers' historical experiences and practices differed fundamentally. Recently Bernd Stöver and David Bankier summed up the profile that emerges from their research: industrial workers were by no means different from the majority of Germans in their readiness to accept if not support Nazi policies, including those against the Jews. In any case, reports on people's behavior from different angles indicate a recurrent disinterest in the treatment and fate of Jews.[5]

1 Detlev Peukert, *Die KPD im Widerstand. Verfolgung und Untergrundarbeit an Rhein und Ruhr 1933 bis 1945*, Wuppertal, 1980.

2 Lutz Niethammer, ed., *"Die Jahre weiss man nicht, wo man die heute hinsetzen soll," Lebensgeschichte und Sozialkultur im Ruhrgebiet 1930–1960*, vol. I, Berlin, 1983; vol II, *"Hinterher merkt man, dass es richtig war, dass es schiefgegangen ist," Lebensgeschichte und Sozialkultur im Ruhrgebiet 1930–1960*, Berlin, 1983; vol. III, Lutz Niethammer and Alexander von Plato, eds., *"Wir kriegen jetzt andere Zeiten," Lebensgeschichte und Sozialkultur im Ruhrgebiet 1930–1960*, Berlin, 1985; especially on peasant workers see Jean H. Quataert, "Combining Agrarian and Industrial Livelihoods. Rural Households in the Saxon Oberlausitz in the 19th Century," *Journal of Family History*, 10 (1985), pp. 145–162.

3 Klaus Behnken, ed., *Deutschlandberichte der Sozialdemokratischen Partei Deutschlands (SOPADE), 1934–1940*, Frankfurt am Main, 1980; see also Bernd Stöver, ed., *Berichte über die Lage in Deutschland. Die Meldungen der Gruppe Neu Beginnen aus dem Dritten Reich 1933–1936*, Bonn, 1996.

4 Gerhard Paul and Klaus-Michael Mallmann, eds., *Die Gestapo — Mythos und Realität*, Darmstadt, 1995.

5 Bernd Stöver, *Volksgemeinschaft im Dritten Reich. Die Konsensbereitschaft der*

"Why?" and "How?" Questions

Historians tend to rephrase questions of "why" as a series of "how" questions.[6] Thus, on the issue of those who accepted and supported Nazism, related questions may investigate how they marked neighbors or others as Jews. Who avoided eye contact or turned greeting rituals into bitter episodes of humiliation? When and how did people insult those they felt entitled to do so? What forms of discrimination were popular among males or females, teenagers and the elderly? Who hurt whom at which occasion? And, ultimately, Who did kill whom where and when? Who stood by and looked the other way, and who derived enjoyment from or turned witnessing these physical attacks into a form of entertainment?

References to "class" or "political camp" have been proven of limited value to explain "why did it happen?", or "how could it happen?" Thus, sociocultural milieu and generation have become prominent theories in the last years. Still, the drive for clear-cut categories and rather unilinear explanations seems uncontested. By this token, fundamental ambiguities that are meaningful to most people in their respective everyday lives are either ignored or discarded. Thus, research time and again ignores crucial features of those practices that people appropriate for organizing both the settings of their everyday lives and their individual trajectories.

Deutschen aus der Sicht sozialistischer Exilberichte, Düsseldorf, 1993; David Bankier, *The Germans and the Final Solution: Public Opinion under Nazism*, Oxford, 1992. Since political culture relies intensely on, and is linked to the practices and culture of the everyday, "close-ups" are most important. In other words, local and regional studies prove particularly useful; see the classical text of William S. Allen (to a certain extent also covering workers) *The Nazi Seizure of Power. The Experience of a Single German Town, 1922–1945*, New York, 1984: and Martin Rüther, *Arbeiterschaft in Köln, 1928–1945*, Cologne, 1990, and Conan Fischer, ed., *The Rise of National Socialism and the Working Classes in Weimar Germany*, Providence RI, 1996.

6 William Dray, *Laws and Explanation in History*, Oxford, 1970.

The Arena of Symbols

In this context an exploration of the arena of symbolic meanings and practices allows for new possibilities of interpretation. Symbols invoke and connect the grand or spectacular with the nonconspicuous and seemingly trivial.[7] Symbols relate the cognitive to the emotive and refer the tangible to the non-tangible. Symbols are not "given" from above, but produced and appropriated in daily encounters and situations. Symbols of work and workers as used or propagated by the Nazi authorities provided the workers with a sense of self-recognition, which in turn led to their increased productivity at each shift, day or night. Also, innovations like new toilets and brighter lighting not only eased the daily hardship, they also invoked the nation's future, promising those experiencing these changes a new and better era.

Symbolic practices were not confined to an "aesthetization of politics" staged "from above." This thesis, formulated in 1935–36 when Walter Benjamin desperately tried to come to grips with the appeal of fascism to the masses, deals only with the spectacular side of symbolic practice. Benjamin insistently drew attention to the "enormous festive processions." But, in contrast to his previous work, he focused on "monster meetings" and "mass sports events;" above all, however, it was the imminence of war that occupied him. According to Benjamin, these mass movements made it possible for the participants "to express themselves," but what he found fundamentally lacking was the chance for them "to exercise their own rights."[8] However, this was precisely what constituted the appeal of marches, rallies, or camps — opportunities hitherto unkown to the many for expressing themselves. Due to his isolation as an exile, Benjamin failed to grasp the political dynamics inherent in the Nazi symbology. At the same time, he underrated the seamless connectedness of the unspectacular everyday practices with the spectacular ones. People used either one to blend "old" and "modern" times in ways of their own.

7 Victor Turner, *The Forest of Symbols. Aspects of Ndembu Ritual*, Ithaca, 1973, pp. 27 ff and pp. 48 ff.

8 Walter Benjamin, "Das Kunstwerk im Zeitalter seiner technischen Reproduzierbarkeit [1935]," in: Walter Benjamin, *Gesammelte Schriften,* Frankfurt am Main, 1974, vol. I, part 2, pp. 431–469, p. 467.

Shopfloor Encounters — and their Ambiguities

In his book *Lingua Tertii Imperii*, Victor Klemperer, until 1935 professor of Romanic languages, describes "one single working day." He refers to working days of forced labor under Nazi rule.[9] Those designated as Jews by Nazi law had been forced into labor since the spring of 1939. Klemperer had been assigned a job in a Dresden factory that produced paper envelopes. He recalls that the atmosphere was not "particularly Nazi." Although the entrepreneur was a member of the SS, "he supported the Jews in the factory wherever it was possible, he talked to them politely and occasionally gave them something from the cantina" (which the letter of the law prohibited). Klemperer also recalls that he is not sure what was more of a consolation — a piece of horse sausage or that once in a while he was called not only by his (last), name but "Herr Klemperer" or even "Herr Professor." According to his recollection the workers too were by no means "Nazi," at least not in the winter of 1943–44, one year after Stalingrad.

One of the workers, a man by the name of Albert, was — according to Klemperer — sceptical of the German (Nazi) Government and not in favor of the war. He had lost a brother at the front. He himself had been exempted from the military because of a stomach ailment, but was anxious to be drafted before "this bloody war comes to an end." Klemperer overheard him talking to another worker, who responded: "But how will this war come to an end? Nobody gives in!" Albert answered: "Well isn't it obvious? The others have to accept that we are invincible; they cannot conquer us, we are so well organized!"

Klemperer describes another worker, Frieda, who occasionally asked about his wife and sometimes brought him an apple. She largely ignored strict orders not to talk to "the Jews." On one such occasion she commented: "Albert says your wife is a German; is she really a German?" Klemperer noted: "Immediately I lost any joy with the apple. This friendly person was not a Nazi at all and had human feelings, but even here the Nazi poison has done its work. She has identified Germanness with the magical notion of Aryan. She could not grasp that my wife could be a German."

9 Victor Klemperer, *LTI. Notizbuch eines Philologen*, 3rd edition, Halle, 1957, pp. 101f.

The second story, specially, illustrates the problem. Frieda was a "nice guy." She was good company and befriended people who were obviously in need of help. This happened in work situations but was extended also to the families of some of the workers (like bringing apples for Klemperer's wife). At the same time she was totally convinced and did not hesitate to express the conviction that there was a fundamental difference between Jews and others, and that Jews were either "not good" or at least inferior to the others, more precisely "Aryans" or Germans. The question, then, is how and to what extent did these conflicting attitudes and practices coincide? Raul Hilberg emphasizes the importance of "bystanders." I believe that the behavior of both Albert and Frieda represents two forms of "standing by," which were not uncommon among industrial workers.[10]

"Work" as the Pivot of Germanness

The symbols of work resonated with concrete practices at work.[11]

10 Cf. Carola Sachse, ed., *Als Zwangsarbeiterin 1941 in Berlin. Die Aufzeichnungen der Volkswirtin Elisabeth Freund*, Berlin, 1996, pp. 54f, 57f, 64, 117, 120 f, 145; Elisabeth Freund had joined forced labor in the spring of 1941. In October 1942 she was among the last people who were allowed to emigrate, and only some weeks later, upon arrival in Cuba, she wrote down her recollections. From April until late May 1941 she was assigned to a large laundry in southeast Berlin. After she had collapsed due to the heavy loads she had to carry and the tremendous heat, she was transferred to a factory producing lamps and other electrical equipment. In both companies Jewish forced laborers worked in separate shifts. Often these shifts were confined to separate rooms. If, however, "Aryan" workers happened to work in the same room a fence demarcated the boundary between them and the Jews; Freund notes that the Jewish workers were treated very differently from their non-Jewish work mates. The female supervisor of the laundry did not miss an opportunity to humiliate and mock the members of the Jewish shift. In the same company, however, she met another female supervisor who treated her very well, giving her advice and acting as a colleague. Some days later Frau Schulz, who evidently had never met Jews before, when realizing that her workers were Jewish "felt like somebody who had been dropped into a lion's cage not knowing what might happen next and how to master the dangerous situation." In the electrical equipment firm she often had to cooperate with "Aryan" workers, mostly men and older people. A female supervisor and several masters were harsh and sometimes brutal, but Freund's immediate colleagues were conspicuously helpful and supportive.

11 For more extended treatment see my article "The Honor of Labor: Industrial Labor

"Work" meant manual dexterity and diligence. The gaze of attentiveness implied physical strength, and validated the claim of "being tough." Moreover, work had been proven time and again to be essential for daily survival. Housework, however, was omitted from such representations. Proper work required not only the working man but also his tools, his machines, which reinforced the value of industry and progress. Thus, "work" was suffused with ideals of a specific "male" appropriation of the world.

Images and notions of "good," "proper" or "quality work" referred to the suggestiveness of a symbol that remained constant, irrespective of changes in one's life situation, such as the shift toward the semiskilled during the 1920s and permanent high rates of unemployment. These symbols had existed for decades not only among the working classes but in other layers of society as well. Here the semiskilled met on common ground with many not of the working class, or with those belonging to the socialist, communist, or nationalist political camp.

For most workers "good" or "quality work" meant the successful product of paid labor: that is producing a usable and "fine" item, and at the same time creating an extra buffer of time for one's next job. Although blueprints were handed to the workers they often had to fill gaps in an incomplete plan. Using their experience they demonstrated to themselves and their superiors that they were not "fools" (it was the American workers who were given tools that were "foolproof," as a union functionary proudly reported to his German colleagues in 1928).

Working meticulously, especially if one's productivity was above average, could pay off in a number of ways. For one thing, the chances of doing well were greater in a wage system based on increasing wage differentials. At the same time this meant that one was spared constant supervision or advice. If the product was deemed satisfactory, workers were granted a certain independence according to their individual rhythm of work. In turn, workers devoted their attention and energy to their job; they took pride in accomplishing goals regardless of hardships or other obstacles, such as breakdowns or inadequate work plans.

and the Power of Symbols under National Socialism," in: *Nazism and the German Society 1933–1945*, David F. Crew, ed., London, 1994, pp. 67–109.

Work was more than just a means to an end. Instrumental orientations were mixed together with meanings, in which work showed itself to be an exhausting, but fascinating "metabolism with nature" (Karl Marx). To endure daily hardships and avoid the risks of an accident occurring at work imbued many workers with a sense of assertiveness. It was this experience that fueled people's *Eigensinn* (obstinate self-reliance) — the ability to carve out niches of space, time and resources for oneself. Not resistance to "above" but distance from everyone — including one's fellow workers — was the preferred way to display *Eigensinn*.

Notions of "German quality work" and related icons had gained momentum in the wake of the First World War. Most people beyond the boundaries of class, gender and generation would agree that revenge for Versailles required ever more German quality work. Across the board, labor organizations subscribed to the call for furthering German quality work. Representatives of the socialist and even of the communist movement envisioned increased production as the only means to improve living conditions, not only of their members but of all working men and women.

Symbols of work enhanced the assumption that being German and taking work seriously was intricately connected. In turn, those who appeared to shy away from hard and preferably manual labor were marked as "alien others."

Motifs which represented "work" in the press of the political left revolved around the image of a competence saturated with experience. This "feel for the work" was admittedly reserved for those who engaged in "trained" activities, even when they were actually only semiskilled. An example is the photograph of a (repair) turner which was printed as the cover picture for the communist-oriented but also commercially successful *Arbeiter-Illustrierte Zeitung*.[12] This manly worker radiated a contolled calm; the perspective and the way the picture is framed emphasizes his concentration on the tools, on the materials and on the task at hand; both orderliness and deftness were signaled. The picture of the confident, experienced machine tender was a citation of the ideal skilled worker counted as the basis upon which colleagues could become "comrades."

12 *Arbeiter-Illustrierte Zeitung*, 31 January 1928.

At the same time, in the 1920s the immigration of East European Jews gave some ideologues the opportunity to cast a stereotyped "Jew" as the counter-figure of the hard-working German, the latter predominantly depicted as a masculine hero. It was a stereotype that the Nazis did not produce but instrumentalized after 1933.[13]

The appeal of the SA to the unemployed and to working-class youth is notorious. The icons (and the symbolic representation in general), of German work and German workers emphasized the primordial importance of bodily might. At least when they employed their bodies and acted violently — especially in 1933 — the SA could claim that they too be counted among German workers.[14]

Work and the Extermination of Others

Evidence from Gestapo files[15] concurs with reports from oppositional sources that industrial workers did not pay particular attention to the discriminatory Nazi policies against Jews. Neither demonstrative violence, like the boycott of 1 April 1933, nor less conspicuous measures of legal and administrative discrimination stimulated strong responses in workshops or working-class neighborhoods.[16]

13 In general, Trude Maurer, *Ostjuden in Deutschland, 1918–1933,* Hamburg, 1986; see also the reactions to the (permanent or recurrent) presence of Polish and Ruthenian migrant workers in the Braunschweig area, Karl Liedke, *"...aber politisch unerwünscht": Arbeitskräfte aus Osteuropa im Land Braunschweig 1880 bis 1939,* Braunschweig, 1993.

14 Christoph Schmidt, "Zu den Motiven 'alter Kämpfer' in der NSDAP," in: *Die Reihen fast geschlossen. Beiträge zur Geschichte des Alltags unterm Nationalsozialismus*, Detlev Peukert and Juergen Reulecke, eds., Wuppertal, 1981, pp. 21–43; Thomas Balistier, *Gewalt und Ordnung. Kalkül und Faszination der SA*, Münster, 1989.

15 See on this type or reports (and also the reports of various branches of the internal administration, the judiciary, and the *NSDAP*) Joachim Kuropka, *Meldungen aus Münster 1924–1944: Geheime und vertrauliche Berichte von Polizei, Gestapo, NSDAP und ihren Gliederungen, staatlicher Verwaltung, Gerichtsbarkeit und Wehrmacht über die politische und gesellschaftliche Situation in Münster und Umgebung*, Münster, 1992.

16 Particularly important are the areas that were less urbanized and also less dominated by large-scale production than, for instance, Berlin, Leipzig, or Nuremberg or — in a different way — the *Ruhrgebiet.* In the 1920s more than fifty percent of industrial workers lived in small towns or villages, see Josef Mooser, *Arbeiterleben in*

To a certain extent Jews fitted the image of the rich if not the capitalist (or the Nazi plutocrat). Such images had also been widely propagated by the socialist press since the 1890s.[17] However, where actual experience with employers nuanced or contradicted such abstract notions, as evidence from southern lower Saxony indicates, more prevalent was the immediate interest in one's job and pay, and the lower prices at a neighboring Jewish retail shop. When and how, then, did these shoppers become "bystanders" — or did some of them become active as fellow citizens and react to, or intervene against, discrimination and exclusion? At this point merely indirect answers are possible. In the first two or three years after 1933 direct support of Nazi policies seems to have been rare among workers and their families. Much more widespread were forms of acceptance and "active passivity."

Although regional economies and, even more, sociocultural *milieus* varied enormously, the younger Germans, particularly, experienced improvements in both material and symbolic terms from 1934–35.[18] Here we can see the life-cyclical aspect: Young people, for example, saw this as a propitious time to get married. There was a clear shift in media coverage and public attention, and for the first time they were given public recognition even though there was no official praise for manual labor. In the context of (relative) recognition of themselves as respectable, again the exclusion of "others" underlined the perception of participating in better times. Such a perception might develop even further if these "others" fitted the principal model of society and history that "German work" offered. However, the focus on "German work" allowed more active participation in excluding "alien others", Jews

Deutschland, 1900–1970, Frankfurt am Main, 1984, p. 169; see also Walter Struve, *Aufstieg und Herrschaft des Nationalsozialismus in einer industriellen Kleinstadt: Osterode am Harz 1918–1945,* Essen, 1992; Lutz Hoffmann, Uwe Neumannn and Wolfgang Schäfer, *Zwischen Feld und Fabrik. Arbeiteralltag auf dem Dorf von der Jahrhundertwende bis heute: Die Sozialgeschichte des Chemiewerkes Bodenfelde 1896–1986,* Göttingen, 1986.

17 Rosemarie Leuschen-Seppel, *Sozialdemokratie und Antisemitismus im Kaiserreich*, Bonn, 1978; Hans-Gerd Henke, *Der "Jude" als Kollektivsymbol in der deutschen Sozialdemokratie 1890–1914*, Mainz, 1994.

18 Michael Zimmermann, *Schachtanlage und Zechenkolonie. Leben, Arbeit und Politik in einer Arbeitersiedlung 1880–1980*, Essen, 1987, pp. 171ff.

but also Gypsies, Poles, Russians, and homosexuals. Accordingly, only those who worked properly deserved human treatment.[19] Above all, to fulfill the German work ideal demanded also doing the "job" of warfaring, or, killing in the death camps (and elsewhere) "properly."

In war production, "German quality work" after 1942 was performed increasingly by prisoners of war. Large numbers of these POWs were regarded as "community aliens" or "subhumans" in the eyes of the National Socialists and were intended to be "destroyed by labor." Yet their products, just like those of the male and female "Aryan" Germans, had to achieve the quality which counted as a precondition for the Final Victory being striven for. In a speech that was part of the propagandistic mobilization for "total war" in the summer of 1943, Armaments Minister Speer brought the collective projection sharply into focus: "Quality will [triumph] over the mass." The message was clear — German work would always be superior to the merely "quantitative" output of the west, it would triumph this time as well.

Warfaring[20]

Several industrial corporations based in Leipzig regularly received letters from soldiers whose peacetime employment had been suspended during the war.[21] The workforce of these companies in 1939 consisted of

19 On the awareness of the treatment of inmates of concentration camps by "ordinary" (young) Germans, not the least apprentices who were trained for various jobs inside the camps see, Isabell Sprenger, *Gross-Rosen. Ein Konzentrationslager in Schlesien*, Cologne, 1996; also, on violence and brutality against seeming "enemies" of the *Reich* that spread from local (sub-) camps into "civilian" neighborhoods, see Peter Koppenhöfer, "Ein KZ als Verhaltensmodell? Mitten im Stadtteil: das Konzentrationslager Mannheim-Sandhofen," *Dachauer Hefte*, 12 (1996), pp. 10–33.

20 The following is based on my article: "The Appeal of Exterminating Others," *Journal of Modern History*, 64 (1992–Suppl.), pp. 46ff.

21 Soldiers' letters from the front had to pass the military censor before they were mailed. The writers were accustomed to orders of the German military command that strongly emphasized: "Field-post letters are weapons, too, comrades," Ortwin Buchbender and Reinhold Sterz, eds., *Das andere Gesicht des Krieges. Deutsche Feldpostbriefe 1939–1945*, Munich, 1982. The command provided further guidance. For instance, guidelines were frequently distributed to the troops, proposing specific formulations that should be used when people wrote field-post letters. The military

five to six hundred, or, in one case, of more than two thousand workers (Rudolf Sack Company, which manufactured agrarian machinery). Some of these soldiers did not have many other people to whom they felt they could write about their life in the military; others mentioned in their letters that they primarily wrote to their kin and friends. Overall however, their letters clearly indicate a sense of commitment to their respective work community.

A close reading of dozens of these letters sent to former employers in Leipzig gives the impression that the writers paid little attention to the rules of confidentiality laid down by military authorities. One topic was the similarity of being a soldier to life as a worker at home. For instance, Emil Caspar wrote on 31 October 1943 that his platoon had just marched three hundred kilometers in nine days. It had been grueling, but "it is as if you are working at home." Another soldier, a worker in a shale mine, wrote in October 1943 from Norway that he had quickly adjusted to the military "and if you only show obedience and good will everything is fine."[22] Another soldier from the Braunkohlenwerk, also a blue-collar worker, wrote in December 1943 that "I never felt as good on my job as I do now with the military."[23]

In some letters the "others" were often mentioned — the soldiers or civilians of enemy countries. Heinz Dübner noted on 21 November 1939 that "the Poles played havoc while we had to restore order and by doing this we became real men."[24] A similar attitude emerges in the letter of Edmund Heinzel who served in November 1940 with the *Reichsarbeitsdienst* somewhere in occupied Poland. He wrote that the houses and streets "are very deficient, that is, houses are built from wood and mud and, to put it in one word, it is really "*polnische*

command aimed at turning field-post letters to "vitamins of the psyche" which would rejuvenate anybody who had become tired. The foremost recommendation was "to display a manly attitude and to write in a strong and clear language."

22 Staatsarchiv Leipzig (hereafter StAL), Braunkohlenwerk 184, Fol. 33 bzw. 37). See also Curzio Malaparte, *Die Wolga entspringt in Europa*, Cologne, 1987, pp. 32 and 44, where he refers to the Russian and German armies, respectively, as "mobile steel mill," and also sees a total identity in both armies as regards the merger of military discipline and industrial discipline.

23 StAL, Braunkohlenwerk 184, Fol. 115, Gerhard Melzig.

24 StAL, Villeroy & Boch, Steingutfabrik Torgau, No. 67.

Wirtschaft."[25] Poles, and after 1941primarily Russians, were depicted as stereotypes, reflecting nationalist and racialist notions about the "natives." For instance, private O. Müller wrote on 27 August 1941 from northeastern Russia that "one sees only huts and not houses and you had better not step into them because of the odor, you don't find curtains, there is neither electric light nor water supply."[26]

During the war in Russia many of those who survived the first weeks remained for one or two years with their unit since leave was granted only rarely. As private Rolf Goebeler wrote on 21 June 1943, "many people develop a stubborn doggedness, it grows during the ongoing fighting, and they aim at crushing the enemy at any rate. The mates swear but this is good !"[27]

The "others" at the distant front, however, were also approaching "home." From 1941, foreign laborers were increasingly being forced to work in German industry. The companies conveyed this information to their employees on the front. Judging from soldiers' responses, there were primarily two issues that concerned them. One was whether the quality of work would suffer. Soldier Roland Gross, however, consoled himself and his mates when he wrote on 18 August 1941 that "although the best quality workers are drafted I think the foreign helpers will not degrade the quality of the machines [that his company produced, A.L.]."[28] In contrast, another displayed furious hatred. Karl Schreiber wrote on 21 July 1942 that "we have too much sympathy with the Russians but they do not have any with us. These foreign workers will not accomplish anything. And if they do not work the best would be to put up a machine gun and shoot them all." We assume that he had participated in some serious battle, as he referred to the Russian soldier with grudging respect: "the Russian fights to the last man, unlike the Tommy." This stood in sharp contrast to the impressions of a cook with the military staff stationed somewhere in the hinterland of the Russian front. His letter had a more optimistic tone. He wrote that he could "imagine lots of trouble at work [at home, A.L.] with foreign workers.

25 StAL, Sack 397, Fol. 157.
26 StAL, Sack 353, fol. 2f.
27 StAL, Sack, 353, fol. 44f.
28 StAL, Sack 397, fol. 193.

But with good will and sign language one can get along pretty well. At least that is what I do with the Russians here."[29]

For sure, these soldiers employed notions and images that had been launched or, more commonly, reshaped by the agents of propaganda. However, they used them not solely because they knew their letters would have to pass the censor. Moreover, the audience they addressed was different from family, relatives, or friends at home. These letters had to impress their work mates. It appears that most of them aimed at striking the pose of an experienced and successful "guy." Nonetheless, the intensity with which most of them expressed their hatred of the enemy reveals a concurrence of public rhetoric and private perception. And it is this conjunction that constituted the support of Nazism — which, of course, it simultaneously triggered.

That soldiering entailed killing or being killed was never a topic in any of the letters. However, the theme and the emotions associated with death were mentioned indirectly. For instance, sergeant Herbert Habermalz, a flight crew member in the air force stationed in southern Poland, had previously worked as a clerk in the sales department of the previously mentioned Rudolf Sack company. In a letter dated 7 August 1943, he gave a detailed account. He mentioned that German authorities had detected a mass grave. The people who had been buried were, in his words, victims of the *GPU* (the Soviet secret police). This grave was in the middle of a "*Volkspark*," only "...ten meters from a swing... Of course, I was eager to see the graves. You really can say that the *GPU* did a very good job — which we, of course, cannot grasp at all. One could see rather well preserved corpses of males, but also of females. All of them with their hands behind their backs. ... Next to the site a group of physicians was at work. The smell was not the best, as you can imagine. In addition, there were many many people who cried and looked for their relatives among the corpses and the physical remains..."[30] A few days earlier he had written a letter in which he described painstakingly the environment of the airbase. It was "very nice, the Vistula is really close ... It is only a pity that this quiet scenery is occasionally disturbed by 'Iwan' with his artillery.

29 StAL, Sack 399, fol. 167 f.
30 StAL, Sack, 353, fol. 31.

Apart from that one could believe one is in a spa."[31] Two weeks earlier Habermalz had sent a letter to the Sack Company in which he described a flight from Cracow to Warsaw in mid-June 1943: "We flew several circles above the city. And with great satisfaction we could recognize the complete extermination of the Jewish Ghetto. There our folks really did a fantastic job [*gute Arbeit*]. There is no house which has not been totally destroyed. This we saw the day before yesterday. And yesterday we took off for Odessa. We received special food, extra cookies, additional milk and butter, and, especially, a very big bar of *Edelbitter* chocolate."[32]

At the same time, though, the letters indicate that the soldiers'anxieties were transformed into an intensified loyalty to their superiors. Even more, the experience of being part of the war machinery itself enhanced the feeling of realizing the goals that the Nazi leadership proclaimed continually. These soldiers tried to get by under enormous hardship and suffering. Thus, they tried to appropriate the given situation, and in the very act of coping and appropriating they turned into actors. Even the privates who wrote angry or bombastic letters home documented how much they had become *victims and accomplices of Nazism alike*. These letters clearly reflect perceptions of being turned into objects of those at the height of command or with power over policy, the economy and society. However, such an interpretation of workers as victims and leaders as the sole agents, challenging as it might be, is not sufficient. The very tone of these letters reveals that the authors did not regard the draft and participation in war as totally alien situations. The intense descriptions of various situations and encounters reflect efforts to eradicate the permanent uncertainties as well as the dangers to one's own life.

These correspondents had been trained in, or at least socialized to, factory life in big cities in Germany. Yet, their self-image seem to have readily integrated the experiences of military life with both the risks and the attractions of war. To withstand the humiliations and rigors of basic training and, in the end, to master the situation provided an enormous boost to their self-esteem.

31 StAL, Sack, 352, fol. 32.
32 StAL, Sack, 352, fol. 46.

For these people, their claim of performing a "perfect" job at home had become increasingly linked to their involvement in the killing operations of the army. In the end, to participate in the extermination of others might have appeared to many as the ultimate fulfillment of "German quality work."

The German-Jewish Relationship in the Diaries of Victor Klemperer

SUSANNE HEIM

To the extent that Victor Klemperer achieved acclaim, it was only as the author of the book *LTI, Lingua Tertii Imperii.*[1] First published in 1947, this study on the language of the Third Reich was considered something of an underground classic primarily among German studies scholars and to a lesser extent among historians. Thus no one could have foreseen the broad-based reaction to the 1995 publication of two thick volumes of his diaries from the Nazi period.[2] The reception was certainly comparable to the tremendous response the film Schindler's List received. The publication was considered the event of the year in the book market, and Klemperer was posthumously awarded the "Geschwister Scholl" prize. Since then, the diaries have gone into six printings — a total of 160,000 copies — and this at a price of DM128. German public television has obtained the rights to film a thirteen-part series on Klemperer's experiences. The publication of Klemperer's *Curriculum Vitae*[3] only a few years earlier, in 1989, barely evoked any response, and yet, when republished following the diaries, they became a public success and led to the publication of further diaries from the Weimar era.[4]

What are the reasons for this unexpectedly immense interest? Or, to put it differently, what do German citizens see in the mirror Klemperer

1 Victor Klemperer, *LTI. Notizbuch eines Philologen*, Berlin, 1947.

2 Victor Klemperer, *Ich will Zeugnis ablegen bis zum letzten. Tagebücher 1933–1945*, vol. I–II, (hereafter: *Tagebücher*), Berlin, 1995.

3 Victor Klemperer, *Curriculum vitae. Erinnerungen 1881–1918*, ed. by Walter Nowopski, Berlin, 1989.

4 Victor Klemperer, *Leben sammeln, nicht fragen wozu und warum. Tagebücher 1918–1932,* vol. I–II, Berlin, 1996.

holds up to them? I will return to this question later in this paper, but will first outline the picture Victor Klemperer has drawn of a cross-section of German society in Dresden from 1933 to 1945.

Klemperer was born in 1881, the son of a rabbi in Landsberg on the Warthe river in what is today Poland. After being forced to apprentice as a businessman, he studied philosophy and Romanic and German philology in Munich, Geneva, Paris and Berlin from 1902 to 1905. Short of money, he interrupted his studies for several years and worked as a writer and journalist, returning to the university only in 1912. He volunteered for service in World War I — an experience that affected him profoundly. In 1919 he became an associate professor in Munich, and a year later obtained a professorship at the Technical College in Dresden. He was often dissatisfied with his professional career and felt unappreciated within his family and among colleagues. He also frequently claimed that he was barred from many opportunities because he was Jewish.

Particularly in the early entries of his diary — and even more so in the writings from the Weimar era — Klemperer comes across as a frustrated, somewhat petty, indeed a typical German professor with a distinct tendency towards hypochondria. Yet in the course of the book one gets a different impression. The painstaking attention to detail, which seems forced in the beginning, comes to represent Klemperer's unusual perceptiveness, a balance between proximity and distance from his object. Perhaps Klemperer was able to see into the heart of the German so clearly, precisely because he perceived himself to be a German and desperately wanted to be accepted as such, yet was not permitted to. On the other hand, he had no desire to view himself as a Jew either. He frequently expressed disdain for "the Jews," particularly Eastern Jewry and Zionists. Thus he was not fully anchored in either a German identity or in Judaism. Perhaps it was this outsider status, together with his meticulousness and a virtually obsessive desire to bear witness, that rendered him a critical, and increasingly self-critical, chronicler.

In 1906 Klemperer married the pianist Eva Schemmer. Together, and with her help, they survived the Nazi period in Dresden. The marriage was considered a "mixed marriage" by Nazi standards, as Eva was not Jewish. Although Klemperer had converted to Protestantism, under the racial laws he was nevertheless considered a Jew. Beginning in May

1940, the Klemperers were forced to live in a so-called *Judenhaus*, in which they shared an assigned apartment with other people. Their own house in a Dresden suburb was given to non-Jewish Germans. The attempt to formally "Aryanize" it or "abort its Jewishness," as Klemperer wrote several times, was drawn out in a positively grotesque bureaucratic procedure that was extremely exhausting for Klemperer, and in the end, unsuccessful.

Because Eva Klemperer, as a non-Jew, did not have to wear the Yellow Star, she could move relatively freely at a time when Jews hardly dared go out on the street, were not permitted to use public transportation, and above all, could not have any contact with "Aryans." This freedom of movement, and the contact with a few non-Jews that it enabled, were important not only to the survival of the Klemperers (and incidentally also to the safety of the diaries), but in many instances also to the other residents of the *Judenhaus*. The Klemperers' mixed marriage was also life saving for another reason: it offered him at least temporary protection from deportation. Of those Dresden Jews who survived the persecutions,[5] most were married to non-Jews. The Allied bombing of Dresden on 13 February 1945 prevented their imminent deportation at the last minute.

After the war Klemperer returned to Dresden and assumed his position at the Technical University. He later taught as professor in several cities of the former German Democratic Republic. Although Klemperer always emphasized in his diaries that he hated communism as much as National Socialism (and, for that matter, Zionism), he joined the Communist Party in the fall of 1945 because he considered it to be the only viable political force with which to overcome the Nazi past. Klemperer also wanted — as he put it — to "pump out the cesspool" of Nazism in German society.[6]

5 Among the 4,675 Jews that census figures indicate to have lived in Dresden in 1933, only 174 still remained just prior to the bombing in February 1945. On the persecution of Dresdener Jews, see Heike Liebsch, "Ein Tier ist nicht rechtloser und gehetzter," in: *Im Herzen der Finsternis. Victor Klemperer als Chronist der NS-Zeit,* Hannes Heer, ed., Berlin, 1997, pp. 73–91, and Nora Goldenbogen "Man wird keinen von ihnen wiedersehen," in: ibid., pp. 92–109.

6 On Klemperers entry into the KPD, see Bernd Greiner, "'Zwiespältiger denn je.' Victor Klemperers Tagebücher im Jahr 1945," in: *Im Herzen der Finsternis,* pp. 149ff.

Victor Klemperer's diaries were both life-threatening and life-saving. He had to hide his writings, and his wife occasionally brought them to a non-Jewish friend for safekeeping. Particularly during the height of Gestapo terror in 1942, when the residents of the *Judenhaus* reckoned every hour with house searches, Jews could be arrested and murdered on any arbitrary pretext. The very acts of writing, storing and transporting the diaries were life-threatening for Klemperer and for those about whom he wrote. Nevertheless, fear for his own life and the lives of others was outweighed by his need to bear witness. Klemperer viewed the writing of the diaries as a task that saved him — it prevented resignation and was often the only thing that staved off total despair. He made a conscious choice to write only marginally about national or international politics and events, and concentrated instead on everyday life, on private events not found in history books. The events we customarily view as decisive dates in the history of Nazism, such as the Nuremberg Laws of 1935, the November pogrom of 1938, the beginning of World War II or the attack on the Soviet Union, even the beginning of the deportation of German Jewry, hardly stand out from the continuum described here, namely, the increasingly oppressive, increasingly hopeless situation of the Jews in Germany.

Starting as early as January 1933 and continuing until the end of the war, Klemperer recorded in his diary every possible indication of an impending collapse of the Nazi regime. He meticulously recorded all expressions of dissatisfaction, any indication of a latent crisis of the system: He interpreted private complaints, rumors, newspaper articles, "gestures of impotent rage"[7] in Hitler's speeches, the mood of the Jews, and the creeping pollution of language by Nazi ideology. He noted terror and intimidation as well as rainy weather that could spoil the harvest, foreign reaction to Nazi policies, and the Wehrmacht's military victories and defeats. The question "What is the true vox populi" was woven like a thread throughout his notes. What backing did the Nazi government have? How long would the horror last? To him, the attitude of non-Jewish Germans toward antisemitic policies and toward the Jews was an important, although by no means the only criterion for estimating loyalty to Nazism, and it helped him to clarify his own relationship to other Germans.

7 *Tagebücher,* vol. 1, p. 43 (20 July 1933).

Klemperer was not a neutral chronicler. He noted not only facts, but also his own subjective fears and feelings. If one uses his diaries as a historical source, two predispositions that probably influenced his perceptions must be considered. First of all, from the very beginning he yearned for the end, and sought desperately for clues that seemed to signal an impending decline. Secondly, Klemperer defended his German identity against both the policy of excluding the Jews from the German nation and against his own doubts about that nation. Even in May 1942, when the terror against the Jews had lasted more than nine years and systematic mass murder had long since begun, he noted of his German identity, "I must hold on to it: I am German, the others are un-German; I must hold on to it."[8] It is likely that his insistent pride in being German, as well as his hope for a swift end to Nazism, led him to overestimate any indications that could help sustain these feelings.This was particularly the case when he wrote about criticisms of Nazism by non-Jewish Germans or their expressions of sympathy for the Jews.

One can read the diaries as a sort of pathogenesis of the Germans. In the early months Nazi rule seemed far from secure to Klemperer; it appeared to be based more on fearful silence, suppression of all opposition, and lack of alternatives than on a broad consensus. In August 1933, he wrote:

> I cannot and will not believe that the mood of the masses really continues to support Hitler. Too many opposing indications. But everything, literally everything is dying of fear. Not a letter, not a telephone conversation, not a word on the street is safe anymore. Each fears that the other is a traitor and a spy.[9]

But a clear change in mood soon became apparent. In 1936 Klemperer acknowledged with resignation:

> The majority of the nation is satisfied; a small group takes Hitler as the lesser evil, no one really wants to be rid of him; everyone sees in him the foreign-policy liberator, fears Russian conditions as a child fears the bogey man, sees it as politically inopportune — to the extent they are not honestly intoxicated — to rebel over such trivialities as the suppression of civil rights, the persecution of the Jews, the falsification of all scientific truth, the systematic destruction of all morality.[10]

8 *Tagebücher*, vol. 2, pp. 83f (11 May 1942).

9 *Tagebücher*, vol. 1, pp. 50f (19 August 1933).

10 Ibid., p. 264 (10 May 1936).

Gradually, Klemperer was becoming "increasingly convinced that Hitler is truly the spokesman of pretty much all Germans."[11] Relating to the war, especially as its consequences became increasingly felt within Germany, Klemperer wrote of a split reaction: on the one hand, there were expressions of sympathy, offerings of food, and comforting words[12] (especially from non-Jewish workers he met during forced labor in 1943–44); and on the other, attacks and open hatred.[13] The few who actually helped the Klemperers, offering more than mere friendly words or handshakes, were almost exclusively (if sometimes only fleeting) acquaintances with whom they had had personal contact for years.[14] In contrast, the Jews lived in fear of open aggression and curses from anonymous passersby such as "You rogue, why are you still alive?"[15] This was one reason why the introduction of the Yellow Star was a torment. In addition, Klemperer documented in his diary the hatred of Jews with which he was indirectly confronted. Thus, interested non-Jews were behind the dogged attempt to "Aryanize" the Klemperer's house. And when, one evening in February 1941, he forgot to darken the windows, he was denounced by a neighbor, arrested and detained for a week.

In early 1945, Klemperer finally noted what was also documented in other memoirs as a typical reaction to the collapse of the dictatorship: the Germans blamed Hitler for the military defeat, while claiming not to have known about the anti-Jewish policies. Above all, they had not

11 Ibid., p. 379 (20 September 1937).

12 *Tagebücher*, vol. 1, p. 653 (21 July 1941), 659 (10 August), 683 (1 November), 688 (24 November), 695 (17 December); vol. 2, p. 9 (12 January 1942), 79 (8 May), 112 (6 June), 126 (13 June), 223 (25 August), 398 (23 June 1943), 406 (19 July), 422 (23 August), 436 (28 September), 493 (4 March 1944), 567 (24 August).

13 Compare *Tagebücher*, vol. 1, p. 683 (1 November 1941), 696 (22 December); vol. 2, p. 65 (18 April 1942), 75 (28 April), 84 (14 May), 186 (27 July), 287 (3 December), 290 (11 December), 398 (23 June 1943), 420 (17 August), 505 (29 April 1944).

14 This phenomenon also resurfaces in other documents and personal recollections as well as in SD reports. In those cases where Jews received assistance from other Germans, the latter were usually personal acquaintances, even antisemites. See David Bankier, *Die öffentliche Meinung im Hitler-Staat. Die "Endlösung" und die Deutschen. Eine Berichtigung*, Berlin, 1995, p. 164.

15 *Tagebücher*, vol. 2, p. 65 (18 April 1942).

the least sense of their own guilt.[16] Greiner commented: "Gestures of offended innocence mixed with aggressive justification. Klemperer met people who supposedly knew nothing and yet in the same breath would remark, there were only convicts in Dachau anyway. Others tried to disqualify the victims of the Holocaust by pointing towards the number of victims of war bombing."[17] In late 1945 Klemperer wrote to a young German, a British prisoner of war, who had asked him for a certificate clearing his name:

> What most upsets me about your letter is the problem of guilt or innocence. ... You, and so many along with you, say over and over: we are innocent, we did not know. But did none of you read Hitler's *Kampf*, where everything that was carried out later was planned in advance with shameless openness? And were all these murders, all these crimes, wherever one turned, apparent only to us — I mean now not just to the Jews, but to all persecutees?"[18]

The question is meant both critically and rhetorically. However, in his diaries Klemperer frequently acknowledged with open astonishment and without rhetoric that even non-Jewish Germans who sympathized with the plight of the Jews did not really know of the severity of their situation — how much was forbidden to them or the quality of the lives they were forced to lead.[19] Among these were Annemarie Kroeger, who hid Klemperer's diary, and Richter, a lawyer, one of the few non-Jews who not only assured Klemperer of his sympathy but also offered him an opportunity to escape. These people, whose sympathy gave Klemperer encouragement, knew that Jews were far worse off than non-Jews. But they had only a very vague idea of the reality of Jewish life under the Gestapo reign of terror. The diaries also often mention non-Jews who did not register until years later, and then with great indignation, that Jews were only permitted to ride streetcars on the way to work, and then only in the front of the platform.

16 See ibid., 807 (28 May 1945). On Germans' attitude toward Jews and the National Socialist Jewish policies at war's end, see ibid., pp. 704, 707, 725, 752, 814. See also the paper of Otto D. Kulka in this volume and Bernd Greiner, *Im Herzen der Finsternis,* p. 148.

17 Bernd Greiner, *Im Herzen der Finsternis*, p. 148.

18 *Tagebücher,* vol. 2, p. 874.

19 *Tagebücher,* vol. 1, p. 57 (19 September 1933), 671 (20 September 1941), vol. 2, p. 66ff (19 April 1942), 102 (29 May), 211 (18 August), 241 (11 September), 324 (30 January 1943), 366 (27 April).

Without analyzing it further, Klemperer alludes to a strange mechanism: the effect even among well-meaning people of psychic barriers on perception, when the subject matter at issue did not affect them personally. Even those who did not agree with the racial exclusion of the Jews stopped short unconsciously before the barrier by which German society separated the people from "enemies of the people." Klemperer misinterpreted the ignorance of the people, wrote Hannes Heer, arguing that he overlooked the fact that the ignorance of the majority was less the result of a blanket effort by the regime and far more a conscious decision within every German not to know more than necessary.[20] Even if this applies to those who sympathized with the fate of the Jews, the questions remain: what were the motives for this repression? Was this the only way in which to reconcile oneself with the existing circumstances?

The well-informed Jews, particularly the Klemperers, stood in crass contrast to this reluctance to acknowledge reality. Despite prohibitions on newspapers and radios, despite isolation and internment in the *Judenhaus*, despite fear of spies and Gestapo terror, Klemperer knew not only about the crimes in his immediate neighborhood; he was also aware, soon after they were committed, of many atrocities that non-Jewish Germans supposedly did not get wind of until after the war, if even then. Often the information was somewhat inexact and was imparted in the form of rumors, but it was basically accurate. Thus, on 17 October 1942 Klemperer wrote of the Auschwitz concentration camp, "which seems to be a rapidly operating slaughterhouse."[21]

In December 1942 he wrote about the "horrible cruelty to Romanian Jews. (Had to dig their mass graves, undress, and were then shot. Just as Eva long since reported from Kiev.)"[22] In early June 1943 Klemperer received news of the uprising in the Warsaw Ghetto, which had been put down shortly before. According to the rumor, the battle had lasted for several weeks and the Germans had shot the residents and burned down the entire Ghetto. That was the accurate part. In addition, there was talk of participation by the Poles and over 3,000 German deserters in the

20 Hannes Heer, "Vox populi. Zur Mentalität der Volksgemeinschaft," in: *Im Herzen der Finsternis,* p. 138.

21 *Tagebücher,* vol. 2, p. 259.

22 Ibid., p. 299 (29 December 1942).

uprising. Klemperer doubted the truth of the news, but remarked, "In any case, the fact that such rumors are circulating is characteristic."[23] In August 1944 he wrote in the diaries, "Jews have been released from Hungary ... after a Hungarian agreement with the USA."[24] In October of the same year, an acquaintance gave him for the first time a figure on the number of victims. According to this astonishingly precise estimate, "six to seven million Jews (of the fifteen million that had existed), have been slaughtered (more precisely, shot and gassed)."[25] In November 1944 he was told yet again of "horrible murders of Jews in the East." The source was a soldier on leave from the Eastern front, who had added that alcohol was distributed to the marksmen at such opportunities.[26] From such reports, Klemperer concluded that none of the Dresden Jews whose deportation he had witnessed would come back alive.

Although he repeatedly pinned his hopes on indications that Germans generally did not agree with Nazi policies, Klemperer had to acknowledge from the beginning the general disinterest in the fate of the Jews and the secret support for anti-Jewish policies that prevailed. Even his descriptions of the academic milieu in which he still moved during the early years reveal a sort of anticipatory obedience. His non-Jewish colleagues anticipated the discrimination against the Jews even before such measures were enacted. In April 1936, a year after his dismissal from the university, Klemperer mentioned a directive for civil servants forbidding them to associate with "Jews, even so-called decent Jews, and disreputable elements."[27] But long before this contact prohibition was enacted, most of his colleagues had turned their backs on him. He had long since been denied any opportunities to publish. In June 1933 a colleague had already thought it advisable to have a Nazi author write for a prestigious collection, rather than a Jew.[28] Publishers no longer honored their contracts with Jewish authors.[29] A

23 Ibid., p. 386 (1 June 1943).
24 Ibid., p. 564 (19 August 1944).
25 Ibid., p. 606 (24 October 1944),
26 Ibid., p. 616 (26 November 1944).
27 *Tagebücher* , vol. 1, p. 259 (28 April 1936).
28 Ibid., p. 34 (30 June 1933).
29 Ibid., p. 47 (10 August 1933).

Jewish colleague of Klemperer's was forced to give up his honorary professorship "voluntarily."[30] By October 1933 philological journals and the university association newspaper already operated "so much in the ethos and jargon of the Third Reich that every page makes one nauseous."[31] Soon students stayed away from the Jewish professor's seminars, and he was removed from the examining board — all this before receiving his dismissal in April 1935. Some university employees expressed their sympathy with the outcast, but there was no open protest against the dismissal of Jewish scholars. Rarely did anyone directly express antisemitic views to him. But the ever more common party badges, the "lukewarm enmity,"[32] and the fact that most took no offense at anti-Jewish rabble-rousing were deeply distressing to Klemperer. He acknowledged the silent withdrawal of acquaintances and colleagues and his gradual isolation, which seems to have hurt him more than the government-ordered harassment. And even among those who expressed to Klemperer their displeasure with Nazi policies, it was impossible to avoid the suspicion that such complaints served primarily as an outlet for them to give vent to their own dissatisfaction in the relative certainty that a Jew would not betray them to the Gestapo.

Opportunism was encouraged by the informal structure. Against the background of state discrimination against Jews, many "Aryan" colleagues apparently developed a sixth sense for which contacts were inopportune and what was expected of a German university professor. This sixth sense — regardless of whether it arose from inner conviction and identification with the new powers, or from a lack of the courage of one's convictions — would become an important element of the dictatorship over the years. It made written orders or threats unnecessary, even when the issue was neither university positions nor publication opportunities, but murder and other crimes. This sixth sense, perhaps more than any consciously articulated opinions, is an indication of the unspoken consensus between the people and their leaders — a silent complicity.[33]

30 Ibid., p. 59 (9 October 1933).

31 Ibid., p. 63 (23 October 1933).

32 Ibid., p. 326 (31 December 1936),

33 See Ian Kershaw, "'Working towards the Führer.' Reflections on the Nature of the Hitler Dictatorship," *Contemporary European History*, 2 (1993), pp. 103–118.

In contrast, according to Klemperer, the Jews developed a premonitory fear, especially after the war began. They had a sure instinct for impending danger, long before they could possibly know of concrete plans. In his first entry, in September 1939, two days after the war began, Klemperer noted, "When I go to sleep, I think: will they come get me tonight? Will I be shot, or sent to a concentration camp?"[34] It is hardly necessary to add that there was no reason for this fear, no offense that could have provided a justification, however flimsy, for his arrest. It was simply the atmosphere of terror that caused such nightmares. On 14 September 1939, the Dresden Jews were ordered, verbally, to fill out a questionnaire on the stage of their emigration. At that, the anxious question appears, "Do they want to deport and exchange us?"[35]

The presentiment of murder and deportation was quite concrete when he wrote in June 1940, "They will put us all up against the wall. Frau Voss [with whom the Klemperers shared an apartment in the *Judenhaus*] said, "we'll all end up in Lublin!"[36] The background to this fear was the deportation of almost 2,000 Jews from Austria to the area around Lublin nine months earlier. On 7 July 1940, the same Frau Voss reported that a friend had heard on the radio of the resignation of the British government. "Now they'll make peace, and we'll be sent to Madagascar."[37] This fear was also real, and it documented how much the Jews knew of the German plans; at that very time, German scientists, at the behest of the Foreign Office, were examining the possibility of deporting six million Jews from Europe to Madagascar.[38] On 12 July, five days after the statement by Frau Voss quoted in the diaries, the General Governor of occupied Poland, Hans Frank, informed his staff of the plan to transport the Jews to a "colony" following the peace treaty, and added, "We are thinking about Madagascar, which France would cede for this purpose."[39]

Aside from such concrete anxieties, Klemperer described the general climate of fear that spread through his surroundings over the years. He

34 *Tagebücher* , vol. 1, p. 483 (3 September 1939).
35 Ibid., p. 488.
36 Ibid., p. 533 (11 June 1940).
37 Ibid., p. 538.
38 See Goetz Aly, Susanne Heim, *Vordenker der Vernichtung*, Frankfurt, 1995, p. 263.
39 Cited in ibid., p. 259.

was tormented from the start by a premonition of death, which becomes increasingly oppressive almost from one page of his diary to the next. He did not know whether he would die of a heart attack because of the terror or be killed in a pogrom; whether he would be murdered in a Gestapo jail or a concentration camp, or be deported or "slaughtered" with the other surviving Jews in the event of a German defeat. But he was almost certain that he, like the other Jews of Dresden, would not live to see the end of the war. In 1942, life in the *Judenhaus* seems to have been completely dictated by fear. Klemperer crept to the window when a car drove by outside, fearing he was about to be taken away. The residents of the *Judenhaus* were terrified when someone rang the doorbell; they no longer expected normal visitors and thought every ring was the Gestapo at the door.

They were afraid not only of house searches and arrests, but also of ordinary Germans. Even if they had less power than the Gestapo, one could not be sure that their hatred of Jews would be any milder. Klemperer hardly dared leave the *Judenhaus* after the introduction of the Yellow Star. But his fear increased with the years. In June 1942 he noted about a trip to the store:

> This waiting in front of the store ... is especially horrible ... the whole world stared at my star. Torture — I can plan a hundred times not to pay attention, it remains a torture. And I never know when someone goes by, drives by, whether he is a member of the Gestapo, whether he will curse me, spit at me, arrest me.[40]

Later he left the house only to go to forced labor, fearing physical attack.[41] And even then, he, like other Jews, ducked into narrow sidestreets away from the main thoroughfares, in order to avoid attacks by non- Jews.[42]

Even though Klemperer describes many expressions of sympathy and friendship he experienced from non-Jewish Germans, the situation in which the Jews were forced to live became more and more horrific. The most banal everyday activities were overshadowed by fear, disgust and depression. Life itself became a torment — and this despite the fact that those who survived were "privileged."

40 *Tagebücher*, vol. 2, p. 117 (9 June 1942).
41 Ibid., p. 500 (2 April 1944).
42 Ibid., p. 505 (29 April 1944).

Such descriptions shed a different light on Klemperer's statements about the German-Jewish relationship. When considered in isolation, three reactions may be discerned in the passages of the diary in which he describes the behavior of Germans toward Jews and anti-Jewish policies. First, he tells of non-Jews who did not support these policies and/or felt sympathy at least with the Jews they knew, treating them with friendliness. Second, were the Germans who, for whatever reason, did not object to the anti-Jewish policies. A typical example was the couple who took care of Klemperer's sister Grete, "The Kemleins ... take the anti-Jewish rabble-rousing as a given, are not disturbed by it, are totally unpolitical, and at the same time are obviously happy with conditions in Germany. Splendor, order, peace."[43] Finally, in the last years of the war, Klemperer more and more frequently met Germans who not only supported the policies toward the Jews, but felt a need to express their hatred of the Jews personally by openly attacking them.

It is difficult to estimate, based on the diaries, how widespread each of the three attitudes was and how close the relationship was between ignorance and silent or open support. At the same time, as mentioned above, the question arises of how representative Klemperer's observations were. Considered in this way, we learn from the diaries no more than that eliminationist antisemitism, of the type Goldhagen considers typical, existed alongside help and solidarity with the Jews, and that many behavioral patterns, such as opportunism, tactlessness, cowardice and ignorance, fell somewhere between the two.

When we take into consideration the description of the Jews' living conditions overall, however, the perspective changes. The majority of reactions then appear as supplements to Gestapo terror. And the examples of friendliness and sympathy that renewed Klemperer's faith show primarily the low expectations he had of non-Jews. Often, what he experienced as a good turn was simply the maintenance of normal behavior — the fact that someone did not immediately address him in the familiar form or shout at him.[44] Even a clap on the back, a few comforting words in passing, or continued greetings from an old acquaintance were seen as rays of hope. The reader gradually identifies

43 *Tagebücher*, vol. 1, p. 430 (9 October 1938).

44 *Tagebücher*, vol. 2, p. 23 (13 February 1942), 189 (29 July), 249 (24 September), 398 (23 June 1943), 411 (26 July), 608 (27 October 1944).

so strongly with the author through his diaries that, given the horrors all around him, we share in the joy at such positive encounters, easily forgetting in the process how pitiful were these examples of "good Germans" — how out of proportion reactions such as a handshake or a gift of potatoes were, in face of the real situation of the Jews. If one reads the diary with the question in mind: were the Germans really that evil, much evidence has been found to the contrary. But if you ask: who would the Jews really rely on to help them in their desperate plight, the truth is that even the most well-meaning interpretation will not find more than two or three such individuals in the aproximately 1,500 pages of Klemperer's diary.

Reviews of Klemperer's books have frequently emphasized the positive behavior on the part of non-Jewish Germans. Especially in the debate over Daniel Goldhagen's book, Klemperer has been used as an authority to prove that German antisemitism was not so severe after all.[45] This exonerating argument lends more complex significance to the extraordinarily strong interest his diaries have engendered in the German public. But even if many people who look in Klemperer's mirror see only a confirmation of their own vanity, this does not mean the mirror is faulty or distorted.

45 For example, Norbert Frei, "Ein Volk von 'Endlösern'? Daniel Goldhagen bringt eine alte These in neuem Gewand," *Süddeutsche Zeitung,* 13–14 April 1996. "Ein Volk von Dämonen?," *Der Spiegel*, 20 May 1996. For a critical response see: Wolfgang Schneider, "Pro Germania. Über Nutzen und Nachteil der Tagebücher Victor Klemperers für die moralische Aufrüstung der wiedervereinigten Deutschen," *Konkret,* Heft 10, October 1996, pp. 18–22; Paola Traverso, "Victor Klemperers Deutschlandbild — Ein jüdisches Tagebuch?" in: *Tel Aviver Jahrbuch für Deutsche Geschichte*, 26 (1997), pp. 307–344.

Jewish Society Under the Nazi System

Reactions of the Jewish Press in Germany to the Nuremberg Laws

JOSEPH WALK

In his typically comprehensive and thoroughgoing article, "The Response of German Jewry to the Nuremberg Laws,"[1] Abraham Margaliot focuses on the practical responses of Jewish organizations to the change in the legal status of German Jewry. Margaliot states that the Nuremberg Laws descended on these (non-Zionist), circles *"like thunder out of a clear blue sky"*[2] [italics mine — J.W.]. This assertion contradicts subsequent remarks in Margaliot's article about members of the non-Zionist camp, who "waged their principal struggle against the revocation of Jews' rights in the spring of 1935" (i.e., about half a year previously), sparing no effort to be allowed to serve in the German army which was then being reestablished. When their efforts failed, they evidently lost all hope of clinging to the remnants of their Emancipation-era rights.[3] Indeed, study of the Jewish press shortly after the Induction Law (*Wehrgesetz*), was gazetted on 21 May 1935 shows that all shades of the Jewish press realized that the exclusion of Jews from active service in the Wehrmacht signaled a decisive turnabout in their legal status, and that they faced "the utter undoing of the emancipation," as Margaliot writes.[4]

Of all publications, it was the representative organ of the "non-Zionists," that of the *Centralverein deutscher Staatsbürger jüdischen Glaubens* (hereinafter, the *CV*), that took note, immediately after the Induction Law was gazetted, of expected developments in the legal

1 In *Between Rescue and Perdition: Studies in the History of German Jewry, 1932–1938*, Jerusalem, 1996, pp. 17–36. The article first appeared in *Yad Vashem Studies*, 12 (1978), pp. 55–76.

2 Ibid., p. 18.

3 Ibid., p. 19.

4 Ibid., p. 18.

status of German Jewry. In a front-page article headlined "Where this law will lead,"[5] the paper bases itself *inter alia* on remarks by Professor Erik Wolf of Freiburg who, as early as November 1934, stressed that a distinction would be made between a "member of the nation" (*Volksgenosse*), and a native or subject (*Staatsbürger*). Admittedly, the Nazi jurist stated with emphasis, this distinction would not diminish the rights of "members of the alien race" (*Artfremde*), as individuals. Two days after the law was gazetted, Dr. Alfred Hirschberg, chairman of the *CV*, also referred to the new statute in a lecture titled "Our Jewish Reality" (*Unsere jüdische Wirklichkeit*), stressing that German Jewry should not be suspected this time of having responded out of fear of losing economic advantages. German Jewry, which had proved its allegiance to, and voluntarism for the Fatherland from the War of Independence (1812), until World War I, felt itself dishonored in view of the sacrifices it had made. The speaker then exhorted his audience to keep up the tradition of "willingness to make sacrifices and display valor" (*Opferbereitschaft und Heldentum*).

About three weeks later, on 29 May 1935, the newspaper published the law and the detailed regulations attached to it under which all non-Aryans liable to induction would be transferred to the second reserve corps of the Wehrmacht. Basing itself on remarks made by the Minister of War, General von Reichenau, the paper stressed that individual Jews would have no chance of being accepted into active service on the basis of their own applications. This warning was addressed to the National Alliance of Jewish Front-Line Soldiers, which considered the new law a stinging insult to its dignity. The National Alliance advised its members to "throw their call-up notices (*Gestellungsbefehle*) into the trash and proclaim their willingness to serve the Fatherland as they had in the past." Thus they sought to assert the ownership of "basic" historical rights (*um fundamentale geschichtliche Rechte geltend zu machen*).

The *Israelitisches Familienblatt*, a neutral family-oriented paper that carefully refrained from identifying with any political stream in German

5 On 30 May 1935, with the title *"Rechtsentwicklungen,"* quoted in the 22 June 1935 issue of *Zur Geschichte des Deutschen Staatsbegriffes*, and remarks by the Nazi Minister of the Interior, Wilhelm Frick, who distinguished between "Staatsbürger" und "Staatsangehörige."

Jewry, also expressed "understanding appreciation" of the feelings of the Soldiers' Alliance (*mitfühlende Achtung*), especially those among its members who had been officers. However, the paper stressed, the new reality should be acknowledged. This reality was expressed with greater vehemence in an article published by the SS journal *Das Schwarze Korps*, unequivocally titled, "There is No Place for Jews in the Army." The Nazi paper also spoke explicitly of the imminent passage of a "citizenship law." The *Israelitisches Familienblatt*, published in Hamburg, corroborated its expectations by citing remarks made by one of the local associations: "A Jew can never become a citizen."[6]

Jüdische Rundschau, the journal of the German Zionist Federation, initially avoided polemics with non-Zionist Jewry and contented itself with analyzing the law and its effects on the legal status of Jewry. Its conclusion: "A profound turnabout in the development of our legal status [has occurred]."[7] Not until the National Association of Front-Line Soldiers issued its protest did the *Jüdische Rundschau* take exception to the association leaders' attempt to urge their members to protest their discrimination — for much the same reason that the *Israelitisches Familienblatt* had — on the grounds that such a protest was hopeless.[8] In the same edition, the paper printed a manifesto from the National Representation of German Jewry, which urged Jews of induction age "to report [for induction ...] and to honor their call-up notices in full."[9] This call was printed in all Jewish newspapers with no further commentary.[10] Today we know that even the National Representation protested to the government about the exclusion of Jews from the Wehrmacht: "We German Jews expect not to be enjoined from participating in compulsory military service as persons with equal rights."[11] It is difficult to determine whether this appeal was meant as a lip-service protest only or to support the stance of the National

6 *Israelitisches Familienblatt* (hereafer *IFB*), 23 May 1935.

7 *Jüdische Rundschau* (hereafter *JR*), 24 May 1935.

8 *JR*, 14 June 1935.

9 "*Zur Musterung zu stellen und dem Gestellungsbefehl in vollem Umfang nachzukommen.*"

10 See, for example, *Breslauer Jüdisches Gemeindeblatt*, 30 June 1935.

11 Central Jewish Historical Archives, A/171: cited in Yitzchak Arad, Yisrael Gutman, and Abraham Margaliot, eds., *Documents on the Holocaust,* Jerusalem, 1981, p. 77–78.

Association of Jewish Soldiers. In sum, all segments of German Jewry were aware that the Induction Law was but a detail that attested to the general trend: the obliteration of German Jews' civil rights.

Two statutes gazetted in June and July of 1935 may have opened the eyes of German Jews who still harbored illusions. On 26 June 1935, the National Service Law (*Reichsarbeitsdienst*), was gazetted, disqualifying "non-Aryans" and those married to "non-Aryans" for enlistment in this organization (which engaged in public welfare projects). "Non-Aryans previously deemed worthy of army service may be accepted, but not as commanders."[12] Which "non-Aryans" were worthy? A detailed regulation attached to the Induction Law, dated 25 July 1935, answers explicitly that "Only non-Aryans who have only one Jew among their forebears may be accepted, pursuant to their application, into active service on an exceptional basis."[13]

Inadvertent loopholes in the Nazi legislation allowed Jews who had converted to Christianity and Jews married to "Aryan" women the possibility of attempting to mask their identity. The Zionist press responded to this shameful behavior with unequivocal rage: "We have absolutely nothing to do with those who call themselves 'non-Aryans',"[14] instead of identifying themselves as full-fledged Jews.

Admittedly, when the Protection of German Blood and German Honor Law, one of the Nuremberg Laws, was gazetted on 15 September 1935,[15] it referred only to "Jews" as persons unmarriageable to persons of German blood, without distinguishing between "full" and "mixed" Jews. It took the legislature another two months, until 14 November 1935, to issue the first complementary regulation to this law, which listed the various kinds of "half-breeds" to which the law would apply leniently or stringently.[16] This regulation coincided with the first regulation of the Citizenship Law[17] which attracted the bulk of Jewish public attention.

12 *Reichsgesetzblatt* 1935, vol. I, pp. 769–771.
13 Ibid., pp. 1047–1049.
14 *Jüdische Volkszeitung*, 16 August 1935.
15 *Reichsgesetzblatt* 1935, vol. I, p. 1146f.
16 Ibid., 1935, vol. I, pp. 1334–36.
17 Ibid., 1935, vol. I, pp. 1333f.

The Citizenship Law, similarly enacted on 15 September 1935,[18] abolished the equal rights of German Jews, revoked their status as "citizens" (*Reichsbürger*), — a status henceforth reserved for "Aryans" only — and redefined them as "subjects" (*Staatsangehöriger*). Although some Jews and Jewish groups had foreseen this, the political spectrum of German Jewry was stunned from end to end. Parenthetically, only one Jewish organization had predicted the impending change in the legal status of German Jewry: On 13 August 1935,[19] this organization, Esra (*Hilfsverein*), had renamed itself (*Hilfsverein der Juden in Deutschland*), instead of *Hilfsverein der deutschen Juden*, while the *Reichsvertretung* and the *CV* were still signing their correspondence with the original expression *Deutsche Juden* until the end of that month.[20]

On 20 September 1935, the *CV-Zeitung* conveyed the response of most German Jews to the loss of equal rights[21] and analyzed the historical watershed that the status of German Jewry had crossed. The editor-in-chief of the paper, Alfred Hirschberg, a *CV* leader, expressed the attitude that he considered desirable by stating, "We are not emerging from the ghetto and we are not returning to the ghetto." After revealing the plan that the National Representation had adopted on the counsel of all its constituent factions, he clashed swords with the Zionists who seemed to be celebrating their victory. His article ends with the slogan: "To live like Jews with dignity and good sense."[22] A week later, the paper continued to stabilize itself in the new realities, stressing that German Jewry had met a unique fate that should not be cited as an indication of what awaited Jewish communities in other European countries.[23] Again, the paper took exception to the idea of establishing a national home in Palestine, considering Palestine but one place of refuge for Jews forced to emigrate from their German homeland. The editorial ends with the clear admission of fear of change in the composition of the National Representation that the

18 Ibid., 1935, vol. I, pp. 1146f.
19 *JR*, 13 August 1935.
20 *JR*, 30 August 1935.
21 *CV*, Nr. 39, S. 1 (A.H.),
22 "in Würde und Anstand als Juden leben."
23 *CV*, No. 40, "Neue Sachlichkeit."

Zionists were demanding; this may be a veiled reference to the Kareski affair, discussed below.

The monthly journal *Der Morgen,*[24] founded by Julius Goldstein, a *CV* member who steered clear of partisan polemics, devoted its editorial "Review" to the term "minority." Basing itself on a statement by the Nazi leadership that the new laws were meant to devise a "tolerant attitude toward the Jewish people," it demanded recognition of the National Representation as a source of authority both internally and externally. However, the author of the "Review" was aware of the "disproportion of forces" — majority and minority — and warned the Jews to avoid rash decisions since the decision was not theirs to make.[25]

The official organ of the Zionist Federation in Germany, the *Jüdische Rundschau*, refrained from disputation with the *CV* journal and addressed its response primarily to the Nazi regime, which was monitoring the discussions at the Zionist Congress in Lucerne at that time. The paper accepted the designation of Jews as a "national minority" in diaspora countries and stressed the Zionist aim to make Jewry a "historical subject" in Palestine rather than a "historical object."[26]

This notwithstanding, the paper, basing itself like the others on the official attitude of the Nazi government which attempted to depict the new legislation as a generous solution (*grosszügig*), to the Jewish problem, demanded that the *modus vivendi* be based on four principles: 1) non-defamation of Jews, 2)Jewish economic freedom, 3) Jewish cultural autonomy, and 4) the possibility of orderly emigration.[27] Addressing itself to the Jewish community, the paper demanded greater Zionist influence in the governing institutions of the National Representation and the *kehillot* (community or congregational organizations).[28] In an editorial titled *"Nahamu, Nahamu, Ami"* ("Comfort, oh comfort My people" — Isaiah 40:1), editor-in-chief Robert Weltsch again displayed his capacity as a thinker who knew how to sustain the morale of

24 Interestingly, it took *Der Morgen* until June 1936 to acquiesce to its renaming from "the monthly of German Jewry" to "the monthly of Jews in Germany."

25 *Der Morgen*, 11. Jahrgang, November 1935, Heft 8, pp. 329–332.

26 *JR*, 17 September 1935.

27 Ibid.

28 *JR*, 24 September 1935.

Jewry in its time of trial and to bolster its psychological and spiritual endurance.[29]

A less representative Zionist newspaper (addressed to Eastern Germany and published in Breslau) ran the proclamation of the Zionist Federation but did not steer clear of internal Jewish polemics. While claiming to have foreseen the results of the Induction Law,[30] the editorial spoke explicitly of a "historical turning point" (*historischer Wendepunkt*), and demanded an internal, not external, response to the new legislation. Hence, it singled out for special emphasis the favorable aspect of the ban on intermarriage.[31]

The problem of "family purity" and its minutiae was the central theme in the response of *Der Israelit*, the Agudath Israel newspaper in Germany. In a series of articles, Dr. Jacob Levy of Berlin discussed the question of "Hereditary Health: the Mission of German Jewry"[32] (*Erbgesundheit: Eine Autgabe der deutschen Juden*). The Association of Orthodox Rabbis warned of an "affront to the purity of virtues" and took exception to "Bolshevism, enemy of the faith" (*Religionsfeindlicher Bolschewismus*), on the one hand (in yet another attempt to find an identity of interests with the Nazi worldview[33]), and the non-religious "Representation" on the other. Among other things, *Der Israelit* categorically ruled out the existence of an ostensible "Jewish flag" under which, according to the Nazi legislature, the Jewish minority would be represented.[34]

A week after the Nuremberg Laws were enacted, the National Representation, terming itself the "future autonomous leadership," expressed its response to the historical change that had occurred in the status of German Jewry.[35] In five paragraphs, it listed its

29 *JR*, 20 September 1935.

30 *"dass man mit ihrem (der Gesetze), Kommen seit längerer Zeit rechnen musste."*

31 "Law for the Protection of German Blood and German Honor."

32 *Der Israelit*, No. 38–39, 19; 26 September 1935.

33 Ibid., No. 39 (26 September 1935). Cf. Rabbi Elie Munk, *Judentum und Umwelt: Sechs Vorträge von Dr. Eli Munk*, Frankurt am Main, 1933.

34 Ibid., No. 38 (19 September 1935), see Article 4(2), of the "Law for the Protection of German Blood and German Honor." As for the matter of the flag, the newspaper devoted a special article to this question in its edition of 10 October 1935 (no. 41–42), under the headline "Jewish Flags and Colors."

35 Most of the "nonpartisan" newspapers, such as those of institutions affiliated with the National Representation and the *kehillot,* merely printed the Central Representation

functions as derived from its authority to represent the bulk of German Jewry: 1) expansion of Jewish educational and cultural autonomy, 2) planning for emigration, 3) assurance of welfare services, 4) efforts to ensure sources of livelihood, and 5) assistance in building Palestine. The response of independent Orthodoxy followed swiftly. The main apprehensions of this faction stemmed from the slogan of the "Uniform School" (*Einheitsschule*), which the National Representation was about to establish in response to "racial segregation" in the German education system.[36] Stressing the "intolerable affront to the conscience" and the "centrality of the Jewish faith," the countrywide Orthodox representative organization demanded "autonomy in religious and cultural life." However, it expressed its willingness to cooperate with the National Representation in economic affairs and social relief.[37]

Indeed, all the Jewish organizations attempted to inspire young Jewish women to take the place of "Aryan" domestic workers (under age 45), whom the new legislation enjoined from working in Jewish homes.[38] Some also proposed that unemployed Jewish men consider "vocational retraining" (*Berufsumschichtung*).[39]

Aware of the regime's hatred of Jewry, all the newspapers restrained their internal polemics with the flagrant exception of the organ of the "National Zionists" (*Staatszionisten*), the German branch of the

memorandum that had been given the consent of most of the political organizations, including the National Association of Jewish Front-Line Soldiers, but not including the Association of National German Jews, the Revisionist Zionists (*Staatszionisten*), and Independent Orthodoxy.

36 This plan, published on 10 September 1935, under the title "Racial Segregation in Public Schools," was not implemented for economic reasons until after *Kristallnacht*. (The order was given on 15 October 1938). The response of the National Union of Jewish Teachers' Associations proves that the Jewish teachers indeed thought in 1935 that the order would cause the Jewish education system to expand.

37 See *Jüdische Schulzeitung, Monatsschrift für Erziehung, Unterricht und Schulpolitik, Organ des Reichsverbandes der jüdischen Lehrervereine*, 11. Jhg., No. 10 (3 October 1935), p. 1–3: "Die Zeit und die Schule" and cf. Ehmann's response to the plea of the *CV* not to secede from organized Jewry at this time of distress.

38 As stipulated in "Law for the Protection of German Blood and German Honor" of 15 September 1935, Article 3.

39 See, for example, *CVZ,* 20 September 1935, *Der Israelit*, 3 October 1935, *Breslauer Jüdisches Gemeindeblatt*, 30 September 1935.

Revisionist movement. The editor of this journal, Max Schulman (who invariably appended "Captain [Res.]" to his name), crowned his editorial with the headline "Avenger of Israel"[40] (*Rächer Israels*). He labeled the Assimilationists "obsequious" (*Speichellecker*), and accused them of "licking the German jackboot." He subjected Jews of the prestigious *Kurfürstendam* to acrid judgment for frequenting resorts instead of helping their needy brethren. Schulman regretted that the censor had not banned the distribution of papers such as the liberal *Allgemeine Zeitung des Judentums*, which had resumed publication, in order to keep them from "spattering their venom" further. Schulman concluded his editorial by expressing nostalgia for the "Jewish avengers" of the Second Temple period, who knew how to apply violence in defense of their people's honor. The secessionist National Zionists brazenly termed the heads of the Central Representation "criminals" and demanded that this institution, which represented the bulk of German Jewry, be reconstituted. Schulman refrained from mentioning the planned appointment of the leader of his movement, Georg Kareski, as the government-sponsored "commissar of Jewish cultural associations."[41]

It is highly doubtful that the Jewish public knew of the Nazi government's intention to install Kareski as the czar of Jewish cultural life. Leo Baeck and Otto Hirsch opposed and eventually frustrated this ploy by threatening to withdraw from the Central Representation leadership. However, the population at large could have discovered it by reading Goebbels's newspaper *Der Angriff*, which ran an interview with Kareski under the headline "A Clean Separation is Highly Desirable." It was the only time that a Jew was interviewed by an official Nazi newspaper, which introduced Kareski as "the man who's just been placed in charge of the Union of Jewish Cultural Associations in the Reich."[42] Kareski sought to avenge the insult done to Jewry in his

40 "Rächer Israels," *Der Staatszionist*, 5. Jhg. No. 26, 23 October 1935.

41 *Selbstwehr*, Zionist newspaper published in Prague, ran the interview in its first edition of 1 January 1936.

42 Various journals, such as the yearbooks of the Leo Baeck Institute (see *Year Books* 21–39, General Index, London, 1995, p. 106), discussed the Kareski affair at length. Here I note only that after Kareski moved to Palestine in 1937, the association of German Immigrants attacked him so viciously that he sued the association for libel. The trial was held in a rabbinical court, which found for the Association on all three counts (Archives of the Leo Baeck Institute, Jerusalem, file 472).

replies to the paper's questions, but his very consent to be interviewed by a Nazi organ was considered by many to be in bad taste.

One response to the Nuremberg laws was exceptional, but it too did not come to public light. This was a prayer written by Leo Baeck approximately three weeks after the Nuremberg Laws were gazetted, which he sent to Jewish congregational leaders to be recited before Kol Nidre on the eve of Yom Kippur. When the authorities discovered this they ordered Otto Hirsch to squelch the prayer, which concluded by urging the congregation to protest the defamation of Jewish values by means of silent devotion.[43]

No one could have imagined then that the very Nuremberg Laws that these German-Jewish newspapers and journals had sought to protest would serve as the infrastructure for a full range of decrees that savaged German Jewry, including confiscation of the property of Jews after they were liquidated in extermination camps.[44] As we give thought to the facts known to us today, our only possible response, like theirs, is silent contemplation.

43 Ernst Simon, *Aufbau im Untergang, Jüdische Erwachsenenbildung im nationalsozialistischen Deutschland als geistiger Widerstand*, Tübingen, 1959, pp. 39–41.

44 Regulation XIII of the Citizenship Law.

Jewish Self-Defense under the Constraints of National Socialism: The Final Years of the Centralverein

DANIEL FRAENKEL

I

The *Centralverein deutscher Staatsbürger jüdischen Glaubens (CV),* the major German Jewish defense organization founded in 1893, continued to exist and to operate under the law well into the sixth year of the Third Reich (it was only shut down by the Nazis in the wake of the November pogrom of 1938). Yet organized Jewish defense as such is usually considered to have come to "an abrupt end" with the advent of the National Socialist regime. As Arnold Paucker, the distinguished historian of German Jewish defense against antisemitism, strikingly formulated it in one of his essays: "[The *CV*'s] so-called defensive battle (*Abwehrkampf*) lasted forty years, and then came unceremoniously (*Sang und Klanglos*) to an end on January 30, 1933."[1] At the time that this dismissive dictum was pronounced more than ten years ago, the *CV*'s extensive documentation, containing many hundreds of files of original correspondence from the thirties, lay buried deep in the cellars of the Osoby archival center near Moscow, virtually unknown and inaccessible to western researchers. Its recent discovery and accessibility to scholarly research — not least through the large microfilming project undertaken by the United States Holocaust

1 Arnold Paucker, "Die Abwehr des Antisemitismus in den Jahren 1893–1933," in: *Antisemitismus. Von der Judenfeindschaft zum Holocaust*, Herbert A. Strauss and Norbert Kampe, eds., Bonn, 1984, p. 143. Paucker partly retracted his position in "Jewish Self-Defense," in: *Die Juden im nationalsozialistischen Deutschland*, Arnold Paucker et al., eds., Tübingen, 1986, p. 61.

Memorial Museum — enables us to undertake a closer look at the final chapter of one of the more important Jewish organizations in the modern era. The particular relevance of the *CV* to a discussion of German society and the persecution of the Jews hardly needs much elaboration. It was the most important representative of that wing in German Jewry, by far the most numerous and most characteristic, which had come to regard itself in the wake of emancipation as an integral part of the German people and the German homeland. Its long defensive battle was predicated on the assumption that antisemitism represented but a temporary and surmountable setback on the long and arduous way of German Jewry to full equality and complete and seamless integration (though not necessarily self-effacing assimilation), into the non-Jewish environment.

I would like to emphasize at the outset that the following analysis is but a first foray into a largely uncharted terrain, based on only a partial examination of extensive and hitherto unutilized archival material. It cannot claim in any sense to be comprehensive or conclusive. I propose to show, based on my reading of the Osoby documentation, that the *CV*'s defense against antisemitism did not come to a sudden halt after Hitler's nomination as chancellor. Although never openly opposing the official antisemitic policy of the government — this would have been tantamount to suicide — the Jewish organization continued against all odds to conduct an energetic everyday defense of Jewish rights and honor. This Jewish activity cannot be categorized as active resistance to the Nazis since it was non-militant in nature and did not openly challenge the authority of the state. But its overall effect was subtly subversive of the Nazi government's policy of isolating the Jews and driving them out of their positions in German society and the German economy. It represented the conscious and organized refusal on the part of a beleaguered ethnic minority to resign itself to the fate of outcasts from society and civilization. In the short run, and within inescapable limitations, this rearguard battle against antisemitism would at times prove surprisingly effective.

II

Let me start by considering briefly the broader historical context. The continued existence of the *CV*, the major Jewish self-defense organization, into the sixth year of the Third Reich must be understood within the framework of the paradoxical autonomy that was enjoyed by the persecuted Jewish minority in Nazi Germany for most of the prewar period. While all other forms of political or social organization that were regarded as inimical to the regime (the *KPD*, the *SPD*, the Labor Unions, even the rightist *Stahlhelm*), were either ruthlessly suppressed or "coordinated" (*gleichgeschaltet*), into the totalitarian state structure in the first few months after Hitler's accession to power, the major Jewish organizations — the *CV, the Zionistische Vereinigung für Deutschland* (*ZVfD*), the *Reichsbund jüdischer Frontsoldaten* (*RjF*), and the umbrella organization, the *Reichsvertretung der deutschen Juden* (*RV*) — continued to operate until the November pogrom of 1938. Until then, needless to say, they were closely watched over by the Gestapo and the SD.[2] It appears as if the very racial incorrigibility of the Jewish enemy in the eyes of the totalitarian regime prevented it for a while from clamping down on Jewish organizational autonomy. In the absence of any direct, conclusive evidence, we can only speculate as to the reasons for this apparent Nazi tolerance of the communal and organizational dimension of Jewish life in Germany, as distinct from the life of Jews as individuals. One plausible explanation, suggested by Hans Mommsen more than thirty years ago,[3] is that the regime used the Jewish organizations in the first years as more or less unwitting tools for tightening its control over the Jewish minority, isolating it from the German environment and driving the Jews out of Germany.

Be that as it may, the specific case of the *CV* is all the more puzzling in view of its pre-1933 record of fighting antisemitism[4] and

2 Cf. Herbert A. Strauss, "Jewish Autonomy within the Limits of National Socialist Policy — The Communities and the Reichsvertretung," in: Paucker, *Die Juden im nationalsozialistischen Deutschland*, pp. 125–152.

3 Hans Mommsen, "Der nationalsozialistische Polizeistaat und die Judenverfolgung vor 1938," *Viertelsjahrshefte für Zeitgeschichte*, 10 (1962), pp. 68–87.

4 Reacting to a police raid of the organization's Berlin main office in the wake of the Reichstag fire, the *CV-Zeitung* issue of 2 March 1933, while strongly rejecting the imputation of clandestine collusion with the communists, declared:

its unbroken and long-standing ideological commitment to defend the Jewish connection to Germany. Here, after all, the regime had to deal with the major Jewish defense organization that was decidedly German in outlook and orientation, and which by no means propagated or encouraged a mass Jewish exodus from Germany in the first years after the Nazi takeover. The organization's very name, the "Central Association of German Citizens of the Jewish Faith" (it was not changed until after the Nuremberg Laws), was calculated to work as a direct provocation to the central ideological fixation of National Socialism: the racially closed *Volksgemeinschaft* in which the Jew as a racial outsider had no share. Its pre-1933 program, which combined the "vigorous protection of the civil and social equality" of the German Jews with "the unswerving cultivation of German convictions"(*Gesinnung*), remained its official public line long after the unfolding antisemitic campaign, and specifically the exclusion laws of spring 1933, had made Jewish equality in Nazi Germany a dead letter.[5]

Although cognizant of the growing gap between its ideological postulates and the reality of the Jewish situation in Nazi Germany, the *CV* leadership refused — until forced by the Nuremberg Laws of September 1935 — either to change its name or to renege on the central premise of the unbroken Jewish connection to Germany. "We have to continue our work so as to secure a living space in Germany, not only for the present generation but also for generations to come" stated the *CV* circular to its individual members as late as 10 January 1935.[6]

Indeed, the belief in the possibility of a Jewish future in Germany was elevated by the organization's leadership in the first years after the Nazi takeover into a central article of ideological faith, a yardstick by which to distinguish between the *CV* faithful and the adherents of the rival Zionist ideology. Acknowledging that the Jewish situation was

"Der Central-Verein ist die Vereinigung der deutschen Juden, deren Aufgabe die Bekämpfung des Antisemitismus ist. Diesen Kamp führt der Central-Verein im vollen Lichte der öffentlichkeit und ausschliesslich auf legalem Wege."

5 See the entry "Centralverein deutscher Staatsbürger jüdischen Glaubens" in the 1935 edition of the *Philo-Lexicon — Handbuch des jüdischen Wissens.*

6 United States Holocaust Memorial Museum Archive, R.G. 1.001M (Osoby Fond #721, Opis 1), Microfilm Reel 97, Folder 54 (Henceforth to be cited as USHMMA + reel number and folder number).

beset with increasing difficulties and complications, the organization's leadership refused to give up hope. As gauged by the *CV* experts in mid-April 1935, more than two years after Hitler's ascent to power and five months before the promulgation of the Nuremberg Laws, the Jewish reality in Nazi Germany did not present a picture of unmitigated gloom. The Berlin head office in its circular letter of the same date, significantly titled "Concerning our Reality," tried to steer a middle way between foolhardy optimism and paralyzing despair. The problems, it reasoned, were too variegated and the overall situation too much in a state of flux to permit any sweeping conclusion. While there were undeniable "difficulties" (as the circular euphemistically termed them), for the Jewish population in certain parts of the country and in some branches of the economy, there were still other sectors where neither legal nor practical exclusion could be observed. It would not do to gloss over the difficulties, it conceded, "but even a primitive ostrich policy is preferable to a deliberate (*zweckbetonter*) pessimism that registers the difficulties with satisfaction, because they seem to confirm one's own Jewish *Weltanschauung*."[7] The latter was an unveiled gibe at the Zionist camp, which was transformed in the wake of the Nazi takeover from a rather marginal minority wing in Jewish life in Germany to a main contender for hegemony. The barely concealed *schadenfreude* displayed by some Zionists after January 1933 was deeply resented by the *CV* activists. German Zionism itself, argued the circular letter, had made in its time full use of the emancipation of the German Jews, of their political equality and the opportunities it offered for spiritual and economic ascent. Attached to the letter was a brief but instructive sample of cases that attested to the practical work of the *CV* in its dealings with various agencies of the Third Reich, which seemed to bear out the impression that all was not lost for Jewish life in Nazi Germany.

Though undoubtedly losing some ground to the Zionists in the wake of the Nazi seizure of power, it would appear that the *CV* continued to enjoy the loyalty of the substantial majority of German Jews. At the beginning of 1935, it still counted no less than fifty thousand active members, organized in 16 regional associations and four hundred local

7 "Um unsere Wirklichkeit," Ortsgruppen Rundbriefe des CV, 4, 15 April 1935, USHMMA, Reel 97, Folder 67.

groups all over Germany.[8] For the same year, 1935, the head office in Berlin could report a scale of activity that included, for Berlin alone, 75,000 written replies and 15,000 individual, oral consultations. As late as December 1937, the *CV-Zeitung* still boasted a circulation of 37,000 copies among the dwindling Jewish population in Germany, claiming to be the most widely read Jewish paper in the German language in any part of the world.[9] The organizational stability of the *CV* was in part a reflection of the fact that — unlike the rival *ZVfD* — it did not have to reckon with a mass exodus of its upper- and middle-echelon leadership following the Nazi seizure of power. Apart from the retirement of its veteran director Ludwig Holländer (Herzfeld claims in his memoirs that Holländer was in a state of collapse after the Nazi seizure of power[10]), and the departure to England of the syndic, Alfred Wiener, the organization did not undergo a major personal reshuffle. Both Julius Brodnitz, the chairman of the *CV* until his death in June 1936, and Ernst Herzfeld, his deputy and successor, were old established leaders. The new syndic Hans Reichmann, and the new editor-in-chief of the *CV-Zeitung* Alfred Hirschberg, had already been among the younger activists before 1933, just as other prominent personalities like Ernst Wallach, Bruno Weil and Rudolf Callmann. Some of the organization stalwarts after 1933 were newly retired German civil servants: Fritz Goldschmidt, Kurt Friedlaender, Richard Joachim and others.

III

In the years 1930–32, at the threshold of the Nazi seizure of power, the veteran Jewish defense organization had made some bold forays into German political life, aligning itself with the democratic parties against the enemies of the republic. This new political mobilization found its expression in activities such as the subsidization of democratic parties and the conducting of anti-Nazi propaganda campaigns. However, even in the context of the pre-Nazi period, the Jewish organization's attempt

8 See note 5.

9 USHMMA, Reel 99, Folder 93.

10 Cf. Ernst Herzfeld, "Meine letzten Jahre in Deutschland," Yad Vashem Archives, R.G. 0.1, File 8, p. 2

to break out of its isolation and find allies among the anti-Nazi political camp was by no means without problem. The Jewish source that funded the *SPD*, for instance, had to be concealed so as not to compromise it in the eyes of its non-Jewish supporters.[11] To pursue the same kind of political opposition to the Nazis after January 1933 would have been suicidal.[12] Thus, the *CV* attempted at first to appease the regime by issuing unsolicited assurances of loyalty and patriotism, clearing the Jewish organization and the Jewish population of any taint of association with either the banned communists or with the so-called "atrocity propaganda" against Germany abroad. During the last days of March 1933 the *CV* functionaries made frantic efforts to convince the new rulers of the loyalty of the Jewish population. On 23 March the chairman of the *CV*, Julius Brodnitz, sent a telegram to Hitler in which he minced no words in condemning the "mendacious and libelous...atrocity propaganda" conducted abroad against the German people and the German government. To reinforce the point, he included the texts of all the dispatches sent by the *CV* to Jewish and non-Jewish leaders abroad in an effort to persuade them to tone down the anti-German campaign.[13] Following a meeting of Jewish leaders with Göring on 25 March, the *CV*, together with the Zionist organization, sent a joint delegation to London in a vain attempt to dissuade Jewish American leaders from holding a mass protest rally in New York's Madison Square Garden.[14] A special touch was added by lawyer Kurt Alexander, a prominent member of the Rhineland regional association, who suggested in an urgent letter to the Berlin head office that the *CV* should issue a public call of support for "the reconstruction work" of the National Socialist government. Such a move, he argued, would accord well with the sentiments of most German Jews, who were "strongly nationalist in their convictions and orientation and who would therefore consider it their obvious duty to rally to the national cause as long as the powers involved in the work of national reconstruction do

11 See Arnold Paucker, "Die Abwehr des Antisemitismus in den Jahren 1893–1933," especially pp. 152–163.

12 Cf. Ernst Herzfeld, "Der jüdische Central-Verein," *CV-Zeitung*, 13 August 1936.

13 Telegram from Julius Brodnitz to Hitler, 23 March 1933, USHMMA, Reel 112, Folder 2485.

14 See Martin Rosenblueth, *Go Forth and Serve*, New York, 1961, pp. 250–251.

not attempt to tamper with Jewish equality." Evidently misjudging the whole racial thrust of Nazi antisemitism, the Jewish lawyer from Krefeld cited some recent promises of official religious neutrality (really meant to calm the fears of the Catholics), as hopeful signs of the Nazi government's willingness to reach some rapprochement with the Jewish population.[15] The reply to anybody within the ranks of the *CV* still entertaining such ill-advised hopes came in the form of the boycott on 1 April and the exclusion laws promulgated in the next weeks. After the shock of the boycott, the *CV* leadership no longer attempted to conduct independent high level negotiations with the Nazi government and, instead, channeled its efforts to the setting up of a representative Jewish umbrella organization, the *Reichsvertretung der deutschen Juden* (*RV*).[16]

The relationship between the *CV* and the *RV* need not concern us in the present context. In fact, the Jewish umbrella organization never realized the purpose for which it was set up, namely the unified political representation of German Jewry vis-à-vis the central Reich authorities. It did achieve, however, a sort of uneasy, inner Jewish truce between the three leading Jewish organizations in Germany: the *CV*, the *ZVfD* and the *RjF*. A rough and nonofficial division of labor was tacitly agreed upon, by which the *RV* was henceforth to take charge of all high level political contacts with the central government; the *RjF* continued to be responsible for special issues concerning Jewish war veterans; the *ZVfD* together with the non-Zionist *Hilfsverein der deutschen Juden* dealt with Jewish emigration from Germany; while the *CV* as such was entrusted with *Rechtsschutz*, a kind of legal, nonpolitical defense of everyday Jewish existence in which it had already specialized and achieved some notable successes before 1933. Here we come to the crux of our problem: how was it possible for a Jewish organization to defend against antisemitism under a regime that had elevated the fight against Jews and Judaism to its primary ideological priority? The very possibility and practice of *Rechtsschutz* seem to have been denied in the

15 Kurt Alexander (Krefeld), to the *CV* in Berlin, 23 March 1933, USHMMA, Reel 100, Folder 2292.

16 Cf. K.Y. Ball-Kaduri, "The National Representation of Jews in Germany — Obstacles and Accomplishments at its Establishment," *Yad Vashem Studies*, 2 (1958), pp. 160–167.

context of what had effectively become an *Unrechtsstaat*, a totalitarian system that negated and perverted the most basic norms of human justice. The *CV*'s pre-1933 fight against antisemitism was premised on the double assumption of the basic equality of the Jew before the law, and the law as entrenching the personal and political liberties of all citizens. The National Socialist conception of the law, however, denied the basic tenet of equality. The Jew as a racial outsider to the German *Volksgemeinschaft* was no longer to be governed by the same set of rules and laws, but by a so-called Jewish *Sonderrecht*. The law itself had lost its primary function of protecting the rights and basic liberties of the individual. It had become an instrument in the hands of the National Socialist leadership for regulating the *Volksgemeinschaft* in line with its views.[17]

IV

By way of a tentative answer, let us examine more closely the rationale and procedure of the defensive work that the *CV* conducted during the early years of the Third Reich. *Rechtsschutz*, as practiced and understood by the *CV* activists after January 1933, had both a narrower and broader scope of application than in the pre-Nazi period. On the one hand, the *CV* lawyers could no longer base their defense against antisemitism and racial discrimination on lofty notions of abstract justice as synonymous with the liberties of the individual and the equality of all citizens under general laws.[18] Thus, they never challenged the constitutionality of the discriminatory paragraphs — the so-called *Arierparagraphen* — of the antisemitic legislation of spring 1933, nor did they ever call in question the legality of the infamous Nuremberg Laws. At the same time, they did not confine their defensive endeavors to actual prosecution before the courts or to strictly judicial issues. The object of *Rechtsschutz* could include any aspect of everyday Jewish

17 See entry "Law" in Christen Zentner and Friedemann Bedürftig, eds., *The Encyclopedia of the Third Reich*, New York (c1976), p. 529.

18 Cf. Brigitte Kelin, *Die CV-Zeitung der Jahrgänge 1925–1935; Zum Problem des Selbstverständnisses deutscher Juden*, Thesis submitted to the Johann Wolfgang Goethe-Universität, Frankfurt am Main, 1969, especially pp. 15–19.

life in Germany before the war: antisemitic signs and posters, offensive songs, economic boycotts, arbitrary dismissals, exclusion of Jews from the professions, individual outrages, discrimination in schools, administrative harassment, religious libel. It could pertain either to issues involving the Jewish collectivity and entire Jewish communities, or to Jewish individuals threatened or harassed on account of their descent. Depending on the nature of the grievance, the authorities to which the appeals for intervention or redress of wrongs were directed could be the local *Bürgermeister* or *Regierunspräsident*, the Ministry of the Interior, the Ministry of Economics, a local police or army commander, the Gestapo headquarters in Berlin, and at one time even the leader of the SA, Röhm, in person. Kurt Sabatzky, the *CV* syndic for the *Mitteldeutschland* regional association, testified after the war: "After the Nazi takeover, I saw it as my main task to offer the Jews legal defense (*Rechtsschutz*), and to find loopholes in the close-meshed net of party and Gestapo through which the Jews could slip." According to Sabatzky's account, one could still find officials inside the German administrative system who were anti-Nazi in their convictions and who were inclined to help the Jews wherever they could. He saw it as his essential duty to track down such individuals and to approach them on behalf of the Jewish cause.[19]

How far can these interventions be regarded as successful? The very notion of success may strike us as incongruous when applied to the Jewish reality inside the Third Reich. This, however, was not necessarily the viewpoint of the people involved. *Erfolge unserer Arbeit* ("Our Work Successes"), was the striking label on the thick folder in which the *CV* functionaries in the Berlin head office filed the resumés of some four hundred cases that they regarded as successful interventions on behalf of the Jewish cause across the length and breadth of Nazi Germany during the years 1933–38.[20] The self-styled "successes" varied widely in their subject matter, scope and geographic location. A proportionately larger number date from the years 1934-36 and are indicative of the confusing interplay between normality and

19 Monika Richarz, ed., *Jüdisches Leben in Deutschland — Selbstzeugnisse zur Sozialgeschichte 1918–1945*, Stuttgart, 1982, p. 293. I am grateful to David Bankier for drawing my attention to Sabatzky's testimony.

20 "Erfolge unserer Arbeit," USHMMA, Reel 99, Folder 190.

exclusion,[21] pressure and relaxation, tightening and untightening of the antisemitic screw, which shaped the Jewish reality in Germany during those years.

In the larger cities in particular, the response of the authorities at times generated the illusion of normality, giving the impression that Germany was still a normal state of law and order, a *Rechtsstaat.* On 2 March 1935, a captain of the Berlin *Schutzpolizei* wrote a polite response to the *CV*'s complaint regarding the posting of antisemitic placards:

> Referring to your letter of 1 March 1935 [i.e. the day before], I have to inform you respectfully that the police officers shall of course prevent *every* unauthorized posting of bills or other notices. Naturally, those who spread them cannot always be caught or found out; however, whenever they are, charges are always pressed against those concerned. I have given instructions to pay special attention to the offensive bills pointed out by you and gave orders to remove those still remaining.

The remarkably friendly letter concluded with the customary greeting "Heil Hitler."[22]

Another successful intervention concerned a Jewish wholesaler in Frankfurt am Main. He had been involved in the egg marketing business in Germany for more than 38 years, but lost his German citizenship following the discriminatory legislation of spring 1933. The now mandatory professional Association for the Utilization of Eggs took advantage of his new "stateless" status to refuse him admission. This, however, had no foundation in the existing law, and the *CV*'s legal experts, after some legalistic bickering, succeeded in forcing the hand of the Association. The latter, in its turn, informed the Jewish wholesaler in March 1935 of its decision to shut down his business temporarily due to the low turnover in the egg trade. An appeal by the *CV* to the parent Union for German Egg Industry proved successful. In accepting the *CV*'s appeal and overturning the decision of the Association, the Union's judgment did not base itself on any abstract notion of the

21 Cf. Fritz Stern, "The German Professionals and their Jewish Colleagues — Comments on the Papers of Konrad H. Jarausch, Geoffrey Cock and Fritz K. Ringer," *LBI Year Book*, 36 (1991), p. 216.

22 "Um unsere Wirklichkeit," Ortsgruppen Rundbriefe des CV, 4, 15 April 1935, USHMMA, Reel 97, Folder 67.

universal rights of man, but invoked the commonsense principle of equal treatment. By the same token, it argued, that the Association's regulations impose on its members equal duties, so they were entitled to equal consideration at a time of economic difficulties.[23]

Most cases of *CV* intervention, however, concerned small and remote localities. Still under the general rubric of "success," the local association of the *CV* in Pomerania, a focus of festering antisemitic agitation, reported to the central office in Berlin on the favorable outcome of its intervention on behalf of the Jewish inhabitants of Lauenburg. Following an appeal to the police, a certain photographer posted at the marketplace — a familiar Nazi tactic to deter potential buyers from entering Jewish shops — was arrested, the photographs taken out of the *Stürmer* stand, and the call for a boycott removed. "Our friends at Lauenburg," concluded the report hopefully, "are very happy with this success and look forward to substantial improvement." At the other corner of the Reich, in Lünen, Westphalia, a canvas was hung across the street warning those passing by against "Jews and pickpockets." Again, a letter from the Berlin *CV*'s office to the state police proved effective and the offensive sign was removed. At Stromberg, East Westphalia, three banners were hung with the following inscription: "The Race question is the key to the history of the world. There can be no redemption for the German people without a solution of the Jewish question." The signs were removed at once following a petition by the local association to the state police at Münster. At the same time at Mansbach, Hessen, the local coal dealers refused to supply the local Jews with coal. The delivery of coal to Jews was renewed following a protest to the government by the chairman of the local *CV* group in Kassel. My last example of "success" is rather macabre but nonetheless highly instructive. The *Oberbürgermeister* of Hirschberg, Rheingebiet, prohibited members of the local Jewish community from holding consecration rites in front of the crematorium, noting that they could take place at the chapel of the Jewish cemetery. An appeal to the *Regierungspräsident* produced the following decision: "...The mayor at Hirschberg/Rheingebiet will no longer prevent Jews from using the consecration hall in front of the crematorium."[24] The last

23 Ibid.

24 "Erfolge unserer Arbeit," USHMM Archive, Reel 99, Folder.

concession, dated January 1936, is in a way especially telling, since the custom of cremation is opposed to Jewish religious law and was only practiced by highly assimilated German Jews. In allowing the Jews to observe their rites outside the bounds of the Jewish cemetery, the responsible *Regierungspräsident* was not just making a humane gesture but signalizing that he regarded the Jew, at least in his death, as an equal member of the general family of man.

V

So much for the self-dubbed successes — what about the failures? It is very difficult to arrive at any quantification as to the proportion of successes versus failures. However, even by the *CV*'s own reckoning, the great majority of interventions it handled must have seemed far more dubious in their outcome. One of the most interesting cases concerns the *CV*'s efforts to obtain a general ban on public singing of crassly antisemitic songs. At the end of April 1934, reacting to an unceasing stream of complaints from local groups, the Berlin head office, initiated a countrywide survey of the incidence of antisemitic songs in the Reich. The regional associations were instructed to collect information on where, by whom, and how frequently songs with blatantly antisemitic texts were being sung. The *CV* intended to use the results of this countrywide survey to support official letters of complaint to be addressed to the Minister of the Interior, to the chief of the SA, Röhm, to the Gestapo headquarters in Berlin, and to the Ministry of Propaganda. The inquiry yielded numerous replies which document the Jewish *Alltag* in Nazi Germany from an unusual angle. The public singing of antisemitic songs appears to have been one of the most popular weapons in the hands of SA gangs and other NSDAP units for harassing and terrorizing the helpless Jewish population, especially in the smaller localities. The *CV* correspondent at Gross-Gerau (Hessen), for instance, reported the following typical text:

> Place the Jews and the big shots against the wall,
> Throw the Jewish gangs out of our German fatherland,
> Send them to Palestine and there cut their throats,
> So will they never be able to come back again.

The antisemitic texts were not only sung by the SA and the Hitler Youth but also by schoolchildren on the streets. Non-Jewish residents disapproved of the songs and expressed dismay. At Merseburg the repertoire of the Storm Troopers also included the old-time favorite: "When Jewish blood squirts from the knife, then will we have it so good once again." It was sung repeatedly whenever the marching troopers came near a known Jewish house, causing consternation and even illness among the residents. Indeed, the inventiveness and sadistic ingenuity of both the writers and performers were truly amazing. The Berlin head office constructed a table containing those parts of the survey relating to the Rhineland, Westphalia and Pomerania. The following details were noted for each locality: name of place, the text of the offensive song, the identity of the performers, when last heard and how often, and special characteristics. It turned out that the most popular by far were the following three doggerels:

1) When Jewish blood squirts from the knife
2) Hang the Jews, place the big shots against the wall
3) Heads rolls, Jews howl (*Kopfe rollen, Juden heulen*),

The most frequent performers were SA units, Hitler Youth and other NSDAP affiliates, but some times also company employees and unorganized youth.

Yet, informative the survey was, it failed to produce any alleviation of the situation. In a sense the initiative even backfired in that it aroused the displeasure of the Gestapo authorities in Berlin. The limits of the Jewish defense organization's ability to act under the National Socialist regime were driven home at a meeting of its two leaders, Brodnitz and Hirschberg, with the head of Gestapo Section II I B 2, Dr. Hasselbacher, in July 1934. In accordance with the draconian rules laid down by the Gestapo officer, neither the *CV* nor any of its branches were permitted to undertake of their own accord any inquiry or survey of anti-Jewish occurrences. They could only function as more or less passive recipients of such reports, transmitting them to the competent local or central authority without taking a position.[25] This of course meant a drastic curtailment of the maneuvering room of the *CV*, but

25 USHMMA, Reel 97, Folder 47; Microfilm Reel 112 , Folder 2499.

did not in effect prevent or deter it from responding to Jewish appeals for help and dealing with them on an individual and local level.

In the economic sphere, the *CV* defense activists had to reckon with all the pre-1933 boycott tactics, which were now reinforced by the semi-official sponsorship of the NSDAP. The array of weapons and ruses that the instigators of the anti-Jewish boycott had at their disposal after January 1933 was indeed formidable. An incomplete list of the more typical ones would include the following tactics: the posting of uniformed SA guards and placing of *Stürmer* stands near Jewish shops, photographing clients and publishing their pictures in the local paper under the title of traitors to the German people, posting of pillory boards (*Prangertafel*) at central locations in town with the names of the offending buyers, threatening NSDAP members with expulsion from the ranks of the party, making recipients of *Winterhilfe* sign sworn declarations not to buy in Jewish shops or be treated by Jewish doctors, excluding patients of Jewish doctors from social benefits, and so on. Against this awesome machinery of enforcement, the obstinate refusal of large sections of the non-Jewish populace to abide by the boycott is sometimes taken as indicative of the extent of popular opposition to the antisemitic persecution. However, in the case of the boycott, it is difficult to disentangle the purely economic from other motives. The very fact that the clientele of Jewish shops could include Nazi bigwigs precludes a simple equation between breaking the boycott and sympathizing with the Jews.[26] The reverse side of the coin is that just as boycott noncompliance cannot be considered per se as a criterion for pro-Jewish sympathies, so boycott compliance cannot be judged as an indication of the extent of popular antisemitism. The truth of the matter lies somewhere between the two.Violating the boycott did not *have* to connote disagreement with the persecution of the Jews; it very well *could*. The behavior of the Aachen public, who on the day of the release of a Jewish butcher from "protective custody" by the Gestapo (April 1935) demonstratively filled up his shop, would be a case in point — though all too rare.[27]

26 Cf. Bernd Stöver, *Volksgemeinschaft im Dritten Reich. Die Konsensbereitschaft der Deutschen aus der Sicht sozialistischer Exilberichte*, Düsseldorf, 1993, p. 254.

27 USHMMA, Reel 113, Folder 2555. The butcher was arrested following the publication of an inflammatory article in *Der Westdeutsche Beobachter* which charged his son with *Rassenschande*.

In endeavoring to defend the economic existence of German Jews against the worst consequences of the post-1933 Nazi boycott, the *CV* legal experts had their hands doubly tied. They could not, as before the Nazi takeover, take the prime instigator of the boycott, the NSDAP and its various affiliates, directly to court. Nor could they challenge discriminatory measures that were part of the official Nazi policy on the Jewish question. They could, however, in their representation of Jewish businesses or individuals threatened by economic extinction, invoke principles of general economic expediency and to a certain extent count on a sympathetic hearing in the Ministry of Economics under Schacht. The latter was commonly identified with the viewpoint that the economic sphere must be isolated from the interference of racial politics and ought to be governed, as far as possible, by considerations of economic expediency alone. Insofar as the *CV* lawyers chose to test the cases of their Jewish clients in court, this was never under penal law, but always — even in cases involving physical assaults against Jews — in courts operating under civil and administrative law.

Here again, it is notable that the dividing line between successful and unsuccessful intervention was not the Nuremberg Laws of September 1935, but the radicalization of the antisemitic campaign in autumn 1937. One cannot discern any obvious break between the defensive work performed by the *CV* before 15 September 1935 and immediately after. To be sure, the formal disemancipation of German Jewry was the occasion of much soul-searching and necessitated a major ideological readjustment on the part of the *CV*. In accordance with the demands of the new racist laws, the name of the organization was changed at first to the "Central Association of the Jews in Germany" (*Centralverein der Juden in Deutschland*), and then to the "Jewish Central Association" (*Jüdischer Centralverein*). The previous references to the civil equality of German Jews and their German *Gesinnung* were carefully expunged from the revised association statutes, and the task of the *CV* was redefined as "the cultivation of Jewish life in Germany as well as the legal and economic care of Jews living in Germany."[28] In a long

28 The letter from the Berlin head office of the *CV* to the *Amtsgericht Berlin-Mitte,* announcing these changes, was sent on 17 September 1935, that is, only two days after the promulgation of the Nuremberg Laws. This demonstrates how well prepared the organization's leadership must have been beforehand. [USHMMA, Reel 99, Folder 140(?)].

programmatic article that appeared in the *CV-Zeitung* issue of 13 August 1936, Ernst Herzfeld, the new chairman, described the reorientation (*Umstellung*) as having been born of "outer and inner necessity." Much of the article was devoted to a discussion of emigration from Germany and its implications for the ideological position of the *CV*. However, one must seriously doubt the sincerity of some of the statements, like the disparaging reference to the old, discarded "slogan of assimilationism" that had such a formative influence on Jewish life in the past. The bottom line of all this ideological repositioning is that despite all the talk on emigration and on the need for deepening Jewish consciousness, there is no indication that anybody within the *CV* ranks (or anywhere else for that matter),[29] seriously considered voluntarily dismantling Jewish life in Germany. The *CV* remained firmly committed to defending the legal and economic basis of Jewish existence in Germany long after September 1935. The interesting thing is that (within the inevitable constraints of National Socialism), such a defense still seemed possible in some measure even after the promulgation of the Nuremberg Laws.

Let me demonstrate the point by two final examples. The first example concerns the ruling, dated 17 January 1936, by the District Labor Court in Breslau on an earlier decision, dated 23 October 1935, the local Labor Court. The latter court had justified the dismissal of a young Jewish apprentice mechanic, arguing that it accorded with the intention of the Nuremberg Laws that favored "a clear separation between 'Aryans' and 'non-Aryans'." One could no longer expect of a public company to undertake the training of a "non-Aryan." In overturning the decision of the lower court and obliging the public company to pay compensation to the Jewish boy, the District Court of Labor ruled that the Nuremberg Laws "concern the preservation of purity of the blood, citizenship rights and civil servants, but have no influence whatever on the position of Jews in the economy." The District Labor Court went on to criticize the lower court for presuming to pronounce a judgment of principle on an extraordinarily delicate question — not least from the foreign policy point of view —

29 The long list of addresses of Jewish organizations preserved in the *CV* files demonstrates how vital and highly ramified Jewish organizational life in Germany was still in summer 1936. See "Adressentafel jüdischer Spitzenorganisationen in Deutschland nach dem Stand von Juni 1936," *USHMMA*, Reel 98, Folder 88.

which ought to remain the prerogative of the Reich leadership. In this tortuous manner, the court sought to justify a commonsense decision of simple justice. My second example is the ruling, dated 5 July 1938, of the District Administrative Court (*Bezirksverwaltungsgericht*), of Frankfurt am Oder on the appeal of a Jewish traveling tradesman against the decision of the *Regierungspräsident* to refuse him a license on account of "political unreliability." In discussing the appeal of the Jewish tradesman, the court admitted that in repeated judgments the Higher Administrative Court had ruled that the assumption of political unreliability or Jewishness was not in itself sufficient ground for refusing a license. One had to adduce specific deeds, words or writings that proved the hostile attitude of the applicant. Such facts, the court added, were "neither proven by the accused [i.e., the *Regierungspräsident*] nor presented by him." But then, in a model piece of judicial illogicality, the court turned to adopt the standpoint of the *Regierungspräsident* that the above-mentioned judgments were outdated and that all Jews without further ado were to be considered suspect of hostility to the state. With this kind of judgment any possibility of legal defense of Jews in Germany effectively came to an end.

Conclusion

Since the Holocaust, the *CV*, the major and most representative organization of German Jewry, has become almost a byname for self-delusion and refusal to face reality.[30] However, the original documentation of the German Jewish defense organization — only a small sample of which has been considered here — refutes this popular caricature. The activity of any political or quasi-political organization similar to the *CV* should be evaluated in the context of its own time — not with hindsight and retrospectively. In the context of prewar Nazi Jewish policy, the *CV*'s strategy of defending the Jewish hold in Germany to the utmost rather than opting for emigration was at the opposite pole of accommodation to the regime. It went against the grain of mainstream Nazi policy and

30 Cf. Fritz Stern's remarks on the negative reaction to German Jewry in "The Burden of Success — Reflections on German Jewry" in, idem, *Dreams and Delusions — The Drama of German History*, New York, 1987, pp. 97–118.

could entail considerable personal sacrifice and risk — as is amply attested to by the repeated arrests of its leading members and their incarceration in concentration camps.[31] Indeed, it may arguably even be regarded as a form of Jewish resistance, though I myself would prefer the term "Jewish defense," which underlines the continuity with the pre-Nazi period.[32]

One may well sympathize with Ernst Herzfeld, the last chairman of the *CV*, who rhetorically asks after the war: "What can a minority do in the face of a deadly assault? Should it defend itself as best as it can, or should it give up without a fight. The answer to this appears to me: honor and duty require us to put up a fight even when the downfall seems inevitable."[33] One may likewise wonder if these short-term practical remedies — as distinct from the ideological perspectives that the Zionist movement offered to the Jews of Germany — were all that more effective. After all, nobody in the Zionist camp really thought in terms of an immediate mass exodus from Germany to Palestine. The development of the Jewish national home was to be a long drawn-out process. In the meantime, what were those remaining in Germany — the vast majority — to do? The German Jews did not have to be Zionists. They had all the justification in the world to regard themselves as no less German than their non-Jewish compatriots, rooted as they were in the German environment and steeped in German culture. We

31 Cf. the moving tributes to Hans Reichmann in the *Leo Baeck Institute Archives*, New York, Collection "Zum Gedenken an Hans Reichmann."

32 On the subject of German-Jewish resistance during the Nazi period see, above all, Konrad Kwiet, "Problems of Jewish Resistance Historiography," in: *The Nazi Holocaust — Historical Articles on the Destruction of European Jews*, Michael R. Marrus, ed., London, 1989, vol. 7, pp. 49–69, and Konrad Kwiet and Helmut Eschwege, *Selbstbehauptung und Widerstand Deutscher Juden im Kampf um Existenz und Menschenwiirde 1933–1945*, Hamburg, 1984. Cf. Michael R. Marrus, "Jewish Resistance to the Holocaust," *Journal of Contemporary History,* 30 (1995), pp. 83–110. Marrus subsumes under the general phenomenon of *Jewish* resistance to the Holocaust, not only Jewish participation in armed struggle against the Third Reich (*offensive resistance*), or revolt in the ghettos and in the camps (*resistance enchained*), but also three variations of non-armed Jewish response: reassertion of Jewish identity and Jewish values in the face of adversity (*symbolic resistance*), underground reporting and documenting of German terror (*polemic resistance*), and help to the persecuted ("defensive resistance").

33 Herzfeld, "Meine letzten Jahre in Deutschland," p. 26

should not therefore fault them for not having been Zionists, whether before 1933 or after.

The stakes as the *CV* activists saw them before 1938 were not physical annihilation versus survival, but Jewish economic survival within the German borders. Open resistance was not a viable proposition for any Jewish group under the conditions of National Socialism. By focusing on the everyday practical aspects of the *CV*'s work rather than on its ideological presumptions and programmatic pronouncements, I have sought to show that the Jewish defense organization was not seized by a sudden paralysis on the advent of the Nazi regime, but continued, to the best of its ability, to defend the Jewish position in Germany against all odds. Viewing themselves as Germans through and through, they were determined to stick it out on German soil.

The *CV*'s ability to perform Jewish defense work within the context of an antisemitic regime was conditioned by three factors. First, there was no unified antisemitic campaign during the early years, and the *CV*'s *Rechtsschutz* activists could thus take advantage of the conflict between the SA rowdyism and the central government's need to maintain a facade of law and order. Second, the subversion of the *Rechtsstaat* and the erosion of its structures did not happen overnight, and even after Hitler's rise to power it was still conceivable, at first for a Jew to obtain a modicum of justice under the relative normalcy of the system of civil and administrative law. We should take note here of the dynamics of the structural development. The relative normality of the civil and administrative law in prewar Nazi Germany was an aspect of the phenomenon that Ernst Fraenkel described long ago as the Dual State: the simultaneous coexistence within one system of the "Prerogative State," characterized by "unlimited arbitrariness and violence unchecked by any legal guarantees" with the "Normative State," characterized by its respect for the courts and the rule of law in general.[34] Now the logic of the National Socialist view of the Jew as the racial foe really required that he be completely subjugated to the "Prerogative State." However, the completion of this process was delayed only as long as the Jews remained integrated into the capitalistic system of the Third Reich. It was finalized as soon as the decision was

34 Ernst Fraenkel, *The Dual State — A Contribution to the Theory of Dictatorship*, New York, 1969, p. 1.

taken to remove them from the German economy.[35] The last factor that accounts for the *CV*'s short-term successes is not structural. It has to do with the fact that even inside a radically evil system like the Third Reich, the *CV* activists could still encounter — at least before 1937 — a certain amount of human decency.

35 Ibid, pp. 87ff.

The "Emigration Effort" or "Repatriation"

The Issue of the Relationship Between Jewish-Polish Emigrants and the Jewish-German Establishment

YFAAT WEISS

One of the characteristic marks of German Jewry, against the background of the events transpiring during the 1930s, was its exceptional organizational ability. Already during the first weeks after Hitler's rise to power, activities were initiated by the Central Committee for Aid and Rehabilitation (*Zentralausschuss für Hilfe und Aufbau*), as of September 1933 a subdivision of the National Representation of German Jews *(Reichsvertretung der deutschen Juden)*. The *Reichsvertretung* incorporated within its ranks most of the segments of German Jewry: liberals, Zionists, orthodox congregations, as well as political and community organizations.[1] The *Reichsvertretung* operated in every sector of Jewish life in Germany — the economy, legal representation, social welfare, and immigration. This alacrity, evidence of the leadership's comprehension of the political situation, proved to be powerful and highly efficient when formulating solutions to the unique problems and difficulties born of the Nazi rise to power. In 1939, upon Nazi orders,

1 Max Grünewald, "Der Anfang der Reichsvertretung," in: *Deutsches Judentum. Aufstieg und Krise. Gestalten, Ideen, Werke*, Robert Weltsch, ed., Stuttgart, 1963, pp. 315–325; Hildesheimer, Ezriel, *Jüdische Selbstverwaltung under dem NS-Regime. Der Existenzkampf der Reichsvertretung und Reichsvereinigung der Juden in Deutschland*, Tübingen 1994; Kulka, Otto Dov, ed., *Deutsches Judentum unter dem Nationalsozialismus*, Bd. 1: *Dokumente zur Geschichte der Reichsvertretung der deutschen Juden*, Tübingen, 1997.

the *Reichsvertretung* changed its character and renamed itself the National Association of Jews Living in Germany *(Reichsvereinigung)*. Membership in the Association, unlike the *Reichsvertretung*, was no longer voluntary and all German Jews were required to join in response to Nazi ethnic classifications.

Many of the German Jewish leadership who survived the Holocaust were quite shocked when, at the beginning of the 1960s, more than a decade after the end of the Second World War, the *Reichsvertretung* as well as its heir the *Reichsvereinigung* were caught in the crossfire of criticism.[2] In 1961, political philosopher Hannah Arendt sharply attacked the *Reichsvertretung* in her *New Yorker* review of the Eichmann trial, which was later published in her book, *Eichmann in Jerusalem.*[3] Arendt distinguished the *Reichsvereinigung* from the *Reichsvertretung* as follows: "The *Reichsvereinigung* — a Nazi-appointed Jewish central organization, not to be confused with the authentically Jewish *Reichsvertretung*, which was dissolved in July 1939."

I would like to illuminate a number of the difficulties entailed with understanding and analyzing the activities of the German-Jewish associations and communities during the 1930s. To do so, I have chosen the issue of the emigration of Polish Jews from Germany during the period 1933–41. Emigration from Germany was arranged within a number of organizational frameworks: The Palestine Office (*Palästinaamt*) coordinated administrative aspects of *aliyah*, that is, immigration directly to Palestine; Relief (*Hilfsverein*) assisted those emigrating to various other countries; while the Bureau of Immigration, under the auspices of the National Representation, assisted foreign Jews to repatriate to their home countries. In retrospect, emigration was the most important of the activities undertaken by the German-Jewish organizations — those who succeeded in emigrating from Germany to countries outside the borders of the German occupation were saved. Furthermore, there is no doubt that the *Reichsvertretung*, the representative body of Germany Jewry, encouraged and supported emigration.

2 F.A. Krummacher, ed., *Die Kontroverse. Hannah Arendt, Eichmann in Jerusalem und die Juden*, Frankfurt am Main, 1964.

3 Hannah Arendt, *Eichmann in Jerusalem. A Report of the Banality of Evil,* New York, 1963.

Although carried out as one of the activities undertaken by German-Jewish organizations, the emigration of Eastern European Jews, was nonetheless performed under conditions totally different from those applicable to the emigration of German Jews from Germany. Like other Jews, many of the Polish Jews in Germany emigrated to Palestine within the framework of the immigration permits granted to *chalutzim*, agricultural pioneers. The proportion of Eastern European Jews immigrating to Palestine was indeed higher than that among the German Jews.[4] In contrast, emigration to Western Europe and other countries was met with many difficulties. For example, Polish Jews living in Germany were permitted to enter the United States under the quota allotted to all Polish nationals, a quota that shrank during the 1930s.[5] The main emigration route open to Jews with active Polish citizenship was the "repatriation" to Poland. I will examine the evolution of this route and, based upon that analysis, deduce a number of conclusions regarding the activities of the German-Jewish associations. I would first like to distinguish between two stages: the voluntary "repatriation" to Poland of 1933–34; and the expulsion of Polish Jews at the beginning of 1940 to the German-occupied areas within Poland, known as the *General Gouvernement*.

The Voluntary "Repatriation" during 1933–34

During the initial months after the Nazi rise to power, only a few thousand Eastern European Jews living in Germany left for their home countries. By the end of 1935, about 9,000 Jews had been repatriated from Germany to Poland; where they were supported by funds distributed by the Joint American Distribution Committee and by local donors.[6] In addition to those who had emigrated directly from Germany were Polish Jews who had chosen to emigrate from Germany

4 Doron Niederland, *German Jews Emigrants or Refugees? Emigration Patterns between the Two World Wars,* Jerusalem, 1996, Hebrew, pp. 183ff.

5 Herbert A. Strauss, *Jewish Immigrants of the Nazi Period in the USA,* New York, 1987, Vol. 6, pp. 206f.

6 Aid to Jews Overseas. Report on the Activities of the American Joint Distribution Committee for the Year 1935, including a Brief Resume for the Year 1936.

to the west, to Belgium, France, and Holland, but had been forced to return to Poland due to difficulties of absorption or, sometimes, expulsion.[7] It is very difficult to estimate the total number of Jews repatriated to Poland from Germany, although, based on data gathered by the Jewish organizations on emigration from Germany, we can ascertain with considerable certainty that most of them emigrated during the early months of 1933, and that by 1934 the number of emigrés had declined.[8]

The term "repatriate" (*Rückkehrer, Rückwanderer*), which was commonly used during that period by the *Reichsvertretung* and the German emigration agencies, is problematic as well as misleading because it creates the impression that the emigrants had been repatriated to Poland of their own free will. The 1930s were characterized by repeated attempts of Western European states like France, Belgium, and the Netherlands, to either repatriate refugees to their countries of origin or close their borders to them.[9] The policies of the German authorities continued this practice forcing Jews with Polish citizenship to return to Poland.

The Intergovernmental Committee for Refugees, an organization appointed by the League of Nations, tried through international charters to limit the extent of the above mentioned phenomena.[10] We should emphasize that, first and foremost, it was the German authorities that forced Jews of Polish origin to return to Poland. This was long-standing German policy, one that had received greater impetus at the end of the First World War with the expulsion of Polish Jews from Bavaria in

7 Special Report of the Joint Foreign Committee 20.7.1933, YIVO Archive, RG 348 Folder 95; Report of Activities for the Months of April to October 1934, November 14, 1934, Joint Distribution Committee Archive (hereafter JDC), Folder 628; High Commission for Refugees (Jewish and other) coming from Germany, April 1934, Central Zionist Archive (hereafter CZA), L 13/154.

8 Council for German Jewry. Statistics of Jewish Emigration from Greater Germany, 1.8.1939, Central Archive for the History of the Jewish People, Inv. 1419.

9 Dan Michman, "Die jüdische Emigration und die niederländische Reaktion zwischen 1933 und 1940," in: *Die Niederlande und das deutsche Exil 1933–1940*, Kathinka Dittrich and Hans Würzner, eds., Königstein/Ts. 1982, pp. 73–85, p. 75; Claudena, M. Skran, *Refugees in Inter-War Europe. The Emergence of a Regime*, Oxford, 1995, pp. 133ff.

10 Ibid.

1923.[11] In 1933, the German authorities adopted a policy of deportation aimed at individuals and, at least at first, justified each case in detail. However, beginning in 1936, the Germans began expelling Russian and Romanian Jews en masse, and later Polish Jews as well.[12]

The Polish government, through its diplomatic missions in Germany, tried to intervene and prevent these deportations.[13] Poland was keen to protect the status of Polish citizens in Germany as part of its overall relationship with Germany. The existence of a sizable German minority in Poland had pushed the issue of minorities onto center stage, allowing Poland to exert a degree of pressure on the Nazi administration.[14] However, the intervention of the Polish diplomatic corps in favor of Polish Jews in Germany was gradually curtailed in response to the signing of the 1934 non-aggression pact between Germany and Poland, Germany's departure from the League of Nations, and the rise of Polish antisemitism during the 1930s. As a result, Polish Jews in Germany realized that their faith in Polish diplomatic protection was misplaced as their position on the Polish policy agenda fell lower from year to year.

The Jewish organizations in Germany were supportive of the "repatriation" policy. Their activities were part of a larger network involving international organizations, which perceived "repatriation"as the best possible solution for refugees without income or work. These activities were coordinated within the framework of attempts to help these people rebuild their lives in their former homelands after their economic situation in Germany had crumbled. Beginning in 1933, the *Hilfsverein*

11 Jozef Adelson, "The Expulsion of Jews with Polish Citizenship from Bavaria in 1923," *Polin*, 5 (1990), pp. 57–73.

12 Sybil Milton, "Menschen zwischen Grenzen: Die Polenausweisung 1938," *Menora*, 1 (1990), pp. 184–208, pp. 189ff.

13 Jerzy Tomaszewski, "Polish Diplomats and the Fate of Polish Jews in Nazi Germany," *Acta Poloniae Historica*, 61 (1990), pp. 115–27; Yfaat Weiss, "'Ostjuden' in Deutschland als Freiwild. Die nationalsozialistische Aussenpolitik zwischen Ideologie und Wirklichkeit," *Tel-Aviver Jahrbuch für Deutsche Geschichte*, 23 (1994), pp. 215–232, pp. 226f.

14 Ressortbesprechung im Auswärtigen Amt über die Behandlung von Ausländern, insbesondere ausländischen Juden am 25.8.1933, Das politische Archiv des Auswärtigen Amtes (hereafter PA), R100211; Emanuel Melzer, *Political Strife in a Blind Alley. The Jews in Poland 1935–1939*, Tel Aviv, 1982, Hebrew, pp. 132ff.

published information about jobs and economic opportunities in different countries.[15] Many of the job offers from Eastern European countries were subject to the individual knowing the local language or having local citizenship. Many of the more attractive prospects came from the German minorities living in Eastern Europe (*Volksdeutsche*) who were interested in exchanging property with Jews living in the Reich's territories. These exchanges were prohibited at a later date by the German authorities, which did not look favorably on the surrender of German status and property in Eastern Europe.[16]

The few thousand Polish Jews who were willing after the Nazi rise to power to be "repatriated" were less willing after the situation in Germany stabilized, especially after they began receiving reports about the difficult economic conditions and the intensification of overt antisemitism in Poland. As a result, the number of returnees declined, many preferring to remain in Germany in the hope of receiving entry permits to other countries.

A comparison of the records of the German emigration agencies, Polish organizations, the JDC and the *Reichsvertretung* indicates that emigration to Poland was forced upon Polish Jews to one degree or another. Official emigration records from Karlsruhe report that the Jewish emigrés from Germany to Poland came from among the poorest strata.[17] The reason cited for emigration was the inability of Jewish social service agencies to assist them due to the greater need of poor German Jews. A year and a half later, officials at the Karlsruhe emigration offices continued to portray "repatriates" as people lacking the financial means that would permit other emigration options.[18] A similar picture emerges from the records of German emigration agencies located in other cities. For instance, in a conversation taken from the records of Cologne emigration offices in 1933, a Jewish welfare worker

15 Vom Reichswanderungsamt anerkannte gemeinnützige Auskunftsstelle für jüdische Durchwanderung und Auswanderung. Zirkularschreiben, CZA, Nr.105, A 142 90/1/3.

16 Auswärtiges Amt an sämtliche Missionen und Berufskonsulate am 4.11.1936, PAAA, Abschrift I B 3 25855/15042.

17 Bundesarchiv Koblenz, Bericht der Auswanderungsberatungsstelle Karlsruhe über die Tätigkeit im I. Vierteljahr 1933 (April, Mai, Juni), p. 7, R 57/21.

18 Bundesarchiv Koblenz, Bericht der Auswanderungsberatungsstelle Karlruhe über die Tätigkeit im III. Vierteljahr 1934/35 (Oktober, November, Dezember), R 57/21.

was reported as stating that the Jewish community was interested in the "repatriation" of East European Jews to their home countries.[19] This supports the German agency's view that East European Jews preferred emigration to the west or to Palestine, rather than Poland, and that the latter option was imposed upon poor Polish Jews by Jewish welfare agencies in Germany who in many cases lacked the resources to assist them. *Klub Polski*, a Polish emigré organization, demanded that the Polish Embassy intervene to prevent the frantic attempts of both the German administration and German Jewish social service agencies in Frankfurt to convince Polish Jews to return home.[20]

The Jewish organizations, headed by the JDC, were aware of the serious difficulties awaiting the Jews of East European origin upon their return "home." Despite this, they saw no other solution and therefore chose to support this policy. A central official stated the following in May 1933:

> We know that of the 80,000 who came from the east, a lot of them will have to be repatriated. What are they to be repatriated to? The hospitality which they will receive in Poland or Russia is, I assure you, very limited. Their life is not any more attractive on this side of the border than on the other side.[21]

This evaluation did not prevent the JDC from supporting and financing the policy of "repatriation" executed by the Jewish organizations in Germany. Already in April of 1933, the *Zentralausschuss* allocated considerable sums for use by those repatriating east, and designated the program as urgent.[22] Immigrants to Germany who had foreign citizenship or no citizenship at all were eligible for the financial support offered by the *Reichsvertretung*. Bernhard Kahn, JDC's director in Europe, justified this policy and heatedly wrote the following:

> Imagine that two men come to you, one a German Jew, to whom all countries are closed, a man who has no country to which he can go, and the other a

19 Tätigkeitsbericht der öffentlichen Auswanderungsberatungsstelle Köln für April, Mai und Juni 1933. I would like to thank Dr. Doron Niederland for this Document.

20 Klub Polski an das Polnische Generalkonsulat am 1.9.1933, Archiwum Akt Nowych, Ambs. Rp. W Berlinie, Akt Nr. 866.

21 JDC, (Warburg) Verbatim Notes, Meeting Held at Home of Mr. Baerwald 14.5.1933, p. 12, Folder 626.

22 Protokoll der Sitzung des "Zentralausschusses für Hilfe und Aufbau" am 29.4.1933, Leo-Baeck Archive-Jerusalem, LBIJ 553/2.

> Polish Jew, who has a country from which he cannot be driven and in which he is forbidden to work. Which of the two would you help? That is the general psychology of the various organizations with which we work, because they have gradually been compelled to renounce making any distinction between German and non-German Jews by us...[23]

There is little doubt that no one dreamed, during those years, of qualifying financial support to German Jews according to any particular destination, and especially to destinations whose value was questionable, such as Eastern Europe.

The Expulsion of Polish Jews at the Beginning of 1940

With the outbreak of World War II on 1 September 1939, 11,500 Polish Jews remained in Germany. Among them were those individuals who had succeeded in evading the mass deportations of Polish Jews to Poland during the last days of October 1938, as well as women and children, deportees whose deportations had encountered difficulties, and those who had been permitted to repatriate to Germany in order to settle their affairs. On 8 September 1939, the Gestapo ordered the arrest of all Polish Jews aged 16 and above, who were now considered to be citizens of an enemy nation, The Gestapo also decreed that their relatives be registered and report to the police for investigation three times a day.[24] The Polish Jewish men found in Germany were sent to Buchenwald, while those found in Berlin were arrested and brought to the Oranienburg prison and from there transferred to the Sachsenhausen concentration camp. During that September, many women began receiving notifications of the deaths of their arrested kin.

Various versions exist regarding the *Reichsvereinigung*'s treatment of those arrested and their families during the final months of 1939. The documentation, based on the testimony of Recha Freier, is both meager and contradictory. In any case, it is clear that during that period

23 Dr. B. Kahn, Chairman of the American Joint Distribution Committee to Mr. Josef Hyman 8.3.1934, Leo Baeck Archive-NY, JDC Box 4 Folder 1.

24 Geheime Staatspolizei an Landräte, Oberbürgermeister [...] am 8.9.1939, Brandenburgisches Landeshauptarchiv, Pr. Br. Rep. 6 B Kreisverwaltung Beerkow-Shorkow 834.

no appropriate solution was found, and attempts to supply the prisoners with emigration permits in order to effect their release were met with delays and other obstacles.[25]

The situation of the Polish Jews jailed in Sachsenhausen continued to deteriorate, and in January 1940, the *Reichsvereinigung* met to discuss their fate. Otto Hirsch, administrative director of the *Reichsvereinigung*, suggested offering the German authorities the option of releasing the prisoners and transferring them to their relatives in Poland or to the *General Gouvernement*.[26] We cannot, of course, reconstruct Hirsch's motives in making that suggestion. Did he believe that the difficulties under the Nazi occupation in Poland were preferable to incarceration in a concentration camp with the highly suspect conditions that were causing an increasing number of deaths each day? However, it is unlikely that he knew of the inhuman conditions in the camps, or of the starvation and disease that faced the deportees who had reached the Polish regions occupied by Germany.[27] On 5 February 1940, the SS ordered the transfer of all Polish Jews and displaced persons from the concentration camps and prisons located in Germany to the *General Gouvernement*.[28] At that time, Hirsch could not envision the fate that awaited them in Poland.

Summary

I have dwelled on these two episodes — the relationship of the *Reichsvertretung* to the "repatriates" and the treatment of the detainees in Sachsenhausen during the winter of 1939–40 — in order to question the validity of the concepts traditionally used in the study of the

25 Testimony of Recha Freier, Yad Vashem Archive, 0–33/85; Testimony of Mr. Ortner, Division of Oral History, Institute of Contemporary Jewry, Hebrew University of Jerusalem.

26 Protokoll der Vorstandssitzung der Reichsvereinigung am 21.1.1940, Archive of the *Reichsvereinigung* der Juden in Deutschland.

27 Gerald Reitlinger, *Die Endlösung. Hitlers Versuch der Ausrottung der Juden Europas 1939–1945*, Berlin, 1979, pp. 45ff.

28 Der Reichsführer SS und Chef der Deutschen Polizei an verschiedene Stellen 5.2.1940, Staatsarchiv Hamburg, Bestand: Senatskommission für die Reichs- und Auswärtigen Angelegenheiten II, Signatur: VI B 1 Fax 49.

responses of the German-Jewish organizations to the Nazis. Hannah Arendt put the issue of Jewish solidarity during the Holocaust to the test when she emphasized the role that Jewish institutions took upon themselves within the framework of the Nazi extermination program. Dan Diner has successfully described the paradox in Arendt's historical judgment when he exposed the duality inherent in her German-Jewish identity.

> A Jewish self-understanding comprising on the one hand the experience of a German Jewess, i.e., the patterns as well as the contents of Jewish emancipation in Germany — the emancipation of Jews in the western sense, i.e., as individuals, as citizens, as *Bürger*, and, on the other hand, a national and collective perception of Jewish existence, a position she accepts during the war and above all after 1945, after the Holocaust.[29]

With regard to the questions posed, we can say that in her critique of the *Reichsvereinigung*, Arendt judged its activities according to the standards of cooperation and collective responsibility which, we may say, were somewhat alien to the principles that actually guided the *Reichsvereinigung*. However, those eager to refute Arendt's contentions have found themselves similarly ensnared in defending that same collective "self" attacked by her. In an attempt to understand the relationship of the German-Jewish associations to the issue of the repatriation to Poland, it makes no sense to use concepts such as "Jewish solidarity" or "collective responsibility" because they do not contribute to understanding the motivations of these organizations.

I contend that a clear linkage exists between the stubborn preference of the *Reichsvertretung*, in conjunction with the JDC, to return Polish Jews to Poland during the years following 1933 rather than assisting them to emigrate to the west — and the *Reichsvereinigung*'s irresolute treatment of the Polish Jews arrested in 1939. In both instances these organizations painstakingly attempted to protect the vital interests of German Jews when responding to the needs of Polish Jews. The *Reichsvertretung* preferred to repatriate the Polish Jews in order to preserve the German Jews' prospects of emigrating to the west. To some degree, then, the Polish Jews' right to repatriation often worked against

29 Dan Diner, "Hannah Arendt Reconsidered. Über das Banale und das Böse in ihrer Holocaust Erzählung," *Babylon,* 16–17 (1996), pp. 94–107, p. 97.

them. Six years later, the *Reichsvereinigung* hesitated in their attempts to release the Polish detainees and to offer them the immediate use of preferential emigration permits, in the absence of another option, i.e., requesting the SS to release the Polish prisoners from the Sachsenhausen concentration camp and to transfer them to the occuped *General Gouvernement*. In both cases, I doubt if there is room for a discussion of solidarity and even less of responsibility. The responsibility of the German-Jewish institutions was, according to their perspective to the fate of the German Jews. The application of different standards to the treatment of foreign Jews was not some sort of "tumbling from grace" as much as a direct continuation of the German-Jewish tradition, which was part of the German-Jewish experience since the *Haskalah* (Jewish Enlightenment) and which strove for civic affiliation rather than ethnic attachment. Moreover, these institutions operated according to the guiding principle of "repatriation." This policy was a direct extension of positions commonly held among German Jews — as well as among Jews living in other western societies — who persisted in their efforts in favor of mass emigration as in the nineteenth century in order to divert Eastern European Jewish immigrants from their borders. On this point, there is no difference between the "repatriation" policy of the *Reichsvertretung* — a voluntary Jewish organization — and the proposals offered by Otto Hirsch within the framework of the *Reichsvereinigung* — an appointed body — in January of 1940. Both were outcomes of the same pattern of thought: Jewish particularism rather than Jewish collectivism. In the extreme circumstances of the 1930s, in the absence of viable emigration objectives and given its incessant competition with the needs of German-Jewish emigration, the repatriation policy toward Polish Jews had the most serious of consequences. However, it is important to understand these acts and repercussions in light of past traditions rather than in terms of later developments, namely, the Holocaust.

Jewish Leadership and Jewish Resistance

ARNOLD PAUCKER and KONRAD KWIET

In the same way that perceptions and interpretations of the Holocaust have shifted in the last half century, so too have the attitudes towards and the evaluations of Jewish self-defense against antisemitism and resistance to Nazi oppression and the "Final Solution." These range from an early neglect of the topic and an underrating of its dimensions to exaggerated claims of its proportions. Long repudiated, at least by historical research,[1] are some constantly reiterated allegations. The first is the image of Jewish leaders as nothing more than the henchmen of the Nazi authorities, or even as collaborators assisting in mass destruction. The second is the picture of German Jews who attempted in vain to maintain their "assimilationist" positions as *jüdische Deutsche* in an increasingly hostile environment. This initial —call it "Zionist" — evaluation ascribed to the Jews a ghetto mentality which rendered them unable to fight back. From here it was only a small step to the portrayal of the Jews as victims blindly submitting to their fate and being led to their deaths like "lambs to the slaughter."

Yet German Jews and their representatives did develop various strategies of defense and survival. They can be divided into two distinct categories — self-assertion defined as protest, acts of defiance and flight, and resistance defined here as politically organized antifascism. Another dividing line can be drawn: the dividing line between the response of the leadership and that of its community. The activities of Jewish leaders restricted themselves to self-assertion, thus excluding any involvement in antifascist campaigns. German Jews in general responded to Nazi persecution with both self-assertion *and* resistance. In this paper we

1 There is a rich literature on all aspects of self-defense and resistance of German Jews under Nazi rule. It is fully listed in the classified Bibliographies of *The Leo Baeck Institute Year Book* I–XLIII, London 1956–1998.

will attempt to shed light on the complex and controversial relationship between the Jewish leadership and Jewish resistance.[2]

The opportunities for Jews to take a stance against the Nazi regime were restricted by many external as well as internal factors. In 1933 some 500,000 Jews experienced the termination of what most felt as their German-Jewish *Lebensgemeinschaft* (co-existence). They found themselves at the mercy of a dictatorship that propagated a *reinliche Scheidung* (a clear parting of the ways of Jews and Germans) — which, in the first years of Nazi rule, still meant either social segregation within Germany or expulsion from its borders.[3] The latter was the preferred Nazi alternative.

2 For a comprehensive account of German-Jewish self-defense and resistance that summarizes research up to 1983, see Konrad Kwiet and Helmut Eschwege, *Selbstbehauptung und Widerstand. Deutsche Juden im Kampf um Existenz und Menschenwürde 1933–1945,* Hamburg 1984 (hereafter Kwiet and Eschwege, *Selbstbehauptung)*; see also the abstract from Konrad Kwiet, "Resistance and Opposition. The Example of the German Jews," in: *Contending with Hitler: Varieties of German Resistance in the Third Reich*, David Clay Large, ed., Washington, 1992, pp. 65–74. For the research undertaken from 1983 onwards, see Arnold Paucker, *Jüdischer Widerstand in Deutschland. Tatsachen und Problematik*, Berlin, 1995; idem, *Jewish Resistance in Germany. The Facts and the Problems*, Berlin, 1991; idem, "Resistance of German and Austrian Jews to the Nazi Regime 1933–1945," *Leo Baeck Institute Year Book,* 40 (1995), pp. 3–20; idem, *Standhalten und Widerstehen. Der Widerstand deutscher und österreichischer Juden gegen die nationalsozialistische Diktatur*, Essen, 1995; idem,"Responses of German Jews to Nazi Persecution 1933–1945," in: *The German-Jewish Dilemma. From the Enlightenment to the Holocaust*, Edward Timms and Andrea Hammel, eds., Lampeter, Wales, 1999, pp. 211–227; idem, " 'Not only Victims'. Reflections on the Resistance of German and Austrian Jews against the Nazi Dictatorship," paper delivered at the international conference 'Olocausto. La Sho'ah tra interpretazione e memoria' held by the Universita degli Studi di Napoli "Federico II" and the Istituto Italiano per gli Studi Filosofici in Naples in May 1997, and to be published in the conference volume in Italian in 1999.

3 General overviews are provided by Arnold Paucker, Sylvia Gilchrist and Barbara Suchy, eds., *Die Juden im Nationalsozialistischen Deutschland / The Jews in Nazi Germany 1933–1945*, Tübingen, 1986; Monika Richarz, ed., *Jüdisches Leben in Deutschland. Selbstzeugnisse zur Sozialgeschichte 1918–1945*, Stuttgart, 1982; Günther Bernd Ginzel, *Jüdischer Alltag in Deutschland, 1933–1945*. Düsseldorf, 1984; Wolfgang Benz, ed., *Die Juden in Deutschland 1933–1945. Leben unter nationalsozialistischer Herrschaft*, Munich, 1993; Saul Friedländer, *Nazi Germany and the Jews*, vol.1: *The Years of Persecution, 1933–1945*, New York, 1997.

In the wake of this drastic change the *Reichsvertretung der deutschen Juden* was formed in Autumn 1933 — a unified representation which constituted a genuine compromise between hitherto opposed Jewish forces and the regional and local communities.[4] Its main driving force were two previously inveterate enemies — the Zionist Federation, very much a minority, albeit a vociferous and intellectually brilliant one, and the majority *Centralverein (CV)*, with its total commitment to Germany. The *Reichsvertretung*, although not a democratically elected body, became a true representative of German Jewry which, under the leadership of Leo Baeck and Otto Hirsch, made every effort to safeguard Jewish rights and to protect the Jewish community. Most significantly, the Jewish leaders made it perfectly clear that their activities would remain strictly within the bounds of legality. This was in keeping with an historically conditioned outlook on the part of German Jewry. All efforts before 1933 to combat antisemitism and Nazism fell within strictly legal parameters, even if some propaganda campaigns were camouflaged.[5] With the Nazi seizure of power the *Rechtsstaat* disappeared and the Jewish community and the new representative institutions it had been permitted to create were subject to the strict supervision of a new *Führerstaat*. Any political activity against Nazism and antisemitism would have been regarded as an attack on dictatorial rule — an onslaught on the State itself. This fight was lost before it could be waged, in the face of the abdication of the liberal *Bürgertum* and the crushing of the labor movement — once supporters of Jewish emancipation.

In 1933 the possibility of *militant resistance* was considered and rejected as futile. Jewish leaders dismissed out of hand a suggestion made by Moshe Shapira, who had hurried across from Palestine to attempt to establish a Jewish self-protection organization to combat

4 Esriel Hildesheimer, *Jüdische Selbstverwaltung unter dem NS-Regime. Der Existenzkampf der Reichsvertretung und der Reichsvereinigung der Juden in Deutschland*, Tübingen, 1994 (hereafter Hildesheimer, *Selbstverwaltung)*.

5 For the first comprehensive study of Jewish defense, see Arnold Paucker, *Der jüdische Abwehrkampf gegen Antisemitismus und Nationalsozialismus in den letzten Jahren der Weimarer Republik*, Hamburg, 1969; idem, "Die Abwehr des Antisemitismus in den Jahren 1893–1933," in: *Antisemitismus. Von der Judenfeindschaft zum Holocaust*, Herbert Strauss and Norbert Kampe, eds., Bonn, 1986ff, pp. 143–171.

antisemitic hostility.[6] In Germany itself there was no armed struggle waged against Hitler's popular regime. Any attempt by Jews to take up arms would have been suicidal. Wherever German Jews were given the opportunity to take up arms, they did so — in 1936 within the ranks of the International Brigades fighting in the Spanish Civil War, and later within the partisan movement emerging in specific regions of Nazi occupied Europe, as well as volunteers in the Allied armies operating at all theaters of World War II. Among the 40,000 brigadists there were some 7,000 Jews representing numerous countries; 400 Jews hastened from Germany to Spain and 120 Jewish volunteers came from Austria.[7] They wanted to wage an armed struggle against Fascism, to engage in a military resistance that was impossible in their own countries. Jewish motivation was certainly subsidiary but it existed, and for many of the survivors it appears stronger in retrospect. Solidarity with the Spanish people in their fight against Fascism was a matter of course for Jewish activists in the German working-class resistance, but it had an impact on the Jewish youth movements also. World Jewry in general supported the legitimate government of the Spanish Republic and it can be safely assumed that most German Jews did so as well. Naturally they could not openly avow animosity to Hitler's ally Franco. Here too there was less restraint in the Jewish youth movements. In both the "assimilationist" and the Zionist youth movement camps there was admiration for the International Brigades. For many young Jews "Spain" was to become a lasting formative experience. Historians of the Jewish youth movements seem to ignore this altogether, perhaps for lack of "documentary" evidence. However, by the end of 1936 the songs of the International Brigade were well known among Jewish youth; in the Zionist-Socialist youth movements they were even sung in Hebrew. There was an entire group of young German Jews who went to Spain via France from a training camp in Holland to volunteer

6 Information obtained by Abraham Margaliot, see Kwiet and Eschwege, *Selbstbehauptung*, p. 59, p. 319 n. 143.

7 The standard work is: Arno Lustiger, *Shalom Libertad. Juden im spanischen Bürgerkrieg*, Frankfurt am Main, 1989; see also idem, "German and Austrian Jews in the International Brigades," *Leo Baeck Institute Year Book*, 35 (1990), pp. 297–320. A comprehensive history of the over 400 German Jews and all the other Jewish volunteers is in progress, initiated by Salman Salzman, Tel Aviv, president of the association of former members of the International Brigades in Israel.

to fight in the Brigades. The Jewish functionaries who had them in their charge totally disapproved of this step. There are other similar episodes. Even after the war surviving Jewish representatives argued that, while they certainly wished well to Spanish Democracy, "we had other worries at the time." It was left to a long-serving President of the State of Israel, the late Chaim Herzog, to assert that the fact that 7,000 Jews had fought in the International Brigades was a glorious page in the annals of the Jewish People.

The International Brigades were dissolved at the end of 1938 and, like so many others, Jewish antifascists crossed into France — to internment — and to other countries. But with the outbreak of World War II, the Brigadists, with their useful military experience, were to play a special role in the European resistance. German-Jewish *Rotspanienkämpfer* can be found throughout the entire spectrum of partisan activities, from the French Maquis, in which they were strongly represented, to Tito's armies of liberation. As to war service,[8] more than 20,000 German Jews and over 15,000 Austrian Jews, largely volunteers, fought against the Nazi regime: the majority in British Forces including the Jewish Brigade, and, to a somewhat lesser degree, in the United States Army, not counting all the others, which include the Red Army, the Free French, the 8th Australian Employment Company and the Homeguard in New Zealand. Generally speaking, most of them felt that by joining the Allied Armies they fulfilled a simple duty like anyone else, even if it meant taking a greater risk in the event of capture, especially if serving in the Commandos or the Special Services, and if discovered to be German Jews. When looking back the volunteers take great pride in their wartime military service, though among them the sentiment prevails that they should not be regarded as resistance fighters.

There was yet another form of defiance that can hardly be classified as resistance. The German-Jewish leaders rejected the advice of Mahatma Gandhi, conveyed to Leo Baeck in the wake of the November Pogrom

8 The first, very early book on the "enemy aliens" in the British Army was written by Norman Bentwich, *I understand the Risks. The Story of the Refugees from Nazi Oppression who Fought in the British Forces in the World War*, London, 1953. See the five essays by Yoav Gelber, John P. Fox and Guy Stern, in *Leo Baeck Institute Year Book*, 35 (1990), and 40 (1995). Much further work is in progress. See also Albert Sternfeld, *Betrifft: Österreich: Von Österreich betroffen*, Vienna, 1990.

in 1938, to call upon German Jews to carry out a *mass suicide* as a spectacular act of protest. Some 10,000 Jews took their own lives but this was not in response to calls from their leaders. The waves of suicide corresponded clearly to the milestones of Nazi persecution, culminating at the time of mass deportation. In suicide the Jews took their leave from a shattered German-Jewish *Lebensgemeinschaft*.[9] It can be left for debate whether these acts of deep despair, committed predominantly by the elderly and the lonely, highly acculturated and assimilated Jews, fall — as the late historian Uri Tal has suggested — within the Jewish religious tradition of *Kiddush-Hashem* (martyrdom).

The Jewish leaders chose to adopt a different course. The attitude towards the Nazi authorities, especially the SS and police with whom they had to negotiate, was determined by the concern that any outright refusal to comply with Nazi measures or open revolt would lead to harsh reprisals, necessarily endangering the Jewish community further. One other basic assumption played a decisive role. In the initial phase of persecution Jewish representatives assumed that the Nazi regime might not remain in power very long, an illusion shared by many non-Jews. The firm belief that such a rapid return to democracy would restore the German-Jewish *Lebensgemeinschaft* deterred them from calling for a mass exodus and working towards the self-dissolution of the Jewish community in Germany. The leadership expressed confidence in their ability to secure a continuing and viable existential basis for the Jews remaining in Germany. They perceived their obligation as falling within the areas of education and retraining, social welfare, and emigration. As in earlier crises and periods of persecution in Jewish history, their response lay in an intensification of Jewish life and in demonstrating Jewish self-assertion. Following are some examples.

In telegrams and letters, resolutions and memoranda, Jewish officials representing all organizations raised their voices against defamation and discrimination. The *CV* persisted, along with the *Reichsbund jüdischer Frontsoldaten (RjF)* and the *Verband nationaldeutscher Juden (VNJ)*, in its pleas to remain in Germany. This in itself represented, paradoxically enough, a gesture of defiance. This strategy earned the disapproval of the Nazi regime. In 1935 all propaganda of an "assimilationist" nature

9 See Konrad Kwiet, "The Ultimate Refuge. Suicide in the Jewish Community under the Nazis," *Leo Baeck Institute Year Book,* 24 (1984), pp. 135–167.

was prohibited. Infringements resulted in a ban on public speaking or writing. The Gestapo's first application to Heinrich Himmler to have the *CV* dissolved ended in failure. As a Gestapo report covering the period from October 1936 until February 1937 reveals,[10] the *Reichsführer-SS* expressed the reservation that "the disbandment of the *CV* would lead to a strengthening of the Jewish opposition." The *Judenexperten* of the Gestapo and the SD did not share this concern. They argued that there were "sufficient unresolved differences existing within the Zionist movement, which could easily serve to detract the attention of the Jews from other political matters." They soon achieved their aim. At the beginning of 1939, in the wake of the November Pogrom, the *CV* was dissolved.

On another and very different level the spiritual caretakers of Judaism reinforced the norms and values of Jewish religion and tradition. Martin Buber and others implemented a program of Jewish education stressing the significance of *spiritual resistance*. His teaching activities were soon prohibited, his appeals silenced. Rabbis frequently dared to preach from their pulpits against injustices being perpetrated. If denounced, they too were quickly silenced. In some cases, specially prepared prayers never reached the ears of those for whom they were intended. The Jewish press, closely monitored and censored, continuously disseminated messages of protests, normally in skillfully veiled language and measured tones. Meetings and cultural events served as venues for articulating criticism and indignation, either directly or indirectly. It should be noted here that only a tiny proportion of these protests came to the attention of the Nazi regime. By mid-1935 the number of registered monthly events in Prussia varied between 2,200 and 2,400. Due to the shortage of Gestapo and SD officials and informers the number of events under surveillance never exceeded seventy.[11]

These early, widespread protests met with little response from within the German population. The overwhelming majority of Germans responded to the persecution and expulsion of the Jews with indifference, or even with approval. Long before the program of the "Final Solution"

10 Lagebericht der Gestapa, 1.10.36–28.2.37, Geheimes Staatsarchiv Berlin, Rep 90-P86.

11 Ibid., Lageberichte April–August 1935, Rep 90-P80-83.

was put into reality, they had found it difficult to respect Jewish existence. From the outset, especially during the early, never-ending debates on Jewish emancipation, the demand had been made that Jews give up their "outdated" traditions and "annoying" traits. Total assimilation was required. By 1941 most Germans were not disturbed when the last Jews were stigmatized with yellow stars, then rounded up and deported to the East. Their departure was even welcomed by many with a feeling of relief. The process of exclusion and expulsion had left behind social outcasts, a *'minorité fatale'* who had come to be regarded as a burden that could be cast off. However, there is no evidence to suggest that the German mass murder of the Jews met, as Daniel Goldhagen maintains,[12] with general understanding, far less with widespread approval. Most Germans preferred to respond to the extermination of Jews with silence and denial.

In the light of this response, Jewish strategists adopted new methods. Protests virtually ceased after the *Kristallnacht* Pogrom of 1938.[13] They were replaced by feverish efforts to foster escape. Jewish officials now dared to go beyond the bounds of legality. Illegal bank accounts were opened to collect donations used to finance rescue operations. The *Reichsvertretung* paid for the release and emigration of imprisoned Jews with special monies from a secret fund established by the Robert Bosch firm in Stuttgart. Between 1938 and 1940, Hans Walz,[14] managing director of Bosch, made 1.2 million Reichsmark available for saving Jewish lives. This considerable sum was, to our knowledge, the only significant financial support from a German source, one which emerged from within the ranks of the conservative resistance movement. Later, when Jews attempted to escape into the German underground, no such financial aid was forthcoming, limiting decisively the possibility of illegal existence. The acceptance and distribution of funds prior to mass deportation constituted one of the few infringements of prevailing law by the Jewish leadership.

12 Daniel J. Goldhagen, *Hitler's Willing Executioners. Ordinary Germans and the Holocaust*. New York, 1996. As to attitudes of the Germans see also David Bankier, *The Germans and the Final Solution. Public Opinion Under Nazism*, Oxford, 1992.

13 See Konrad Kwiet, "Gehen oder bleiben? Deutsche Juden am Wendepunkt," in: *Der Judenpogrom 1938. Von der "Reichskristallnacht" zum Völkermord*, Walter H. Pehle, ed., Frankfurt am Main, 1994, pp. 132–145.

14 Akte Hans Walz, Yad Vashem Archives, Jerusalem (hereafter YV).

Other illegal rescue operations, however, met with internal opposition. A striking illustration of this is the bitter controversy surrounding the *Youth Aliyah* organizer Recha Freier, a controversy that continues to elude our full understanding. The Berlin-based Jewish Agency affiliated to the *Reichsvertretung/Reichsvereinigung* served Recha Freier as an organizational base for planning and facilitating her rescue operations. Conflict emerged when she was confronted with guidelines set by the German-Jewish leadership. According to these, priority was to be given to German Jews in the question of emigration to western countries. For the many Polish Jews who had been taken hostage at the outbreak of the war and incarcerated in concentration camps, repatriation to Poland was the option preferred. Recha Freier provoked the final break when she apparently "misused" official forms of the *Reichsvereinigung* for the release and emigration of Polish and stateless Jews. Moreover, children of Polish parents who had been imprisoned were smuggled from Poland to Vienna en route to Palestine. The *Reichsvereinigung* refused to support the transport. Only when Recha Freier pretended to be in possession of valid certificates was a green light given to the operation. The transport reached Yugoslavia safely. One group, however, was detained and their forged papers discovered. It was only with great difficulty that Recha Freier managed to obtain valid certificates from Palestine. At the same time her position in Berlin became untenable. The *Reichsvereinigung* forbade her to enter the Jewish Agency, and it did not hesitate to draw the Gestapo into the affair. Recha Freier succeeded in escaping in time. In her account, written years later and entrusted to Yad Vashem,[15] bitterness and indignation about the behavior of and the role played by the Jewish leadership are expressed in no uncertain terms. She refers to the "ausserordentlich freundliche Beziehungen," the "extraordinarily friendly relations," that existed between the *Reichsvereinigung* and Adolf Eichmann and his *Judenreferat*. In particular, Leo Baeck is the butt of vehement criticism. Recha Freier did not hesitate to express her longing for the day when "this man celebrated as a hero has his halo removed." While she preferred to keep her bitter resentments to herself, others have been more outspoken.

15 Statement by Recha Freier, YV, 03/3455.

There can be no doubt that even after 1939 the Jewish leadership keenly felt the obligation to further secure the increasingly threatened existential basis of the community. Following the events of the November pogroms, one can detect a shift of direction on the part of the leadership. It was now its intention to embark on a course of self-dissolution of the community in Germany. Jewish leaders believed this winding-up would take only a few years to complete. Their pleas "not to lose a minute" in seizing the last opportunities to leave the country were unmistakable. They called for donations, sponsorships and visas. A mood of depression took hold after the Nazi regime imposed a ban on emigration in October 1941. At that time there were still some 164,000 Jews in Germany, one-third of the Jewish population of 1933. Most of them still intended to emigrate. The familiar assumption, or old accusation, that the remaining Jews in Germany were unwilling to leave falls into the realm of historical legend.

From 1939 the leadership, however, was forced to take on tasks which turned the intended role of protector into its very opposite. Shortly before the outbreak of the war the *Reichsvertretung* was transformed into the *Reichsvereinigung* and compelled to furnish administrative assistance in paving the way for the gradual implementation of the program of the "Final Solution." Jewish officials were instructed to assist with registration, forced labor and group housing, the marking out of Jews and finally deportation.[16] In so doing, the "Jewish apparatus" became inextricably entangled in the wheels of the Nazi machinery of destruction from which there was no escape, except through suicide or flight. The *Reichsvereinigung* played its role as unenviable conveyor of Nazi orders until the bitter end. Until its liquidation in 1943 it remained caught in the trap of legality.

There was still strong resistance to the first deportations. In February 1940 concerted efforts were made to halt the deportation of the Jews of Schneidemühl and Stettin to occupied Poland. In October 1940 some 7,000 Jews in Baden and the Saar Palatinate were arrested and sent to

16 See H. G. Adler, *Der verwaltete Mensch. Studien zur Deportation der Juden aus Deutschland,* Tübingen, 1974; Wolf Gruner, *Der Geschlossene Arbeitseinsatz deutscher Juden. Zur Zwangsarbeit als Element der Verfolgung 1938–1943,* Berlin, 1996; Avraham Barkai, *From Boycott to Annihilation: The Economic Struggle of German Jews 1933–1943*, Hanover, NH, 1989.

southern France. Jewish officials hurried to trace Jews currently away on journeys and to warn them about the perils of returning home. Otto Hirsch lodged a protest with the RSHA and demanded the return of the deportees. In order to add weight to the demand, members of the board of the *Reichsvereinigung* threatened to resign collectively. The foreign press was secretly informed about what had transpired. A circular letter urged officials to observe a day of fasting and remembrance, to cancel all events of the *Kulturbund* for one week, and to pray and hold sermons on behalf of the deportees.

The RSHA forced the *Reichsvereinigung* to revoke its instructions and, as on earlier occasions, the Jewish leadership bowed to its will. This time the RSHA wished to send a clear signal that such opposition would not be tolerated any longer. Julius Seligsohn, author of the circular letter, was arrested and put to death in Sachsenhausen. Otto Hirsch was removed from his post and murdered in Mauthausen. With these acts of reprisal, the back of the resistance was broken. In Autumn 1941 the *Reichsvereinigung* and the subordinate branch offices of the Jewish communities followed without protest the directives of the RSHA and the Gestapo stations to distribute the Yellow Stars — a model designed by Goebbels and approved by Hitler in August 1941. This public stigmatization completed the process of social isolation; it also signaled the beginning of mass deportation. Jewish officials sent out notices and detailed information sheets, and were responsible for ensuring that transportation took its "proper course." This meant, among other things, that they strongly advised against any refusal to comply with deportation orders.

Between 10,000 and 12,000 German Jews still found the strength to resist Nazi orders for wearing the yellow star and ultimate deportation. Most of them tried to find hiding places in Berlin. In 1943 there were probably about 5,000 Jews living in hiding — some 7 percent of the Jewish population of Berlin in 1941. At the end of the war 1,402 Jews surfaced. In other words: three out of every ten Jews who went underground survived. We must presume that there were some 25,000 Germans who distinguished themselves by offering shelter in an attempt to save Jewish lives. Among the survivors were members of a small Zionist youth group that has become known by the name of *Hug*

Halutzi (Pioneer Circle).[17] On its way into the Berlin underground this *Hehalutz* group also had to overcome barriers erected by the Jewish leadership. Initially, even officials of the Jewish Agency rejected any flight into illegality, with the admonition that such steps would be at odds with "Jewish honor" and "Jewish dignity." It was only in the summer of 1942 — in the wake of the news filtering through about genocidal campaigns carried out in the East and about deportations starting in western Europe — that such ideas were pushed aside. *Hehalutz* organized rescue operations in many places in Europe.

When the German Jews embarked on their final journey to the East, virtually all of them trusted the official proclamations that feigned a program of "resettlement" or "evacuation" for purposes of "labor deployment." The systematic extermination of the Jews, unprecedented in history, defied all human imagination. It was just as difficult to give credence to the news or rumors that filtered through about mass shootings and gassings. By 1941 Leo Baeck had already received word about the murderous campaigns, including the deployment of mobile gas vans. Like representatives of Jewish councils elsewhere, he clung to the hope that forced labor would still offer a chance of survival. He maintained this view until the very end. Nonetheless, Leo Baeck stopped short of conveying his knowledge to the community. Even in August 1943 in Theresienstadt, when he was informed about murder by poison gas in Auschwitz, he preferred to keep silent — with this explanation, which has given rise to much debate: "To live in the expectation of death by gassing would have been even more difficult. And this death did not threaten all. There was the selection for labor deployment. So I arrived at the difficult decision not to say a word to anyone."[18]

In whatever light one chooses to see this "difficult decision" taken by Leo Baeck, many questions remain about his contradictory and

17 Christine Zahn, "'Nicht mitgehen, sondern weggehen!' Chug-Chaluzi — eine jüdische Jugendgruppe im Untergrund," in: *Juden im Widerstand. Drei Gruppen zwischen Überlebenskampf und politischer Aktion 1939–1945*, Wilfried Löhken and Werner Vathke, eds., Berlin, 1993, pp. 159–205; see also Jizchak Schwersenz and Edith Wolff, "Jüdische Jugend im Untergrund. Eine zionistische Gruppe während des Zweiten Weltkrieges," in: *Bulletin des Leo Baeck Instituts,* 12 (1969), pp. 5–100.

18 Albert H. Friedlander, *Leo Baeck: Leben und Lehre,* Stuttgart, 1973, p. 59.

puzzling behavior; even contemporary close observers, such as Herbert A. Strauss, do not claim to have a ready answer.[19] It is, however, an irrefutable fact that neither Leo Baeck nor the *Reichsvertretung/Reichsvereinigung* was in a position to stop the destructive course of the National-Socialist racial policies on their own. They were dependent on the help of others. Little solidarity was forthcoming from the German population. Even within the German resistance movement, far too little attention was paid to the persecution of the Jews. At no time were the various resistance groups able or willing to place the special plight of the Jews and later the struggle against the "Final Solution" at the center of their campaigns.

Insurmountable barriers prevented any alliance between the Jewish leadership and the Communist resistance. Long before 1933 the Communists had propagated a "solution" to the "Jewish Question" which was to be identical with the dissolution of Judaism, a perspective unacceptable to the great majority of the Jewish community. In the course of emancipation, most Jews had found their place within the ranks of the bourgeoisie, manifest in their liberal convictions and conservative lifestyle, religious ties, and social and economic status. As such they came under fire from the Communists in the course of their class struggle. At the same time the Communists' anticapitalist (and by its implication and in its effects also at times anti-Jewish) propaganda and anti-Zionist campaigns, as well as their entrenched stance against the Weimar Republic, only served to deepen the rift further. (It is however fair to state that the Jewish adherents of the Communist Party — despite some discernible anti-Jewish features — at no time perceived it as an antisemitic party; and they also subscribed to the idea that the Jewish problem would be solved and discrimination and antisemitism end with the emancipation of the proletariat.) At any rate, 95 percent of all Jews displayed clear anticommunist sentiments prior to 1933. This hardly changed in the wake of the Nazi seizure of power. In 1935 Communist programs and strategies changed course slightly.[20] Three

19 Herbert Strauss has now published his memoirs: *Über dem Abgrund. Eine jüdische Jugend in Deutschland 1918–1943,* Frankfurt am Main, 1997. This is not just an autobiography, but an historian's shrewd and sober assessment of his own years in Weimar and Nazi Germany.

20 See David Bankier, "The German Communist Party and Nazi Antisemitism, 1933–1938," *Leo Baeck Institute Year Book,* 32 (1987), pp. 325–340.

years later, faced with the massive outburst of Jew-hatred, the exiled party leaders signaled solidarity with the persecuted Jews, documented in the remarkable protest, "Against The Disgrace of the Jew-Pogrom," published in the illegal newspaper *Die Rote Fahne*. And, undoubtedly, from the very beginning the Communist resistance, along with other leftist groups, offered Jewish party members or sympathizers a political and organizational platform for taking up the antifascist struggle. It must be stressed that for all these Jewish antifascists in the left-wing resistance, antifascism was the priority.

The decision to join the various resistance groups was based solely on political convictions. In other words, Jewish antifascists entered the struggle against the Nazi regime as convinced Communists, Socialists, Social Democrats, Trade Unionists, Trotskyites or Anarcho-Syndicalists. Still, when evaluating this resistance, one has to distinguish between the two major "Jewish" groups engaged in illegal activities. The much larger contingent — some 2,500 — consisted of Jewish Socialists and Communists who after the Nazi takeover took up underground work as part of the cadres of the various organizations. Once most underground groups had been crushed by the Gestapo by 1937/1938, Jewish representation in all resistance activities diminished drastically. In the initial years of the Nazi regime the concentration camps were full of Jewish antifascists. Most of these Jewish resisters fall within a category which was already termed "Red Assimilation" by the Jewish community in the Weimar Republic: antifascists first and foremost, and largely outside the organized Jewish community. The degree of their Jewish consciousness remains difficult to assess. It was certainly flexible and underwent changes as the persecution of the Jews increased and became murderous. Under the conditions of illegality and terror their eyes were opened to the fact that as Jews they were branded. This realization served in many cases to rekindle a Jewish awareness, giving their antifascism a distinctly Jewish element. But it is also true that the organized Jewish community exercised hardly any influence on this "contingent."

It was otherwise with the younger "contingent" — some 500 to 600 who operated within the Jewish youth movements.[21] They certainly

21 These estimates have been repeatedly discussed in the literature listed in note 2. For a general assessment of the behavioral patterns of Jewish youth under

were "in the care" of the official Jewish representation, which was responsible for their behavior. That these Jewish functionaries judged what they called the "antics" of this very small minority among organized Jewish youth (at the very most 1–2 percent) as foolhardy, naive and a danger to all Jews in Germany (a community of hostages) has been stated many times. Added to this was the accusation levied against them then, and in retrospect, that their motivation was hardly Jewish. It is quite correct that the major influence on these young people's behavior was political opposition to Nazism in general. They adhered to whatever political philosophy their various German underground movements professed, and most of them — though not all — had been enrolled by Jewish activists of the various illegal underground groupings. Naive and reckless many of these young Jews may have been, but to dismiss their activities as bereft of any Jewish concerns is something that can barely be sustained.

First of all there were some Jewish groups, such as the *Borochow-Jugend* with their *Anti-Stürmer* underground journal, which quite clearly acted from Jewish motivation.[22] Moreover, there is sufficient evidence that Jewish motives were even prevalent among young Jewish communists. When Jewish boys and girls painted out the "*Un*" from the notorious antisemitic slogan to read "*Die Juden sind unser glück*," or when Jewish antifascists distributed leaflets during the 1936 Olympic Games in Berlin telling gullible foreign visitors not to be taken in by Nazi propaganda, as the capital of the Reich had only been cleansed of antisemitic slogans and ordinances for the duration — the Jewish motivation speaks for itself.

The attitude of the Jewish leadership to any form of active and militant anti-Nazi work of Jewish antifascists was and remained entirely negative. Even in the light of later knowledge — and the destruction of German Jewry — surviving Jewish representatives have not wavered in their condemnation of this antifascist militancy. Officially,

repression, see now Arnold Paucker, "Zum Selbstverständnis jüdischer Jugend in der Weimarer Republik und unter der nationalsozialistischen Diktatur," in: *Jüdische Selbstwahrnehmung in Mitteleuropa*, Hans Otto Horch and Charlotte Wardi, eds., Tübingen 1997.

22 Israel Getzler, "Der 'Anti-Stürmer': Kampfblatt gegen Antisemitismus und Rassenhass," *Jüdischer Almanach des Leo Baeck Instituts, 1994,* pp. 44–48.

the *Reichsvertretung* ignored antifascist campaigns until 1939, and afterwards the *Reichsvereinigung* disapproved of them and sought to prevent them. Warnings were given not to engage in any "illegal" or "subversive" endeavors, if only for reasons of security. Surviving Jewish antifascists recalled that they felt so desperately frustrated under Nazi oppression that they had to do something — anything. They did not regret their anti-Nazi propaganda and later acts of sabotage. They felt contempt for the Jewish establishment, not sharing its concern that their activities would have drastic repercussions for the Jewish community. The Herbert Baum group is a classic example of this.[23]

The antifascist struggle carried out by this Jewish-Communist group reached its peak in a spectacular act of sabotage. In May 1942 members of the group attempted to destroy the Nazi propaganda exhibition "The Soviet Paradise," in the Berlin *Lustgarten*, with incendiaries and bombs. This subversive action was seen by many Jews still living in Berlin in 1942, and by their leaders, as a fatal step. Even in retrospect it has been condemned as purely pro-Soviet motivated. A munitions factory, a military installation, and above all Gestapo headquarters or deportation offices would have been far more suitable targets of sabotage. Leaving aside the question as to whether such targets were even within the realm of possibility, it can be shown convincingly that "The Soviet Paradise" exhibition sought to propagate anti-Jewish and anticommunist sentiments, providing the group with a clear motive for attacking it. The abortive coup had disastrous results both for the group and the Jewish community. The Gestapo was swift to take revenge. Within a few days the group was liquidated. Before their execution in the Berlin Plötzensee prison, group members sang Jewish and working-class songs, including the Zionist anthem "Hatikva" and the "Internationale." This was indeed the final expression of their sense of belonging to both the Jewish and communist worlds. In Berlin 500 Jews were taken hostage and put to death, 250 were shot in Sachsenhausen, 250 were executed in the SS barracks in Berlin-Lichterfelde. Relatives

23 See Kwiet and Eschwege, *Selbstbehauptung*, pp. 114–139. For many illuminating details of the history of the Baum Group, see also Eric Brothers, Red Flags and Yellow Stars: Jews in the Resistance against Nazism, unpublished manuscript, New York, 1988 and 1989. A book edition with the title *The Herbert Baum Group: Jewish Resistance against Nazism* has not yet been published.

of the victims as well as Jewish officials were compelled to witness the murders. Representatives of the *Reichsvereinigung*, as well as of Austrian and Czechoslovakian Jewry, were ordered to appear at the RSHA without delay. Adolf Eichmann informed them in no uncertain terms that the Jewish community and its leaders would be held accountable for any illegal activities of its members, and that further action would meet with even more draconian measures. The Jewish representatives were instructed to inform their communities accordingly and to make clear to them the consequences of their actions for the entire Jewish population. A few days later a proclamation was drafted to be issued by the *Reichsvereinigung*:[24]

> Every Jew is responsible for our community. Everyone of us must remember this always and everywhere, in his deeds and his utterances, at home, in the street, in his place of work. The behavior of every individual counts as he carries the responsibility not only for himself and his family, but for all Jews. Not for one moment must it be forgotten that every one of us is responsible for all of us, and that the acts of every single individual has implications for this entire community.

This draft is marked for publication in the *Jüdisches Nachrichtenblatt* in early June 1942, the only journal the Nazis permitted the German Jews — though there is no definite proof that it was ever published as no complete set of the journal exists.

Shocked about the mass executions of hostages and deeply concerned about the threat of new sanctions, the *Reichsvereinigung* established contact with the Baum group for the first time. It was only with some difficulty that a go-between was found, Norbert Wollheim, who was able to trace one member of the Baum group, Richard Holzer. The meeting took place during the small hours of the night, close to Berlin Alexanderplatz. Two very opposing accounts of the dialogue exist. Robert Holzer maintains that he told Wollheim that the Baum group had already been disbanded, thus no further acts of sabotage could be expected. He added that some members had opposed the action, concerned with the repercussions for the Jewish community. Norbert Wollheim, on the other hand, recalls a curt, dismissive answer: "What you are telling us is of no interest to us. If we believe we

24 Quoted from Hildesheimer, *Selbstverwaltung*, p. 228.

have to act, then we do so. The only thing that matters to us is what serves our purpose."[25] When Wollheim conveyed this message to the *Reichsvereinigung*, Leo Baeck is supposed to have responded: "Quite frankly, I have never believed that under these circumstances reason would prevail. What they have undertaken was pure madness from the outset. Now at least we know it. There is nothing that we can do."

While most young Jews opted for the Left, Jewish leaders preferred to maintain links not only with the liberal[26] but in particular with the national conservative resistance. This was something quite in keeping with their own more conservative leaning and a result of their contacts with conservative elements in the state apparatus opposed to Nazism. An alliance between the two unequal partners emerged, one that did not result in active Jewish involvement with any conservative or military conspiracy, or in any kind of putsch. This would not only have been out of keeping with the character of those representing the Jewish community, in their isolation it would in fact have been a technical impossibility. Furthermore, in 1933 there was no outcry from conservative quarters when Jewish emancipation was revoked. Germany's national-conservative elites joined forces with the National Socialists in calling for a "traditional" solution of the "Jewish Problem," envisaged in the parting of the way of Jews and Germans. Their opposition in general against Hitler did not emerge until just before the war, at the time when the Jews had already been effectively excluded from society. Certainly, an overthrow of the Nazi regime, especially a successful military coup at an early stage, would have put an end to the genocidal campaigns unleashed against the Jews and other victim groups. However, the "new order" to be established would not have welcomed a return to the full emancipation of Jews.[27] Out of the

25 See Kwiet and Eschwege, *Selbstbehauptung*, p. 129.

26 Horst R. Sassin, *Liberale im Widerstand. Die Robinsohn-Strassmann-Gruppe, 1934–1942*, Hamburg, 1993; idem, "Liberals of Jewish Background in the Anti-Nazi-Resistance," *Leo Baeck Institute Year Book*, 37 (1992), pp. 381–396; idem, *Widerstand, Verfolgung und Emigration Liberaler 1933–1945*, Bonn, 1983.

27 Christof Dipper, "Der deutsche Widerstand und die Juden," *Geschichte und Gesellschaft*, 9 (1983), pp. 349–380; idem, "Der 20. Juli und die Judenfrage," *Die Zeit*, (1 July 1994). See also Peter Steinbach, "Der deutsche Widerstand und die Judenverfolgung," in: *Die Macht der Bilder. Antisemitische Bilder und Mythen*, Jüdisches Museum der Stadt Wien, ed., Vienna, 1995, pp. 305–320.

question was a rebirth of a shattered German-Jewish "symbiosis." What survivors of the "Final Solution" could have expected was support in moving to Palestine. Naturalized German Jews wishing to return to Germany would be granted the status of aliens. Despite this perspective Jewish representatives sought and found access to a handful of Hitler's opponents who, indeed, provided information, advice and, above all, financial and humanitarian aid. There are only a few episodes recorded, largely based on testimonies given after the war. They are still shrouded in mystery, and it seems that the lack of historical sources will prevent any attempt to fully explore the relationship between the Jewish leadership and the conservative resistance.

It was only in 1955, shortly before his death, that Leo Baeck announced that the time had come to write about his relations with the resistance. This plan was not realized. However, he did talk in London with four people about his contacts.[28] These were Hans Liebeschütz, Robert Weltsch, and Hans and Eva Reichmann, well-known representatives of German Jewry who were convinced of the truth of his late revelations. Leo Baeck recalled that he was approached by Carl Goerdeler in 1942 to participate in a competition, set up by the opposition. As the representative of German Jewry he was asked to submit a proclamation to be published after the liberation, entitled "To the German People." Baeck's "Manifest" was chosen by the selection committee. The draft is regarded as lost. All intensive investigations to find the text have been fruitless to date. To our knowledge there is no historical document or any other eyewitness account confirming the existence of this "Manifest." There are historians who incline to the belief that it was in fact never written.

Another manuscript, however, has been preserved: a multi-volume transcript entitled "The Legal Position of German Jewry throughout Centuries."[29] This work, also known as the *Rechtslage* manuscript, was

28 Arnold Paucker held several interviews with those concerned in London in the years 1960 to 1965.

29 Albert H. Friedlander, "A Muted Protest in War-time Berlin. Writing on the Legal Position of German Jewry throughout the Centuries, Leo Baeck — Leopold Lucas — Hilde Ottenheimer," *Leo Baeck Institute Year Book,* 37 (1992), pp. 363–380; see also Arnold Paucker, "Preface and Introduction", in, *ibid.,* pp. XIII–XIV; idem, *Standhalten und Widerstehen,* pp. 16–20, 51–53.

written by Leo Baeck in close cooperation with Rabbi Dr. Leopold Lucas and the sociologist Dr. Hilde Ottenheimer. Both co-authors fell victim to the "Final Solution," Lucas in Theresienstadt, Ottenheimer in Riga. Leo Baeck maintained that this study was written in secrecy between the years 1939/1941, at the suggestion of the conservative opposition and, after completion, handed over to an emissary of the resistance. Like the "Manifest" it was to be published after the liberation with a view to informing the German population about the history of the German Jews. Doubts have been raised as to whether in fact conservative opponents of Hitler commissioned the work, as well as to its suitability for the audience for whom it was presumably intended.

Gestapo documents have resurfaced that attest to an order by the Nazi authorities in March 1942 to furnish them with a scholarly work about the history of the Jews in Europe. The deadline for its completion was set for December 1942. Permission was sought by Baeck to consult publications held in German libraries. Sections of this work were submitted on time. Based on this documentary evidence there are compelling grounds to assume that Leo Baeck was indeed acting here on Nazi orders. This would seem to stamp him as either a liar or ashamed to tell the truth, or as someone suffering from psychological stumbling blocks or confused memories.

The evidence can, however, be interpreted in quite a different light. The project commissioned by the Gestapo had nothing to do with the original *Rechtslage* manuscript. By March 1942 this multi-volume study had definitely been completed. Moreover, it could not have been written in the few months before Baeck's deportation to Theresienstadt, and the Gestapo documentation does not mention Dr. Ottenheimer but another female co-worker. The internal evidence of the original manuscript does not point to a Gestapo commission. The study is a very dignified record, with no attempt to pander to Nazism. Unresolved is a problem relating to a special marking code. The footnotes are interspersed with the capital letter "J." Set in brackets, the letter is placed after all Jewish authors and sources quoted. Similar classifications can be detected in Jewish publications that appeared after 1933 under Nazi censorship, such as the popular *Philo-Lexikon*. Moreover, even before the letter "J" was stamped on passports or other documents belonging to Jews, from 1935 onwards Gestapo and SD officials placed this special mark after the names of suspected or detained Jewish resisters.

Several copies of the *Rechtslage* transcripts were made and distributed, and for many years they were regarded as lost. The original was taken by Leo Baeck to Theresienstadt, and after liberation was eventually entrusted to the Leo Baeck Institute. Two copies have resurfaced. One copy was found recently in the personal papers, of Dr. H.G. Adler, the chronicler of Theresienstadt and author of a monumental study on the deportation of German Jews. H.G. Adler obtained the copy in the mid-fifties from Dr. Richard Korherr,[30] once Himmler's chief statistician, who on request from the *Reichsführer-SS* produced the well-known report on "The Final Solution of the Jewish Question in Europe." After Auschwitz, Richard Korherr presented himself as an opponent of Hitler. It is not known whether he is the "Nazi-renegade" recalled by Baeck as one of the recipients of the transcript.

In 1990 the second copy was found in the Military Archives in Prague. Archival inquiries revealed that the bundles of transcript, tied together and kept in two boxes, were handed to the Secret Military Archives in March 1946 from the "Memorial to the Liberation," which also served as a depot for Nazi documents captured at the end of World War II. It is unknown whether the Prague copy originates from the SS war archives that had been set up in the "Castle Zasmuky," in reality a manor house close to the city Kolin, or from another Nazi institution operating in the *Reichsprotektorat*.[31] At any rate, the *Rechtslage* manuscript fell into the hands of the Nazi authorities. No evidence has come to light as to whether it was written under their supervision. A handwritten note in German attached to the Prague copy confirms that the research for this large-scale and collective project commenced after 1935.

It is also plausible that initially neither the conservative opposition nor the Gestapo had commissioned Leo Baeck with the writing of this monumental study, which appears to be a real labor of love. Leo

30 Arnold Paucker received this information from the son of H.G. Adler, Professor Jeremy Adler, London, in 1995.

31 As chief historian of the Australian War Crimes Commission (SIU), I (Konrad Kwiet) was one of the first western historians to conduct extensive archival research in the Military Archives, Prague. I came across the copy more or less by coincidence, and with the help of the archivist Suzanne Pivcova, to whom I am very grateful for all the assistance received.

Baeck and his co-workers perhaps saw themselves obliged to start recording the history of the *Rechtslage* of the Jews after the enactment of the Nuremberg Laws. Soon afterwards, the November pogrom of 1938 triggered a profound sense of shock in the Jewish community. Most Jews abandoned the notion that they still had any rights as citizens of their German homeland. A new Jewish homeland had to be established: the Jewish state in Palestine. Towards the end of the *Rechtslage* manuscript special emphasis is placed on the notion that the future of the Jewish people was now in the Middle East. Leo Baeck belonged to the Jewish Agency wing of the *CV* and surely by 1939–41 reflected only the beliefs of a great many German Jews who had reached similar conclusions. While this work was still in progress, he may well have been approached by the conservative resistance and encouraged to intensify his research. (Handed over to an emissary, the study provided the conservative resistance not only with a scholarly account of the legal history of the Jews but also with a place where — after the destruction of the German-Jewish *Lebensgemeinschaft* — Jews could be resettled; Conservative opponents to Hitler promised to support their emigration to Palestine.) Once the *Rechtslage* manuscript was finished, and even Gestapo officials had obtained knowledge of it, Leo Baeck was instructed to provide them with a scholarly work on the history of the Jews in Europe.

These two interpretations are not mutually exclusive if one accepts the proposition that there were two *Auftraggeber* commissioning Leo Baeck's studies at different times. Undoubtedly, the initial *Rechtslage* manuscript can be — as Albert Friedlander suggests — interpreted as "a muted protest in war-time Berlin," as a scholarly attempt to document and maintain Jewish "dignity and identity as destruction moved upon Jewish life."[32]

In conclusion, prior to and during World War II there were many opportunities to save Jewish lives, but only a few were taken up.[33] It is easy today, in hindsight, to criticize the behavior of Jewish victims and the role played by their leaders, a trend that has gained increasing popularity in both public and academic discourse. However justified this criticism may be in some cases, it all too frequently overlooks — and

32 Friedlander, "Muted Protest," p. 376.

33 Konrad Kwiet, "Resistance and Opposition," p. 74.

for obvious reasons — one decisive factor. Even if the Jews and their representatives had overcome their own misgivings and shortcomings, their internal disputes and diverging attitudes, it would by no means have cleared the way for an effective response to Nazi persecution. Their strategies of defense and survival encountered many obstacles erected by the German society in which they were living and in which they once had felt at home. The limits of German-Jewish resistance and the ineffectiveness of Jewish protests and rescue efforts should therefore not be attributed to those who initiated them, but rather to those who ignored or sought to abort them. In 1965 — two decades after the one thousand-year-old history of German Jewry had come to an end —the Council of Jews from Germany, based in England, published a volume in memory of the Jewish representatives who had been murdered by the Nazis. They gave it the title *Bewährung im Untergang.*[34] Those in charge of the community during the Holocaust were Jewish representatives who prior to the outbreak of World War II had had the opportunity to seek refuge abroad. Leo Baeck himself returned from England in 1939 to be with those who were left behind. Functionaries and rabbis who had accompanied the *Kindertransporte* came back to Nazi Germany to stay with their imperiled flock. They were deported with the remnants of the community and most of them perished in the East.

In a recent survey of the responses of the German Jews to Nazi persecution, by one of the present authors, the following conclusion about the behavior of the Jewish leadership was reached:

> All these men and women — with their virtues and failings in conditions of intolerable stress — had been brought up in surroundings of middle-class respectability and decency, with a firm belief in the rule of law which protected them and which, in their turn, they obeyed. They found themselves facing a Nazi regime and a German society which had rapidly wiped out every vestige of civilized law and behavior and which swept them aside as no more than rubbish. And yet, despite this, they were not broken entirely as people. There was a *Bewährung im Untergang.*[35]

34 E. G. Lowenthal (ed.), *Bewährung im Untergang. Ein Gedenkbuch*, published for the Council of Jews from Germany, London, 1965.

35 Arnold Paucker, "Responses of German Jewry," p. 225.

This essay is by no means an uncritical assessment of the actions of the Jewish leadership when the great catastrophe befell the community, but we felt it right that these words should be repeated here.

Jewish Daily Life in Wartime Germany

MARION KAPLAN

Even before the war, Jews found themselves in a war-like situation. They had experienced full-scale expropriation, almost complete "racial" segregation, the beginnings of forced labor and forced ghettoization, in sum, social death in German society.[1] But once Germany went to war, the Nazis accelerated the economic descent and social isolation of the remaining Jewish population. The general agony of an ever-aging Jewish community — one that in 1941 registered two-thirds of its population as past middle age — intensified rapidly with the war, which provided the occasion for massive isolation, expulsion and ultimate annihilation.

Curfews, Rations and Judenhäuser

When Germany unleashed the war, the government placed a curfew on all Jews. Although by this time few Jews ventured out after dark, these legal restrictions magnified their social isolation. Jews could no longer

1 Orlando Patterson introduced the term "social death" to describe the slave condition. He pointed to three features which add up to the social death of slavery: personal domination, excommunication from the legitimate social or moral community," and a perpetual condition of dishonor. A social history of Jews in Germany illustrates many similarities (with important differences, such as freedom to emigrate, at least until the war). While they did not face *personal* domination in the sense Patterson intends, they did forced labor for the state whose agents had the power of life and death over individual Jews. See, *Slavery and Social Death*, Cambridge, 1982 and *Freedom: Freedom in the Making of Western Culture*, New York, 1991.

even visit friends. Some people disobeyed the curfews, but they ran great risks doing so.[2]

The issue of food, however, plagued Jews far more than did the curfews. On 28 August 1939, three days before Germany started the war, the government imposed food rationing on all Germans.[3] From a pre-war average of 3,000 calories per person a day, by 1944 normal consumer intake gradually dropped to about 2,000 calories.[4] Even then, "the looting of a continent (and the government's concern about the hunger in World War I being repeated), made sure that German rations were by far the highest in Europe."[5] For Jews (but not for "first degree *Mischlinge*"), caloric intake plummeted immediately.[6]

Many Jews feared starvation. Starting in 1939, the government limited purchase hours and stores where Jews were allowed to shop. In some cities, like Kassel, these stores also charged Jews ten percent more than other consumers.[7] Shortly after the government forcibly drafted

2 Rolf Kralovitz defied the curfew often, attending his beloved, and also forbidden, opera. His anxious mother spent evenings worrying that she would have to cover for him if the Gestapo spontaneously inspected the *Judenhaus* in which they lived, to check that all residents were indoors during the curfew: "Although my mother was happy that I was interested in opera, at the same time she was very worried when I returned home late from the performance." Bernd Lutz Lange, ed., *Davidstern und Weihnachtsbaum. Erinnerungen von Überlebenden*, Leipzig, 1992, pp. 31, 33.

3 *Deutschland-Berichte der Sozialdemokratischen Partei Deutschlands, 1934–1940*, Frankfurt, 1980, vol. 1940, pp. A40–71.

4 That is, official food rations to "Aryan" consumers did not fall below subsistence until very late. Manfred Enssle, "German Everyday Life after World War II," *Central European History*, 26 (1993), p. 9.

5 Gerhard L. Weinberg, "Iconoclasm: German Plans for Victory, 1944–45," *Central European History,* 26 (1993), p. 218.

6 Gerdy Stoppleman, memoirs, Leo Baeck Institute Archives, New York (hereafter *LBI*), suggests that the rations for Jews were half those for Aryans, p. 3. Moreover, concentration camp rations were even more deficient. Her husband's daily rations in the Sachsenhausen concentration camp, where he was interned after the November pogrom, included: "... a watery cup of *Ersatzkaffee* (malt coffee), and two slices of dry *Kommisbrot* (dark army bread). This was to last from 5 a.m. till 5:30 p.m. when a watery soup, in which fatty pieces of meat — very few — were swimming, was doled out. Sometimes another slice of bread was added." p. 4.

7 Report of 17 March 1942, in: Sybil Milton and Frederick Bogin, eds., *Archives of the Holocaust: An International Collection of Selected Documents*, vol. X, *American Joint Distribution Committee, New York*, London, 1995, part I, p. 216.

Jews to work, it cut their food rations, which led to malnutrition and disease.[8] Jews (mostly women), had to go to special offices for their ration cards that were stamped with the word "Jew," while "Aryans" received their ration cards at home from their block warden. By January 1940, Jews received less meat, fruit and butter than did non-Jews, and no legumes, cocoa or rice. Jewish heavy laborers received 200 grams of meat a week compared to 1000 for "Aryans." Jews were forced to race from shop to shop in the one hour that was alotted for food shopping in order to gather what little remained after "Aryans" had filled their needs.[9] Then Jewish women had to make the food stretch.

Moreover, the list of forbidden foods grew ever longer. In 1941, in addition to the already prohibited foods, the list included: canned foods, fish, poultry, coffee, milk (even skim milk), and cigarettes and tobacco. Jews could no longer buy apples or tomatoes and were limited to particular vegetables.[10] When a shortage of potatoes occurred, stores displayed signs that "Foods in short supply are not sold to Jews." Jewish parents could purchase milk only if their children were very young;[11] Jewish children could not purchase candy or even artificial honey.[12] If one managed to acquire forbidden goods on the black market, it was dangerous to store them since the authorities conducted sporadic house searches to ensure that Jews did not have forbidden foods in their homes.[13]

To make matters even harder, some non-Jewish women appointed themselves guardians of the food pantry. For example, an enthusiastic Nazi in Berlin regularly terrified her Jewish neighbor's child. The little girl, on her way to the grocer, "...came out of our entrance with a shopping bag. This woman stood right in front of it. Diagonally across

8 Elisabeth Freund, memoirs, LBI, p. 29.

9 By January 1940 rationing for Jews became ever more stringent as they were denied legumes, most fruit and meat. Only Jews who did heavy labor were still allotted 200 grams of meat per week compared to 1000 grams per week for "Aryans" doing heavy labor. *Deutschland-Berichte der Sozialdemokratischen Partei Deutschlands*, vol. 1940, p. 49. The average "Aryan" worker received 500 grams of meat per week. The reports give the rations for meat, bread and fat for "Aryans."

10 Elisabeth Freund, memoirs, pp. 49–50.

11 Ibid., p. 29.

12 Ibid., p. 30.

13 Ibid., p. 74.

from us hung the pharmacist's large round clock. It was shortly before 4 and she said, 'You're not allowed to go shopping yet, I won't let you out of here'."[14] Erna Becker-Kohen, a convert to Catholicism in a "privileged" mixed marriage, tried sending her young son for milk in her Berlin neighborhood: "The women railed mercilessly that the Jew-woman had sent her child shopping when she is forbidden to do so; therefore they don't want to wait on the little fellow anymore. ..." Like other Jews, she attempted to shop in another part of town where she would not be so easily recognized and could do so successfully — if no one commented on her dark hair and dark eyes.[15]

The dire food situation of the Klemperers, an "unprivileged mixed" couple, illustrates the plight of many Jews, except that the Klemperers had more "Aryan" contacts and, therefore, a potentially better situation than most "full" Jews. The chase to find scarce foods, sometimes causing Eva Klemperer to hunt from early morning to late at night, began by the second year of the war. Victor Klemperer noted in his diary how gaunt his friends looked and how he and his wife's hunger was never satisfied at mealtime. They bartered, did favors and carried out extra chores for food. By August 1942, as the deportations were progressing, Klemperer noted his own "typical hunger stomach," swollen like a "drum." He regularly stole potatoes and bread from one of his *Judenhaus* neighbors. He justified this behavior to himself by explaining that she received so many extra provisions from non-Jewish relatives that her supply was spoiling. By the war's end the Klemperers were surviving on food they had begged from their non-Jewish friends.[16]

The government soon forbade Jews from buying new shoes, lingerie and clothing, nor could they buy the material with which to make or darn clothing or repair their shoes. Public laundries were forbidden to Jews and only designated Jewish shoemakers could repair the shoes of Jews. Even teenagers who continued to grow could not buy clothing and had to wear threadbare and outgrown garments. In Hamburg,

14 Hazel Rosenstrauch, *Aus Nachbarn wurden Juden. Ausgrenzung und Selbstbehauptung 1933–1942*, Berlin, 1988, p. 118.

15 Erna Becker-Kohen, memoirs, LBI, pp. 31–32.

16 Victor Klemperer, *Ich will Zeugnis ablegen bis zum letzten. Tagebücher 1933–1945*, Berlin, 1995, vol. I, p. 679; vol. II, pp. 52, 87, 112, 114, 138, 147, 152, 158, 175, 189, 192–93, 203, 227, 541, 651.

one destitute mother, appealing to the Jewish community, managed to acquire a new winter coat for her growing son. The community also provided a pair of shoes for him in May 1940, exchanged his coat for a used one, and allowed him to have his shoes repaired for the last time in January 1941.[17] After the deportations began, needy Jews sometimes received the hand-me-downs of their neighbors who had committed suicide or were deported to concentration camps. This was patently illegal, since the government insisted on confiscating all Jewish property.[18]

When Jews had to wear the yellow Star of David, trying to shop at off-hours or in stores not designated for Jews meant removing the star and, hence, gambling with one's life. In Leipzig, one Jewish woman who had taken her yellow star off in order to shop noticed the Gestapo entering. Dreading a search, she quickly grabbed the star and tried to swallow it, choking to death.[19] Similar incidents occurred in Berlin.[20]

In addition to the scarcity of food for Jews, the Nazis succeeded in turning Jews into refugees within Germany. Government agencies forced Jews to move out of their homes and into new ones on short notice, and kept them moving from one place to another. Each time, they had to sell more furniture because each move meant smaller and smaller quarters.[21] The poet Gertrud Kolmar, sharing an apartment with her father and several strangers, wrote to her sister: "Since my bed is in the dining area, I actually have no refuge anymore, no space to myself, and the feeling of homelessness ... has grown ever more powerful."[22] In Leipzig, the Nazis forced a widow whose four children had emigrated, but whose own attempts had met with failure, to leave her apartment in April 1940 for a one-room sublet. In February 1941 they compelled her to leave that room for an unheated sublet and in

17 Staatsarchiv Hamburg, Jüdische Gemeinde: 992n Band 4.

18 Klemperer, *Ich will Zeugnis*, vol. I, pp. 541, 550, 562, 572, 576, 689–90; vol. II, pp. 59, 140, 443, 614.

19 Rolf Kralovitz in Lange, *Davidstern,* p. 35.

20 Manfred Fackenheim-Field, memoirs LBI, p. 9.

21 Rolf Kralovitz in Lange, *Davidstern,* pp. 31–32. On furniture, see also, Elisabeth Freund, memoirs, p. 74.

22 Gertrud Kolmar in: *Briefe an die Schwester (1938–1943),* Johanna Zeitler, ed., Munich, 1970, quoted by Beatrice Eichmann-Leutenegger, "Die Dichterin Gertrud Kolmar, 1894–1943," *Leo Baeck Institut Bulletin*, 85 (1990), p. 30.

September they made her move yet again to a room in a *Judenhaus* which she shared with a stranger. These moves preceded the final one, to Riga, from which she never returned.[23] In Berlin, Jews received five days notice to evacuate their apartments and could rent rooms only in houses still owned by Jews. People had to find new lodgings without taking time off from their long shifts at forced labor.

The new lodgings were underheated and overcrowded. In the winter, frost formed inside the rooms as fuel deliveries were never adequate.[24] Often an entire family was squeezed into a small room; sometimes complete strangers were jammed together.[25] Many made do with tight quarters in old buildings where the rooms were often infested with bedbugs. Ruth Klüger wrote of the dark, bug-ridden room she shared with her mother: "You turn off the light and imagine the bugs crawling out of the mattresses. Then you get bitten, turn on the light and wail loudly, because this disgusting vermin is actually walking around in the bed."[26]

By 1943, most of the few remaining Jews lived in *Judenhäuser*, the last stop before their deportation. In some cities these houses were located in a single neighborhood, concentrating Jews in a ghetto-like area. Indeed, Jews who lived there often referred to it as a "ghetto." Most of these houses accommodated only Jewish families. Some, however, separately housed "non-privileged" mixed marriages and Jewish members of mixed marriages (particularly where the "Aryan" spouse had died or had divorced the Jewish spouse), while others lumped them together with all-Jewish families.

Dreaded spot-checks by the Gestapo were an integral part of daily life in many *Judenhäuser*. The Dresden Gestapo, spitting at and beating the inhabitants, regularly burst into Jewish apartments, destroyed whatever furniture or bedding was left, and stole money and food. Disregarding the taboo against hurting old people, especially women, they kicked,

23 "Briefe einer Mutter, 1939–1942," Luise Stern Collection, LBI.

24 Klemperer, *Ich will Zeugnis*, vol. II, pp. 15, 18.

25 Lange, *Davidstern*, p. 209. See also, Manfred Fackenheim-Field, memoirs LBI, p. 14. Max Stein interview in, Douglas Morris, "The Lives of Some Jewish Germans who lived in Nazi Germany and Live in Germany Today: An Oral History," B.A. Thesis, Wesleyan University, 1976, p. 154.

26 Ruth Klüger, *weiter leben*, Göttingen, 1992, p. 60.

beat or punched elderly women, or smeared their faces and clothing with food. In 1942, Gestapo members attacked women between the ages of 70 and 85 in Dresden's Jewish old age home.[27] Jews lived in terror on the streets and at home. "Fear and hunger fill the day," wrote Victor Klemperer in June 1942: "Will I be beaten up and spat at today?"[28] Whereas in other *Judenhäuser,* survival rather than brutality, were immediate overarching concerns, for Klemperer daily life had evolved into fear of everything.

The inability of many Jews to find adequate living quarters did not concern the government, which considered barracks acceptable. In Cologne, for example, two thousand Jews, who were given three days notice to leave residences owned by non-Jews, moved into barracks erected for Russian prisoners-of-war during World War I. Klara Caro wrote:

> They reminded me of the Roman catacombs, except that here it was a matter of sheltering living human beings, not dead ones. Due to the dripping water, the damp odor of mold spread. Everything needed to serve the most primitive needs was missing. ... 20 persons ... crammed together in one room. Everyone could bring along a bed, table and chair, that meant separating from the last things to which one was attached. All other remaining possessions were expropriated by the Gestapo. How touching it was, that those affected understood, even in this miserable little spot, that it was within their power to smuggle in something tasteful, whether a vase with a flower, a colorful cloth, a small picture.[29]

In Dresden, those crammed together considered themselves lucky: "it was not Poland, it was not a concentration camp!"[30]

Despite the dire situation of Jews in *Judenhäuser* and barracks, with the cacophony of voices and the impossibility of privacy, the Jews created a community of connection and concern, some even finding a new "extended family." Holding on to their bourgeois values and way of life was a matter of integrity and identity, of resistance against "Aryan" dehumanization. Jews shared and bartered food with each

27 On house searches, see: Klemperer, *Ich will Zeugnis*, vol. II, pp. 19–20, 41, 46, 51, 57, 61, 94, 102, 121, 142. On attack against old women, see: vol. II, pp. 72, 79, 82, 95, 111–12, 121, 199, 228; against old people: pp. 111, 151.

28 Ibid., vol. II, pp. 141, 143.

29 Klara Caro Collection, LBI, "Der Untergang des deutschen Judentum," p. 2.

30 Klemperer, *Ich will Zeugnis*, vol. II., p. 285.

other, gave gifts and services and consoled each other after the arrests of friends and family members. No longer integrated into German neighborhoods, and no longer allowed to frequent German shops, ride on public transportation,[31] or work with German workers, most "full" Jews were spared much of the public enmity they had previously faced and could aid and comfort each other. In Dresden, an elderly woman left a suicide note to the members of her *Judenhaus* thanking them deeply for their "heartfelt courtesy" toward her while she lived there. Her careful words exemplify most of these relationships: not chosen friendships but bonds forged out of necessity and commiseration. Else Behrend-Rosenfeld, in charge of the 320 Munich Jews crammed into the barracks at Berg am Laim, commended the internees:

> Orthodox and Liberals, those baptized as Catholic and Protestant, the formerly rich and poor, the highly educated and those from very simple social circles had to live and get along with each other. And, naturally, not everyone demonstrated good will ... we did our best to mediate, and then it became clear ... that we had been successful...: In Berg am Laim we had become a true community.

Parents continued, even with limited means, to provide some of the remnants of bourgeois education to their children. Anneliese Winterberg fondly recalled the six months of piano lessons she received as a child in Bonn, where 474 Jews were squeezed into a former cloister during their last months before deportation. Only nine ultimately survived. In some *Judenhäuser*, younger residents created a small theater and staged performances. In Leipzig, teenagers gathered to listen to a forbidden gramophone that belonged to an "Aryan" woman married to a Jewish man. They danced to old records on Sundays: "We were more carefree than the adults, who suffered greatly from the persecution."[32]

While most turned to the community for social support, many also turned to religion for moral sustenance. During these years, Rabbi Joseph Carlebach received hundreds of questions regarding Jewish ritual and Jewish law, with the queries to him increasing dramatically

31 Joseph Walk, *Das Sonderrecht für die Juden im NS-Staat*, Heidelberg, 1981.

32 Suicide note in Klemperer, *Ich will Zeugnis*, vol. II., p. 216; Behrend Rosenfeld in Konrad Kwiet, "Nach dem Pogrom: Stufen der Ausgrenzung," in: *Die Juden in Deutschland, 1933–1945*, Wolfgang Benz, ed., Munich, 1988; Bonn in "Erinnerungen von Anneliese Winterberg," in: *Frauenleben im NS-Alltag*, Annette Kuhn, ed., Pfaffenweiler, 1994; Leipzig in Lange, *Davidstern*, p. 43.

as other rabbis fled. Thus, even as the situation deteriorated around him, his wife and children, he felt compelled to stay on to serve the religious needs of the remaining Jews in Germany. As late as the winter of 1943, regular prayer services continued in Hamburg and the community was attempting to rebuild a *mikvah* (ritual bath). In Bonn, regular religious services took place in the *Judenhaus*, including a wedding right before a deportation, and outside Munich, Orthodox Jews prayed in the cloister of a nunnery where they had been herded.

Memoirs and letters do not dwell on religious life in the *Judenhäuser*, perhaps because religious Jews took their observance so for granted that remarking on it would have seemed superfluous. Even Salomon Samuel, a rabbi, only rarely mentions "Sabbath" in his letters. Yet, documentation exists that the Sabbath and holidays were commemorated even in the Jewish Hospital in Berlin — which may be characterized as the last official residence of Jews in Germany. Furthermore, a description of Jews from Cologne conducting a Passover Seder in the Theresienstadt concentration camp suggests that such observances surely took place in the less horrifying atmosphere of the *Judenhaus*. In Theresienstadt in 1943, Rabbi Caro gathered between twenty and thirty people in a room intended for five. "The women and men sat on the floor. "The Seder plate consisted [of] a carrot, a little bit of [inedible] green, a bone and salt water. ... The Rabbi ... celebrated the Seder, reading the Haggadah and a Chazan [cantor]from Prague ... chanted the well-known songs. It was in keeping with the satanic tricks of the Nazis that on Jewish holidays they invented especially cruel punishments. So all of a sudden the lights went out ... But the Rabbi went on saying the Haggadah by heart. ... Never [had] "*Leschana Habaa Birushalayim*" [Hebr. for "next year in Jerusalem"] been said with more fervor. ...[33]

33 Carlebach in Miriam Gillis-Carlebach, *Jedes Kind ist mein Einziges*, Hamburg, 1992, pp. 224–25, 252; Bonn in Kuhn, *NS-Alltag*, pp. 294–95; Samuel in Angela Genger, ed., *Durch unsere Herzen ziehen die Jahrtausende*, Düsseldorf, 1988; hospital in Rivka Elkin, "Kinder zur Aufbewahrung im jüdischen Krankenhaus," *Tel Aviver Jahrbuch für deutsche Geschichte*, 1994, p. 264; Caro coll., LBI, "Seder to Remember."

The Star of David

From 19 September 1941 onward, Jews over the age of six had to identify themselves by wearing a large yellow Star of David on which the word *Jude* was written in black, Hebrew-like letters on it. The introduction of the yellow star signaled a new stage in persecution. "This was the most difficult day in the twelve years of hell," according to Victor Klemperer. Every person wearing a Star "carried his ghetto with him, like a snail its house."[34]Up to this point, with the exception of the November Pogrom, the Nazis had used a low-key, sometimes secretive, approach. For example, the decrees that forbade Jews from attending public entertainment, and those that blocked the wealth of Jews, were relatively concealed. In the first case, Jews simply "disappeared" from audiences; in the second, few people besides the bureaucrats and bankers responsible witnessed the confiscation of property. Certainly, shopkeepers knew of all the rules limiting purchases by Jews, neighbors watched Jews emigrate or saw them evicted or herded into *Judenhäuser*, and parents and children heard about or witnessed the expulsion of Jewish children from school.

The yellow star, however, was qualitatively different for Germans and evoked some shock among them. Some responded with sympathy, others with hostility, most with indifference. Many, having promoted and become accustomed to the social death of the Jews, were surprised that "so many" Jews were still around. That Jews were easily identifiable was now woven into the daily lives of Jewish and non-Jewish Germans.[35] Jews themselves, according to Ruth Klüger, often date the moment they had to wear the star further back than the actual event: "That is because the isolation of Jews was already in full swing before September 1941."[36] Most Jews felt the full torment intended. Klaus Scheurenberg recalled: "The star seemed as big as a plate and to weigh a ton."[37] While some tried to hide the star by holding a brief case

34 Victor Klemperer, *LTI. Die unbewältigte Sprache. Aus dem Notizbuch eines Philologen*, Munich, 1947, pp. 176, 178.

35 Ibid., chapter 25.

36 Klüger, *weiter leben*, p. 48.

37 Klaus Scheurenberg, *Ich will leben*, Berlin, 1982, pp. 79–80..

or shopping bag in front of their chest when they went out — also a punishable offense — few dared to go without it.

Although the yellow star was yet another form of persecution, many Jews had already been recognized as such by their non-Jewish neighbors. Even Jews in "privileged" mixed marriages, who did not have to place a star on their clothing or residences, were shunned by "Aryan" neighbors who sometimes even reported them to the Gestapo. In Krefeld, for example, neighbors complained that Jews were gathering in the home of an "Aryan" man married to a Jewish woman. The husband explained that his wife had many relatives in town and that these were visits by relatives, not meetings. Still, he had to promise that the visits would cease. Neighbors then proclaimed that the couple had acquired illegal furniture. Fortunately, the couple could prove that the old clothing and chest of drawers that they had recently received were legally inherited from the wife's sister. Other neighbors informed the Gestapo that the couple had ten baptized, Catholic children. Four had been born after the Nuremberg Laws, thus giving the local party leader pause: "...We have no interest in having even more half-Jews result from this marriage."[38] Erna Becker-Kohen faced similarly vicious neighbors in Berlin. Her "Aryan" husband worried that, in their enthusiasm for the war, his neighbors might beat his "racially" Jewish (though Catholic), wife and *Mischling* child to death. As a result, he brought them to a convent. They could remain there for only a few weeks because a female guest refused to live near a Jew, and a nun, who felt very "German," did not want to encounter her either. No one even sympathized with the baptized child. She commented on her neighbors: "To be sure, we live in a completely 'respectable' neighborhood, where... they do not believe they should leave the Jewish woman in peace. Their hatred is boundless. When these people think they can cast their good upbringing aside, they are surely even more dangerous than the gangsters around the Alexanderplatz."[39] Becker-Kohen's neighbors, however, did not have a monopoly on odious behavior. In October 1941, the members

38 Hauptstaatsarchiv Düsseldorf, Gestapo files, RW 58 65442.

39 Erna Becker-Kohen, memoirs, LBI, p. 5.

of her Catholic church choir refused to sing with a "Jew." This was not an isolated incident.[40]

The Bombings: Popular Attitudes and Jewish Ambivalence

During the war popular attitudes increasingly hardened towards the Jews. As bombings took their toll, the government repeatedly shifted responsibility for the war onto the Jews, dubbing the bombings "Jewish sky terror."[41] The war became the "Jewish war."[42] Primed by antisemitic propaganda since 1933, the population was not slow in picking up this theme. Even many who disliked or opposed the Nazis were confused or poisoned by the atmosphere. "The Jews are responsible for this," proclaimed Lilly Wust in March 1943, surveying the rubble around her home in Berlin. A few weeks later, she helped to hide her Jewish lover and aided other Jews in hiding.[43] Victor Klemperer reported that after surviving air raid attacks with workers who opposed the war, one declared, "...they are getting rich as a result of this war, these few swinish Jews (*Saujuden*). It is really the 'Jewish war."[44] Disheartened, Klemperer concluded, "None were Nazis, but all were poisoned."[45]

Antisemitism found its most intense expression in bomb shelters where Jews, despite their official pariah status, were nonetheless required by the government to hide. But Jews were to remain segregated from "Aryans" even in these shelters, isolated in dark, cramped spaces.[46] When the bombardments started, Erna Becker-Kohen grabbed her small

40 David Bankier, *The Germans and the Final Solution. Public Opinion Under Nazism*, Oxford, 1992, p. 122.

41 *Völkischer Beobachter*, 3 March 1943.

42 Klemperer entitled one of his *LTI* chapters, "The Jewish War," noting Nazi usage; also see his *Ich will Zeugnis*, vol. II, pp. 8, 541, 638–39, 690.

43 Erica Fischer, *Aimée und Jaguar; Eine Liebesgeschichte*, Berlin, 1943, Cologne, 1994, p. 53.

44 Klemperer, *LTI.*, p. 102.

45 Ibid., p. 103.

46 Elizabeth Bamberger, for example, hid in a "dirty hole stuffed full of junk" while the "Aryan" tenants went to the "laundry room which had been fixed up for this purpose." Andreas Lixl-Purcell, *Women in Exile: German-Jewish Autobiographies Since 1933*, Westport, Conn., 1988, p. 97.

child, wrapped him in a blanket, and rushed into the shelter. There, her neighbors made nasty comments about her, even though she remained in a separate section. She wrote: "I fear the people more than the bombs."[47]

After the war when Germans recalled the Nazi era, they stressed the very real horrors of the bombings. The bombings — whether as a result of their guilt or embarrassment about the genocide or as a reminder of their own victimization, or all of these — stood out as the German civilian war experience.[48] Jews, on the other hand, did not recall the bombings in great detail. When a bomb hit their neighborhoods some Jews lost their homes and their few remaining possessions, and the Jewish communities tried, where possible, to alleviate immediate needs.[49] Although Jews did suffer and die in the bombings, these attacks threatened Jewish lives in an arbitrary manner; the deportations threatened them in a more systematic way. Elizabeth Freund remarked: "I'm not afraid of the bombings, even if it isn't exactly pleasant, and one never knows whether one will survive until the next morning. That is a danger we ... share with many millions. ... We are only afraid of the Gestapo."[50]

Thus, the anonymity of the bombings were a relief to Jews who feared more personal attacks. "Ruth Fleischer" recalled: "The war's outbreak was something else altogether from Crystal Night because Crystal Night touched our personal life as Jews. ... I took the war indifferently because it was a general circumstance. ... Other Germans were shook up ... they had to send their sons and husbands off to fight. The war touched their personal lives".

But most importantly for Jews, the bombs held out hope of a German defeat and the end of the Nazi nightmare. Many Jews only

47 Erna Becker-Kohen, memoirs, p. 9. Strangely enough, Jewish observers described these neighbors in gender-neutral terms, although, in fact, women probably outnumbered men on the "homefront."

48 Annemarie Tröger noted how quickly women focused on their own suffering during the bombings when interviewed about their lives under Nazi rule. "German Women's Memories in World War II," in: *Behind the Lines: Gender and the Two World Wars*, Margaret Randolph Higonnet et al., eds, New Haven, 1987, p. 299.

49 Staatsarchiv Hamburg, Familie Plaut D38.

50 Elisabeth Freund, memoirs, pp. 58–59. Klemperer, too, feared the Gestapo more than the bombings. Klemperer, *Ich will Zeugnis*, vol. II, pp. 474, 606, 656.

hoped they could hold out as long as it would take for an Allied victory. "Fleischer" reflected: "Probably it was completely normal that I thought that perhaps this war would bring us luck and be our rescue."[51]

Jewish Social Life in Wartime

By the start of the war most families were already split in many directions. Trapped in Germany, the elderly were intensely lonely. In 1940 a mother wrote to her grown son of her dream: "Last night I had a wonderful dream. Walter, you appeared in person, took both of my hands in yours and said: 'Why are your fingers so rough?' 'That's from all the house work,' I said and then you stroked my two little fingers. It was the first time that I dreamed of one of my children and saw them so alive before me. I was very happy."[52]

Children left behind also experienced pain of a different sort. There was no respite from the harshness of daily life. School, which Jewish children were allowed to attend only until June 1942, was hardly a source of relief. Due to mass emigration, the school situation was in constant flux. The deportations, that began in October 1941, made the situation even more unstable. As the number of students and teachers dwindled, schools closed down and the remaining children were crammed into another school — and yet another. The new classrooms became increasingly more dilapidated just as the children's clothing got thinner and more shabby.[53]

And, what happened to children during school breaks? "Where was one to put them, these poor, overly nervous children, who after these last years with their terrible experiences needed a holiday rest especially badly?"[54] Public parks were already forbidden to Jews, and in 1941 the

51 "Ruth Fleischer" — a pseudonym — in: Douglas Morris, "The Lives of some Jewish Germans", p. 106.

52 Letter from Gertrud Grossmann, 7 February 1940, p. 1. Thank you to Atina Grossmann for sharing these letters.

53 Klüger, *weiter leben*, pp. 13–14.

54 Elisabeth Freund in Monika Richarz, ed., *Jewish Life in Germany: Memoirs from Three Centuries*, Bloomington, 1991, p. 416.

Gestapo forbade Jews from taking excursions in the forests.[55] When the non-Jewish neighbors of Jewish daycare centers, objected to noise if the children played outdoors, the Jewish community came up with a solution: "...transforming every free spot in the Jewish cemeteries into playgrounds with sand boxes for the smaller children." The bigger children were put to weeding around the graves, and in this way the children were exposed to fresh air and kept occupied. The graves remained in good repair, something for which no extra Jewish workers were available and which, inexplicably, had been demanded by the Gestapo. "That is what things have come to now: In Germany the cemeteries are not only the final resting place for the old people, but also the only spot where Jewish children can play."[56]

Nor did high-strung children or teenagers find peace at home, where parents, most of whom worked at forced labor, manifested enormous stress.[57] Ruth Klüger recalled that "Death, not sex was the secret about which grown-ups whispered, about which one would have liked to have heard more." She reflected that most children understood what threatened them: "On the street below, Nazi rascals ran around with their small pointed daggers and sang the song about Jewish blood spurting from the knife. One didn't have to be very clever to understand, rather it took more than minor mental acrobatics to misunderstand..."[58]

In spite of the inability of families to stave off disaster, many still clung to traditional notions of marriage and family. Jews continued to marry up until their own deportations, perhaps as a form of silent protest or defiance, perhaps determined to survive — or die — with a committed partner. In November 1941, Hermann Samter, an official in the Berlin Jewish community, wrote: "Characteristic for the present

55 Most park benches had been forbidden since the outbreak of war, but in some cities, like Berlin, they had been forbidden even earlier. In 1937 one Berlin district forbade 92 of its 100 benches to Jews. Wolf Gruner, "Die Reichshauptstadt und die Verfolgung der Berliner Juden 1933–1945," in: *Jüdische Geschichte in Berlin*, Reinhard Rürup, ed., Berlin, 1995, pp. 235.

56 On Berlin, see: Elisabeth Freund, in: Richarz, *Jewish Life*, p. 416. Ruth Klüger writes about playing as a child in the Jewish cemeteries of Vienna *weiter leben*, p. 58), and Klemperer notes this for Dresden as well *Ich will Zeugnis*, vol. II, pp. 376, 389, 403).

57 Klüger, *weiter leben*, p. 59.

58 Ibid., pp. 7–8

time is not only the high number of suicides (among us), but even more the flood of marriages. Shortly before our end, almost every relationship leads to marriage." His last letter of 7 February 1943 announced that he had just married his fiancée.[59]

Most Jews turned to family and friends to provide sustenance, information and evaluation of the situation. A sense of solidarity in misery prevailed: "Each one trembled with the other's news ... A readiness to help each other arose which only perilous times and a merging of fates can create."[60] For the few who retained non-Jewish friends, they, too, became a source of solace and, for some, a means of survival in hiding.[61]

What often struck Jews about Germans was how little they seemed to know or admit about the extremes of official antisemitism. They reacted with feigned or real surprise to Jewish adversity. Victor Klemperer's own close friend, an "Aryan" woman who stored his diaries at great risk to herself, offered to buy furniture from him well after Jews were no longer allowed to sell their own property. As late as June 1944, an "Aryan" factory worker wished Klemperer an enjoyable summer. When he responded that he avoided long walks because of the yellow star, she rejoined, "Then I wouldn't wear it outdoors!" She was surprised when he informed her that such an infraction could cost him his life.[62]

"Aryan" complaints about their own suffering impressed Jews even more than "Aryan" obliviousness. Shortly after the German attack on the Soviet Union, Elisabeth Freund was sitting on a boat next to an "Aryan" woman. Not aware that Freund was Jewish, the woman grumbled about the war with Russia, anxious for her 17-year-old son and angry at the untrustworthy Russians. She added: "the Führer surely knows better!" Even when non-Jews acknowledged the plight of Jews, they relativized it or told Jews how lucky they were to leave

59 Hermann Samter, Yad Vashem Archives, Wiener Library Collection, 02/30, letters of 30 November 1941 and 7 February 1943.

60 Ilse Rewald, "Berliner die uns halfen die Hitlerdiktatur zu überleben," Berlin, 1975, p. 6.

61 Elisabeth Freund, memoirs, p. 53. Ilse Rewald stressed the importance of her non-Jewish friends, not only for their solidarity, but also for the practical aid they provided. Ultimately, they helped her survive in hiding. Ilse Rewald, "Berliner die uns halfen," p. 5.

62 Klemperer, *Ich will Zeugnis*, vol. II, pp. 66–67, 324, 536.

their homeland. When Freund's clothing began to look threadbare, a non-Jewish co-worker asked about them. She explained that Jews had not received ration cards for clothing since the beginning of the war. Surprised, he thought about this predicament and concluded: "Actually, the difference is not really so great. You have no clothing ration cards and get no socks — we have some [cards] but there are no socks to be bought. It comes to the same thing..."[63]

She finally received permission to emigrate in October 1941. While buying glasses before she left, the salesman, learning of her destination, exclaimed: "What, you're going to America, a land without war! I wish I could switch places with you!"[64] The salesman never acknowledged the extreme persecution of the Jews and perceived the Jews as luckier than he. This denial of Jewish suffering and emphasis on German suffering extended into and permeated the postwar era. American military administrators confirmed this widespread belief in German suffering. One report noted: "Perhaps the most common mechanism by which the German masses avoid a sense of guilt for the fate of the ...six million Jewish dead, is to convince themselves that they too, have been victims of Nazism, and possibly in greater measure than any other people."[65]

Postwar historians have noticed that as soon as German interviewees are asked about the uncomfortable issue of National Socialism, they promptly recall the war.[66] The "Jewish war" is remembered as a disaster for the German people as victims. This is not the place to analyze how such victim status alleviated responsibility, guilt, or embarrassment regarding the genocide, nor how much serious damage was actually wrought. However, it is worth noting simply that our information regarding the deprivations that Jews endured during the war comes almost entirely from German decrees and from the Jewish victims — not from "Aryan" shoppers who saw them discriminated

63 Elisabeth Freund, memoirs, pp. 91–92.

64 Ibid., pp. 178.

65 After the war, claims of German victimization abounded. Frank Stern, *The Whitewashing of the Yellow Badge. Antisemitism and Philosemitism in Postwar Germany*, Oxford, 1992, p. 92.

66 Annemarie Tröger quoted by Elaine Martin, "Autobiography, Gender, and the Third Reich," in: *Gender, Patriarchy and Fascism in the Third Reich*, Elaine Martin, ed., Detroit, 1992, pp. 188–90.

against in groceries, not from "Aryan" workers who could observe their increasingly shabby clothing, not from those who averted their eyes as someone with a yellow star came into view, and not from neighbors who saw Jews evicted from their homes or who banished them to separate areas in the bomb shelters.

Responses of the Churches

The Catholic Anti-Jewish Prejudice, Hitler and the Jews

WALTER ZWI BACHARACH

Numerous and diverse anti-Jewish elements can be identified in the statements and writings of the minor clergy and in homiletic literature. Anti-Jewish theology was transformed into political ideology, whose aim was to serve non-ecclesiastical interests. The sum total of charges against the Jews and Judaism voiced in Germany reflected universal Catholic views and were not unique to Germany. But it was in Nazi Germany that the practical conclusions were drawn from centuries of consecutive vilification, conclusions which culminated in the planning and implementation of the mass murder of Jews. Thus, it is worth examining the impact of the Catholic outlook on Nazi antisemitism. The question is whether historical and ideological continuity is discernible between Christian antisemitism and the atrocities committed by the Nazis.

At first glance, the question appears irrelevant. There are great differences between the attitudes of Nazism and Christianity towards Jews. In contrast to Nazi ideology, Christianity was interested in the survival of the Jews, in the hope that they would some day abandon their religion and convert to Christianity, thereby fulfilling Christianity's religious mission. It is a historical fact that very few Jews responded to Christian missionary efforts. The Jew's adherence to his tradition and his refusal to accept Christianity brought down on his head the wrath of the Christian church, which perceived him as the ugly and corrupt Jew, setting himself against all that was good on earth. As long as Jews refused to acknowledge their error, the church attacked them furiously, degrading and insulting them, but did not seek their death. This is the essence of Christian antisemitism; it is not true of Nazism. The proclaimed aim of the Nazis was the physical annihilation of the Jews and the eradication of Judaism in general. There was an additional striking difference between the approach of the two ideologies towards racist theories. The church totally refuted these theories, thereby creating a rift with the Nazi regime.

German Catholics were unwilling to be included in the organized antisemitic camp — either under the Second or the Third Reich. This was already true in Bismarck's day: Catholics joined the Center Party but avoided being officially denoted antisemites. They dissociated themselves from the antisemitic sector since, as a liberal-antisemitic group, it adopted a blanket stand against the Jews, the *Junkers* (the landowning and officer class), and the Jesuits. Any Catholic who joined their ranks would have been obliged to oppose his fellow Christians, the Jesuits, thereby acting counter to his religious principles. Nor was there political justification for such a move. The Center Party did not openly declare its identification with antisemitism, in accordance with the policy laid down by its leader Windthorst. At the same time, many of its members were antagonistic towards the Jews, and their views were reflected in their newspaper *Die Wahrheit*. An article entitled "Antisemitism among German Catholics" stated:

> We did not wish to be known by this name (antisemites Z.B.) ... There is no contradiction here, since we do not dissociate ourselves from the objective identified with this name, but from what has been done in Germany in the name of this objective. This is what rouses our opposition. ... We have no sympathy for Jews ... we can sum up our attitude towards the Jewish question by saying: not hatred of Jews but protection of Christians.[1]

This diplomatic statement, which camouflaged anti-Jewish feeling under the guise of protection of Christians, and which fitted the dominant mood in German society, particularly at the end of the nineteenth century, was relevant for many Catholics during the Third Reich as well. There was an additional reason why many Catholics preferred not to be known as antisemites. The explanation lies in contemporary events. One should distinguish between the period of the *Kulturkampf* and the period from the end of the 1880s onward. At the beginning of the *Kulturkampf* Catholics denounced the "hostile attitude towards the Jews" (*Judenfeindlich*), seeking to dissociate themselves from the political and racial antisemitism of the newly emerged antisemitic

1 *Die Wahrheit*, vol 2, Munich, 1896, pp. 346, 347, 348.

parties. They still considered the racial element to be indicative of "un-Christian antisemitism."[2] It would certainly be a misstatement to claim that the entire Catholic camp supported Nazism. However, protection of Christians and promotion of the interests of the Catholic church undoubtedly took precedence over humanitarian concern for the fate of Jews.

Influential German Catholics did not usually take the risk of protesting against the persecution of Jews. A typical example is the attitude of Cardinal Faulhaber. When requested by the Gestapo in Munich to clarify his attitude towards anti-Jewish racial policies, he replied evasively that he had indeed defended biblical Jewry in his sermons, but had expressed no views whatsoever on the modern Jewish question.[3] But even when the rumors of atrocities perpetrated against Jews were verified, the Catholic bishops did not take to the barricades. Cardinal Faulhaber realized that the church must raise its voice in protest. He approached his colleague, Cardinal Bertram of Breslau, and proposed that they compose a manifesto protesting the murder of Jews. Bertram's reply reflects the Catholic approach, namely that the church leadership should wield its influence, which he considered to be minimal, only on matters "of greater importance in the long term," particularly the burning issue of how to stem the destructive influence of anti-Christian and anti-ecclesiastical forces on the education of German Catholic youth.[4] This order of priorities demonstrates the place of the Jews in the German Catholic consciousness.

It would, as noted above, be difficult to prove the existence of a direct link between Catholic anti-Jewish actions and Nazi antisemitism, nor can Catholics be held directly responsible for the Nazi atrocities perpetrated against Jews. But the Catholics did play an important part in disseminating the negative image of the Jew, fostering unbridled hatred of Jews among Germans in particular and in world public opinion in general. There was nothing new in Nazism's antisemitic

2 Uriel Tal, *Christians and Jews in the 'Second Reich' 1870–1914*, Jerusalem, 1985 (Hebrew), pp. 58–59, Werner Jochman, *Gesellschaftskrise und Judenfeindschaft in Deutschland 1870–1914*, Hamburg, 1988, p. 24.

3 Georg Denzler and Volker Fabricius, *Die Kirchen im Dritten Reich. Christen und Nazis Hand in Hand?*, Frankfurt am Main, 1984, vol. 1, p. 143.

4 Denzler-Fabricius, *Die Kirchen*, p. 153.

charges. Its racist ideology could just as well have been grounded on traditional antisemitism.[5] And not only was there nothing innovative in this propaganda. It should be clarified emphatically that there was an affinity between traditional anti-Jewish Christian theories and secular antisemitism in general and Nazi antisemitism in particular. This affinity reflects the ideological continuity between Nazism and anti-Jewish Christian doctrines. It is true that Christians were not partners in racist ideology or in mass murder. But where antisemitism and anti-Jewish incitement are concerned, not only should the two ideologies be linked together, but — and this is even graver — one cannot understand the Nazi anti-Jewish viewpoint outside the Catholic-Christian context. Marcel Dubois, the Christian philosopher, has stated:

> While I consider it a distortion of fact to say that the Holocaust was the work of Christians — even though many of its perpetrators were *de facto* Christians — I admit that there is ample evidence that the centuries-old Christian anti-Judaism prepared the soil for modern antisemitism and the Holocaust.[6]

Prof. Jacob Katz, in his scholarly study on antisemitism, has underlined the old Christian motivations for the hatred of Jews:

> The key to the understanding of what happened in the nineteenth and twentieth centuries in Jewish-Gentile relations, including its catastrophic climax in the Holocaust is not to be found in the immediate past, but in the course of Jewish history, at least since its entanglement with the history of Christianity.[7]

What happened in this entanglement with Christianity? Here, I believe, we should stress the guilt of Christianity, of Catholicism and later Protestantism, in shaping and disseminating the everlasting prejudices against Jews. In his study *The Nature of Prejudice*, Gordon W. Allport defined prejudice as an antipathy based upon a faulty and inflexible generalization. It may be felt or expressed. It may be directed toward

5 Zwi Bacharach, *Racism — The Tool of Politics. From Monism Towards Nazism*, Jerusalem, 1985, p. 93.

6 Marcel Dubois, "The Challenge of the Holocaust and the History of Salvation," in: *Judaism and Christianity under the Impact of National Socialism* , Otto D. Kulka and Paul R. Mendes-Flohr, eds., Jerusalem, 1987, p. 512.

7 Jacob Katz, "Christian-Jewish Antagonism on the Eve of the Modern Era," in: Kulka and Mendes-Flohr, *Judaism and Christianity,* p. 34.

a group as a whole, or toward an individual because he is a member of that group.[8]

In Christian-Jewish relations there developed during the course of history an anti-Jewish prejudice that led from verbal aggression to violence, from rumor to riot, from gossip to genocide. When dealing with Hitler's antisemitism we should not oversee this vital component. The mass murder of the Jews, the Nazi atrocities — as an unprecedented crime — have, naturally, attracted the interest of historical research, but research did not focus enough on Christian responsibility.

Catholicism shaped the image, the concept of a degraded wicked Jew. The very existence of Jews was a nuisance to Christians. The degradation of the Jew on grounds of theology paved the way for future persecutions and discrimination of the Jew among the nations. Actually, it shaped the background for the deep-rooted prejudice against the Jew in world history. The Jew was identified with the absolute Evil that rose against the absolute Good. No compromise is possible, the choice is final. The prejudice of the malicious Jew in person came into existence. The meaning of this process lies in its emphasizing the momentum of Jewish might and power. The one who is capable of crucifying God or God's son can only be an evil and mighty power — the diabolic Jew. It is exactly the nature of every prejudice: to judge somebody according to assumptions, impressions and images instead of relying on proven facts. The effectiveness of prejudice becomes a threat when it is accepted by a majority, no matter if that majority is composed of Christians or anti-Christian antisemites. Once accepted in public, the distinction between imagined concept and real fact is blurred. The total negation of the Jew and his Jewishness destined his place in the history of mankind as the anti- type.

Long before the rise of the Nazis, the harsh and hostile pronouncements of the church prepared German public opinion — from all strata of society — to absorb anti-Jewish slander and to identify with it. Hitler himself noted the connection between Catholic antisemitism and his policies towards the Jews:

> I have been attacked for my treatment of the Jewish question. For 1500 years, the Catholic church regarded the Jews as pests (*Schaedlinge*), and dispatched them

8 Gordon Allport, *The Nature of Prejudice*, New York, 1958, p. 10.

> to ghettoes, etc. They then recognized what the Jews were. Under liberalism this danger was not yet acknowledged. I am returning to the deeds of that period 1.500 years ago ... Perhaps I am doing Christianity the greatest service.[9]

I do not know whether the church, for its part, considered Hitler's deeds to be "the greatest service." It may be assumed that it deplored the acts of genocide he committed against the Jews. But Hitler was operating on ground prepared for him by the church, and harvesting what Catholicism had sown. This is not to say that Hitler considered himself to be carrying out the church's policies.[10] He abhorred its teachings, which he perceived as the total opposite of Nazi ideology. It was not the doctrines of the church but its organization that he admired, and he was ready to emulate its tactics in his war on the Jews. He himself attested to the fact that he adopted those ideas and methods which were useful for the implementation of his policies. "We absorbed our ideas from every twig and branch on the road of life, and we no longer know the origins of these ideas."[11] On his future plans, and to what extent he intended to learn from the church, he said:

> What can we ourselves do? Precisely what the church did when it forced its faith on the pagans: we will preserve what can be preserved, but will change the meaning. We will march backward: Easter is no longer the festival of the resurrection, but the eternal renewal of our nation. Christmas is the birth of our savior and this is the spirit of courage and liberty of our own nation. ... The Catholic church is indeed a great institution. What organization! It has survived for two thousand years, and we must learn from it. ... The church did not content itself with the image of Satan; it felt the need to translate it into a tangible enemy ... the Jew ... it is easier to fight him as flesh and blood that as an invisible demon.[12]

9 Hans Müller, *Katholische Kirche und Nationalsozialismus*, Munich, 1965, p. 129.

10 Despite his basic objections to Catholic dogmas and his proclaimed abhorrence of Christianity, one cannot ignore the fact that Hitler was a Catholic, remained such and never left the church. Moreover, despite his persecutions of churchmen, he was never excommunicated. Friedrich Heer calls Hitler "an atheist Catholic," See: Friedrich Heer, *Gottes Erste Liebe. Die Juden im Spannungsfeld der Geschichte*, Munich, 1986, p. 383ff.

11 Hermann Rauschning, *Hitler Speaks*, London, 1940, p. 45.

12 Rauschning, *Hitler Speaks*, pp. 58, 60, 234; Werner Jochmann, *Adolf Hitler. Monologe im Führer-Hauptquartier 1941–1944. Die Aufzeichnungen Heinrich Heims*, Hamburg, 1980, p. 321.

Thus Nazism learned a lesson in tactics from the church but with the intention of altering the objective of the struggle.

There is a general tendency in certain circles to differentiate between the anti-clericalism which characterized racist-nationalist circles and Nazi ideology, and traditional Christian antisemitism. The conclusion is that because of the contrast between them they cannot be compared. It is more valid to say that "the Aryan-Semitic conflict is not a denial of the Christian-Jewish conflict but rather presumes its prior existence and absorbs it." Voelkisch circles in Germany were anti-ecclesiastical rather than anti-Christian. Anti-Jewish prejudices stemmed from the Christian heritage and remain imprinted on the public consciousness. The drift away from the ecclesiastical organization and establishment as a result of modern trends does not necessarily imply departure from Christian elements.[13] In this context, one cannot ignore the link between theological antisemitism and Nazi antisemitism, and Christianity cannot evade its responsibility for the existence of the interrelation between them.[14] In 1963, Cardinal Bea put his case bluntly:

> The things which are being revived ... are rendered particularly acute by the cruel slaughter of millions of Jews by the Nazi regime, and it is not within our authority to give exact figures. Special attention should be paid to this issue by the Second Vatican Council ... This activity was accompanied by strong and highly effective propaganda; all this was made possible because this propaganda swept up believing Catholics, who were influenced by arguments originating in the New Testament and the annals of the church.[15]

In 1964, at the Second Vatican Council, one of the participants, Bishop Elchinger of Strasbourg, speaking of church sermons, admitted:

> ...that we cannot deny the fact that not only in our own century, but also in previous ones, crimes were committed against the Jews by sons of the church, and often falsely in the name of the church. ... and we also cannot deny that to the present day errors have often crept into sermons and catechestic literature, which are in contravention of the spirit of the New Testament.[16]

13 Hermann Greive, *Theologie und Ideologie. Katholizismus und Judentum in Deutschland und Oesterreich, 1918–1935*, Heidelberg, 1969, p. 16; Tal, *Christians and Jews*, p. 82 n. 105.

14 Günter Lewy, *The Catholic Church and Nazi Germany*, New York, 1964, p. 269.

15 *Freiburger Rundbrief*, XV (January 1964), No. 57/60, p. 79.

16 J. Hoefer and K. Rahner, eds., *Lexikon für Theologie und Kirche*, Freiburg, 1957, vol. II, p. 445.

Raul Hilberg, in his important book *The Destruction of European Jews*, sought to examine the bureaucratic apparatus that the Nazis employed in order to execute their murderous plans. At the beginning of his work, he drew a comparison between the ecclesiastical bureaucracy which had operated for centuries, and the apparatus put into action by the Nazis. He justified this comparison with the following words:

> If precedents have already been formed, if a guide has already been constructed, invention is no longer a necessity. The German bureaucracy could draw upon such precedents and follow such a guide, for the German bureaucrats could dip into a vast reservoir which church and state had filled in fifteen hundred years of destructive activity.[17]

In the sphere of antisemitic ideology, the Nazis were again able to draw on a reservoir of traditional hatred, which freed them from the need to invent hatred anew and enabled them to follow in the footsteps of others while aspiring to different objectives. The Catholic ideological precedent, like the bureaucratic precedent, constituted a basis for comparison which enables us to understand the readiness of the German public to absorb Nazi antisemitism.

Let us now examine some of the similarities. Taking the Nazi attitude towards the ancient classical world for example, one discovers that it was envisaged as a world of perfect, of total perfection, whose aesthetic value far surpassed that of the spiritual worlds of both Judaism and Christianity. Hitler believed the pagan nations in the classical world to have been tolerant, because they did not worship one universal god as did Judaism and Christianity. This demonstrates the inferiority of the Jew to the Greek and Roman.[18] Catholicism takes the opposite view. Paganism arrived at monotheistic belief through Judaism, but achieved perfection only when it accepted Christianity. The Jews were culturally superior to the pagans, but in their turn yielded place to the Christians who were superior to them. For Hitler, the Jew was less than the pagan; for the Catholic, Judaism was inferior to Christianity. One way or another, the Jew is always inferior.[19]

17 Raul Hilberg, *The Destruction of the European Jews*, Chicago, 1967, p. 4.

18 Werner Jochmann, *Adolf Hitler*, pp. 96, 97.

19 The devaluation of the Jews became a dominant component in the eyes of Christian believers.

The Nazi theory strove to prove that Jews were inherently corrupt, and, in doing so, employed methodology similar to that of the German Catholic catechism.[20] In the 1920s Nazi nationalist literature describes "the secret of Judaism" as the heritage of the Old Testament. Verses such as, "For the soul of the flesh is in the blood, and therefore have I given it to you upon the altar to effect atonement for your souls, for the blood means: which one's soul maketh one atonement" (Leviticus 17, 11), and the sacrifice of Isaac, were distorted by the Nazis. As far as they were concerned, these events demonstrated the murderous inborn traits of the Jew since — thus they interpreted — non-Jewish sacrifices would be offered up in place of Isaac.[21] Hitler referred to the destructive character of the Jew. This description was common in nineteenth century sermons as well.[22] With Hitler, the theological accusation had now become racist and biological in character, and hence more absolute. In any event, the idea of the corrupt destructive Jew, the murderous sinner, was by no means unfamiliar to the general public, in all walks of life.

Additional, more fundamental motifs that are present in the Catholic catechism appear in new guise in Hitler's outlook. The idea of the chosen people was central to both ideologies. Christianity — both Catholic and Protestant — saw itself as the heir to the birthright of the Jewish people. It allotted the Jews the role of a superfluous, debased, and accursed people amidst the other nations of the world. Hitler adopted the idea of the invalidation of the Jewish people's status as chosen people, and his outlook, with its pagan manifestations, was based on it. "There cannot be two chosen peoples. We are God's people." A Catholic preacher declared: "The birthright has been revoked ... and handed over to the Catholics for we are now the chosen people."[23]

20 The praise lavished on the books of the Bible as the source of Christian morality has served as the pretext in modern times for the differentiation between the biblical Jew and the so-called corrupted and therefore despised modern Jew, the "Talmudic" Jew.

21 Hermann Greive, *Geschichte des Modernen Antisemitismus in Deutschland*, Darmstadt, 1983, p. 107; Jochmann, *Adolf Hitler*, p. 158.

22 Catholics abhorred the Reformist Jews, who emerged in the nineteenth century, because, as was claimed, they had distanced themselves from the messianic ideal.

23 Rauschning, *Hitler Speaks,* p. 238.

Hitler believed that there was a polarity between "the people of the Devil" and "the people of God." Sermons and catechestic literature also propounded the theme of the demonic nature of the Jews. For Hitler, the Jew was the antithesis of all that was human in contrast to the "Aryan", while Christian teaching confronted Satan with Jesus. Those who reject Jesus are fighting the forces of good, and are identified with evil, just as the enemy of the "Aryan" is, as Hitler said, "outside nature and alien to it."[24]

The catechism charged the Jews, inter alia, with materialism. Our research has shown, on the basis of sermons and homiletic literature, that the catechism deduced Jewish materialism from the legalistic tradition. According to this argument, strict adherence to the letter of the law had stifled all aesthetic spirit in the Jew.[25] Over the centuries, there grew the image of the "Mammon Jew," characterized by his covetous nature, worship of worldly things, and greedy exploitation of others. The literature on this theme is extensive and a few examples will suffice to illustrate it.[26] Hitler, as was his wont, absorbed the message and transformed it, in the spirit of Nazism, into an anti-Jewish diatribe: "The Jew Mordechai-Marx, being a good Jew, awaited the coming of the Messiah. He placed the messianic idea within the framework of historical materialism, assuming that worldly riches are a component in the almost endless process of evolution." And elsewhere,"the deification of money," "Jewish profit," "Jewish materialism" are common expressions. In his monologues, he announced: "The Americans ... when they receive gold in return for manual labor, store it in the cellar and assume that the world will follow this economic method, which originates in the Jewish spirit." "The Jew has no economic grasp, his thoughts are solely capitalistic." In general, Hitler often used the expression "moneyed Jewry"(*Finanzjudentum*).[27]

Jewish artistic creativity was also denounced. The Jewish ability to contribute to the arts was denied, since, it was claimed, Jews had

24 Christian sermons confronted Satan with Jews.

25 Jesus, the divine figure, took on the form of a man in order to reveal himself to the people, who were groaning under the yoke of law and *Mitzwot*, the Jewish legalistic tradition.

26 *Christlich-Soziale Blätter*, 1 (1872), p. 20; 12 (1875), p. 8.

27 Adolf Hitler, *Mein Kampf*, 10th edition, Munich, 1942, pp. 163, 212, 339, 702.

no aesthetic sense. These theories were grounded on the theological view of the Jews. Here again, a few examples can suffice to illustrate. Preachers declared that "the Jew has little interest in artistic and scientific aspirations." A Catholic journal cited Richard Wagner, who argued that it was impossible to conceive of a tragic hero or loving character being portrayed on stage by a Jew. If this were done, the audience would immediately sense the absurdity of the portrayal. The Catholic author admits that the Jews have nonetheless taken over the theaters, and are presenting Jewish operettas that violate the spirit of Christian morality. Jewish talent is best expressed in comedies, since this genre is suited to the Jewish temperament and character whose power lies in imitation and pretense. After all, it was argued, in everyday life as well, the Jew employs these skills to deceive and cheat, since "all their aspirations are theater. For the Jews life is a comedy, while for Christians it is a great tragedy." A local church periodical complains that the true sense of art (*echter Kunstsinn*), and true interest in science have been lost, since all has been devoured by Jewish materialism.[28] From the church sermons, this anti-Jewish motif evolved until it was rediscovered in anti-ecclesiastical and non-ecclesiastical literature. In his well-known essay "On the Jewish question," the Protestant Bruno Bauer expresses the opinion that the Jew lacks the flexibility and the liberal spirit required for artistic and scientific creativity. Ernest Renan, the nineteenth century French linguist and orientalist, also expressed emphatic views on the artistic sense of Jews. Writing of the "Semitic spirit," he claimed that the Semites lacked all creative imagination and were devoid of fictitious creativity. Their culture was identifiable by its negative characteristics: their works contain neither mythology, nor epics, nor science, nor fiction, nor philosophy, nor plastic arts. All these omissions stem, to his mind, from the Jewish-Semitic monotheistic conception.[29]

There is no evidence in favor of the theory that Hitler drew inspiration from the Catholic catechism or the writings of Bauer and Renan;

28 *Die Wahrheit*, p. 564.

29 Ernest Renan, *Histoire General et Systeme Comparee des Langues Semitiques*, Paris, 1800, pp. 11–12; 18.

nonetheless, his remarks echo the *Zeitgeist*.[30] His views on the artistic talents and aesthetic spirit of the Jews could have been copied from theories prevalent before his time. In *Mein Kampf*, we read:

> There was never a Jewish art, nor does it exist today. Judaism has made no original contribution whatsoever to the two queens of the arts — architecture and music. Its achievements in art ... are spiritual theft. The Jews lack those qualities which mark the creative and the cultural elements in gifted races ... The Jew is usually found in that art where the skill of self-invention is not evident — namely the art of the theater. Here, he is revealed, at most, as a mimic ... a pathetic comedian.

In his monologues, he declared: "I have always said that the Jews are the most foolish devils who exist. They have not a single true musician. They have no art, they have nothing. They are liars, forgers and cheats."[31]

From Catholic sermons and literature and from Hitler's statements, one can draw up a list of the negative characteristics attributed to the Jews. The list augurs the Holocaust to come. The central themes are focused on the nullification of the status of the Jews as the chosen people, their satanic character, intolerance, inferiority, corruption, thirst for blood, destructive character, materialism, worship of Mammon, greed, lack of aesthetic and artistic sense, mimicry, and cheating. We can but reiterate Hilberg's original statement in the context of the possible affinity between Nazi and Catholic ideologies: "Necessity is said to be mother of invention, but if precedents have already been formed, if a guide has already been constructed, invention is no longer a necessity."[32]

Hitler drew practical conclusions from the venomous denunciation of the Jews. There were no precedents for this genocide, and its occurrence may be regarded as the horrific innovation of Nazi antisemitism. And if indeed no precedent for the Holocaust can be found in Christian antisemitism, indirect sanction is implied in the sermons which nurtured public opinion. There it was said: "God did not wish this people —

30 Karl D. Bracher, *Die deutsche Diktatur. Entstehung, Struktur, Folgen des National-Sozialismus*, Berlin, 1966, p. 66: "Hitler never gave concrete information on the literature he read."

31 Hitler, *Mein Kampf*, p. 332; Jochmann, *Adolf Hitler*, p. 131.

32 Hilberg, *Destruction of the European Jews*, p. 4.

which deserved to be annihilated more than any other people — to be totally destroyed, in order that we should have living testimony of the truth of our holy religion."[33] The "true religion" was now faith in Nazism, which had no further need of living testimony provided by the humiliation of the Jew. "This people deserves to be annihilated," but not because of Catholic-Christian considerations. Through their annihilation, Hitler sought to achieve his final aim: the establishment of a new world order.

The terminology used by Catholic preachers and writers was permeated with images taken from death, from the demonic world, and from the insect kingdom, doomed to extermination. Hitler readily absorbed these ideas. He himself attested that "for one thousand five hundred years the Catholic church considered the Jews to be pests."[34] It is easy to imagine the force of the impact on the imagination and spirit of unlearned people and even educated believers, when they heard such descriptions as the following: "They (the Jews), were truly revealed to be cunning serpents, who, from their place of concealment, stung with their fatal venom; the descendants of their forefathers are a nest of vipers."[35] This identification of the Jew with demonic forces, with the Devil, is the expression of a latent wish, an unspoken desire to bring about the death of the Jew. Since, as the proverb says: "In the battle against Satan, all means are justified."[36]

From the Middle Ages on, the church disseminated anti-Jewish propaganda, focusing on the motif of the demonic Jew, who is the Devil's partner, and his struggle against Jesus. A scholar who devoted a special study to the medieval Christian conception of the Jew and the Devil, wrote, inter alia, that the church inculcated in its flock the belief "that his followers must destroy the agents of the Devil ... Christianity was summoned to a holy war of extermination, of which the Jews were only incidentally the objects. It was Satan whom Christian Europe sought to crush."[37]

33 Joseph Deharbe, *Hilfsbuch für den Katechetischen Unterricht in der Schule und in der Kirche*, Paderborn, 1869, Vol. 4, p. 150.

34 Müller, *Katholische Kirche,* p. 129.

35 Georg Patiss, Kurze Homelien, Insbruck, 1882, p. 696.

36 Heer, *Gottes Erste Liebe*, p. 338.

37 Joshua Trachtenberg, *The Devil and the Jews. The Medieval Conception of the Jew and its Relation to Modern Antisemitism*, New York, 1966, p. 21f.

This tradition of demonization and dehumanization of the Jew is ever present in the sermons delivered by priests to their congregations. Hitler translated the following declaration (from a sermon), into the language of action, with the passive and active cooperation of numerous Christians:

> This satanic generation was not destroyed when the Old Testament was forced to yield place to the New Testament; this hell's spawn (*Ausgeburt der Hoelle)* still lives ... It sneaked from the Old Testament into the New, and spreads like poisonous weeds which cannot be eradicated within the Christian community.[38]

Nazi propaganda films tried to present a visual image of the despised Jew. In the notorious *Der Ewige Jude*, a parallel is drawn between the Jews, crowding together, and a flock of rats darting about among sacks of flour. The associative intention is clear, and one might be excused for thinking that only the Nazi mind could have invented so perverted a comparison. But these images are to be found in nineteenth century Catholic writings as well. In one source, we find the statement that in order to understand the true meaning of a certain liberal article, one should translate each term into the opposite meaning. The following example is given: "In the language of the great stock exchange, a priest equals a rat. But the opposite of the priest is the Jew. Hence — Jew equals rat."[39]

One might ask what difference there is between the language of the churchmen and that of Hitler? Poisonous serpents, vipers, hell's-spawn and rats are transformed in Hitler's lexicon into vampires, germs, bloodsuckers, parasites.[40] It has been said regarding Hitler's assertions that "the language indicates the method" (*Und so legte schon die Sprache die Methoden nahe*). This remark is valid to the same extent for Catholic manifestations and the statements of anti-Christian German nationalists in the nineteenth century. The words of Paul de Lagarde may be regarded as the link between Christian hatred of Jews and Nazi antisemitism. He attacks those who are too cowardly to "...trample the spreading insects ... one cannot negotiate with tapeworms and

38 *Philothea. Blätter für religiöse Belehrung und Erbauung durch Predigten*, Jhrg. 15, (Würzburg 1851), p. 394.

39 *Miscellen der Deutschen Landeszeitung — Die Sittenlehre des Talmud und der zerstoerende Einfluss des Judenthums im Deutschen Reich* (3. Aufl. 1876), p. 178.

40 Hitler, *Mein Kampf*, pp. 331, 334

germs, nor can they be educated. They must be stamped out as soon as possible." The manifesto of the Association of Antisemitic Parties, published in Hamburg in 1899, contains a clear allusion to the extermination of the Jewish people: "Since the Jewish question, in the course of the twentieth century, will become a world problem, it must be solved finally (*endgültig*), by the removal of the Jews. ... and in the end by the extermination of the Jewish people."[41]

Yet another parallel may be drawn. The Nazi leaders, including Hitler himself, tried to justify the murder of Jews on grounds of self-defense. The argument was that if the Germans did not rise up at once and eradicate the Jewish people, the Jews would turn on the Germans and destroy them. A Catholic periodical presented this idea in Christian guise: "Both the Book of the *Zohar* and the *Shulkhan Arukh* exhort the Jew explicitly to destroy Christians (*die Christen auszurotten*), and they perceive the advent of the Messiah as dependent on the extermination of the Christians." The fear of Jewish domination of Christians is also implicit in the statements quoted above.[42] The Jews, "like poisonous weeds, which cannot be eradicated" are depicted as a negative force threatening Christianity. In present-day Germany, a bitter debate is raging on revisionism of the understanding of the history of the Third Reich. Prominent among the revisionists is the well-known historian Ernst Nolte. The "defensive" element is central to his strange arguments. Nolte does not claim that the murder of the Jews was justified on grounds of self-defense against the Jewish threat, but, to his mind, it was permissible for Hitler to incarcerate the German Jews as prisoners of war, since Chaim Weizmann had declared in 1939 that the Jews intended to fight on the allied side. Even stranger is his statement, which is ostensibly related to the theme of the present study:

> Auschwitz is not *essentially* the outcome of traditional antisemitism [Italics mine Z.B], and was not in essence mere 'genocide.' What we have here is a reaction

41 Paul de Lagarde, *Ausgewählte Schriften*, Munich, 1924, p. 209. On Lagarde's remarks see: Fritz Stern, *The Politics of Cultural Despair. A Study in the Rise of German Ideology*, New York, 1965, p. 93. Nor did the National Socialists forget this prophecy. In 1944, when they were carrying out their policy of extermination, an anthology of Lagarde's work was distributed by the army, and contained Lagarde's demand for murder.

42 *Philothea. Blätter für religiöse Belehrung und Erbauung durch Predigten* (see note 38).

> born out of fear at the destructive processes of the Russian revolution. This copy was far more irrational than the preceding original (since it would be a delusion to believe that 'the Jews' ever intended to destroy the German bourgeoisie or the German people), and it is hard to attribute to them so distorted an ethos. The copy was worse than the original because it perpetrated the destruction of human beings in almost industrial fashion ... This explains the singular quality, but does not change the fact that what was known as the extermination of the Jews in the Third Reich was but a reaction or distorted copy, and was neither a primary nor an original act.

Nolte sees no continuity between traditional antisemitism and the Nazi horrors, and explains the murder of the Jews as a response and a copy of the Russian atrocities. We are not concerned here with the debate as such. But it is important to indicate the trend to liberate hatred of Jews from its traditional roots and sources, and to explain it by considerations of self-defense which have nothing to do with the Jews themselves. Such revisionism, whatever its reasons, not only distorts the historical truth of the annals of the Holocaust, but also twists and distorts the history of the development of antisemitism from ancient Christianity through the policies of the church and its dissemination of its catechism, to Hitler's death camps.[43] The connection between the Catholic attitude towards Judaism and the Jews and Nazi anti-Jewish policy is a tragic one. James Parkes has pointed it out from a universal viewpoint, and his remarks enhance understanding of the German aspect of the problem:

> That which changed the normal pattern of Jewish-Gentile relations was the action of the Christian church. The statement is tragic but the evidence is inescapable. What is still more tragic is that there is no break in the line which leads from the beginning of the denigration of Judaism in the formative period of Christian history, from the exclusion of Jews from civic equality in the period of the Church's first triumph in the fourth century, through the horrors of the Middle Ages, to the death camps of Hitler in our own day.[44]

And indeed, under Hitler's tyranny, the cross collapsed, yielding place to the swastika.

43 Hitler, *Mein Kampf*, p. 702. Rudolf Hoess, *Kommandant in Auschwitz,* Munich, 1978, p. 157; *Historikerstreit. Die Dokumentation der Kontroverse um die Einzigartigkeit der nationalsozialistischen Judenvernichtung*, Munich, 1987, pp. 24, 32f.

44 James Parkes, *Antisemitism*, London, 1963, p. 60.

"The Jewish Problem Becomes a Christian Problem"

German Protestants and the Persecution of the Jews in the Third Reich

URSULA BÜTTNER

I

In recent years, the attitude of German Protestants towards the persecution of Jews during the Third Reich has aroused considerable interest — in research, the media, and within the church. This was not always the case. For several decades after 1945, research on the history of the churches during the National Socialist period concentrated on the *Kirchenkampf* (Church Struggle). Much of this research was undertaken by theologians who had been involved in those conflicts, and they were still mainly concerned with the then-prevailing controversies regarding the rights and obligations of the church in a totalitarian dictatorship.[1] The persecution of the Jews was not considered. These eyewitnesses, almost all of them belonging to the *Bekennende Kirche* (Confessional Church), had no doubts about the distribution of guilt. The *Deutsche Christen* (German Christians) had supported the Nazi policy against the Jews and also made strenuous efforts to expel congregants of Jewish origin from the church. The Confessional Church, on the other hand, was regarded as having opposed these violations of Jewish rights. The first scholarly correction of this euphemistic picture was a doctoral

1 Martin Greschat, "Die Bedeutung der Sozialgeschichte für die Kirchengeschichte. Theoretische und praktische Erwägungen," *Historische Zeitschrift*, 256 (1993), pp. 97–103; Carsten Nicolaisen, "Zwischen Theologie und Geschichte. Zur 'Kirchlichen Zeitgeschichte' heute," *Der evangelische Erzieher*, 42 (1990), pp. 410–419.

thesis that was completed in 1970 but was not accepted for publication in Germany until 17 years later.[2] Its new findings were first recognized and published in England.[3] In the meantime, the results of this new approach have been confirmed by other research and supplemented by additional information.

The question how the German churches behaved with respect to the Nazi persecution of Jews has gained new importance following the challenge of Daniel Jonah Goldhagen's provocative book.[4] In reaction to a school of research which concentrates so heavily on socioeconomic structures that intellectual and ideological developments tend to be overlooked, Goldhagen makes antisemitism the central factor in his explanation of the Holocaust. In his opinion the Christian churches played a decisive role in the emergence and consolidation of anti-Jewish traditions in Germany. With his one-sided argument and its exaggerated emphasis, however, he is in danger of reverting to the old simplistic thesis that the German murderers of the Jews stood in a long line of continuity going back to Luther. Unsatisfactory as this explanation may be, it should not simply be rejected as outdated as many of his opponents have done. Instead, it is necessary to reexamine thoroughly the role and spread of antisemitism in German society and to reconsider the attitude of the churches towards the persecution and murder of Jews, especially since by 1933 ninety-five percent of the German population were members of Christian churches.

The state of affairs within the German Protestant Church was particularly difficult. Germany's defeat in World War I and the 1918 German revolution had led to a deep sense of insecurity among many Protestants who suddenly felt thrown into a dangerous unknown world. They had to find a new way of organizing their church and, even more pressing, cope with the blow to their theology and ideology. Having prayed so long and so fervently for the success of the "just

2 Wolfgang Gerlach, *Als die Zeugen schwiegen. Bekennende Kirche und die Juden*, Berlin, 1987; Ph. D. thesis, Hamburg 1970; distributed as typoscript under the title *Zwischen Kreuz und Davidstern. Bekennende Kirche in ihrer Stellung zum Judentum im Dritten Reich*, Hamburg, 1972.

3 Richard Gutteridge, *Open Thy Mouth for the Dumb! The German Evangelical Church and the Jews 1879–1950*, Oxford, 1976.

4 Daniel Jonah Goldhagen, *Hitler's Willing Executioners. Ordinary Germans and the Holocaust*, New York, 1996.

German cause" and having been assured over the years by their pastors that God would reward their sacrifices by granting victory to Germany, they were bewildered by the unexpected defeat in 1918. Only small groups of young academics, influenced by Karl Barth,[5] managed to make a fresh start. They concluded from these experiences that in future all historically based theological speculations should be rejected and that the Bible was to be accepted as the one and only source of divine revelation. The great majority of German Protestants, however, tried to find another way out. For them the destruction of the German Empire meant that no longer was it the nation or state that could be regarded as divinely protected but the *Volk*. Popularized by the writings of Wilhelm Stapel,[6] this *Volkstumstheologie* gained considerable influence. Like marriage and family, the *Volk* was now considered a *Schöpfungsordnung Gottes* (order of divine creation). From there it was only one step towards claiming this quality for "race" as well.

With the downfall of the monarchy German Protestants had lost not only the rulers of their various states but also the heads of their churches.[7] Although the privileges enjoyed by the churches were guaranteed in the democratic constitution, only a few saw the new situation as a liberation from the chains of state patronage. The majority feared that without the accustomed support of the *Obrigkeit* (authorities) they would not be able to hold their own against the antireligious and anti-ecclesiastical ideology of liberalism and socialism. They regarded democracy and universal suffrage as a danger. Against these threats Adolf Stoecker, a court chaplain and the Protestants' most influential spokesman in imperial Germany, had already used antisemitism as a

5 There is a huge literature on Karl Barth and his theology, cf. the bibliography in the newly published book: Eberhard Busch, *Unter dem Bogen des einen Bundes. Karl Barth und die Juden 1933–1945*, Neukirchen, 1996.

6 Wolfgang Tilgner, *Volksnomostheologie und Schöpfungsglaube*, Göttingen, 1966.

7 Jonathan R. C. Wright, *"Über den Parteien." Die politische Haltung der evangelischen Kirchenführer 1918–1933*, Göttingen, 1977; Jochen Jacke, *Kirche zwischen Monarchie und Republik. Der preussische Protestantismus nach dem Zusammenbruch von 1918*, Hamburg, 1976; Kurt Nowak, *Evangelische Kirche und Weimarer Republik. Zum politischen Weg des deutschen Protestantismus zwischen 1918 und 1932*, Weimar, 1981.

weapon.[8] Mainly through his efforts, political antisemitism had infiltrated into the German Protestant church, transforming and strengthening traditional Christian anti-Judaism. Many church leaders during the Weimar Republic and the National Socialist period were substantially influenced by Stoecker. Like him they wished for a strong national church, but the twenty-eight regional churches (*Landeskirchen*), which were only loosely joined in a church league (*Kirchenbund*), were far removed from this.

Thus, National Socialism held considerable appeal for a large number of German Protestants, promising to foster a "positive Christianity" (*positives Christentum*) and to provide favorable conditions within a strong state for the foundation of a uniform Protestant Reich church.[9] It follows that Hitler's coming to power was generally welcomed within the Protestant church. In the church elections in July 1933, German Christians with the help of the *NSDAP* won an overwhelming victory in the new unified Reich Church (*Reichskirche*) and in most regional churches. But still relations remained complicated.[10] Out of protest against the ecclesiastical, political and theological efforts of the German Christians, the Confessional Church was born. Both directions fell into different groups, and a third direction the *Mitte* (center) emerged which tried to provide an equilibrium with the state. The "center" included among others the three big Lutheran churches of Hanover, Bavaria and Württemberg, which were designated as "intact," i.e., not controlled by the German Christians. The differences and conflicts existed even in individual congregations. Also, the government's church policy continued to oscillate between oppression, efforts at pacifying, and

8 Günter Brakelmann, Martin Greschat and Werner Jochmann, *Protestantismus und Politik. Werk und Wirkung Adolf Stoeckers*, Hamburg, 1982.

9 Klaus Scholder, *Die Kirchen und das Dritte Reich*, Frankfurt am Main, 1977; Werner Jochmann, "Antijüdische Traditionen im deutschen Protestantismus und nationalsozialistische Judenverfolgung," in: Werner Jochmann, *Gesellschaftskrise und Judenfeindschaft in Deutschland 1870–1945*, Hamburg, 1988, pp. 265–281.

10 Georg Denzler and Volker Fabricius, *Christen und Nationalsozialismus*, Frankfurt am Main, 1993; Kurt Meier, *Der evangelische Kirchenkampf. Gesamtdarstellung in drei Bänden*, Göttingen, 1976, 1984; Kurt Meier, *Kreuz und Hakenkreuz. Die evangelische Kirche im Dritten Reich*, Munich, 1992; Kurt Meier, *Die Deutschen Christen. Das Bild einer Bewegung im Kirchenkampf des Dritten Reiches*, Göttingen, 1964.

disinterest,[11] with the result that the course of the church leaders swayed correspondingly.

The same diversity characterized the attitude of the German Protestant church towards the Nazi persecution of the Jews. Nevertheless, particularly with regard to this question, the different groups had more in common than they would have admitted. Since the German Christians generally advocated a vicious antisemitism, the National Socialist anti-Jewish policies met with their full approval at all phases. Like the state, they wanted to rid the church of all "Jews", i.e. of all Christians of Jewish origin as well as "non-Aryans." The Confessional Church rejected these demands; indeed their opposition to these "heretic" efforts was an important reason for its foundation. Resentment of the Jews was more moderate among its members, but certainly not absent.

There were theological and political reasons for this. From the very beginning Christians had set out their own doctrine in contrast and opposition to Judaism, and this in turn determined Christian attitudes to Jews. Thus, according to this tradition, the Jews' rejection of Jesus as the Messiah had cost them their privileged status. The distinction of a "chosen people" granted by God to the Jews had been transferred to the Christians; the old covenant had been substituted by a new one, this time with the Christians. For the Jews, the history of salvation had come to an end; for the Christians, post-biblical Jewry was therefore of no further interest. At best their fate of being in exile served as a warning example of divine judgement. This dismissal of the Jews created the conditions in which political, socioculturally founded antisemitism could take root.

The large majority of the Protestant theologians shared the antipathy against Jews that was common among their stratum — the conservative, educated middle class.[12] Three examples serve to illustrate this — in the realm of theological science, church leadership and church bureaucracy. In 1923, at the peak of the social and political crisis caused

11 John S. Conway, *Die nationalsozialistische Kirchenpolitik 1933–1945. Ihre Ziele, Widersprüche und Fehlschläge*, Munich, 1969.

12 Martin Greschat, "Die Haltung der deutschen evangelischen Kirchen zur Verfolgung der Juden im Dritten Reich," in: *Die Deutschen und die Judenverfolgung im Dritten Reich*, Ursula Büttner, ed., Hamburg 1992, pp. 273–292; Jochmann, "Antijüdische Traditionen."

by hyperinflation, Berlin University professor Reinhold Seeberg voiced his concern for European intellectual culture. In a brochure he described Jewry as "an international power, as a subversive direction of thought." To fight against the Jews was a duty "for everyone who intends to preserve German ways and traditions and the Christian religion for our people."[13]

Hans Meiser, who was to be bishop of Bavaria from 1933 to 1955, wrote a series of articles in 1926 explaining why the Germans had to defend themselves against the undermining power of the Jews in the economy, in politics and in culture.

> Those who are aware of the egalitarian, leveling Jewish intellect, which, excessive and even lascivious as it is, is destroying the moral fundaments of our people, can appreciate the threat looming over its future, if this intellect went on spreading among German society. Against this Jewish corruption of our people we cannot fight vigorously enough. [...] God has not given every people its specific *völkisch* character and its racial peculiarities to have it dissolved in worthless racial mixtures. Our *Volkstum* is a talent [unit of ancient money] entrusted to us by God for which we once shall have to give account on Doomsday.[14]

The fateful consequences of the *Volkstumstheologie* are apparent in these statements.

The third example involves senior officials of the church league and the largest regional church, that of the Old Prussian Union. In

13 Reinhold Seeberg, *Zum Verständnis der gegenwärtigen Krisis in der europäischen Geisteskultur*, Leipzig, 1923, pp. 102f. Seeberg described Judaism as *"eine internationale Macht, eine zersetzende geistige Richtung. Sie zu bekämpfen, sei für jeden Pflicht, [...]der deutsche Art und Sitte und christliche Religion unserem Volke erhalten will."*

14 Eberhard Röhm and Jörg Thierfelder, *Juden-Christen-Deutsche*, Stuttgart, 1990, vol. 1: 1933–1935, pp. 350–362, quotations pp. 357f. *"Wer den alles nivellierenden, die sittlichen Grundlagen unseres Volkstums zersetzenden, bis zur Laszivität ausschweifenden jüdischen Geist kennt, [...] der kann sich ein Bild davon machen, was unserem Volk drohte, wenn dieser Geist noch weiter als bisher schon um sich griffe [...]. Gegen diese Art der 'Verjudung' unseres Volks können wir nicht energisch genug ankämpfen. [...] Gott hat jedem Volk seine völkische Eigenart und seine rassischen Besonderheiten doch nicht dazu gegeben, damit es seine völkische Prägung in rassisch unterwertige Mischlingsbildungen auflösen lässt. Auch unser Volkstum ist ein anvertrautes Pfund, mit dem wir wuchern sollen, und für das wir einst Rechenschaft schuldig sind."*

July 1932 a delegation of American Christians visited Berlin to assess the situation of the Jews in Germany and, in particular, "the attitude of the Hitler movement towards Jewry." Dr. Jeremias told them that "National Socialism had many aspects to be welcomed by the Church" (*vom kirchlichen Standpunkt aus viel Begrüssenswertes habe*). The Church was "conscious of its mission towards the Jews, but it was no less conscious of its duty towards its own people which it had to protect against the notoriously harmful Jewish influence." *Oberkirchenrat* D. Schreiber added traditional antisemitic allegations about the extraordinary power of the Jews in the money market and public life. The Jews, he said, had used the war to secure unjust advantages for themselves and had afterwards played a leading role in the German revolution. "Admittedly the pamphlet *Protocols of the Elders of Zion* published in 1920, had been a fake, but it had nevertheless correctly denoted the Jewish striving for power."[15]

In view of such convictions it is not surprising that in the campaign for the Prussian Church elections in autumn 1932, the German Christians were not discouraged from using a platform containing passages like the following:

> We regard race, *Volkstum* and nation as divinely created orders of life entrusted to us by God. To maintain these orders is divine law. Mixing the races, therefore, has to be prevented. We reject the mission among the Jews in Germany as long as they own German citizenship and because of these rights the danger of camouflaging the race and creating bastards exists.[16]

One-third of the voters supported this platform. However, they were not

15 Minutes of 15 July 1932, Evangelisches Zentralarchiv (EZA), Berlin: 1/C3/170, vol. 1a. Jeremias: *Die Kirche sei "sich ihrer Missionspflicht dem Judentum gegenüber bewusst, ebenso aber auch ihrer Pflicht gegen das eigene Volk, das sie gegen schädliche Einflüsse, die notorisch vom Judentum ausgehen, [...] schützen müsse."* Schreiber: *"Die 1920 erschienene Schrift 'Geheimnisse der Weisen aus Zion' sei zwar eine Fälschung gewesen, hätte aber die jüdischen Herrschaftstendenzen richtig gekennzeichnet."*

16 Röhm and Thierfelder, *Juden-Christen-Deutsche*, vol. 1, p. 70. *"Wir sehen in Rasse, Volkstum und Nation uns von Gott geschenkte und anvertraute Lebensordnungen, für deren Erhaltung zu sorgen uns Gottes Gesetz ist. Daher ist der Rassenvermischung entgegenzutreten. [...] Wir lehnen die Judenmission in Deutschland ab, solange die Juden das Staatsbürgerrecht besitzen und damit die Gefahr der Rassenverschleierung und Bastardierung besteht."*

the only ones who believed in the necessity of fighting the Jews. Many of those who preferred another list of candidates shared that opinion. With the utterances made by leading theologians and in particular the Sunday papers that were distributed in the millions, Protestants in Germany had become accustomed to antisemitic statements.[17] Hence it was neither the victory of the German Christians in the church elections of 1933 nor the pressure of the National Socialist state that determined the attitude of the Protestant Church towards the persecution of Jews; the course had been set long before.

II

This was apparent during the first months of the Third Reich. The Church officials, all of whom had been appointed during the Weimar Republic and were still in office, saw no reason for the Protestant Church to protest or even reconsider their attitude towards the new regime following the serious attacks of violence against Jews in March 1933. On the contrary, in a radio speech broadcasted to America, the General Superintendant of the *Kurmark*, Otto Dibelius, justified and played down the state-organized boycott of Jewish businesses on 1 April, claiming that this act of resistance against the anti-German campaign of foreign Jews had "taken place in an absolute calm and orderly way." By removing Jews from the civil service and law courts, he asserted, the government had no other aim but to return to earlier conditions. What was happening in Germany, he added, would lead to a situation "which all who love and honor the German way of life will be grateful for," and it will "be for the best of the world."[18]

Dibelius was not a man who willingly submitted to the new political regime. A short time later he became a leading member of the

17 Ino Arndt, *Die Judenfrage im Lichte der evangelischen Sonntagsblätter von 1918–1938*, Ph. D. thesis, Tübingen, 1968.

18 I am grateful to Professor Werner Jochmann for a complete copy of the speech. Extracts are printed in Gerlach, *Zwischen Kreuz und Davidstern*, p. 40 and quoted in Scholder, *Kirchen*, pp. 340f.: *"Sie werden es erleben, dass das, was jetzt in Deutschland vor sich geht, zu einem Ziele führen wird, für das jeder dankbar sein kann, der deutsches Wesen liebt und ehrt. Und dass es nicht nur Deutschland, sondern der Welt zum Besten dienen wird."*

Confessional Church and was dismissed from his office because of his defence of the church against state pressure. Nonetheless, he was, as he had written to his pastors in 1928, an antisemite, convinced "that the Jews played a leading role in the destructive appearances in modern civilization."[19]

However, there were other Protestants, laymen as well as clergymen, who believed it was the obligation of the church to condemn the persecution of Jews. A pastor in Frankfurt, Rudolf Wintermann, even publicly appealed to the church authorities to protest against the maltreatment of German Jews. In a newspaper article published in Easter 1933, he stated that "the Jewish problem has become a Christian problem in that it challenges the genuineness and seriousness of our Christianity."[20]

During the early months of the Third Reich many appeals were made to church leaders to condemn the anti-Jewish policy. These came both from lay people who held no particular church office[21] as well as from prominent members of the church community: for example, representatives of the Protestant Women's Associations,[22] the Regional *Kirchenamt* Kassel,[23] and Wilhelm Freiherr von Pechmann, former President of the *Deutscher Evangelischer Kirchentag* (German Protestant Church Assembly).[24] But their efforts were in vain. Although more sensitive to the distress of Jews than most, they were but a powerless minority within the German Protestant church.

19 Circular letter no. 2, 3 April 1928 (EZA: 50/R19). Dibelius thought that *"bei allen zersetzenden Erscheinungen der modernen Zivilisation das Judentum eine führende Rolle spielt."* He repeated his statement literally in his Easter circular letter 1933, quoted by Gerlach, *Zwischen Kreuz und Davidstern*, p. 28.

20 "Die Judenfrage und das Christentum. Ein Osterwort," *Frankfurter Zeitung*, 16 April 1933: *"Die Judenfrage wird zur Christenfrage, d.h. zu der Frage nach der Echtheit und dem Ernst unseres Christentums."*

21 Some letters of protest are printed in Röhm and Thierfelder, *Juden-Christen-Deutsche* vol. 1, p. 364–368 and in Hans-Joachim Fliedner, ed., *Die Judenverfolgung in Mannheim 1933–1945. Dokumente*, Stuttgart, 1971, pp. 355–357.

22 Marikje Smid, *Deutscher Protestantismus und Judentum 1932/1933*, Munich, 1990, p. 328.

23 Letter of the Regional *Kirchenamt* Kassel of 5 May 1933, quoted by Gerlach, *Zeugen*, pp. 46f. The regional church office at Kassel dealt in particular with the distress of Christians of Jewish origin as they had no representation; it also expressed its concern over the persecution of the Jews.

24 Friedrich Wilhelm Kantzenbach, ed., *Widerstand und Solidarität der Christen in*

This became apparent on 26 April 1933 at a meeting of the Church Executive Committee (*Kirchenausschuss*), the highest executive body in the Protestant Church. Pechmann proposed a resolution that the church issue a public statement declaring that it not only reaffirms its solidarity with its members of Jewish origin, but also "asks for justice and Christian love for our Jewish national comrades" (*aber auch für unsere jüdischen Volksgenossen Gerechtigkeit und christliche Liebe verlangen*). Using the term *Volksgenossen* for Jews was an open challenge to Nazi ideology. Pechmann was given no support.[25] It is important to note that those who rejected his resolution had been elected during the Weimar Republic. The discussion following his proposal revealed the same prejudices and tactical considerations that would later define the attitude of church leaders towards the persecution of Jews. Several arguments were put forward: That "a terrible infiltration of some professions by alien elements" had taken place; that certain phrases of the proposed declaration, once taken out of context, could be used against the church; that in view of "the immense danger which the church at present found itself in, it was bound to silence;" that such a "declaration would be misused by Germany's foreign enemies against her;" that the church was not the appropriate institution to admonish the state, or even more clearly, that it was

> against the Christian faith to stop the secular sword from striking, in particular on a matter which was not of mere peripheral importance for the government, but was a central point of its platform. [...] For one thousand seven hundred years the Jews had been submitted to special discriminatory laws, with the full approval of the church. [...] Ideas of progress were not to be identified with Evangelical values.

Those who claimed to safeguard the teachings of the Bible knew what the correct path was: It did "not conflict with God's commandment," they declared, "if Jews in their relationship with the state were treated differently to Germans. Accordingly there was no need for the Christian conscience to be burdened, but at most it might feel concern that a sense

Deutschland 1933–1945. Eine Dokumentation zum Kirchenkampf aus den Papieren des D. Wilhelm Freiherrn von Pechmann, Neustadt a.d. Aisch, 1971, pp. 37ff.

25 Pechmann quoted his motion in a letter to the Swedish Lutheran Dr. Per Pehrsson of 10 May 1933, printed in Kantzenbach, *Widerstand*, p.42.

of humanity might suffer." To ask for favorable treatment of "Jewish Christians" would also be a problem "as this might enlarge the influx of Jews into Christianity in a dangerous way."[26] Rejected in all his efforts to change the attitudes of the leading churchmen, Pechmann drew his own conclusions, and in Easter 1934 he declared his withdrawal from the German Protestant church.[27]

The Jews could expect nothing from the Protestant church; this was already quite clear at the beginning of the National Socialist regime. It was not until late in the war that a few clergymen and laymen took a stand on behalf of the Jews. This involved great personal risk, especially since there were so few of them and they had no widespread support from the church. This became obvious in 1936 when the Second Provisional Leadership (*Zweite Vorläufige Leitung*), that is the small radical wing of the Confessional Church, produced a memorandum to denounce among other grievances, the deification of "blood, peoplehood, race and honor" (*Blut, Volkstum, Rasse und Ehre*),

26 The minutes of the meeting are printed in Armin Boyens, *Kirchenkampf und Ökumene 1933–1939. Darstellung und Dokumentation*, Munich, 1969, pp. 295–299. The arguments are: There is *"eine Überfremdung fürchterlicher Art in einzelnen Berufen."* The church is *"bei der ungeheuren Gefahr, in der sie sich z. Zt. befinde, der Mund gebunden." "Eine Kundgebung werde von den Feinden im Auslande gegen Deutschland mißbraucht werden." It is "gegen den Glauben, dem weltlichen Schwert in den Arm zu fallen, zumal es sich für die Regierung nicht um eine peripherische Sache, sondern um einen zentralen Punkt ihres Programms handele. [...] 1700 Jahre hätten die Juden unter Ausnahmerecht gestanden unter völliger Billigung der Kirche. [...] Die Fortschrittsgedanken dürften nicht mit evangelischen Normen identifiziert werden."* It is *"nicht wider Gottes Wort, wenn Juden in ihren Beziehungen zum Staat anders behandelt würden als Deutsche. [...] Daher könne das christliche Gewissen in der gegenwärtigen Lage nicht beschwert sein und lediglich besorgen, dass die Menschlichkeit leiden möchte."* The church leaders did not want better conditions for "Jewish Christians," *"da dann der Zustrom zum Christentum in verhägnisvoller Weise verstärkt werden könnte."*

27 Pechmann gave three reasons for his resignation: He wanted to protest against the forcible unification of the Protestant churches in Germany, against their surrender to the Nazi striving for totalitarian power (*Totalitätsanspruch*) and "against their silence with regard to too much injustice and to all the distress and deep sorrows which have been brought into many non-Aryan hearts and houses, Christian as well as Jewish" (*gegen ihr Schweigen zu viel Unrecht und zu all' dem Jammer und Herzeleid, das man [...] in ungezählte 'nichtarische' Herzen und Häuser, christliche und jüdische, getragen hat*). (Letter of 2 April 1934, printed in Kantzenbach, *Widerstand*, p. 80).

as well as the injunction to hate Jews. Their legal adviser, Friedrich Weissler, was murdered in a concentration camp because he was said to have passed the text on to the foreign press.[28] Since Weissler was of Jewish origin, proof of his "betrayal" appeared not to be necessary.

That individual supporters of the Jews put themselves in danger was again evident after the pogrom of November 1938. Many Christians reacted with dismay at the destruction of synagogues, shops, lodgings and other Jewish property. But very few clergymen dared to protest from the pulpit. One who did was the vicar Julius von Jan from Württemberg, and he paid for his courage. He was subjected to severe maltreatment, several months imprisonment and finally banishment from his parish. Although he belonged to an "intact" church, which was not under the control of the German Christians, his superiors evaluated his penitential sermon as an unjustified intervention in politics and only gave him their half-hearted support.[29] The leaders of the Confessional Church went a step further and revealed to their followers their disapproval of the violence perpetrated against Jews. At that time under severe political pressure, however, they refrained from a public declaration and restricted themselves to a proposal for a prayer of intercession on the Day of Repentance. In this prayer they lamented the destruction of the Jews' human dignity, affirmed the Jews' right to live, and expressed their solidarity with their fellow Christians of Jewish descent.[30]

28 Martin Greschat, ed., *Zwischen Widerspruch und Widerstand. Texte zur Denkschrift der Bekennenden Kirche an Hitler (1936),* Munich, 1987; Röhm and Thierfelder, *Juden-Christen-Deutsche*, vol. 1, pp. 165–186.

29 Eberhard Röhm and Jörg Thierfelder, *Juden-Christen-Deutsche 1933–1945*, vol. 3: 1938–1941, Stuttgart, 1995, part I, pp. 69–92; Gerhard Schäfer, *Dokumentation zum Kirchenkampf. Die Evangelische Landeskirche in Württemberg und der Nationalsozialismus*, Stuttgart, 1986, vol. 6, pp. 116–158; Theodor Dipper, *Die Evangelische Bekenntnisgemeinschaft in Württemberg 1933–1945*, Göttingen, 1966, pp. 262–267.

30 The text is printed in Röhm and Thierfelder, *Juden-Christen-Deutsche* , vol. 3/I, p. 48. In the proposed prayer the church leaders said: "Take care of the distress of all Jews amidst us who, because of their blood, are losing their human honor and their possibility to live. Help so that nobody will take revenge on them. [...] In particular do not allow the bond of love to be torn to pieces with those who with us cling to the same dear faith and by this faith are your children just like us." (*Nimm Dich der Not aller der Juden in unserer Mitte an, die um ihres Blutes willen Menschenehre und Lebensmöglichkeit verlieren. Hilf, dass keiner an ihnen rachsüchtig handle. [...] In Sonderheit laß das Band der Liebe zu denen nicht zerreißen, die mit uns in*

Some Christians, among them the same Baron von Pechmann, went further.[31] They knew that by its silence the Protestant Church had become partly responsible for the ever-increasing persecution of Jews. In their opinion, public protest was the only means to prevent further injustice. Dr. Elisabeth Schmitz, a member of the congregation of Berlin pastor Hellmut Gollwitzer, responded to his sermon on the Day of Repentance by writing a letter in which she expressed her concern for the Jews. She wrote that since the official boycott of Jewish shops on 1 April 1933 the Confessional Church had compounded its guilt by remaining silent; after the November 1938 pogrom, it was the duty of the church to speak out and protest against the measures already planned to totally separate Jews and non-Jews before it was too late. She especially urged the church to oppose the introduction of a sign on Jews' clothing about which rumors were already circulating in 1938. "Once the orders are there, it is too late." Clearsighted, Elisabeth Schmitz prophesied with uncanny accuracy:

> We have seen the destruction of property, to make this possible the shops had been marked that summer; if one begins to mark human beings, this would lead to a probable conclusion which I do not want to contemplate in detail, and nobody can claim that such orders will not be carried out with the same prompt, unscrupulous, stubborn, wicked and sadistic effort as the present instructions. Can the church tolerate this?[32]

demselben teuren Glauben stehen und durch ihn gleich uns deine Kinder sind.) This prayer contains a fine example of camouflaged language. The word "*rachsüchtig*" was not meant to accuse the Jews of any atrocities for which it was justified to take revenge. On the contrary, the Confessing Church leaders referred to the pretext for the pogrom in the official Nazi propaganda as an outburst of people's anger (*Volkszorn*) in order to stress that it was against God's will to avenge oneself. In this way they condemned all violent actions against the Jews without mentioning the pogrom.

31 Pechmann wrote to his Bavarian bishop Hans Meiser on 15 November 1938: "Whether today the Christian Church keeps silence or raises its voice is extremely important not least for the souls of the Jews who have to suffer unbearable hardships." (*Davon, ob heute die christliche Kirche schweigt oder spricht, hängt nicht zuletzt für die Seele der bis zur Unerträglichkeit schwer geprüften Juden unausdenkbar viel ab.*) Kantzenbach, *Widerstand*, p. 263.

32 The letter is printed in Röhm and Thierfelder, *Juden-Christen-Deutsche* vol. 3 / I, pp. 67f. "*Wir haben die Vernichtung des Eigentums erlebt, zu diesem Zweck hatte man im Sommer die Geschäfte bezeichnet. Geht man dazu über, die Menschen zu*

Elisabeth Schmitz's warning was not heeded. Instead of defending the Jews, the leaders of the Protestant church chose to adapt themselves to the politics of the state by emphasizing their detachment from the victims of Nazi persecution. This became particularly obvious in the spring of 1939 during the preparation of the so-called Godesberg Declaration. Minister for Ecclesiastical Affairs Kerrl had arranged for this paper to be drawn up by representatives of the German Christians and the "Center" in order to serve as a basis for the unified Reich Church, which he was still trying to establish. The central statement regarding the Jews was simply: "The Christian faith is the irreconcilable religious opposite of Judaism."[33] Eleven of the regional churches dominated by the German Christians immediately agreed with the Declaration. Those who opposed did so not because of the discriminatory nature of the statements regarding Jews. Quite the reverse: in a proposal intended as a compromise by the Ministry for Ecclesiastical Affairs, these statements were even intensified. In another version produced by the Church Leaders' Conference (*Kirchenführerkonferenz*), to which the bishops of the "intact" churches (Marahrens, Wurm and Meiser) had agreed, it was stated: "As for beliefs a sharp contradiction exists between the Gospel of Jesus Christ and his apostles and the Jewish religion of the law. As for national life a stern and responsible racial policy is necessary to keep our people pure."[34] Large groups of Protestants were united in their hostility to Jews, and the only point criticized by the more moderate bishops was the use of violence.

bezeichnen, so liegt ein Schluss nahe, den ich nicht weiter präzisieren möchte. Und niemand wird behaupten wollen, daß diese Befehle nicht ebenso prompt, ebenso gewissenlos und stur, ebenso böse und sadistisch ausgeführt würden wie die jetzigen. Darf die Kirche das zulassen?"

33 Joachim Beckmann, ed., *Kirchliches Jahrbuch für die Evangelische Kirche in Deutschland 1933–1944*, Gütersloh, 1948, pp. 293–295: *"Der christliche Glaube ist der unüberbrückbare religiöse Gegensatz zum Judentum."* For further details compare: Meier, *Kirchenkampf*, vol. 3, pp. 73–86.

34 Beckmann, *Kirchliches Jahrbuch*, pp. 300f.: "*Im Bereich des Glaubens besteht der scharfe Gegensatz zwischen der Botschaft Jesu Christi und seiner Apostel und der jüdischen Religion der Gesetzlichkeit [...]. Im Bereich des völkischen Lebens ist eine ernste und verantwortungsbewusste Rassenpolitik zur Reinerhaltung unseres Volkes erforderlich.*"

The intensification of the persecution of Jews during the war did not lead to a basic change in attitude of the Protestant church. The German Christians welcomed the measures introduced by the state, and the church on the whole adhered to its apathy. Not until the institution of genocide did individual leading churchmen and theologians raise their voices against the serious violation of the Fifth Commandment. Eventually, in 1943, two Lutheran bishops, Wurm and Marahrens, representing the "Center," felt obliged to warn the government to respect the right of Jews to life. Even so, they were extremely cautious, choosing to use secret petitions couched in very moderate language.[35]In October 1943 the twelfth Confessional Synod of the Old Prussian Union went a step further; its members did not merely protest against the murder, but reminded those responsible for carrying out the extermination policy of their personal responsibility before God, which they could not unburden onto any of their superiors.[36] In fact, for some Protestant Christians the state-organized mass murder became an important incentive to join the resistance movement against National Socialism.

While the purpose of these actions was to put an end to the mass murder, for most Protestant opponents of the Nazis this did not imply a change in their basic attitude towards Jews. This is evident from plans developed by a Protestant resistance circle attached to Carl Goerdeler for the treatment of Jews in a future German state, which are today embarrassing to read. In their view, the perpetrators of crimes against Jews were to be punished and the Jews compensated as far as possible for the damages done to them; but Jewish survivors,

35 Petition of Landesbischof Marahrens, Hannover, 19 January 1943, printed in Eberhard Klügel, *Die lutherische Landeskirche Hannovers und ihr Bischof 1933–1945. Dokumente*, Berlin, 1965, pp. 202f.; letters of *Landesbischof* Wurm, Württemberg, to the *Reichsstatthalter*, 8 February 1943; to the Reich Minister of Ecclesiastical Affairs, 12 March 1943; to the Reich Minister of Interior, 14 March 1943; to Hitler 16 July 1943, printed in Gerhard Schäfer, *Landesbischof D. Wurm und der nationalsozialistische Staat 1940–1945. Eine Dokumentation*, Stuttgart, 1968, pp. 159–169.

36 Printed in Georg Denzler und Volker Fabricius, *Die Kirchen im Dritten Reich. Christen und Nazis Hand in Hand?* vol. 2: Dokumente, pp. 183–188; Beckmann, *Kirchliches Jahrbuch*, pp. 399–402; Wilhelm Niesel, *Kirche unter dem Wort. Der Kampf der Bekennenden Kirche der Altpreussischen Union 1933–1945*, Göttingen, 1978, pp. 275f.

including German Jews, were to be treated as foreigners. In this memorandum under the title "An Attempt at Self-Examination of the Christian Conscience" (*Versuch zur Selbstbesinnung des christlichen Gewissens*), author Constantin von Dietze attempted to justify his proposal by enumerating the whole gamut of traditional anti-Jewish arguments. Von Dietze was an eminent economist, a pious Christian and a man of high moral principles. In his memorandum von Dietze reiterates the religious conviction that Jews be condemned on the grounds of their rejection of Christ, and expresses the well-known prejudices about their social positions of power since the emancipation. Even allegations about racial differences are found here.[37]

Only a few theologians reached the conclusion that the Jewish catastrophe and the involvement of the church necessitated reconsidering the relationship between Jews and Christians. Foremost among them was Dietrich Bonhoeffer, who had wrestled with the problem since 1933 and in 1940 had already formulated an impressive confession of the church's guilt towards Jews.[38] In Easter 1943 another theologian, Hermann Diem, together with a circle of laymen in Munich urged their bishops Wurm and Meiser to publicly denounce the persecution of Jews either in their sermons or in a special message. The church, they claimed, should bear in mind the insoluble connection between Jews and Christians and regard the "attack directed at Israel" (*den gegen Israel gerichteten Angriff*) as an attack against themselves and their Lord Jesus Christ.[39] But, despite their sincerity, these endeavors to create a new theology and the declarations of protest against murder were initiated by only a few individuals.

III

Prejudice against Jews was so powerful within the German Protestant church that it even influenced the attitude towards its own members of Jewish origin. It is not generally known, even by scholars, that during

37 Helmut Thielicke, ed., *In der Stunde Null. Die Denkschrift des Freiburger "Bonhoeffer-Kreises,"* Tübingen, 1979, appendix 5, pp. 146–151.

38 Eberhard Bethge, ed., *Dietrich Bonhoeffer, Ethik*, Munich, 1958, p. 50.

39 Hermann Diem, *Sine vi, sed verbo*, Munich, 1965, pp. 108–111.

the Third Reich Christians, too, became victims of racial persecution.[40] I can only elaborate on this with a few remarks. For the Nazis, baptism was of no importance and only the alleged "racial" origin counted. Christians with three or four Jewish grandparents were Jewish in their view and were treated as such. Only when the extermination policy was instituted were some of these Christians spared the worst treatment, such as being forced to live in crowded *Judenhäuser* (Jewish houses), being robbed of valuable possessions, having to wear the Yellow Star and, ultimately, deportation and murder. They were exempted not because they were Christians — they were racially classified as Jews — but they did have a better chance of survival as they had usually chosen Christian spouses, most of whom were "Aryans," and therefore frequently lived in so-called "privileged mixed marriages." Whereas a "mixed marriage" was exceptional for Jews, it was normal for Christians of Jewish origin and meant some protection for them during the war years. But their situation was still precarious.

"Jewish Christians" — the name they themselves preferred to be known by during the Nazi period — were often regarded as aliens within the church. In 1933 at a meeting of the Church Executive Committee for instance, one member expressed his concern that preferential treatment of "Jewish Christians" would lead to an undesirable influx of Jews into the church; he was not contradicted.[41] Later, the resistance group already mentioned intended that Christians of Jewish origin undergo a special procedure of naturalization.[42] Despite their attempts to distance themselves emotionally, German Protestants could not entirely ignore the plight of "Jewish Christians" as easily as they could for Jews. A short time after the fruitless discussion in the Church Executive Committee, the problem of the "Jewish Christians" was placed on the agenda of the Protestant Church — not through the endeavors of their friends but through the attacks of their enemies.

Buoyed by their victory in the church elections in July 1933, the German Christians immediately began to ban "Jews" — who were of

40 Cf. Ursula Büttner,"Die Verfolgung der 'Judenchristen' im Dritten Reich und die deutsche evangelische Kirche," in: *Krisen und Umbrüche in der Geschichte des Christentums. Festschrift für Martin Greschat*, Wolfram Kurz, Rainer Lächele and Gerhard Schmalenberg, eds., Giessen, 1994, pp. 21–50.

41 See note 26.

42 See note 37.

course Christians of Jewish origin — as well as anything described as Jewish, from the Protestant Church. The radical wing even tried to get rid of the Old Testament. Following the example of the state, they began by introducing the "Aryan clause" for office bearers in the Reich Church and for church officials in several regional churches. This decision met with considerable opposition. For the German Christians the "Aryan clause" was a self-evident need derived from the *Volkstumstheologie*. For many, though not all members of the Confessional Church however, the exclusion of "Jewish Christians" from holding church offices was a serious violation of the sacrament of baptism and, beyond that, a violation of the fundamental principles of Christian faith and the very essence of the church.

In expert memoranda, articles and pamphlets, theologians argued about the right of the church to introduce the "Aryan clause." The Theological Faculty of Marburg University vigorously denied this right, whereas the theologians of the University of Erlangen defended the "Aryan clause."[43] A number of specialists of the New Testament referred to the Bible to refute the opinion "that any official activity within the congregation should be regulated according to someone's *völkisch* or racial identity."[44] Their renowned colleague Gerhard Kittel, on the other hand, advocated "such an administrative measure" considering "the singularity of Jewish Christianity in the history of salvation;" he was even in favor of "separate Jewish-Christian congregations."[45] Theologians who were themselves of Jewish origin emphasized other aspects. Hans Ehrenberg, on the one hand, strongly condemned any diminution of the legal position of "Jewish Christians" within the church, claiming, "there are no half Christians."[46] Paul Leo, on the

43 Kurt Dietrich Schmidt, ed., *Die Bekenntnisse und grundsätzlichen Äusserungen zur Kirchenfrage des Jahres 1934*, Göttingen, 1934, pp. 178–186.

44 Memorandum of 23 September 1933, printed in: Schmidt, *Bekenntnisse*, pp. 189–191, quotation p. 190. They were against the opinion "*dass eine amtliche Betätigung in der Gemeinde nach dem Gesichtspunkt völkisch-rassischer Zugehörigkeit zu regeln sei.*"

45 Gerhard Kittel, *Kirche und Judenchristen*, Stuttgart, 1933, NEK-Archiv Kiel, earlier Church Archives Hamburg: DC 4. Kittel justified "*eine solche Verwaltungsmassnahme*" because of the "*heilsgeschichtliche Einzigartigkeit des Judenchristentums.*"

46 Hans Ehrenberg, 72 Leitsätze zur judenchristlichen Frage, July/ August 1933,

other hand, agreed with Ehrenberg in principle, but was prepared to accept a *numerus clausus* for "Jewish Christian" pastors.[47]

Against the background of this general lack of clarity, it is not surprising that the Barmen Synod in May 1934 kept silent on their relationship towards Jews and "Jewish Christians." At this gathering the representatives of the church opposition wanted to assure themselves about the confessional foundations of their church, with respect to the question of Jews and "Jewish Christians" they were not sure at all. This had serious consequences. In the years that followed, the Confessional Church often appeared to be more interested in the defense of the Old Testament than in the protection of their fellow Christians of Jewish origin.

In contradiction to their theoretical positions, members of the Confessional Church advised the "Jewish Christian" pastors to take their "special position" into account. They should avoid causing offense (*Ärgernis*) in their congregations, be inconspicuous by practicing self-restraint, and if this was not possible, "out of regard for the weakness" of their parishioners and out of love for them, they should resign from office.[48] This suggestion enabled racist fanatics to enforce the resignation of "non-Aryan" pastors by provoking turmoil in parish congregations. Sometimes, in exceptional cases, those attacked were given moral support by their colleagues in the Assembly of Pastors; their superiors, however, tried at best to secure for them some financial support, but did not defend their rights. By 1939 all "non-Aryan" pastors had been removed from office.[49]

printed in: Schmidt, *Bekenntnisse*, pp. 66–73, quotation p. 72. ("*Halbe Christen gibt es nicht.*")

47 Klügel, *Landeskirche Hannovers*, p. 492.

48 Letter from the head of the Westphalian Church Präses Karl Koch to Reich Bishop Ludwig Müller, dated 19 September 1933, quoted from Gerlach, *Zeugen*, p. 68. Martin Niemöller also demanded of the "Jewish Christian" pastors "to avoid trouble in their congregations by showing the necessary self-restraint." (*durch die gebotene Zurückhaltung in ihren Gemeinden Ärgernis zu vermeiden*). Cited in Christine-Ruth Müller, *Dietrich Bonhoeffers Kampf gegen die nationalsozialistische Verfolgung und Vernichtung der Juden*, Munich, 1990, p. 28.

49 A survey of the fate of the "non-Aryan" pastors and a description of several particular cases can be found in Röhm and Thierfelder, *Juden-Christen-Deutsche*, vol. 3/I, pp. 341–354. On p. 350f. is the notable declaration of solidarity that the

The protest by the Confessional Church was directed against the introduction of state legislation into the church. It was not a protest against the anti-Jewish policy as such. The struggle was about equal rights for Christians of Jewish origin only within the church; beyond that they received no protection from discrimination or persecution. Revealing of this attitude was the way members of the Confessional Church actually dealt with the "Aryan clause." Pastors refused to answer questions concerning their parents and grandparents to church authorities. At the same time, however, they declared their willingness to provide this information to the state authorities.[50] Most sympathizers even of the Confessional Church, conceded to the state the right to change the position of Jews and "non-Aryans" within society, accepting the legitimacy of laws that removed the legal, political, economic and social equality of this group. A narrow understanding of the Lutheran *Zweireichelehre* ("teaching of the two realms"), which was perverted by the glorification of the state, prevented the mainly conservative members of the church opposition from standing up for their "non-Aryan" fellow Christians plunged into misery by the government, by the *Obrigkeit*. Their reluctance was strengthened by the fact that many of them were in agreement with the aim of the state to eradicate the allegedly damaging influence of Jews and their kin. Those who did not share this assumption argued quite differently. This was the case for Bonhoeffer's "Jewish Christian" friend Franz Hildebrandt. As early as 1937 Hildebrandt spoke of the guilt of the church, describing it as follows: "The Church has given the impression that obedience to the state requires of it to say a welcoming 'Yes' to the handling of the Jewish question."[51]

On the whole, "non-Aryans" among Protestant Christians, with the exception of a few church employees, received little and belated

pastors" convent (*Pfarrerausschuss*) of the Lutheran Church of Hanover distributed in defence of two colleagues dismissed from office.

50 Such declarations by pastors of the Confessing Church are available for Bremen and Saxony. EZA Berlin: 1/A4/220.

51 Quoted from Eberhard Röhm and Jörg Thierfelder, *Juden-Christen-Deutsche*, vol. 2: 1935–1938, part I, Stuttgart, 1992, p. 294. *"Sie hat aber auch den Anschein erweckt, als fordere ihr Gehorsam gegen die Obrigkeit das freudige Ja zu der Behandlung der Judenfrage."*

support. They shared the fate of the Jews in every respect. In September 1935 a synod of the Confessional Church refused to occupy itself with their precarious situation. It only reaffirmed its lasting obligation to baptize Jews, and even this was too much for some synodalists.[52] There were already many congregations that rejected the baptizing of Jews. Pastors who nevertheless felt obliged by their ordination vow to baptize Jews found it increasingly difficult to have them registered in the congregation records as required by law.[53] No church leader, either in the Confessional Church or one of the "intact" churches, protested against the marriage prohibitions of the Nuremberg Laws, although they refrained from blessing Christian marriages if "non-Aryans" were involved. Absurdly, the discrimination of Christians of Jewish origin extended even beyond their death. In some towns already in the thirties they could not be buried in Christian cemeteries. After the introduction of the Yellow Star in 1941 graves sometimes had to be sought in a Jewish cemetery because, it was said, "Aryan" mourners could not be expected to tolerate them next to their own beloved dead.[54]

52 Wilhelm Niemöller, ed., *Die Synode zu Steglitz. Die dritte Bekenntnissynode der Evangelischen Kirche der Altpreussischen Union. Geschichte-Dokumente-Berichte*, Göttingen, 1970, pp. 17–21, 183–184, 278–280, 300–308. The synod was supplied with an impressive memorandum on the misery of Christian "non-Aryans" compiled by Marga Meusel head of a Protestant district welfare office at Berlin-Zehlendorf, (pp. 29–58). Although some leading representatives of the Confessional Church, among them Martin Niemöller, supported the memorandum, others successfully prevented its discussion. Mission Director Siegfried Knak advocated, against the majority of the synod, the prohibition of baptising Jews. He had already earlier condemned the neglect of the "racial differences" as a "sin against blood," using the title of a novel by Arthur Dinter, one of the most rabid German antisemites.

53 Präses Gerhard Jacobi, loc. cit., p. 279. In Hamburg Bishop Franz Tügel advised Jews who wished to be baptised to apply to the Irish Presbyterian "Jerusalem Church" until its closure by the Gestapo at the end of 1938. In his opinion it was not worth "risking one's office for such a thing" (*Es lohne nicht "sein Amt um einer solchen Sache willen aufs Spiel zu setzen"*). (Tügel to Superintendent Böhme, Meissen, 21 January 1938, NEK-Archiv Kiel, earlier Church Archives Hamburg: B IX b 12.4). After the introduction of the Yellow Star many congregations throughout Germany refused to register recently baptised Jews (Röhm and Thierfelder, *Juden-Christen-Deutsche*, vol. 3/II, pp. 278f.).

54 Röhm and Thierfelder, *Juden-Christen-Deutsche*, vol. 2/I, pp. 106–109 concerning Fulda and Leipzig; vol. 3/II, pp. 104–109 concerning Munich and Breslau; another case at Dresden is documented in the EZA Berlin: I/C3/172, vol. 3.

"Jewish Christians" remained "aliens" despite their baptism and their assimilation into the German people. This became apparent on many occasions. Protestant charitable institutions, such as hospitals and homes for children, the aged or the disabled, refused to take on unemployed "Jewish Christians" not only out of fear of losing public funds but also for fear of their identity being undermined by "foreigners" (*Angst vor Überfremdung*).[55] In 1933 the president of the Church Executive Committee had declared that the Protestant church could not tolerate a coercive transfer of Christian pupils to Jewish schools. When this transfer was enforced at the beginning of 1939, however, the church remained silent. Only on the private initiative of a few individuals who were affected by the new regulations was a small "Family School" for "Jewish Christian" children founded in Berlin.[56]

During the early years of persecution, Protestant "non-Aryans" received some assistance from small organizations that they themselves had managed to establish, but their ability to help was limited. In addition, a few German fellow Christians and a number of church representatives from abroad tried to support them in their daily misery, but they, too, could do very little for them. Only in 1938 did the Confessional Church commit itself to contribute funds to a central relief organization, the *Büro Heinrich Grüber* in Berlin, with affiliated organizations in twenty-four German towns.[57] Its main objective was to foster emigration, and it indeed found refuge abroad for about 2,400

55 Jochen-Christoph Kaiser, "Protestantismus, Diakonie und 'Judenfrage' 1933–1941," *Vierteljahrshefte für Zeitgeschichte,* 37 (1989), pp. 673–714.

56 Röhm and Thierfelder, *Juden-Christen-Deutsche* vol. 3/II, pp. 145–157.

57 Röhm and Thierfelder, *Juden-Christen-Deutsche* vol. 2/II, pp. 258–276; vol. 3/I, pp. 93–107, 121–133, 155–159, 226–252; vol.3/II, pp. 294–330. Hartmut Ludwig, "Zur Geschichte des 'Büros Pfarrer Grüber'," *Beiträge zur Berliner Kirchengeschichte*, Günter Wirth, ed., Berlin, 1987, pp. 305–326; Hartmut Ludwig, "Als Zivilcourage selten war. Die evangelische Hilfsstelle 'Büro Pfarrer Grüber,' ihre Mitarbeiter und Helfer im Rheinland 1938 bis 1940," in: *Mut zur Menschlichkeit. Hilfe für Verfolgte während der NS-Zeit*, Günther B. Ginzel, ed., Cologne, 1993, pp. 29–54; Helmut Baier, *Kirche in Not. Die bayerische Landeskirche im Zweiten Weltkrieg*, Neustadt a.d. Aisch, 1979, pp. 227–230; Schäfer, *Wurm*, p. 149. The Bavarian Church entrusted two pastors with the special task of looking after their Christian "non-Aryans"; this relief work was undertaken under the roof of the "Home Mission" and financed by subsidies of 10,000 *Reichsmark* per year. In contrast, in Württemberg the relief center was run by a voluntary worker from the ranks of the

Protestant "non-Aryans." Moreover, it paid for the *Familienschule*, helped people find work, and offered financial aid to those in dire need. The *Büro Grüber* acquired the necessary funding from private donations, from subsidies of the Confessional Church and the "intact" churches of Bavaria and Württemberg, and the largest contribution by far from the *Reichsvereinigung der Juden in Deutschland* to which "Jewish Christians" were forced to belong after July 1939. As long as the Nazi regime aimed at the expulsion of "non-Aryans" from Germany the *Büro Grüber* enjoyed official support. After these policies were discontinued, the office was closed in 1940 and Heinrich Grüber was arrested and sent to a concentration camp. Some of his assistants — all of whom were either "Jewish Christians" or of partial Jewish descent — fled abroad, others became victims of the Holocaust.

For the "non-Aryan" Protestant Christians, the liquidation of the *Büro Grüber* meant the loss of the only efficient relief organization of their church. Once again they found themselves in a situation where they depended on individual men and women who, by helping them, put themselves at great risk. We know of a few such cases in 1941: For example, when the Yellow Star was enforced, vicar Katharina Staritz, who was in charge of the "Jewish Christians" in Breslau, sent a circular to the congregations in the town urging them to look "with particular love" after their stigmatized members.[58] She was heavily attacked in Nazi journals, dismissed from office by the church, and sent to a concentration camp. Another case involved a congregation of the Confessional Church in Bremen, whose members took the opportunity of a prayer service to publicly bid farewell to some of its members who had received their deportation orders. Soon after the pastor was called up for the army, and three women on the board of the congregation who

"non-Aryan" Christians themselves and subsidized with only 1,200 *Reichsmark* per year.

58 Ernst Hornig, *Die Bekennende Kirche in Schlesien 1933–1945. Geschichte und Dokumente*, Göttingen, 1977, pp. 297–307; Gerlind Schwöbel, "*Ich aber vertraue.*" *Katharina Staritz, eine Theologin im Widerstand*, Frankfurt am Main, 1990; Karol Jonca, "Schlesiens Kirchen zur 'Lösung der Judenfrage'," in: *Das Unrechtsregime. Internationale Forschung über den Nationalsozialismus*, Ursula Büttner, ed., Hamburg 1986, vol. II, pp. 123–147, in particular pp. 138f.

were teachers had to face disciplinary action by the school authorities.[59] Bonhoeffer, together with some friends, and also a group of pastors in Württemberg, established illegal networks to smuggle Jews and "Jewish Christians" out of the country.

No doubt there were other instances of personal courage, but the majority of German Protestants, felt no obligation to resist the anti-Jewish policy of the state, even when the fate of their Jewish-born fellow Christians was at stake. In fact, among regional churches dominated by the German Christians, every increase in the persecution of Jews led to even further efforts to exclude "Jewish Christians" from the church. In the spring of 1939, a few months after the November 1938 pogrom, five regional churches — in Anhalt, Thuringia, Mecklenburg, Saxony and Lübeck — promulgated laws prohibiting the admission of "Jews" into the church or any ministration to them.[60] After the Yellow Star was introduced in September 1941 the German Christians redoubled their efforts to rid themselves of their "Jews." New laws were issued,[61] and

59 Almuth Meyer-Zollitsch, *Nationalsozialismus und Evangelische Kirche in Bremen*, Bremen, 1985, pp. 279–282; Diether Koch, *Christen in politischen Konflikten des 20. Jahrhunderts*, Bremen, 1985, pp. 202–224.

60 Röhm and Thierfelder, *Juden-Christen-Deutsche* vol. 3/II, pp. 15–18. The account of Heinz Brunotte who, during the National Socialist period, was in charge of the legal department of the Church Main Office, is in parts apologetic and misleading: Heinz Brunotte, "Die Kirchenmitgliedschaft der nichtarischen Christen," *Zeitschrift für evangelisches Kirchenrecht,* 13 (1967), pp. 140–174.

61 On 17 December 1941, after the start of the systematic mass deportations of Jews, seven regional churches governed by the German Christians (Saxony, Nassau-Hessen, Schleswig-Holstein, Thuringia, Mecklenburg, Anhalt and Lübeck) explicitly approved of the Nazi persecution policy. According to them Germany fought a just "defensive struggle" against the Jews who had "initiated the war in its worldwide dimensions" (*"Abwehrkampf" gegen die Juden, die den "Krieg in seinen weltweiten Ausmassen [...] angezettelt" hätten.*) Christian baptism, they said, did not alter "the racial characteristics of a Jew, his belonging to a certain people and his biological nature. A German Protestant Church has to care for and promote the religious life of the German *Volks*-comrades. There is no room in it and no right for racially Jewish Christians." (*Durch die christliche Taufe wird an der rassischen Eigenart eines Juden, seiner Volkszugehörigkeit und seinem biologischen Sein nichts geändert. Eine deutsche evangelische Kirche hat das religiöse Leben deutscher Volksgenossen zu pflegen und zu fördern. Rassejüdische Christen haben in ihr keinen Raum und kein Recht.*), Beckmann, *Kirchliches Jahrbuch 1933–1944*, p. 481.

these were crowned by one actually barring "Jewish Christians" from attending services or other church events and from entering church buildings, parish premises and even cemeteries.

Four examples demonstrate the ruthlessness of some German Christian leaders. The provost of Stormarn (Schleswig Holstein) asked the pastors of his church district "to inform baptized Jews at the beginning of the service that they should worship in their own 'Jewish Christian' community [which in fact did not exist, U.B.] as our Church is a German national Church."[62] In Breslau the board of a congregation forbade "wearers of the star" to enter its two houses of worship, and all church premises and cemeteries had notices to this effect affixed to the doors.[63] The third example involves a "fully Jewish" member of a congregation in Hindenburg (Upper Silesia) who was terminally ill. Even before his death the board inquired how they could prevent serious damage if "the family should demand an ecclesiastical burial." The SS was said to be already "waiting for this case" (*lauere schon auf diesen Fall*). The entire family was "fully Jewish" according to the Nazis, but had belonged to the congregation for thirty years and had "until the order concerning the Star of David" faithfully shared its life.[64] Finally, a pastor in Dresden asked a former teacher, who "earlier had rendered her good services" to the congregation, not to attend his Bible classes and other church events any longer since complaints had been lodged after she had been obliged to wear the Yellow Star. As she had to live in a *Judenhaus*, the congregation was probably the last connection to her former life.[65] Many Christian "wearers of the badge"

62 Circular letter of 27 May 1942, NEK-Archiv Kiel, earlier Church Archives Hamburg: B.V.6. The pastors were instructed, "*getaufte Juden [...] vor Beginn des Gottesdienstes darauf aufmerksam zu machen, dass sie ihre judenchristliche Gemeinschaft aufsuchen müssen, weil unsere Kirche eine deutsche Volkskirche ist.*"

63 The three pastors of the congregation who had not been present at the meeting sent a letter of protest against the resolution of 24 November 1941 to their superiors, the *Evangelische Konsistorium* of the church province of Silesia. (Letter of 5 December 1941, Wojewodschaftsarchiv Wroclaw: Evangelisches Konsistorium I/2439). A similar decision is known from Berlin-Charlottenburg. (Gerlach, *Zeugen,* p. 296).

64 Letter to the Evangelische Konsistorium Breslau of 16 January 1942, Wojewodschaftsarchiv Wroclaw: Evangelisches Konsistorium I/2439.

65 Letter from the pastor of the Lukas church to the Regional Church Office (Regional *Kirchenamt*) of 12 November 1941, EZA Berlin: 1/C3/172, Bd.3.

had the same experience; exclusion from the church also meant the severance of personal relationships.

The orders and actions aiming to remove "non-Aryans" from the church were in line with the program that the German Christians had advocated from the very beginning. But a new development, and one with serious consequences, occurred when the *Kirchenkanzlei* (Church Main Office) and representatives of the "Center" came around to this course. Two days before Christmas 1941 the *Kirchenkanzlei* called upon the regional churches to "take suitable precautions that baptized non-Aryans should stay away from the ecclesiastical life of the German congregation."[66] The leaders of the Confessional Church and the Wurttembergian bishop Wurm did protest,[67] but theirs was a lone voice. On 9 January 1942, the "intact" Lutheran Church of Hanover promulgated a law excluding "Jews" — in reality Christians of Jewish origin — from its ranks.[68] Even those who were in favor of the "Jewish Christians"and tried to help them as best they could felt entitled to draw parallels with the Foreign Mission where, for example

66 Circular letter of the Church Main Office (*Kirchenkanzlei der Deutschen Evangelischen Kirche*) to the central offices of the Protestant regional churches, dated 22 December 1941, repeatedly printed, e.g., Kurt Meier, *Kirche und Judentum. Die Haltung der evangelischen Kirche zur Judenpolitik des Dritten Reiches*, Göttingen, 1968, pp. 116f. The regional churches were asked, *"geeignete Vorkehrungen zu treffen, dass die getauften Nichtarier dem kirchlichen Leben der deutschen Gemeinde fernbleiben."*

67 Letter of the *Evangelische Oberkirchenrat* at Stuttgart, dated 27 January 1942, and letter of Bishop Wurm of Württemberg, dated 6 February 1942, to *Deutsche Evangelische Kirchenkanzlei*; furthermore joint declaration of the *Konferenz der Landesbruderräte* and the second *Vorläufige Leitung* of the Confessional Church, printed in: Beckmann, *Kirchliches Jahrbuch 1933–1944*, pp. 482–485. Letters of protest with a great number of signatures came also from Confessional Church congregations in Pomerania, Potsdam and Berlin-Babelsberg. (Evangelisches Zentralarchiv Berlin: I/C3/172, vol. 3).

68 Klügel, *Landeskirche Hannovers*, p. 498, denies the existence of a regulation excluding "Jewish Christians." The wording of the law of 9 January 1942, however, seems clear to me, "Jews" as defined by the First Implementation Decree of the Citizenship Law, should no longer be obliged to pay church taxes, because they "cannot be regarded as members of the Lutheran Church of Hanover as a corporation under public law." (*weil sie nicht als Mitglieder der Evangelisch-lutherischen Landeskirche Hannover als Körperschaft des öffentlichen Rechts angesehen werden können*). Quoted from Gerlach, *Zeugen*, p. 327.

in Africa, blacks and whites worshipped separately. Thus they had no objections to the division, according to "racial difference," into separate congregations if it was advantageous for the church, considering the state's politics. So argued the director of the *Betheler Anstalten* Friedrich von Bodelschwingh, and the director of the *Lobethaler Anstalten* Paul Braune.[69] They, too, regarded the "Jewish Christians" as members of a foreign *Volk*. Nevertheless, because the "Jewish Christians" were scattered all over the country and because their numbers were too small, the establishment of special congregations did not in fact come about in Germany. They did though in Theresienstadt, where, "Jewish Christian" congregations were formed, bringing together Protestants and Catholics who, as "Jews," had been deported to the ghetto.[70]

IV

One fact becomes patently clear with regard to the acceptance of "Jewish Christians": For the majority of German Protestants, Jews were and always would be strangers no matter how assimilated they were. Moreover, many Protestants, even members of the Confessional Church, shared the widespread prejudices that not only were Jews too powerful they were dangerous to the German nation; and as their *völkisch* peculiarities were regarded as intrinsic, this aversion was extended to include the "Jewish Christians." To underline this argument

69 Röhm and Thierfelder, *Juden-Christen-Deutsche* vol. 3/I, pp. 252–257.

70 H.G. Adler reports of a growing number of Christians in Terezin who had been deported there after the dissolution of their "mixed marriages": H.G. Adler, *Theresienstadt 1941–1945. Das Antlitz einer Zwangsgemeinschaft*, Tübingen, 1960, p. 308.

	Catholics	Evangelicals
Dec. 1943	1321	830
May 1944	1439	1084
Dec. 1944	943	1198
20 Apr. 1945	2014	1808

About 800 Protestants joined the parish which was initiated and headed by Arthur Goldschmidt, a former Hamburg judge, of whom between 150 and 200 regularly attended the services. (Arthur Goldschmidt, *Geschichte der evang. Gemeinde Theresienstadt 1942–1945*, Tübingen, 1948, p. 13.).

I would like to conclude by citing a particularly striking example: The church of Baden issued a memorandum meant to be in favor of "Jewish Christians" which contained the following advice: "The Church expects nevertheless, that our alien racial Christian brothers and sisters should make serious efforts to give up those characteristics they have inherited from their fathers which are alien to the German and to integrate themselves in our German *Volkstum*. In public life they must show wise reticence, so that no obstacles may arise to the exercise of brotherly love."[71]

From this quotation and this survey as a whole, it is apparent that for German Protestants, with a few praiseworthy exceptions, Jews not only adhered to a foreign religion, they belonged to a foreign people. So deeply rooted was the notion that their *Wesen* (essence) differentiated them from other Germans, that it survived the Third Reich. True, the specific, racially founded Nazi antisemitism disappeared after the collapse of the regime and the widespread sociocultural prejudices against the Jews became a taboo. But the traditional ecclesiastical definition of the relationship between Christians and Jews was not questioned.

Not until the seventies did a change gradually come about. The significance of this change is considerable — and this does in fact lead me to end on a positive note after all. Today the Protestant Church fully acknowledges its failure with regard to the murder of Jews, and this recognition has important consequences. In contrast to the relationship that had been determined over hundreds of years by hostility and hatred, or at best by lack of respect and apathy, Protestant theologians are now for the first time showing interest in the Jewish religion and in the *Wesen des Judentums* (*The Essence of Judaism*), as Leo Baeck titled his celebrated book. Some synods are making efforts to describe the Christians' insoluble bonds with the Jews with gratitude and respect. In 1924, long before the mass murders of the Holocaust, Franz

71 Fliedner, *Judenverfolgung*, pp. 358–360, quotation p. 359 "*Die Kirche erwartet dabei allerdings, dass diese unsere fremdstämmigen Glaubensbrüder und -schwestern ernstlich versuchen, die ihnen von ihren Vätern her angeborenen deutschfremden Eigenschaften abzulegen, sich unserem Volkstum einzugliedern und sich im öffentlichen Leben einer weisen Zurückhaltung zu befleissigen, damit die Ausübung der brüderlichen Liebe nicht gehindert [...] werde.*"

Rosenzweig had complained about the "deathly silence" (*Totenstille*) between Christians and Jews that had lasted for some three to four hundred years.[72] This deathly silence seems to have been overcome at last. While attempting not to overestimate the influence of the churches in modern society, this new approach gives us reason to hope — for the Jews in Germany, for the church, and for German political culture.

72 Franz Rosenzweig to Martin Buber, 19 March 1924, in Grete Schaeder, ed., *Martin Buber. Briefwechsel aus sieben Jahrzehnten*, Heidelberg, 1973, vol. 2: 1918–1938, p. 189.

Responses of German Resistance

The German Resistance to Hitler and the Jews

PETER HOFFMANN

A methodical approach to the subject of German resistance to Hitler requires firstly a consideration of how the position of "the German resistance" concerning the persecution of the Jews could be determined. Secondly, since resistance to the National Socialist regime was offered by individuals and one cannot determine the mentality and actions of individuals from a putative mentality of the social stratum to which they allegedly belonged, an individual-biographical method must be followed.[1] Its application to the cases of thousands of individuals would make the topic unmanageable.

For the purposes of this paper, the most controversial member of the conspiracy of 20 July 1944 will be the focal point. A more comprehensive estimate concerning the other participants in the failed insurrection will conclude the paper, based on the findings of the Gestapo investigating commission that interrogated hundreds of conspirators, and based also on records independent of the police interrogations.

Carl Goerdeler, the Mayor of Leipzig (1930–36), and Reich Prices Commissioner (1931–32, 1934–35), became the civilian head of the conspiracy against Hitler during the Second World War. He actively pursued it from 1937 to 1944. His position on the "Jewish Question" has led some researchers to negative assessments of Goerdeler.[2] A new,

1 Cf. Lothar Graf zu Dohna, "Vom Kirchenkampf zum Widerstand. Probleme der Widerstandsforschung im Brennspiegel einer Fallstudie," in: Ralph Melville, Claus Scharf, Martin Vogt, Ulrich Wengenroth, eds., *Deutschland und Europa in der Neuzeit. Festschrift für Karl Otmar Freiherr von Aretin zum 65. Geburtstag*, Stuttgart, 1988, pp. 857–858.

2 For controversial discussions see Nicholas Reynolds, *Treason Was No Crime. Ludwig Beck, Chief of the German General Staff*, London, 1976, p. 54; Christof Dipper, "Der Deutsche Widerstand und die Juden," *Geschichte und Gesellschaft,*

more detailed examination of the record than they have made, however, will reveal a more differentiated position.[3]

Goerdeler maintained in 1944, after he had been sentenced to death and while awaiting execution, that he had initially worked loyally with the National Socialist government and its functionaries. He may have referred to his meeting with Hitler in 1935, when he had seemingly won the dictator's support for his own view on economic policy against a powerful rival, Economics Minister Hjalmar Schacht. From then on, Goerdeler was under the illusion that, given an opportunity, he would be able to persuade Hitler to see reason, and later, to end the war.[4] When he wrote down these thoughts in prison, however, he also wrote them for the eyes of the heads of the Gestapo and the SS, suggesting that he could help to end the war.

But he had not in fact worked loyally with the National Socialist government in matters concerning Jews. On 1 April 1933 he had intervened, in full formal dress and accompanied by his Deputy Mayor Ewald Löser, against the National Socialists' party militia, the SA, when they harassed and attacked Jews and businesses belonging to Jews during the government-organized nationwide boycott, and he had personally protected Jewish furriers in Leipzig-Brühl against SA thugs

9 (1983), pp. 349–380; Daniel J. Goldhagen, *Hitler's Willing Executioners*, New York, 1996, pp. 114–116.

3 Dipper, pp. 349–380, fails to cite anything conclusive, disregards a substantial body of evidence, and relies on supposition; Martin Broszat, "Plädoyer für eine Historisierung des Nationalsozialismus," *Merkur*, 39 (1985), pp. 382–383, relies on Dipper. Klemens von Klemperer in conference discussion, "Christianity and Resistance. National Socialist Germany 1933–1945," University of Birmingham, UK, 22 April 1995, maintained that Goerdeler had signed a "decree" in 1936 restricting the use of public baths in Leipzig by Jews; there is no evidence that Goerdeler ever signed such a decree. In response to the author's questions, Klemperer replied (letter 15 August 1996), that according to his notes Goerdeler's typed signature appeared under a decree dated 19 September 1936 restricting the use of public baths by Jews, but Klemperer cannot produce or identify the "decree." See details below at p. 466.

4 [Carl Goerdeler], *Unsere Idee*, typescript, Berlin, November 1944, Bundesarchiv Koblenz, Nl Goerdeler 26, pp. 10–11; Gerhard Ritter, *Carl Goerdeler und die deutsche Widerstandsbewegung*, Stuttgart, 1956, pp. 77–78, 430–431, 434–440.

and looters.[5] Also, in the first weeks after Hitler's appointment as Chancellor, Goerdeler used the Leipzig police to liberate Jews who had been detained and beaten by the SA.[6]

In January 1935 Goerdeler had to accept the creation of a "Race Authority" within the Municipal Health Commission, which was required by a national law.[7] On 9 April 1935 he received a complaint from the *Landesverband Mitteldeutschland des Centralvereins deutscher Staatsbürger jüdischen Glaubens* (Saxon Association of the Central Association of German Citizens of Jewish Faith). The complaint was directed against Goerdeler's new Deputy Mayor Rudolf Haake, a National Socialist, who had warned civil servants against consulting any Jewish physicians. A government decree of 22 April 1933 had excluded Communist physicians and "non-Aryan" physicians who were not World War veterans or sons or fathers of World War veterans from practicing under public health insurance plans.[8] A decree of 17 May 1934 had excluded physicians from approbation if they were descended from one or more Jewish grandparents, or if they were married to a "non-Aryan." But physicians who had previously been admitted to practice under medical insurance plans did not lose their approbation. The decree also stipulated exceptions similar to those in the decree of 22 April 1933.[9]

5 Goerdeler, *Unsere Idee*, p. 12; Ritter, p. 68 uses this source without specific reference; Marianne Meyer-Krahmer, *Carl Goerdeler und sein Weg in den Widerstand. Eine Reise in die Welt meines Vaters*, Freiburg im Breisgau, 1989, p. 73.

6 Meyer-Krahmer, *Carl Goerdeler*, p. 73.

7 Verhandlungen der Stadtverordneten zu Leipzig 1935, Stadtarchiv Leipzig, Band I, 30 Jan. 1935; Gesetz zur Vereinheitlichung des Gesundheitswesens, 3 July 1934, *Reichsgesetzblatt, Teil I*, Berlin, 1934 (RGBl. I 1934), no. 71, pp. 531–532; Erste Durchführungsverordnung zum Gesetz über die Vereinheitlichung des Gesundheitswesens, 6 February 1935, (RGBl. I 1935), no. 13, pp. 177–180.

8 Verordnung über die Zulassung von Ärzten zur Tätigkeit bei den Krankenkassen, 22 April 1933, RGBl. I 1933, p. 222.

9 Verordnung über die Zulassung von Ärzten zur Tätigkeit bei den Krankenkassen, 17 May 1934, RGBl. I 1934, pp. 399–410. Veterans who had been severely wounded were exempt from certain conditions of approbation. Physicians (the decree did not distinguish here between "Aryan" and "non-Aryan" physicians), who had practiced medicine from a date before 1 October 1921 were also exempt from certain preconditions for approbation to practice under medical insurance plans.

The Association asked Goerdeler to put a stop to the unlawful boycott of Jewish physicians. On 11 April 1935 Goerdeler signed an internal memorandum which listed "non-Aryan" physicians who were permitted by law to treat patients under the terms of the public health insurance authority, and which listed those who were not permitted to do so.[10] Goerdeler confirmed the legal position that the Association had invoked, protecting those who were legally entitled to practice. He protected them against the efforts of National Socialists to exclude all Jews from practice. He followed a similar procedure concerning dentists.

The files of the Leipzig city archives further contain correspondence and minutes concerning restrictions for Jews on the use of public baths. Almost all the documents on this issue, which originated in the Leipzig city administration, bear the signature of the National Socialist Deputy Mayor, Rudolf Haake. In a reply to a complaint, Haake wrote under the date of 19 August 1935 that he (he used the pronoun "I"), had accepted the justification for prohibiting Jews from the use of public baths in which they would come into contact with non-Jewish users.[11] Goerdeler has been accused of antisemitism for allegedly sanctioning restrictions on the use of public baths by Jews.[12] Goerdeler's involvement in the matter — although his ultimate responsibility as Mayor is clear — is revealed in the records of the Leipzig city archives as limited to answering, on 19 September 1936, an inquiry from the Saxon section of the National Council of Municipalities. Goerdeler wrote, using the passive voice in the third person, that from the end of July 1935 Jews had been prohibited from using the Leipzig municipal summer baths, indoor pools and other communal baths.[13]

Meanwhile for years, and most urgently in the spring of 1936 before the summer Olympiad in Berlin, local Party leaders, especially the National Socialist Deputy Mayor, had been pressing Goerdeler to permit the removal of the statue outside the Gewandhaus at Leipzig, which had been erected in 1892 in honor of its former director, Felix Mendelssohn-Bartholdy. The National Socialists considered that

10 Stadtarchiv Leipzig, Kap. 1 Nr. 122.

11 Ibid.

12 Klemens von Klemperer in conference discussion, see note 3.

13 Stadtarchiv Leipzig, Kap. 1 Nr. 122.

Mendelssohn-Bartholdy, a Christian whose ancestors had been Jewish, was a Jew according to the Nuremberg Laws of 1935. Goerdeler refused to permit the removal of the statue. He agreed that the question might be discussed, but he postponed discussion until after the summer, *sine die*. In the autumn of 1936 Goerdeler accepted an invitation of the German Chamber of Commerce to travel to Helsingfors in Finland. Before he left, he secured Goebbels' and Hitler's support for his decision to leave the monument in place, and he instructed Deputy Mayor Haake accordingly.[14] But on 9 November 1936, while Goerdeler was out of town, Deputy Mayor Haake had the statue removed. When Goerdeler returned to Leipzig, he demanded an explanation. Haake accused him in a written deposition on 16 November 1936 of not sharing the Party's view on the Jews.

On 25 November 1936 Goerdeler resigned as Mayor. In a statement on 4 December justifying the city's acceptance of Goerdeler's resignation, Haake said that Goerdeler had criticized and opposed most National Socialist policies since 1933, and that "Dr. Goerdeler's attitude in the Jewish Question had been revealed particularly clearly in the matter of the Mendelssohn-Bartholdy statue."[15] This had indeed been Goerdeler's intention.

Haake's explanation might be considered self-serving, since he had committed an act of insubordination. But this was clearly not Haake's own view. Haake was convinced that he had acted in the interest of the racial doctrine of the Party which superseded all other considerations. Goerdeler, in his own explanation for his resignation, cited Haake's insubordination, and explained that he had found in consultation with the Saxon Ministry of the Interior and the district Party leader that they were not willing to discipline Haake. Therefore he had had no choice

14 Goerdeler to Reichsstatthalter Martin Mutschmann, 23 November 1937, Stadtarchiv Leipzig, Kap. 10 G Nr. 685 Bd. 2.

15 Acta, das Felix Mendelssohn-Bartholdy-Denkmal btr. Ergangen vor dem Rathe der Stadt Leipzig 1859–1947, Stadtarchiv Leipzig, Kap. 26A Nr. 39; Goerdeler personnel file Stadtarchiv Leipzig, Kap. 10 G Nr. 685 Bd. 1 and 2. Manfred Unger, "Die 'Endlösung' in Leipzig. Dokumente zur Geschichte der Judenverfolgung 1933–1945," *Zeitschrift für Geschichtswissenschaft,* 11 (1963), p. 944 cites Goerdeler as saying only that the matter could be examined; Unger who was head of the Stadtarchiv and had full access to the records suppressed Goerdeler's true position and Haake's denunciations.

but to resign since he would otherwise have lost his authority.[16] But there is ample evidence to show that Goerdeler's position regarding the statue was also rooted in his "attitude in the Jewish question."

After his resignation Goerdeler continued to concern himself with the mistreatment of the Jews. As Arnold Paucker and Konrad Kwiet have shown, Goerdeler arranged for Leo Baeck to obtain 1.2 million Reichsmark "for saving Jewish lives."[17] In a memorandum of 1 December 1937 intended for publication in America, Goerdeler said he was disturbed by the equanimity with which many outside Germany received the news of the Hitler regime's atrocities.[18] At the request of the head of the British Foreign Office, Sir Robert Vansittart, the British industrialist A.P. Young, who had business and personal links with Robert Bosch in Stuttgart, met with Goerdeler on 6 and 7 August 1938 in Rauschen Dune, when the Hitler government was intensifying its anti-Jewish policies. Goerdeler urged the British government, through A.P. Young, to express their disgust forcefully at the National Socialist methods and to refuse to discuss the vital issues Germany was interested in if the practices against the Jews continued.[19] According to laws enacted in 1933 and 1934, this constituted treason against the country.[20] After German authorities had driven 10,000 Polish Jews across the Polish-German frontier, three days before the November 1938 pogrom, Goerdeler again met with A.P. Young in Switzerland on 6 and 7 November 1938. Goerdeler predicted "a great increase in the persecution of the Jews and Christians."[21] At the same meeting, he was "greatly perturbed that there is not yet in evidence any strong reaction

16 Goerdeler to Mutschmann, 23 November 1937, Stadtarchiv Leipzig, Kap. 10G Nr. 685 Bd. 2.

17 Arnold Paucker and Konrad Kwiet, "Jewish Leadership and Jewish Resistance," in this volume, p. 369.

18 Ritter, pp. 167–168. Ritter, p. 484 note 22, wonders why Goerdeler did not explicitly write of the "Judenverfolgung noch von den Schrecken der Konzentrationslager;" but "Greueltaten" covered both.

19 A.P. Young ed., *The "X" Documents*, London, 1974, pp. 45–49, 59.

20 Verordnung des Reichspräsidenten gegen Verrat am Deutschen Volke und hochverräterische Umtriebe, 28 February 1933, RGBl. 1933 I no. 18, pp. 85–87; Gesetz gegen heimtückische Angriffe auf Staat und Partei und zum Schutz der Parteiuniformen, 20 December 1934, RGBl. 1934 I no. 137, pp. 1269–1271.

21 Young, *The "X" Documents*, p. 136.

throughout the democracies, in the press, the church, and in parliament, against the barbaric, sadistic and cruel persecution of 10,000 Polish Jews in Germany."[22] Meeting A.P. Young in Switzerland again, between 4 December 1938 and 15 January 1939, Goerdeler deplored "the cruel and senseless persecution of the Jews" and "the way in which the Nazi leaders enriched themselves by stealing Jewish property."[23] He warned that Hitler was determined to conquer the world and had "decided to destroy the Jews — Christianity — Capitalism." Goerdeler urged the British government to apply strong pressure on Hitler's government "to save the world from this terrible catastrophe."[24] When Goerdeler met A.P. Young on 16 March 1939, the day after the occupation of Bohemia and Moravia by German troops, Goerdeler listed "three milestones of great historical importance" that Hitler had already passed, the first being "the pogrom against the Jews on November 9 and 10" which, he said, Hitler had ordered. Goerdeler "spoke with burning indignation," especially of how small children were driven from their homes in the night, and of young Nazi gangsters raped Jewish women.[25]

In 1941 the persecution of the Jews led Goerdeler to draft a memorandum for a solution to the "Jewish Question." He has been accused of antisemitism because of it: namely, because in this draft he used the term "race" for the Jewish people, and because he proposed that Jews be treated as foreign nationals and as citizens of the yet-to-be-founded Jewish state if they or their ancestors had not lived within the borders of the German Empire before 1 July 1871. Equally, Goerdeler has been accused of antisemitism because he acknowledged a state's right to determine who could be a citizen of the state, and because he supported the idea of a Jewish state.[26]

22 Ibid., p. 139.
23 Ibid., pp. 154-160.
24 Ibid., pp. 161-162.
25 Ibid., p. 177.
26 [Carl Goerdeler], "Das Ziel", *Beck und Goerdeler. Gemeinschaftsdokumente für den Frieden 1941–1944*, Wilhelm Ritter von Schramm, ed., Munich, 1965, pp. 105–107; cf. Hans Mommsen, "Gesellschaftsbild und Verfassungspläne des deutschen Widerstandes," in Walter Schmitthenner and Hans Buchheim, eds., *Der deutsche Widerstand gegen Hitler. Vier historisch-kritische Studien*, Cologne, 1966, pp. 133, 266–267, 269–270; Goerdeler, *Idee*, p. 12. Christof Dipper, "Der 20. Juli und die 'Judenfrage'," *Die Zeit* , 1 July 1994, p. 20, contrives to see Goerdeler's case in particularly dark colors because, writes Dipper, Goerdeler

In his 1941 memorandum, Goerdeler's suggestion to deprive naturalized German Jews of their citizenship — after years of injustices and cruelties committed by German authorities against German and non-German Jews — appears shockingly insensitive.[27] At the same time, Goerdeler's critics ignore the fact that he comprehensively condemned the National Socialists because they had "overthrown God with their racial madness." They equally ignore the fact that Britain controlled Jewish immigration to Palestine.[28] In fact, in view of Goerdeler's actions on behalf of German Jews (and of Polish Jews), it is impossible to suggest, that he ever intended to make their position worse. On the

had "especially not" mentioned Palestine; but Dipper ignored the account which Goerdeler wrote in prison in which Goerdeler mentioned Palestine as a territory for a Jewish state. Dipper, "Der deutsche Widerstand," p. 368, finds "Goerdeler's influence" in a memorandum by Constantin von Dietze [Constantin von Dietze], "Vorschläge für eine Lösung der Judenfrage in Deutschland," in: *In der Stunde Null. Die Denkschrift des Freiburger "Bonhoeffer-Kreises:" Politische Gemeinschaftsordnung. Ein Versuch zur Selbstbesinnung des christlichen Gewissens in den politischen Nöten unserer Zeit*, introduction by H. Thielicke, Ph. von Bismarck, ed., Tübingen, 1979, pp. 146–151) and offers as evidence Dietze's introductory remark that "various proposals had been made;" Goerdeler was in Freiburg on 17 November 1942 in order to discuss the memorandum, but on that day it was only agreed that an appendix on the Jewish Question was to be prepared later; Christine-Ruth Müller, *Dietrich Bonhoeffers Kampf gegen die nationalsozialistische Verfolgung und Vernichtung der Juden. Bonhoeffers Haltung zur Judenfrage im Vergleich mit Stellungnahmen aus der evangelischen Kirche und Kreisen des deutschen Widerstandes*, Munich, 1990, p. 276 and note 178, based on Christine Blumenberg-Lampe, *Das wirtschaftliche Programm der "Freiburger Kreise." Entwurf einer freiheitlich-sozialen Nachkriegswirtschaft. Nationalökonomen gegen den Nationalsozialismus*, Berlin, 1973, p. 25. Broszat, p. 383, readily accepted Dipper's ill-founded use of sources to convict Goerdeler of antisemitism.

27 Eberhard Bethge, *Dietrich Bonhoeffer. Theologe, Christ, Zeitgenosse*, Munich, 1970, pp. 796, 836–837.

28 [Carl Goerdeler], *Gedanken eines zum Tode Verurteilten über die deutsche Zukunft*, typescript [Berlin September 1944], Bundesarchiv, Koblenz, Nl Goerdeler 26, p. 25. In 1939, Britain's published policy provided for the immigration of 75,000 Jews during 1939–44. In the autumn of 1944, there were still 14,000 places open while Jews from Bulgaria, Rumania and Hungary tried, mostly unsuccessfully, to escape from the SS via the Black Sea; Peter Hoffmann, "Roncalli in the Second World War: Peace Initiatives, the Greek Famine and the Persecution of the Jews," *Journal of Ecclesiastical History,* 40 (1989), pp. 83–84.

contrary, he had been desperately seeking to persuade the murderers to accept a relatively less harmful alternative. The purpose of his memorandum was to try to wrench the weapon out of the murderer's hands and to secure a status for the Jews that allowed them to survive.

Although the persecution of the Jews did not motivate Goerdeler exclusively — there were also the murders of the mentally ill, Polish priests and intellectuals, and great numbers of Russian civilians and prisoners of war; the numerous perversions of justice; and the war itself — the persecution of the Jews received Goerdeler's strongest expressions of condemnation, both before and during his imprisonment. In his "Thoughts about the German Future by One Condemned to Death," written in the days after he had been sentenced in September 1944, Goerdeler felt it necessary to point out what he called "the great guilt of the Jews who had intruded themselves into our public life in ways which lacked all appropriate consideration," and almost in the same breath he declared: "And I am not an antisemite."[29] Goerdeler wrote further that Hitler's hands were "dripping with the blood of innocent Jews, Poles, Russians and Germans who were murdered and starved to death, with the blood of millions of soldiers of all nations who are on his conscience." He maintained that one must not allow the Germans to cover up what had happened; and he wrote that around a million German Jews and an unknown number of Polish and Russian Jews had been "murdered with a bestiality unheard of in world history."[30] And: "We must not deny the Jews the rights which God gave to all humans." The Secret State Police reported that Goerdeler, in prison after 20 July 1944, "again and again expressed his outrage about the great massacres of Jews in Poland."[31] Goerdeler justified his leadership in the conspiracy against the National Socialists as an attempt to liberate the world of "those monsters who sought to upset all

29 Goerdeler, *Gedanken*, pp. 37–38; Goerdeler, *Idee*, pp. 12, 14, 19–22, 24; *Beck und Goerdeler*, pp. 105–107; Carl Goerdeler, *Im Gefängnis Weihnachten 1944*, typescript, Christmas 1944, Bundesarchiv Koblenz, Nl Goerdeler 26, p. 2.

30 Goerdeler, *Gedanken*, pp. 25, 37–38.

31 Ritter, p. 613; *Spiegelbild einer Verschwörung. Die Kaltenbrunner-Berichte an Bormann und Hitler über das Attentat vom 20. Juli 1944. Geheime Dokumente aus dem ehemaligen Reichssicherheitshauptamt*, Stuttgart, 1961, p. 474.

values and who elevated the fatherland to a moloch, who had dethroned God with their racial madness."[32]

The Secret State Police interrogation records, which survive incompletely, show that at least fifteen members of the anti-Hitler conspiracy stated during interrogation that their main motive, or one of their main motives for their opposition to National Socialism, was the persecution of the Jews: they were Klaus Bonhoeffer, Admiral Wilhelm Canaris, Hans von Dohnanyi, Carl Goerdeler, Franz Kempner, Hans Kloos, Professor Adolf Lampe, Heinrich Count Lehndorff-Steinort, Brigadier Hans Oster, Colonel (GS) Alexis Baron von Roenne, Rüdiger Schleicher, Franz Sperr, Professor Alexander Count Stauffenberg, Berthold Count Stauffenberg, and Peter Count Yorck von Wartenburg (all except Kloos, Lampe and Alexander Stauffenberg were executed). Twenty-three other anti-Hitler plotters are on record as having been equally motivated: General Ludwig Beck, Dietrich Bonhoeffer, Major Axel Baron von dem Bussche, Professor Constantin von Dietze, Colonel (GS) Eberhard Finckh, Brigadier Rudolf-Christoph Baron von Gersdorff, Eugen Gerstenmaier, Lieutenant-Colonel (GS) Helmuth Groscurth, Hans-Bernd von Haeften, Ulrich von Hassell, Julius Leber, Carlo Mierendorff, Helmuth James Count Moltke, Johannes Popitz, Adolf Reichwein, Ulrich Count Schwerin von Schwanenfeld, Colonel Wilhelm Staehle, Colonel (GS) Claus Count Stauffenberg, Lieutenant-Colonel Theodor Steltzer, Brigadier Helmuth Stieff, Brigadier Henning von Tresckow, Adam von Trott zu Solz, and Josef Wirmer.[33] There were also a number of Catholic priests and Lutheran ministers, and twenty-eight members of the White Rose student group who made the same declaration.[34]

32 Goerdeler, *Gedanken*, p. 25.

33 Beck and Tresckow committed suicide; Bussche, Dietze, Gersdorff, Steltzer and Gerstenmaier survived; Groscurth died as a prisoner of war; Mierendorff was killed in an air raid; the others were executed.

34 The names of the White Rose group include Alexander Schmorell, Hans Scholl, Willi Graf, Christoph Propst, Professor Kurt Huber, Helmut Bauer, Heinrich Bollinger, Eugen Grimminger, Heinrich Guter, Falk Harnack, Hans Hirzel, Susanne Hirzel, Traute Lafrenz, Franz Josef Müller, Gisela Schertling, Katharina Schüddekopf, Harald Dohrn, Manfred Eickemeyer, Wilhelm Geyer, Josef Söhngen, Willi Bollinger, Lieselotte Dreyfeldt, Wolfgang Erlenbach, Valentin Freise, Marie-Luise Jahn, Hans Leipelt, Hedwig Schulz, Franz Treppesch, Jürgen Wittenstein. Cf. Willi Graf, *Briefe*

und Aufzeichnungen, Anneliese Knoop-Graf and Inge Jens eds., Frankfurt am Main, 1988. *Spiegelbild*, pp. 110, 199–202, 420, 431, 443, 450, 471–474, 501, 520; Veit Osas, *Walküre. Die Wahrheit über den 20. Juli 1944 mit Dokumenten*, Hamburg, 1953, p. 98. On Dohnanyi see also Bethge, *Bonhoeffer*, pp. 702–11, 838–44; Ulrich von Hassell was appalled by the Nuremberg Laws, as his daughter noted in her diary on 18 September 1935. He condemned the laws as signifying "for our country the end of its culture"; Fey von Hassell, *Niemals sich beugen. Erinnerungen einer Sondergefangenen der SS*, Munich, 2nd edition 1991, p. 32. Hassell recorded his outrage at the November 1938 pogrom in his own diary on 25 November 1938: "But my chief concern is not with the effects abroad, not with what kind of foreign political reaction we may expect – at least not for the moment. I am most deeply troubled about the effect on our national life, which is dominated ever more inexorably by a system capable of such things." Ulrich von Hassell, *The von Hassell diaries 1938–1944*, London, 1948, p. 20. Hassell's published diary – thus far only the portions from September 1938 to July 1944 have been published – refers to the situation of the Jews 43 times; Hassell, pp. 76, 140, 198, 219, 272; Ulrich von Hassell, *Die Hassell-Tagebücher 1938–1944. Aufzeichnungen vom Andern Deutschland*, Berlin, 1988, p. 281; Heinz Eduard Tödt, "Judenverfolgung und Kirchenzerstörung im Spiegel der Hassell-Tagebücher 1938–1944," in, *Die Hebräische Bibel und ihre zweifache Nachgeschichte. Festschrift für Rolf Rendtorff zum 65. Geburtstag*, Erhard Blum et al., eds., Neukirchen-Vluyn, 1990, pp. 707–715. On Goerdeler see also Lautarchiv des Deutschen Rundfunks, ed., *Volksgerichtshof-Prozesse zum 20. Juli 1944: Transkripte von Tonbandfunden*, Frankfurt am Main, 1961, p. 119; on Oster also Fabian von Schlabrendorff, *Begegnungen in fünf Jahrzehnten*, Tübingen, 1979, p. 183; Alexander Stahlberg, *Die verdammte Pflicht*, Berlin, 1987, pp. 314–315, 377; on Yorck also Theodor Steltzer, *Sechzig Jahre Zeitgenosse*, Munich, 1966, p. 147; Eberhard Bethge, *Dietrich Bonhoeffer. Theologian, Christian, Contemporary*, London, 1970, p. 613; *Trial of the Major War Criminals before the International Military Tribunal Nuremberg 14 November 1945—1 October 1946*, vol. XXXIII, Nuremberg 1949, p. 424; Philipp Freiherr von Boeselager, *Der Widerstand in der Heeresgruppe Mitte (Beiträge zum Widerstand 1933–1945*), Gedenkstätte Deutscher Widerstand, Berlin, 1990, p. 10; Dietrich Bonhoeffer, *Gesammelte Schriften*, Munich, 1959, Volume II, pp. 44–53, 115–117, 144; Dietrich Bonhoeffer, *Werke*, Volume 6, Munich, 1992, pp. 93–95, 98–100, 113–115; Bethge, *Bonhoeffer* (German edition), index "Juden"; Eberhard Bethge, "Dietrich Bonhoeffer und die Juden," in: *Konsequenzen. Dietrich Bonhoeffers Kirchenverständnis heute* (Internationales Bonhoeffer-Forum, Nr. 3), Ernst Feil and Ilse Tödt, eds, Munich, 1980, pp. 171–214; Peter Hoffmann, *Widerstand, Staatsstreich, Attentat. Der Kampf der Opposition gegen Hitler*, Munich, 1985, pp. 334–335, 399; Dietze, pp. 146–151; Ritter, pp. 523–524, note 71; Stahlberg, pp. 342–345; Ivar Anderson, diary 14 Dec. 1942, Kungliga Biblioteket, Stockholm, Ivar Andersons paper L 91; Fabian von Schlabrendorff, ed., *Eugen Gerstenmaier im Dritten Reich. Eine Dokumentation*, Stuttgart, 1965, pp. 42–43; Inge Scholl, *Die*

Hitler's few opponents in Germany were unable to intervene against the mass extermination of the Jews, even though they rescued a few individuals. This is part of the tragedy of the German resistance. But many of Hitler's opponents in Germany were motivated by the persecution of the Jews above all other consideration.

On the day after the failed 20 July 1944 insurrection, Hitler and his propaganda minister broadcast the version that "a small clique of ambitious, unscrupulous and criminal, stupid officers" had plotted to eliminate the Führer and "to exterminate the staff of the German Armed Forces leadership."[35] The Secret State Police soon discovered, however, that the conspiracy was deeply rooted and widely ramified, and that its motives were not as portrayed by the official propaganda.

After the first two weeks of investigations following the attempted insurrection, the head of the Secret State Police investigating commission, SS Lieutenant-Colonel Walter von Kielpinski, wrote in a

weisse Rose, Frankfurt am Main, 1952, passim; *The White Rose. The Resistance by Students against Hitler. Munich, 1942/43*, Munich, 1991, p. 60; Hassell (1988), pp. 62–63, 67–68, 130, 330; *Spiegelbild*, p. 501; Dr. Theodor Haubauch in his People's Court trial on 17 Jan. 1945, *Volksgerichtshof-Prozesse*, p. 100; Benedicta Maria Kempner, *Priester vor Hitlers Tribunalen*, Gütersloh, n.d., pp. 231–233; *Spiegelbild*, p. 501; Michael Balfour and Julian Frisby, *Helmuth von Moltke. A Leader against Hitler*, London, 1972, p. 218; Freya von Moltke, Michael Balfour, Julian Frisby, *Helmuth James von Moltke 1907–1945. Anwalt der Zukunft*, Stuttgart, [1975], p. 215; [Helmuth] James von Moltke, *Briefe an Freya 1939–1945*, ed. Beate Ruhm von Oppen, Munich, 1988, pp. 317–319; Hassell (1988 German edition), pp. 70, 330; report on Popitz's trial, Princeton University, A.W. Dulles Papers, IV g 10 b 57/44 gRs 4 Oct. 1944; Detlef Graf von Schwerin, *"Dann sind's die besten Köpfe, die man henkt." Die junge Generation im deutschen Widerstand*, Munich, [1991], p. 426; Ger van Roon, *Wilhelm Staehle. Ein Leben auf der Grenze, 1877–1945*, Munich, 1969, p. 88; Peter Hoffmann, *Stauffenberg. A Family History, 1905–1944*, Cambridge, 1995, pp. 133, 151, 226; Hans Rothfels, ed., "Ausgewählte Briefe von Generalmajor Helmuth Stieff (hingerichtet am 8. August 1944)," *Vierteljahrshefte für Zeitgeschichte*, 2 (1954), pp. 300, 303; Stahlberg, p. 380; Henry O. Malone, *Adam von Trott zu Solz. Werdegang eines Verschwörers 1909–1938*, Berlin, 1986, pp. 143, 160, 209; Diana Hopkinson, *The Incense Tree. An Autobiography*, London, 1968, p. 163; *Spiegelbild*, pp. 199–202; Osas, p. 98; Gerhard Schäfer, *Landesbischof D. Wurm und der nationalsozialistische Staat 1940–1945. Eine Dokumentation*, Stuttgart, 1968, pp. 159–160, 164–165.

35 *Völkischer Beobachter*, 21 July 1944, p. 1.

preliminary report dated 7 August 1944, under the heading "Criticisms of National Socialism:"

> Besides the treatment of the churches and of Christianity in the National Socialist state, certain points of view recur consistently in the statements of almost all persons now under investigation. a) Commonly they say that initially they had no objections to National Socialism, and had in fact observed its assumption of power with sympathy. But in subsequent years there had been a disillusionment [...] The implementation of National Socialism in reality had often been in strong contrast with proclaimed principles, which they always illustrate with personal experiences. Regularly they accuse the top brass of a lack of integrity. b) A number of conspirators opposed to the National Socialist State approved of antisemitism in principle but rejected the methods of its enforcement. Partly they emphasize humanitarian motivations, such as that the enforcement procedures had not been sufficiently humane and had not corresponded to the German character, partly they question the political expediency of causing severe tensions with the rest of the world by the rapid and rigorous elimination of Jewry.[36]

Since several conspirators had already declared the persecution of the Jews their chief motive, this was a distortion of the available evidence.

After three months of intensive investigations, on 16 October 1944 the Secret State Police Commission reported that the arrested conspirators "either reject in principle fundamental parts of the [National Socialist] program, or they dilute them to such an extent that hardly anything remained of the fundamental point [*grundsätzlichen Forderung*], the removal of the Jews." The Commission also wrote a nine-page report (dated 28 October 1944), dealing only with the anti-Hitler conspirators' attitudes "on the Racial Question, particularly the Jewish Question." The Commission summarized the results of the investigation: "The entire inner alienation from the ideas of National Socialism which characterized the men of the reactionary conspiratorial circle expresses itself above all in their position on the Jewish Question. [...] they stubbornly take the liberal position of granting to the Jews in principle the same status as to every German."[37]

There is no reason to doubt the accuracy of the police reports, which quote verbatim the rejection of anti-Jewish measures by a number of conspirators. The resisters articulated openly their reproof of the regime's core policy (its "*grundsätzlichen Forderung*"). This could

36 *Spiegelbild*, p. 168.
37 Ibid., pp. 449–450, 457, 471.

only diminish the resisters' prospects of escaping with their lives. Some did try to present themselves as supportive of the ideas of National Socialism, though in some disagreement with its practice; some revealed their anti-Jewish bias while opposing mass murder. The resisters had little control over the terminology the police employed in their reports. The more remarkable is the comprehensiveness of the Secret State Police's conclusion about the views of the conspirators.

There is, on the other hand, substantial independent evidence that confirms the Secret State Police summary, in the form of public lectures, administrative and private correspondence, diary entries, testimony in the "People's Court", and policy statements prepared for the day of the insurrection.

In spite of this evidence, some maintain that all or most of Hitler's opponents in Germany were antisemites, and that they supported Hitler's anti-Jewish policies.[38] These critics cite certain resisters' alleged approval of a "racial principle," or of restrictions on the influence of Jews in economic, professional and cultural occupations. But the critics either cite such expressions without citing also the resisters' condemnation of the National Socialist practice, or they treat these condemnations as insignificant. Others deduce the mentality of individuals from the fact that the individuals belonged to social strata in which that mentality was current. Only an individual-biographical method can produce reliable information on the issue.[39] An absence of evidence of overt manifestations of opposition to anti-Jewish policies cannot be interpreted as evidence of antisemitism. An overt response, on the other hand, such as either support of, or opposition to anti-Jewish measures, must be scrutinized within its historical context.

If the critics were right that Hitler's German opponents were as antisemitic as the rest of German society and therefore co-responsible for "Auschwitz," and that they objected to anti-Jewish policies only when such policies were pursued with public "rioting and force,"[40] the

38 Dipper, "Der Deutsche Widerstand," pp. 349–380; Unger, pp. 941–957. Dipper spent a great deal of time discovering the "influence" or the "handwriting" of this or that resister whom he seeks to convict of "antisemitism," without offering substantiating evidence; Reynolds, p. 54.

39 Cf. Dohna, pp. 857–858.

40 Dipper, "Der 20. Juli;" Dipper, "Der Deutsche Widerstand," pp. 349, 354.

resisters' references to anti-Jewish outrages and mass murder, which were treated as state secrets and kept out of the public's view, as arguments in the struggle against Hitler would have been singularly unsuited to win over confederates. But Bonhoeffer, Dohnanyi, Oster, Tresckow, Beck and Stauffenberg all used these references to convince potential military allies to try to obstruct the deportations and atrocities, and to speed up the preparations for the overthrow of National Socialism.[41] The fact that these references were constantly made in the search for supporters of Hitler's overthrow means that the persecution of the Jews was a fundamental motive of resistance to Hitler's rule.

41 Bethge, *Bonhoeffer* (German edition), pp. 835–836; Hoffmann, *Stauffenberg*, pp. 210–212.

*20 July and the "Jewish Question"**

CHRISTOF DIPPER

Marion Gräfin Dönhoff recounted in her memoirs[1] that regarding the events of 20 July 1944 she is often asked whether the conspirators, many of whom she knew very well, were "real democrats." She would answer that the question was worded incorrectly, because for those who were involved in the 20 July conspiracy it was not the political belief that was crucial, but rather the willingness to oppose Hitler unconditionally. Gräfin Dönhoff points to something very important with this statement: the question should be asked not from the vantage point of life in the Federal Republic, but from the context of the contemporary situation.This is true not only for the resistance, but for the Third Reich as a whole.

Everyone who examines the Third Reich today recalls "Auschwitz." This is understandable and legitimate. But it is a view that is determined by hindsight and is thus ahistorical. One cannot understand the Third Reich if only Auschwitz is considered. One cannot even — and this will be argued in this paper — understand resistance. A historicization of National Socialism, first called for by the late Martin Broszat some years ago[2] as a responsibility of our time, must be able to explain the following:

* As Professor Hoffmann's paper for this conference is to a very large extent identical to what he wrote in the *Frankfurter Allgemeine Zeitung* in July 1994 in which he criticized me severely, I thought it therefore justifiable to put to discussion my own article in the German weekly *Die Zeit* published two weeks earlier. I add, however, some bibliographic information. My comments are to be found at the end of the article. Translation by Julia Brüggemann and Marline Otte.

1 Marion Gräfin Dönhoff, *Um der Ehre willen. Erinnerungen an die Freunde vom 20. Juli*, Berlin, 1994.

2 Martin Broszat, "Plädoyer für eine Historisierung des Nationalsozialismus," *Merkur*, 39 (May 1985), pp. 373–385.

- regarding the Third Reich as a whole: the coexistence of criminal energy and destruction on the one hand and success and mobilization of masses on the other.
- regarding resistance: the coexistence of participation and renunciation, of collaboration (*Bündnispolitik*), and conspiracy.

I

During the past fifteen years German historiography has attempted to dismantle a construct that it had itself created since 1945 — the ahistorical monumentalization of the German resistance, which admittedly was important as a founding idea of the Federal Republic.[3] Many, in fact most taboos have been broken. All historians have begun to emphasize that the conspirators not only worked toward the fall of Hitler, but were also instrumental in his rise to and consolidation of power. It is evident that in this context "resistance" only refers to those groups of national conservatives who governed Germany since Brüning. They needed the NSDAP in order to hold onto power themselves, especially after Brüning's successors and the National Socialists realized that they would not succeed without a coalition. Hence, their tactical alliance with the national conservatives in 1931 called the *Harzburger Front*. The term "tactical" here refers both to the inner reservations each party harbored about the alliance and to their reluctance to commit themselves to a particular program. Their shared wish to abolish the Weimar Republic based on political and cultural resentments sufficed for their cooperation.

In a larger sense this alliance of enemies of the "Weimar system" also includes the churches. Both confessions never succeeded in overcoming their aversions to the Weimar Republic. It would be wrong to suggest that this implied a general affinity with National Socialism; in fact the Catholic episcopate continually emphasized their ideological, and after 1933 also their politico-cultural differences, while Protestants,

3 Latest surveys by Gerd R. Ueberschär, ed., *Der 20. Juli 1944. Bewertung und Rezeption des deutschen Widerstandes gegen das NS-Regime*, Cologne, 1994. Wolfgang Benz and Walther H. Pehle, eds., *Lexikon des deutschen Widerstandes*, Frankfurt, 1994.

especially Lutherans, more or less avoided investigating the ideology and program of the National Socialists. In addition, the theory that Hitler as the ultimate anti-Bolshevik would serve as a bulwark and thus deserved sympathy, coupled with the traditional anti-Judaic theology, helped tear down the walls that had previously separated the parties.

Nobody today doubts the broad antisemitic consensus of these forces which held unrestricted power after 1933. The National Socialists as well as the conservative nationalist élites saw the "Jewish question" as a problem that needed a "solution." Details, however, had not been agreed upon before Hitler took power, so that the partners here as well as in many other areas cooperated and even competed in various anti-Jewish measures. This explains why the anti-Jewish policies of the Third Reich — which began with the tumultuous removal of most Jews from the Prussian and Bavarian justice systems at the end of March 1933 and the boycotts of Jewish-owned stores on 1 April 1933 — were only categorically rejected by those who later emerged as the opposition if the riots and the use of force were not politically motivated. The Law for the Reestablishment of the Professional Civil Service, issued on 7 April 1933, with its anti-Jewish elements, however, corresponded to old demands of the right-wing parties and thus initially did not generate criticism from that camp. It surprised even Hitler that the Minister of War, Blomberg, on 2 February 1934 ordered the adoption of this law with its "Aryan clause" for the army. This did not affect the contempt most officers felt toward antisemitism of the Streicher kind. The Nuremberg Laws of 1935 also show that the increasing exclusion of Jews, as long as it proceeded within proper legal channels, originated at the top levels of the bureaucracy. One of the initiators, Minister of Economics Schacht, explained in typically obscure language that this was to ensure that "the program of the NSDAP could be implemented" without letting "the lawless drifting" determine the atmosphere.[4]

Similarly, the new regime did not attempt to force the churches to adopt the Aryan clause. Whenever such initiatives were introduced, they originated with the organizations themselves. The Catholic church

4 Minutes of a conference in the Ministry of Economics, 20 August 1938, cited by Otto Dov Kulka, "Die Nürnberger Rassengesetze und die deutsche Bevölkerung im Lichte geheimer NS-Lage- und Stimmungsberichte," *Vierteljahrshefte für Zeitgeschichte,* 32 (1984), p. 617.

remained unaffected, the concordat of 20 July 1933, longed-for since decades realized the separation of the secular and religious spheres. On the Protestant side, however, right wing "German Christians," called for the introduction of an "Aryan clause" as well as coordination (*Gleichschaltung*), leadership principle (*Führerprinzip*), and a state church even before the decree of the Law of the Professional Civil Service. This motion, however, was contrary to the fundamental principles of Christianity and threatened to undermine the autonomy of the Church. This was one of the reasons for the founding of the *Pfarrernotbund*, which led to the imminent church struggle. Yet neither the Protestant nor the Catholic leaders raised an objection to these state-sponsored measures. In an essay published at the beginning of April 1933, it was Dietrich Bonhoeffer, thus acting in a semi-public arena who conceded the state's right to "pursue new paths" on the "Jewish question." But he impressed upon the church to remind the state that its competence in these matters had limits, and that the church should help the victims regardless of their confession, and even sabotage the process, if necessary.[5]

The above brief sketch of the behavior of the German élites at the beginning of the Nazi period is important because it illustrates the dilemma of the conservative forces that cooperated with the regime while keeping a certain distance. This dilemma continued to determine the attitudes of the resistance toward the anti-Jewish policies.[6] Their conviction that there was indeed a "Jewish question" begging a solution from the state weakened their ability to be critical and to resist. There was no clear veto of these policies, but the official measures were deemed worthy of discussion. They did not reject the renunciation of Jewish emancipation and this had far-reaching consequences. The trend — and not just with respect to the anti-Jewish policies — that can be followed through the history of the slowly emerging conservative resistance, was already discernible at the beginning: namely, the attempt to differentiate between policies of which they generally approved, and what they used to qualify as intolerable "excesses."

5 Dietrich Bonhoeffer, "Die Kirche vor der Judenfrage" (April 1933), in his *Gesammelte Schriften*, Eberhard Bethge, ed., Munich, 1965, vol. II, p. 45.

6 For detailed information cf. Christof Dipper, "The German Resistance and the Jews," *Yad Vashem Studies,* 16 (1984), pp. 41–76.

Until 1938 Hitler's allies believed they could control the political development. In that year they suffered a double defeat. First they had to realize "with horror"[7] on 10 November after a night of pogroms that mob antisemitism, which was supported by the SA and had been organized by Goebbels, could run wild in the streets without any intervention by the state. This moral defeat was coupled with a foreign policy disaster. Moreover they believed it would have negative military ramifications as well — a characteristic way of thinking for them. They were so focused on the idea that politics was dominated by disciplined élites that they failed to recognize the emergence of the SS as a new, and soon to be more powerful competitor. The SS initially continued the policy of repression and expropriation — more quietly than before but also more radical and more "efficient" — and in 1941 made the extermination of the Jews its primary function.

It was during this year that the later conspirators formed loose associations of resistance. According to their memoranda, letters and diaries, they reached this decision primarily based on foreign policy and military considerations. They realized that they had lost almost all their influence at the level of "high" politics. They believed Hitler's policies after 1938–39 to be a "foolish" (*leichtfertig*)[8] gamble of previous achievements. The moral illegitimacy of the regime was merely the trigger for a minority of resisters to pursue active opposition. This is not to say that the conspirators did not have moral standards, but as people with a rigorous ethic of Christian conservatism, they believed the state itself was a moral institution that was held to different standards than those of individuals. As long as the bureaucracy brought about the dissimilation of the Jews according to the rule of law, as it had done since 1933, they believed in the legality of these measures. The relative ease with which the consequences of *Kristallnacht* were handled by the administration confirmed the illusion of the resisters that the state was once again in control of the excesses of the vulgar party. Because the foreign policy developments had accelerated so drastically, the

7 The Diary of Ulrich von Hassell, 27 November 1983. Friedrich Freiherr Hiller von Gaertringen, ed., *Die Hassell-Tagebücher 1938–1944. Aufzeichnungen vom Andern Deutschland*, Berlin, 1988, p. 63.

8 *Die Hassell-Tagebücher*, 29 September and 10 October 1938, 30 and 31 August and 11 October 1939.

problems of a minority, that by 1939 had been decimated to 218,000 persons or 0.35 percent of the population of the *Altreich*,were hardly perceived.

This would change dramatically with the beginning of the war against Poland and the attack on the Soviet Union. The war in the east had always been declared as a *Volkstumskampf* and marked the inception of the "Final Solution." The argument that the excesses were the work of individuals was no longer plausible, because the opposition, which was moving closer and closer together, found out about the various orders and the reports of the *Einsatzgruppen* — sometimes even through the official channels. Even those who were not directly involved were aware of the extent of the extermination by the end of 1941, as we know from the diary of Ulrich von Hassell who was retired.[9] The deportation of Jews from Berlin happened before the very eyes of the political élites and von Hassell was correct when he suspected that "these people were killed, because one never hears from them again."[10] By the fall of 1942, not long after completion of the trial phase with extermination gas, the conspirators were aware of the existence of, and the techniques employed in, the industrial operation of the mass extermination of European Jews in the camps in the east. Even the churches, which depended on others for information and could not immediately assess the crimes in the east, were aware of the situation by 1943.

The systematic mass extermination heightened the urgency for action among the resistance. The immoral character of the regime could now no longer be doubted. The news from the East was, however, so incredible that it was accepted reluctantly. This was especially true for the older generation. The younger among the later conspirators, who were all soldiers and thus had inadvertently been eyewitnesses to the atrocities, spontaneously decided to interfere with the state's interests. It is difficult to establish to what extent knowledge about events in the east influenced the planning and activities of the enemies of the regime. Firstly, there are only incomplete records about the last years of the resistance. Secondly, schemes for the removal of Hitler began to take priority over plans for Germany after day X. The activities of the

9 *Die Hassell-Tagebücher*, 1 November 1941.

10 *Die Hassell-Tagebücher*, 4 August 1943.

Kreisau Circle are the most fully documented. It appears that after they learned of the mass exterminations in 1942–43 they agreed to an active fight against the regime; they also established contact with a group of military men whom they had previously avoided, as well as with the group around Beck and Goerdeler.

The same cannot be claimed for Beck and Goerdeler, who were the organizational and intellectual leaders of the old conservatives. Goerdeler's memorandum *Das Ziel* (The Goal), written before the inception of the "Final Solution" in 1941 and never changed despite the new situation, was determined by the traditional primacy of foreign politics. This is also true for other memoranda that were written later. Two reasons can be cited for this. Firstly, such texts took the reasoning of the target group into account. In this case Goerdeler and Beck wanted to reach men at the highest levels; even Himmler was considered a possible ally in the struggle against Hitler until the end. Secondly, Goerdeler and von Hassell notoriously considered the mass murder of the Jews a foreign policy disaster. This betrays a hierarchy of norms and values that reflected a loss of sense of scale. Even in 1944 the "Final Solution" was considered both a moral and foreign policy catastrophe that prevented Germany from attracting foreign allies, a key concept of the ruling lites since Bismarck's time.

These tactical considerations were completely ineffective, because the generals, who were actively involved in the *Volkstumskampf* in the east, could not be convinced to join the resistance simply by knowing about the events either through official channels or through memoranda of the conspirators. The group of men around Beck, Goerdeler, von Hassell, and Popitz therefore lost the initiative to the younger generation in 1944. Their motives were a good deal more of a moral nature. The knowledge of new details of the mass murder in Poland hastened their actions. Stauffenberg, for example, was convinced of the need to quickly eliminate Hitler when he heard in the spring of 1944 from Yorck that Kaltenbrunner issued an order to "give 40,000 to 42,000 Hungarian Jews 'special treatment' in Auschwitz."[11] Tresckow's reaction to the renewed doubts by Stauffenberg in July 1944 is well known. In his eyes

11 Cited by Christian Müller, *Oberst i.G. Stauffenberg. Eine Biographie*, Düsseldorf, 1971, p. 382.

the assassination and coup were imperative for moral reasons alone, even if success was doubtful.[12]

Unlike these officers — who only turned into enemies of the regime after they witnessed, with horror, the extermination practices, a regime they had previously ardently admired — Bonhoeffer did not need these experiences. Racial antisemitism was completely alien to him. He realized the illegitimacy of the regime as soon as the persecution of the Jews began in 1933 or a little later. This was also the central motivation for his decision to join the political resistance — first (1938), in a passive role, later (after the French offensive), as co-conspirator. Political considerations were secondary. Bonhoeffer's intrusion into state politics did not yet have a theological foundation. Protestantism traditionally did not provide arguments in this situation. In his attempts to find dogmatic (theological) justification, Bonhoeffer was ahead of his time. Already in 1940 he called the Jews his "brethren."[13] His critique was thus not only directed against the state, but also against his church which was not able or willing to follow him.

The sparse primary sources give the impression that Bonhoeffer was only able to explain and gain acceptance of his theological views when he was physically present at church meetings. In November 1941, he succeeded in convincing the tenth *Altpreussische Bekenntnissynode* to draw up a text on the fifth commandment. It was completed after several drafts in early 1943 and to great extent written by Bonhoeffer himself. In October 1943 in an internal memorandum, it prompted the twelfth *Altpreussische Bekenntnissynode* to denounce extermination and liquidation of fellow men.[14] A sermon on the occasion of the Day of Repentance (*Busstag*), in 1943 urged publicly: "Woe us and our people ... if we consider it just to kill people, because they are considered unworthy of life or because they belong to a different race ..."[15] Here euthanasia and the extermination of Jews were mentioned in the same

12 Cited by Fabian von Schlabrendorff, *Offiziere gegen Hitler*, Frankfurt, 1962, p. 138.

13 In his magnum opus which he could not complete, entitled *Ethik*, cited by Eberhard Bethge, "Dietrich Bonhoeffer und die Juden," in *Konsequenzen. Dietrich Bonhoeffers Kirchenverständnis heute*, Ernst Feil and Ilse Tödt, eds., Munich, 1980, p. 202.

14 Cf. Eberhard Bethge, *Dietrich Bonhoeffer. Eine Biographie*, Munich, 4th edition 1978, pp. 795–798.

15 Cit. ibid., p. 797.

breath, but this should not obscure the fact that both churches merely protested against euthanasia in a formal way. Conversely, according to the existing sources, euthanasia did not play any role in the rhetoric of the resistance.

The results were different outside of Bonhoeffer's reach. A memorandum, that he initiated at the turn of 1942–43 with the knowledge of Goerdeler was of a different nature. It was supposed to be presented to the ecumenical movement by the Confessional Church after the war. This text is of particular importance because it was drawn up without consideration for high-ranking officials inside the Nazi regime. The memorandum of the so-called "Freiburg Circle" was called *Politische Gemeinschaftsordnung. Ein Versuch zur Selbstbestimmung des christlichen Gewissens in den politischen Nöten unserer Zeit* (The Polity. An Attempt at Self-Examination of the Christian Conscience in View of the Political Problems of Our Time). Its section No. 5 with the title *Vorschläge für eine Lösung der Judenfrage in Deutschland* (Suggestions for a Solution of the Jewish Question in Germany), was drawn up by the economist Constantin von Dietze and shows that traditional antisemitism did not lose influence even in light of the "Final Solution." On the one hand von Dietze considered self-evident both the racial barriers as practiced by the churches — "they exist in all Christian churches of the world" — and racial politics of the state — "to fight the dangerous influences of a certain race on the *Volksgemeinschaft*." On the other hand, he was horrified that National Socialism "systematically killed hundreds and thousands of people just on the basis of their Jewishness." Compensation (*Wiedergutmachung*), was the responsibility of the state. Von Dietze suggested three alternatives for the solution of the "Jewish Question." The first was that it be solved on the international stage in the form of a "convention" for the protection of the rights and duties of Jewish citizens. The second recommendation described a special "Jewish status", guaranteed by international law, which would unite the Jews and give them representation, as well as the right to education and the right to be economically active in return for their expatriation. The third suggestion applied to Germany alone. Von Dietze considered it unnecessary to have special regulations for Jews. "The number of surviving returning Jews would be so small as to not pose a threat to the German people."[16] The renunciation of future

16 The document has been reprinted in *In der Stunde Null. Die Denkschrift des*

legal discrimination was purely of a pragmatic nature, being dependent upon the size of the Jewish community. Von Dietze thus reproduced the classical position of the German nationalist (*deutschnational*) middle classes, which can be traced back to Treitschke.

Saying this, we are already dealing with the resistance's plans for the future. Goerdeler unequivocally castigated the genocide in his memorandum, calling the systematic and hideous elimination of the Jews an abomination. For him compensation was also self-understood. Shortly before the assassination attempt on Hitler, he drew up the "Government Policy Statement No. 2" and stated laconically: "The persecution of the Jews, which proceeded in the most inhuman and deeply shameful manner and can never be compensated, has stopped."[17] However, this did not fully solve the problem for him. His long-term goal — resulting from the truism that "the Jews belonged to a different race" — was to establish a Jewish state "under decent circumstances either in parts of Canada or South America" — not in Palestine. He believed that the majority of German Jews should become a part of this community. Only a small group of Jews who were willing to assimilate completely would be allowed to keep full German citizenship. This plan would also offer a solution to the "problem of mixed marriages."[18]

The parallels with the program of the "Freiburg Circle" are so evident that one can exclude any tactical considerations on Goerdeler's part. Here we also encounter a concept that had been circulating in the national conservative milieu for decades, and not only there. According to this approach, the Jews were divided into two groups with differing legal status: a well-established elitist minority and a majority of recently immigrated Eastern Jews. Thus assimilation and dissimilation formally

Freiburger "Bonhoeffer-Kreises": Politische Gemeinschaftsordnung. Ein Versuch zur Selbstbesinnung des christlichen Gewissens in den politischen Nöten unserer Zeit, Philipp von Bismarck, ed., Tübingen, 1979, pp. 146–151.

17 Third Version reprinted in Archiv Peter, ed., *Spiegelbild einer Verschwörung. Die Kaltenbrunner-Berichte an Bormann und Hitler über das Attentat vom 20. Juli 1944*, Stuttgart, 1961, p. 149.

18 Carl Goerdeler "Das Ziel" (Memorandum finished 1941), in Wilhelm Ritter von Schramm, ed., *Beck und Goerdeler. Gemeinschaftsdokumente für den Frieden 1941–1944*, Munich, 1965, pp. 105–107.

received a legal status, which related to the perceived dangers that the Jews posed to the German people.

The documents of the Kreisau Circle differed considerably from these perspectives and prejudices. In the summer of 1943, the final statement of the Kreisau Circle demanded the complete restoration of emancipation. However, it remains open to what extent Moltke's editing obscured the various opinions, since the participants had strong Christian ties and as such must have been influenced by prejudice against Jews. Nevertheless, their distance from the national conservative resistance remained substantial.[19] This explains Moltke's continuing reservations toward the group of conspirators around Beck, Goerdeler and von Hassell. The resistance thus did not come to a unitary view of the "Jewish Question." Their opinions varied too widely. They only agreed on a rejection of the rowdy antisemitism of the SA (and of course the extermination practices of the SS). This should not be surprising in view of the social distance between the élites involved in resistance, and the party, which they perceived as vulgar.

Against their better judgement, the Gestapo evaluated the standpoints of the conspirators after their interrogations regarding 20 July: "They stubbornly held on to liberal ideas, which placed Jews on par with all other Germans."[20] This may have held true for members of the Bonhoeffer, Schleicher and von Dohnanyi families, for whom the illegitimacy of the Third Reich was evident from the start. For the majority, the anti-Jewish policies of National Socialism did not present a motive for resistance until 1938 or even 1940. Their resistance can be traced to other causes and generally terminated a loyal cooperation with the regime, a cooperation that had never been free from doubts. They continued the cooperation solely for tactical reasons. Knowledge of the mass murder of Jews did not have a catalytic effect, since the decision of the national conservative élites of the older generation to attempt a coup preceded the beginning of the "Final Solution." The news of the mass murder reinforced their disgust with the regime but

19 Cf. the documents reprinted in Ger van Roon, *Neuordnung im Widerstand. Der Kreisauer Kreis innerhalb der deutschen Widerstandsbewegung*, Munich, 1967.

20 Report of the interrogations, 28 October 1944; reprinted in *Spiegelbild* (note 17), p. 471.

did not influence their political plans and goals. Without a doubt this was a "rebellion of tradition."

It is remarkable in this context that the "Final Solution" also led to a "rebellion of conscience." It was their outrage at witnessing the murder that led the most determined of the planners of the assassination to resistance, namely Tresckow, Stauffenberg, Yorck, Schulenburg and von dem Bussche. This was a generational question. As ardent supporters of National Socialism initially, they hoped to realize an idealistic renewal of Germany. Antisemitism was not alien to them. But the existence of some doubts, coupled with personal confrontation with the "Final Solution," shattered their dream and forced them to act. The murder of the Jews drove them to action, although — unlike the older generation — they already knew that everything was lost.

II

To conclude these remarks and return to the problem of historicization of the German resistance that I raised earlier, it should be clear that Gräfin Dönhoff was correct in her assumption that the question about the democratic convictions of the resisters was posed incorrectly. Moral questions are harder to answer. While democracy can be considered an attribute of political modernization — and thus cannot be demanded of those conspirators who had not been professional politicians before 1933 and who were confined by their social prejudices — moral standards are timeless. But this is only partially true, since the relationship between morality and law as well as between morality and politics undergoes constant change. Murder remained murder even for the German opposition. But the majority did not consider the exclusion of Jews from the civil service and the free professions as a breach of the law — not yet. Quite the contrary, anybody who assumed that a "Jewish Question" existed — which was certainly true for the national conservative élites — felt obliged to find its solution. Even if some measures, albeit formulated by the bureaucracy and legally decreed, violated justice, one could accept the shortcomings of discrimination especially if the alternative was a "wild" solution by the party, something that was inherent in Hitler's "dual state."[21] One of the typical characteristics of the National Socialist regime was that even nonconformists partially cooperated — because temptation and force, seduction and violence, achievement and destruction were always coupled. Secondly, nobody could predict the future. Hitler had avoided clear programmatic declarations before 1933 and the antisemitic dimensions of his campaigns since 1928 were not taken all too serious. *Mein Kampf* was read — if at all — only by Hitler's opponents. As a party platform it has been overrated in hindsight. Moreover, in modern political systems, success in mobilization can be attributed more to techniques of persuasion than to clear programmatic statements. Finally, it was a new political experience in Germany to have a notorious criminal in the top position of the state. In Germany, the state still represented the manifestation of a moral idea.

Let us return to the predictability of the future. The National Socialist themselves did not have a clear vision as to how the "Jewish Question" should be solved. They merely agreed on the fact that the Jews had to "disappear." It was a matter of opportunity to determine the procedure. This increased their ability to act, allowed for potential interventions by their allies, and left everybody uncertain about the future, including Jews. Even the leading Jewish representatives in 1933 believed that the period of assimilation had ended and that they would be able to accommodate themselves in the new state on a lower level. They encouraged only the younger generation to emigrate. This was welcomed by the National Socialists, who even came to an agreement with the Zionists to accelerate the stagnating exodus. Until 1939–41 the regime pursued a policy of deprivation of rights and encouraging emigration. When they began to use violence after 1938 things picked up again. Dissimilation and emigration were accepted, indeed demanded by the majority of Hitler's national conservative allies, although the anti-Jewish policies did not have the same meaning for these circles as they did for the National Socialists.

The political successes and the extraordinary extent of the consensus for Hitler between 1938 and 1940 led people to ignore the increasing radicalization of antisemitism by the regime, especially since it took

21 Ernst Fraenkel, *The Dual State. A Contribution to the Theory of Dictatorship*, New York, 1941.

place outside the *Altreich* — first in Austria, then in the Protectorate and finally in the *Generalgouvernement*. The methods of the SS, which was in charge of Jewish affairs since 1938, increased in brutality. Until the summer of 1941 the regime still believed in a "solution" via emigration, or increasingly, expulsion to the east. Already from 1939, expulsion was accepted even though it involved a large number of deaths. The failure of the *Blitzkrieg* strategy in the war with the Soviet Union destroyed the hopes of deporting European Jewry past the Urals. Nevertheless, the orders to the *Einsatzgruppen* concerning Russian Jews were not modified. In the other countries the overflowing ghettos and the beginning of the relocation of *Volksdeutsche* necessitated a search for a quick "solution." By the turn of 1941–42 the locations of the extermination camps, the annihilation methods, the responsibilities and the priorities for the target areas had been determined and were ratified at the *Wannsee* conference. The decision to commit mass murder, however, remained secret. The initial steps were such that people could understand them as either legal measures or as excesses of individuals or specific organizations. Hitler's allies, particularly, were caught in this perspective as they partially shared the goals. Up to this point there was no problem of morality. It only appeared when the "excesses" were increasing to such an extent that the diabolical nature of the system became transparent. By this time, the opposition had already decided to resist actively for other reasons.

The relationship between morality and resistance was more complicated than many admit. Hannah Arendt had called the German opposition immoral, which caused a storm of indignation.[22] Of course, she only reacted to the German historiography, which for years had indiscriminately spoken of a "rebellion of conscience." Such a simplistic view obscures the complexity of historical reality. There is a threefold answer to the question of the role that moral considerations played in the decision to act by different groups at different times. Men like Bonhoeffer, Dohnanyi and Moltke on principle did not accept the argument of conflict between ethics and political actions. It was their moral outrage that forced them into the resistance. The

22 Hannah Arendt, *Eichmann in Jerusalem. A Report of the Banality of Evil*, New York, 1963.

so-called younger generation of military conspirators[23] who had served the regime with dedication during the first years of the war reacted differently. Only when they became aware of the criminal nature of the regime, did they recognize their moral delusions and try to compensate for it. The plans of Schulenburg, Tresckow and Stauffenberg for a coup and even more for an assassination have to be interpreted as an act of self-criticism, where the act took precedence over the result. This "Damascus experience" was denied to the so-called older generation which was allied with Hitler, whom they saw as the lesser evil. What determined the behavior of Beck, Halder, Goerdeler, Hassell, Popitz and Canaris were not primarily moral considerations but considerations of political power. They did not need moral arguments to resist. The "Final Solution" reinforced their judgement of National Socialism as a regime that was unable to uphold ethical norms, even when it served their purposes.

The national conservative resistance encompassed the entire range from "rebellion of conscience" to "rebellion of tradition." This repeatedly reduced its effectiveness. This was not the reason for its failure however; it did not succeed because the military leaders, except for a few individuals, did not cooperate with the conspirators. Neither morality nor tradition prompted the generals to act — they had become too much a part of the system. The historical achievement of the resistance is that it acted in spite of the hopeless situation. The resistance, therefore, has to be judged just as the many other Germans who tried to save Jews for moral reasons are judged. Both were considered resisters by the National Socialists, and most conspirators and many other lifesavers ended on the scaffold.

Comments to Peter Hoffmann

Professor Hoffmann is certainly one of the leading experts on the July 1944 plot against Hitler. Thanks to his lifelong research activities he

23 Cf. Wolfgang Schieder, "Zwei Generationen im militärischen Widerstand gegen Hitler," in: *Der Widerstand gegen den Nationalsozialismus. Die deutsche Gesellschaft und der Widerstand gegen Hitler*, Jürgen Schmädeke and Peter Steinbach, eds., Munich, 2nd edition, 1986, pp. 436–459.

established excellent relationships with many of the survivors, their relatives, their collaborators, their friends and others. They gave him an abundance of material and interviews — not always without disinterest of course (for example he was given access to the Goerdeler papers, whereas neither Hans Mommsen nor Hans-Ulrich Thamer nor myself had this opportunity). He gave us the most detailed history of the plot and a valuable portrait of the Stauffenberg family.[24]

Yet though Professor Hoffmann is an excellent historian of the plot, his judgments concerning the German resistance as a whole are, in my opinion, less valuable. The reason is that he approaches historiography in a manner which in Germany would be characterized as *voraussetzungslos* (unconditional). In other words, the "facts" he discovered in the documents he used are isolated and it is Professor Hoffmann who gives them their significance.

It is my opinion that facts can only be qualified as part of the whole. We have to integrate the history of the resistance movement into the history of the Third Reich. To do this some elementary questions must be answered, namely: How did Nazism work as a political system? What were the functions of the later conspirators in the system? How did they think in general about racial, social, national or other kinds of discrimination? When and why did those involved decide to start a resistance movement? Who did they think would be a possible ally? What were their plans for the day after? What was discussed strictly within the conspirators' group and what did they say to others, for instance for tactical reasons? And finally, given the isolation in which the conspirators had to act, why did they risk the plot?

Summing up my own position I would like to stress four crucial points. First, in 1933 most of the July 44 plotters acted as partners of the Nazis. They were members or sympathizers of the *DNVP*, a party as antidemocratic as it was antisemitic. Consequently one cannot but state that the conspirators had had — up to a certain limit — aims that were identical to those formulated by the Nazis. The national conservatives, who then comprised the German élite, regarded the Nazis as vulgar and brutal, and therefore unable in the long run to keep themselves in

24 His best-known books are *Widerstand, Staatsstreich, Attentat. Der Kampf der Opposition gegen Hilter*, Munich, 3rd edition, 1979, and *Claus Schenk Graf von Stauffenberg und seine Brüder*, Stuttgart, 1992.

power. This, as we know, was a common but terrible mistake. It caused the conservatives to make one compromise after the other — in order to avoid the worst as they constantly said — such that they were unable to say: This far and no further. In most cases the conservatives would accept one kind of policy and criticize or reject another. Cases of total disunion were late and rare. The dissent was usually as partial as the collaboration.

Second, it must be admitted that there were persons who did not fit this description. The Dohnanyi, Bonhoeffer and Schleicher families, Count Moltke and others never considered the Nazis as possible coalition partners, nor did they support their ideology. This is especially true with regard to racial discrimination. It is therefore not surprising that they were extremely reluctant to collaborate with the national conservative resistance movement. When they finally decided to join them, they did so with reservations and preferred to stay in the background, knowing that the generals and former high officials were severely compromised. On the other hand, it was their accurate information about what was happening in the east that changed their minds.

Third, in order to understand the twisted road that led to the plot one must recognize that there were two different generations involved. The conspirators themselves knew this: in the von Hassell diary there are many entries dealing with the "older" and the "younger ones." "Generation" in this respect does not strictly mean the biological span of time but rather two groups with different life experience. Many of the younger generation were, at the beginning of the Third Reich, fanatic supporters of the regime. This was especially the case for the Stauffenberg brothers, for Tresckow, for Schulenburg. They were Nazis in the idealistic sense, carried away by the nationwide enthusiasm in 1933. They trusted in Hitler's promises to create the *Volksgemeinschaft*, they supported his battle against bolshevism, and of course they profited from the expansion of civil and military personnel. Antisemitic thinking was not unknown to them. When the war began, the younger among them mostly served as front officers in the east. There Tresckow, Claus Stauffenberg, Schulenburg, Gersdorff, Yorck, von dem Bussche and others saw the mass killings with their own eyes. Shocked, they decided to organize a coup even after most of their superiors had declined to take part. The generals, having organized the assassination of the so-called Russian "commissars" and other suspected groups, and tolerating, even helping the ethnic purges, were not swayed by the ghastly news their subordinates told them. And finally, the motives differed between the two groups. For the younger group, killing Hitler was not so much a precondition for the establishment of an alternative political system as it was a symbolic act, and as such it had to be done even if one knew or had the presentiment that the plot would fail.

The fourth point regards the so-called Kaltenbrunner report.[25] Professor Hoffmann says he trusts the wording concerning the attitudes of the conspirators toward the Jews. I myself doubt whether Kielpinski, who led the interrogation, really believed what he wrote. It must be remembered that there were two reports of the interrogations taped for Hitler. In the first one, Kielpinski related truly what the conspirators had said, namely that they had not opposed the anti-Jewish policy of the Nazis but of course were against the barbaric treatment of the Jews and, especially, the "final solution." It was in Kielpinski's second report, however, that his famous phrase appears: that the conspirators believed in absolute equality of all human beings. Why did he change his argument? My hypothesis is that in the meantime the SD had discovered the real dimensions of the conspiracy, that there were many more conspirators than the Nazis had previously thought. Kielpinski thus had to describe the resistance movement as being far more radical and therefore far more dangerous. From the Nazi point of view, accepting that all human beings are equal is more dangerous than having some anti-Jewish resentment, as stated in the first interrogation. I do not believe Kielpinski was telling the truth about the conspirators, but he had to justify why the SD had first underestimated the resisters' network and why they were really as dangerous as the *Führer* had previously claimed.

In his 1994 article countering mine, Professor Hoffmann chose as the title "They Rose Against Hitler Because They Could Not Tolerate the Killing Any Longer."[26] This is perfectly true regarding the younger generation. The problem, however, is that Professor Hoffmann does not make this distinction, and that, besides Stauffenberg and

25 Cf. note 17.

26 Peter Hoffmann, "Sie erhoben sich, weil sie die Morde nicht dulden wollten. Die Verfolgung der Juden als Motiv des 20. Juli," *Frankfurter Allgemeine Zeitung*, no. 162, 15 July 1994, p. 6.

Bonhoeffer, he focuses on Goerdeler and Beck. Yet these two had decided to resist Hitler long before they knew of the "final solution." Of course they were appalled when they heard about the destruction of European Jewry, and of course they would have stopped it had the plot been successful. But that goes without saying. More important is that Goerdeler, the intellectual and political leader of the older generation, was convinced that there was a "Jewish question." He was by no means an exception. On the contrary, this was a common argument within the right-wing groups and the Protestant churches. Goerdeler therefore made several proposals concerning the "solution" of the "Jewish question," whose fundamental premise was to establish a kind of "apartheid" antisemitism, that is, dissimilation and a different legal status. A minority of old, assimilated families, however, could keep their citizenship. I do not believe there is evidence that Goerdeler changed his mind substantially during the war.

I therefore find it difficult when Professor Hoffmann argues the opposite. In my view, an antisemite is not only one who physically attacks Jewish businesses, and a person is not necessarily a partisan of emancipation if he is greatly perturbed by the barbaric persecution of ten thousand Polish Jews in Germany in 1938–39. What were the reasons for Goerdeler's resignation as Mayor of Leipzig in 1936? Was it the defense of his Jewish fellow countrymen? That seems rather unlikely, since Mendelssohn-Bartholdy whose statue had been removed contrary to Goerdeler's order was never a Jew! Only the Nazis declared him as such. Should Goerdeler have argued in the Nazi manner? I doubt it. He resigned because of the clear — and repeated — insubordination of the deputy mayor who was backed by the party.[27] Between 1936 and 1938 numerous representatives of the national conservatives resigned, either because they saw no alternative or because they were simply compelled to leave their posts.

Lastly, a few words about racial and social prejudice in Germany. The Nazi persecution was not directed exclusively at Jews; their vision of a biological purge included other groups — Gypsies, persons with genetic diseases or defects, and last but not least the so-called asocial people. What did the resistance movement think about this? We don't

27 Cf. now Ines Reich, *Carl Friedrich Goerdeler: ein Oberbürgermeister gegen den NS-Staat*, Cologne 1997.

know. There is not a single document that mentions the elimination of socially unfit or maladapted persons. How should we interpret this? Can we conclude from the absolute silence a general disinterest, prejudice, consent or whatever else? Professor Hoffmann does not pose the question. I instead prefer to embed the history of the German resistance into the whole history of the Third Reich, which consists not only of force and control but also — and in large measure — of approval and willing participation.

Responses of the Bystanders

American Diplomatic Records regarding German Public Opinion During the Nazi Regime

RICHARD BREITMAN

Despite the quantity and importance of Nazi official reports on German public attitudes, there is no way to derive a representative sample of the population from them.[1] As a result historians have turned to non-Nazi sources to enhance our picture of the German public under the Nazi regime. The extensive data compiled by the Socialist underground and smuggled abroad (*Sopade* Reports), represent one major source of nonofficial evidence of German public attitudes. Reports by foreigners in Germany provide another valuable perspective and, occasionally, a source of detailed information on changes in German public attitudes during the 1930s.

Foreign diplomats, responsible for sending accurate information to their governments, represent a special category of foreign observers — at their best, providing running and expert observations of changes in the political and social climate over time. To be sure, not all foreign diplomats had an interest in the Jewish question. Moreover, many diplomats lacked sufficient contact or familiarity with German society to make observations of significant historical value (or of immediate use to their governments). But American diplomatic records and private correspondence by some American consular officials stationed in Germany offer some corroboration of other sources on German public opinion, as well as some insights into the strength of German antisemitism during the years 1933–39.

All reports sent by Embassy and Consular officials to the State Department (and correspondence from Washington to the field), are

1 David Bankier, *The Germans and the Final Solution. Public Opinion Under Nazism*, Oxford, 1992, pp. 4–9.

available in the Central Decimal File in Record Group 59 of the United States National Archives branch in College Park, Maryland. American officials in Germany, as elsewhere, gathered much more information than they actually sent to Washington. These original records (often called post records) of the Embassy and consulates were supposed to have reached Record Group 84 of the National Archives. Although some original records of the American consulates in Germany survive, most of what was of political significance was apparently sent to Berlin, where a fire during World War II gutted the collection. So we are left largely with the materials sent to Washington, supplemented by private papers.

In theory, American Embassy officials had charge of political reporting, while the consulates specialized in economic analysis, promotion and protection of American interests and citizens, and a range of other matters such as issuance of visas. In actuality, the distinctions between the American diplomatic service and the consular service had begun to break down, which was an advantage in the case of Germany.[2] Key consular officials in Germany consistently provided more detailed and more valuable political reports than their Embassy counterparts.

The Embassy in Berlin lacked strong direction. American Ambassador to Germany Frederick H. Sackett, Jr. resigned before the March 1933 inauguration of President Roosevelt, and his successor, former history professor William E. Dodd, did not arrive at his post until July 1933. Although admirably anti-Nazi, Dodd lacked diplomatic experience and self-confidence and failed to develop good contacts within German society, let alone among Nazi officials during 1933–37.[3]

2 Jesse H. Stiller, *George S. Messersmith. Diplomat of Democracy*, Chapel Hill, 1987, pp. 29, 35.

3 Contemporary appraisals of Dodd's weakness are legion. See Moffat's comment "Dodd may know the situation in Germany but has no power to describe it or keep the Department fully informed" in Wilbur Carr's Diary, 19 April 1935, Library of Congress. Geist's appraisal of Dodd's ineffectiveness can be found in Wilbur J. Carr's memorandum, 5 June 1935, Box 12, Carr Papers, Library of Congress. See the excellent article by Franklin L. Ford, "Three Observers in Berlin: Rumbold, Dodd and Francois-Poncet," in: *The Diplomats, 1919–1939*, Gordon A. Craig and Felix Gilbert, eds., Princeton, 1953, pp. 437–76. See also the assessment of Dodd by Robert Dallek, *Democrat and Diplomat. The Life of William E. Dodd*, New York, 1968, which is not convincing.

Dodd's successor at the start of 1938 was Hugh Wilson, who decided that a softer line against Nazism might be less confrontational. Wilson was recalled after *Kristallnacht*,[4] and there was no American ambassador in Germany during the nine months preceding the outbreak of war. An early counselor at the Embassy (and chargé des affaires during the *Gleichschaltung*) was George A. Gordon, who was snobbish and weak.[5]

Meanwhile, Consul General George S. Messersmith had served in Berlin since 1930 and was fluent in German, having been raised in a middle-class Pennsylvania Dutch family where German was a second language.[6] Messersmith also had an extremely talented subordinate and protegé in Consul Raymond H. Geist, a Harvard Ph.D. who also spoke German fluently and quickly became the most valuable American representative in Berlin.[7] He eventually became not only consul general, but also first secretary in the embassy. Geist's contacts within the German government and Nazi movement made it possible for American lawyer George Rublee to negotiate with Germany on behalf of the Intergovernmental Committee on Refugees in early 1939.[8]

In my research for this article I looked at a broad array of American diplomatic and consular reporting. Since Messersmith and Geist provided the most detailed and consistent accounts, I have focused on them here. A broader account would not, I believe, significantly alter the conclusions drawn from Messersmith's and Geist's views.

Almost from the beginning of the Nazi regime Messersmith began to supply Washington with lengthy reports of dramatic and not so

4 Messersmith to Secretary of State, 14 November 1938, Messersmith Papers, item 1075. Robert Dallek, *Franklin D. Roosevelt and American Foreign Policy, 1932–1945*, New York, 1979, pp. 167–68.

5 Stiller, *Messersmith*, pp. 28–29.

6 Ibid., pp. 1–5, 17.

7 In 1935 Messersmith described Geist as the most valuable officer the U.S. had in Berlin, and the Assistant Secretary of State Carr agreed. Carr Diary, 24 April 1936, Library of Congress. On Geist generally, Richard Breitman and Alan M. Kraut, *American Refugee Policy and European Jewry, 1933–1945*, Bloomington, 1987. Also, Stiller, *Messersmith*, pp. 27–28.

8 Because all of Messersmith's official dispatches and private letters are included in his papers, I have used and cited the Messersmith Papers below, rather than the National Archives. All the official reports, however, are also in the National Archives.

dramatic events. Not for nothing did he have the nickname "forty-page George."[9] In a manner that must have occasionally infuriated his busy superiors, but which benefited historians later, Messersmith relayed very detailed information about the antisemitic movement in Germany, as well as his own interpretation and analysis. Messersmith also took to writing lengthy personal letters to Jay Pierrepont Moffat, who headed the European division in the State Department, and Undersecretary of State William Phillips. When Messersmith left Berlin to take up the post of American minister in Vienna in 1934, his interest in the changes in Germany persisted and he continued to write about them.

Geist followed his example in writing dispatches and letters, although in better prose and not to the same length. Geist also corresponded with Messersmith, especially after the latter became Assistant Secretary of State in 1937. The result is two continuous series of reports from perceptive and involved observers in Germany, both of whom paid considerable attention to the evolving Nazi policies toward Jews and both of whom deplored them. Messersmith provided early warning (in August 1933!) that the Nazi regime was working on, and intended to issue a law stripping German Jews of their citizenship, and that it wanted eventually to eliminate Jews from German life.[10] In a letter to Undersecretary of State William Phillips, who was himself a social antisemite, Messersmith did not gloss over the political and moral problem of Nazi antisemitism:

> There has been nothing in social history more implacable, more heartless and more devastating than the present policy in Germany against the Jews. We cannot permit the public statements in Germany ... and the propaganda which is being carried on abroad by the Germans to blind us to the real facts. ...[11]

Phillips spoke to President Roosevelt about this letter and sent him a copy.[12]

9 Stiller, *Messersmith,* p. 5.

10 Messersmith to Secretary of State, 24 August 1933, confidential, "Further Development of the Anti-Semitic movement in Germany," and Messersmith to William Phillips, 29 September 1933, Messersmith Papers, items 270 and 312, University of Delaware.

11 Messersmith to William Phillips, 29 September 1933, Messersmith Papers, item 312. On Phillips, see Breitman and Kraut, *American Refugee Policy,* pp. 36–37.

12 Phillips to Messersmith, 14 October 1933, Additions to Collection, Messersmith Papers.

Initially Messersmith viewed the Nazi leaders as having infused antisemitism into their followers over a number of years, promising them benefits from the takeover of power and the forthcoming actions against Jews. Thus, the party and SS members, according to Messersmith, represented a force for radicalism on the Jewish question.[13] He wanted to believe that the party leaders were more moderate and opportunistic. He soon came to recognize, at least as far as Hitler and Goebbels were concerned, that the appearance of moderation was a complete illusion. It was only the realization that antisemitic actions could injure Germany's interests that exerted a check on the regime's actions against Jews.[14]

Geist was even more pessimistic (and more accurate) in his appraisal of Hitler and other party officials. In late 1935 Geist regarded Himmler as probably the second most powerful individual in the Nazi regime after Hitler; he also forecast a German move eastward in about two years. Geist sensed that in spite of divisions between moderates and radicals on the Jewish question, Hitler would align with the radical camp, which would win out in the end. In December 1938 Geist urged a major new American effort to save larger numbers of German Jews who were "condemned to death."[15] Toward the end of his tenure, in April 1939, Geist warned that once the efforts of the Intergovernmental Committee yielded limited results, the Nazi leaders would proceed to solve the Jewish question in their own way:

> It will, of course, consist in placing all the able-bodied Jews in work camps, confiscating the wealth of the entire Jewish population, isolating them, and putting additional pressure on the whole community, and getting rid of as many as they can by force.[16]

13 Messersmith to Secretary of State, 14 March 1933, 21 March 1933, 28 March 1933, 17 June 1933, items 118, 123, 128, 195.

14 Messersmith to Secretary of State, 17 June 1933, strictly confidential; Messersmith to Secretary of State, 1 November 1933, "Present Status of the Anti-Semitic Movement in Germany," strictly confidential, Messersmith Papers, items 195 and 325.

15 William Phillips Diary, 22 December 1935; notes on conversation with Geist in Berlin, Phillips Papers, Houghton Library, Harvard University. Breitman and Kraut, *American Refugee Policy*, p. 67.

16 Geist to Messersmith, 4 April 1939, Messersmith Papers, item 1187.

Both Messersmith and Geist observed with surprising accuracy what was happening within the regime in the area of anti-Jewish policy.

Given their track record, their views of German public opinion are of considerable interest. Both men initially distinguished sharply between the Nazi movement and the German public. Messersmith believed that Nazi actions against Jews in the professions and in business were not acceptable to the majority of the German people.[17] The reason, however, was not moral principle, but rather a distaste for Nazi methods combined with concern about the practical effects. Messersmith reported that the boycott of 1 April 1933 was not popular with the German public, because it damaged both the economy and Germany's image abroad. At the same time, many Germans came to accept Nazi propaganda that the boycott was necessary to convince foreign countries to stop their own "boycotts" and propaganda against Germany. Messersmith included a detailed memorandum written by one of two American vice consuls who had toured Berlin on 1 April, reporting that many Germans had treated the boycott as a joke and had continued to shop at their favorite stores.[18]

Messersmith also sent a very detailed summary of a private conversation with Hermann Bücher, head of the huge electrical power concern AEG, who was under pressure to dismiss those of his department heads who were Jewish.

> Dr. Bücher informed me that his attitude was as follows: It was evident that the problem of the Jews in Germany had for many years been a serious one, as on account of their industry, intelligence and application they had been able in extraordinarily large numbers to make places for themselves in the government administrations, in the professions, in business and in banking. He said that probably because there was a prejudice against them, not only here but elsewhere, the Jews applied themselves to whatever they did with greater zeal and with a greater singleness of purpose than those who did not have such a prejudice to contend with, and with this zeal in addition to native intelligence they had succeeded in Germany in getting into a preponderant position in many

17 Messersmith to Secretary of State, 1 November 1933, "Present Status of the Anti-Semitic Movement in Germany," strictly confidential, Messersmith Papers, item 325.

18 Messersmith to Secretary of State, 3 April 1933, strictly confidential, Messersmith Papers, item 133. William E. Beitz Memorandum Concerning Boycott of Jewish Stores in Berlin on 1 April 1933, Messersmith Papers, item 124.

> activities of German life. He pointed out that in one hospital, for example, 84% of the physicians were Jews and that while this percentage was large the number of Jews in the professions was much higher than their relative percentage of the population ... While in his opinion as a non-Jew he believes that Jews hold relatively too large a place in the government, business, professional and financial structure of the country, and while something could be done and should be done to bring about a better relative position [for non-Jews], he does not believe that this should be done in the way it is being attempted under the present government.[19]

Despite some sympathy for Jewish achievements and considerable resentment of Nazi interference with his firm, Bücher lacked principled opposition to early Nazi Jewish policy. After an apparent conversation with Hitler on the subject, he went along with the creation of a party screening committee within the firm to review personnel appointments.[20] Messersmith concluded from this and other examples that members of the German elites would not oppose the regime on the Jewish question; either they would express enthusiasm or they would bottle up their concerns. Perhaps they had little choice.

Both Messersmith and Geist focused on the attitudes of German youth. Although not fully "Nazified," more and more youths became swept up in the enthusiasm for the regime and its goals and were highly susceptible to Nazi propaganda. Geist warned in June 1934: "The younger hordes massed into the Hitler Youth, which flourish in every township and hamlet in the country, will make European history of the gravest importance, if not world history, if they continue under the present regime."[21] A few months later Geist reported that German youth was being inculcated with a sense of militarism to an unprecedented degree.[22]

In May 1933 Messersmith believed that the Nazi movement had aroused mass prejudices against Jews to such an extent, that even if official persecution ceased, professional and private life for Jews would

19 See especially Messersmith to Secretary of State, 22 June 1933, strictly confidential, Messersmith Papers, item 199.

20 Messersmith to Secretary of State, 3 April 1933, Messersmith Papers, item 133.

21 Messersmith to Secretary of State, 22 June 1933, strictly confidential; Messersmith to Phillips, 28 October 1933; Messersmith Papers, item 186 and 324. Quote from Geist to Moffat, 9 June 1934, Messersmith Papers, item 376.

22 Geist to Moffat, 15 September 1934, Messersmith Papers, item 417.

be difficult for years to come. Moreover, those opposed to antisemitic measures because of their consequences for the economy were, on balance, afraid to raise their voices.[23] A little more than a year later Geist warned against the conclusion that Germans as a whole shared the rabid antisemitism of the Nazis. He believed that the persecution of the Jews was purely the result of Nazi action. Although the public (in contrast to German youth) was tired of and disgusted by it, they were not much concerned with Jewish suffering. Those who might gain something from it would continue to victimize Jews, and they could certainly appeal to authorities to get their way, but otherwise actions and direction came from above.[24]

Geist did not, however, give a positive appraisal of German attitudes generally. He saw the public as increasingly enthusiastic about Pan-German ideas and willing to follow Hitler wherever he might lead. (Geist noted that the most significant reservations were held by German workers, who already feared that the Nazi course would lead to war.)[25] During a 1935 visit to Germany Messersmith, too, got the impression that the combination of Hitler's successes and propaganda had unleashed dangerous sentiments:

> ...there is a certain amount of popular hysteria in Germany. It is the psychology of a defeated nation which is frantically trying to get out of its inferiority complex. The Germans are a docile people, easily led, but now completely disorganized and disoriented with respect to practically every social and economic problem, and with respect to the outside world. It is not only the controlled press, but the daily diet of Nazi propaganda which is responsible for this.[26]

He did not comment at all at this time on popular antisemitism.

In early 1937 Geist reinforced his claim that the German people were tired of hearing Nazi propaganda about the Jews. Shortly before

23 Messersmith to Secretary of State, 23 May 1933, Messersmith Papers, item 186. Messersmith to Secretary of State, 1 November 1933, "Present Status of the Anti-Semitic Movement in Germany," strictly confidential, Messersmith Papers, item 325.

24 Geist to Moffat, 9 June 1934, Messersmith Papers, item 376.

25 Geist to Moffat, 9 June 1934, 10 August 1934, and 15 September 1934, Messersmith Papers, item 376, 398, and 417.

26 Messersmith Memorandum on Trip to Germany, 21–25 March 1935, Messersmith Papers, item 495.

Christmas a booklet was printed in Breslau listing the names of all the shops owned and operated by Jews. Many of the inhabitants, however, used it as a shopping guide, and the Jewish merchants did a fine business. Geist even wrote explicitly that only Nazi laws and other actions could harm the Jews, not public sentiment. However, because of the structure of the regime and its commitment to antisemitism and anti-Bolshevism, there was and would be no improvement in the situation of the Jews. Moreover, the regime did not lack energetic followers who had faith in Germany's destiny under Hitler.[27]

Geist's reports in 1938 and 1939 tended to concentrate more on the refugee problem, the Intergovernmental Committee on Refugees, and the approach of war than on German public opinion. There is little, however, to indicate that he changed his appraisal. The driving force behind antisemitism in Germany was clearly the Nazi regime. There was some quiet discontent with the constant flow of antisemitic propaganda, but the German public did not object, neither did they regard the problem as pressing. On the other hand, German youth solidly supported antisemitism, and the regime had more than enough active supporters to implement its program. Hitler was determined to get his way in any case.

On balance, Messersmith had a slightly more negative view of German prejudices toward Jews than did Geist, although Messersmith also believed that Nazi agitation had instilled many prejudices, not reinforced them. Since neither man had spent significant time in Germany before the Nazi movement became powerful, both of them tended to assume that the Nazis had originated much of the antisemitism. Nonetheless Messersmith and Geist certainly appreciated that a good number of German professionals and some businessmen had benefited from antisemitic measures, that Nazi propaganda had spread a demonic image of Jews to some of the lower socioeconomic classes and the youth, and that even many "good Germans" were willing to put up with this for the sake of Germany's increased strength.

Their reporting had significant limitations. Neither man traveled frequently throughout the country, so, although both received information from elsewhere, they probably exaggerated the conditions in Berlin and other major cities. Finally, in spite of Geist's occasional comments

27 Geist to Messersmith, 11 January 1937, Messersmith Papers, item 817.

about German workers, both men most likely drew heavily on their personal acquaintances from the middle and upper classes. In short, if the SD reports and other official Nazi sources have characteristics that make them difficult to use, these American diplomatic reports and letters are an even cruder gauge of German public opinion. Still, they are not inconsistent with other sources.

In 1943 an analyst in the (American) Office of Strategic Services summarized two diametrically opposed theories about recent antisemitism in Germany. Socialist Paul Hagen had argued that antisemitism was purely a Nazi creation, and that many Germans had made gestures to Jews from 1933 onward to express their disagreement with the Nazi policy. German writer Emil Ludwig, however, had claimed that the German people were inherently and irretrievably antisemitic, and that Nazi antisemitism had a tremendous popular following. The Office of Strategic Services analyst suggested that the Nazis had initiated much, but that previous animosity toward Jews must have existed in some sectors of the population, especially the upper bourgeoisie and the free professions. The working class was not enthusiastic about antisemitism to start with and had benefited little from Nazi measures against Jews. Those who became disillusioned with Nazi antisemitism during the 1930s, however, were more than outweighed by the new generation which had been raised on a steady diet of antisemitic propaganda. It was the German youth that represented the largest base of support for antisemitism.[28]

Some rough conclusions are permissible from the American diplomatic/consular sources. There is no doubt that the Nazi takeover and Nazi propaganda intensified prejudices against Jews and spread them to wider segments of the population. Second, two observers highly sensitive to the significance of Jewish policy for the Nazi regime did not see Nazi treatment of Jews either as a major reason for, or as an obstacle to, the increasing popularity of Hitler and the government. Finally, there is no indication whatsoever that either Messersmith or Geist observed or sensed popular antisemitism so intense that the Germans were ready and eager to murder Jews at the slightest sign of encouragement from above.

28 Current Status of Anti-Semitism in Germany [1943], National Archives, Record Group 200, Box 29, Folder 361.

German Social Democrats and the Jewish Question

DAVID BANKIER

I

The attitude of German socialism to the Jewish question is a topic that has prompted considerable scholarly research, yet historians have focused primarily on the attitudes to antisemitism in the Wilhelmine empire and in the Weimar Republic, with relatively little written on the years of the Third Reich.[1] The present paper seeks to partly fill this gap by exploring the responses of exiled German social democrats to Nazi antisemitism. It will attempt to establish whether the worsening situation of the Jews in the Third Reich changed the attitude of social democrats in exile to the Jewish question.

Historians have pointed out that the organized movement of German workers consistently defended Jewish rights and, from the last years of the nineteenth century onwards adopted a clear and unequivocal stand against political antisemitism. This approach also characterized, to a large extent, German social democracy during the Weimar Republic. Anti-Jewish feelings were rarely manifested publicly in the *SPD*

1 Edmond S. Silberner, *Sozialisten zur Judenfrage*, Berlin, 1962; Helmut H. Knütter, *Die Juden und die deutsche Linke in der Weimarer Republik 1918–1933,* Düsseldorf, 1971; Donald L. Niewyk, *Socialist, Antisemite and Jew: German Social Democracy Confronts the Problem of Anti-Semitism 1918–1933*, Baton Rouge, 1971; Rosemarie Leuschen-Seppel, *Sozialdemokratie und Antisemitismus im Kaiserreich*, Bonn, 1978; H. G. Henke, *Der "Jude" als Kollektivsymbol in der deutschen Sozialdemokratie 1890–1914*, Mainz, 1994; George L. Mosse, "German Socialists and the Jewish Question in the Weimar Republic," *Leo Baeck Institute Yearbook*, 16 (1971), pp. 123–50; Peter Pulzer, *Jews and the German State*, Oxford, 1992, pp. 261ff.

mainstream, and when they appeared they were promptly silenced as offshoots of immature anticapitalist resentment.[2]

Examination of the Weimar years has shown that with the notable exception of a few who correctly assessed the magnetic appeal of myths and racist utopias to the German public, socialists generally underestimated the integrative potential of irrational elements. The majority of them also played down the seriousness of Hitler's intentions and belittled the Nazi movement as an unstable conglomerate of masses misled by the demagogic manipulations. The same ideological lens that blunted the socialists' understanding of the Nazis' strength also led them to underplay the centrality of racial antisemitism in their ideology. It is apparent that they did not realize the qualitative difference between previous Jew hatred and modern Nazi antisemitism. They only noticed its political functionality and consequently submerged it under the general category of means of oppression used by reactionary forces. Thus, by viewing it as merely a political tool to undermine the Republic, they underrated the ideological commitment of the Nazis. The question I would like to consider is whether the institution of an antisemitic policy by the Nazis, which culminated in the destruction of European Jewry, modified the socialists' optic.

As it is known, the collapse of the Weimar Republic forced the majority of the party leadership to flee and find temporary shelter in Prague. A short time after it recuperated from its traumatic defeat, the émigré executive (known by its acronym *sopade*) broke with the Germany-based *SPD* and renewed publication of the party organ, the *Neuer Vorwärts*. The first issue of this weekly appeared in June 1933 and from the second issue onwards it was distinctly outspoken in its criticism of Nazi antisemitism. Nonetheless, it is evident that the attitudes of social democracy to the Jewish question cannot be determined by a quantification of articles dealing with Nazi antisemitism alone; a more adequate analysis that examines their content in depth is needed.

2 For a more subtle analysis, see Ingrid Belke, "'Antisemitismus habe ich nur in den Zeitungen zu spüren bekommen, im Leben nie.' Tucholsky und der Antisemitismus bis 1933," *Jahrbuch für Antisemitismusforschung*, 5 (1996), pp, 67–86. Cf. The comments of Thomas Hartwig, former president of the International Proletarian Freethinkers Union that "even within the Freethinkers Movement — especially in Germany and Austria — there was an explicit antisemitism," *Sozialistische Warte*, 11 March 1938, p. 236.

The socialist doctrine dismissed the importance of Jew hatred considering it a marginal phenomenon linked to the economic interests of the bourgeoisie. The capitalists, it was argued, pulled the strings behind the antisemitic agitation and exploited demagogically the anti-Jewish sentiments of the masses in order to divert their attention from their real problems. This explanatory model also typifies the social democrats' interpretation of Nazi anti-Jewish policy in the thirties. To their mind it was no different from earlier manifestations of anti-Jewish campaigns, being simply an instrument of oppression in the service of German capitalism that concealed behind a facade of antisemitism its true intentions — the destruction of democratic institutions. Hence, social democracy's commitment to fight antisemitism was certainly based on a moral obligation to defend its victims, but it was motivated primarily by political expediency because it realized that Jew-hatred functioned as an instrument to strengthen and consolidate Hitler's dictatorship.

As to the immediate causes behind the antisemitic waves in the Third Reich, social democrats gave competing interpretations. Some construed the anti-Jewish policy as the lightning rod of a regime that was unable to fulfil its promises and extricate itself from economic difficulties. Others reasoned that it was propped up by the conflicts among party members who wished to expand their power. However diverse the interpretations, antisemitism was ignored as an issue in its own right and only understood as a policy that reflected the need of a regime to find an enemy image. Typical of the socialist misunderstanding of the specifically anti-Jewish drive of the Nazis is the statement "the essence of fascism is not the destruction of the Jews but the oppression of the working class."[3]

This conception underlay the articles in the *Neuer Vorwärts* that dealt with the racial laws of September 1935. The serious implications of the laws were not yet comprehended, since the reports on the Nuremberg rally centered on the conflict between party and state; the racial laws were a secondary issue. To the columnists of the socialist weekly, the real significance of the event was the victory of the alleged masters

3 "Das Wesen des Faschismus ist ja nicht Judenausrottung, sondern Unterdrückung der Arbeiterklasse," Julius Civilis, "Verdächtige Judenfreunde," *Neuer Vorwärts*, 1 September 1935; Otto Wels, "Gegen die Rassenhetze," *Neuer Vorwärts*, 8 September 1935; "Antisemitismus und Nationalsozialismus," *Neuer Vorwärts*, 19 January 1936.

of the Third Reich — the army and high finance — which made the Nazi party an instrument of domination in their service. It was in this context that the racial laws were explained as a side issue — an attempt to placate Streicher and prevent further rioting of the Nazi radicals.

A distinctive feature of the articles carried by the *Neuer Vorwärts* was the emphasis on the pornographic nature of the *Stürmer*. It is plain that this theme was purposely exaggerated to denigrate the Nazis. The writers presumed that pointing out the Nazis' sexual perversions would ridicule the irrational sources of Jew hatred, and in this way also expose the true face of its antisemitic policy. A case in point is a comprehensive discussion of Jewish emancipation, where the entire racial doctrine was reduced to a pseudoscientific construction invented by people who suffered from sexual disorders and tried to conceal their perversions behind this ideology.[4] Yet, apart from the political aim — to mock the Nazis — this manner of writing seems to reflect the difficulty the left had in coming to terms with the Nazi anti-Jewish policy. They sincerely believed that antisemitic racism originated in the psychological needs of perverted individuals seeking confirmation for their belonging to the ruling class, or in weak groups trying to achieve social advancement through antisemitic activism.

This was not merely political rhetoric employed for the general reader of the socialist press. The *Zeitschrift für Sozialismus* — the prestigious journal of the German left, which aimed at a more sophisticated audience — addressed the topic in a similar fashion. In its analysis too, the significance of antisemitism was its functionality — that is, an instrument to accelerate the dictatorial process, or a means to condition public opinion for the discrimination of further segments of German society. Both the exclusion of Jews from the German economy and the "Aryanization" policy were explained on the basis of this theoretical model. It was practical to remove the Jews in order to create jobs for party members or for different segments of society to ensure their dependence on the Nazis' good will.

Whereas the *Neuer Vorwärts* seldom commented on the Nazi policy of 1936–37, the litany of antisemitic measures in 1938 generated a greater sensitivity to the Jewish fate. The Anschluss of Austria

4 Andreas Howald, "Das Ende der Judenemanzipation. Von der Humanität zur Sexualpathologie des Dritten Reiches," *Neuer Vorwärts*, 20 October 1935.

added a drastic new aspect to the refugee problem, and the exiled social democrats displayed considerable interest in arbitrary arrests, "Aryanization" and discriminatory legislation through their newspaper and periodic reports on the internal situation in the Reich. The party executive protocols also show that the plight of the Jewish refugees and related issues, such as the Evian conference and antisemitism in Poland, were discussed, albeit briefly, in the party's executive meetings.[5] Nevertheless, the new reality hardly affected the basic understanding of Nazi antisemitism. The revived offensive against the Jews was not seen as Hitler's main objective but simply as a testing balloon which anticipated the oppression of the rest of German society.

In stark contrast to the commitment to fight antisemitism that appeared in the publications of the social democrats in exile, during the prewar years, I could not find any illegal material on the Jewish question, either printed by their underground in the Reich itself or smuggled into it from abroad. Was it because the Jewish question was irrelevant to the clandestine social democrats who had more pressing problems to deal with? Or was it because the underground suspected that it would not be politically wise to raise the Jewish theme, which might alienate part of the working class that supported the antisemitic policy? The present stage of research does not allow a clear answer to these questions. Yet, the recollections of Jews, like Inge Deutschkron for example, hidden by social democrats attest to the fact that many sympathized personally with the Jews and expressed their compassion for human suffering and misery by helping them. A few surviving documents on the organized resistance of the social democrats, however, show that anti-Nazi activities and helping individuals were not incompatible with political opportunism.[6]

A case in point is a leaflet disseminated in Berlin in December 1942 signed by the underground *SPD* which, inter alia, also broached the extermination of the Jews. In response to the wave of propaganda orchestrated by Goebbels around Theodore Kaufman's pamphlet *Germany Must Perish*, the authors felt duty bound to inform the German population that the reason for the Jewish demands for revenge was the

5 Marlis Buchholz and Bern Rother, eds., *Der Parteivorstand der SPD im Exil*, Bonn, 1995, p. 155.

6 Martin Broszat et. al., eds, *Bayern in der NS-Zeit*, Munich, 1982, vol. V, pp. 411–14.

enormous scale of the Jewish extermination in Russia and Poland.[7] It told its readers that "tens of thousands of Jews, aged, men, women and children are daily machine-gunned or gassed in special barracks" in the east. These events are termed "the most horrible atrocity hereto seen by world history." The policy that led to the death of more than two million Jews is labeled "*the heaviest moral burden that the German people had carried until now*." [emphasis in original, D.B.] The mentioning of the figure two million matches the estimate given by the report of the Allied commission in December 1942 and broadcast over the BBC. Nonetheless, while genuinely appalled by the extermination of the Jews, the writers of the leaflet were at the same time also sensitive to the prevailing antisemitic sentiments and therefore carefully adapted their discourse to the German climate of opinion. Thus, when referring to Goering's deputy Erhard Milch, the leaflet terms him "*schwerreiche Halbjude*" to ridicule the genuineness of the Nazis'antisemitic persecution. Here the old allegation of the left, that only poor Jews are persecuted while the rich ones enjoy immunity, reappeared. More disturbing is the usage of racial and antisemitic language:

> We want the war between fraternal people of the white race to stop. ... We want friendship and cooperation with the racially related Anglo-Saxon nations and not with the Japanese, the enemy of the white race. ... We don't want Jews to have influence in State affairs and culture, but we find the idea that hundreds of thousands of them are murdered repugnant.[8]

At worst this document may indicate that antisemitic stands were not absent in the *SPD*; at best it reveals either an accommodation to the racial and antisemitic intoxication of German society in the Third Reich, or British Intelligence estimate of the *SPD* spirit at the time.

7 *Germany Must Perish* was the private work of a Jewish pharmacist from Newark, New Jersey, which suggested that the Germans be sterilized to immunize the world forever against Germanism. It was successfully used by Goebbels in a campaign to revive antisemitism at the beginning of the invasion of the Soviet Union.

8 Bundesarchiv Berlin (hereafter BA), NS/479, fol. 1, p. 78. I am grateful to Haim Rosen who called my attention to this document, and to Hans Mommsen for its criticism.

II

Let me now return to the main topic. Following the *Kristallnacht* pogrom, the social democratic party executive in exile instructed its contacts in Germany to immediately begin a propaganda campaign on the significance of the new twist in Nazi policy and to furnish it with details on the persecution of Jews.[9] The reason for the prompt and determined response was a combination of true concern and political tactics. Apart from being honestly outraged at Nazi criminality, the party leadership rightly sensed that the orchestrated vandalism perplexed a good many in the German population and such an opportunity to discredit the Nazis should not be wasted.

In addition to the reports on the propaganda campaign, which gained momentum in Germany in the face of *Kristallnacht*, there is ample evidence that important initiatives were taken in exile. Confronted with the mass exodus of Jews fleeing the Reich, the party executive raised the refugee problem in international forums. Thus, for instance, the former *SPD* politicians Rudolph Breitscheid and Philipp Scheidemann appealed to the Danish Minister of Justice to lift the barriers to the immigration of German Jews to Denmark. Parallel to these efforts, German social democrats issued a joint statement with the French socialists against the Nazi atrocities,[10] and the foreign committee representative of the German trade unions in exile also brought up the Jewish question during the consultations that took place in Copenhagen and in the arena of the Second International.[11]

Yet, to fight antisemitism was one thing, to have a selective perception of Jews and attribute them negative traits as a group, quite another. For that reason, a deeper understanding of the issue at hand must go beyond public declarations, and if we distinguish between actions and attitudes

9 Gestapo, Jahresbericht über die Sozialdemokratie 1938, BA, R58/412; Gestapo Berlin, Lagebericht über die marxistische Bewegung, November 1938, Yad Vashem Archives (hereafter YVA), JM/2834.

10 Appeal of antifascist Germans to the French left to protest against the Kristallnacht, Archiv der sozialen Demokratie der Friedrich-Ebert-Stiftung, Bonn (hereafter AdsD), ISK, Box 36.

11 Gestapo Berlin, Lagebericht über Kommunismus, November 1938, BA, R58/584; Gestapo Berlin, Lagebericht über die marxistische Bewegung, YVA, JM/3448.

the historical picture becomes more complex. This methodological distinction is valid not only when dealing with socialists. In the writing of other political exiles as well we find that a resolve in principle to defend the Jews from discrimination could coexist with a personal dislike of them because of their alleged unpleasant peculiarities. Consider for example the case of the communist Alfred Kantorowicz — himself of Jewish origins. His description of Jews does not leave room to speculate what his stereotypes were. When meeting a group of Jews in August 1936 he did not mince his words, referring to them as: "disgusting, insolent, coarse, clumsy, waddling, flat-footed, noisy, vulgar, deserve to be detested as they are described by the *Stürmer*."[12] It was also he who wrote the chapter on the persecution of the Jews in the anti-Nazi Brown Book on Hitler's terror.[13]

By the same token, socialists were a far cry from the antisemites of their times; but a close examination of their writings on the Jewish question reveals that the ambivalence towards Jews was not uncommon in the socialist camp. First, there was a measure of resentment among some of the political exiles that Jewish refugees received preferential treatment. Although the politicals were aided by the League for Human Rights, the Secours Rouge or the Comité Matteoti, they felt that more organizations were caring for Jews than non-Jews.[14] Besides, Jews could, to some extent, prepare their emigration, sell their property, get support from Jewish agencies for their emigration and somehow resume a new life abroad. All this was by no means possible for the politicals who had to leave in a hurry.

Second, socialist writings reflect the distrust of Jews as a capitalist. More than once the denunciation of antisemitism was coupled with assertions that only a minority among the Jews recognized and appreciated the socialist efforts undertaken on their behalf, while the majority persisted in its unfriendliness to the workers' movement. This

12 Ursula Büttner and Angelika Voss, eds., *Alfred Kantorowicz, Nachtbücher. Aufzeichnungen im französischen Exil 1935 bis 1939*, Hamburg, 1995, entry of 4 August 1936, p. 170.

13 *Braunbuch über Reichstagbrand und Hitlerterror*, 1933.

14 In France, for example, they were supported by the Comité National d'Aide et d'Acceuil aux Refugiés, Comité National de Secours aux Réfugies Allemands victimes de l'Antisemitisme and Comité d'assistance aux Refugies — established by Jewish organizations — and later by the Joint Distribution Committee.

tension — between commitment to fight discrimination and attribution of negative traits to the discriminated — was fully articulated by Friedrich Stampfer in an article on Judaism and Social Democracy.[15] Stampfer, a totally assimilated Jew, a member of the party executive, and until 1935 editor of the *Neuer Vorwärts*, contrasted the generosity of German socialism, and its eagerness to fight for Jewish interests, with Jewish ingratitude. Only destitute Jews supported the *SPD*, he affirmed, while the bourgeois majority remained antagonistic, or at best, indifferent to socialism. It could be argued that Stampfer had set his hopes on Jewish help, and by making this comparison he was only spurring the Jews to support anti-Nazi activities. It appears, however, that he was voicing the common reservations about Jews by socialist circles. The fact that the *SPD* and Jewish organizations, especially the *CV*, had collaborated before 1933 did not change these images. Even if it were true that in the last years of the Weimar Republic most of the Jews casted their votes for the *SPD* — and the evidence on this line of conduct is still inconclusive[16] — both sides understood that the affinity linking Jews and socialists was very fragile. The differences had been merely glossed over to forge an ad hoc alliance in the urgency to fight a common enemy.

This distrust can also be inferred from the response of Hans Vogel, chairman of the Union of German Socialist Organizations in Great Britain, to Leon Kubowitzky, head of the department of European Jewish Affairs of the World Jewish Congress. When approached in November 1943 to issue a statement on the policy towards the Jews to be adopted by post-Hitler Germany, Vogel replied that the attitude, in principle, of German social democracy to the Jewish question did not change as a result of the tragic events of the last decade. It was contained in the programmatic declaration of January 1934 and reaffirmed in the condemnation of the extermination issued in December 1942. After Hitler's fall, he said, a democratic Germany will revoke all forms of discrimination and compensate those who were persecuted on the grounds of their religion, political convictions or racial origin. At

15 Friedrich Stampfer, "Rasse, Christentum, Sozialismus, Judentum und Sozialdemokratie," *Neuer Vorwärts*, 4 September 1938.

16 Arnold Paucker, *Der jüdische Abwehrkampf gegen Antisemitismus und Nationalismus in den letzten Jahren der Weimarer Republik*, Hamburg, 1969, 87ff.

the end of his letter he added, however, that "it would also depend on the conduct of the German Jews. When they return to Germany after the war they would have to show by their political stands and practical deeds that they feel themselves attached to the progressive and democratic forces of the German people."[17] From the wording it is plain that Vogel was actually alluding to the Jews' alleged past support of reactionary parties.

Aside from the image of Jews as supporters of reactionary forces, the competition for victim status was to become a chronic source of friction between Jews and political exiles. Most of the latter's reports on Nazi antisemitism were printed within the context of the persecution of the illegal opposition and other segments of German society. This style of writing not only aimed at granting political meaning to the Nazi oppression of Jews by seeing it as another case of a universal phenomenon. In the rivalry over victim status it was crucial to highlight that others were oppressed as well, in order to prevent the impression that Jews were Hitler's main victims. This was not exclusive of social democrats. The above-mentioned communist Kantorowicz reacted to *Kristallnacht* by writing: "it is abominable but no more abominable than the pogrom against the communists in the face of which the world keeps silent."[18]

Closely linked to this were differences over the question of the prominence of antisemitism in anti-Nazi propaganda. Many of the political émigrés did not minimize the significance of antisemitism but insisted on playing down the Jewish question in their propaganda, because they genuinely believed that singling out the Jews from the repression of other groups would imply acceptance of the Nazi theory that the Jews are indeed a different category and constitute a problem. Others were concerned with political tactics and suggested that the Jews' plight be played down, warning that the Jewish issue was over-represented in the anti-Nazi campaign and would damage the exiles' cause. Even a staunch fighter against antisemitism such as Heinrich Mann thought that the exiles' propaganda expended too much

17 See correspondence between Hans Vogel and Leon Kubowitzki, AdsD, sopade, Mappe 142. Reprinted in a slightly changed form in *Neue Volkszeitung*, 12 February 1944.

18 Op. cit., entry of 4 December 1938, p. 195.

time and energy on antisemitism. At anti-Nazi meetings, he said, Jewish organizations should not be the only ones to speak because there were others who suffered as well.[19]

His nephew Klaus was even more explicit. Reviewing Chaplin's film *The Great Dictator*, Klaus Mann relativized the suffering of the Jews, weighing it against other victims' tragedies. He wrote:

> Nothing could be more fallacious than to present the Nazi ordeal as an unpleasant experience exclusively for the Jews. Hitler's heinous antisemitism has already played too predominant a part in our propaganda. I have always considered it a dangerous mistake to overemphasize this one particular angle. ... What the Führer has done to the Poles and Greeks is at least as bad as what he does to the Jews.[20]

It appears that Klaus Mann did not revise his views even in 1945 when the magnitude of the Holocaust became common knowledge. In his letter to Hermann Kesten of March 1945 he affirmed that the tragedy that befell the Jews was not unique and not even significant.

> Why write a novel about the Jews? It's such a melancholy subject! Was not the Jewish Question just one of Hitler's ugly inventions? And shouldn't we drop the matter — now, with Hitler being nearly defeated? I think we should! Let's write about more pleasant things! Why don't [you] write a novel about a circus, or about Toulouse-Lautrec, or about Confucius, or a book about Voltaire? Leave the Jews to Schalom Asch! The Jews are dreary.[21]

It is perplexing that Klaus Mann seems to have felt no discomfort or moral unease when he wrote these lines, and that he continued playing down the Jewish question even when his belief could not be squared with the facts of the Holocaust. This letter is significant not only because Mann was articulating a fundamental concept held by German exiles that the Jewish question was a secondary issue which was receiving more attention than it rightfully deserved, but also because

19 Heinrich Mann, "Aufgaben der Emigration," *Die neue Weltbühne* (1933), pp. 1556–57; reprinted in: Heinrich Mann, *Verteidigung der Kultur. Antifaschistiche Streitschriften und Essays*, Berlin, 1960, p. 12. See also Sigrid Bauschinger, "Kultur gegen Barbarei," in: *Wider den Faschismus. Exilliteratur als Geschichte*, Sigrid Bauschinger and Susan L. Cocalis, eds., Tübingen, 1993, p. 114.

20 Klaus Mann, "What is Wrong with Anti-Nazi Films," *Decision*, 2 (August 1941), p. 33.

21 Klaus Mann, *Briefe und Antworten*, Munich, 1987, pp. 533–34.

it shows the extent to which people do not allow new information to influence their judgments. In Mann's case, this mental conservatism was instrumental in generating moral distancing in the face of news on the mass extermination of European Jewry.[22]

Exiles of Jewish origin who were active in exile politics were unusually apprehensive over a "correct" dosage of the Jewish theme in anti-Nazi publications. These sensitivities shed light on Anna Seghers' refusal to be included in an anthology of Jewish authors banned by the regime,[23] and on Franz Schonauer's concern that the abundance of Jews writing in the exile publication *Die Sammlung* might create the erroneous impression that all exiles were Jews, thereby damaging the anti-Nazi camp.[24] But also non-Jews felt that the large number of Jews in the exiled anti-Nazi camp was counterproductive for the anti-Nazi camp. Exiled social democrat Wilhelm Sollmann, for example, wrote that the very fact that half of the fifty members of Willi Münzenberg's committee in Paris were Jews was detrimental to the exiles' interests. Equally harmful was the prominence of Jewish journalist Georg Bernhard in anti-Nazi propaganda activities. Although, he said, this phenomenon could be understood considering the composition of emigré intellectuals, it was not wise to have so many Jews in the front as it provided Hitler with ammunition that the émigrés were part of the world Jewish conspiracy against Nazi Germany.[25]

III

Why was it that even assimilated Jews were seen as a problem even in the German socialist community? To begin with, it is plain that economic, academic, or professional accomplishments of German Jews

22 Mann was absolutely open with Kesten because he considered *him "Der Einzige von den hiesigen deutschen Kollegen zu dem ich noch irgend sympathie und Vertrauen habe*," in: Joachim Heimannsberg, ed., Klaus Mann, *Tagebücher*, Hamburg, 1995, entry of 22 September 1940.

23 Hermann Kesten, ed., *Deutsche Literatur im Exil. Briefe europäische Autoren 1933–1949*, Vienna, 1964, pp. 48–49.

24 Ibid., p. 58–60.

25 Wilhelm Sollmann to Paul Hertz, 20 January 1936, Stadtarchiv Köln, Nachlass Sollmann, IV–4–24, a, b.

are not to be equated with social integration in German society. By the same token, whether or not Jews were integrated in the socialist party cannot be established by statistics on how many Jews were in the *SPD*, or how many of its Reichstag members were of Jewish origin. Their presence in the parties of the left in numbers far exceeding their proportion of the German population made them highly visible and their prominence in the top leadership made them even more conspicuous.[26] Moreover, the fact that party members did not usually know who was of Catholic or Protestant origin, but knew who was of Jewish origin, is also telling. Second, although articulating anti-Jewish sentiments was anathema in ordinary times, the normative discourse and the politically correct attitudes collapsed in times of crisis. There is some evidence that German political parties, sensitive to charges of supporting Jewish interests, at times avoided presenting Jewish candidates in elections.[27] The left was not an exception. The Communist Party was even ready on certain occasions to adopt antisemitic stands,[28] and politicians in the *SPD* also succumbed to the temptation of broadening its basis by giving in to antisemitic prejudices.[29] Wilhelm Sollmann confessed in his correspondence that political prudence would not have allowed him to appoint Paul Hertz, a member of the party executive, as Minister of Finance in the Weimar Republic because of Hertz's Jewish origins. "The German people would never have accepted this and it would have been bad for the SPD," he wrote.[30] It seems, however, that in the critical months of March-June 1933 some social democrats went even further in subordinating their socialist ethos to political interests.

Hitler's assumption of power cracked the political fabric of German social democracy. One faction, led by Otto Wels, decided to keep on

26 According to Eduard Bernstein, 10 percent of the social democratic representatives in the Reichstag were of Jewish origin, and in Roberto Michels estimate between 20 and 30 percent of Jewish intellectuals adhered to social democracy, see Enzo Traverso, *Les Marxistes et la question juive*, Montreuil, 1990, p. 53.

27 Niewyk, *The Jews in Weimar*, p. 72; Hans Rosenberg, *Grosse Depression und Bismarckzeit*, Berlin, 1967, p. 112; Knütter, pp. 131, 212.

28 David Bankier, "The German Communist Party and Nazi Antisemitism 1933–1938," *Yearbook of the Leo Baeck Institute*, 32 (1987), pp. 325–40.

29 Knütter, pp. 131, 212.

30 I am grateful to Dr. Ursula Langkau-Alex for her comments on this issue and for sending me pertinent documents.

fighting the Nazis from exile while another, led by Paul Löbe with the support of the trade unions, decided to swim with the tide and reach some sort of accommodation with the Nazi regime. Immediately after the elections the *Gewerkschaftszeitung* adopted a nationalist tone and the executive committee of the General Federation of German Trade Unions informed Hitler's government that they were ready to break off the long-established association with the SPD. Since Gauleiter Wagner and von Papen — who conducted the talks on the Nazi side — issued an ultimatum that they would not allow international connections nor Jewish officials in the unions,[31] the adoption of this collaborationist course was accompanied by an outburst of anti-Jewish feelings. When the General Federation of German Trade Unions met in April 1933 to discuss collaboration with the Nazis, Siegfried Aufhäuser, the only Jew among their leaders who favored the disbandment of the Federation rather than giving in to the Nazi demands, was also the only one who vigorously opposed the collaboration. The antisemitic unions demanded to be rid of Aufhäuser and he was forced to resign. In their eagerness to strike a deal with the Nazis, several party members took practical steps to purge socialist organizations of Jews. The correspondence of Fritz Naphtali with *sopade* leaders attests to the caustic anti-Jewish climate in the *SPD*. The disenchantment and bitterness that this experience left on Naphtali transpire in a letter to Erich Ollenhauer of the party executive, then exiled in Prague: "Let's be honest," Naphtali wrote, "not only rank and file but official leaders of the *SPD* had antisemitic stands and for that reason between March and July we, [the Jews in the party, D.B.] had experiences that were more painful than the insults of the Nazis."[32] Paul Hertz backed this allegation, affirming that in the discussions following the break-up of the workers' movement in the spring of 1933 the claim was put forth that the Jews had obtained far too great an influence in the movement. This argument, he said, was advanced far more among the leaders than among the mass of supporters.[33]

31 Interview with Siegfried Aufhäuser in the Dutsche Rundfunk on 1 May 1967.

32 Nachlass Paul Hertz, Internationaal Instituut voor Sociale Geschiedenis, Amsterdam (hereafter IISG).

33 Ibid.

It would be wrong to attribute these stands only to the atmosphere of emergency of those months. Gustav Noske's autobiography makes it clear that it was not the crisis of 1933 that set the stage for feelings of estrangement towards Jews. It has often been said that favorable contacts with individuals do not necessarily imply a change of attitude towards the group from which the individual comes; similarly, the negative traits ascribed to a group need not apply to its individual members. This accounts for the warm words of praise that Noske had for "good" German Jews, such as Ludwig Frank or Hugo Haase, and the xenophobic estrangement he displayed towards what he called the *"Ausländerei"* in the socialist party who came from Poland and Russia. He portrays the Eastern European Jews as unpleasant types who arrived in Germany with the pretension to teach socialism to the Germans. And since, he claims, they had a particular talent to transform socialism into a dogma and convert commonplaces into articles of faith, their dogmatic Marxism was never understood by the German workers.[34] He does not name them, but it is clear that he had in mind socialists of Jewish origin such as Rosa Luxembourg, Alexander (Parvus) Helfand, and Karl Radek. To Noske these were, to borrow Hanna Arendt's concept, intellectual pariahs who had suffered the consequences of uprootedness and found in internationalism a substitute for their Jewish identity. They came to social democracy — where antisemitism was seldom voiced publicly, although it was present under the carpet — because they saw it as an agency for their assimilation. They considered their Jewish origins a liability and a source of embarrassment, which is why they became irritated when the topic of Judaism came up in party discussions.

Socialists like Noske would not subscribe to the crude stereotypes that placed the Jews outside the universe of moral obligation. Yet by viewing Jews as uprooted, hypersensitive, pessimistic, full of hatred, arrogant and aggressive, they were actually viewing them as a category that was separate from their realm, perpetuating the myths of Jewish otherness. No matter how progressive and open-minded Noske claimed to be or how many Jewish friends he may have had, it is clear that he suffered from the "some of my best friends are Jewish" syndrome,

34 Gustav Noske, *Erlebtes aus Aufstieg und Niedergang einer Demokratie*, Offenbach, 1947, pp. 27, 148.

which allowed him to both relate to Jews on an individual level and to viewing Jews as "others." In his attempts to explain their behavior by reference to group properties Noske was stereotyping them, and it is immaterial that he attributed the Jews' negative traits to socioeconomic factors rather than to their inherent makeup as an antisemite would have done. From this perspective it is easier to understand that such deeply rooted sentiments could not just melt away when the opportunism of early 1933 dissipated. Moreover, it made it easier for some to believe that the Jews had themselves to blame for their persecution since they provoked it by their behavior.

Reading the *sopade* surveys on the public mood in Hitler's Germany we come across clear examples of the tendency to find confirming evidence of self-fulfilling stereotypes of Jews and see their persecution as their own doing. For example, some reports refer to former members of the *SPD* who blamed the Jews for the party's failure. These were people who probably opposed persecution of Jews but found it an "understandable" reaction considering the irritation they caused. There were those who voiced the view that the Jews who had led the party in the Weimar era had only a frivolous interest in socialism, they were bourgeois *Salonsozialisten* and it was their fault that the workers had voted for the Nazis. The comments of others suggest that the "well-earned" type of antisemitism — that Jews deserved to be discriminated against and forced to pay for their behavior — had also spread its roots among socialists. Reacting to the Nuremberg Laws, former *SPD* supporters expressed the view that the Jews had always pushed to the top and were now paying for their arrogance during the Weimar Republic.[35]

To what should we attribute this *Schadenfreude*: To the erosion of class consciousness in the face of Nazi propaganda? To scapegoating and rationalized displacement of frustrations? To be sure, the antisemitic atmosphere in the Third Reich certainly influenced these stands, but this explanation is insufficient because it does not account for the choice of target. Why were the Jews to be blamed for the party's failure to stop Hitler? It is clear that such opinions were voiced by people who started out with anti-Jewish feelings of their own, and adherence to the

35 *Sopade*, September 1935 (Bayern) A12; January 1936 (Bayern) A19; February 1936, A5.

well-earned-punishment theory made the Jews the preferred substitute target of frustration.

For certain, labeling Jews with negative collective traits was not exceptional in German society, but what is notable is that such uncritical acceptance of these prejudices found fertile soil in socialist circles as well. Stereotypes and derogatory language on irritating Jewish practices and on the pernicious effects of "Jewish" traits are not absent in socialist writings. Undeniably, these would never attribute racial peculiarities to Jews, but would indeed ascribe them negative behavioral characteristics stemming from Jewish society, culture, and alleged psychological makeup. Consider, for instance, the representations of Jews in terms of their personality traits which surfaced in a debate on the Jewish question that appeared in the exiles' periodical *Freies Deutschland.* The Jews, affirmed one writer, have a special facility for journalism and psychology; they are gifted with a talent for mimicry; they think in the abstract and lack feeling for sentimental values. Consequently, the socialist theory formulated by Jewish intellectuals could not be understood by the proletarians and led to the alienation of the working class.[36] This view was endorsed by another socialist exile who maintained that Jews had enjoyed excessive power in the party, their demands for leadership stemming from their intellectual arrogance.[37] For these writers, no matter how assimilated Jewish socialists felt, they still carried the negative marks of the society from which they wanted to detach themselves. In the light of these attitudes it is hardly surprising that the *SAP* activist Boris Goldenberg confided to his comrades that he, like other Jews in socialist parties, suffer from an inferiority complex which is compensated by a tendency to hyper-intellectualism and cosmopolitanism.[38]

Georg Reinbold's stereotypes (although probably not typical) provide factual testimony to an overlapping of discourses that transcended the

36 Esch, "Zur Judenfrage," *Freies Deutschland,* Cf. K. Singer, "Antisemitische Bekämpfer des Antisemitismus," Ibid., 9 September 1937; Thomas, "Zur Diskussion der Judenfrage," Ibid., 9 December 1937.

37 E. P., "Arbeiterbewegung und Judenproblem," 26 August 1937.

38 Boris Goldenberg, 18 November 1935, AdsD, Box 25, Mappe 246. See also the comments of Theodor Hartwig, former president of the International Proletarian Freethinkers, in: *Weltgericht über den Judenhass. Eine internationale Rundfrage über das Wesen des Antisemitismus*, Prague, 1933, pp. 51–52.

dividing lines of left and right as far as the representations of Jews were concerned. To him, no matter how assimilated they felt, Jewish socialists still carried the pejorative traits of the society from which they wanted to remove themselves. If the overwhelming majority of the Jewish community during the monarchy and the Republic was branded as bourgeois and conservative, those who distanced themselves from it and became socialists were still "Jews" in Reinbold's eyes.

Reinbold who had been a senior *SPD* official in Baden, emigrated to Luxembourg where he became a border secretary and representative of the *sopade*. In a letter to the party executive on October 1935 Reinbold reacted to the analysis of fascism made by the socialist of Jewish origin Richard Loewenthal in the *Zeitschrift für Sozialismus*. Loewenthal had gained fame in leftist circles as a brilliant theoretician whose unique analysis of fascism influenced the writings of both Otto Bauer and Franz Neumann. Loewenthal, however, was too much an internationalist for Reinbold's taste, and in a letter to the party leaders Reinbold complained:

> How can we tolerate that everything German should be trampled to the floor by a troop of Jewish intellectuals, only because these people cannot think in terms of a nation and its needs. We [meaning the *SPD*] suffer from the poison of disintegration of un-German tendencies which sink in by a band of intellectuals who can think only as Jews. ... What I suffered most was when I had to see our disenfranchised German comrades who came from the working class in the company of such Jews.[39]

When asked to comment on these views, the previously mentioned social democratic leader Wilhelm Sollmann diminished their importance, attributing them to the old resentment in the party organization against

39 *"Es kann es nicht geben, dass durch einer Schar jüdischer Intellektueller alles, was deutsches Emfinden ist zu Boden getrampelt wird, nur weil diese Kreise nicht im Sinne einer nation und ihre Bedürfnisse zu denken vermoegen. ... Wir leiden an einem Gift der Zersetzung durch undeutsche Strömungen, die hineintragen werden durch eine Schaar Intellektueller, die meistens nur als Juden denken koennen. Man sehe sich mal die Verfasser der Verschiedenen Artikel in der vorliegenden Zeitschrift an. Mir tut der arme Sollmann leid, dass er mit seiner gesunden deutschen Ansicht in einer solchen Gesellschaft erscheinen muss. Das schmerzlichste war mir immer, wenn ich bei Ausbürgerungen unserer prächtigen deutschen Genossen, die aus dem Arbeiterstand hervorgegangen sind sie in der Gesellschaft von all den Veilchenbaum und Apfelblüte usw. Sehen musste."* 26 October 1935, AdS, Sopade, Mappe 91.

intellectuals, many of whom were of Jewish origin. It is true that there had been tensions between the Jewish intellectuals on the one hand, most of whom were of bourgeois origin, had university educations and worked as journalists and writers, and the German proletarians who had worked themselves up from the factory machines, on the other. The writings of Wilhelm Hasselmann particularly mirrored this sort of anti-Jewish prejudice against the Jews in the party. It is also true that social democratic leaders such as Eduard David and Karl Kautsky pointed in their writings to negative Jewish stereotypes, and even August Bebel had depicted Jews as frivolous, ostentatious, tactless and pushy in their relations with gentiles. The standing of these figures in the party undoubtedly legitimized the prejudice by adding further validity to it. All this notwithstanding, it cannot be claimed that Reinbold's stereotypes of Jews drew from these sources. His feeling of unease among Jews, his view of them as the antithesis of anything German, and his accusations that Jews were foreign agents of decomposition mirror the appropriation of the most common representations of Jews from the antisemitic discourse. These images were employed, for example, by conservatives in the 1892 antisemitic platform of Tivoli and play a major role in the writings of Hans Blüher, Paul de Lagarde, Julius Langbehn and other notorious racist figures. So anchored were these stereotypes, they could not be neutralized by abstract socialist ethics.

Reinbold's tone and his depiction of Jews as the personification of internationalism and opposed to the German nation's interests could hardly be ignored. It triggered a sharp reaction among some party members who called Reinbold a fascist, but it is significant that no official response was issued. The *sopade* did not call Reinbold to account for voicing such views, despite demands to do so, and when this topic was raised at the party executive meeting in May 1936 the leadership simply decided to restrict the number of those who would read the letter.[40] To Paul Hertz the refusal to express open repudiation was not insignificant. While for the leadership it was simply an infringement of political correctness which needed no reprimand, for Hertz it was a tacit official sanction of latent antisemitic

40 Marlis Buchholz and Bern Rother, eds., *Der Parteivorstand der SPD im Exil*, Bonn, 1995, p. 155. Eventually, Reinbold managed to escape occupied Europe and reach the USA with the help of the Jewish Labor Committee.

prejudices that had moved from the private to the public domain. I would surmise that this response of the party executive came in order not to exacerbate anti-Jewish prejudices in the émigrés camp, the existence of which becomes apparent in the correspondence between Paul Hertz and Wilhelm Sollmann. Both concurred that while there was no antisemitism in the illegal *SPD* in the Reich, a sort of racial separation was taking place in the party in exile and antisemitic tendencies among former party functionaries had markedly increased. Sollmann exemplified his assertion by citing from letters complaining that it was mainly Jews who express themselves in the socialist organs *Sozialistische Aktion* and *Neuer Vorwärts*.[41]

It is against this background that the confidential "Memorandum on the Future of the Jews in a Post-Hitler Germany" written by Paul Hertz in March 1940 is best viewed.[42] The circumstances surrounding the writing of this document are unknown and therefore can only be a matter of conjecture. In any event, Hertz takes issue with two affirmations of the exiled socialists. One, that the Nazis failed to transform Germans into antisemites. Two, that after Hitler's fall, the restoration of rights to Jews would be an easy task. Regarding the first point, Hertz contends that, through antisemitism, Hitler managed to connect racism with nationalism and that his propaganda influenced the new generation in particular. Consequently, those between the ages of eighteen and forty did not regard Jews as members of the national community. Also, the education of the youngsters converted them into sworn antisemites. Hertz is very keen in his observation that criticism of Nazi methods, in the responses to *Kristallnacht*, should not be overestimated. He attributes this criticism to the embarrassment of the bourgeois population over the brutal methods used by the Nazis to implement political measures; hence it lacked political significance. His conclusion is therefore unequivocal: since antisemitism became a component of the political thought of the German people, not only will

41 Hertz to Sollmann, 14 February 1938, Nachlass Sollmann, Stadtarchiv, Köln, IV–4–19, 19a, b; Hertz to Sollmann, 14 January 1936, Ibid., Nr. 420, Brief 9; Sollmann to Hertz, 20 January 1936, Ibid., IV–4–24, a, b.

42 Nachlass Paul Hertz, IISG. On Hertz, see Ursula Langkau-Alex, "Paul Hertz," in: Peter Lösche, Michael Scholing, Franz Walter, eds., *Vor dem Vergessen bewahren*, Berlin, 1988, pp. 145–69.

it not disappear by itself but the fall of Hitler will not signify the return of rights to Jews.

More relevant to our discussion is Hertz's affirmation that among Hitler's opponents of the left there were proponents of antisemitism who hoped in the event of his fall to make some concessions in this direction in order to gain popularity. Alluding to the above-mentioned letter of Georg Reinbold, Hertz added that had these been the expressions of a private person who found the Jews unpleasant on a personal and social level, they would be of little importance, but other socialist leaders, he claimed, shared Reinbold's views. These leaders maintained quite openly that they considered the Jews to be a distinct race that had dominated the Germans intellectually. The Jews were a minority and must be handled as such. They warned against the danger of Jewish competition and urged that it be combatted with stringent measures and laws. In a post-Hitler Germany, these socialist leaders claimed, the restoration of civic rights to the Jews should not be considered. Hertz's conclusion is therefore very pessimistic: antisemitism will not disappear when Hitler falls. His only consolation was that the younger and more active members of the socialist camp made as little concession to antisemitism as they did to nationalism.

Hertz's harsh indictment — difficult to ascertain due to the fragmentary state of documentation and lack of research — is open to dispute. But even if he does exaggerate, his allegation is still startling for it shows how a totally assimilated Jew placed at the top of the party executive assessed the opinions on Jews by socialist circles. If we are to trust Hertz I would suggest that despite all the differences, when it came to stereotypes of Jews there was a distinct overlapping of opinions by the socialist left and the nationalist right.

Summing up, it is not my intention to argue that there was an antisemitic tradition in German social democracy. Socialists never harbored the vulgar stereotypes and claims of antisemites that placed the Jews beyond human society. Quite the contrary, they sharply criticized these views, were unreservedly against political antisemitism, and put their best efforts towards finding a solution to the refugee problems and alleviating the Jewish plight. Reinbold's views, which reveal an underlying racial antisemitism, seem in no way indicative of the majority. The vast majority of socialists continued the tradition of the enlightenment — namely that emancipation meant assimilation and the disappearance of antisemitism concomitant with the disappearance of the Jews. Nonetheless, the fight against antisemitism is only one aspect, albeit an important one, of the approach of social democracy to the Jewish question. No less important is the assessment of images of Jews as a group. To obtain a full historical picture these images should be put on an equal footing with the commitment to oppose discrimination. Having done so in the present paper it becomes apparent that feelings about Jewish "otherness" were hardly monopolized by the right's behind-the-scenes prejudice, since offensive language against Jews was also heard in the socialist camp. A good many in the socialist camp believed that Jewish culture, which took its cue from religion and persecution, led to Jewish insularity which, in turn, was partly responsible for their predicament. The rooted images of Jewish frivolity, arrogance and aggressiveness applied equally to Jews who had detached themselves from Jewish society and had joined the ranks of the socialist camp. These sentiments made it possible to generate the "serves them right" attitudes that can be found lurking behind comments on Nazi antisemitic legislation. Finally it should be emphasized that the motivations of those who held these views are irrelevant. Even if their motives were noble and all they aspired to was a "progressive" solution to the Jewish question — the creation of a homogeneous society and the assimilation of Jews therein — what is historically significant is that beyond the differences of diametrically opposed ideologies there was a common ground of shared Jewish representations that crossed the political divisions of right and left.

British Policy, Allied Intelligence and Zionist Dilemmas in the Face of Hitler's Jewish Policies

SHLOMO ARONSON

A major influence on Nazi policy toward the Jews of Europe in 1939–41 was Hitler's perception of British, American and Soviet behavior. Hence British behavior toward the Jews of Europe, and toward Palestine as a haven for European Jews, might have played a role in his decision later on to abandon his forced emigration policy altogether. Instead he ordered the physical annihilation of Soviet Jews at first, and then the "Final Solution," all the way to Auschwitz. These decisions were made in the larger context of the transformation of World War II from a series of what seemed to have been limited campaigns in east and west to a global war by the end of 1941. The role of Palestine for Hitler in this context must have been pretty limited anyway, and later he saw in the Jewish community there also a target for annihilation, among the rest of the Jews residing in the Arab-Moslem Middle East. In between Nazi Germany toyed with various "territorial solutions" to the "Jewish Question," among them the so-called "Madagascar Plan," which however required British collaboration. Another Nazi "bonus" in this regard was the use of the deported Jews to Madagascar as hostages to restrain "their brethren in America." Having decided on their side to fight Nazi Germany to the end, for British Palestine was, and remained later on an important — and troublesome — asset, which dictated in their eyes a variety of actions vis-a vis the Zionists. In the period under consideration here, the British — having lost France as a major ally — had to mobilize the Americans to support them as best as they could, without making concessions to the Zionists.

The role of the Middle East, especially Palestine, in the British overall policy during the period 1939–41 had far-reaching repercussions. The closure of Palestine's gates to Hitler's refugees by the British on 17 May 1939 due to Arab military and political pressure was — and still is — one of the historical sources of the Israeli-Arab conflict. Furthermore, the issue of Zionist behavior at the time, during World War II, and after, was and continued to be a source of British-influenced anti-and post-Zionist arguments in the sense that the Arabs of Palestine were the helpless victims of European antisemitism and Zionist exploitation.

The Problem

The British government under Chamberlain officially abandoned the Zionist cause in May 1939 as part of its effort to prepare for war with Nazi Germany.[1] This act was followed by the closure of the British Isles to Jewish refugees after 1 September 1939.[2] For the mainstream, largely Labor-oriented Zionists such as David Ben-Gurion, this seemed to be a part of the "appeasement" policy itself, rather than a possible departure from it.[3]It took them quite some time to understand that their moral, historical and political arguments for Jewish immigration to Palestine without Arab consent were overshadowed by the coming war, and that their social-pioneering endeavors in Palestine began increasingly to

1 A large body of scholarly literature exists on British policy toward Zionism and Palestine. One of the relatively recent works is: Ronald W. Zweig, *Britain and Palestine during the Second World War*, Woodbridge, Suffolk, 1986.

2 Increasing data on British behavior toward the Jews as a domestic and refugee problem are added to Bernard Wasserstein's pioneering work, *Britain and the Jews of Europe, 1939–1945*, London, 1979. Among them, see Tony Kushner, *The Persistence of Prejudice, Antisemitism in British Society during the Second World War*, Manchester, 1989, and cf. Bryan Cheyette, *Constructions of "the Jew" in English Literature and Society, Racial Representations, 1875–1945*, Cambridge, 1993.

3 Yehuda Bauer's, *Diplomacy and Underground in Zionism 1939–1945*, Jerusalem, 1966, (in Hebrew) recently reissued in English, remains an important discussion of the topic, from which Ben-Gurion's initial view of the "White Paper" is taken. More works on Ben-Gurion during that period should be mentioned here: Michael Bar-Zohar, *Ben-Gurion*, vol. I, Tel-Aviv, 1975, pp. 417ff, (in Hebrew) and Shabetai Teveth, *The Burning Ground*, Tel-Aviv, 1988, (in Hebrew) and cf. also Teveth's *Ben-Gurion and the Holocaust*, New York, 1996, and Meir Avizohar, ed., *David Ben-Gurion, Memoirs*, vol. VI, January–August 1939, Tel Aviv, 1987 (in Hebrew).

resemble "National-Socialism" in the eyes of British officials during a war aimed at destroying Nazism.

At the time that Hitler's forced emigration policy was underway, other options were considered including the imprisonment of German Jews in military facilities; and deportations to Poland, improvised and bloody as they were, were experimented with but abandoned for practical reasons. Finally came "Barbarossa," which signified the beginning of the "Final Solution" on Soviet soil. This was rationalized in Nazi eyes by the very transformation of the limited war of 1939 as perceived by Hitler and threatened by him in his Reichstag speech of 30 January 1939. This so-called "prophecy" speech threatened to the destruction of European Jewry as a direct result of the Jews inciting another world war.[4] This new drama was allegedly imposed on Germany by three factors: the continued British struggle, American aid to the British — both seen as Jewish inspired or Jewish related, and the need to strike a blow at Stalin's empire before it joined the two other powers. In between these dynamics the Jews of Europe were caught from all sides.

The embattled British, perceiving Jewish refugees and Jewish-related issues as an embarrassment at home, wanted to avoid the impression that the life and death struggle in which they found themselves was a "Jews' war." What motivated British officials were a Nazi spy scare and "fifth column" scare, while in the Middle East the Jewish immigration seemed to be a major threat to their relations with the Moslems in general, and the Arabs in particular, after the Arab rebellion of 1936–39 and in view of the pro-Axis role of the Palestinian leader, Hajj Amin el Husseini and other Arab and Moslem figures.[5]

Hitler viewed the British as an instrument of Jewish ideas and Jewish interests, and the Americans — whose immigration policy remained largely unchanged — as a tool in the hands of Franklin "Rosenfeld," the

4 In this speech Hitler publicly warned that should the world's *"Finanzjudentum"* trigger a second world war, the outcome would not be the "bolshevization" of the earth, but "the annihilation of the Jewish race in Europe." Thus the Polish, the French and other campaigns, which did not yet trigger a full scale annihilation program, were not yet perceived as a "Second World War."

5 This is a rather simplified, but basically correct, description of Arab realities by 1939. For a detailed analysis see Yehoshua Porath, *In the Test of Political Action, Palestine, Arab Unity and British Policy 1930–1945*, Jerusalem, 1985, esp. pp. 49–53, 68, 72, 84–85 (in Hebrew).

man who mobilized the U.S. Navy and resources behind the British.[6] Furthermore, Hitler believed that Stalin, who personally might have been rather antisemitically inclined, not only used Jewish Bolshevism to inspire foreign nations but also made unacceptable demands in Europe, while threatening to emerge from his current troubles as a future strategic threat to join the British and the United States.[7] "Barbarossa" — and with it the beginning of the "Final Solution" — was the outcome of all this and more, including the perception of the Soviet Union as easy prey, trapping the Jews further from all sides.[8]

In this paper I shall deal not with Nazi policy in the early stages of World War II leading to the above-described climax, which also encompasses General Franco's refusal to join the Germans against the British and thus prevented a full-scale German offensive in the Mediterranean, but with British policies between 1939 and 1941, and with the Zionist dilemmas and activities at this early stage. This discussion is not only relevant to the "rescue debate" — partially a political controversy and partially a contested issue in Jewish-Zionist history requiring serious research for its own sake — but also to its

6 For a recent analysis of Roosevelt's policies in the period under consideration here in the largest possible framework, see Gerhard L. Weinberg, *A World at Arms, A Global History of World War II*, New York, 1994, pp. 153–154. Weinberg believes that Hitler intended to invade the USSR anyway and did not take the Americans seriously at that stage or even later; yet one of Weinberg's most important contributions to the history of the Second World War was his emphasis on Hitler's naval planning — aircraft carriers included — to deal with the Americans sooner rather than later.

7 This issue has been dealt with very extensively in the scholarly literature on the origins of "Barbarossa." On my part I do not accept Weinberg's intentionalist theory regarding the Soviets. In this paper I call the reader's attention to the American moves to help the British, limited as they were, in relationship to British belligerent actions and Soviet moves to consolidate and expand their gains in the west, plus other related developments. A useful timetable can be found in Andreas Hillgruber and Gerhard Hummelchen's chronology of events from October 1939, and 31 July 1941, the date Göring gave Heydrich the order to complete the preparations for the overall solution of the Jewish question in the German areas of influence in Europe, in: Percy E. Schramm, ed., *Kriegstagebuch des Oberkommandos der Wehrmacht*, vol. II, Bonn, no date, pp. 1149–1243. In it both authors underline not only Hitler's activities but those of the British, the Soviets and the Americans, together with Japan's.

8 This is discussed in detail in my forthcoming study, entitled: *The Quadruple Trap — Hitler, the Allies, the Arabs and the Jews*.

political ramifications ever since. I shall concentrate on the British aspect, and its Palestine policy from May 1939 until "Barbarossa" by citing previous scholarship and largely unused primary sources. I will focus on Jewish-Zionist responses and dilemmas that emerged from the initial triple trap in which the Jews found themselves after their former, reluctant allies — the British — closed the gates of Palestine under Arab pressure in order to fight the Jews' arch enemies, the Nazis.

The Periodization and the Sources

The above mentioned "catch 22," or rather "catch 44," was in the making since May 1939, with the British resolve to fight Hitler, should he further break his previous commitments — particularly not to invade Poland. That would mean an unavoidable war with Germany and possibly with Mussolini's Italy, its Mediterranean ally. The British decision resulted in their "abandonment" of Jewish aspirations and actual rescue options in Palestine; at the same time Hitler blamed the Jews for British actions which were divorced from Jewish interests.

Given the complexity of the subject, the period under discussion can be divided into the following chapters:

- From the publication of the British "White Paper" on Palestine until the outbreak of World War II.
- The "Phony War."
- From the fall of France until after the "Battle of Britain."
- From the defeat of Italy in the North African campaign to the fall of Yugoslavia and Greece leading to "Barbarossa."
- From "Barbarossa" to Pearl Harbor. This last chapter is pivotal to understanding the American position at the time; British views related or unrelated to Jews; and Zionist efforts in both Great Britain and the United States leading to the "Biltmore Conference" of mid-1942, which called for free Jewish immigration into an independent "Jewish Commonwealth" in Palestine, as the "Final Solution" was already underway in occupied Soviet territories. Since this last chapter and related matters are beyond the scope of this paper it will be mentioned only briefly.

The dimensions of the analysis should include the following: First, British policies at the cabinet level with regard to Palestine and especially Jewish emigration from Europe. This aspect has been researched and analyzed by others, and will be mentioned in short on the basis of their works.[9] The related issue of Jewish immigration into the United Kingdom itself after the outbreak of World War II will also be mentioned in some detail. Second, the intelligence activities of the British in the Middle East and in Palestine. I will relate mainly to this point, including pertinent intelligence reports, by verifying and explaining existing scholarship findings. Third, the Zionist response to British actions and to the situation in Europe itself will be dealt with in brief. Fourth, British influence on American views of the Palestine question, for which I will cite unpublished sources.

The relevant records can be found in the considerable bulk of research already done by others on these issues, based on Foreign Office (FO), Colonial Office (CO), and Cabinet papers (CAB) stored in the British Public Record Office (PRO) at Kew, and in other official and private papers used by other scholars. Research on antisemitic and anti-Zionist views prevailing among British officials at the time was recently added by British historians to the strictly political-diplomatic analyses existent before.[10] Zionist sources such as the Central Zionist Archives (CZA), Ben-Gurion's Archive (BGA) and others were also extensively used, but this article — in terms of primary sources — will be limited to relatively unused records. These include British intelligence reports on the Palestine Jews, recently released into the custody of the *Haganah* Archive in Tel Aviv, whose nature and significance require a short

9 See in addition to already mentioned works by Zweig and Porath, Gavriel Cohen, "Churchill and the Genesis of the Cabinet Committee on Palestine (April–June 1943)," *ha'Zionuth,* 4 (1975), pp. 259–336; *The British Cabinet and the Palestine Question, April–July 1943*, Tel-Aviv, 1976 (in Hebrew); and Michael Cohen, "The British White Paper on Palestine, May 1939, Part 2: The Testing of a Policy, 1942–1945," *Historical Journal*, 19 (1976), pp. 727–58.

10 See Kushner, *Persistence of Prejudice*.

discussion,[11] and the *Haganah*'s own records.[12] Established in the twenties, the *Haganah* was the military arm of the mainstream *Yishuv* (the Jewish community in Palestine). Immigration activists and rescue operatives, as well as local and foreign intelligence and underground operators came from its ranks or were associated with it. I will also cite American intelligence reports from the recently released files at the United States National Archive (NA), now located at College Park, Maryland.[13] These include U.S. Army G-2 and OSS — Office of Strategic Services, the central American intelligence agency operating during World War II.

11 Late in 1947 the staff of the British government's Criminal Investigation Department (CID) started filming the CID's archive, while destroying the original files toward the evacuation of Palestine by the mandatory regime. The filming was done by a Jewish employee of the British mandatory government. Copies of his filmed records reached Israeli Intelligence and were found in the late eighties in one of its storerooms and transferred to the Israel Defense Force's Central Archive and later to the *Haganah* Archive as Record Group 47. About 100,000 negatives were thus released for research, but only about 80,000 are legible. About 25,000 records dealt with Jewish affairs, and about 55,000 with Arab issues.

12 The *Haganah* created its own Counterintelligence (*RN*) organization on a national scale in 1940, following local initiatives within the Political Department of the Jewish Agency, under David Shealtiel. Later the *RN* became the *Shai* — the *Haganah*'s Intelligence. About 500 files from the *Shai*'s archive were transferred to the *Haganah* archive in Tel Aviv. Here I have used files from Record Group 112, *Shai-Porshim*, i.e., *Shai*'s intelligence gathered on the Stern Group and the *IZL*.

13 My primary source collection at the National Archives, Washington used in this paper is divided into the following main groups: Record Group (RG) 226, Office of Strategic Services (OSS), the U.S. Army's Military Intelligence Division (MID), and the Army's Military Intelligence G-2 and its Counter Intelligence Corps (CIC), stored in RG 165 (Records of the War Department, General and Special Staffs), RG 338 AMET G-2 (AMET was first abbreviated USAFIM — U.S Army Forces in the Middle East). Also U.S. Army's Judge Advocate General (JAG), International Affairs Division, War Crimes Office 1944–49 files were used, whose origin was in intelligence agencies in many cases, collected in RG 135, and other military intelligence files pertaining to Jews, to the Holocaust, to rescue efforts and to Palestine, located at the time in the National Archives's branch in Suitland, Maryland. These sources also contain captured German documents and interrogation of German POWs only released recently, as well as censorship intercepts and intelligence from British or combined British-American authorities and specifically from Palestine.

British Intelligence in the Middle East and its Significance

Any analysis of Zionist behavior since May 1939, that is not based on the obstructing role of the British authorities vis-a-vis both Zionist political aspirations and the actual rescue of Jews from Hitler's hands and their subsequent absorption in Palestine, misses the focus of Zionist intentions at the time. From the British point of view, the problem was a simple reversal of the same: how to prevent Jews from "flooding" Palestine, and how to prevent the Zionists from helping them or organizing them to get there. At the same time they had to control possible Zionist and Arab violence, deal with resistance to their policies in various areas as declared by the "White Paper," such as land purchases, and block possible Zionist efforts in America without losing vital American aid and growing support.

The American factor was essential for the isolated British after the fall of France. The issue of American-British cooperation on the intelligence level can be cited here as an example of British — and American — views of the Middle East and of Jewish immigration in the period under consideration. Not least, the ensuing increasing aid given by Washington to the British should be added here to suggest Hitler's response to it — which in my view plays a role in the "Final Solution."

The Departments of State and War, like American ambassador to London Joseph Kennedy, were pessimistic about Britain's chances of survival. After the fall of France, President Roosevelt sent his close friend William J. Donovan — retired World War I Colonel and later Brigadier General, and future OSS director — overseas to ascertain the chances of the British.[14] Wherever he went, including the Balkans and the Middle East, which he toured from Cairo to Baghdad as we are told by historian Bradley F. Smith, Donovan arrived and left as a strong supporter of Britain's chances and interests. Yet already then, very much under British influence, he warned the President that the Arabs could cause incredible harm, if the United States intimidated them. Donovan's SIS friend in New York, the wealthy Canadian industrialist William (later Sir William) Stephenson, who helped arrange Donovan's

14 For Donovan's trip in 1940, see Bradley F. Smith, *The Shadow Warriors, O.S.S and the Origins of the C.I.A*, New York, 1983, pp. 46–53.

tour and red carpet reception from Churchill downward, cabled MI6 headquarters that Donovan helped bring about the American destroyer deal. This deal preceded the Land-Lease Act of March 1941, a factor leading in my view to the "Final Solution" of the Jewish question in Europe. This tragic-ironic development obviously cannot be, and should not be ascribed to Churchill, nor to his American friends, whose main — legitimate — problem at the time was to keep Britain afloat. This objective was held even at the price of threatening the government's fall, the rise of a "Quisling government" in London, that may have delivered the British Navy to the Third Reich, and other threats of that kind. Yet only a "Quisling government" in London could have negotiated with the Germans a "Madagascar-like" solution of the "Jewish question."

Like a Greek tragedy, the protagonist's fate or that of his brethren is determined by superior forces, which he has to accept or not effectively resist. If the Jews did support a government that might have negotiated with Germany, having taken Hitler's "prophecy" of 30 January 1939 seriously, the Jews might have done the right thing from Hitler's point of view. But they could not: the "prophecy" seemed crazy, aimed at the Allies as a warning not to wage a global war. Furthermore, If they did not, they would have been seen as traitors to the anti-Nazi cause on both sides of the Atlantic, and as a tool in Hitler's hand to undermine the — still weak but growing — Atlantic bond. Notwithstanding, MI5, and less so SIS, as well as other British agencies suspected at least a Zionist-Nazi common denominator: to get the Jews into Palestine even during the war, which was perceived by these intelligence agencies as damaging to the war effort. British attitudes to the Zionists were not necessarily uniform, nor did they remain unchanged when Churchill, a declared Zionist and enemy of the "White Paper" policy, became Prime Minister and Minister of Defence in mid-1940. Yet the closure of Palestine's gates to Jewish refugees remained in force after Churchill's ascendance, due both to his minority status in his own cabinet on the subject and the input of the bureaucracies in charge of foreign and security policies. It was given up to an extent only late in 1943, a period not discussed in this paper.

One of the reasons for the difficulties, as claimed by British politicians and historians ever since, was Zionist terrorism, especially the terror activities of the "Stern Gang" (or the "Stern Group") under Avraham

"Yair" Stern.[15] However, it was not only Stern himself or his followers that were regarded by the British as ultranationalists, indeed something akin to the Nazis, and collaborators with the Axis. Major Labor-Zionist leaders, such as David Ben-Gurion, Chairman of the Jewish Agency for Palestine since 1935, were perceived and described in British official correspondence as "National-Socialists" and possibly, tools in Nazi hands. Conspiracy theories about Gestapo-Zionist collaboration circled among British intelligence operatives and were initiated, adopted or echoed by Colonial Office and Foreign office members in key positions not only in the period considered here, but later on as well.

Tony Kushner correctly points to the attitude of the security forces in the United Kingdom itself. According to Kushner, "it must be suggested that in the conspiratorial world of the security forces, being Jewish and anti-Nazi was no proof of loyalty to the British cause." The officer in charge of counterespionage at MI5, Maxwell Knight, "could distrust an agent simply because she had a Jewish lover,"[16] while "the security forces had been in the forefront to link Jews with international Bolshevism in the post-war world, and it does not seem that their views had totally changed in the Hitlerite period."[17] Since the British were a major, if not the only source of American military and civilian intelligence organizations after the fall of France, we should not be surprised to find similar notions among the heads of G-2, the U.S. Army's regular intelligence arm, and CIC, its Counter Intelligence Corps. The OSS was not yet fully born in 1940, and even that rather unusual outfit harbored astonishing ideas about Jews and Zionists, while employing many Jews at the time.

For British officials, Hitler's forced emigration of Jews, and the Holocaust itself, was a most troublesome matter. Kushner added to the previous research the relationship between the government and

15 For a recent, comprehensive, analysis of the history of the *IZL* and the Stern Group, see Joseph Heller, *LEHI — Ideology and Politics, 1940–1949*, Jerusalem, 1989, vol. I, esp. pp. 83–184 (in Hebrew).

16 Ibid. p. 143 and 143n.

17 Ibid. Knight's paranoia and methods of fighting his alleged traitors and enemy agents finally discredited him to such an extent that his future warnings against Soviet spies in Britain remained unnoticed, while those "moles" were very real indeed, see Bernard Porter, *Plots and Paranoia, A History of Political Espionage in Britain 1790–1988*, London, 1992, pp. 177ff.

public opinion on the immigration of Jews to Great Britain counting the number of Jewish refugees allowed to enter the British isles after 1 September 1939.[18] There were several thousands, among the total of 70,000 who were allowed entry since 1933. The policy was primarily based on security grounds since the government believed that any refugee arriving after the start of the war would have needed the approval of the Germans, specifically the Gestapo, as the latter was in charge of all Jewish affairs at that time and in direct control over the border police under Gestapo Chief Heinrich Müller. Worse still, Müller's boss — Reinhard Heydrich, was the chief of the SD as well, the intelligence organization of the Nazi party and the SS. The Gestapo, the criminal police (merged under Heydrich to the so-called Security Police) and the SD — were combined to a large extent in 1939, in the framework of the Reich Security Main Office (RSHA).[19]

Thus the refugees who Hitler tried to push out could have been perceived as his agents. And in the background loomed the larger conspiracy theory, namely that Hitler was using the Jews to foster antisemitism in Britain. Foreign Office officials agreed that "National Socialism had gained many supporters merely by exploiting anti-semitism."[20] In other words this "earned or justified trap" was in the mind of British officials, some of whom even blamed the Jews for their own troubles in Germany and, it follows, refused to allow them to generate similar conditions in Britain, which would have jeopardized the war effort against Germany. When Herbert Morrison became Labour-Party Home Secretary in October 1940, "the domestic antisemitism argument became even more powerful against the entry of Jewish refugees in the war."[21]

The Colonial Office produced its own version of the conspiracy theory. The head of its Middle East Department, H.F. Downie, went further, claiming that Jewish illegal immigration into Palestine (beyond

18 Kushner, *The Persistence of Prejudice*, p. 152.

19 For the structure and field units of the RSHA 1941–1943, see Raul Hilberg, *The Destruction of the European Jews*, London, 1961, pp. 184–186.

20 Kushner, *The Persistence of Prejudice*, p. 153n.

21 Ibid. And see Cheyette, *Constructions of "the Jew,"* p. 125n: The dialectical proximity created between alleged Jewish values and Nazism or similar theories can be found in H. G. Wells', *The Outlook for Homo Sapiens*, London, 1942 and cf. his, *Anatomy of Frustration* (1936).

the restricted quotas allowed by the British White Paper of May 1939) was "a conspiracy," "facilitated by the Gestapo and the Jewish Agency."[22]. Indeed, an eager SD officer, Adolf Eichmann, had been pushing Jews out since the Anschluss of Austria early in 1938, and later he, the hard-working chief emigration officer, continued the deportations from occupied Czech regions and Germany proper in the framework of a newly created "Central Authority for Jewish Emigration" under Heinrich Müller and Reinhard Heydrich. But in fact what he was doing was implementing — relentlessly and with great efficiency — the declared German policy since 1933, carried out by the more ruthless arm of the Nazi government. It was not an espionage affair, neither was it a "conspiracy" conceived by the SD and the Jewish Agency, unless we accept the dialectically opposed common ground between Hitler and western officials — that the absorption of Jewish refugees anywhere was serving the aims of Nazi Germany.[23] For Hitler, and for that matter Eichmann, it was irrelevant at that stage where the Jews went, especially since Hitler calculated that wherever they went their arrival would generate more antisemitism. In fact more German Jews emigrated to the United States between 1938 and 1939 than before, when they were allowed to fully use the (in itself insufficient) quota allotted to Germans since the mid-twenties. Jewish immigration remained extremely unpopular in America according to the polls. Since Hitler himself had not yet decided on his mass murder policy, the issue would not have been publicly seen as a matter of life and death, in which the FDR administration could be blamed for passive collaboration in sentencing the poor *St. Louis* passengers to death.[24]

22 See Kushner, *The Persistence of Prejudice*, p. 152.

23 Regarding the priority given by the SD itself to Palestine as a possible haven for German Jews, at first, and Eichmann's trip with his superior Herbert Hagen to Palestine in 1937 to meet among others (a possible Arab connection) a Zionist activist named Feivl Polkes, see Michael Wildt, *Die Judenpolitik des SD 1935 bis 1938*, Munich, 1995, p. 43–45. The British refused them entry, and the missions' failure might have, as Wildt maintains, dampened SD expectations from Palestine and the Zionists. This may have been partially true also due to the Arab rebellion and Lord Peel's partition plan of the same year, which forsaw a sovereign Jewish state in Palestine. But according to Wildt Hitler early in 1938 "underlined again his decision of Spring 1937, to continue the emigration policy, paying no attention to the host country," Ibid. p. 44.

24 According to Breitman and Kraut, *American Refugee Policy and European Jewry,*

After the fall of France the Zionists realized that the war had become a life and death struggle for the British. Yet despite Britain's hostile attitude to the Zionists and their complete indifference to the fate of Jews under Hitler's control, the Zionists understood that Britain was essential to fight Nazi Germany. Thus the Zionists mobilized to the British Army, hoping to use British intelligence agencies to fight Nazi Germany in various arenas and at the same time enhancing Jewish interests and goals. The role of intelligence agencies was important due to the presence of various, prevailing myths that worked against Jewish and Zionist interests, and because of the Axis control over Europe since summer 1940.

At this point I would like to specify the British intelligence gathering and security intelligence organizations in the Middle East, since they were established, streamlined, and coordinated to a certain degree, starting in summer 1939, in anticipation of a coming war with the Axis. Further, we can assess whether their reports and actions could be used to learn more about the Zionists, the British themselves, and the rescue dilemmas and options in this period.

1933–1945, Bloomington, 1987, p. 55, Raymond Geist, the very able number two man in the American Embassy in Berlin, was told by "an SS official named Karl Hasselbacher, head of Security Service Department IIF2 in charge of Jews, Freemasons, Lodges and emigrants, sometimes in 1938... that Germany was to be made 'judenrein' and that those Jews unable to leave the country would be exterminated." This statement is inaccurate regarding the man, at least. Dr. Hasselbacher was the veteran "Jewish Referent" of the Gestapo, not the SD. The Gestapo retained at that stage a degree of traditional German police character, even when it fully collaborated with the SD, which had no executive power of its own, but like other police officials in Nazi Germany Hasselbacher may have held also an SS rank even before the amalgamation in 1939 of the Gestapo and the SD into one SS-Hauptamt (RSHA). At that time Adolf Eichmann, a nontraditional, ambitious and ruthless SD man (the SD being the party's and the SS' own racist oriented Security Service and home intelligence), grabbed an executive job in annexed Austria and overshadowed Hasselbacher by enhancing the forced emigration policy from that country, which was further extended in the framework of a "Central Migration Office" under Gestapo Chief Müller with Eichmann as executive director to the *Altreich* and the Czech Protectorate. It seems Hasselbacher pushed Geist to impress upon his superiors in Washington the need to help facilitate the forced emigration policy of that period, possibly in order not to fall behind Eichmann.

In fact, British Intelligence was a hybrid, and rather uncoordinated structure in the thirties, with SIS (MI6) operating abroad, MI5 operating at home and in the Empire, and various agencies created to deal with local situations in areas such as the Middle East, sometimes under the control of the Royal Air Force. According to Christopher Andrew, SIS Berlin agent Frank Foley, a Zionist sympathizer since the First World War, built up an intelligence network of well-placed Jewish businessmen, among them Wilfried Israel, the British-born heir to a famous business dynasty, who maintained "clandestine contacts with a number of Nazi administrators during the early years of the Third Reich." Foley, like Harold Gibson, SIS Station Chief in Prague and later in Istanbul during the war, sympathized with the plight of Jewish refugees, and helped many German Jews to emigrate.[25] But Foley's espionage activities among German Jews, and the later use of refugees to obtain military information on the Axis powers, officially supported by the Jewish Agency, could have been a security risk to the Nazi policy of forced emigration. This policy was nonetheless maintained due to Hitler's expectations of reaching a general understanding with the European Allies under his hegemony.[26] Still, some of the MI6

25 See Foley, *Her Majesty's Secret Service. The Making of the British Intelligence Community*, London, 1986, p. 379. Claude Dansey, chief of SIS "Z" Organization (the SIS operation against Germany) recruited the retired Royal Navy Commander Kenneth Cohen as his assistant already in 1937. Wilfried Israel was a Zionist, and operated a rescue network in Portugal later during the war.

26 For a very interesting remark in this regard see: R. V. Jones, *Most Secret War*, Hebrew translation, Tel Aviv, 1984, p. 76. Dr. Jones was the chief scientific officer of British air intelligence, shared by both MI6 and the air staff. Among other achievements, he was responsible for the British effort to block German navigation beams guiding the Luftwaffe to its targets during the "Battle of Britain." His lower middle class, conservative background, which made Jones a "militarist" in the eyes of his fellow Oxford students even in the late thirties, was mixed with an extremely sharp yet insular mind. Jones recounts one of his side duties during the "phony war;" when he was ordered to join a committee devised by Sir Henri Tizard, the government's scientific adviser at the time, to "milk" Jewish immigrants for information about German scientific developments. The committee comprised English and German Jews and Jones, "the sole Anglo-Saxon," and the chairman. Simon Marx (later Sir Simon, finally Lord Marx, a department store magnate) was a member, but the most imposing one was Chaim Weizmann, who had a "fantastic oriental" aura about him. The only man Jones had ever encountered with such an aura about him, wrote Jones in his memoir, was "the Mehdi." At

officers, in what came to be known as ISLD (Inter-Service-Liaison Department) in the Middle East, held different opinions about Jews, refugees, and Zionists, as we shall see below. The counterespionage section of MI6 under Felix Cogwill and later Tim Milne, that worked in close cooperation with representatives of the Foreign Office, was active in Cairo under the umbrella of ISLD and worked with the so-called XX Committee in London.[27] In Egypt both the ISLD and "Section 5," in the framework of a specific Middle East security organization, were dealing with the Holocaust in Hungary. This was probably the so-called Combined Services Detailed Interrogation Center (CSDIC), established in 1940 and stationed in Fayid, in the Canal Zone.[28] This was made possible by the "Purple Primers," which contained all that was known about active members of the Nazi SD, and Abwehr. This material heavily influenced their US counterparts.[29]

any rate, nothing came out of this committee, due also to British bureaucratic squabbles. "Later on several of the Jewish refugees helped the Intelligence in the most courageous fashion when they secretly returned to Germany." This remark requires attention, once the relevant files would be opened. Jones' superviser at MI6, Group Captain [Frederick] Winterbotham, was however "very critical of the intelligence... provided [by the refugees]," according to Christopher Andrew, *On His Majesty's Secret Service*, London, 1985, p. 382.

27 See Robert Cecil, "Five of Six at War: Section V of MI6," in *Intelligence and National Security*, 9 (1994), pp. 345–353. The author was one of the wartime representatives of the Foreign Office in Section V. Kim Filby, the Soviet agent, also became a senior member of Section V, having first served at SOE, to be described below; during Cogwill's absence from the UK in the spring of 1944, he left Filby in charge. See Cecil, op. cit. p. 349. Cecil quotes Cogwill in regard to the "Fifth Column" scare of 1940, having attended a meeting of the Home Defence Security executive. He recalled later how the Home Office representative demanded that the invasion of refugee-carrying small boats should be turned back. "Lord Swinton, who was in the chair, asked the Admiralty representative how he thought this could be done. 'Sink 'em!' Mercifully the majority of those present were not prepared to go that far." Ibid.

28 David A. Charters, "British Intelligence in the Palestine Campaign, 1945–47," *Intelligence and National Security*, 6 (1991), pp. 115–140, esp. p. 116.

29 See for example a relatively late OSS report on rescue efforts from Hungary, in which American Jewish officials and Jewish Agency operatives were involved: "[American Patriotic considerations may have consciously or subconsciously received secondary consideration *where strong racial sympathy obscured hidden motives of ardent Zionists under SD pressure* (my underlining S.A.)." "The Jews who already consider

MI5, the counter-intelligence organization whose main activity was concentrated within the British Isles and Empire, had been suspicious of alien Jews for decades. It expanded rapidly after the outbreak of the war and was joined by intellectuals of all colors. However, it is important to distinguish between MI5's activities within the British Isles and its operation in various regions of the Empire, where MI5 "stations" known as DSO's (Defence Security Offices) may have developed a rather autonomous character due to the distances, the wartime strain, and the local and regional nature of their operations.[30] After to the MI5 "stations," which necessarily dealt with counterespionage and any possible rescue schemes of Jews from Nazi Germany, the Palestine Police Force was an important intelligence source.[31] The Political

themselves a nation, though still without a home or legal status, are probably even now casting about for future allies in the post-war period. That Britain will very likely not be one of these is already apparent. It is possible the Zionists consider the war already won, and are viewing all problems in a post-war light. From the Zionist viewpoint: unity of America and Russia with Great Britain might be less likely to further Zionist aims than would be a disagreement of these powers. Therefore any arrangement with the enemy for the rescue of the remaining Jews in Europe could hardly be expected to be discriminated against by Zionists on security grounds, especially when the deal implies that the enemy himself believes the jig is up. Zionists are playing a purely Palestine game. They will therefore welcome any force that could be brought to bear against opponents of the Jewish National Home (for one, the British). For an American Zionist to be anti-British, even in a war in which Britain and America are allies is not difficult. *This sentiment plays into German hands*." (Underlining added S.A.) Source: NA, RG 226, Entry 120 Box 20, X-2 (counterintelligence), declass. 7-1989. Comment on the Brand-Grosz rescue mission in Hungary.

30 About the DSO's see Charters, op. cit. p. 117.

31 The main archival source, which became available to historians only recently, is the abovementioned RG 47, CID, at the *Haganah* Archive in Tel Aviv. Also see Charters, ibid. It is interesting, but not our point here, to follow Charter's analysis of the decline of the rather effective British wartime intelligence network in Palestine and in the Middle East after the war, which the author ascribes also to the decline of British imperial power and the British economy. The "success" of the combined "two front war" waged by the *Haganah* and *IZL*/Stern against the mandatory power on Israel's road to independence is ascribed also — after London's hesitant policy toward the Jews of Palestine — to serious intelligence failures, but not at all to the impact of the Holocaust upon the Jews, the Americans, and maybe even on the British themselves.

Branch of the Criminal Investigation Department (CID) operated under the British High Commissioner for Palestine, in cooperation with MI5 and MI6 local "stations" and with their regional networks. In addition, two specific British regional military intelligence bodies for the Middle East as a whole, with Palestine given top priority, were set up in 1939, with headquarters in Cairo. These were the MEIC (Middle East Intelligence Center) and SIME (Security Intelligence Middle East), to be mentioned below. Later on, a third, quite important body was set up, PICME (Political Intelligence Centre Middle East), under the General Officer Commanding in Chief (GOC in C), Middle East.[32] All of them dealt, in various ways, with Palestine, the Zionists, and with rescue efforts as interpreted by them. They obviously reported on enemy activities, direct and indirect of both the Arab elite and the masses; for example, pro-Axis activities in the region and later anti-Allied and antisemitic propaganda broadcasted from Berlin and many other Axis stations to the Middle East that were fostered by Palestinian leader, Hajj Amin el Husseini.[33] These British intelligence units further supplied detailed information on the right-wing organizations in the Zionist movement in Palestine and abroad, the so-called Revisionists, under Vladimir Jabotinsky. After his death in 1940 they collaborated with several of his successors, while reporting on them and using information obtained from them on other Zionist outfits, until the arrival of Menahem Begin from abroad and his decision to launch his rebellion against the British.[34] They certainly dealt with the Sternists, on a weekly, ad hoc, sometimes daily and immediate basis, as reflected very well in US-Army G-2 and OSS reports and cable traffic.

The Middle East Intelligence Centre (MEIC) was set by the Committee of Imperial Defence upon recommendation of the Joint Intelligence Committee (JIC), following the initiative of Deputy Chiefs of Staffs of the armed services on 27 June 1939. MEIC began operating in

32 For exact dates and details, see H. O. Dovey, "The Middle East Intelligence Center," *Intelligence and National Security*, 4 (1989), pp. 800–812, and cf. F. H. Hinsley et. al., *British Intelligence in the Second World War*, Vol. I, London, 1979, esp. pp. 26–30.

33 See for an American sample thereof, NA, RG 165, Entry 77, Director of Intelligence, War Department, G-2 Regional File 1933–1944, Palestine, box 3027.

34 See in the same collection, same box 3027.

Cairo in August, about a month before the outbreak of the war. MEIC was meant to furnish the Commanders in Chief of the British Army, RAF and Royal Navy and representatives of the Civil Departments in the Middle East with "coordinated intelligence and provide the Joint Planning Staff in the Middle East with the intelligence necessary for the preparation of combined plans." The "planning euphoria" of those days is reflected quite clearly in this charter. Later a British Minister of State was sent to Cairo to provide the political aspects of military planning, in cooperation with a "Middle East War Council." The "Council" comprised key British diplomats and Arab experts in the area, such as Sir Miles Lampson, the British envoy in Egypt; his colleague in Baghdad, Sir Kennan Cornwallis; Bill Smart, an important Arab expert; and the British High Commissioner for Palestine, Sir Harold MacMichael. The Minister Resident was usually in the chair.

In early December 1939, a Security Intelligence Section of the GOC in C, ME, Cairo was established to "collect information regarding, and to keep all concerned informed of, movements and activities of enemy agents."[35] The War Office thus established Security Intelligence Middle East (SIME) on 9 December. SIME played a key role in a specific rescue case, the "blood for trucks deal" regarding the rescue of Hungarian Jewry. SIME was also an important source of political information on Arabs and Jews, which also reached the American military authorities before and during the peak years of the Holocaust. According to Dovey, "the volume of information in the periodical summaries — from MEIC and SIME — show that SIME had a large network of informants throughout the region." MEIC, also had quite good information, gathered by ISLD and other sources, as reflected in American reports fed by it, or directly by ISLD. The December 1942 Diary of MEIC shows that Brigadier I.N. (later Sir Iltyd) Clayton was then commanding the Center and that it had a Syrian detachment. The April 1943 Diary, according to Dovey, shows that Clayton was posted to the office of the Minister of State as Arab Adviser. The bulk of the staff moved to a new organization, the Political Intelligence Centre Middle East (PICME), which in fact replaced MEIC following a decision of the Political Committee of the Middle East War Council

35 See Dovey, op. cit. p. 803.

on 31 March 1943.[36] Brigadier C.D. Quilliam was in command. This, however, important as it may have been in torpedoing Zionist efforts in London and America, goes beyond the premises of this paper. As we have seen, SIME was under the GOC in C, Middle East, since 1940, in Cairo.[37] Several SIME officials were old SSO hands (Special Service Office, a RAF attached unit in charge of counterintelligence in the thirties), some of whom knew the Zionists well, were free of absurd ideas about them, and were ready to cooperate with them to expose Nazi spies and prepare for a possible Axis occupation. RAF intelligence officers were also active in creating ties between the Zionists and MI6, or SIS, but others were more suspicious. The latter calculated that the Zionists would do whatever they could to save Jews, including collaboration with the Nazis who were willing to use Jews for their own purposes. These included espionage, using Jews as hostages to get Zionist cooperation or simply as a source of troublesome immigration into a highly sensitive region, the only one in which the British were waging war directly against the Axis during and after the "Battle of Britain." Furthermore, the logic of Nazi-Zionist cooperation on the basis of their common interests was a kind of a political wisdom prevailing among several intelligence officers from the beginning to the bitter end.

Fear prevailed, paradoxically but not surprisingly, among the British top military. Fear of a renewed Arab rebellion in Palestine, if not of a general Arab revolt across the Middle East if the "White Paper" policy was to be abandoned, or if British Army units stationed in Palestine would be sent to subdue the pro-Nazi regime in Iraq. Although it proved to be very successful. General (later Field-Marshal) Sir Archibald P. Wavell himself the GOC in C, was totally opposed to the Iraqi venture, fearing an Arab rebellion in Palestine and trouble in Egypt.[38] In fact Churchill had to compel him to restore British control over Iraq in 1941. At the same time however, due to strong opposition at home and in the region, the Prime Minister had to abandon his own idea of

36 Ibid.

37 See also Michael Howard, *British Intelligence in the Second World War*, Vol. V, New York, 1990, pp. 31–32.

38 See Churchill, *World War II Memoirs*, Hebrew translation, Vol. III, Tel-Aviv, 1957, pp. 222–223.

arming the Jews of Palestine and thus free the British troops stationed in that country so that they could participate in real fighting elsewhere.[39] The fear of trouble with the Arabs and Moslems in general remained very much in the mind of Wavell's successors, Sir Claude Auchinleck, Sir Harold Alexander, and Sir Henry Maitland "Jumbo" Wilson, who inherited this traditional view with the officials who had adopted it. There are several reasons to explain this — besides the elitist fear of primitive masses, that may go back to the Mehdi's rebellion in the Sudan — such as Wavell's own experience in fighting the rebelling Palestinian Arabs in the late thirties, and the Moslem question in India, including the problem of Moslem soldiers in the British Indian Army. Both the Foreign and the Colonial Offices in London shared what Churchill called a "pro-Arab and an anti-Jewish" view, which may be attributed to the mixture of prejudices, images and reputations of Jews, combined with imperial interests and security considerations, some of them having a typical conspiratorial nature.

Writing in 1990, a distinguished contemporary historian, Michael Howard, describes British fears: "the British were based in countries whose populations were elements in a Levantine society extending around the shores and throughout the islands of the eastern Mediterranean, bound together by commercial and family links dating back over millennia; a society whose complexity foreign security authorities could barely comprehend...the region might be described as an intelligence officer's paradise and a security officer's hell."[40] Michael Howard's wit of the nineties is of course just a reminiscence of British security officers' fears regarding a possible Nazi-Zionist collaboration that could explode the Arab-Iranian-Turkish-Maghreb ocean. Such calculations were fed by a basic perception of Jews — especially Zionists — as bearing similar hypernationalistic, egotistical, unfair and inhuman characteristics of fascism itself. These views were held by Herbert Downie of the Colonial Office, and sometimes by Sir John Shackburgh of the Foreign Office, who were in charge of the Palestine sections, respectively, during the period under consideration.[41] Hence, among

39 Ibid., Vol. II, p. 336.

40 Howard, *British Intelligence*. p. 31.

41 See Zweig, *Britain and Palestine*. pp. 133, 180.

themselves and especially in dealing with the Americans, the British officials involved would use the intelligence reports and arguments which would associate the Zionists with the Nazis, in Downie's tradition.

Zionist hopes centered on SOE (Special Operations Executive) — the British intelligence unit aimed at subversion and at active warfare on enemy soil.[42] According to Christopher Andrew, Whitehall's initial interest in sabotage and subversive operations against Germany, harbored in SIS, "stemmed chiefly from an exaggerated belief in Germany's economic vulnerability." Accordingly, both Neville Chamberlain and Lord Halifax — his right hand man — began the war believing that economic pressure rather than military defeat would bring Germany to its knees. "Time," Halifax is quoted to have quipped, "is on our side." Yet another reason not to enter into any deals with the seemingly doomed Hitler. Hitler had a similar view of the British, unless they accepted his hegemony. Since the German war effort was believed to be critically dependent on two imports, Swedish iron ore and Rumanian oil, SIS planned subversive operations in both countries, which failed miserably. The failure of the Swedish scheme and the British Norway campaign — in which Churchill played an important but not very successful role — may have helped prompt the occupation of Denmark and Norway by the Germans and the fall of Chamberlain in Churchill's and the national coalition's favor. The Rumanian scheme as described by Christopher Andrew, was an extremely amateurish, poorly conducted operation. German agents managed to trick the crews of Rumanian explosive-carrying barges, that were supposed to be sunk next to the Iron Gates, the most vulnerable Danube narrows.[43] The Germans made the story public on 8 April 1940. Andrew did not mention a follow-up operation initiated by the SIS against German oil shipping on the Danube. The Zionists, however, responded positively to SIS overtures: a number of *Haganah* executives, among them David Hacohen and Yehuda Arazi, went to Bucharest to organize the sabotage act with local Jewish aid, but nothing came out of this endeavor, either.

These early schemes, however, tell us something about the thinking of both the British and the Zionists; the British dreamed of victory due to Germany's economic distress, which explains their inactivity on the

42 Ibid., pp. 472–476.
43 Ibid. p. 475.

Western Front during the "Phony War;" and the Labor Zionists tried to help the British abroad, by using their local Jewish connections. Whether they calculated the risk inherent in this for Rumanian Jewry or for Jews under Hitler's direct or indirect control, is not known. "Rescue" of Jews at this stage did not entail life or death, yet. But once the Germans won the six-week Blitzkrieg in the west, which began on 10 May 1940, the British developed high hopes with regard to guerrilla warfare behind the Germans' back. As Andrew puts it: "the failure of regular warfare was now to be redeemed by irregular warfare." As a result , Andrew tells us, the adoption of guerrilla warfare strategy removed it from SIS control. The Joint Chiefs reported to the War Cabinet on 25 May 1940 that, if France fell, "Germany might still be defeated by economic pressure, by a combination of air attack on economic objectives in Germany and on German morale and the creation of widespread revolt in her conquered territories."[44] None of these options related to the Jews, which, if they had, might have provoked the Arabs to a rebellion of their own. On the contrary, thought the British, "German morale" could hardly be undermined, if they perceived the bombing of German targets as serving Jewish interests. The conquered European nations would rise against the Nazi yoke for the sake of their own interests and values, supported per se by the British. Once, however, these illusions were swept aside and the British could focus on the defense of the British Isles proper (and the Middle East), the support of the British masses, who bore most of the burden, and the maintenance of domestic morale became an utmost priority, which in turn excluded alien Jews, as Kushner told us. Yet the idea of conducting a sabotage warfare behind German backs, paradoxically nourished by the alleged initial success of Nazi "fifth column" tactics due to the expected, overwhelming mass resistance in the occupied countries, survived and was adopted by Hugh Dalton who became Minister of Economic Warfare in Churchill's cabinet. The outgoing Foreign Secretary, Lord Halifax, was told by one of his colleagues that he would "never make a gangster." Andrew, who quotes this, says that "Dalton had the appearance of a man who would." He was confident "that by the end of the year, 'the slave lands which Germany had overrun' would rise in revolt, and that Nazism might then

44 See Andrew, op. cit., pp. 475–6.

'dissolve like the snow in the spring.' 'Regular soldiers, he complained, are not the men to stir up revolution, to create social chaos or to use all those ungentlemanly means of winning the war which come so easily to the Nazis.'" Although "ungentlemanly" methods in the security and intelligence organizations had been used in World War I, perceived already then as a "total war," Nazi Germany had infested its enemies with a degree of inhumane attitude to winning a war, manifested in the treatment of the Jews by MI5 operators such as Maxwell Knight.[45] The Zionists, in turn, were also infused with the guerrilla warfare mania, and subsequently mobilized and trained hundreds of *Haganah* commandos to be parachuted into occupied Europe. For this they needed British — and American — tools and political support, and finally found allies even among otherwise not very friendly British officials such as Brigadier I. N. Clayton himself.[46] But very little came out of this, due to other British and American priorities, and mainly to German and allied German countermeasures. In fact the whole idea was far removed from the realities on the ground. But myths were born, which would in turn explode in the face of their creators during the "Kasztner Trial" in independent Israel.[47]

Traditional suspicions of Jews and Zionists at SIS and SOE were not necessarily as negative as those typical of MI5, SIME and PICME, but carried out high political preferences regarding wartime dilemmas and priorities, also related to the postwar future of the region. The web of British intelligence in the Middle East included also the branch of the "Imperial Censorship" — i.e. censorship of mail, radio and telegraph — which reported to Whitehall and other interested offices across the Empire, such as India because of the Moslem element in the subcontinent, and also to the American censorship bureau. Its censors, several dozens of whom worked in Jerusalem (later during the war under the future Viscount Samuel, the son of the liberal politician

45 See Porter, *Plots and Paranoia*. pp. 168–171

46 For the British, see Wasserstein, *Britain and the Jews*. pp. 290–291 and his official sources.

47 The *Yishuv* parachuted several commandos into occupied Europe in 1944, with SOE's help. The operation in Hungary, where three commandos, including the legendary Hannah Szenes were sent, ended in catastrophe which was ascribed by right-wing Zionists during that trial to the Labor Zionist operative in Budapest, Dr. Israel Kasztner. The operation itself had little chance of succeeding.

and first British High Commissioner in Palestine), opened all relevant foreign letters from and to Palestine, monitored cables, and submitted regular reports including samples to the Allied Joint Censorship Board in Bermuda. An American censor, actually a G-2 captain, joined the British censorship office in Jerusalem later in the war.[48]

The *Yishuv* leadership was thus under a kind of a siege, of which it became very conscious. Meanwhile the British Palestine authorities and their counterparts in Whitehall perceived *themselves* to be under a sort of Jewish siege due to Zionist influence "in high places." The reference here is to Churchill's own traditional Zionist inclinations and the personal relations that existed between the Prime Minister, a few cabinet ministers and Chaim Weizmann (the President of the World Zionist Organization who resided in Britain). These connections did not suffice to prevent measures undertaken from time to time by the Palestine authorities against the *Yishuv* for its rescue efforts ("illegal immigration") and periodically also against its illegal military preparedness, meager as it in fact was.[49] At the same time, the *Yishuv* mainstream leadership searched for common denominators with the Allies wherever they could find them. The general Jewish public was torn between its views of the British — known for their hostile policy toward Jewish refugees from Europe and the sometimes harsh measures against the *Haganah* and its illegal arms hideouts — and the *Yishuv*'s leadership call to mobilize to the British Army to help fight the Nazis. The initial response to the call was very enthusiastic to the dismay of the British authorities in the area, who viewed the Jewish volunteers

48 See for details on Palestine censorship, NA, Entry 190, General OSS Correspondence, Cairo-SI-OP-15.

49 See for this, Ronald Zweig, "The political use of military intelligence: evaluating the threat of a Jewish revolt against Britain during the Second World War," in: *Diplomacy and Intelligence During the Second World War, Essays in Honor of F.H. Hinsley*, Cambridge, 1985, pp. 109–125, 286–293. Zweig argued in this article that the use of inflated numbers of *Haganah* members and of threats of Jewish violence against the British, based on British intelligence sources, in fact played into Zionist hands and enhanced cabinet deliberations in their favor, e.g., the return to the partition idea of Palestine by the cabinet late in 1943 and early 1944. I do not accept this interpretation, as I believe that Churchill was motivated by both the improved war situation and his traditional Zionist views, which however were finally torpedoed by the Middle East and Whitehall's officialdom.

as future troublemakers and even enemies, assigning them with Arabs to auxiliary units of the British armed forces. Thus the initial drive dissipated, after a while, and had to be pursued by the *Yishuv* leadership again and again, with limited success.

The leadership's own bids for military cooperation with the Allies assumed several dimensions. One of the less known among them was its cooperation with Allied intelligence in the interrogation of Jewish refugees for military purposes. These were first conducted in cooperation with the *Haganah*, the *Yishuv*'s semi-legal military arm, and later institutionalized in two refugee centers — Atlit near Haifa, and Homs in Syria. The CID, the British Police Intelligence, and other agencies involved in this common effort did not restrict themselves to the interrogation of these refugees; they monitored the *Yishuv* leadership and the *Haganah*, especially after the limited cooperation aimed at subduing the Palestinian revolt of 1936-39 ended in 1940, and later, following the limited military cooperation against a German invasion of Palestine in 1942 once Rommel's threat in the Western Desert seemed to be under control. The *Yishuv* leaders became extremely cautious as a result of this. Ben-Gurion himself left Palestine for longer periods in 1940 and late in 1941 to London and to the United States — before the "Final Solution" became known to him — absences that future observers regarded as negligence. Moreover the leaders' later official meetings, protocolled in the Central Zionist Archive, may well have been self-censored, especially with regard to secret rescue schemes later in the war.[50]

50 Hence the protocols of such meetings, in which Ben-Gurion, for example, grew rather reserved and mentioned security leaks several times (see for example CID report on Labor leaders meeting at the home of Moshe Shertok Sharett, on 12 November 1942, PRO, FO 921/7, and cf, Zweig, "The political use," p. 289n.) do not suffice as the only source for studying his rescue efforts, nor for his general Zionist strategy, as this was done by several of his critics such as Amos Elon. See Elon, *Timetable*, Jerusalem, 1980 (in Hebrew); Yigal Elam, *The Executors*, Jerusalem, 1990 (in Hebrew), and Tom Segev, *The Seventh Million, The Israelis and the Holocaust*, Jerusalem, 1991 (in Hebrew) and others. Instead, one should consult also other sources, such as Ben-Gurion's personal archive sources at Sde Boker (ABG) quoted by Tuvia Friling, also by Shabetai Teveth, and our own, foreign collections, put together.

SOE and Allied Propaganda Warfare

The Zionist problem at this stage, i.e. 1939–41 was to impose itself on a rather reserved network of foreign political, military and intelligence bodies. British intelligence agencies such as the Palestine government's CID, MICE and SIME, were in fact organs opposing the Zionists and the rescue of Jews into Palestine combined.

More research is needed on the activities of the Political Warfare, or "black propaganda" agency, under the Ministry of Information, which was active in this and other arenas. This agency later worked together with Elmer Davies' American foreign propaganda machine OWI (Office of War Information) and with the OSS's own "black propaganda" outfit, which steered away from Jews as best they could.[51] Sometimes it even

51 This policy might have originated among members of the Central European Section of OSS, such as Franz Neumann, the celebrated author *of Behemoth*: — an analysis of Nazi Germany completed in 1941. Neumann became a leading analyst in William L. Langer's Research & Analysis (R&A) Branch of the Office of Strategic Services, established in 1940 as the Office of Coordination of Information under Colonel William J. Donovan. Several members of the "Frankfurt School" joined Neumann at the Europe-Africa Division of OSS, and with others created the main "brain" of its Central European Section, such as Herbert Marcuse, Otto Kirchheimer, Hajo Holborn, Felix Gilbert, Walter Dorn, Sherman Kent and many others who served on the various boards created to define, edit and finally adopt the various reports issued by R&A during the war following a serious, multi-staged, semi-academic process. For a detailed analysis of the behavior of the "Frankfurter" among them, as OSS analysts and "Frankfurt School" ideologues, based on R&A reports, see Barry M. Katz, "The Criticism of Arms: The Frankfurt School Goes to War," *Journal of Modern History,* 59 (1987), pp. 439–478, esp. p. 472. And cf. Petra Marquardt-Bigman, "Amerikanische Geheimdienstalasysen des nationalsozialistischen Deutschlands," *Tel Aviver Jahrbuch für deutsche Geschichte*, 23 (1994), pp. 325–344. Neumann's "functionalist," or rather neo-Marxist interpretation of the Holocaust — which he had hardly foreseen due to the same "functionalist" method — as a "spearhead" aimed at the oppression and destruction of others besides Jews was maintained by him until after the war. Neumann blamed the democracies for offering Wilsonian values to the Germans after World War I but failing to back them up, for not stopping Hitler on time in the thirties, and especially for not offering a socially just solution to the problems of Germany but political equality, i.e., formal democracy. In this context the Jewish question was in his view marginal, but it was successfully inflated by Nazi propaganda to overshadow Germany's real problems, What was needed was not only the destruction of the Nazi grip over the German masses by war, in which the Jewish question should remain marginal in order to

used antisemitic fabrications to discredit high-ranking Nazis, that might have returned to the Allied camp as intelligence.[52]

It was mostly the SOE, also called MO4, the already mentioned British foreign sabotage and guerrilla organization in the Middle East and the Balkans, working under the Ministry of Economic Warfare in the Middle East under several names — such as ISSU6, SPOC, "A-Force," and the like — that was willing to mobilize the Zionists for the war against Germany and cooperate with official Zionist bodies. Several years after the outbreak of the war, SOE even transmitted

avoid any Allied inputs to the already inflated and useful — for the Nazis — side issue, but the creation of a socially successful democracy in a united, in itself not thoroughly nazified Germany, once the Nazi grip was broken; cf. NA, RG 59, R&A report 1113.9, Weekly Roundup, Central European Section 5/18–5/24 1943, and Franz Neumann, *Psychological Warfare*, in which he cited Goebbels' pledge (in *Das Reich*, May 1943) to exterminate Jews in the East, and *New York Times* report of the destruction of the Warsaw Ghetto. Neumann asserted, with examples, his "spearhead theory" of antisemitism, following a critique of democracies' behavior toward Germany in the late thirties. In his view the anti-Jewish measures of late 1938 were partly the result of the democracies' refusal to resist Hitler's expansionism such as the destruction of Czechoslovakia, construction of the Western Wall, the Anschluss of Austria, which paved the way for Hitler's more aggressive moves that required a united home front. Neumann then asserted the concept of collective guilt used by the Nazis to preclude the German populace from leaving "the Nazi boat," and non-Nazi members of the ruling class from attempting separate peace negotiations. Finally, under the heading "Use," the above "prevents us from making anti-antisemitic propaganda. It would be futile, wouldn't be believed anyway, and also dangerous to praise Jews for contribution to civilization." In other words, since the Nazis made the Jews a central issue — aiming thereby at other goals — the Jewish issue itself became self-defeating, if the Allies concentrated on it. The "collective guilt" argument, which I regard as Hitler's "bonus" and regard to the "Final Solution," was discussed by me in my forthcoming "Quadruple Trap." In addition to Neumann a much more developed theory of antisemitism is that offered by Hannah Arendt, who explains the catastrophe of the European Jews (as possibly divorced from their future in America) by a variety of arguments, many related to Jewish traits and behavior as explanatory variables, some that she picked up from Heinrich Heine and Neumann himself, without giving them due credit. In the scholarly literature on antisemitism this may be debated as the scapegoat versus interactionist, or convergence explanation of antisemitism. Cf. Arendt's *Origins of Totalitarianism*, Cleveland, 1963, especially pp. 5–10, 22–25, 74–75.

52 See, for example, NA, RG 226, Entry 190, Director's Office and Field Stations, box 31, Bern, MO ("black propaganda").

Jewish Agency cables from London to the Head Office in Jerusalem, averting the censors, but was ordered to stop the cable traffic late in 1942. The Agency developed a kind of illegal radio traffic with its representatives in London and in the U.S. already in 1941, but had no similar radio contact with continental Europe.[53]

The Palestine Home Front 1939–1942

Ben-Gurion's initial concept — during the period outlined above, May 1939 to September 1939 until his departure to London in May 1940 following the proclamation and implementation of the "White Paper" policy in spite of or rather because of the outbreak of World War II — was of a large-scale protest campaign against the "White Paper" policy, together with legal or illegal immigration, as well as the creation of a Jewish army within Allied ranks once the war broke out.[54] Ben-Gurion made a distinction between the government of Palestine, whose policy of curbing immigration was to be resisted as far as possible without risking an open rebellion, and the *Yishuv,* which at the same time was supposed to be morally and practically mobilized to join the British against Nazi Germany. He even suggested to SIS and SOE, and later to OSS, that they use the *Yishuv*'s training and immigration network in Europe to fight the Germans, collect intelligence and help the Allies in any other way.[55]

All kinds of unrealistic ideas were circulating during that phase, such as a network of radio stations based in Zionist outposts in

53 Testimonies of Shlomo Lavi and Menahem Yitzhaki, the pioneers of the *Haganah*'s illegal communication service, which first operated from Kibbutz G'vat and then had an operator in London as well, in private communications to the *Haganah* Archive and in G'vat newsreel, #1553, courtesy of *Haganah* historian Gershon Rivlin.

54 See Tuvia Friling, "David Ben-Gurion and the Catastrophe of European Jewry 1939–1945," Ph.D. dissertation, Hebrew University, 1990, pp. 1–40, and in his book, *Arrow in the Dark*, Jerusalem, 1998, and cf. Bauer, *Diplomacy and Underground*, pp. 62–84.

55 Arthur Goldberg, COI New York, Labor Desk, to Allen W. Dulles, COI New York Office Director, following a meeting between the two and Emanuel Neuman, a Zionist operative, suggesting a meeting between Allen Dulles, Ben-Gurion and Weizmann upon their anticipated arrival in New York in Autumn 1940, NA, RG

occupied Europe, stretching from Austria to Salonica in Greece to British headquarters in Cairo. Once examined, however, they were abandoned by Zionists and British intelligence officers. These ideas were conceived in typically romantic fashion — based on the Labor Zionist view of anti-fascist forces of the time, nourished by the myth of the Spanish civil war, and inspired by the legend of mass resistance to fascist tyranny together with guerrilla and clandestine activities — with the *Yishuv* wanting its share while pursuing Zionist claims at the peace conference. The relevance of potential Jewish resistance to Hitler's decisions about Jews when he overran most of central, western and southern Europe, was not known then and is unclear now. And whether a pro-Allied letter sent by the Zionist Organization's President Chaim Weizmann late in August 1939 to the British Prime Minister[56] enraged Hitler and rationalized his future moves is doubtful. What we do know is that this same letter is being used today by German historian Ernst Nolte to justify Hitler's countermoves. Clearly, Hitler was not motivated by Zionist statements.

Once the situation in Europe deteriorated, the Zionist immigration envoys left for Palestine or neutral countries. This was later viewed as an act of serious moral negligence, although no one could have known at that juncture that Hitler himself had not yet decided to kill the Jews. Most of the European Jews however, paralyzed and shocked by the events of 1939-40, would not go to British Palestine — closed as it was by the British and threatened by Arabs as it seemed to be — until it was too late. Indeed for many, Palestine still seemed less attractive and more dangerous than their own ghettos or more normal habitats in the Balkans or in occupied western Europe, and they refused to listen to Zionist pleas to leave everything behind and go to Palestine — in spite of British counteractions.[57] On the other hand, the *Yishuv* tried to maintain contact, through the neutral countries, with the Zionist youth movements and work together with Zionist individuals in countries

226, Entry 106, Secret Intelligence Operations, New York, box 42; next Goldberg advised Dulles about their arrival; no answer was available in this file. Goldberg also mentioned Zionist-British intelligence cooperation as a Zionist asset.

56 See Norman Rose, *Chaim Weizmann, A Biography*, New York, 1986, pp. 354–355.

57 See Menahem Bader's memoirs, *Sad Missions*, revised edition, Tel-Aviv, 1958, pp. 14–32 (in Hebrew).

allied to Germany to enhance illegal immigration to Palestine, which had been closed by the British to large scale, free immigration.

The *Haganah*-SIS-SOE secret cooperation continued, on several levels, mainly with regard to intelligence gathering in the pro-Axis Middle Eastern countries such as Syria, (under Vichy France, which was occupied by the British with some *Haganah* support in summer 1941 due to Churchill's insistence), but also in Turkey and Iran, where *Yishuv* emissaries were asked by the British to build intelligence cells among local Jews, should these countries come under Axis influence or be lost altogether.[58]

As mentioned previously, the right-wing opposition to the mainstream leadership of the *Yishuv*, organized within the New Zionist Organization (NZO) and its military wing *Irgun Tzvai Leumi* (National Military Organization - NMO, abbreviated *IZL* in Hebrew) lost their leader, Vladimir Ze'ev Jabotinsky, who died in mid-1940 in the United States. Under David Raziel, Jabotinsky's followers split, and Raziel concluded a formal agreement of cooperation with Allen Saunders, Inspector General of the Palestine Police. Raziel's followers, such as Yitzhak Berman, a future cabinet minister under Menahem Begin, were ready to cooperate with the British, supply them with information and fight pro-Axis elements in the Balkans, the Baltics, and Middle Eastern countries such as Iraq.[59] Raziel eventually died in a British mission against the pro-Nazi nationalists under Rashid Ali el Qeillani, who assumed power in Baghdad for a short while in 1941 in cooperation with Hajj Amin el Husseini, the former Mufti of Jerusalem. Thus, as

58 One of them was Eliahu Epstein-Elath, a member of the Jewish Agency's Political Department, and later the first Israeli ambassador to Washington, and cf. his (not always reliable) memoir: *The Struggle for Statehood*, Washington, 1945–1948, Tel Aviv, 1979 (in Hebrew). Elath indeed cooperated with ISLD's (in fact MI6) Palestine station under John Teague, who mobilized him for a variety of intelligence operations in Iran, Iraq and Turkey, according to detailed testimony given to me. Cf. Eldad Haruvi, *British Intelligence and Secret Cooperation with the Yishuv during World War II*, M. A. Thesis, Haifa University, 1993, pp. 40–72.

59 For the Saunders-Raziel agreement of October 1939, see Heller, *LEHI*, pp. 90–91. The CID's reports stored in RG 47 do not reveal names of *IZL* informants, but Raziel and NZO activists such as Dr. Arie Altmann, who strongly supported cooperation with the British, were in regular touch with the British authorities. Berman even joined SIS Istanbul later in 1942 as an active MI6 officer.

Yehuda Bauer wrote,[60] a high degree of cooperation existed between *IZL* and the British Palestine Police and the CID — the police intelligence of the Palestine British government. In language not unlike the antisocialist credo of Jabotinsky's followers, the CID colored their reports on the Labor Zionists by equating *Mapai*'s civilian militia with the Gestapo (probably confusing it with the Nazi SA). I would argue, on the basis of the recently released reports from the CID and *Shai* (the intelligence network of the *Haganah*), that the information came from NZO officials, via variety of paid and otherwise recruited informers, among them non-Jews married to Jews who entered the country legally, from telephone monitoring, and indeed from *IZL* sources.

A minority in *IZL*, under the influence of Avraham "Yair" Stern, continued to view the British as the main enemy, rather than the Axis powers with whom they hoped to find a common language. Stern even tried to negotiate with Italian and German diplomats before the "Final Solution" was decided upon, and reach an agreement with them against the British in order to facilitate the mass departure of Jews from Europe to Palestine.[61] But the British apprehended him and shot him on the spot, obviously without trial. Moreover, the Palestine Government and the British Palestine experts in Cairo did not concentrate solely upon Stern's group. In fact there were serious ups-and-downs in the treatment by British mandatory authorities of the *Yishuv*'s elected and semi-legal institutions after the outbreak of World War II. This began with the very harsh implementation of the "White Paper" policy as a whole, including a military crusade against the *Haganah*. This was

60 See Bauer, *Diplomacy and Underground*, pp. 112–113.

61 See Inspector General [Palestine Police A. Saunders to Chief Secretary, Palestine Government, 11.9.1940, Subject: Disturbances at Herzlia, secret, pertaining to the robbery by Stern Gang members of *Haganah* weapons, to which the Inspector General added a summary of the Gang's background and previous activities such as bank robberies in Jerusalem and Tel Aviv to finance its illegal activities. See further most secret memo 59/1809/GS, dated 10 October 1940, an internal CID document carrying the header Giles Bey (Arthur F. Giles, the CID's chief, who used the Egyptian title "Bey") on Stern's connections with Fascist Italy, and about Stern's letter of understanding, to the Italian mission in Syria recommending the arrest of the group. Similar British intelligence sources were disseminated at the time about Stern's efforts to create a viable working collaboration with Fascist Italy, in conjunction with Stern's own takeover in Palestine, once "liberated" from the British, found in the CID's files, *Haganah* Archive, RG 47.

followed by a period of relaxation that was related to Axis threats in the whole Mediterranean basin, and a degree of military cooperation was reestablished between the *Yishuv* and the British military on the ground in preparation for Axis onslaughts. When the fronts stabilized, the mainstream Zionists led by Ben-Gurion proclaimed a new policy at a public conference held at the Biltmore Hotel in New York in mid-1942. This policy called immediate independence in western Palestine and its opening to free Jewish immigration. This was followed, as we are told by Ronald Zweig and his sources,[62] by a new phase: the British High Commissioner for Palestine, with the support of members of the Minister of State's Office in Cairo and various intelligence and censorship agencies, launched a crusade to abolish the Jewish Agency itself, describing the leadership's political behavior as working toward the creation of a "national-socialist [that is, Nazi] state," using terms like "Zionist Juggernaut," and "Organization Todt" (the Nazi slave labor organization). Neither side yet comprehend the magnitude of the "Final Solution," which would penetrate their minds a little later.

The Intelligence Pictures

Even before the outbreak of the Second World War the British authorities in Palestine itself and in Cairo targeted the following Zionist outfits and persons:

- Those involved in all kinds of illegal immigration at home and abroad. Illegal immigrants who entered the country were targets for prosecution as well.
- Those who might have been enemy agents proper, or collaborated with the enemy for their own purposes, or sought some kind of collaboration with Mussolini's Italy and Nazi Germany, falling under the category of "fifth columnists." Sternist activists in particular were perceived to belong to that category, which finally led to Stern's murder at British hands. Later on, Sternists who escaped from British jails and renewed their terror activities were of great concern to the British authorities, who knew very well the differences between them and

62 Op. cit., pp. 152–167.

Labor Zionists. Yet, at the same time, the British realized that the Sternists and their *IZL* sympathizers were a major tool in their hands to both discredit the Zionists as a whole in American eyes and awaken American fears of Arab Moslem violence in the whole region stretching from North Africa to Iran, to India and even to the Far East if Jewish immigration to Palestine was to be allowed. Finally, the mainstream Labor leadership were described as "National-Socialists."

- *Haganah* and *IZL* activists, weapon hideouts, the purchasing and smuggling of weapons, military training, which were continuously targeted.
- Political parties, the *Yishuv*'s elected bodies, Zionist organizations abroad, developments within the *Yishuv* in its relations with Arabs and with Jewish communities abroad, which were reported about with a relatively high degree of accuracy. Also the economic situation in Palestine, and the *Yishuv*'s trade relations with foreign countries, were under constant surveillance.

The CID's network of informers included enlisted men, among them Jewish officers, or paid agents or people maneuvered by the CID to collaborate by various means. British civilian and military intelligence networks became large enough to deal with the small (about 500,000 strong) Jewish community in Palestine. They were effective and largely accurate, if we compare CID and military intelligence reports to the actual developments on the ground as reflected in Zionist sources, among them the *Shai* archive, the *Haganah*'s own intelligence service and its counterintelligence (*RN*) archive.

The picture of the Zionist situation at the time, including Zionist rescue efforts emerging from these sources can be summed up thus:

- Due to the *Yishuv*'s inner divisions, ideological schisms and relatively small numbers, the British were able to successfully penetrate its organizations and use its inner rivalries for British purposes. One of the results of these divisions was a relatively high degree of collaboration between NZO officials and the British, against the Sternists and their bid to find a common language with Mussolini's Italy and even with Nazi Germany. This bid was based upon Stern's assumption that the Zionists and the Axis powers shared a common interest regarding a territorial solution of the Jewish question outside of Europe, such as the "Madagascar Plan" which became publicly known in 1940, and upon a further assumption that the Axis powers would concentrate on the Middle East, once Britain lost its grip on Europe and the Germans failed in their direct offensive against the British Isles. Thus the next German target would be the British presence in the Middle East. To achieve this, Sternist terrorism against the British as well as against the *Yishuv*'s "collaborationist" leadership would have to merge with the alleged common Zionist-German interest in a territorial solution to the Jewish question outside of Europe. But it was not only NZO officials — regarded both then and later by the Sternists as traitors and British tools — who were outraged by Stern's minority views and terror activities. The mainstream Zionist leadership, viewing Stern's behavior as political blindness bordering on treachery against the Jewish cause, tried to limit the Sternist influence as best they could, including cooperation with the British authorities, a well-known fact that seems to have been more than justified on the basis of the newly opened records. At the same time, the British exploited this domestic tragedy for gathering information by all sides on the others in order to discredit the Zionist cause in American eyes.

Perhaps the best example of the *Yishuv*'s inner divisions that could have been exploited by the British was the case of Malkiel Gruenwald, a religious fanatic who had fought the secular Labor Zionists in his native Vienna in the thirties, collaborating with the fascist Dollfuss regime in Austria. In November 1940, Gruenwald informed the British CID that enemy agents were among the passengers of the "*Patria*," an illegal immigrant ship sent by the *Yishuv* to Palestine and interned at Haifa harbor by the British.[63] This denunciation was even more painful for the *Yishuv* leadership, who had no choice but to authorize a sabotage act in the vessel's hull to prevent the British from banishing the ship and its passengers to Mauritius — a British crown colony in the Indian Ocean. This was not uncommon practice by the British in order to enforce the "White Paper" policy. The sabotage act, aimed at immobilizing the ship only, resulted in a great loss of life, which needless to say did not prevent the British from pursuing their policy as before. This view of illegal immigrant vessels destined for Palestine as "spy ships" was maintained by Downie at the Colonial Office even later, when

63 Gruenwald file, *Shai* collection, *Haganah* Archive.

the British succeeded in sending yet another vessel, the *Struma*, back to the Black Sea, whereupon it was torpedoed and sunk, leaving only one survivor.[64] The *Struma* tragedy resulted in a storm of protests at home and abroad against the British authorities, which brought about some changes in the British attitude toward the refugees. This change in attitude was also influenced by the news of the Holocaust, but that goes beyond the scope of this paper.[65]

Because of this, and due to the inner rivalries typical of the *Yishuv* at that time, a growing quest emerged for better cooperation within and control over the *Yishuv*'s future behavior, which was demonstrated later during the war under *Mapai*'s leadership. This may be perceived today as *Mapai*'s historical "Bolshevism," described as "National-Socialism" by the British mandatory authorities on the one hand, and as *Mapai*'s "collaboration" with the British on the other, based on the mainstream Zionist leadership's refusal to use force against the British and its alleged negligent behavior with regard to rescuing the Jews of Europe. As elaborated above, during most of the period considered here the Nazis themselves had not yet decided what to do with the Jews under their control, nor did most of the European Jews anticipate their coming doom, or opt for the Zionist solution, which would mean leaving their homes to a dangerous unstable environment in which the Zionists seemed to have lost British protection and good will since the publication of the "White Paper."

The intelligence picture reveals both a growing reluctance among American Jews from May 1939 to support the seemingly hopeless Zionist cause, and the unfolding of a giant world drama beginning in September 1939. It is not surprising then that Whitehall's calculations regarding American Jewish support of their cause and British behavior in Palestine were free of doubt. This confidence was not even shaken by America's noninvolvement. It was not until Pearl Harbor and Hitler's declaration of war against the United States three days later that

64 See Kushner, *The Persistence of Prejudice*, pp. 152–153.

65 Malkiel Gruenwald would play another role in independent Israel — that of denouncing *Mapai*'s man in Hungary as if he — Kasztner — collaborated with the Nazis, prompting the famous "Kasztner Trial" in the early fifties, and becoming the hero of the extreme Israeli right and of other radicals at the time, and possibly legitimizing them on *Mapai*'s account.

America entered as a full ally, which sanctioned the global war, a war in which the "Jewish race would be annihilated, this time," as Hitler had publicly threatened on 30 January 1939. When the Germans began to pursue the "Final Solution" in Soviet-occupied territories in summer 1941, the isolated Zionists in Palestine could do nothing to rescue them, except possibly to try and help the Rumanian Jews deported to Transnistria via neutral Turkey, where the British did their best to block such Zionist activities. This, and other efforts aimed at rescuing Jews from other German allied nations and from the Polish Ghettos directly required German collaboration to begin with — which at that time was out of the question, and British consent — which during the period under consideration was not forthcoming. In fact, Jewish immigration into Palestine was even perceived as war damaging, and described in such terms to the Americans. British intelligence efforts and censorship intercepts were geared not only to pursue this view, but to fight the meager rescue efforts undertaken by the Zionists. This included the persecution of illegal immigrants even when they entered Palestine. The widespread local and regional intelligence network that fed this information to the British was also responsible for deportation of Jewish refugees on their way to Palestine to the crown colony Mauritius. These actions as well as various operations undertaken against the *Haganah* and its weapon hideouts, once Rommel's threat was checked, led the mainstream *Yishuv* leadership to use the *Haganah*'s military power in Palestine as an inflated threat. The decision by David Ben-Gurion to leave Palestine late in 1941 and concentrate on American Jewry — by that stage aroused and horrified by the deteriorating conditions of the Jews in Europe and by British actions against those who tried to reach Palestine — culminated in the "Biltmore Conference" of mid-1942. This marked the beginning of a unified American-Jewish effort toward a Zionist solution of the Jewish question in Europe. But this response turned out to be too late to rescue most of the Jews trapped in Europe, not because of official Allied reluctance to absorb them, but because of Hitler's growing resolve to exterminate European Jewry per se, and in reaction to the Allied war against Nazi Germany, which he had brought about.

The lessons of the "abandonment" of the Jews by the British beginning in May 1939 in the face of Arab military actions, British calculations, American reservations and the Nazi challenge combined, were not forgotten, however. In fact this was the beginning of emancipated, possibly autonomous, even independent, Jewish political-military thinking, which would pursue Jewish interests in a world in which the Jews were helplessly caught from all sides. This new thinking would not abandon the moral-political, socialist and western-oriented values of Ben-Gurion and other Labor leaders. The legacy of the behavior of the Sternists' and the *IZL* in 1939-42, detached from each other but competitive, is blurred. It survived in various and peculiar interpretations and remained — plus other inputs related to the Holocaust — a driving force in Israeli politics ever since, and partially explains its dynamics vis-a-vis Labor's tradition, the Arabs, and the world until today.

List of Contributors

Aronson, Shlomo, Professor of political science at the Hebrew University of Jerusalem. He has studied history, the Holocaust and political science at the Hebrew University, the University of Munich and the Free University of Berlin. His publications include: *The Beginnings of the Gestapo System — The Bavarian Model*; *Reinhard Heydrich and the Early History of Gestapo and SD* and his forthcoming study *The Quadruple Trap. Hitler, the Allies, Arabs and Jews.*

Bacharach, Walter Zwi, Professor Emeritus and incumbent of the Samuel Braun Chair for the History of the Jews of Prussia at Bar-Ilan University. Among his publications: *Anti-Jewish Prejudices in German Catholic Sermons* and *The Human Image in Nazi Weltanschauung.*

Bajohr, Frank, Historian at the Institute for the history of National Socialism in Hamburg. Dr. Bajohr has written several publications on the German labor movement, the resistance to National Socialism and regional aspects of Nazi rule. Among his publications *"Arisierung" in Hamburg. Die Verdrängung der jüdischen Unternehmer 1933–1945.*

Bankier, David, Head of the section of Holocaust Studies at the Institute of Contemporary Jewry of the Hebrew University. Dr. Bankier has published extensively on modern Latin American Jewry, antisemitism and the Holocaust. His publications include *The Jewish Emancipation*; *Zionism and the Palestinian Question*; *The Holocaust*; *The Germans and the Final Solution.*

Bauer, Yehuda, Director of the International Center for Holocaust Studies of Yad Vashem and founder of the Vidal Sassoon International Center for the Study of Antisemitism at the Hebrew University of Jerusalem. His many works include: *Jews for Sale?*; *Out of the Ashes*; *History of the Holocaust*; *The Jewish Emergence from Powerlessness.*

Breitman, Richard, Professor of history at American University in Washington, chief editor of *Holocaust and Genocide Studies*. Author of several books related to the Holocaust. His study: *The Architect of Genocide — Himmler and the Final Solution* won the Fraenkel Prize for Contemporary History and has been translated into German and Italian.

Büttner, Ursula, Historian at the Institute for the History of National Socialism in Hamburg and professor at the Institute for Social History of Hamburg University. Dr. Büttner has written about German society in the Weimar Republic, the Third Reich and the years of occupation (1945–1949). Her many studies include *Das Unrechtsregime. Internationale Forschung über den Nationalsozialismus* and studies on the problems of reintegrating Nazi victims into German society after 1945.

Dipper, Christof, Graduate of the University of Heidelberg. Since 1990 professor of Contemporary History at the Technical University of Darmstadt, and Editor-in-Chief of the journal *Neue Politische Literatur*. His many publications include a seminal article on the attitude of German resistance to Nazi antisemitism. In 1998/9 Dr. Dipper was a Fellow at the Historisches Kolleg, Munich.

Fischer, Albert, Member of the Department of Economics and Business Administration of the University of Jena. Dr. Fischer researched the role of the state banks in the interwar period. On the politics of Hjalmar Schacht he published his book *Hjalmar Schacht und Deutschlands "Judenfrage." Der "Wirtschaftsdiktator" und die Vertreibung der Juden aus der deutschen Wirtschaft*.

Fraenkel, Daniel, For many years Dr. Fraenkel was an archivist in the Israel National Archives. Since 1994, he is in charge of documentation and cataloging of archival material at the Yad Vashem Archives. Dr. Fraenkel is author of the book *On the Edge of the Abyss*, which discusses Zionist Policy and the plight of the Jews in Germany 1933–1938.

Gerstenberger, Heide, Incumbent of the chair on theory and history of the modern state and society at the University of Bremen. Among her books *Revolutionary Conservatism*; *History Workshops and Analysis of Fascism*, as well as many articles on conditions for the functioning of dictatorships.

Gruner, Wolf, Was a fellow of the International Center for Holocaust Studies in Yad Vashem and is presently involved in a project analyzing techniques of persecution in the 19th and 20th centuries at the Center for the Research of Anti-Semitism of the Technical University in Berlin. Among his publications *Judenverfolgung in Berlin 1933–1945*; *Der Geschlossene Arbeitseinsatz deutscher Juden. Zur Zwangsarbeit als Element der Verfolgung 1938 bis 1943*.

Heim, Susanne, Was a fellow of the International Center for Holocaust Studies in Yad Vashem. She presently works at the Max-Planck-Institute of History of Science in Berlin in a research project on the Kaiser-Wilhelm-Gesellschaft in the Third Reich and is also preparing a major study on Jewish emigration and international refugees policy. Dr. Heim has co-authored the book, *Vordenker der Vernichtung*.

Hoffmann, Peter, William Kingsford Professor of history at McGill University in Canada. Author of many publications on German resistance, among them: *The History of the German Resistance 1933–1945*; *Widerstand, Staatsstreich, Attentat: Der Kampf der Opposition gegen Hitler*; *Stauffenberg und der 20. Juli 1944*.

Kaplan, Marion A., Professor of History at Queens College and the Graduate Center, City University of New York. Prof. Kaplan's publications have focused on German Jewish history. Her books include: *When Biology Became Destiny, Women in Weimar and Nazi Germany*; *The Jewish Feminist Movement in Germany*. Her new book, *Between Dignity and Despair. Jewish Life in Nazi Germany*, won the 1998 National Jewish Book Award.

Kulka, Otto D., Professor of Modern History at the Hebrew University of Jerusalem and incumbent of the Rosenbloom Chair of Jewish History. Dr. Kulka has published i.a. *Deutsches Judentum unter dem Nationalsozialismus* and co-edited *Judaism and Christianity under the Impact of National Socialism, 1919–1945*.

Kwiet, Konrad, Professor of German and Deputy Director of the Center for Comparative Genocide Studies at Macquarie University, Sydney. Professor Kwiet also serves as Chief Historian of the Australian War Crimes Commission. He published many articles and a seminal study with Helmut Eschwege, *Selbstbehauptung und Widerstand. Deutsche Juden im Kampf um Existenz und Menschenwürde 1933–1945*.

Ladwig-Winters, Simone, Graduate of the Free University, Berlin. Her book *Wertheim — ein Warenhausunternehmen und seine Eigentümer*, is a product of her studies of the "aryanization" of department stores based on unknown sources of the German banks in the central archive of the former DDR. Her current research is on the elimination of Jewish attorneys in Berlin after 1933.

Lohalm, Uwe, Since 1997 director at the foundation Forschungstelle für Zeitgeschiche Hamburg. His many publications include essays on welfare policy and local administration in the Weimar Republic and the Third Reich. Among his books, *Die Weimarer Republik 1918–1933. Quellen und Kommentar*; *Hamburgs nationalsozialistische Diktatur: Verfassung und Verwaltung 1933 bis 1945* and *Fürsorge und Vervolgung. Öffentliche Wohlfahrtsverwaltung und nationalsozialistische Judenpolitik in Hamburg 1933 bis 1942*.

Lüdtke, Alf, Research fellow at the Max-Plank-Institut für Geschichte in

Göttingen and Professor at the University of Hannover. His publications include studies on forms of domination and state-making in modern history, practices and symbols of (industrial) work, the inner fabric of dictatorship and the history of everyday life.

Meyer, Beate, Since 1990 affiliated with the Institute for the History of German Jewry in Hamburg. Established the oral history archives of biographical interviews with Nazi victims at the Forschungstelle für Zeitgeschichte in Hamburg. Wrote several publications on regional history in the nazi period and a study on *Jüdische Mischlinge. Rassenpolitik und Verfolgungserfahrung 1933 bis 1945*. Dr. Meyer is presently working at the Stiftung Neue Synagoge — Centrum Judaicum in Berlin.

Obenaus, Herbert, Professor of History at the University of Hanover. He is presently conducting a research project of Jewish communities in Lower Saxony in conjunction with the Hebrew University and Yad Vashem. Prof. Obenaus has published extensively on German social, constitutional and political history. His publications include *"Schreiben wie es wirklich war"*, the edition of Karl Dürkefelde's diaries of WWII and *Im Schatten des Holocaust.*

Paucker, Arnold, Since 1959 Director of the Leo Baeck Institute, London and editor of its *Yearbook* between 1970 and 1992. Author of many studies on general German-Jewish history and Yiddish popular literature and on Jewish self-defense and resistance in Germany, e.g. *Der jüdische Abwehrkampf gegen Antisemitismus und nationalsozialismus in den letzten Jahren der Weimarer Republik*. Editor and Co-editor of nine symposium volumes on German-Jewish Studies 1965–1998.

Walk, Joseph, Professor Emeritus of Bar-Ilan University and former Director of the Leo Baeck Institute in Jerusalem. Recipient of the Dushkin Prize, Buber-Rozenzweig medal and many other awards. Dr. Walk is author of many articles and books on Jewish life in Nazi Germany, e.g., *Das Sonderrecht für die Juden in NS-Staat*; *Jewish Schools and Education in the Third Reich*; *As Yesterday: Essays and Reminiscences.*

Weiss, Yfaat, Studied at the universities of Tel Aviv and Hamburg, taught at the University of Munich and presently teaches at Haifa University. Dr. Weiss has written on Eastern European Jewry in Germany. Among her publications, *Schicksalsgemeinschaft im Wandel. Jüdische Erziehung im NS Deutschland* and a forthcoming book on the encounter between German and Polish Jewries in the Third Reich.

Wickert, Christl, Graduate of the Georg-August University, Göttingen. Dr. Wickert was Assistant Professor at the Free University of Berlin and the Technische Universität Berlin. She is presently doing research at the Friedrich Ebert Institute in Bonn.

Wildt, Michael, Research Fellow at the Institute for the History of National Socialism in Hamburg. Dr. Wildt has edited *Die Judenpolitik des SD 1935 bis 1938* and co-edited *Himmler's Kalendarium 1941/42*. His current research is on the leaders of the Reich Main Security Office.

Yahil, Leni, Professor Emeritus of Haifa University and a member of the editorial board of *Yad Vashem Studies*. Dr. Yahil is author of *The Rescue of Danish Jewry — Test of Democracy*; *The Holocaust — The Fate of European Jewry* and numerous articles on the Holocaust period.

Index of Names and Places